Frommer's®

1st Edition

Provence
&
the Riviera

by Darwin Porter
& Danforth Prince

Macmillan • USA

ABOUT THE AUTHORS

France and its southern tier are "second home" to **Darwin Porter,** a native of North Carolina, and **Danforth Prince,** who lived in France throughout most of his 20s. Darwin, who has worked in television advertising and as a bureau chief for the *Miami Herald* and who hopes someday to create a perfect bouillabaisse, wrote the original version of *Frommer's France.* Dan, who began his association with Darwin in 1982, worked for the Paris bureau of the *New York Times* between renovations of a historic building in the Loire Valley and bicycle trips through Provence and the Camargue. Both writers know southern France well, as they've made countless trips there, for both work and R&R.

MACMILLAN TRAVEL

A Simon & Schuster Macmillan Company
1633 Broadway
New York, NY 10019

Find us online at **www.frommers.com**
or on America Online at Keyword: **Frommers**

ISBN 0-02-861659-6
ISSN 1094-7647

Editor: Ron Boudreau
Production Editor: Michael Thomas
Design by Michele Laseau
Digital Cartography by Roberta Stockwell, Raffaele Degenarro, and Ortelius Design

SPECIAL SALES

Travel Discount Coupon

This coupon entitles you to special discounts
when you book your trip through the

RESERVATION SERVICE

Hotels ♦ Airlines ♦ Car Rentals ♦ Cruises
All Your Travel Needs

Here's what you get: *

♦ A discount of $50 USD on a booking of $1,000** or more for two or more people!

♦ A discount of $25 USD on a booking of $500** or more for one person!

♦ Free membership for three years, and 1,000 free miles on enrollment in the unique Travel Network Miles-to-Go® frequent-traveler program. Earn one mile for every dollar spent through the program. Redeem miles for free hotel stays starting at 5,000 miles. Earn free roundtrip airline tickets starting at 25,000 miles.

♦ Personal help in planning your own, customized trip.

♦ Fast, confirmed reservations at any property recommended in this guide, subject to availability.***

♦ Special discounts on bookings in the U.S. and around the world.

♦ Low-cost visa and passport service.

♦ Reduced-rate cruise packages and special car rental programs worldwide.

> Visit our website at http://www.travelnetwork.com/Frommer or call us globally at 201-567-8500, ext. 55. In the U.S., call toll-free at 1-888-940-5000, or fax 201-567-1838. In Canada, call at 1-905-707-7222, or fax 905-707-8108. In Asia, call 60-3-7191044, or fax 60-3-7185415.

* To qualify for these travel discounts, at least a portion of your trip must include destinations covered in this guide. No more than one coupon discount may be used in any 12-month period, for destinations covered in this guide. Cannot be combined with any other discount or promotion.

**These are U.S. dollars spent on commissionable bookings.

***A $10 USD fee, plus fax and/or phone charges, will be added to the cost of bookings at each hotel not linked to the reservation service. Customers must approve these fees in advance. If only hotels of this kind are booked, the traveler(s) must also purchase roundtrip air tickets from Travel Network for the trip.

Valid until December 31, 1999. Terms and conditions of the Miles-to-Go® program are available on request by calling 201-567-8500, ext 55.

PRO234

Contents

4   Languedoc-Roussillon & the Camargue   73

5   Provence: In the Footsteps of Cézanne & van Gogh   115

6 | **The Western Riviera: From St-Tropez to Cannes to Cap d'Antibes 191**

List of Maps

AN INVITATION TO THE READER

In researching this book, we discovered many wonderful places—hotels, restaurants, shops, and more. We're sure you'll find others. Please tell us about them, so we can share the information with your fellow travelers in upcoming editions. If you were disappointed with a recommendation, we'd love to know that, too. Please write to:

Frommer's Provence & the Riviera, 1st Edition
Macmillan Travel
1633 Broadway
New York, NY 10019

AN ADDITIONAL NOTE

Please be advised that travel information is subject to change at any time—and this is especially true of prices. We therefore suggest that you write or call ahead for confirmation when making your travel plans. The authors, editors, and publisher cannot be held responsible for the experiences of readers while traveling. Your safety is important to us, however, so we encourage you to stay alert and be aware of your surroundings. Keep a close eye on cameras, purses, and wallets, all favorite targets of thieves and pickpockets.

WHAT THE SYMBOLS MEAN

✪ Frommer's Favorites

Our favorite places and experiences—outstanding for quality, value, or both.

The following abbreviations are used for credit cards:

AE	American Express	EURO	EuroCard
CB	Carte Blanche	JCB	Japan Credit Bank
DC	Diners Club	MC	MasterCard
DISC	Discover	V	Visa
ER	enRoute		

FIND FROMMER'S ONLINE

Arthur Frommer's Outspoken Encyclopedia of Travel (www.frommers.com) offers more than 6,000 pages of up-to-the-minute travel information—including the latest bargains and candid, personal articles updated daily by Arthur Frommer himself. No other Web site offers such comprehensive and timely coverage of the world of travel.

The Best of Provence & the Riviera

As you're heading to the south of France to luxuriate in life along the sunny and sexy Mediterranean—not to exhaust yourself making difficult decisions—we've searched out the best deals and once-in-a-lifetime experiences for this book. What follows in this chapter is our roster of the best of the best, the kind of discoveries we'd share with our closest friends.

1 The Best Travel Experiences

- **Dining and Drinking Provence Style:** Believe it or not, chasing after gorgeously bronzed bodies isn't the major quest of all who are bound for the south of France. Many people flock here specifically to enjoy *cuisine provençale,* a Mediterranean mix of bold flavors with an emphasis on garlic, olive oil, and aromatic local herbs, like thyme and basil. The world's greatest bowls of bouillabaisse are made here, especially in Marseille; Provençal lamb is among the best in France; and the vegetables (such as asparagus, eggplant, tomatoes, and artichokes) will make you realize that this is France's market garden. The regional wines, though not equaling those of Bordeaux and Burgundy, are the perfect accompaniment, ranging from the warm, full-bodied Châteauneuf-du-Pape to the rare, choice Bellet, produced on Nice's hill slopes. See "A Taste of Provence" in chapter 2.
- **Partying in the Land of Festivals:** Provence is called the Land of Festivals with good reason: It hosts some 500 festivals that include an astonishing 4,000 events. Of course, the ultimate example is the you-won't-believe-it-until-you've-seen-it Cannes Film Festival in May. July and August are the busiest months, as Aix-en-Provence, Toulon, and Nice host jazz festivals and Nîmes and Arles stage theater and dance performances. On May 16, St-Tropez's riotous *bravades* in theory honor the saint but are really just an excuse for revelry. Many festivals have roots deep in Provençal folklore, honoring the bounty of earth and sea: the wine harvest in numerous villages, the rice harvest in Languedoc's Camargue, and the apple harvest in Peyruis. Everything seems to end in a feast where the wine and pastis flow. Contact any tourist office for the free booklet *Provence—Terre de Festivals* and check out "Provence Calendar of Events" in chapter 3.

- **Breaking the Bank at Monte Carlo:** Few other casinos can match the excitement generated at the Monte Carlo Casino. The world's wealthy flocked to Monaco when the casino by Charles Garnier opened in 1878. But since 1891 much of the nonwealthy world has followed—even those who couldn't afford losses. During a 3-day gambling spree that year, the American Charles Deville Wells turned $400 into $40,000, an astonishing amount back then. His feat was immortalized in the song "The Man Who Broke the Bank at Monte Carlo." Even if you do no more today than play the slot machines, a visit to this casino will be a highlight of your trip, as you bask amid the extravagant decor and under the gilded rococo ceilings. (Some not as lucky as Wells have leaped to their deaths from the casino windows or the "Suicide Terrace.") See chapter 7.

- **Sunning and Swimming on the Riviera Beaches:** There are greater beaches but none more fabled, overcrowded though they are. Most of them are sandy, except those stretching from Antibes to the Italian frontier, including Nice's. These are shingled (covered with coarse gravel), but that doesn't stop the world from flocking to them. A beach mattress fits just fine on the shingles, and there are umbrellas to rent when you want to escape the relentless sun. Along the Riviera toplessness is now almost universally accepted. Legend has it that it began with Brigitte Bardot, who pulled off her bra and said, "Let's wake up sleepy St-Trop." There are also nudist beaches, notably at Cap d'Agde and Port Cros. If you decide not to go topless or bottomless, you can still wear your most daring bikini or thong. Also see "The Best Beaches," later in this chapter.

- **Following in the Footsteps of the Great Artists:** Modern art wasn't born in Provence, but artists from all over came here to paint its "glaring festive light." The good news is that most of them left behind fabulous legacies. Perhaps it all began when Monet arrived with Renoir in 1883. In time they were followed by a host of others, including Bonnard, who took a villa in St-Tropez. Van Gogh arrived in Arles in 1888, and Gaugin showed up a few months later. Even the Fauves sought out this region, notably Matisse, whose masterpiece is his chapel at Vence. Not long afterward, Picasso arrived at Antibes. Deeply jealous of Picasso and Matisse, Chagall moved to Vence and was later infuriated that the street on which he lived was renamed avenue Henri-Matisse. He got over it and lived and painted on the Riviera until he died at 97.

- **Spending a Day in St-Rémy-de-Provence:** Our favorite town in Provence is St-Rémy. We're not alone in our enthusiasm, for we've spotted Princess Caroline here several times. Long before us, St-Rémy was known to Nostradamus, who was born here. Gertrude Stein and Alice B. Toklas liked to come down for tranquil visits. Tragically, van Gogh spent his last year near here in an asylum; his "cell" was later occupied by an interned German during World War I—Albert Schweitzer. Many artists who could live anywhere have chosen St-Rémy as their home today. To wander St-Rémy's streets is to recapture Provence's essence, especially its Vieille Ville (old town). After exploring its alleys, pause on one of its immaculate leafy squares. Then go in search of an art gallery or two and perhaps reward yourself with a painting and a memory. See chapter 5.

- **Having Fun Day and Night:** If nothing else, the Riviera is about the art of entertainment, both high and low. The Côte d'Azur offers not only beaches and race cars and yachts but also fêtes and festivals and even bullfights, real Spanish-style ones where the animals are killed in the old Roman arenas at Arles and Nîmes. Glittering casinos are seemingly everywhere—Monte Carlo, Cannes, Cassis, and Beaulieu, to name a few. Many have discos and elegant restaurants. There's even a cultural side to the merriment, especially in Nice, Monte Carlo, Avignon,

Montpellier, and Marseille, which boast their own opera houses with resident companies. But mainly the Riviera offers white-hot nightclubs and dance clubs for all sexes and sexual orientations, especially in Cannes, Nice, Monte Carlo, and St-Tropez. See chapters 6 and 7.

- **Absorbing a Unique Lifestyle:** Provence and Languedoc share a uniquely Mediterranean lifestyle. Compared to the rest of France, the air here is drier, the sun beats down stronger, and the light beloved by so many painters appears clearer. Nothing could be more typical than a game of boules played under shade trees on a hot afternoon in a Provençal village. This is a place that respects time-honored crafts; Picasso might have arrived here a painter, but he left a potter. And nothing is finer in life than to be invited into a Provençal kitchen—the heart of family life—and smell the aroma of herbs and wines cooking with the catch of the day. To walk in the gardens, filled with vegetables, flowers, and fruit trees, is reason enough to go, as is to attend a harvest, not just grapes, but perhaps linden blossoms. It's a land of ingrained traditions and a dramatic landscape that somehow seems at its most romantic when hit with the dreaded mistral winds blowing north from Africa. Discovering this land and making it your own is one of the great rewards of all European travel, especially if you go in the best months: May and September.

2 The Best Romantic Getaways

- **Les Baux** (Provence): Occupying the most spectacular position of any town in this guide, Les Baux stands on a promontory of sheer rock ravines. In the distance across the plain you can view the Val d'Enfer (Valley of Hell). After a turbulent history, the town today is one of the great escapes for the savvy French who can gaze from their windows onto thousands of olive trees (many planted by the Greeks) that produce the best oil in France. Les Baux is a pocket of posh, with some of the country's grandest inns and finest cuisine. The most notable is **L'Oustau de Beaumanière,** Maussanel-les-Alpilles (☎ 04-90-54-33-07), with one of France's best restaurants. After you and your loved one sample the ravioli with truffles, you'll understand why. See chapter 5.
- **Iles d'Hyères** (Provence): If an off-the-record weekend is what you have in mind, there's no better spot than what the people of the Renaissance called the Iles d'Or, because of a golden glow sometimes given off by island rocks in the sun. This is a string of enchanting little islands 24 miles east/southeast of the port of Toulon. The largest and westernmost of the islands is Ile de Porquerolles, thickly covered with heather, eucalyptus, and exotic shrubs. Ile de Port-Cros is hilly and mysterious, with spring-fed lush vegetation. The best spot for a romantic retreat is **Le Manoir** on Ile de Port-Cros (☎ 04-94-05-90-53), an 18th-century colonial-style mansion set in a park. See chapter 5.
- **Mougins** (Western Riviera): Only 5 miles north of Cannes, the once-fortified town of Mougins is a thousand years old, but never in its history has it been so popular as a place to enjoy the good life. Picasso, who could afford to live anywhere, chose a place nearby, Notre-Dame-de-Vie, to spend his last years. The wonderful old town is known for its cuisine, and Roger Vergé reigns supreme at his elegant **Le Moulin de Mougins,** Notre-Dame-de-Vie (☎ 04-93-75-78-24); however, you can live for less at more secluded and less publicized oases. See chapter 6.
- **Peillon** (Eastern Riviera): Of all the "perched" villages (*villages perchés*) along the Côte d'Azur, this fortified medieval town on a craggy mountaintop, 12 miles

northeast of Nice, is our favorite. It stands 1,000 feet above the Mediterranean. Peillon is the least spoiled of the perched villages and still boasts its medieval look, with covered alleys and extremely narrow streets. Tour buses avoid the place, but artists and writers flock there (we once spotted Françoise Sagan) to escape the mad carnival of the Riviera. For a cozy hideaway with your significant other, try the **Auberge de la Madone** (☎ 04-93-79-91-17). Dinner for two on the terrace set among olive trees is the best way to start a romantic evening. See chapter 7.

- **Roquebrune and Cap-Martin** (Eastern Riviera): Along the Grande Corniche, Roquebrune is one of the most charming of the Côte d'Azur's villages, and its satellite resort of Cap-Martin occupies a lovely wooded peninsula. Between Monaco and Menton, these two have long been romantic retreats. We learned that when we once spotted Princess Grace having lunch here with a handsome young man whom we later learned was her lover. But that was before paparazzi started crawling all over the Côte hoping to capture on film some celebrity toe-sucking or whatever. Long before Grace, Empress Eugénie and her monied crowd used to winter here. The best choice for hiding away with that certain someone is the **Vista Palace,** Grande Corniche (☎ 800/223-6800 in the U.S., or 04-92-10-40-00), a modern luxury hotel clinging giddily to a cliffside over Monte Carlo. See chapter 7.

3 The Most Dramatic Countryside Drives

- **From Carcassonne to Albi** (Languedoc-Roussillon): From the walled city of Carcassonne, D118 takes you north into the Montagne Noire (Black Mountains), which are both arid and lush in parts, marking the southeastern extension of the Massif Central. You can spend a full day here exploring the Parc Régional du Haut-Languedoc, crowned by the 3,700-foot Pic de Noire. You can base in the old wool town of Mazamet and have lunch here before continuing northwest on N112 to Castres with its Goya Museum. Then you can continue exploring the surrounding area or head for Albi, 25 miles away, the hometown of Toulouse-Lautrec. For more details, see the box "A Countryside Drive" in chapter 4.
- **From St-Rémy-de-Provence to Eygalières** (Provence): A 40-mile drive northeast of Arles takes you into some of the most dramatic and forlorn countryside in Provence, even to the Val d'Enfer (Valley of Hell). At the beginning of the tour you pass Roman monuments before climbing into the hills with their distant views of the Parc Naturel Régional de la Camargue and Mont Ventoux. The tour also takes you to Les Baux, the most dramatically situated town in Provence and to-day a gourmet citadel. At Fontevieille you can view the famous windmill immortalized by the 19th-century author Alphonse Daudet. After many turns and twists, you eventually reach the ancient village of Eygalières, with its medieval castle and church. For more details, see the box "A Countryside Drive" in chapter 5.
- **Along the Ours Peak Road** (Western Riviera): The best driving tour in the area starts in St-Raphaël and lasts for only 35 miles, but because the terrain is so rough and torturous allow at least 3 hours. The views are among the most dramatic along the Côte d'Azur, as you traverse a backdrop of the red porphyry slopes of Rastel d'Agay. Along the way you'll go through the passes of Evêque and Lentisques. Eventually, hairpin bends in the road lead to the summit of Ours Peak (Pic de l'Ours) at 1,627 feet, and you're rewarded with a superb panorama. For more details, see the box "A Drive in the Hills" in chapter 6.
- **From Vence to Grasse** (Western and Eastern Riviera): After calling on the Matisse chapel in Vence, you can take D2210 through some of the most luxuriant

countryside along the French Riviera, taking in views of the Gorges du Loup and stopping over in the artisans' village of Tourrettes-sur-Loup. Here its main street is filled with the ateliers of craftspeople. As you continue, follow the signs to Point-du-Loup and you'll be rewarded with a panorama of waterfalls, and will later pass fields of flowers that eventually will lead you to the perfume center of Grasse. For more details on the gorge, see the box "Exploring the Gorges du Loup" in chapter 7.

- **From Nice to Mont Chauve** (Eastern Riviera): The hilltops surrounding Nice have long been known for their colorful villages and rural scenery. In our view, the best countryside and the best panoramas unfold by driving to Mont Chauve (Bald Mountain) across a circuit that traverses 33 miles. Though the trip is short in mileage, you can spend a worthwhile afternoon taking it. You can stop at several villages along the way, including Aspremont and Tourette-Levens. You'll even pass the Gorges du Gabres, with its sheer walls of limestone, before passing through the enchanting village of Falicon. Eventually you'll reach Mont Chauve. Allow at least 30 minutes to hike to the summit. For more details, see the box "Two Countryside Drives" in chapter 7.

4 The Best Beaches

- **La Côte Vermeille** (Languedoc-Roussillon): In contrast to the eastern Riviera's pebbly beaches, the Côte Vermeille is filled with sand stretching toward Spain's Costa Brava. The best place for fun in the sun is the 6-mile beach between the resorts of Leucate-Plage and Le Barcarès in the Pyrénées-Orientales district. The "Vermilion Coast" takes its name from the backdrop of red-clay soil studded with the ubiquitous olive groves, giving the land a vermilion tint. Henri Matisse was so taken with the light of this coast that he painted it. See chapter 4.
- **Beaches of Ile de Porquerolles** (Provence): These beaches lie 15 minutes by ferry from the Giens peninsula east of Toulon. One of the Iles d'Hyères (see "The Best Romantic Getaways," earlier in this chapter), Porquerolles is only 5 miles long and some 1¹/₄ miles across and enjoys national park status. Its beaches, along the northern coast facing the mainland, get 275 days of sunshine annually. There are several white-sand beaches, the best of which are Plage d'Argent, Plage de la Courtade, and Plage de Notre-Dame. The waters lapping up on this beach have been compared to those in the French Antilles, such as Martinique. See chapter 5.
- **Plage de Tahiti** (St-Tropez, Western Riviera): And God created woman and man and all the other critters found on this sizzling sandy beach outside St-Tropez. Tahiti is France's most infamous beach, mainly because of all the topless or bottomless action going on, with the Japanese snapping souvenir pictures. Ever since the days of Brigitte Bardot, this beach has been a favorite of movie stars. It's very cruisy, very animated, with a French nonchalance about nudity. If you bother to wear a bikini, it should be only the most daring. See chapter 6.
- **Plage Port Grimaud** (St-Tropez, Western Riviera): This long golden-sand beach is set against the backdrop of the urban architect François Spoerry's *cité lacustre,* facing St-Tropez. Spoerry created this 247-acre marine village inspired by an ancient fishing village—"the most magnificent fake since Disneyland." The world has since flocked to Port Grimaud and its beach, including homeowners like Joan Collins, who comes here to hide from the paparazzi. Some of the Riviera's most expensive yachts are tied up in the harbor. This beach isn't as decadent as those at St-Trop, but it does pick up the "overflow" on the see-and-be-seen circuit. See chapter 6.

- **The Beaches at Cannes** (Western Riviera): From the Palais des Festivals and west to Mandelieu, the beach at Cannes has real sand, not pebbles as at Nice. This beach resort offers a movable feast of high-fashion swimsuits, particularly skimpy bikinis. If you look like Demi Moore or JFK Jr., so much the better. Ever since the 1920s, the word on the beach here has been: "Menton's dowdy. Monte's brass. Nice is rowdy. Cannes is class!" Along the fabled promenade, La Croisette, the white sands are littered with sunbeds and parasols rented at the beach concessions. The beach is actually divided into 32 sections, our favorites being Plages Gazagnaire, Le Zénith, and Waikiki. Some of the beaches are privately run, but the best public beach is in front of the Palais des Festivals. See chapter 6.
- **Monte-Carlo Beach** (at the Monaco border, Eastern Riviera): This beach, once frequented by Princess Grace, is actually on French soil. Of all the Riviera's beaches, this is the most fashionable, even though its sands are imported. The property adjoins the ultra-chic **Monte-Carlo Beach Hotel,** 22 av. Princesse-Grace (☎ 04-93-28-66-66). The great months to be here are July and August, when you never know who's likely to be sharing the sands with you—perhaps Luciano Pavarotti or Claudia Schiffer. The main topic on the beach? Both legal and funny money. See chapter 7.

5 The Best Offbeat Experiences

- **Spending a Night in Aigues-Mortes** (Languedoc-Roussillon): Once St. Louis sailed from this port to fight in the Crusades to the east. He died in Tunis in 1270, but his successor, Philip III, held this port, the only stretch of the Mediterranean in French hands at the time. Great walls were built around the town, and ships all the way from Antioch used to anchor here. But beginning around the mid–14th century, Aigues-Mortes began to live up to its name of "dead waters," as the harbor filled with silt and the waters receded. Today it sits marooned in time and space right in the muck of the advancing Rhône delta. Nothing along the coast is as evocative of the Middle Ages as this town, where you can walk along its walls and slumber in one of its inns. See chapter 4.
- **Checking In and Stripping Down** (Cap d'Agde, Languedoc-Roussillon): Some people have been arrested for walking around a town without their clothes or even for wearing too skimpy a swimsuit. But not so at a holiday town on the outskirts of Cap d'Agde. Along the Languedoc coast, between the Rhône delta and Béziers, Cap d'Agde was constructed like a pastiche of a local fishing village, similar to Port Grimaud near St-Tropez. At its outskirts is a town with supermarkets, nightclubs, a casino, and rooms for 20,000 bodies—nude bodies. Except in foul weather, it's compulsory to walk around nude. You'll definitely have to check your apparel at the gate. *Vive la France!* See the box "Liberté, Egalité, Fraternité . . . Nudité" in chapter 4.
- **Exploring Les Calanques** (between Marseille and Cassis, Provence): At the old fishing port of Cassis, with its white cliffs and beaches that were a favorite of Fauve painters, you can rent a boat and explore the Calanques, small fjords along the rugged coast. Covered with gorse and heather, the white cliffs form a backdrop for this adventure. By car from Cassis you can drive to the creek of Port Miou, with its rock quarries. To reach the Port Pin and En Vau creeks farther west you must travel on foot (trails are well signposted). You can, however, take one of the boat excursions that leaves regularly from Cassis. If you go on your own (not on the boat) you can take a picnic and spend the day skinny-dipping in these cool crystal waters. See the box "Exploring the Massif des Calanques" in chapter 5.

- **Searching for the Unknown Masterpiece of Edith Wharton** (Hyères, Provence): *The Age of Innocence* was Miss Wharton's best-known masterpiece, but her relatively unknown masterpiece, La Solitude, stands in Hyères, the oldest of all Côte d'Azur resorts, dating from the 18th century. Over the years the resort attracted everybody from Napoléon to Queen Victoria before falling from fashion. Miss Wharton fell in love with Hyères and stayed there to create 28 terraced acres of gardens that you can visit today. See the box "The Unknown Masterpiece of Edith Wharton" in chapter 5.
- **Visiting a Tycoon's Island** (Bendor, Provence): West of Toulon, Bandol is a small resort that was visited by Katherine Mansfield and D. H. Lawrence in the 1920s. It's still stylish, with a yacht marina and a trio of sandy beaches, but virtually overlooked by foreigners. However, there's a nugget here worth the trip. Less than a mile off the coast is the tiny rocky island of Bendor, owned by Paul Ricard, the pastis tycoon and an eccentric philanthropist. He has re-created a Provençal fishing port, with shops for artisans who paint, sculpt, make jewelry, or whatever. At the harbor in Bandol, you can catch a boat over to the tiny island created in a moment of whimsy by the flamboyant Ricard. See the box "Checking Out a Tycoon's Private Island" in chapter 5.

6 The Best Small Towns

- **Cordes-sur-Ciel** (Languedoc-Roussillon): Perched like an eagle's nest on a hilltop, Cordes is an arts-and-crafts town, its ancient houses on narrow streets filled with artisans plying their trades. Once fabled in France for the brilliance of its silks, today it's a sleepy town 15¹/₂ miles northwest of Albi, the city of Toulouse-Lautrec. Ideally, you should visit Cordes as a side trip from Albi, but you may become enchanted with the place, as did François Mitterrand and Albert Camus before you, and decide to stop over in this town of a hundred Gothic arches. See chapter 4.
- **Uzès** (Provence): It's with good reason that this town of lofty towers and narrow streets was selected for the location of Jean-Paul Rappeneau's *Cyrano de Bergerac,* starring Gérard Depardieu. Uzès is a gem, a bit of a time capsule. Jean Racine once lived here and was inspired by the town to write his only comedy, *Les Plaideurs.* André Gide also found a home in this "dream of the Middle Ages." Once Louis XIII called Uzès "the premier duchy of France." You can see why by staying at the stately 18th-century Château d'Arpaillargues. See chapter 5.
- **Gordes** (Provence): One of the best known of Provence's hill villages, Gordes, east of Avignon, is deservedly called *le plus beau village de France.* Today an escape for in-the-know Parisians, it's a town of silk painters, weavers, and potters. The setting is bucolic, between the Coulon valley and the Vaucluse plateau. Houses built of golden stone rise to the Renaissance château crowning the top. Victor Vasarély, the late artist, lived here in a fortified château that has been turned into a museum displaying much of his work. See chapter 5.
- **Roussillon** (Provence): Northeast of Gordes, Roussillon stands on a hilltop in the heart of "ocher country," where the earth is a bright red, as are rocks jutting out for miles around. (*Roussillon* means "russet.") This village is ancient, boasting houses made in every shade of burnt orange, dusty pink, and russet red—they take on a particular brilliance at sunset. Roussillon, however, is no longer the sleepy village described in Laurence Wylie's 1961 *Village in the Vaucluse.* Artists, writers, and trendy Parisians have discovered its charms, and today many use it as their second home. See chapter 5.

- **Roquebrune** (Eastern Riviera): This medieval hill village southwest of Menton is the finest along the Côte d'Azur. It has been extensively restored, and not even the souvenir shops can spoil its charm. Steep stairways and alleys lead up to its feudal castle, crowning the village. But before heading here, take in rue Moncollet, flanked by houses from the Middle Ages. This castle, dating from the 10th century, is the oldest in France—in fact, it's the only Carolingian castle left standing. See chapter 7.

7 The Best Châteaux & Palaces

- **Château d'If** (off Marseille, Provence): One of France's most notorious fortresses, this was the famous state prison whose mysterious guest was the Man in the Iron Mask. Alexandre Dumas père's *Count of Monte Cristo* made the legend famous around the world. It doesn't really matter that the story was apocryphal: People flock here because they believe it, just as they go to Verona to see where Romeo and Juliet lived and loved and died. The château was built by François I in 1524 as part of the defenses of Marseille. To reach it, you take a boat in the harbor to the islet 2 miles offshore. See chapter 5.
- **Palais des Papes** (Avignon, Provence): This was the seat of Avignon's brief but golden age as the capital of Christendom. The popes lived here during the period that the Romans called the Babylonian Captivity. And they lived with pomp and circumstance, knowing "fleshly weaknesses." The Italian poet Petrarch denounced the palace as "an abode of sorrows, the shame of mankind, a sink of vice." From 1352 to 1377 seven popes ruled there, all of them French. Even after Gregory XI was persuaded to return to Rome, some cardinals remained, electing their own pope or "antipope." Thus from the Palais des Papes the Great Schism of the West was launched. The antipope was finally expelled by force in 1403. See chapter 5.
- **Château de La Napoule** (La Napoule, Western Riviera): The Riviera's most eccentric château is also the most fascinating. This great medieval castle was purchased in 1917 by the American sculptor Henry Clews, heir to a banking fortune. He lived, worked, and was buried here after dying in Switzerland in 1937. During that time, he produced an unmatched collection of works. In this castle Crews created his own grotesque menagerie—scorpions, pelicans, gnomes, monkeys, lizards, whatever came to his tortured mind. His view of feminism? A distorted suffragette depicted in his *Cat Woman*. He likened himself to Don Quixote. See chapter 6.
- **Palais du Prince** (Monte Carlo, Monaco, Western Riviera): The world has known greater palaces, but this Italianate one on The Rock houses the man who presides over the tiny but incredibly rich principality of Monaco, Europe's second-smallest state. As head of the House of Grimaldi, Prince Rainier III (alas, without his Princess Grace) sits on the throne, wondering if his heir apparent, Prince Albert, now in his 40s, will ever get married and produce an heir. (Without a male heir, Monaco will revert back to France.) When the prince is here, a flag will be flying and you can watch the changing of the guard. The throne room is hung with pictures by Holbein, Brueghel, and others, and in one wing of the palace is a museum devoted to souvenirs of Napoléon. See chapter 7.
- **Villa Kérylos** (Beaulieu, Eastern Riviera): This villa is a faithful reconstruction of an ancient Greek palace, built between 1902 and 1908 by the archaeologist Théodore Reinach. Designated a historic monument of France, it's filled with luxury and architectural detail, including white, yellow, and lavender Italian marble. Reinach, a bit of an eccentric, lived here for 20 years, preferring to take

baths and eat and dress with his male friends (who pretended to be Athenian citizens), while segregating the women to separate suites. With its ivory and bronze copies of vases and mosaics, Kérylos is a visual knockout, and the parties that went on here are legendary. See chapter 7.

8 The Best Museums

- **Musée Toulouse-Lautrec** (Albi, Languedoc-Roussillon): This museum displays the world's greatest collection from this crippled genius, who immortalized can-can dancers, cafe demimonde, and prostitutes. In the brooding 13th-century Palais de la Berbie in the artist's hometown, the "red city" of Albi, this museum takes you into the special but tortured world of Toulouse-Lautrec. Especially memorable are the posters that marked the beginning of an entirely new art form. When he died, his family donated the works remaining in his studio—posters, pastels, drawings, lithographs, sketches, the works. See chapter 4.
- **Musée Picasso** (Antibes, Western Riviera): After the bleak war years in Paris, Picasso returned to the Mediterranean in 1945. He didn't have a studio, so the curator of this museum offered him space. Picasso labored here for several months—it was one of his most creative periods. At the end of his stay, he astonished the curator by leaving his entire output on permanent loan to the museum, along with some 200 ceramics he'd produced at Vallauris. This museum reveals Picasso in an exuberant mood, as evoked by his fauns and goats in a cubist style, his still lifes of sea urchins, and his masterful *Ulysses et ses Sirènes*. A much-reproduced photograph displayed here shows him holding a sunshade for his lover, Françoise Gilot. See chapter 6.
- **Musée Ile-de-France** (St-Jean-Cap-Ferrat, Eastern Riviera): Baronne Ephrussi left a treasure trove of art and artifacts to the Institut de France on her death in 1934. Sometimes known as the Villa Ephrussi, the 1912 palace that contains these pieces reveals what a woman with unlimited wealth and highly eclectic taste can collect. It's all here: paintings by Carpaccio and other masters of the Venetian Renaissance; canvases by Sisley, Renoir, and Monet; Ming vases; Dresden porcelain; and more. An eccentric, she named her house after the ocean liner *Ile de France* and insisted that her 35 gardeners dress as sailors. The baronne lived here for only 3 years before moving to Monaco. See chapter 7.
- **Musée des Beaux-Arts** (Nice, Eastern Riviera): In the former home of the Ukrainian Princess Kotchubey, the collection comes as an unexpected delight, with not only many belle époque paintings but also modern works, including an impressive number by Sisley, Braque, Degas, and Monet, plus Picasso ceramics. There's whimsy too, especially the sugar-sweet canvases by Jules Chéret, who died in Nice in 1932. Well represented also are the Van Loo family, a clan of Dutch descent whose members worked in Nice. The gallery of sculptors honors Rude, Rodin, and J. B. Carpeaux. See chapter 7.
- **Fondation Maeght** (St-Paul-de-Vence, Eastern Riviera): One of Europe's greatest modern-art museums, this foundation is remarkable for both its setting and its art. Built in 1964, the avant-garde building boasts a touch of fantasy, topped by two inverted domes. The colorful canvases virtually radiate with the joy of life. All your favorites are likely to be here: Bonnard, Braque, Soulages, Chagall, Kandinsky, and more. Stunningly designed is a terraced garden that's a setting for Calder murals, Hepworth sculptures, and even the fanciful fountains and colorful mosaics of Miró. A courtyard is peopled with Giacometti figures that look like gigantic emaciated chessmen. See chapter 7.

- **Musée National Fernand-Léger** (Biot, Eastern Riviera): Ridiculed as a Tubist, Léger survived many of his most outspoken critics and went on to win great fame. This museum was built by Léger's widow, Nadia, after his death in 1955, and it became one of the first in France dedicated to a single artist. It owns some 300 of Léger's highly original works. You wander into a dazzling array of robotlike figures, girders, machines, cogs, and cubes. The museum allows you to witness how he changed over the years, dabbling first with impressionism, as shown by his 1905 *Portrait de l'oncle*. Our favorite here—and one of our favorite artworks along the Riviera—is Léger's *Mona Lisa*, contemplating a set of keys with a wide-mouthed fish dangling at an angle over her head. See chapter 7.

9 The Best Cathedrals & Churches

- **Basilique St-Sernin** (Toulouse, Languedoc-Roussillon): Consecrated in 1096, this is the largest and finest Romanesque church extant. It was built to honor the memory of a Gaulish martyr, St. Sernin, and was for a long time a major stop on the pilgrimage route to Santiago de Compostela in Spain. The octagonal bell tower is particularly evocative, with five levels of twin brick arches. Unusual for a Romanesque church, St-Sernin has five naves. The crypt, where the saint is buried, is a treasure trove of ecclesiastical artifacts, some from the days of Charlemagne. See chapter 4.
- **Cathédrale St-Jean** (Perpignan, Languedoc-Roussillon): In 1324, Sancho of Aragón began this cathedral, but the consecration didn't come until its completion in 1509. Despite the different builders and architects over the decades, it emerged as one of Languedoc's most evocative cathedrals. The bell tower contains a great bell that dates from the 1400s (it's held in a wrought-iron cage from the 1700s). The single nave is typical of church construction in the Middle Ages, and it's enhanced by the altarpieces of the north chapels and the high altar, the work of the 1400s and the 1500s. See chapter 4.
- **Cathédrale St-Just** (Narbonne, Languedoc-Roussillon): Though construction on this cathedral, begun in 1272, was never completed, it's one of Languedoc's most enduring landmarks. Construction had to be halted 82 years later to preserve the city's ramparts, as architects would've had to breach the ramparts to make room for the nave. In the High Gothic style, the vaulting in the choir soars to 130 feet. Battlements and loopholes crown the towering arches of the apse. The cathedral's greatest treasure is appropriately in its treasury, the evocative *Tapestry of the Creation*, woven in silk and gold thread. See chapter 4.
- **Cathédrale Notre-Dame** (Avignon, Provence): Next to the Palais des Papes, this was a luminous Romanesque structure before baroque artists took over. It was partially reconstructed from the 14th to the 17th century. In 1859 it was topped by a tall gilded statue of the Virgin, which earned it harsh criticism from many architectural critics. The cathedral houses the tombs of two popes, John XXII and Benedict XII. You'd think this cathedral would be more impressive because of its role in papal history, but it appears that far more time and money went into the construction of the papal palace. Nevertheless, the cathedral reigned during the heyday of Avignon. See chapter 5.
- **Basilique St-Victor** (Marseille, Provence): This is one of France's most ancient churches, first built in the 5th century by St. Cassianus. He was honoring St. Victor, a 3rd-century martyr. The saint's church was destroyed by the Saracens, except for the crypt. In the 11th and 12th centuries a fortified Gothic church was erected, looking like a fortress. The catacombs of the crypt have both pagan and

early Christian sarcophagi. The sarcophagi depicting the convening of the Apostles and the Companions of St. Maurice are justly renowned. See chapter 5.

10 The Best Vineyards

Southern France is home to thousands of vineyards, many of which are banal-looking, somewhat anonymous agrarian bureaucracies known as *cooperatives.* Employees at these cooperatives tend to be less enthusiastic about their product and care less about showing it off to newcomers than those who work at true vineyards, where the person pouring your *dégustation des vins* might be the son or daughter of one of the owners. At least in southern France, don't assume that just because the word *Château* appears in the name that there'll be a magnificent historic residence associated with the property. In some cases, the crenellated battlement you're look-ing for might be nothing more than a feudal ruin.

We selected the vineyards below because of the emotional involvement of their (private) owners, their degree of prestige, and in many cases, their architectural interest.

- **Château de Simone,** 13590 Meyreuil (☎ **04-42-66-92-58**): Simone is less than a mile north of Aix-en-Provence (take N7 toward Nice, then follow the signs to Trois Sautets). Its 40 acres of vineyards surround a small 18th-century palace that might've been transported unchanged from *La Belle du bois dormant.* You can't visit the interior, but you can buy bottles of vintages 3 years old or older for less than 100F ($20). The minimum purchase is six bottles of red, white, or rosé. Ad-vance notification is important.

- **Château de Virant,** R.D. 10, 13680 Lançon-de-Provence (☎ **04-90-42-44-47**): Set 14 miles east of Aix-en-Provence and named after a nearby rock whose ruined feudal fortress is barely standing, this property produces Appellation d'Origine Contrôlée–designated Coteaux d'Aix-en-Provence as well as a translucent brand of olive oil from fruit grown on 40 of the 200 acres associated with the vineyards. The English-speaking Cheylan family, who cooperate with North American educational-exchange programs involving both wine and aviation, showcase a labyrinth of cellars dating from 1630 and 1890. Tours, tastings, and sales can all be arranged. Advance notification is wise.

- **Château de Calissane,** R.D. 10, 13680 Lançon-de-Provence (☎ **04-90-42-63-03**): On the premises is a substantial 18th-century château, an outbuilding of which sells the white, rosé, and red produced by this property's 110 acres of vine-yards and olive groves. The white-stone house sports very old terra-cotta tiles and a sense of the *ancien régime.* Even older is the Gallo-Roman *oppidum Constantine,* a sprawling ruined fortress that you can visit if you obtain a special pass from the sales staff. Set amid the vineyards, it, along with the two grades of olive oil sold by the staff, evokes old Provence. Advance reservations are vital.

- **Château de Fonscolombe** (☎ **04-42-61-89-62**) and **Château de LaCoste** (☎ **04-42-61-89-98**), 13610 Le Puy Ste-Réparade: These vineyards are adjacent to each other, 12¹/₂ miles north of Aix-en-Provence. Fonscolombe controls 400 acres of vineyards and offers tours of a modern facility that's of interest to wine-industry professionals; LaCoste is smaller and less state-of-the-art but offers an exterior view of a stone-sided villa that was built for a cardinal during the reign of the popes in Avignon. You can buy their red, white, and rosé wines. Advance notification is needed.

- **Château de Coussin,** R.N. 7, 13530 Trets (☎ **04-42-29-26-32**): This property, 10 miles east of Aix-en-Provence, is centered around a 16th-century château whose stone facade bears geometric reliefs associated with Renaissance-era construction in Provence. The 600 acres of vineyards scattered over three neighboring regions have been owned by the same family for nearly a century. You can visit the château's interior only by special request, but the overview of the wine-making industry is worth the trip.

On adjacent properties, two amiable competitors also offer wine tours to those who phone in advance: **Château de Grand'Boise,** 15350 Trets (☎ **04-42-29-22-95**), whose venerable château you can admire from the outside; and **Mas Cadenet Negrel,** 13530 Trets (☎ **04-42-29-51-59**), where a substantial Provençal farmhouse is the centerpiece for modern wine-making equipment that has produced many well-respected vintages.

11 The Best Luxury Hotels

- **Hôtel du Cap–Eden Roc** (Cap d'Antibes, Western Riviera; ☎ **04-93-61-39-01**): Looming large in F. Scott Fitzgerald's *Tender Is the Night,* this is the most stylish of the Côte's luxury palaces, standing at the tip of the Cap d'Antibes peninsula in its own 22-acre manicured garden. The hotel reflects the opulence of a bygone era and has catered to the rich and famous since it opened in 1870. Everybody has shown up here: from Haile Selassie to Betty Grable, from George Bernard Shaw to John F. Kennedy, from John Travolta to Madonna. See chapter 6.
- **Hôtel Carlton Intercontinental** (Cannes, Western Riviera; ☎ **800/327-0200** in the U.S., or 04-93-06-40-06): A World War II Allied commander issued orders to bombers to avoid hitting the Carlton "because it's such a good hotel." The 1912 hotel survived the attack and today is at its most frenzied during the annual film festival. Taste and subtlety aren't what the Carlton is about—it's all glitter, glitterati, and glamour, the most splendid of the area's architectural "wedding cakes." The white-turreted doyenne presides over La Croisette like some permanent sand castle. See chapter 6.
- **Grand Hôtel du Cap-Ferrat** (St-Jean-Cap-Ferrat, Eastern Riviera; ☎ **04-93-76-50-50**): The Grand Hôtel, built in 1908, competes with the Hôtel du Cap–Eden Roc as the Riviera's most opulent. Set in a well-manicured 14-acre garden, it was once a winter haven for royalty and was totally refurbished in 1990. This pocket of posh has it all, including a private beach club with a heated seawater pool and a Michelin-starred restaurant utilizing market-fresh ingredients. See chapter 7.
- **Hostellerie du Château de la Chèvre d'Or** (Eze, Eastern Riviera; ☎ **04-93-41-66-66**): In striking contrast to the palaces above, this gem of an inn lies in a medieval village 1,300 feet above sea level. All its elegant rooms open onto vistas of the Mediterranean. Everything here has a refreshingly rustic appeal, not false glitter. Following in the footsteps of former guests like Roger Moore and Elizabeth Taylor, you can stay in this artistically converted medieval château. As the paparazzi catch you sipping a champagne cocktail by the pool, you'll know you've achieved Côte d'Azur chic. See chapter 7.
- **Hôtel de Paris** (Monte Carlo, Monaco, Eastern Riviera; ☎ **92-16-30-00**): The 19th-century aristocracy flocked here, and though the hotel isn't quite that fashionable anymore, it's still going strong. Onassis, Sinatra, and Churchill long ago checked out, but today's movers and shakers still pull up in limousines with tons of luggage. This luxury palace boasts two Michelin-starred restaurants, the more celebrated of which is Le Louis XV, offering the sublime specialties of Alain Ducasse. Le Grill boasts Ligurian-Niçois cooking, a retractable roof, and a wrap-around view of the sea. See chapter 7.

- **Hôtel Négresco** (Nice, Eastern Riviera; ☎ **04-93-16-64-00**): An aging Lillie Langtry sitting alone in the lobby, her once-great beauty camouflaged by a black veil, is but one of the many memories of this nostalgic favorite. Self-made millionaires and wannabes rub shoulders with one another at this 1906 landmark. We could write a book about the Négresco, but here we'll give only two interesting facts: The carpet in the lobby is the largest ever made by the Savonnerie factory (the cost was about one-tenth the cost of the hotel), and the main chandelier was commissioned from Baccarat by Tsar Nicholas II. See chapter 7.

12 The Best Hotel Bargains

- **Hôtel Renaissance** (Castres, Languedoc-Roussillon; ☎ **05-63-59-30-42**): In the quaint town of Castres, with its celebrated Goya Museum, 26 miles south of Albi, this hotel is a good introduction to the bargains awaiting you in provincial France. Built in the 1600s as a courthouse, it was long ago converted from a dilapidated site into a hotel of discretion and charm—all at an affordable price, even if you opt for a suite. Some rooms have exposed timbers, and you'll sleep in grand but rustic comfort. See chapter 4.
- **Hôtel du Donjon** (Carcassonne, Languedoc-Roussillon; ☎ **800/528-1234** in the U.S. and Canada, or 04-68-71-08-80): Built into the solid bulwarks of Carcassonne, one of France's most perfectly preserved medieval towns, is this small-scale hotel whose well-appointed furnishings provide a vivid contrast to the crude stone shell that contains them. A stay here truly allows you personal contact with a site that provoked bloody battles between medieval armies. See chapter 4.
- **La Réserve** (Albi, Languedoc-Roussillon; ☎ **05-63-60-80-80**): La Réserve's design approximates a *mas provençal,* the kind of severely dignified farmhouse usually surrounded with scrublands, vineyards, olive groves, and cypresses. It's less expensive than many of the luxurious hideaways along the nearby Côte d'Azur and has the added benefit of lying just outside the center of one of our favorite fortified sites in Europe, the medieval town of Albi. See chapter 4.
- **Hôtel Danieli** (Avignon, Provence; ☎ **04-90-86-46-82**): Built during the reign of Napoléon, this 29-room gem is classified a historic monument. Small and informal, it has Italian flair but Provençal furnishings. The acquisitive owner scans the countryside for antiques to fill the place. The tile floors, chiseled stone, and baronial stone staircase add style in a town where too many budget hotels are bleak. See chapter 5.
- **Hôtel d'Arlatan** (Arles, Provence; ☎ **04-90-93-56-66**): At reasonable rates you can stay in one of Provence's most charming cities at the former residence of the comtes d'Arlatan de Beaumont, built in the 15th century on the ruins of an old palace ordered by Constantine. Near the historic place du Forum, this small hotel has been run by the same family since 1920. The rooms are furnished with Provençal antiques, and the antique tapestries are grace notes. The best rooms overlook the garden. See chapter 5.
- **Hôtel Clair Logis** (St-Jean-Cap-Ferrat, Eastern Riviera; ☎ **04-93-76-04-57**): The real estate surrounding this converted 19th-century villa is among Europe's most expensive; nonetheless, this hotel manages to keep its prices beneath levels that really hurt. If you opt for one of the pleasant rooms (each named after a flower that thrives in the 2-acre garden), you'll be among prestigious predecessors: Even General de Gaulle, who knew the value of a *centime* and *sou,* selected it for his retreats. See chapter 7.

13 The Best Luxury Restaurants

- **La Barbacane** (Carcassonne, Languedoc-Roussillon; ☎ 04-68-25-03-34): In this walled medieval city, Christophe Turquier may not be as famous as the Riviera legends, but he's on his way. He has brought to his cuisine (based on seasonal ingredients) a refinement rarely known in this town, where much of the cuisine is based on great-grandmother's recipes. He's daring and imaginative with many dishes, though some of his platters would've pleased Escoffier. Opt for his more experimental food, including green ravioli perfumed with seiche, a species of octopus. See chapter 4.
- **Jardin des Sens** (Montpellier, Languedoc-Roussillon; ☎ 04-67-79-63-38): Twins Laurent and Jacques Pourcel have set off a culinary storm in Montpellier. Michelin has bestowed two stars on them, the same rating it gives to Ducasse at his Monaco citadel. Postnouvelle reigns supreme, and both men know how to take the bounty of Languedoc and turn it into meals sublime in flavor and texture. Though inspired by other chefs, they now feel free to let their imaginations roam. The results are often stunning, like the fricassée of langoustines and lamb sweetbreads. See chapter 4.
- **Christian Étienne** (Avignon, Provence; ☎ 04-90-86-16-50): In a house as old as the nearby papal palace, Étienne reigns as Avignon's culinary star. A chef of imagination and discretion, he has a magical hand with French cuisine, reinterpreting and improving when necessary. He deliberately keeps a short menu so that he can give special care and attention to each dish. His menu is often themed—one might be devoted to the tomato. Save room for his chocolate/pine-nut cake, something of a local legend. See chapter 5.
- **L'Oustau de Beaumanière** (Les Baux, Provence; ☎ 04-90-54-33-07): This Relais & Châteaux occupies an old Provençal farmhouse. Founded in 1945 by the late Raymond Thuilier, the hotel's restaurant was once touted as France's greatest. It may long ago have lost that lofty position, but it continues to tantalize today's palates. Thuilier's heirs carry on admirably as they reinvent and reinterpret some of the great Provençal recipes. At the foot of a cliff, you dine in Renaissance charm, enjoying often flawless meals from the bounty of Provence. See chapter 5.
- **Le Louis XV** (Monte Carlo, Monaco; ☎ 92-16-30-01): Michelin may have lowered Alain Ducasse's rating here from three stars to two, but this regal restaurant is as fine or finer than ever. Perhaps Ducasse got a lower rating because he now divides his time between here and his eponymous three-star restaurant in Paris. Attracting a flashy clientele, the kitchen specializes in the ultimate blending of the flavors of Liguria with the tastes and aromas of Provence and Tuscany. Yes, Ducasse dares grace the local macaroni gratin with truffles. See chapter 7.
- **Chantecler** (Nice, Eastern Riviera; ☎ 04-93-16-64-00): The most prestigious restaurant in Nice, and the most intensely cultivated, Chantecler is currently in the hands of Alain Llorca, who's attracting the area's demanding gourmets and gourmands. You dine in a monument to what the extravagance of the turn-of-the-century could produce, and the menu is attuned to the seasons and to quality ingredients. A true taste of the country is evident in the fresh asparagus, black truffles, sun-dried tomatoes, and beignets of fresh vegetables—all deftly handled by a chef on the rise. See chapter 7.

14 The Best Deals on Dining

- **Brasserie des Beaux-Arts** (Toulouse, Languedoc-Roussillon; ☎ 05-61-21-12-12): This turn-of-the-century brasserie with its authentic art nouveau decor is operated by the country's most successful directors of brasseries, many classified as national historic monuments. The owners don't depend on decor alone. They turn out a savory cuisine that discreetly combines old-time southwestern dishes like cassoulet and magret of duckling with modern and innovative recipes—all at an affordable price with good-value fixed-price menus. See chapter 4.

- **Le Bistro Latin** (Aix-en-Provence, Provence; ☎ 04-42-38-22-38): The economic virtue of this Provençal restaurant lies in its fixed-price menus, whose composition is something of an art form. The prices are low, the flavors are sensational, and hints of Italian zest pop up frequently in such dishes as risotto with scampi. See chapter 5.
- **Bar/Hôtel/Restaurant des Arts** (St-Rémy-de-Provence, Provence; ☎ 04-90-92-08-50): In our favorite town in all of Provence, this place hasn't changed much since Albert Camus used to hang out here, a drink in hand and a cigarette dangling from his mouth. Don't mind the often long wait for dinner—it'll give you a chance to hang out at the bar with the locals. The menu hasn't changed much since Alice and Gertrude passed through, and that's the way the habitués like it. We're talking rabbit terrine, pepper steak with champagne, and tournedos with mushrooms—all that good stuff. See chapter 5.
- **L'Echalotte** (St-Tropez, Western Riviera; ☎ 04-94-54-83-26): A reasonably priced restaurant in St-Tropez sounds like a contradiction, but there are a few. This is the most affordable and charming. Though the dining room is simple, it offers a tiny garden as a grace note. Post-moderne never made it here, for the cuisine is solidly bourgeois—the chefs serve recipes presumably taught them by their mothers. Many of southwestern France's classic dishes appear, like magret of duckling. But the true Côte devotee will opt for fresh fish, especially the delectable sea bass in a salt crust. See chapter 6.
- **Le Monaco** (Cannes, Western Riviera; ☎ 04-93-38-37-76): Restaurant tabs on La Croisette often resemble the annual budget of an Ivory Coast country. But believe it or not, pricey Cannes has working people who have to eat, and they often go to Le Monaco, a blue-collar eatery with great food served bistro style. You eat as the locals do, devouring couscous, roast rabbit with mustard sauce, and even grilled sardines. It's hearty and robust fare and completely affordable. See chapter 6.
- **Le Safari** (Nice, Eastern Riviera; ☎ 04-93-80-18-44): This ever-popular, ever-crowded brasserie overlooking the cours Saleya market soaks up every ray of Riviera sun. Dressed in jeans, waiters hurry back and forth, serving the habitués and visitors alike on the sprawling terrace. This place makes one of the best salade niçoise concoctions in town, as well as a drop-dead spring lamb roasted in a wood-fired oven. See chapter 7.

15 The Best Shopping Bets

- **Caves de l'Hôtel de France** (Auch, Languedoc-Roussillon; ☎ 05-62-61-71-71): Southwestern France is fabled for its Armagnac brandies produced in the foothills of the Pyrénées. Armagnac has been produced here since 1422, making it older than cognac. The best selection of this fire water, representing the output of some 100 distilleries, is found in this off-the-beaten-path shop. See chapter 4.
- **Galerie Sant Vicens** (Perpignan, Languedoc-Roussillon; ☎ 04-68-50-02-18): This region of France is next door to Catalonia, whose capital is Barcelona. Catalan style, as long ago evoked by Antoni Gaudí, is modern and up-to-date here—at affordable prices. Textiles, pottery, and furnishings in forceful geometric patterns are displayed at this showcase. See chapter 4.

- **Véronique Pichon** (Avignon, Provence; ☎ **04-90-85-89-00**): This is the best outlet for a reasonably priced porcelain manufacturer who has been turning out quality wares since the 18th century. Decorative urns, statues, lamps, and tableware—all manufactured in the nearby town of Uzès—are displayed in designs that reveal fine craftsmanship. Shipping can be arranged virtually anywhere. See chapter 5.
- **Les Indiens de Nîmes** (Avignon, Provence; ☎ **04-90-86-32-05**): Provence has long been celebrated for its fabrics, and one of the best, most original, and affordable selections is found here. Open since the early 1980s, this outlet went back into the attic to rediscover old Provençal fabrics and to duplicate them in a wide assortment. The fabric is sold by the meter and can be shaped into everything from clothing to tableware. See chapter 5.
- **Les Olivades Factory Store** (St-Etienne-du-Grès, Provence; ☎ **04-90-49-19-19**): About 7¹/₂ miles north of Arles on the road leading to Tarascon, this store features the region's most fully stocked showroom of art objects and fabrics inspired by the traditions of Provence. You'll find fabrics, dresses, shirts for both men and women, table linen, and fabric by the yard. Part of the Olivades chain, this store has the widest selection and the best prices. See chapter 5.
- **Santons Fouque** (Aix-en-Provence, Provence; ☎ **04-42-26-33-38**): Collectors from all over Europe and North America purchase *santons* (figures of saints) in Provence. You'll find the best ones here, cast in terra-cotta, finished by hand, and decorated with an oil-based paint. The figures are from models made in the 1700s. See chapter 5.
- **Shopping for *Brocante*** (Provence): *Brocante*—items sold in French flea markets—is sold all over Provence, but the little village of Isle-sur-la-Sorgue, 14 miles east of Avignon, has long been known as the best center. The market, selling items not only from Provence but also from all over Europe, takes place on Saturday and Sunday mornings. Few customers come away without a purchase of some sort.
- **Verrerie de Biot** (Biot, Eastern Riviera; ☎ **04-93-65-05-85**): Biot has long been known for its unique pottery, *verre rustique*. Since the 1940s artisan glassmakers here have been creating this bubble-flecked glass in brilliant colors like cobalt and emerald. They're collector's items but sold at affordable prices on home turf. The Verrerie de Biot is the best outlet, though there are dozens of others. If you arrive at this shop on any day except Sunday, you can actually see the glassmakers creating this unique product. See chapter 7.

Introducing the South of France

2

Provence is one of the world's most evocative regions—both the western area, known as Provence, whose landscapes and magical light have seduced innumerable artists, and the eastern coastal area, known as the Riviera, whose beach resorts have seduced innumerable hedonists. Provence and the Riviera are beautiful, diverse, and culturally rich, offering everything from fabulous beaches to amazing art museums to white-hot nightlife to a distinctive cuisine that blends the best of the mountains and the sea.

A land of gnarled olive trees, cypresses, umbrella pines, almond groves, lavender fields, and countless vineyards, the western section of **Provence** is more like Italy, its Mediterranean neighbor, than it is the rest of France. Its curse is the dreaded mistral that blows through the region.

This has long been a land of writers and artists, the latter particularly attracted to the brilliant light. You'll find that one of the major joys of Provence is seeking out the scenery and locations depicted in the canvases of Cézanne and van Gogh. The best place to start is the Montagne Ste-Victoire area east of Aix-en-Provence.

As Provence was once a stronghold of the Roman Empire, it's rich in Roman ruins, and much of its Mediterranean flavor still dates from the Romans. The most impressive ruins are the theater and triumphal arch at Orange, the ruined houses in and around St-Rémy, and the grand arena at Arles.

Though Provence is hardly the region Edith Wharton discovered long ago, it hasn't been irretrievably spoiled. Overpopularity and overbuilding and the summer hordes descending on such cities as Avignon have made the province less desirable in parts, especially if you're driving behind a mile-long line of cars in summer heat. The once-sweet disposition of its citizens is a bit taxed by their endless tourist pressure. But the vast hilly hinterland remains relatively intact, there are still vast pockets of rural area, and, yes, old men still play a leisurely game of boules on a hot afternoon, preferably under shade trees.

Every habitué has a favorite oasis along the **Riviera** and will try to convince you of its merits: Some say "Nice is passé." Others maintain that "Cannes is queen." Others shun both in favor of Juan-les-Pins, and still others would winter only at St-Jean-Cap-Ferrat. If you have a large bankroll you may prefer Cap d'Antibes, but if money is short you can try the old port of Villefranche.

Each resort on the Riviera, known as the Côte d'Azur (Azure Coast)—be it Beaulieu by the sea or eagle's-nest Eze—offers its unique flavor and special merits. Glitterati and eccentrics have always been attracted to this narrow strip of fabled real estate, less than 125 miles long, between the Mediterranean and a trio of mountain ranges.

A trail of modern artists attracted to the Côte d'Azur have left a rich heritage: Matisse in his chapel at Vence, Cocteau at Menton and Villefranche, Picasso at Antibes and seemingly everywhere else, Léger at Biot, Renoir at Cagnes, and Bonnard at Le Cannet. The best collection is at the Maeght Foundation in St-Paul-de-Vence.

The corniches of the Riviera stretch from Nice to Menton. The Alps here drop into the Mediterranean, and roads were carved along the way. The lower road, about 20 miles long, is the Corniche Inférieure. Along this road are the ports of Villefranche, Cap-Ferrat, Beaulieu, and Cap-Martin. Built between World War I and the beginning of World War II, the Moyenne Corniche (Middle Road), 19 miles long, also runs from Nice to Menton, winding spectacularly in and out of tunnels and through mountains. The highlight is at mountaintop Eze. The Grande Corniche—the most panoramic—was ordered built by Napoléon in 1806. La Turbie and Le Vistaero are the principal towns along the 20-mile stretch, which reaches more than 1,600 feet in elevation at Col d'Eze.

Provence and the Côte d'Azur are more fabled, but **Languedoc** is another compelling region sending out its siren call. Much of the landscape, cuisine, lifestyle, and architecture of Languedoc is similar to that of its neighbor, Provence. Since the Middle Ages the dividing line between Provence and Languedoc has been the mighty Rhône. Even today the river marks the political boundaries between the two regions—that of Provence–Côte d'Azur and that of Languedoc-Roussillon. Much of Languedoc is so similar to its neighbor that the city of Nîmes appears to be more Provençal in character, though officially it's in Languedoc.

Languedoc was ruled until the 13th century by the powerful comtes de Toulouse, whose lands swept from the Rhône to the Garonne. Today, the former holdings vastly shrunk, Languedoc-Roussillon consists of only the eastern *(bas)* region along the coast, stretching from Carcassonne to Montpellier, taking in the district of Roussillon, the French version of Catalonia, far more linked to Barcelona than to Paris.

1 History 101: A Few Thousand Years in Provence

THE GREEKS

During the Bronze Age, Provence was inhabited by primitive tribes whose art legacy began around 6000 B.C. in the form of etched pottery (see "Art & Architecture from Paleolithic to Postmodern," later in this chapter). By around 700 B.C. traders from Greek-speaking colonies in Greece and around the Aegean established colonies at Antipolis (Antibes), Nikaia (Nice), and Massilia (Marseille). Mediterranean wines, grains, and ceramics were exchanged, it's believed, for pewter and livestock from west-central France.

The Regions of France

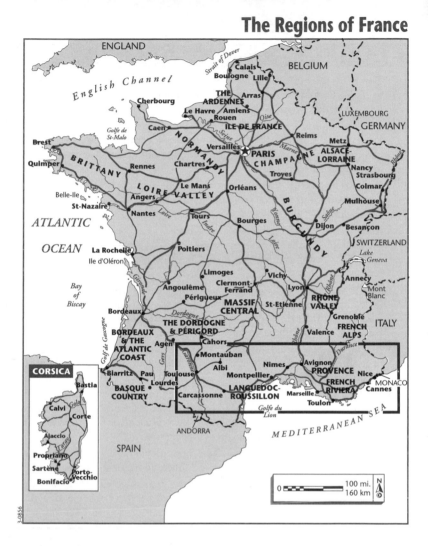

The Greeks even sailed up the Rhône, trading with the Celtic and Ligurian tribes and influencing them with their sophisticated ways. They introduced both the grape and the olive, which would play vital roles in the Provençal economy for millennia to come. The stopping-off point for much of the traffic coming from the Aegean to Provence was Sicily, sections of which at the time were Greek-speaking strongholds known for their vital commerce and culture.

In 600 B.C. Protis, captain of a group of Greek traders, was the guest of honor at a Provençal celebration in honor of Gyptis, daughter of a local tribal leader. Swept away by the charm of her father's guest (and perhaps the pawn in one of the region's many political machinations), she selected Protis as her husband. Her dowry included the harborfront of what is now Marseille, the gateway through which massive amounts of matériel and ancient warriors and weapons later poured.

Around the same time, waves of migration from the Celtic north added to the non-Mediterranean population. The Celts intermarried easily with the native Ligurians and eventually formed a fierce force that opposed the expansionist efforts of the Greeks. In 218 B.C. some of the tribes supported Hannibal during his passage across

❓ Did You Know?

- Two weeks before the Armistice in November 1918, Vita Sackville-West eloped to Monte Carlo with Violet Trefusis. Vita appeared dressed as a soldier named Julian, her hair covered with a khaki bandage.

- The most expensive party in the history of St-Tropez cost $1 million in 1988. Prince Léon de Lignac, a Dutchman, transformed a beach here into the Château of Versailles to celebrate his 70th birthday and his 30 years together with his longtime companion, Hans.

- Crippled by arthritis, Colette spent each spring and summer from 1950 until she died in 1954 at the Hôtel de Paris in Monte Carlo. She called its charm "paperweight."

- In the wake of the 1956 film *And God Created Woman,* starring Brigitte Bardot, the first topless bathers at St-Tropez were arrested. The police didn't know what to do with the women since they'd put Coca-Cola bottle caps over their nipples for modesty.

- The 1956 wedding of Grace Kelly and Prince Rainier III attracted 600 guests, including some reporters disguised as cassocked priests and a few jewel thieves who robbed the princess's mother and a bridesmaid and made off with a Rembrandt and a Rubens (shades of *To Catch a Thief*).

- F. Scott Fitzgerald warned his editor, Maxwell Perkins, not to mention the Riviera in advertising copy for his books: "Its very mention invokes a feeling of unreality and unsubstantiality," he cautioned.

- In 1948, Joseph Kennedy's daughter Kathleen (nicknamed Kick), then Lady Hartington, died with her husband in a chartered plane that was flying off the Riviera. (The marquis of Hartington was a Protestant, and the devout Rose Kennedy had disowned her daughter at the marriage.)

- On her role as duenna of cultural affairs in Monaco, Princess Caroline has proclaimed, "People do not come to live in Monaco for cultural reasons."

- When Onassis invited Churchill in his later years to go aboard his yacht in Monte Carlo, the Greek shipowner had to hand-feed the aging World War II leader caviar.

the Alps and his destructive advance on Rome, an alliance that Rome would severely punish several generations later. As the local forces (Celts and Ligurians and, later, Teutonic tribes from the north) faced off against the Greeks in the south, tensions grew to the point where the Greeks called on the rapidly emerging Roman Empire to subdue the threat to their colonial power. The resulting genocides and annihilations helped define the future racial and cultural makeup of Provence.

THE ROMANS

In 125 B.C., flexing his empire's muscles after its spectacular victories over the Carthaginians, the Roman general Sextius massacred thousands of Celts and Ligurians at Egremont, north of Aix-en-Provence. This action was duplicated less than a quarter century later on an even larger scale when the Roman general Marius massacred as many as 200,000 Teutonic, Celtic, and Ligurian tribespeople during their attempts at southward incursions. Ever after, because of the need for a cultural buffer between

Rome and the savages of Gaul and of the fertility of Provence itself, Rome considered the Mediterranean coastline of what is today known as France as one of its most treasured provinces.

The Romans named their new possession Provincia Transalpina, which was later bastardized into Provence. Gallia Narbonensis (now Narbonne) was the administrative center. By 55 B.C. Julius Caesar had conquered all of Gaul and even invaded Britain, an act that suddenly diminished Provence's importance in the context of the Roman Empire. But despite Roman influence throughout the rest of Europe, few other regions received as concentrated a dose of Romanization. Evidence of this remains in grandiose construction: amphitheaters, bath houses, temples, and stadiums at Arles, Orange, Nîmes, Glanum (near St-Rémy), Fréjus, and Cimiez (near Nice). The pont du Gard—a masterpiece of civil engineering and one of France's most frequently photographed sites—was completed in 19 B.C. Marseille, whose pedigree predated that of virtually every other Roman site in Provence, was bypassed during this explosion of Roman building because of its alliance with the losing side in the civil war between Pompey and Caesar.

Later, as the scope of the empire diminished and its far reaches became frayed and tattered, Provincia Narbonensis remained staunchly Roman. Even after the empire's East-West schism and long after Paris and the Rhône valley became centerpieces for Frankish resistance, Provence remained a beneficiary of trade and attention from whomever happened to rule the empire at the time.

THE EARLY MIDDLE AGES

Such scholars as Gore Vidal have claimed that the conversion of the emperor Constantine to Christianity marked the beginning of the end for Rome. Despite Constantine's obsession with the Middle East (especially Constantinople), he designated Arles his favorite city in the western empire and built a palace there; ironically, faced with the pressures of his position, he rarely visited it. In 400 A.D. the short-lived emperor Honorius launched Arles into a fleeting role as the capital of the Three Gauls—Britain, Spain, and France. Meanwhile, Provence and much of the rest of the empire rushed headlong toward Christianization. You can see some of the earliest evidence of the spread of this inflammatory new religion in Marseille at the oft-repaired Basilique St-Victor.

Arles's preeminence didn't serve it well after the empire's collapse. In 471 it was sacked by the Visigoths, and a few years later it, and many of the other important Provence settlements, were sacked by other barbarians. From 600 to 800 the devastations were duplicated by Saracen (Moorish) navies and occasional Viking raids along the Rhône. Charles Martel himself, one of the patriarchs of modern France, led his Frankish troops through Provence between 736 and 740 on orgies of appalling brutality. In the aftermath of these, local politics wavered between instability and anarchy.

The only exception to this chaos was the brief ascendency of the Merovingians around A.D. 500. But because their strongholds lay in what is now northeastern France, they didn't focus a lot of creative energy on Provence. Later, Charlemagne passed through Provence en route to Rome, where he was crowned Emperor of the West by the Roman pope. After Charlemagne's death, when his empire was split among three feuding grandsons, Provence was bequeathed to Lothair, the eldest. Lothair placed his own son, Charles, on the throne of Provence, designating it as a kingdom in its own right. By 879 Provence was ruled jointly with Burgundy by the medieval ruler Boson, brother-in-law of Charles the Bald.

THE MIDDLE AGES

In 1032, with its capital at Aix-en-Provence, the eastern half of Provence joined the Holy Roman Empire, a loose configuration of duchies and kingdoms unified mainly by fear and loathing of the Moors. The area west of the Rhône came under the control of the comtes de Toulouse. Romanesque architecture, poetry, music, and verse flourished for almost 300 years, a cultural high point that represents the flowering of the troubadour and the beginnings of literature and popular entertainment as we know them today.

By around 1125 most of the power in Provence was controlled by the comtes de Toulouse and the comtes de Barcelona. It even appeared for a time that they (through marriage and treaties against their enemy, the French) might have succeeded at uniting their kingdoms. By 1246, though, control of Provence tipped in favor of the French kings thanks to marriages among the family of St. Louis, the rulers of Barcelona, and the royal residents of Provence. Today the village of Barcelonette derives its medieval name from the influence of those counts.

The Paris-based kings realized Provence's strategic importance as a starting point for conquests of other Mediterranean kingdoms. St. Louis ordered the construction of one of the most remarkable sites in southern France, the fortified town of Aigues-Mortes, as a bulwark against the Moors and other interlopers. In 1248 he, along with a doomed army of soldiers, sailors, and priests, set sail from that city on the Seventh Crusade, only to die en route in Tunis.

In 1307 the French-born pope Clement V caused one of the most bizarre political imbroglios in European history. Fearful of the instability in Rome, he decided to move the official seat of the papacy to Avignon. Surrounded by an army of courtiers, priests, soldiers, and purveyors of luxury goods, the papacy remained for 70 years under the protection of the kings of France and the comtes de Provence. Avignon thus became a vibrant and prosperous city. The papacy was eventually moved back to Rome after violent politicking and even armed conflicts between the factions.

Plagues decimated the population of Provence beginning in 1348, with even more severe outbreaks in 1375. At the same time, extortion, plundering, and highway robbery by small-time feudal despots, including the rulers of the much-dreaded Les Baux, added to a general sense of confusion, unrest, and despair.

In 1409 the University of Aix was founded as southern France's answer to the thriving Sorbonne in Paris. In 1434 René d'Anjou was designated count of an independent Provence, and he fostered economic development and the arts. Shortly after René's death, his nephew and heir signed a pact with Paris-based Louis XI, who immediately used it to annex Provence into the orbit of the French monarchs.

THE WARS OF RELIGION

Provence has always been fertile ground for offshoot religions. The Cathar heresy, whose strongholds had thrived in Languedoc but whose adherents also lived in Provence, was a threat to the French monarchs and thus violently obliterated. The rallying cry for French forces during their slaughter of the Cathars, "Kill them all, and God will decide who is guilty," lives in infamy even today.

In the 1500s the Reformation changed Europe forever. Influenced by the thriving community of Protestants under John Calvin whose stronghold lay in Geneva, Huguenots (Protestants) in Provence grew in number and power. One of the most extreme of these sects was the Vaudois. Founded in the 1200s by a wealthy merchant, Valdès or Vaudès, from Lyon, the sect rejected the idea of an ecclesiastical hierarchy, preached the virtues of poverty, and denied the authenticity of the sacraments. This was greeted with horror by the church. When in 1545 the Vaudois responded to their persecutors by attacking several Catholic churches near their stronghold in the Luberon hills, the armies of François I massacred more than 3,000 of them over a 4-day period and sent 600 into the French navy as slaves.

However, Protestantism continued to flourish in Orange, Uzès, and especially Nîmes. For 40 years beginning in 1560, religious battles occurred regularly. Chief of State Richelieu, whose obsession was the unification of all aspects of French society into a form approved by Paris, eventually suppressed or destroyed Huguenot communities throughout France. The bloodiest of these skirmishes was in the Atlantic coast port of La Rochelle, but also affected were the Provençal strongholds at Uzès and Les Baux.

In 1720 a devastating plague was imported through the harbor of Marseille, killing what is conservatively estimated at 100,000 people. Despite that and similar setbacks, Provence had become one of France's wealthier regions. An aesthetic had developed that was distinct to the region and is today emulated by decorators around the world, as noted in the majestic town houses and *mas* (country estates) prized by real-estate investors.

Some scholars argue that the revolutionary fervor that swept over France in 1789 was greatly influenced by popular philosophers in Provence. One of the most articulate (and inflammatory) members of Paris's Etats-Généraux (the radical committee that helped inaugurate the Revolution) was the comte de Mirabeau, elected by Aix-en-Provence. In 1790 the Revolutionary government divided France and Provence into a labyrinth of political districts (*départements*) that shattered the country's medieval boundaries and political networks. In the process, the once-autonomous region of Provence was carved into three, and later five, subdivisions.

In 1792 a corps of volunteers from Marseille marched through the streets of Paris, heading toward the Tuileries, singing a call to arms written by Rouget de Lisle. Its original name was "L'Hymn de Bataille de l'Armée du Rhin" ("Battle Hymn of the Army of the Rhine"), but that was later changed to "La Marseillaise." In 1793 the emerging career of the Corsican general Napoléon Bonaparte received an enormous boost after he masterminded a victory at the siege of Toulon.

THE 19TH CENTURY

Partly because of its strategic dominance of more than half of France's Mediterranean ports, Provence gained enormous prosperity during the 19th century. In 1815 Napoléon used a minor seaport near Cannes, Golfe-Juan, as the site of his return to France after his exile on Elba. The enthusiasm his armies received in Provence set a precedent for welcomes in non-Provençal towns along the route of his march to Paris. (The route he followed—now Route N85 through Dignes and Sisteron—has been known ever since as "La Route Napoléon.") He managed a short-lived return to power but was soon defeated by Wellington at Waterloo.

In 1854, fearing the demise of the Provençal language and culture, a group of cultural luminaries founded Félibrige, an organization devoted to the dessemination of Provence's medieval literary forms. Five years later the artistic patriarch Frédéric Mistral published his Provençal poem *Mirèio*, which was met with widespread approval.

In 1864 a railway line linked Provence with the rest of France, encouraging increased travel. The 1869 opening of the Suez Canal and the expansion of French influence into Morocco, Algeria, Tunisia, and Egypt thrust Provence's ports into international prominence and helped develop Marseille into one of the greatest seaports in the world.

The development of Nice and the Riviera into international resorts was largely a result of the unemployment caused by the phylloxera epidemic in Provençal vineyards and the collapse of the silkworm industry. Tourism was a logical answer to the economic deprivations of pestilence and economic dislocations. In 1822 the expatriate British colony in Nice helped finance their namesake promenade. In 1830 Lord Brougham bought an estate in Cannes and promoted it to the aristocracy as a suitably hedonistic place to escape from the fog, the cold, and the Victorian repressions of England. In 1860 the region around Nice, whose administration by the House of Savoy represented an anachronistic holdover from the feudal age, was fully integrated into France. Then, a few years later, the ruler of one of western Europe's least prosperous territories, Monaco, built the most opulent casino in the world. Thanks to the patronage granted to the site by the haut monde, profits came pouring in.

THE WORLD WARS & THE POSTWAR YEARS

Fortunately for Provence, most of the bloodshed and destruction of World War I occurred in other areas of France, particularly the northeast and east. During World War II, Provence and Languedoc were part of the territory controlled by the collaborationist Vichy government. In 1940, after Nazi-dominated North Africa fell to the Allied forces, the Nazis retracted their pledge not to occupy the zones controlled by Vichy and moved into Provence with heavy artillery. Two years later, when the Nazis moved to confiscate the French navy's warships, French saboteurs sank most of the Mediterranean fleet in the harbor at Toulon. Many martyrs were created by these conflicts, most notably Jean Moulin.

On August 15, 1944, Allied forces landed on the Provençal coast between St-Raphaël and St-Tropez as part of a successful attempt to regain control of Europe from Nazi domination. All of Provence was liberated in 14 days, with some of the most dramatic liberation scenes occurring in Marseille.

Few other regions of the world have zoomed into the international consciousness the way Provence has since 1945. In 1947 Cannes initiated its role as Europe's film capital with its first film festival, which has since grown to almost mythic proportions. Beginning around 1950, both farming and industry were modernized to keep pace with the rest of Europe. Tourism, which had been a recurrent theme since the 19th-century days of the English expats in Nice, took a giant leap forward. Celebrity watching seemed to go hand-in-hand with voyeurism and exhibitionism, as the Riviera's topless beaches caused a stir as far away as Chicago and as stars like Brigitte Bardot elevated St-Tropez to its role as sybaritic capital of the most sybaritic country.

In 1953 the Socialist Gaston Defferre, a pivotal figure in the region's politics, was elected mayor of Marseille, a post he held for 33 years. His ardent appeals for the semiautonomy of Provence finally came to fruition in 1981, 2 years before his death, with the approval, under Mitterrand, of a limited form of self-government. To Defferre's chagrin, this culmination of his life's work helped usher in right-wing opponents to a political landscape that had long been dominated by leftist politics.

In 1962 the collapse of the French government in Algeria led to a flood of newly impoverished, newly homeless French citizens who arrived by the thousands in Provence. Mainlanders called them *pieds-noirs* (blackfeet). Many opted to relocate here, where their noteworthy business acumen helped revitalize the local economy.

Transit among Provence, Paris, and the rest of world was greatly facilitated in 1970 with the opening of the A6/A7 high-speed autoroute between the French capital and Marseille. Between 1970 and 1977, the year the Marseille subway opened, two major national parks (Parc Naturel Régional de la Camargue and Parc Naturel Régional de Lubéron) were created for the preservation of Provence's native ecology. And in 1981 the high-speed Train à Grande Vitesse (TGV) was launched between Paris and

Marseille, with other branches opening in following years. Transit time by train between Paris and Cannes was reduced to less than 4 hours.

Around 1985 Provence emerged as the national stronghold for anti-immigrant sentiments, perhaps in reaction to its thousands of non-French newcomers, legal and illegal. Voters supported Jean-Marie Le Pen's anti-immigration platform, Le Front National, or FN, giving a wider approval (23% of the popular vote in the 1992 elections) than they had to the region's traditional vote-getter, the Socialist party. Since then, Provence's regional assembly, though dominated by the center-right, has been forced to rely on FN support to avoid being overwhelmed by other voting blocs, like the potent alliances from the Socialist, Communist, and "green" party representatives.

Late in 1995 the creation of a Euro-Mediterranean free-trade zone by the year 2010 was announced in Barcelona. A vast financial aid program, which will be funded by the European Union by loans, was also announced. This huge amount, a projected $14 billion, bodes well for Marseille and other ports of Provence just when it seemed that decay was inevitable. This massive development should have enormous impact, allowing the region to tap into a market of some 360 million consumers. Marseille by 1997 already stood as the largest port on the Mediterranean, with nearly 90 million tons handled annually.

2 Art & Architecture from Paleolithic to Postmodern

ANCIENT ORIGINS

The sense of timelessness that permeates Provençal architecture has ancient origins. Though Paleolithic remains and artifacts have been found in Provence, there's a lot less prehistoric art here than in such neighboring sites as Lascaux in the Dordogne. Despite that, excavations like Terra Amata, above the old port in Nice, have unearthed remants of circular huts *(bories)*, each with a central fire pit, that were adjacent to what was at the time a freshwater spring. Tombs from the late Paleolithic age have unearthed skeletons covered in sea shells strung together into necklaces.

Around 6000 B.C. sheep and other livestock began to be domesticated, and bories were erected from flat stones laid on top of one another without mortar. None of these bories survives, though many sociologists believe that the later development of the rural farmhouse *(mas)* in Provence was based on them. Dating from around the same time are a series of dolmens (mysterious standing stones) and scattered rock carvings—poised on their ends and raised into vertical positions, for reasons that no one really understands.

For about 400 years beginning in the 4th century B.C., Celtic tribes migrated into Provence, bringing a skill for carving rock with iron tools. Their greatest legacy is a network of fortified *oppidi* (fortresses on hilltops). (The best remaining example is Oppidum de Nages, at Nages-et-Solorgues, 6 miles southeast of Nîmes. Another example is the Plateau d'Entrement, 1^1/2 miles from the center of Aix-en-Provence.) The trading links that mariners from the Greek-speaking eastern Mediterranean developed around 600 B.C. was with this new breed of Celts, who had by that time intermarried with the local Ligurians. The ports established by the Greeks (Antibes, St-Tropez, La Ciotat, Nice, and Hyères) soon adopted many of the aesthetics of the Greek world, though on a relatively small scale. Very little of the Greek era survives in Provence today.

Because of Provence's status as a buffer zone between Italy and savage Gaul, the Romans lavished it with a comprehensive assortment of public buildings. Examples are the arenas at Nîmes and Arles; aqueducts, such as pont du Gard, that are some of the finest examples of civil engineering in the ancient world; and the triumphal arches at St-Rémy-de-Provence, La Turbie (La Trophée des Alpes), and Orange. You can still see remains of ruined villas at Vaison-la-Romaine. Maison Carré in Nîmes is the most oft-copied monument, after the Parthenon in Athens and the Pantheon in Rome. The Romans passed on their knowledge of the arch, the barrel vault (a masonry technique in which individual stones were so carefully cut that mortar was unnecessary), and a primitive form of concrete. Since Provence, because of its proximity to Rome, was Christianized before virtually any of the other regions of Gaul, it's honored with one of the oldest Christian basilicas in France, the Basilique St-Victor in Marseille. Inaugurated in the 400s and enlarged and modified many times since, it's unique in France for its associations with the early Christian church.

After Rome's collapse, when Provence was torn among a rapidly changing parade of feudal anarchies in the Dark Ages, very little of enduring value was built, with the exception of a handful of octagonal baptisteries. Combining aspects of classical Roman design with Frankish motifs from northeastern France, they still exist in Fréjus, Aix-en-Provence, and the hamlet of Venasque. Other than these, few buildings of any kind remain in Provence from the 300-year Merovingian dynasty.

PROVENÇAL ROMANESQUE & GOTHIC

Beginning around 1100, a revitalized interest in building, usually by monks, began to enrich Provence. Consistent with the explosion of Romanesque architecture in Italy, church floor plans were usually laid out in a cross shape, with soaring pillars and barrel vaulting, small severe-looking windows, and facades (especially western-facing facades) that were allegorically sculpted with scenes of redemption, salvation, punishment for sins, or other religious themes. The best examples of Provençal Romanesque are Aix's Cathédrale St-Sauveur (interior), Arles's Eglise St-Trophime, and St-Rémy's and Montmajour's village churches.

As Provence was pulled more tightly into France's orbit, it began to depend more on artistic and architectural inspiration from areas like Normandy, especially this region's Gothic style. The Gothic's larger windows and more elaborate decoration derived from a more sophisticated use of pointed arches, ribbed vaulting, and (as a means of counterbalancing the outward thrust of heavy roofs that rested on sometimes alarmingly delicate pillars) flying buttresses. The sense of verticality that resulted contrasted directly with the more horizontal and rounded lines of Romanesque architecture. You can best see Provençal Gothic in the newer part of Avignon's Palais des Papes, St-Maximin's basilica, Béziers's cathedral, and Fréjus's cloisters. The best examples of Flamboyant Gothic, the final, most ornate, and most decadent phase of the movement, are the Eglise St-Siffrein in the village of Carpentras and the facade of the Cathédrale St-Sauveur in Aix.

THE ART OF FORTIFICATION

The most memorable aspect of Provence's architecture is its fortified towns and villages. Testimonials to their residents' determination to survive repeated sieges, they're perched atop jagged hills or cliffs, meticulously crafted from chiseled blocks of stone and punctuated with crenellated battlements and/or a moat. Many have openings through which boiling oil or molten lead could be poured on attackers. The designs of many, like Les Baux, Sisteron, and Tarascon, emerged spontaneously, after decades of brutish labor. A handful of others, like the rigidly symmetrical quadrangle of Aigues-Mortes, were commissioned and elaborately designed before the first stone was laid. Carcassonne is less rigidly symmetrical but more impregnable.

So great was the fear of attack from assorted enemies that many Provençal churches incorporated fortifications into their designs. In the event of attack, the church could provide physical as well as spiritual shelter, which early medieval prelates used as a means of eliciting cheap or free labor from the faithful who built them. Examples are the village church in Les Stes-Maries and the redbrick Cathédrale Ste-Cécile in Albi.

The development of large-scale cannons in the 1400s made many of the above-mentioned fortifications obsolete, but by that time defensive warfare had evolved so drastically that the fortress-style churches and towns were left intact. Not only did they serve a useful function, but also they evoked the obsessions of earlier centuries.

THE RENAISSANCE & THE RISE OF SECULAR ART

In terms of painting and architecture, the Renaissance had more of an effect in Italy than in Provence, though it left two distinct legacies in Nice and Avignon. In Nice, beginning in the late 1400s, a school of design spearheaded by Louis Bréa produced a wide assortment of painted altarpieces. They proliferate around Nice, most notably in the village church at Lucéram.

An equivalent school flourished in Avignon, a result of the need to adorn the network of churches built during the "Babylonian exile" of the papacy. The leading artist was Enguerrand Charenton, also known as Quarton. Completed in Avignon and later moved to Villeneuve, his *Coronation of the Virgin* is the era's best-known painting. A worthy colleague was Nicolas Froment, appointed painter to the court of King René. His most famous work is *The Burning Bush,* which adorns the interior of Aix's Cathédrale St-Sauveur. Charenton and Froment were the founders of the Avignon school of painting, which survived until the 1800s. Members of the school during the 1600s included Nicolas Mignard and members of the Parrocel family, whose works you can see in museums and churches throughout Provence.

Beginning around 1650, artists began to abandon a reliance on purely religious subjects, opting for themes from antiquity or everyday secular life. The works of Pierre Puget (1620–94), a native-born Marseillais and Provence's greatest sculptor, evoke the exalted drama of Bernini. The best places to see his works are Paris, Toulon, and Marseille. The Dutch-born Van Loos painted from bases in Aix and Nice during the 17th century, with some of their best works displayed in Nice's Musée Cheret. Though he more or less abandoned Provence at an early age for more sophisticated climes near the court in Paris, Jean-Honoré Fragonard (1732–1806) was born in Grasse. Few other artists captured the frivolity of life during the *ancien régime* as effectively. Regrettably, few of his works are exhibited in Provence.

Neoclassicism made much more of an impact in Italy, but you can see 17th- and 18th-century examples of the style's appeal in the many private mansions in Montpellier, Aix-en-Provence, and Avignon.

INDUSTRIALIZATION & IMPRESSIONISM

During the 1800s Europe's increasing industrialization produced increased wealth, frequently displayed in the form of architectural showcases. Public buildings and private villas, commissioned by the wintering rich, were erected in styles that ranged from classical revival to mock-feudal to neo-Byzantine. Provençal examples of the latter are Marseille's Cathédrale de la Major and Basilique Notre-Dame de la Garde. The casino and the Hôtel de Paris in Monte Carlo were lavished with gilded stucco and ornamentation equivalent to that used for some of Paris's most extravagant monuments. Charles Garnier, the quintessential designer of the belle époque, designed some aspects of the building boom in Monte Carlo. A few years later the Hôtel Négresco in Nice captured the essence of the Gilded Age with elaborate beaux arts ornamentation. Around 1910 the lavish construction boom continued in the form of the Hôtel Carlton at Cannes.

At the same time a core of devoted painters and aesthetes influenced the way the world interpreted light and color. Under the streaming sunlight of Provence, they evolved their theories of luminosity and color. Paul Cézanne (1839–1906) was born in Aix and spent large parts of his career depicting the area's terra-cotta roofs and verdant cypresses. One of his repeated subjects was Mont-St-Victoire. Vincent van Gogh (1853–90) lived in Arles for many years, depicting the starry heavens and fiercely vibrant landscapes before spending his final years in a mental hospital near St-Rémy. Ironically, very little work of Cézanne or van Gogh is exhibited in Provence's museums. By around 1900, Paul Signac (1863–1935), a neo-impressionist, retreated to St-Tropez and established a mania for "Le Trop" that has existed ever since, attracting both Matisse and Bonnard for "paint fests."

Auguste Renoir (1841–1919) spent his final years near Cagnes-sur-Mer, painting and sculpting despite bouts of agonizing arthritis. Henri Matisse (1869–1954) lived at Cimiez, near Nice, and at Vence beginning in 1917, remaining there until his death. Pablo Picasso (1881–1973) came to Antibes in 1945 and spent two of the most prolific and pivotal years of his career. Later he was instrumental in reviving the pottery traditions of Vallauris, whose output of ceramics is among France's most prolific. Marc Chagall (1887–1985), master of the dreamlike power of artistic free association, moved to the Riviera and created his world-acclaimed *Biblical Message,* now displayed in his namesake museum in Nice. Others to flock here were Dufy, Braque, Vlaminck, Léger (who has a namesake museum in Biot), and Vaserély (whose works are exhibited in Gordes and Aix). Even Jean Cocteau (1889–1963), known for frivolity in his earlier years, reached a more intense level of spirituality during his final years in Provence, as proven by his frescoes in Villefranche's Chapelle St-Pierre.

THE PROVENÇAL *MAS*

No review of Provençal art and architecture would be complete without mention of the region's utilitarian rural architecture. Farmhouses *(mas)* built as late as 1910 were directly influenced by the Middle Ages and their obsession with fortification and a sensitivity to the local climate. Thick masonry walls, undersize windows, and solid stocky doors were crafted from local lumber, clay, mud, soil, and stone. North-facing walls were often designed with curved sides and without windows as a means of deflecting the harsh mistral, and roofs were pitched at low angles to reduce the possibility of tiles breaking loose and sliding off. Hinged shutters could be opened or closed as protection against heat, wind, and sun; chimneys were deliberately low and squat, never rising high enough to risk being demolished during windstorms. Evergreen cypresses were usually planted as windbreaks on a farmhouse's north side, and deciduous broad-leaved trees like sycamores provided midsummer shade to the south but let in the warming sunshine in winter. The construction techniques for walls, made of coarsely chiseled stone and often sheathed with stucco or plaster, was roughly equivalent to what had been developed 2,000 years before by the Romans. Virtually every farmhouse and outbuilding in Provence was capped with rounded terra-cotta roof tiles *(tuiles romaines)* that derived both their name and their inspiration from materials used during the Roman conquest.

Though many of Provence's *mas* were ignored or even scorned by aristocratic 19th-century newcomers, the primal appeal of their age-old stonework has since entered the mainstream consciousness of Europe's real-estate investors. Today the boxy-looking old farmhouses, along with the olives, vines, and cypresses that traditionally surround them, are prized and fetch awesome sums, especially when they're sited in ways that afford at least some privacy. Of the thousands of technically sophisticated buildings erected in Provence since the end of World War II, an enormous percentage were designed along lines inspired by the timeless allure of the Provençal *mas*.

THE POSTWAR BOOM

Since World War II a building boom has transformed many of the suburbs of such cities as Aix-en-Provence, Avignon, and Arles into urbanized landscapes with their attendant banality. Traffic congestion, especially noticeable during July and August, has diminished much of the charm of roadside neighborhoods. As the need for holiday villas and housing for service personnel has risen, vast blocks of apartment houses—some stylish, some ordinary—have been erected. Many have at least tried to emulate the age-old Provençal farmhouse design. A handful, however, including Le Corbusier's 1952 design for a massive apartment block in Marseille (L'Unité d'Habitation) and J. L. Sert's design for the Fondation Maeght at St-Paul-de-Vence, are cited for their intelligent application of age-old styles in bold new ways.

3 The Rise & Fall of Provençal

Part of the identity of Provence derives from a language that, though deliberately suppressed by the French monarchs and now in great decline, used to thrive as an evocative tongue in its own right. Though only a handful of Provençaux, most of them professional scholars, are familiar with the language today, you'll hear hints of the old ways in modern speech patterns throughout the south. Only in the "Deep South" is *maintenant* pronounced "mangtenang," *demain* "demang," and *vin* "vang," and the speed with which you'll hear these sounds makes everyday communication more difficult than you might have expected.

THE LATIN INFLUENCE

During the Roman occupation of what is now France, the Celtic, Ligurian, and Teutonic dialects were gradually replaced by the more specific, and more universally understood, Latin. This was not the erudite, cadenced form of Latin as perfected by classical writers like Virgil, but the "vulgar Latin" used by soldiers, administrators, and colonists who had moved north from Italy. But as was inevitable in a landmass as huge as the Roman Empire, vulgar Latin was gradually transformed into the wide roster of tongues that now dominate many of the former Roman strongholds. Known today as Romance languages, they include Romanian, Catalán, all the dialects of Italian, Portuguese, Spanish, and two distinctly different languages that soon developed in what is now France.

In the north of France, where greater influences remained from the Frankish and Teutonic tribes, the dialect that developed was the *langue d'oïl*. In the south, where the influence of the ancient Romans was more deeply entrenched, the name of the dialect that developed was the *langue d'oc*, which is also identified as either Occitanian or Provençal. Today France's Mediterranean coastline west of the Rhône (Languedoc) derives its name from the early medieval language that developed here. Both *oïl* and *oc*, used in the north and south, respectively, were the words for what later developed into the modern French *oui*, or "yes."

After the Roman Empire tottered and collapsed, southern France was fragmented into chaotic, semiautonomous fiefdoms, each of which survived thanks to the confusing set of heirarchies and conflicting loyalties known as feudalism. By around A.D. 700 the differences between the dialects of north and south were in full bloom and eventually evolved into separate languages.

By around 1000 it was in the more sophisticated south, a wide belt that stretched from Bordeaux along the Atlantic coast to Nice, close to the modern-day Italian border, that literature and poetry were much better developed than in the less lyrical north. Why? Some historians theorize that it was a result of southern France's, and especially Provence's, early exposure to the civilizing aspects of the ancient Greeks and Romans, a process that began 600 years before the "taming" of northern Gaul.

TROUBADOURS & THE ORAL TRADITION

Feudal power was concentrated in a network of fortified castles, where life was tenuous and anxiety-ridden. Banquets were the main form of amusement, and every banquet needed some kind of entertainment. Troubadours (named after the Provençal verb *trobar,* "to seek and find") filled the need for amusing popular entertainment. The best composed their own sonnets and poems; others drew on a repertoire that grew rapidly into an impressive literary inventory. Accompanying themselves with music from a harp, nomadic minstrels did more to unify popular tastes and perceptions within southern France than any other force except the Catholic church. Members of a linguistic community all their own, they migrated freely across political frontiers between northern Italy and the Pyrénées, entertaining exclusively in the *langue d'oc* and performing at court affairs en route. In some cases they collected valuable strategic information for one or more patrons, sometimes selling the information to whomever paid the highest price. Often they became entangled in romantic imbroglios and had to flee for their lives. Despite these complications, troubadours embodied the courtly aspects of chivalry and, in occasional cases, were of noble birth themselves. Their poems, delivered in melodic patterns whose nuances can only be imagined today, were divided into stanzas, often with sophisticated rhythms and rhyming. Famous names from the era include Peire Vidal de Toulouse, Bertran de Born, Joffroy Rudel, Raimbaut d'Orange, Raimbaut de Vaqueiras, Folquet de Marseille, Jaufré de Blaise, and Bernard de Ventadour. A limited number of poems even survive from a female poet, the comtesse de Die.

Recurrent themes involved the medieval interpretation of courtly love, wherein the ardor of a knight or minstrel for a lady would eventually win over her reservations. This artistic reinforcement of the heirarchical systems of court life continued to develop in France until they culminated in the late 1700s at Versailles with some of the most elaborate court rituals in the history of Europe.

PROVENÇAL'S PEAK

Changing tastes and religious persecution of divergent forms of Provençal religion—most obviously the genocidal crusade to stamp out the Albigensian heresy—led to the decline of the troubadour tradition around 1280. Despite that, there were strong incentives for the continued use of Provençal as the language of choice. Other than Latin, it was the only written administrative language in Europe. It was the everyday tongue of the papal court at Avignon during the 70 years of the Catholic church's "Babylonian exile," and it's believed that Dante (1265–1321) came very close to selecting it as the language for his *Divine Comedy.* Later Petrarch (1304–74) occasionally deviated from his use of Latin and Italian to compose sonnets in Provençal. Based on his experiences in exile in Avignon, his *Canzonière* was composed in Provençal after the death of his beloved, Laura de Noves, in 1348.

By around 1300 strongly defined subdivisions of the *langue d'oc* had developed as separate dialects, some of them appearing in written form, across the face of southern France. Examples included the Nissard dialect of Nice, the Dauphinoise dialect of the French Alps, the Rhodanien Provençal of the Rhône valley, the Languedocien dialect of the region around Toulouse, the Gascon dialect used around Bordeaux, the Auvergnat used around Clermont-Ferrand, and the North Occitanian dialect, used around Limoges, that mingled aspects of the *langue d'oc* with the northerly *langue d'oïl*. Even today, despite the homogenization of modern-day French, occasional words from these medieval dialects still appear in popular slang and even names of some food items.

ONE GOVERNMENT, ONE LANGUAGE

As the power of the monarchs to an increasing degree became centered in Paris and the Loire Valley, the *langue d'oïl* (the precursor of modern standardized French) began to replace the widespread use of *langue d'oc*.

The beginning of the end for Provençal and the other dialects of France came in 1539 through a Parisian edict, Villers Cotterêts, that has been interpreted ever since as one of the most visible proofs in history of Paris's cultural imperialism. Impressed with the difficulty of governing a linguistically fragmented nation, it decreed that the official administrative language of France would be the language as it was used in Paris and the Ile de France. Thanks to this and the later efforts of a chauvinistic corps of government-sanctioned academics, the Académie Française, France emerged as one of the most linguistically consistent countries in the world.

Despite these setbacks, *langue d'oc,* which to an increasing degree was identified as Provençal because of its strongholds in that region, continued to be respected and admired. A soldier-poet who helped revive literary interest in the tongue was Bellaud de la Bellaudière, born in 1534 in Grasse. An ardent opponent of Protestantism, he composed 160 personalized and subjective sonnets, *Oeuvres et Rimes,* while in prison. Writers who emulated his style around the same time included Raynier de Briançon, François de Bègue, and Claude Bruey.

In the 1600s Nicolas Saboly composed a roster of simple poems called *Noëls* in Provençal. In 1661 Racine complained that during a trip through the south of France, no one in Uzès understood him, as the entire town spoke only Provençal. Mme de Sévigné, the quintessential arbiter of 18th-century French taste and gossip, was surrounded by a mostly Provençal-speaking staff during her sojourns in Grignan. Even the Catholic church, noteworthy for clinging to Latin longer than any other entity in history, often conducted masses and church services throughout Provence and parts of the Midi in Provençal up until the end of the 19th century.

The Revolution, whose thousands of edicts were invariably composed in standardized French, contributed to a whittling away of the Provençal language. Later the military campaigns of Napoléon and the conscriptions of the Franco-Prussian War and World World I drew many men of the Midi into military life where administrative communications were conducted in mainstream French. In modern times the centralized French state and the intrusion of radio and television into even the most isolated of communities has all but obliterated the use of Provençal.

PROVENÇAL REVIVAL

Provençal experienced the first in a series of modern-age revivals in 1795 after the publication of Abbot Favre's satirical poem *Siège de Caderousse,* critiqued by some scholars as derivative of Rabelais. In 1847, concurrent with a rebirth of interest in the national origins and culture of subcultures across Europe, Joseph Roumanille (1818–91) published *Lie Margarideto,* an epic poem in Provençal. Although it wasn't widely distributed outside his hometown of Avignon, it inspired the linguistic nationalism of Provençal's greatest modern-day patriarch, Frédéric Mistral (1830–1914), who began composition of the 12 cantos of his Provençal epic *Miréio* in 1851. In

1854 Mistral, along with half a dozen other Provençal writers, founded Le Félibrige, a group of cultural nationalists whose goal involved the restoration of the Provençal language and the codification of its grammar and spelling.

In 1859 *Miréio* was published to wild acclaim by such critics as Lamartine and the composer Charles Gounod, who shortly thereafter reconfigured it into an opera. Between 1878 and 1886 Mistral painstakingly compiled the world's first Provençal dictionary, *Lou Trésor du Félibrige,* and welcomed an impressive roster of important French writers, including Rostand, Zola, Daudet, and Alcard, into membership in the increasingly prestigious Félibrige. In 1904 he was awarded the Nobel Prize for literature for at least a half-dozen major works, all written in Provençal.

Professional academics appreciate the resonancy and lyricism of medieval Provençal sonnets and the idealistic blend of cultural nationalism and literary skill shown by the 19th-century revivalists. Ironically, despite the increasing favor it has enjoyed as an intriguing yet abstract intellectual pursuit, Provençal has all but disappeared as a spoken language.

Meanwhile, the sense of regional identity in Provence is strong. Directions throughout the south of France are being signposted both in mainstream French and their Provençal counterparts, and the ancient language is now included as an elective in the curricula of some schools. But faced with the appeal and sheer practicality of English as a viable second language within France, it's doubtful that the intensely esoteric Provençal language will ever be revived, other than as an intellectual oddity, outside scholastic circles.

4   A Taste of Provence

LA CUISINE DU SOLEIL

Pungent and earthy, Provençal cuisine is generally high in vitamins and fiber and low in saturated fat. The flavors of southern France incorporate the liberal use of olive oil; herbs like basil, garlic, rosemary, and sage; and a sophisticated blend of products from the mountain areas, such as lamb from the Alpilles, and the bounty of the Mediterranean. This is *la cuisine du soleil,* infused with warmth and sunshine, based on a wealth of produce and raw ingredients that spring from soil whose richness is belied by its parched, often stony surface.

THE BOUNTY OF PROVENCE

As much of the allure of Provençal cuisine derives from its raw ingredients, menus are likely to state the source of what you're about to consume. To see this wealth firsthand, head for any of the open-air markets where vast amounts of meat, cheese, produce, wine, and herbs with evocative names like purple hyssop and *sarriette* (summer savory) are sold from simple kiosks.

FRUITS & VEGETABLES   Strawberries from the village of Carpentras or the district of Bouches-du-Rhône have a special cachet. Melons, especially ogen melons, from the town of Cavaillon were so famous that in 1864 civic leaders opted to present a dozen perfect melons each year to the French novelist Alexandre Dumas *père* as a sign of their ongoing respect. He later wrote that he hoped that the readers of Cavaillon would always find his books as charming as he found their melons. Apricots are delicious anywhere, but if they're from the slopes of the Roussillon, your menu will usually let you know. *Mousserons,* one of many varieties of wild mushrooms you'll see in local markets, evoke frissons among gastronomes when they're from the Ardèche, west of the Rhône. Lots of species of onions are for sale; one of the most intriguing is the banana-shaped *échalotes-bananes.*

OLIVES   Along with bread and wine, olives were practically the staff of life for many centuries in Provence. Look for varieties like *olives cassées* from Les Baux and fennel-flavored *picholines du Gard*. Any resident of Nice might rebel at the idea of making a *salade niçoise* with anything other than nut-brown *olives de Nyons*.

CHEESE   Sophisticated gastronomes consider a well-selected cheese tray to be one of the symbols of civilization, and in the south of France you could spend hours choosing among the varieties of *chèvre* alone. A Provençal folk saying likens goats to "the poor man's cow," but over the centuries, goat-milk cheese has attained gourmet status. Merchants who deal in the creamy delicacies are proud of the variety and will provide details about any cheese's origin. Looking for something esoteric? Ask for a rare *tomme de Camargue*, a firm but creamy cheese that combines milk from both goats and sheep and whose dislike surface is embedded with sprigs of rosemary. There's also *Banon vrai*, a goat-milk cheese made in the hamlet of Banon in northern Provence. During its fermentation, it's marinated in *eaux de vie*, aged in clay pots on dried chestnut leaves, and wrapped with raffia string. Equally delicious is *lou pevre*, a goat cheese whose pungency is enhanced by a black-pepper coating.

BREAD   Almost as varied as the cheeses are the shapes and ingredients of the bread. You can buy it as long and thin *ficelles*, marvelously crusty, and as *gibassiers*, baked with a dollop of olive oil for flavor. These aren't to be confused with *pain d'olives*, with the flesh of the olive in the dough; *pain de raisins*, flavored with dried raisins; *pain à l'anis*, aniseed bread; and earthy *pain au levain*, sourdough bread. In Aix you'll find a regional recipe for *pain d'Aix*, a double-mounded staple that resembles women's breasts. The most democratic of Provençal breads is *pain d'égalité*, developed in response to an edict during the Revolution declaring that only one kind of bread, composed of one part rye flour and three parts wheat, could be consumed in an egalitarian society. Today this is scorned as something akin to generic supermarket bread, but it's still occasionally available in Provençal markets. Beware of Provençal witches, who, according to legend, will come to dance on any loaf of bread that's turned upside down.

PASTRIES & SWEETS   As far as pastries go, southern France is expert at turning out *calissons*, rectangular sweets concocted from almond paste; they invariably taste best when baked in Aix-en-Provence. There are more recipes for *nougat*, honey-sweetened chewy candy flavored with either almonds or pistachios, than anyone could possibly document. Nougat from the industrial-looking town of Montelimar seems to have a slight edge. A variety of almond-and-honey cookies, *croque moines* (crusty monks), were named for the monks who baked them to raise money for their causes. *Une galette provençale*, a tartlet filled with pralines, almond cream, and grated orange zest, is a perennial childhood favorite in Arles and St-Rémy.

A MENU OF CHOICES

CASSOULET & BOUILLABAISSE   What dish should you be especially alert for in the southwest? The magic word is *cassoulet*, not to be confused with a cassolette, a fancy word for a small stewpot and whatever ingredients someone might be tempted to throw into it. *Cassoulet*, which is to Toulouse what bouillabaisse is to Marseille, is a succulent mixture of slow-cooked white beans flavored with a herbed combination of roasted lamb, mutton, goose, sausages, duck, and various forms of pork.

Bouillabaisse is Provence's most famous dish. Traditionally, it combines a trio of fish: rascasse, grondin, and congre (the spiny red hogfish, gurnet, and conger eel). The original recipe from Marseillaise kitchens actually called for a dozen kinds of fish, including fielan, rouquier, and sard. Increasingly, mussels are added, or, when one is elegant, spiny lobsters. The kettle of fish is cooked rapidly in bouillon, flavored with olive oil and various seasonings such as bay leaf, saffron, onion, and fennel. We always toss in some cognac or white wine. A paste of Spanish peppers, called a rouille, sharpens the sauce, giving it an extra reddish color. The cooking time is 10 minutes.

VEGETARIAN DISHES   Provence is delightful with its emphasis on vegetarian dishes, each of which seems to bring a transcendent earthiness from deep within the soil. Examples are succulent grilled eggplant with basil-tomato sauce and grilled vegetables garnished with zucchini flowers (stuffed with a purée of zucchini and herbs, they're coated with batter and deep-fried). No one denies the international appeal of room-temperature *ratatouille,* the soothing combination of eggplant, onions, peppers, and herbs slowly stewed in olive oil.

The perfect accompaniment for any of these dishes is *aïoli,* the garlic-laced mayonnaise that's the appropriate foil for fish, grilled vegetables, and plain or toasted bread. Incidentally, *aïoli* can also refer to an entire meal composed of poached salt cod, boiled vegetables, and (in some cases) roasted snails; the garlic mayonnaise binds the disparate ingredients together.

Also look for specialties like *pissaladière,* a doughy form of onion pizza; *mesclun,* assorted wild greens that make divine salads; and *pistou,* a rich basil-infused soup similar to minestrone.

GOOSE & DUCK   Southwestern France is the world's headquarters of dishes boasting fattened goose and duck. The appreciation of *foie gras* from either bird has been elevated to something approaching a cult, and many dishes gain a noteworthy unctuousness when fried in *graisse d'oie* (goose fat). Thighs of both species are cooked in large quantities of their own ample fat to create tender *confits,* and the breast of ducks *(magrets)* are often grilled over charcoal or oak fires. *Aiguillettes* (long, thin strips carved from the duck's back) are prepared according to a varied repertoire of techniques. Pâtés made from the by-products of duck, and sometimes studded with truffles, figure high on everyone's favorite appetizer list. Goose, at least in Gascony, might be flambéed in armagnac, then slowly braised with wine and vegetables for the classic *daube d'oie.*

HEARTY STEWS   A specialty remembered (sometimes fondly, sometimes not) from many Provençaux childhoods is *pieds et paquets,* a combination of mutton or lamb tripe and lambs' feet cooked with cured, unsmoked pork, garlic, wine, and tomatoes. This classic is much appreciated by adventurous gastronomes. An equally prized variation is a *gratin de pieds de porc aux truffes* (gratin of pigs' feet with truffles). *Civit de lapin* is wild rabbit stewed with herbs and red wine, with rabbit blood added to the stew at the last minute as a thickener. *Daube de boeuf à la provençale* is an unusual combination of stewed beef marinated in garlic purée with red wine. Bourride, a succulent fish stew, is Languedoc's answer to the world-famous bouillabaisse of Provence. Baudroie is a simple but flavorful mix of monkfish, thin-sliced potatoes, garlic, onions, herbs, and an unexpected ingredient—the zest of navel oranges.

GAME   If you're planning a trip to the deep south in autumn, you'll discover many game dishes at your disposal. These include *perdreau* (partridge), *sanglier* (wild boar), *chevreuil* (venison), *faison* (pheasant), and *lièvre* (wild hare). Often the meat will be marinated in herbs and wine, roasted with acute care by experts, and served with vibrant red wine from grapes grown in the Rhône Valley.

BULL   Throughout the south, but especially in the flat wetlands and bull-raising terrain of the Camargue, look for *gardiane de taureau.* Concocted from tough and somewhat fibrous bull flesh and flavored with olives and red wine, it's invariably served with *riz de Camargue*—rice from the lowlands of the delta of the Rhône.

LES VINS DE PROVENCE

For wine-making purposes, Provence is defined as the area between Cannes, not far from the Italian border, and the eastern banks of the Rhône. This is distinctly different from the area connoisseurs have designated around Avignon, Châteauneuf-du-Pape, and Orange. Despite the fact that these towns are historically and culturally a part of Provence, their wines fall into a separate district, the Côtes-du-Rhône. That district begins at Avignon and extends about 140 miles northward up the valley of the Rhône to just south of Lyon, near Côte Rotie.

Wine produced west of the Rhône, within a band of real estate that extends about 40 miles north of the Mediterranean coast all the way to the Spanish border, belongs to a different entity, Languedoc-Roussillon.

Most of the wines from these three districts are red and tend to be strong, solid, and flavorful, usually with a potent level of alcohol (a by-product of the high sugar content of the varieties of grape that thrive in the heat and constant sunlight).

The pleasure of Provence's wine is undeniable. A disadvantage, however, is the insecurity of local vintners concerning adequate rainfall in a region known for its droughts. Consequently, the vintners have traditionally relied on a complicated blending of grapes. Strains of this grape have, since the phylloxera epidemic of the late 19th century, included varietals from Italy and Spain. The result, according to many connoisseurs enamored with the more aristocratic vintages of Burgundy and Bordeaux, is an occasional inconsistency and confusion about the way the wines might age. However, massive investments in recent years have helped elevate many of the region's vintages to international repute.

THE REDS, THE WHITES & THE ROSÉS

In 1923 a distinguished Provençal landowner, Baron Le Roy de Boiseaumarie, inaugurated a series of quality controls from his lands near Châteauneuf-du-Pape. His efforts were instrumental in the imposition of standards on vintners and helped launch what later evolved into the national Appellations d'Origine Contrôllées (A.O.C.).

Despite the appeal of southern French wines as an accompaniment for such strongly flavored foods as anchovies, sardines, and bouillabaisse, the region has a lower percentage of wines that oenophiles call "great" than do more temperate regions. So pride is taken by vintners with lands in designated A.O.C. districts. This, while no guarantee of quality, is a beginning point for newcomers who want to distinguish prestigious vintages from ordinary *vin de table*. Many A.O.C. designations are relatively new—upstarts compared to the more venerable designations in Burgundy and Bordeaux. Côtes du Provence, producer of more than 100 million bottles annually, was designated A.O.C. as recently as 1977.

The two best Provençal whites are produced near Aix, most notably the delicate Cassis and the more forthright Palette. Bellet, a relatively small wine-growing district in the hills above Nice, produces intensely fashionable reds, whites, and rosés.

Impressions

An optimistic description of Provence wines always mentions the sun-baked pines, thyme, and lavender, and claims that the wine takes its character from them. This is true of some of the best of them. . . . Others get by on a pretty colour and a good deal of alcohol. "Tarpaulin edged with lace" is a realistic summing up of one of the better ones.
—Hugh Johnson, *World Atlas of Win*

The Pleasure of Pastis

The proper start to a Provençal meal is a glass or two of the unpretentious local apéritif, a translucent yellow liqueur, *pastis,* that becomes cloudy when you add water or ice. Although it's usually associated with truck drivers and dockyard laborers in Marseille, you might really appreciate it once you develop a taste for it. It's scented with anise, fennel, mint, and licorice, but in the case of France's most popular brand name (Ricard, beneficiary of millions of francs' worth of ad campaigns, or its sweeter rival, Pernod), it contains some additional secret ingredients as well.

Particularly strong reds are Gigondas and Vacqueras, whose alcohol content sometimes exceeds 13%. Names to look for on a wine list are Côtes de Provence (Pierrefeu and Château Minuty are two important producers) from the dry hills north of Toulon, Côtes du Rhône Villages, Côtes du Vivarais, and Châteauneuf-du-Pape, the only wine in the world that's allowed to bear the crest of the long-ago popes of Avignon. Any bottle of this last wine, because of the vagaries of rainfall and the growing season, may be composed of more than a dozen grapes from around the district. A memorable sweet wine from the Côtes du Rhône, favored by pastry chefs as a foil for their concoctions, is Baumes de Venise.

The two most famous rosés of the south are Tavel, a name that's been used by several novelists as the wine of choice of their dashing heros, and Bandol, a worthy producer of which is Château Simone. A recent contender rapidly growing in repute is Listel, a cloudy rosé produced on the sunbaked plains of the Camargue.

The vineyards of Languedoc-Roussillon represent more than a third of France's total acreage devoted to grapes. The fields around Nîmes, Béziers, and Narbonne produce rivers of ordinary table wine, which, thanks to newfangled methods of cultivation and harvesting, have of late been more favorably regarded by wine scholars. Aristocratic vintages from Languedoc include unusual sweet wines like Banyuls and Muscat de Rivesaltes and the reds from towns on the eastern foothills of the Pyrénées, Côtes de Roussillon.

SAMPLING THE VINTAGES

A cost-effective means of trying ordinary table wines is bringing your own container (usually a plastic jug sold on the premises or in hardware stores) to some large-scale producers. At bargain-basement prices, they'll use a gas pump–inspired nozzle to pump wine from enormous vats directly into your container. In a restaurant such a vintage would be sold in a glass carafe or ceramic *pichet* at a low price. If you're driving through the vineyards and see one of the many signs announcing *vente au détail,* it means that you'll be able to buy estate-bottled wine by the bottle, invariably at lower prices than in retail wine shops.

If you opt to visit some of Provence's vineyards, don't be disappointed by the overuse of the word *château.* Only in rare instances will you discover aristocratic or baronial homes and showcase architecture. In unpretentious rural Provence, most of the wine is produced by small or medium-sized farms on family-owned plots that have thrived for many generations under the same bloodlines. In fact, nearly half the wine of southern France is produced by cooperative wineries. However, most of the places in chapter 1's list of "The Best Vineyards" just happen to have an impressive château associated with their lands.

Planning a Trip to the South of France

3

This chapter is devoted to the where, when, and how of your trip. It covers everything from what you'll need to do before leaving home and how you'll get to the south of France to where you can begin your adventures in Languedoc, Provence, and along the Côte d'Azur.

1 Visitor Information, Required Documents & Money

SOURCES OF INFORMATION
TOURIST OFFICES

IN THE UNITED STATES Your best source of information—besides this guide, of course—is the **French Government Tourist Office,** 444 Madison Ave., 16th Floor, New York, NY 10022; 676 N. Michigan Ave., Suite 3360, Chicago, IL 60611-2819; or 9454 Wilshire Blvd., Suite 715, Beverly Hills, CA 90212-2967. To request information at any of these offices, call the **France on Call** hot line at ☎ **900/990-0040** (50¢ per minute). For the office's Web site, see below.

IN CANADA Write or phone the **Maison de la France / French Government Tourist Office,** 1981 av. McGill College, Suite 490, Montréal, H3A 2W9 (☎ **514/288-4264**).

IN THE UNITED KINGDOM Write or phone the **Maison de la France / French Government Tourist Office,** 178 Piccadilly, London, W1V 0AL (☎ **0891/244-123;** fax 0171/493-6594).

IN AUSTRALIA OR NEW ZEALAND Write or phone the **French Tourist Bureau,** 25 Bligh St., Sydney, NSW 2000 (☎ **02/9231-5244;** fax 02/9221-8682).

IN IRELAND Write or phone the **Maison de la France / French Government Tourist Office,** 35 Lower Abbey St., Dublin 1 (☎ **01/703-4046**).

INTERNET WEB SITES
- **French Government Tourist Office:** http://www.fgtousa.org
- **Maison de la France:** http://www.franceguide.com
- **Relais & Châteaux:** http://www.integra.fr/relaischateaux
- **FranceScape:** http://www.france.com/francescape
- **WebMuseum:** http://sunsite.unc.edu/wm

TRAVEL TO MONACO

Information on travel to Monaco is available from the **Monaco Government Tourist and Convention Bureau,** 565 Fifth Ave., 23rd Floor, New York, NY 10017 (☎ **212/286-3330;** fax 212/286-9890). Although most of its facilities (along with its consulate) are in New York at the above address, Monaco maintains a branch office at 542 S. Dearborn St., Suite 550, Chicago, IL 60605 (☎ **312/939-7863**). In London, the office is at 3/18 Chelsea Garden Market, The Chambers, Chelsea Harbour, London SW10 OXF (☎ **0171/352-9962;** fax 0171/352-2103). Document requirements for travel to Monaco are exactly the same as those for travel to France, and there are virtually no border patrols or passport formalities at the Monégasque frontier.

REQUIRED DOCUMENTS

PASSPORT   All foreign (non-French) nationals need a valid passport to enter France (check its expiration date).

VISA   The French government no longer requires visas for **U.S. citizens,** providing they're staying in France for less than 90 days. For longer stays, U.S. visitors must apply for a long-term visa, residence card, or temporary-stay visa. Each requires proof of income or a viable means of support in France and a legitimate purpose for remaining in the country. Applications are available from the Consulate Section of the **French Embassy,** 4101 Reservoir Rd. NW, Washington, DC 20007 (☎ **202/944-6000**), or from the visa section of the **French Consulate** at 10 E. 74th St., New York, NY 10021 (☎ **212/606-3689**). Visas are required for students planning to study in France even if the stay is for less than 90 days.

Visas are generally required for **citizens of other countries,** though Canadian, Swiss, and Japanese citizens and citizens of EU countries are exempt (but check with your nearest French consulate, as the situation can change overnight).

DRIVER'S LICENSE   U.S. and Canadian driver's licenses are valid in France, but if you're going to tour Europe by car you may want to invest in an **International Driver's License.** Apply at any branch of the American Automobile Association (AAA). You must be 18 years old and include two 2- by 2-inch photographs, a $12 fee, and your valid U.S. driver's license with the application. If the AAA doesn't have a branch in your hometown, send a photograph of your driver's license (front and back) with the fee and photos to **AAA,** 1000 AAA Dr., M/S28, Heathrow, FL 32746-5063 (☎ **800/222-4357** or 407/444-4300; fax 407/444-4247). Always carry your original license with you to Europe, however.

In Canada, you can get the address of the **Canadian Automobile Club** closest to you by calling its national office (☎ **613/226-7631**).

INTERNATIONAL INSURANCE CERTIFICATE   In Europe, you must have an international insurance certificate, called a green card *(carte verte).* The car-rental agency will provide one if you're renting.

MONEY

France is one of the world's most expensive destinations. But to compensate, it often offers top-value food and lodging. Part of the problem is the value-added tax (VAT—called TVA in France), which tacks anywhere from 6% to 33% on top of everything.

CURRENCY   The basic unit of French currency is the **franc (F),** which consists of 100 **centimes.** Coins are issued in units of 5, 10, 20, and 50 centimes, plus 1, 2, 5, and 10 francs. Notes are denominated in 20, 50, 100, 200, 500, and 1,000 francs. The new 200F note honors Gustave Eiffel on the front.

The French Franc

For American Readers   At this writing, $1 = approximately 5F (or 1F = 20¢), and this was the rate of exchange used to calculate the dollar values given in this book.

For British Readers   At this writing, £1 = approximately 8.33F (or 1F = 12p), and this was the rate of exchange used to calculate the pound values in the table below.

Note: Because the exchange rate fluctuates from time to time, especially in France, this table should be used only as a general guide.

F	U.S.$	U.K.£	F	U.S.$	U.K.£
1	.20	.12	150	30.00	18.00
5	1.00	.60	200	40.00	24.00
10	2.00	1.20	250	50.00	30.00
15	3.00	1.80	300	60.00	36.01
20	4.00	2.40	400	80.00	48.02
25	5.00	3.00	500	100.00	60.02
30	6.00	3.60	750	150.00	90.04
40	8.00	4.80	1,000	200.00	120.05
50	10.00	6.00	1,250	250.00	150.06
75	15.00	9.00	1,500	300.00	180.07
100	20.00	12.00	2,000	400.00	240.10

All banks are equipped for foreign exchange, and you'll find exchange offices at the airports and airline terminals. Banks are open Monday to Friday from 9am to noon and 2 to 4pm. Major bank branches also open their exchange departments on Saturday from 9am to noon.

When converting your home currency into francs, be aware that rates may vary. Your hotel will offer the worst rate. In general, banks offer the best, but even they charge a commission, often $3, depending on the transaction. Whenever you can, stick to the big banks of France, like Crédit Lyonnais, which usually offer the best rates and charge the least commission. Always make sure you have enough francs for *le weekend.*

If you need a check denominated in French francs before your trip (for example, to pay a deposit on a hotel room), contact **Ruesch International,** 700 11th St. NW, 4th Floor, Washington, DC 20001-4507 (☎ **800/424-2923**). Ruesch performs a wide variety of conversion-related services, usually for $3 per transaction. You can also inquire at a local bank.

CREDIT & CHARGE CARDS   Credit and charge cards are useful in France. Both **American Express** and **Diners Club** are widely recognized. The French equivalent for Visa is **Carte Bleue.** A **EuroCard** sign on an establishment means that it accepts MasterCard.

Of course, you may make a purchase with a credit card thinking it'll be at a certain rate, only to find that the U.S. dollar or British pound has declined by the time your bill arrives and you're actually paying more than you bargained for. But those are the rules of the game. It also can work in your favor if the dollar or pound should unexpectedly rise after you make a purchase.

What Things Cost in Nice	U.S. $
Taxi from the airport to the city center	36.00
Public transportation for an average trip within the city limits	1.60
Local telephone call	.20
Double room at the Hôtel Négresco (deluxe)	260.00
Double room at the Hôtel Busby (moderate)	100.00
Double room at the Hôtel du Centre (budget)	48.00
Lunch for one, without wine, at La Toque Blanche (moderate)	29.00
Lunch for one, without wine, at l'Estocaficada (budget)	11.60
Dinner for one, without wine, at Chantecler (deluxe)	79.00
Dinner for one, without wine, at Chez Michel (moderate)	37.00
Dinner for one, without wine, at La Baron Ivre (budget)	20.00
Glass of wine	3.00
Coca-Cola	1.80
Cup of coffee	3.00
Roll of ASA 100 film, 36 exposures	6.50
Admission to the Musée Masséna	5.00
Movie ticket	6.50
Tickets to the opera	8.00–64.00

Some ATMs in France accept U.S. bankcards like Visa and MasterCard. The exchange rates are often good, and the convenience of obtaining cash on the road is without equal. Check with your credit-card company or bank before leaving home.

ATM NETWORKS   Plus, Cirrus, and other networks connecting ATMs operate in France. If your bankcard has been programmed with a Personal Identification Number (PIN), it's likely you can use your card at French ATMs to withdraw money as a cash advance on your credit card. Always determine the frequency limits for withdrawls and check to see if your PIN must be reprogrammed for use in France. For **Cirrus** locations abroad, call ☎ 800/424-7787; for **Plus** usage abroad, dial ☎ 800/843-7587.

TRAVELER'S CHECKS   Most large banks sell traveler's checks, charging fees of 1% to 2% of the value of the checks, though some out-of-the-way banks charge as much as 7%. If your bank wants more than a 2% commission, call the traveler's check issuers directly for the address of outlets where this commission will be less.

American Express (☎ 800/221-7282 in the U.S. and Canada) doesn't charge a commission to AAA members or holders of certain types of American Express cards. For questions or problems arising outside North America, contact any of the company's regional representatives. There's also **Citicorp** (☎ 800/645-6556 in the U.S. and Canada, or 813/623-1709, collect, from elsewhere). **Thomas Cook** (☎ 800/223-7373 in the U.S. and Canada) issues MasterCard traveler's checks. And **Interpayment Services** (☎ 800/732-1322 in the U.S. and Canada, or 212/858-8500, collect, from elsewhere) sells Visa checks issued by a consortium of member banks and the Thomas Cook organization.

Each of these agencies will refund your checks if they're lost or stolen, provided you have sufficient documentation. Of course, carry your documentation in a safe place—never along with your checks. When purchasing checks from one of the banks listed, ask about refund hot lines; American Express and Bank of America have the most offices around the world.

Sometimes you can purchase traveler's checks in the currency of the country you're visiting, thereby avoiding a conversion fee. American Express, for example, issues checks in French francs. Foreign banks may ask up to 5% to convert your checks into francs. Note, also, that you always get a better rate if you cash traveler's checks at the banks issuing them.

MONEYGRAMS   If you find yourself without money, a wire service provided by American Express can help you tap willing friends and family for emergency funds. Through **MoneyGram,** 6200 S. Quebec St. (P.O. Box 5118), Englewood, CO 800155 (☎ **800/926-9400**), money can be sent around the world in less than 10 minutes. Senders should call the above toll-free number to learn the address of the closest MoneyGram outlet. Cash, credit card, or a personal check (with ID) are acceptable forms of payment. AMEX's fee for the service is $10 for the first $300, with a sliding scale for larger sums. The service includes a short Telex message and a 3-minute phone call from sender to recipient. The beneficiary must present a photo ID at the outlet where the money is received.

2 When to Go

In terms of weather, the most idyllic months are May and June. Though the sun is intense, it's not uncomfortable. The coastal waters have warmed by then so swimming is possible, and all the resorts have come alive after a winter slumber but aren't yet overrun. The flowers and herbs in the countryside are at their peak, and driving conditions are ideal. In June and July there's light until around 10:30pm.

The most overcrowded times—also the hottest, in more ways than one—are July and August, when seemingly half of Paris shows up in the briefest of bikinis, often topless. Reservations are difficult, the discos are blasting, and space is tight on the popular beaches. The worst traffic jams on the coast occur all the way from St-Tropez to Menton.

Aside from May and June, our favorite time is September and even early October, when the sun is still hot, at least during the day, and the greatest hordes have headed back north. This is also a good time for seeing all the art museums along the Côte d'Azur and the cultural attractions of Provence, such as those in Avignon.

In November the weather is often pleasant, especially at midday, though some of the restaurants and inns you'll want to visit might take a sudden vacation. It's the month that many chefs and hoteliers elect to go on their own vacations after a summer of hard work catering to masses of people.

Winter hasn't been the fashionable season since the 1930s. In the early days of tourism, when Queen Victoria came to visit, winter was when all the fashionable people showed up, deserting the Côte by April. Today it's just the reverse. However, winter on the Riviera is being rediscovered, and many visitors (particularly retired people or those with leisure time) elect to visit then. If you don't mind the absence of sunbathing and beach life, this could be a good time to show up. However, some resorts, like St-Tropez, become ghost towns when the cold weather comes, though Cannes, Nice, Monaco, and Menton remain active year-round.

WEATHER

France's weather varies considerably from region to region and sometimes from town to town as little as 12 miles apart. It can be sunny in Nice but cold and rainy in Avignon at the same time.

The Mediterranean coast has the driest climate. When it does rain, it's usually heaviest in spring and autumn. (Surprisingly, Cannes sometimes receives more rainfall than Paris.) Summers are comfortably dry—beneficial to humans but deadly to much of the vegetation, which (unless it's irrigated) often dries and burns up in the parched months.

Provence dreads *le mistral* (a cold, violent wind from the French and Swiss Alps that roars south down the Rhône Valley), which most often blows in winter for a few days, but which can blow for up to 2 weeks.

For up-to-the-minute **weather forecasts,** dial ☎ **900/WEATHER** in the United States (95¢ per minute). This report comes from the cable TV station Weather Channel. Listen to the recorded menu, pressing the appropriate buttons on your Touch-Tone phone. The 24-hour service reports on conditions in Provence and the Riviera.

HOLIDAYS (*JOURS FERIES*)

In France, holidays are known as *jours feriés.* Shops and many businesses (banks and some museums and restaurants) close on holidays, but hotels and emergency services remain open.

The main holidays—a mix of secular and religious ones—include New Year's Day (Jan 1), Easter Sunday and Monday (early April), Labor Day (May 1), Ascension Thursday (40 days after Easter, May 21 in 1998), V-E Day in Europe (May 8), Whit Monday (mid May), Bastille Day (July 14), Assumption of the Blessed Virgin (Aug 15), All Saints' Day (Nov 1), Armistice Day (Nov 11), and Christmas (Dec 25).

PROVENCE CALENDAR OF EVENTS

January
- **Monte Carlo Motor Rally.** The world's most venerable car race. For more information, call ☎ **92-16-61-66.** Usually mid-January.

February
- **Fête de la Chandeleur (Candlemas),** Basilique St-Victor, Marseille. A procession brings the Black Virgin up from the crypt of the abbey. Navettes (orange-flower–flavored biscuits baked in the shape of a boat to evoke the boat that brought the two St. Marys to Provence) are traditionally sold. For more information, call ☎ **04-91-13-89-00.** Mid-February.
- ✪ **Carnival of Nice.** Float processions, parades, confetti battles, boat races, street music and food, masked balls, and fireworks are part of this ancient celebration. The climax follows a 113-year-old tradition where King Carnival is burned in effigy, an event preceded by Les Batailles des Fleurs (Battles of the Flowers), during which members of opposing teams pelt one another with flowers. Come with proof of a hotel reservation. For information or reservations, contact the **Nice Convention and Visitors Bureau,** 1 esplanade Kennedy (BP 4079), 06302 Nice CEDEX 4 (☎ **04-92-14-48-00;** fax 04-92-14-48-03). Mid-February to early March.

April
- **Férla Pascale (Easter Bullfighting Festival),** Arles. This is a major bullfighting event that includes not only appearances by the greatest matadors but also *abrivados* and *bodegas* (wine stalls). For more information, call ☎ **04-90-18-41-20.** Easter.
- **Festival des Musiques d'Aujourd'hui (Festival of Contemporary Music),** Marseille. This festival presents the works of very young French and European composers in music and dance. For more information, call Experimental Music Groups of Marseille at ☎ **04-91-39-29-00.** Throughout April.

May

- **La Fête des Gardians (Camargue Cowboys' Festival)**, Arles. This event features a procession of Camargue cowboys through the streets of town. Activities feature various games involving bulls, including Courses Camarguaises, in which competitors have to snatch a rosette from between the horns of a bull. For information, call ☎ **04-90-18-41-20**. Early May.
- ✪ **Cannes Film Festival.** Movie madness transforms this city into the kingdom of the media-related deal, with daily melodramas acted out in cafes, on sidewalks, and in hotel lobbies. Great for voyeurs. Reserve early and make a deposit. Getting a table on the Carlton terrace is even more difficult than procuring a room. Admission to some of the prestigious films is by invitation only. There are box-office tickets for the less important films, which play 24 hours. For information, contact the Direction du Festival International du Film, 99 bd. Malesherbes, 75008 Paris (☎ **01-45-61-66-00**; fax 01-45-61-97-60). Two weeks before the festival, the event's administration moves en masse to the Palais des Festivals, esplanade Georges-Pompidou, 06400 Cannes (☎ **04-93-39-01-01**). Early to mid-May.
- **Fête de la Transhumance (Move to Summer Grazing)**, St-Rémy. This event celebrates the now-abandoned custom of shepherds presenting their flocks to the public before moving them to higher ground for summer. Today goats from Le Rove and Provençal donkeys are also shown. In this mock event, the flocks move off as if genuinely going up to the mountains. For more information, call ☎ **04-90-92-05-22**. Mid- to late May.
- **Monaco Grand Prix.** Hundreds of cars race through the narrow streets and winding corniche roads in a surreal blend of high-tech machinery and medieval architecture. For more information, call ☎ **92-16-61-66**. Late May.
- **Le Pélerinage des Gitans (Gypsies' Pilgrimage)**, Stes-Maries-de-la-Mer. This festival is in memory of the two Marys for whom the town is named (Mary, the mother of James the lesser, and Mary Salome, the mother of James the greater and John). A model boat containing statues of the saints is taken to the seashore and blessed by the bishop. A statue of St. Sarah, patron saint of Gypsies, is also taken to the sea. For more information, call ☎ **04-90-97-82-55**. Last week of May.

June

- **Festival de la St-Eloi (St. Eloi Festival)**, Maussane-les-Alpilles. For this festival, wagons are decorated and raced in the Carreto Ramado, followed by mass, a procession in traditional dress, and a benediction. Special events are held and local produce and handcrafts sold. For more information, call ☎ **04-90-54-52-04**. Mid-June.
- **Festival Aix en Musique ("Aix in Music" Festival)**, Aix-en-Provence. Concerts of classical music and choral singing are held in historic buildings, such as the Cloisters of the Cathédrale St-Sauveur and the Hôtel Maynier d'Oppède. For more information, call ☎ **04-42-21-69-69**. Mid-June to early July.
- **Festival d'Expression Provençale (Festival of Provençal Language)**, Abbaye St-Michel de Frigolet, Tarascon. At this festival, homage is paid to the region's language with works by Provençal writers that are acted in French and Provençal. For more information, call ☎ **04-90-95-50-77**. Late June to early July.
- **Fête de la Tarasque**, Tarascon. The town relives St. Martha's victory over the dragon known as the Tarasque, which was believed to live in the Rhône in the 1st century. There's a procession of horsemen, an archery competition, historical events, a medieval tournament, a Tarasque procession, Novilladas (young bull-fighters), and an orchestral concert with fireworks. For more information, call ☎ **04-90-91-03-52**. Late June.

- **Feu de la St-Jean (St. John's Fire),** Fontvieille. This event features folk troupes and Camargue cowboys who gather in front of the Château de Montauban. For more information, call ☎ **04-90-54-67-49.** June 24.
- **La Fête des Pêcheurs (Fishermen's Festival),** Cassis. The local "Prud'hommes" (members of the elected industrial tribunal) walk in procession wearing traditional dress, and a mass is held in honor of St. Peter, followed by a benediction. For more information, call ☎ **04-42-01-71-17.** Late June.
- **Les Nuits d'Eté de La Magalone (Summer Nights at La Magalone),** Bastide of La Magalone, Marseille. Concerts given in the manor house feature early, baroque, and contemporary music. For more information, contact Cité de la Musique at ☎ **04-91-39-28-28.** Late June to early July.
- **Reconstitution Historique (Historical Pageant),** Salon-de-Provence. This pageant held in honor of Nostradamus includes a cast of 700 in historical costume and is followed by a son-et-lumière at the Château d'Empéri. For more information, call ☎ **04-90-56-77-92.** Late June to early July.

July

- **St-Guilhem Music Season,** St-Guilhem le Désert, Languedoc. This festival of baroque organ and choral music is held in a medieval monastery. For information, call ☎ **04-67-63-14-99.** July to early August.
- **Festival International d'Art Lyrique et de Musique d'Aix (Aix International Festival of Opera and Music),** Palais de l'Archévêche and Cathédrale St-Sauveur, Aix-en-Provence. This highly prestigious festival presents operas, particularly of Mozart, as well as concerts and recitals. For more information, call ☎ **04-42-17-34-00.** Throughout July.
- ✪ **Bastille Day.** Celebrating the birth of modern-day France, the festivities in the south reach their peak in Nice with street fairs, pageants, fireworks, and feasts. The day begins with a parade down promenade des Anglais and ends with fireworks in the Vieille Ville. No matter where you are, by the end of the day you'll hear Piaf warbling "La Foule" (The Crowd), the song that celebrated her passion for the stranger she met and later lost in a crowd on Bastille Day. Similar celebrations also take place in Cannes, Arles, Aix, Marseille, and Avignon. July 14.
- **Festival Mosaïque Gitane (Festival of Gypsy Music),** Arles. This festival features concerts presenting world and folk music and Gypsy and flamenco music. For more information, call ☎ **04-90-93-24-75.** Mid-July.
- **Nuit Taurine (Nocturnal Bull Festival),** St-Rémy-de-Provence. At this festival the focus is on the age-old allure of bulls and their primeval appeal to roaring crowds. Abrivados involve bulls in the town square as "chaperoned" by trained herders on horseback; encierros highlight a Pamplona-style stampeding of bulls through the streets. Music from local guitarists and flaming torches add drama. For more information, call ☎ **04-90-92-05-22.** Mid-July.
- ✪ **Grand Parade du Jazz (Nice Jazz Festival).** This is the biggest, flashiest, and most prestigious jazz festival in Europe, with world-class entertainers. Concerts begin in early afternoon and go on until late at night (sometimes all night in the clubs) on the Arènes de Cimiez, a hill above the city. Reserve hotel rooms way in advance. For information, contact the Grand Parade du Jazz, ℅ Abela Regency Hotel, 223 promenade des Anglais, 06200 Nice (☎ **04-93-37-17-17**), or the Cultural Affairs Department of the city of Nice (☎ **04-93-13-25-90;** fax 04-93-80-53-64). Mid-July.
- ✪ **Festival d'Aix-en-Provence.** This musical event par excellence features everything from Gregorian chant to melodies composed on computerized synthesizers. The audience sits on the sloping lawns of the 14th-century papal palace for operas and

concertos. Local recitals are performed in the medieval cloister of the Cathédrale St-Sauveur. Make advance hotel reservations and take a written confirmation with you when you arrive. Expect heat, crowds, and traffic. For more information, contact the Festival International d'Art Lyrique et de Musique, Palais de l'Ancien Archévêche, 13100 Aix-en-Provence (☎ 04-42-17-34-00; fax 04-42-96-12-61). Mid- to late July.

- **Les Chorégies d'Orange,** Orange. One of southern France's most important lyric festivals presents oratorios and choral works by master performers whose voices are amplified by the ancient acoustics of France's best-preserved Roman amphitheater. For more information, call ☎ 04-90-34-24-24. Mid-July to early August.

✪ **Festival d'Avignon.** One of France's most prestigious theater events, this world-class festival has a reputation for exposing new talent to critical acclaim. The focus is usually on avant-garde works in theater, dance, and music by groups from around the world. Mime, too. Make hotel reservations early. For information, call ☎ 04-90-27-66-50 or fax 04-90-27-66-83. Edwards and Edwards can order tickets to virtually any of the musical or theatrical events at the Avignon festival, as well as at other cultural events throughout France. Its address is 1270 Ave. of the Americas, Suite 2414, New York, NY 10020 (☎ 800/223-6108). Mid- to late July.

- **Festival Marseille Méditerranée.** This festival features concerts and recitals of music and song from the entire Mediterranean region. Theater and dance are also presented, along with special exhibitions in the city's main museums. For more information, call ☎ 04-91-55-02-03. Second 2 weeks in July.

- **Fête de la St-Eloi (Feast of St. Eloi),** Gémenos. Some hundred draft horses draw a procession of traditional flower-decked wagons. Folk troupes also perform. For more information, call ☎ 04-42-32-18-44. Late July.

August

- **Fêtes Daudet (Daudet Festival),** Fontvieille. At this festival, mass said in Provençal is held in the avenue of pine trees. There's folk dancing outside Daudet's mill and a torchlight procession through the streets of town to the mill. For more information, call ☎ 04-90-54-67-49. Mid-August.

- **Feria de St-Rémy (Bullfights),** St-Rémy-de-Provence. This event features a 4-day celebration of bulls with abrivado and encierro (see the Nuit Taurine entry above), branding and Portuguese bull fighting (matadors on horseback). For more information, call ☎ 04-90-92-05-22. Mid-August.

September

- **Fête des Olives (Olive Festival),** Mouriès. A mass is held in honor of the green olives. There's a procession of groups in traditional costume, an olive tasting, and sales of regional produce. For more information, call ☎ 04-90-47-56-58. Mid-September.

- **Féria des Prémices du Riz (Rice Harvest Festival),** Arles. Bullfights are held in the amphitheater with leading matadors, and a procession of floats makes its way along boulevard des Lices; there are also traditional events with cowboys and women in regional costume. For more information, call ☎ 04-90-18-41-20. Mid-September.

- **Journée de l'Olivier en Provence (Day Celebrating the Olive in Provence),** Salon-de-Provence. This event is attended by producers of olive oil, Marseille soap, olive-wood articles, booksellers, and pottery and earthenware makers. Special events are held in the history center. For more information, call ☎ 04-90-56-27-60. Late September.

Christmas in Provence

In Provence, Christmas remains the year's most important festival. Celebrations begin on December 4 with the Feast of St. Barbe, when the people sprinkle grains of wheat and lentils onto moistened cotton-wool in a saucer. If the seeds germinate profusely by December 25, there'll be a good harvest (and thus more cash). Throughout December, fairs selling *santons* (figures of saints) are held all over. Much importance is placed on the crèche and the number of santons it holds. The authentic crèche is supposed to represent a Provençal village and its little world, but the purely religious symbol has been given a secular twist. At the pastrage, one of the many ceremonies held in the villages, a newborn lamb is presented during midnight mass.

In another ceremony, shepherds cross the hillside pastures to come to midnight mass, which is enriched by folk troupes who perform traditional songs, living cribs, or the nativity play. Performances of the play, which narrates the journey to the stable and the adoration of the newborn child, begin in late December and continue through January.

In 1844 Antoine Maurel created the best-known version of the Nativity play, which has changed little since. The Christmas Eve meal or *gros souper* (great supper) is traditionally meatless. The table, still a spectacular sight, is decorated with at least three cloths and festooned with red-berried holly. The meal includes fish and vegetables, plus the traditional Provençal 13 desserts, consisting of fougasse (oil-based bread), raisins, dried figs, almonds, walnuts, winter pears, preserves, white nougat, black nougat, and fresh fruit, representing the guests at the Last Supper.

Christmas celebrations continue through Twelfth Night (Epiphany), when people eat the King's Crown, a cake covered with crystallized fruit with a dried bean and a miniature santon baked inside, and end at Candlemas on February 2 when the crib is dismantled.

- **Perpignan Jazz Festival.** Musicians from everywhere jam in what many visitors consider Languedoc's most appealing season. For more information, call ☎ **04-68-35-37-46.** Late September.

November

- **Les Semaines Gastronomiques (Cookery Weeks),** Gémenos. This celebration of Provençal cuisine opens with a notable spice fair. For more information, call ☎ **04-42-34-18-44.** First 2 weeks in November.

December

- **Biennale de l'Art Santonnier (Biannual Santon Festival),** Aubagne. At this festival there's a procession of living santons, a torchlight procession with a cast of 500 in traditional costume, and a nativity play. For more information, call ☎ **04-42-03-49-98.** Early December in even-numbered years.
- **Fête des Bergers (Shepherds Festival),** Istres. This festival features a procession of herds on their way to winter pastures. There are cowboys, a Carreto Ramado, a blessing of the horses, an all-night Provençal party with shepherds and Provençal storytellers, and folk troupes. For more information, call ☎ **04-42-55-51-15.** First 2 weeks in December.
- **Midnight Mass,** Fontvieille. A traditional midnight mass is held, including the pastrage ceremony. There's a procession of folk troupes, Camargue cowboys,

and women in traditional costume from Daudet's mill to the church, followed by the presentation of the lamb. For more information, call ☎ **04-90-54-67-49.** December 24.

- **Noël Provençal (Provençal Christmas),** Eglise St-Vincent, Les Baux. The procession of shepherds is followed by a traditional midnight mass, including the pastrage ceremony. For more information, call ☎ **04-90-54-34-39.** December 24.
- **Fête de St-Sylvestre (New Year's Eve),** nationwide. Along the Riviera it's most boisterously celebrated in Nice's Vieille Ville around place Garibaldi. At midnight the city explodes. Strangers kiss strangers and place Masséna and promenade des Anglais become virtual pedestrian malls. December 31.

3 Health & Insurance

STAYING HEALTHY

If you need a doctor, your hotel will locate one for you. You can also obtain a list of English-speaking doctors from the **International Association for Medical Assistance to Travelers (IAMAT):** in the United States at 417 Center St., Lewiston, NY 14092 (☎ **716/754-4883**); in Canada at 40 Regal Rd., Guelph, ON N1K 1B5 (☎ **519/836-0102**). Getting medical help is relatively easy. Don't be alarmed, even in rural areas. You can find competent doctors in all parts of the country.

INSURANCE

Insurance needs for the traveler abroad fall into three categories: health and accident, trip cancellation, and lost luggage.

First, review your present policies—you may already have adequate coverage between them and what's offered by your credit- and charge-card companies. Many card companies insure their users in case of a travel accident, providing the ticket was purchased with their card. Sometimes fraternal organizations have policies protecting members in case of sickness or accidents abroad.

Incidentally, don't assume that Medicare is the answer to illness in France. It only covers U.S. citizens who travel south of the border to Mexico or north of the border to Canada.

Many homeowners' insurance policies cover theft of luggage during foreign travel and loss of documents—your Eurailpass, passport, or airline ticket, for instance. Coverage is usually limited to about $500 U.S. To submit a claim on your insurance, remember that you'll need police reports or a statement from a medical authority that you did suffer the loss or experience the illness for which you're seeking compensation. Such claims, by their very nature, can be filed only when you return from France.

Some policies (and this is the type you should have) provide advances in cash or transfers of funds so you won't have to dip into your precious travel funds to settle medical bills.

If you've booked a charter flight, you'll probably have to pay a cancellation fee if you cancel a trip suddenly, even if the cancellation is caused by an unforeseen crisis. It's possible to get insurance against such a possibility. Some travel agencies provide this coverage, and often flight insurance against a canceled trip is written into the cost of tickets paid for by credit/charge cards from such companies as Visa and American Express. Many tour operators and insurance agents provide this type of insurance.

The following companies offer such policies:

Access America, 6600 W. Broad St., Richmond, VA 23230 (☎ **800/284-8300**), offers a comprehensive travel insurance/assistance package, including medical and on-the-spot hospital payments, medical transportation, baggage insurance, trip cancellation/interruption insurance, and collision-damage insurance for a car rental. Its 24-hour hot line connects you to multilingual coordinators who can offer advice on medical, legal, and travel problems. Packages begin at $34. Varied coverage levels are available.

Wallach & Co., 107 W. Federal St. (P.O. Box 480), Middleburg, VA 20118-0480 (☎ **800/237-6615** or 540/687-3166), offers a policy called Healthcare Abroad (MEDEX). It covers 10 to 120 days at $4 per day; the policy includes accident and sickness coverage to the tune of $250,000. Medical evacuation is also included. Provisions for trip cancellation can also be written into the policy at a nominal cost.

Travel Guard International, 1145 Clark St., Stevens Point, WI 54481 (☎ **800/826-1300**), offers a comprehensive 7-day policy that covers basically everything, including emergency assistance, accidental death, trip cancellation/interruption, medical coverage abroad, and lost luggage. It will waive exclusions for preexisting medical conditions if the insurance is purchased within 7 days of your initial trip payment.

4 Accommodations Options

French hotels are rated by stars: from four-star luxury and four-star deluxe (no five stars) down through three star (first class), two star (good-quality "tourist" hotel), and one star (budget). In some of the lower categories the rooms may not have private baths; instead, many have what the French call a *cabinet de toilette* (hot and cold running water and a bidet), whereas others have only sinks. In such hotels, bathrooms are down the hall. Nearly all hotels in France have central heating, but in some cases you might wish the owners would turn it up a little on a cold night.

Most hotel rates quoted in France are for double occupancy, since most rooms are doubles; if you're traveling solo, be sure to ask about rates for a single. Some of these rooms contain twin beds, but most have double beds, suitable for one or two.

RELAIS & CHATEAUX

Now known worldwide, this organization of deluxe and first-class hostelries began in France for visitors seeking the ultimate in hotel living and dining, most often in a traditional atmosphere. Relais & Châteaux establishments (numbering about 150 in France) are former castles, abbeys, manor houses, and town houses that have been converted into hostelries or inns and elegant hotels. All have a limited number of rooms, so reservations are imperative. Sometimes these owner-run establishments have pools and tennis courts. The Relais part of the organization refers to inns called *relais,* meaning "posthouse." These tend to be less luxurious than the châteaux, but they're often quite charming. Top-quality restaurants are *relais gourmands.* Throughout this guide we've listed our favorite Relais & Châteaux, but there are many more.

For an illustrated catalog of these establishments, send $8 to **Relais & Châteaux,** 11 E. 44th St., Suite 704, New York, NY 10017 (for information and reservations of individual Relais & Châteaux, call ☎ **212/856-0115;** fax 800/860-4930 or 212/867-4968). Check out its Internet Web site at **http://www.integra.fr/relaischateaux.**

BED & BREAKFASTS

Called *gîtes–chambres d'hôte* in France, these accommodations may be one or several bedrooms on a farm or in a village home. Many of them offer one main meal of the day as well (lunch or dinner).

There are at least 6,000 of these accommodations listed with **La Maison des Gîtes de France et du Tourisme Vert,** 59 rue St-Lazare, 75009 Paris (☎ **01-49-70-75-75**).

Sometimes these B&Bs aren't as simple as you might think: Instead of a barebones farm room, you might be housed in a mansion deep in the French countryside.

In the United States, a good source for this type of accommodation is **The French Experience,** 370 Lexington Ave., New York, NY 10017 (☎ **212/986-1115;** fax 212/986-3808). It also rents furnished houses for as short a period as 1 week.

CONDOS, VILLAS, HOUSES & APARTMENTS

If you can stay for at least a week and don't mind cooking your own meals and cleaning house, you might want to rent a long-term accommodation. The local French Tourist Board might help you obtain a list of real-estate agencies that represent this type of rental (which tends to be especially popular at ski resorts). In France, one of the best groups of real estate agents is the **Fédération Nationale des Agents Immobiliers,** 129 rue du Faubourg St-Honoré, 75008 Paris (☎ **01-44-20-77-00**).

In the United States, **At Home Abroad,** 405 E. 56th St., Apt. 6H, New York, NY 10022-2466 (☎ **212/421-9165;** fax 212/752-1591), specializes in villas on the French Riviera, as well as places in the Provençal hill towns. Rentals usually are for 2 weeks. For a $25 registration fee (applicable to any rental), it will send you photographs of the properties and a newsletter.

A worthwhile competitor is **Vacances en Campagne,** British Travel International, P.O. Box 299, Elkton, VA (☎ **800/327-6097;** fax 540/298-2347). Its $4 directory contains information on more than 700 potential rentals across Europe, including the south of France.

If renting an apartment in the south of France is what you're looking for, the **Barclay International Group,** 150 E. 52nd St., New York, NY 10022 (☎ **800/845-6636** or 212/832-3777), can give you access to about 3,000 apartments and villas scattered throughout Languedoc, Provence, and the Riviera, ranging from modest modern units to among the most stylish. Units rent from 1 night up to 6 months; all have color TVs and kitchenettes, and many have concierge staffs and lobby-level security. The least-expensive units cost around $89 per night, double occupancy. Incremental discounts are granted for a stay of 1 week or 3 weeks. Rentals must be prepaid in U.S. dollars or by a major U.S. credit or charge card.

If after reading Peter Mayles's *A Year in Provence* and *Toujours Provence* you want to follow in his footsteps, at least for a week or two, you can contact **Provence West Ltd.,** P.O. Box 2105, Evergreen, CO 80437 (☎ **303/674-6942;** fax 303/674-8773; e-mail: http://ProvenceW@aol.com). This outfit specializes not in villas but in *gîtes* (rural cottages), many in Provence and Languedoc. It advises travelers about rental possibilities and processes the reservation with French *gîte* offices. Its owner, Lida Posson, has visited some 100 properties in France and can offer personal advice. She also publishes a quarterly journal and newsletter, *Window on France—An Insider's View of French Country Life.*

HOMESTAYS

If you'd like a more personal encounter with the French people, **Friends in France Ltd.,** 40 E. 19th St., 8th Floor, New York, NY 10003 (☎ **212/260-9820;** fax 212/228-0576), arranges homestays in more than 60 private residences, ranging from farmhouses to manors and châteaux, many in the south of France. The host families have been carefully selected to assure the friendliest and most comfortable stay. The program's 90-page *Guide to Host Families* describes the homes, the hosts, and other necessary details; it's available by sending a check for $15 (including postage) to the above address. The staff will personally assist you in selecting just the right hosts to match your interests and needs. They'll help you plan a more comprehensive vacation that may include bookings at hotels, apartments, or villas between your stays at private residences.

HOTEL ASSOCIATIONS

Hometours International, Inc., P.O. Box 11503, Knoxville, TN 37939 (☎ 800/ 367-4668 or 423/690-8484), offers beautiful Riviera villas, all with pools, at reasonable rates. For budget travelers, this organization offers a prepaid voucher program for the Campanile hotels, a chain of about 350 two-star family-run hotels throughout France. Rates begin as low as $70 per night double. This is an excellent alternative to B&B hotels because all chain members provide a buffet breakfast for only 35F ($7) per person. B&B catalogs for $8 or apartment brochures for $4 are available from the address above.

Others wanting to trim costs might want to check out the **Mercure** chain, an organization of simple but clean and modern hotels offering attractive values throughout France. Even at the peak of the tourist season, a room at a Mercure in Languedoc or Provence rents for $79 to $109 per night. For more information on Mercure hotels and a copy of a 100-page directory, call **RESINTER** at ☎ 800/221-4542 in the United States.

Formule 1 hotels are barebones and basic though clean and safe, offering rooms for up to three at around $30 per night. Built from prefabricated units, these air-conditioned soundproof hotels are shipped to a site and reassembled. There's a coterie of 150 of these low-budget hotels throughout France. (Formule 1, a member of the French hotel giant Accor, also owns the Motel 6 chain in the United States, to which Formule 1 bears a resemblance.)

While you can make a reservation at any member of the Accor group through the RESINTER number above, the chain finds that the low cost of Formule 1 makes it unprofitable and impractical to prereserve (from the States) rooms in the Formule chain. So you'll have to reserve your Formule 1 room on arrival in France. Be warned that Formule 1 properties have almost none of the Gallic charm for which some country inns are famous, but you can save money by planning your itinerary at Formule 1 properties. For a directory, contact Formule 1 / ETAP Hotels, 6/8 rue du Bois Bernard, 91021 Evry CEDEX (☎ 01-69-36-75-00).

Other worthwhile economy bets, sometimes with a bit more charm, are the hotels and restaurants belonging to the **Fédération Nationale des Logis de France,** 83 av. d'Italie, 75013 Paris (☎ 01-45-84-70-00). This is a marketing association of 3,828 hotels, usually simple country inns especially convenient for motorists, most rated one or two stars. The association publishes an annual directory. Copies are available for $23.95 from the **French Government Tourist Office,** 444 Madison Ave., 16th Floor, New York, NY 10022 (☎ 212/838-7800), and also from stores specializing in travel publications, including the **Traveller's Bookstore,** 22 W. 52nd St., New York, NY 10019 (☎ 800/755-8728 or 212/664-0995; fax 212/397-3984).

5 Tips for Travelers with Special Needs

FOR TRAVELERS WITH DISABILITIES

Facilities for travelers with disabilities are certainly above average in Europe, and nearly all modern hotels in the south of France now provide rooms designed for persons with disabilities. However, older hotels (unless they've been renovated) may not provide such important features as elevators, special toilet facilities, or ramps for wheelchair access.

The new high-speed TGV trains are wheelchair accessible; older trains have special compartments for wheelchair boarding. Guide dogs ride free. Some stations don't have escalators or elevators, so these present problems.

There are agencies in the United States and France that can provide advance-planning information. Knowing in advance which hotels, restaurants, and attractions are wheelchair accessible can save you a lot of frustration—firsthand accounts by other travelers with disabilities are the best.

The **Association des Paralysés de France,** 17 bd. Auguste-Blanqui, 75013 Paris (☎ 01-40-78-69-00), is a privately funded organization that provides wheelchair-bound individuals with documentation, moral support, and travel ideas. In addition to the central Paris office, it maintains an office in each of the 90 *départements* of France and can help find accessible hotels, transportation, sightseeing, house rentals, and (in some cases) companionship for paralyzed or partially paralyzed travelers. It's not, however, a travel agency.

The **Travel Information Service** of Philadelphia's MossRehab Hospital serves as a telephone resource for travelers with physical disabilities. Call ☎ **215/456-9600** (voice) or 215/456-9602 (TTY).

You can obtain **"Air Transportation of Handicapped Persons"** by writing to Free Advisory Circular No. AC12032, Distribution Unit, U.S. Department of Transportation, Publications Division, M-4332, Washington, DC 20590.

The **Society for the Advancement of Travel for the Handicapped,** 347 Fifth Ave., Suite 610, New York, NY 10016 (☎ **212/447-7284;** fax 212/725-8253), can provide information for people with disabilities and for the elderly, as well as listings of specialized tour operators. Yearly membership dues (which include quarterly issues of *Open World* magazine) are $45, or $30 for seniors and students.

One of the best organizations serving the needs of persons with disabilities (especially those assisted by wheelchairs and walkers) is **Flying Wheels Travel,** 143 W. Bridge (P.O. Box 382), Owatonna, MN 55060 (☎ **800/525-6790**), which offers various escorted tours and cruises internationally and private tours using a minivan with a lift.

For $25 annually, consider joining **Mobility International USA,** P.O. Box 10767, Eugene, OR 97440 (☎ **541/343-6812** voice and TDD; fax 541/343-6812). It answers questions about facilities for persons with disabilities at various destinations and offers discounts on videos, publications, and the programs it sponsors.

FOR GAY & LESBIAN TRAVELERS

Ever since the days of Somerset Maugham, gays and lesbians have flocked to the Côte d'Azur. The Riviera doesn't boast the gay activity associated with Paris, but plenty goes on here. There are even gay nude beaches, such as Jetée du Port at Nice. The gay scene in Nice is located near the port and the old city. Cannes is the other gay mecca in the south of France, with a popular and cruisy nude beach, La Plage de La Batterie. The final magnet for gays and lesbians is St-Tropez, where everyone converges on Plage de Tahiti.

PUBLICATIONS   Before going to France, men can order *Spartacus,* the international gay guide ($32.95), or the new *Paris Scene* ($10.95), published in London but available in the States. Also helpful is *Odysseus, the International Gay Travel Planner* ($27). Both lesbians and gays might want to pick up a copy of *Gay Travel A to Z* ($16).

These books and others are available from **A Different Light Book Store,** 151 W. 19th St., New York, NY 10011 (☎ **800/343-4002** or 212/989-4850), or **Giovanni's Room,** 1145 Pine St., Philadelphia, PA 19107 (☎ **215/923-2960;** fax 215/923-0813).

Our World, 1104 N. Nova Rd., Suite 251, Daytona Beach, FL 32117 (☎ **904/ 441-5367;** fax 904/441-5604), is a magazine devoted to gay and lesbian travel worldwide; it costs $35 for 10 issues. *Out & About,* 8 W. 19th St., Suite 401, New York, NY 10011 (☎ **800/929-2268;** fax 800/929-2215), has been hailed for its "straight" reporting about gay travel. It profiles the best gay or gay-friendly hotels, gyms, clubs, and other places. Its cost is $49 per year for 10 information-packed issues. Aimed at the more upscale gay traveler, it has been praised by everybody from *Travel & Leisure* to the *New York Times.*

TRAVEL AGENCIES   A company called **Our Family Abroad,** 40 W. 57th St., Suite 430, New York, NY 10019 (☎ **800/999-5500** or 212/459-1800; fax 212/ 581-3756), operates escorted tours that include about a dozen European itineraries. In California, a leading option for gay travel arrangements is **Above and Beyond,** 300 Townsend St., Suite 107, San Francisco, CA 94107 (☎ **800/397-2681** or 415/ 284-1666; fax 415/284-1660).

AN ORGANIZATION   The **International Gay Travel Association (IGTA),** P.O. Box 4974, Key West, FL 33041 (☎ **305/292-0217,** or 800/448-8550 for voice mail), is an international network of travel-industry businesses and professionals who encourage gay/lesbian travel worldwide. With around 1,200 members, it offers quarterly newsletters, marketing mailings, and a membership directory that's updated quarterly. Membership often includes gay and lesbian businesses but is open to individuals for $125 yearly, plus a $100 administrative fee for new members. Members are kept informed of gay and gay-friendly hoteliers, tour operators, and airline and cruise-line representatives, plus such ancillary businesses as the contacts at travel guide publishers and gay-related travel clubs.

FOR SENIOR TRAVELERS

Many discounts are available in France for seniors—men and women who've reached the "third age," as the French say. For more information, contact the French Government Tourist Office (see section 1 in this chapter).

DISCOUNT RAIL CARD   At any rail station in the country, seniors (men and women 60 and older—with proof of age) can obtain a **Carte Vermeil** (silver-gilt card). There are two types of Carte Vermeil: The Carte Vermeil Quatre Temps costs 145F ($29) and allows a 50% discount on four rail trips per year. A Carte Vermeil Plein Temps goes for 279F ($55.80) and is good for a 50% discount on unlimited rail travel throughout a year.

There are some restrictions on Carte Vermeil travel—for example, you can't use it between 3pm Sunday and noon Monday and from noon Friday to noon Saturday. There's no Carte Vermeil discount on the Paris network of commuter trains. Holders of the Plein Temps card sometimes receive discounts of up to 30% on rail trips to other countries of Western Europe. Carte Vermeil also delivers reduced prices on certain regional bus lines, as well as theater tickets in Paris and half-price admission at state-owned museums.

AIRFARE DISCOUNTS   The French domestic airline **Air Inter Europe** honors "third agers" by offering a 25% to 50% reduction on its regular nonexcursion tariffs. Restrictions do apply, however. Also, discounts of around 10% are offered to passengers 62 or over on selected Air France flights. These include some flights between Paris and Nice, as well as many international flights, including some on the Concorde.

ORGANIZATIONS   The **American Association of Retired Persons (AARP),** 601 E St. NW, Washington, DC 20049 (☎ **202/434-AARP**), is the nation's leading organization for people 50 and older. It serves their needs and interests through advocacy, research, informative programs, and community services provided by a network of local chapters and experienced volunteers throughout the country. The organization also offers members a wide range of special membership benefits, including *Modern Maturity* magazine and the monthly *Bulletin*.

Elderhostel, 75 Federal St., Boston, MA 02110-1941 (☎ **617/426-8056**), arranges numerous study programs around Europe, including France. Most courses, lasting about 3 weeks, represent great value since they include airfare, accommodations in student dormitories or modest inns, all meals, and tuition. The courses involve no homework, are ungraded, and often focus on the liberal arts. These are not luxury vacations, but they're fun and fulfilling. Participants must be 55 or older. Write or call for a free newsletter and a list of upcoming courses and destinations.

Mature Outlook, P.O. Box 10448, Des Moines, IA 50306 (☎ **800/336-6330;** fax 847/286-5024), is a travel organization for people over 50. Members are offered discounts at ITC-member hotels and receive a bimonthly magazine. Annual membership is $14.95 to $19.95, which entitles members to discounts and often free coupons for discounted merchandise from Sears.

SAGA International Holidays, 222 Berkeley St., Boston, MA 02116 (☎ **800/ 343-0273;** fax 617/375-5951), is well known for its inclusive tours and cruises for those 50 and older.

The **National Council of Senior Citizens,** 8403 Colesville Rd., Suite 1200, Silver Spring, MD 20910 (☎ **301/578-8800**), a nonprofit organization, offers a newsletter six times a year (partly devoted to travel tips) and discounts on hotel and auto rentals; annual dues are $13 per person or couple.

FOR STUDENT TRAVELERS

Students can usually obtain a wide array of discounts. The largest travel service for students is **Council Travel,** a subsidiary of the Council on International Educational Exchange (CIEE), 205 E. 42nd St., New York, NY 10017 (☎ **212/822-2700;** fax 212/822-2699), which provides details about budget travel, study abroad, work permits, and insurance. It also publishes helpful materials and issues the International Student Identity Card (ISIC) for $19 to bona-fide students. For a copy of *Student Travels* magazine, with information on all the council's services and CIEE's programs and publications, send $1 in postage. Council Travel offices are located throughout the States; call ☎ **800/GET-AN-ID** to find out where the closest office is. There's an office in Aix-en-Provence at 12 rue Victor-Leydet (☎ **04-42-38-58-82;** fax 04-42-38-94-00) and an office in Nice at 37 bis rue d'Angleterre (☎ **04-93-82- 23-33;** fax 04-93-82-25-59).

Hostelling International / IYHF (International Youth Hostel Federation) was designed to provide bare-bones accommodations for serious budget travelers. Regular membership costs $25 annually; those under 18 pay $10 and those over 54 pay $15. For information, contact Hostelling International–American Youth Hostels (HI-AYH), 733 15th St. NW, Suite 840, Washington, DC 20005 (☎ **202/ 783-6161;** fax 202/783-6171).

6 The Active Vacation Planner

Provence and the Côte d'Azur are especially well organized for many sports. Most clubs will accept temporary members and activities are wide ranging, from biking through the countryside to golfing on the pine-fringed fairways of Provence to swinging a tennis racquet close to Mediterranean waters. If you like your activities offbeat, you can even go barging along the lowlands of the Camargue.

Of course, if you want to go really local, you'll forsake all the activities below and take up boules and its local variant, pétanque. The game is relatively simple to learn—any local can teach you—and it's played with small metal balls on earth courts in every dusty village square.

BARGING

Before the advent of the railways, many of the crops, building supplies, raw materials, and finished products of France were barged through a series of rivers, canals, and estuaries. Many of these are still graced with their old-fashioned locks and pumps, allowing shallow-draft barges easy access through some of the most idyllic countryside. Many companies offer wonderful barging tours.

The **Crown Blue Line,** c/o Fenwick & Lang, 100 W. Harisson, Suite 350, Seattle, WA 98119 (☎ **206/216-2903**), acts as a clearinghouse for the chartering of at least 400 cruise craft, each with a shallow draft, that can slowly navigate the locks and channels of France's waterways. You choose from among 27 kinds of boats, each suitable for between two and about a dozen passengers. Rentals last for a week and can be arranged with a staff or without. Plan on cruising no more than 5 hours a day, then devoting the rest of your holiday to exploring the countryside, perhaps on bicycle. A 7-day rental of any of the vessels ranges from $1,290 to $4,620, depending on its capacity and the season.

With **Kemwel's Premier Selections,** 106 Calvert St., Harrison, NY 10528 (☎ **800/234-4000** or 914/835-5555; fax 914/835-5449), you'll discover the secret corners of France as you wind your way along waterways on board a luxury hotel barge. Enjoy fine wines and cuisine, bicycling, walking, and exploring. Its fleet can accommodate individuals as well as groups and offers a wide array of cruising areas, including the south of France. Inclusive fares per person for 3 nights (double occupancy) begin at $1,160, with 6 nights beginning at $1,490.

Le Boat, 215 Union St., Hackensack, NJ 07601 (☎ **800/992-0291** or 201/342-1838), focuses on regions of France not covered by many other barge operators. The company's pair of barges are luxury craft of a size and shape that fit through the relatively narrow canals and locks of the Camargue, Languedoc, and Provence. Each 6-night tour involves no more than 10 passengers in five cabins outfitted with mahogany and brass, plus meals prepared by a Cordon Bleu chef. Prices range from $14,000 per person off-season to $16,500 per person in summer.

BICYCLING

A well-recommended company that has led cyclists through the provinces since 1979 is the California-based **Backroads,** 801 Cedar St., Berkeley, CA 94710 (☎ **800/462-2848** or 510/527-1555; fax 510/527-1444). Its well-organized tours of Provence last between 5 and 8 days and include stays in everything from Relais & Châteaux hotels to campgrounds where staff members prepare most meals featuring local cuisine. All tours include an accompanying vehicle that provides liquid refreshments and assists in the event of breakdowns. Per-person rates range from $1,100 to $3,100, depending on the territory, the duration, and the degree of luxury.

Holland Bicycling Tours, Inc., P.O. Box 6485, Thousand Oaks, CA 91359 (☎ **800/852-3258;** fax 805/495-8601), is the North American representative of a Dutch-based company that leads a 10-day tour through Provence, past Roman ruins, van Gogh's sunflowers, and fields pungent with lavender, thyme, and basil. The trip begins in Avignon and concludes with a 2-day stay near Gordes, a charming town with vaulted passageways. The price is $1,750 per person. Occupants of single rooms pay a supplement of $325.

Bridges Tours, 2855 Capital Dr., Eugene, OR 97403 (☎ **800/461-6760**), offers several regional biking and walking tours. All tours feature groups of eight, escorts, van support, and stays at inns and small hotels, costing $200 or $300 per person per day. **Châteaux Bike Tours,** P.O. Box 5706, Denver, CO 80217 (☎ **800/678-2453**), promotes luxury tours of France with small groups, van support, two guides, and stays in châteaux. Tours (usually for 5 to 18 people) range from 5 to 9 days and cost $2,000 to $3,000 per person, double occupancy.

FISHING

The Mediterranean provides a variety of fish and fishing methods. You can line fish from the rocks along the coast or from small boats known as *pointu.* Local fishers often take visitors along when fishing in the sea for tuna. The rivers provide sea trout, speckled trout, and silver eel, and the sandy shores of the Camargue offer the tellina or sunset shell, which are small shellfish. For more information on regulations and access to fishing areas, contact the **Comité Régional PACA de la Fédération des Pêcheurs en Mer** (☎ **04-91-72-63-96**) or the **Fédération Départmentale pour la Pêche et la Protection du Milieu Aquatique,** Espace la Beauvalle, Hall B, rue M.-Gandhi, 13084 Aix-en-Provence 2 (☎ **04-42-26-59-15**).

GOLFING

The area around Bouches-du-Rhône has many fine golf courses, with seven 18-hole courses, five 9-hole courses, and several practice courses in the Provence area. A few of the 18-hole courses are **Golf-Club d'Aix-Marseille,** Domaine Riquetti, Chemin Départmental 9, 13290 Les Milles (☎ **04-42-24-20-41**); **Golf de la Salette,** impasse des Vaudrans, 13011 Marseille (☎ **04-91-27-12-16**); and **Golf de l'Ecole de l'Air,** Base Aérienne 701, 13300 Salon-de-Provence (☎ **04-90-53-90-90**). A 9-hole course is **Set Golf le Pey Blanc,** chemin de Granet, 13090 Aix-en-Provence (☎ **04-42-64-11-82**).

Golf International, Inc., 275 Madison Ave., New York, NY 10016 (☎ **800/833-1389** or 212/986-9176; fax 212/986-3720), offers the Golfing Epicurean package: a week-long trip based in the historic hilltop village of Mougins, a 10-minute drive from Cannes and the bustle of the Riviera. Mougins is the golfing capital of the south of France and provides a wealth of fine dining opportunities. As part of this package you spend 6 nights at the four-star Les Mas Candille, a 200-year-old converted farmhouse in the village. The price includes golf on four of the best courses in the area: Royal Mougins, Cannes-Mougins, Valbonne, and Cannes-Mandelieu. Also included is a car rental with collision-damage waiver insurance and unlimited mileage. The cost is $1,795 for golfers, with a $247 reduction for nongolfers. You can request a copy of Golf International's *Complete Golfing Vacation Guide* by calling the number above.

For more information on the options available, contact the **Fédération Française de Golf,** 69 av. Victor-Hugo, 75116 Paris (☎ **01-44-17-63-00**).

HIKING

The Bouches-du-Rhône area is a walker's heaven, whether you enjoy a stroll or a strenuous long-distance hike or even mountain climbing. The walking challenges include the wetlands of the Camargue, the semi-arid desert of La Crau, and the mountainous hills to the wild rocky inlets of Les Calanques. Long-distance hiking paths, **Sentiers de Grande Randonnée** (GRs), join the area's major places of interest. GR6 starts in Tarascon, runs along the foot of the Lubéron Hills, and crosses the Alpilles Hills. GR9 goes down the Lubéron, past Mont Ste-Victoire, and ends in Ste-Baume. GR98 is an alternative path linking Ste-Baume with Les Calanques and ends in Marseille. GR51 links Marseille and Arles via La Crau. GR99A links GR9 to the highlands of the Var département.

Spring and autumn are the best for hiking, as many of the paths are closed in summer because of forest fires. Be sure to check with the département before you begin your walk. For information, call the **Comité Départemental de Randonnée Pédestre** (Bouches-du-Rhône Hiking Committee), M. Busti, 24 av. du Prado-Immeuble B, Bureau 401, 13008 Marseille (☎ **04-91-81-12-08**), or **Comité Départmental Mont-Alp-Escalade** (Bouches-du-Rhône Mountaineering & Climbing Committee), Daniel Gorgeon, 5 impasse du Figuier, 13114 Puyloubier (☎ **04-42-66-35-05**).

The **Adventure Center,** 1311 63rd St., Suite 200, Emeryville, CA 94608 (☎ **800/227-8747**), sponsors 15-day hiking/camping trips in Provence, beginning and ending in Nice. The cost of an outing, exclusive of airfare and other travel-related expenses, is $805 per person, $135 of which is a local fee added in France. Included are 14 nights of campground accommodations and 1 night of bush camping. Eight evening meals are provided; the other seven are usually purchased in Provençal restaurants along the way. Campers are also expected to purchase three lunches. The company offers six trips per year, and though dates may vary, these include one departure in May and September and two departures in June and August.

Another company known for its adventure trips is **Mountain Travel Sobek,** 6420 Fairmount Ave., El Cerrito, CA 94530 (☎ **800/227-2384**), which offers two tour packages during summer. Trip dates vary, but both are offered three times a year between May and September. The upscale "Luxury Walking in the South of France" is $2,890 per person (travel not included), which covers a 6-day, 57-mile trek with accommodations provided in luxury hotels. The fee also includes five dinners at fine restaurants and one gourmet picnic lunch. Starting in Fontvieille, the hike encompasses the immediate environs of the lower Alpilles, St-Rémy, Les Baux, and Gordes. The more moderate "Hike in France's 'Grand Canyon'" is an 8-day journey following the Verdon River through the Grand Canyon du Verdon. The fee of $2,090 per person (exclusive of travel) includes accommodations in small hotels and inns, eight lunches, and four dinners. The itinerary begins in Marseilles, ends in Nice, and includes stops at Riez, Moustiers-Ste-Marie, La Palud, Point Sublime, Castellane, and St-André-les-Alpes.

HORSEBACK RIDING

One of the best ways to see the wildlife, salt swamps, and marshlands of the Camargue or the wooded hills around Alpilles, Ste-Baume, and Mont Ste-Victoire is on horseback. For more information, contact the **Délégation Nationale des Sports Equestres** (National Equestrian Sports Board), Centre Equestre Les Décanis, chemin Collavery, 13760 St-Cannat (☎ **04-42-57-35-42**); the **Comité Départemental de Tourisme Equestre** (Bouches-du-Rhône Equestrian Tourism Committee), M. Coulomb, Quartier Peyre-Bas, 13122 Ventabren (☎ **04-42-28-82-89**); the **Association Professionnelle du Tourisme Equestre** (Equestrian Tourism Trade Association), M. Dewavrin, La Provence à Cheval Quartier St-Joseph, 19350 Cadolive (☎ **04-42-04-66-76**); or the **Association Camarguaise de Tourisme Equestre** (Camargue Equestrian Tourism Association), Centre de Ginès–Pont de Gau, 13460 Stes-Maries-de-la-Mer (☎ **04-90-97-86-32**).

A clearinghouse for at least eight French stables is **Equitour FITS (Fun in the Saddle),** P.O. Box 807, Dubois, WY 82513 (☎ **800/545-0019** or 307/455-3363). It can arrange 9-day cross-country treks through Provence and the Camargue regions, with prices ranging from $750 to $2,200 per person.

7 Gourmet Tours & Language Schools

GOURMET TOURS

The **Annemarie Victory Organization,** 136 E. 64th St., New York, NY 10021 (☎ 212/486-0353), specializes in gourmet tours like the World of Alain Ducasse. This 12-day deluxe gourmet and wine tour begins in Nice and continues through Antibes, St-Paul-de-Vence, Monte Carlo, Mougins, Grasse, Haute Provence, Moustiers, Sisteron, Grenoble, and Lyon, and finally ends in Paris, where Ducasse will personally prepare a sumptuous farewell dinner. The price is $6,800 per person, double occupancy.

Cuisine International, P.O. Box 25228, Dallas, TX 75225 (☎ 214/373-1161), offers a week-long culinary experience in Provence. Accommodations are in hotels and private homes, such as the one overlooking a lake in Provence that houses the school. Classes are arranged to allow time for sightseeing, and meals are eaten in restaurants and private homes. Rates are inclusive, except for airfare: The price is $1,600 to $2,600. A tour by **European Culinary Adventures,** 5 Ledgewood Way, no. 6, Peabody, MA 01960 (☎ 800/852-2625), touts culinary vacations during which you stay in an 18th-century farmhouse (also the school) between Bordeaux and Toulouse. The price of a 7-day/6-night tour is $2,450 per person, including lodging, cooking classes, most meals, touring, and local transportation. In addition, four people can charter an 85-foot barge for a week of cooking, dining, and touring.

Endless Beginnings Tours, 12650 Sabre Springs Pkwy., Suite 207, San Diego, CA 92128 (☎ 800/822-7855), specializes in food and wine tours, garden and villa visits, and art programs. Small groups of 10 to 15 travel with knowledgeable guides. Accommodations are in four-star hotels and occasionally in charming three-star lodgings. The 16-day tour of Provence and the Côte d'Azur (beginning and ending in Nice) is $4,500 per person, double occupancy.

LANGUAGE SCHOOLS

A clearinghouse for information on French-language schools is **Lingua Service Worldwide,** 211 E. 43rd St., Suite 1303, New York, NY 10017 (☎ 800/394-LEARN or 212/867-1225; fax 212/983-2590). Its programs cover Antibes, Aix-en-Provence, Avignon, Cannes, Juan-les-Pins, Montpellier, and Nice. Courses can be both long- or short-term, the latter with 20 lessons per week. They range from $200 to $990 per week, depending on the city, the school, and the accommodations.

The **National Registration Center for Studies Abroad (NRCSA),** 823 N. 2nd St., Milwaukee, WI 53201 (☎ 414/278-0631), has a $2 catalog of schools in France, including the International House in Nice and Provence Langues and CELA (Centre d'Etudes Linguistiques d'Avignon) in Avignon. It'll register you at the school of your choice, arrange for room and board, and make your airline reservations—all for no extra fee. Ask for a free copy of its newsletter. Prices vary greatly depending on the university and the course length, from $1,171 to $34,158.

8 Getting to the South of France from North America

BY PLANE

Nonstop flights to Paris (sometimes on airlines you might not think of automatically) are available from such North American hubs as Atlanta, Chicago, Cincinnati, Houston, Miami, New York, and St. Louis.

A Note on Flight Routing

Although if you've bought this book you're obviously headed to the south of France, your flight will be routed through Paris. In rare instances, the flight will merely stop in Paris and then continue on to, say, Marseille or Nice. Most frequently, you and your luggage will have to change planes in Paris. However, Delta offers one flight per day direct from New York to Nice.

Flying time to Paris from New York is about 7 hours; from Chicago, 9 hours; from Los Angeles, 11 hours; from Atlanta, 8 hours; from Miami, 8¹/₂ hours; and from Washington, D.C., 7¹/₂ hours.

Hardcore Paris hands consider its two airports—Orly and Charles de Gaulle—as almost even bets in terms of convenience to the city's core, though taxi rides from Orly might take a bit less time than those from de Gaulle. Orly, the older of the two, is 8 miles south of the center, while Charles de Gaulle is 14 miles northeast. In April 1996 the last of Air France's flights to Paris from North America was routed away from Orly and into Charles de Gaulle (Terminal 2C). Air France's U.S.-based competitors tend to focus on both airports in equal measure.

Most airlines divide their year roughly into seasonal slots, with the lowest fares between November 1 and March 13. Shoulder season, between the high and low seasons, is only slightly more expensive and includes mid-March to mid-June and all of October, which we think is the ideal time to visit France.

THE MAJOR U.S. CARRIERS

All the major airlines fly to Paris from the U.S. cities listed below. Once you fly into Orly or Charles de Gaulle, you must take **Air France** or **Air Inter** (☎ 800/ 237-2747), a division of Air France, to reach your destination in Languedoc, in Provence, or on the Riviera. From Orly and Charles de Gaulle there are 20 flights per day to Marseille and to Nice, 16 to Toulouse, and 4 Monday to Friday and 2 Saturday and Sunday to Avignon.

American Airlines (☎ 800/433-7300) offers daily flights to Paris from Dallas / Fort Worth, Chicago, Miami, Boston, and New York. **Delta Airlines** (☎ 800/ 241-4141) is one of the best choices for those flying to Paris from the southeastern United States or the Midwest. In fact, Delta offers the greatest number of flights to Paris from the United States. From cities like New Orleans, Phoenix, Columbia (S.C.), and Nashville, Delta flies to Atlanta, connecting every evening with a non-stop flight to Paris. Delta also operates daily nonstop flights from both Cincinnati and New York. All these flights depart late enough in the day to permit transfers from much of Delta's vast North American network. Note that Delta is the only airline offering nonstop service from New York to Nice.

Continental Airlines (☎ 800/231-0856) provides nonstop flights to Paris from Newark and Houston. Flights from Newark depart daily, while flights from Houston depart four to seven times a week, depending on the season. **US Airways** (☎ 800/428-4322) offers daily nonstop service from Philadelphia to Paris.

TWA (☎ 800/221-2000) operates daily nonstop service to Paris from New York. In summer, several flights a week from Boston and Washington, D.C., go through New York; several times a week there are nonstop flights from St. Louis; and three times a week there are flights from Los Angeles, connecting in St. Louis or New York. In winter, flights from Los Angeles and Washington are suspended, and flights from St. Louis are direct, with brief touchdowns in New York or Boston en route.

THE FRENCH NATIONAL CARRIER

Aircraft belonging to the **Air France** (☎ 800/237-2747) fly frequently across the Atlantic. Formed from a merger combining three of France's largest airlines, the conglomerate offers routes that, until the merger, were maintained separately by Air France, UTA (Union des Transports Aériens), and France's internal domestic airline, Air Inter (now Air Inter Europe).

The airline offers daily or several-times-a-week flights between Paris and such North American cities as Newark; Washington, D.C.; Miami; Chicago; New York; Houston; San Francisco; Los Angeles; Montréal; Toronto; Mexico City; and Los Angeles. Flights to Paris from Los Angeles originate in Papeete, French Polynesia.

THE MAJOR CANADIAN CARRIER

Canadians usually choose the **Air Canada** (☎ 800/776-3000 in the U.S. and Canada) flights to Paris from Toronto and Montréal that depart every evening. Two of Air Canada's flights from Toronto are shared with Air France and feature Air France aircraft.

OTHER GOOD-VALUE CHOICES

Consolidators (known as "bucket shops") act as clearinghouses for blocks of tickets airlines discount and consign during normally slow periods of air travel. Tickets are usually priced 20% to 35% below the full fare. The terms of payment vary—from 45 days before departure to last-minute sales. You can purchase tickets through regular travel agents, who usually mark up the price 8% to 10%, maybe more, thereby greatly reducing your discount. But using such a ticket doesn't qualify you for an advance seat assignment, so you're likely to be assigned a "poor seat" at the last minute.

Most flyers estimate their savings at $200 per ticket off the regular price. Nearly a third of the passengers reported savings of up to $300 off the regular price. But—and here's the hitch—many people reported no savings at all, as the airlines sometimes match the consolidator ticket by announcing a promotional fare. The situation is a bit tricky and calls for some careful investigation to determine how much you're saving.

Bucket shops abound from coast to coast. Look for their ads in your local newspaper's travel section; they're usually very small and a single column in width. (*Note:* Since dealing with unknown bucket shops might be a little risky, it's wise to call the Better Business Bureau in your area to see if complaints have been filed against the company from which you plan to purchase a ticket.)

Here are some recommendations:

One of the biggest U.S. consolidators is **Travac,** 989 Sixth Ave., 16th Floor, New York, NY 10018 (☎ 800/TRAV-800 in the U.S., or 212/563-3303), which offers discounted seats from throughout the United States to most cities in Europe on airlines like TWA, United, and Delta. Another Travac office is at 2601 E. Jefferson St., Orlando, FL 32803 (☎ 407/896-0014).

In New York, try **TFI Tours International,** 34 W. 32nd St., 12th Floor, New York, NY 10001 (☎ 800/745-8000 in the U.S. outside the New York City area, or 212/736-1140 inside New York City). This tour company offers services to 177 cities worldwide.

From anywhere, explore the possibilities of **Travel Avenue,** 10 S. Riverside Plaza, Suite 1404, Chicago, IL 60606 (☎ 800/333-3335 in the U.S.), a national agency. Its tickets are often cheaper than those at most shops, and it charges only a $25 fee on international tickets, rather than taking the usual 10% commission from an airline. Travel Avenue rebates most of that back to you—hence, the lower fares.

In Minnesota, a possibility is **TMI (Travel Management International),** 1129 E. Wayzata Blvd., Wayzata, MN 55391 (☎ **800/245-3672** in the U.S.; fax 612/ 476-1480), which offers a wide variety of discounts, including youth fares, student fares, and access to other kinds of air-related discounts.

800-FLY-4-LESS is a nationwide airline reservation and ticketing service that specializes in finding the lowest fares. For information on available consolidator airline tickets for last-minute travel, call ☎ **800/359-4537.** When fares are high and advance planning time low, such a service is invaluable.

BY PACKAGE TOUR

For package tours that offer adventure and activity, see "The Active Vacation Planner," earlier in this chapter. For other types of tours, see "Gourmet Tours & Language Schools," also earlier in this chapter.

The French Experience, 370 Lexington Ave., New York, NY 10017 (☎ **212/ 986-1115;** fax 212/986-3808), offers prearranged package tours lasting 6 or 7 days in Languedoc, in Provence, and on the Riviera. Stops are arranged in hotels and hostelleries in Provence and on the Riviera and in private homes that might be a farmhouse or a small castle or manor house in Languedoc. Typical prices: a 7-night stay at Hostellerie des Agassins ouside Avignon at $588 per person or a 6-night stay at several hotels/châteaux in the Provence/Riviera area at $628 per person.

American Express Vacations (as operated by Certified Vacations, Inc.), P.O. Box 1525, Fort Lauderdale, FL 33302 (☎ **800/446-6234** in the U.S. and Canada; fax 954/357-4682), is the world's most recognizable tour operator. Its offerings in France are more comprehensive than those of many other companies. Highlighting the unparalleled variety are more than 40 "go-any-day" city packages (6 nights from $2,731 to $3,991, double occupancy, depending on season), 9 freelance vacations ($1,079 per person for land package only), and 18 escorted tours ($1,199 per person for land package only). If you have a clear idea of what you want and it's not already available, this operator can arrange an individualized itinerary.

Trafalgar Tours, 11 E. 26th St., New York, NY 10010 (☎ **800/854-0103**), offers cost-conscious packages with lodgings in unpretentious hotels. Its Best of France is a 14-day trip starting and ending in Paris, with stops on the Riviera and in Lourdes, Nice, Monaco, and others. Most meals and twin-bed accommodations in first-class hotels are part of the package, which is $1,499 per person for the land package only. Call your travel agent for more information (Trafalgar takes calls only from agents).

For top-of-the-line travel, try **Travcoa,** P.O. Box 2360, Newport Beach, CA 92658 (☎ **800/992-2003**). All its tours are fully escorted, with stays in four-star hotels and three à la carte meals a day. The 28-day Exotic France begins and ends in Paris and takes 28 days to circle the country going down the west coast, then up the east side back to Paris and visiting numerous historic sites; prices range from $1,177 to $1,285 per person, double occupancy.

9 Getting to the South of France from the United Kingdom

BY PLANE

If you're in the United Kingdom and don't want to go to Paris before flying to the south of France, you'll find a number of flights offered to the Nice–Côte d'Azur Airport and the Marseille-Provence airport. A number of daily flights are offered by

A Note on British Customs

On January 1, 1993, the borders between European countries were relaxed as the European markets united. When you're traveling within the EU, this will have a big impact on what you can buy and take home with you for personal use.

If you buy your goods in a duty-free shop, then the old rules still apply: You're allowed to bring home 200 cigarettes and 2 liters of table wine, plus 1 liter of spirits or 2 liters of fortified wine. But now you can buy your wine, spirits, or cigarettes in an ordinary shop in France or Belgium, for example, and bring home *almost* as much as you like. (Excise law does set theoretical limits.) If you're returning home from a non-EU country, the allowances are the standard ones from duty-free shops. You must declare any goods in excess of these allowances. British Customs tends to be strict and complicated in its requirements.

For details, get in touch with **Her Majesty's Customs and Excise Office,** Dorset House, Stamford Street, London SE1 9PY (☎ **0171/202-4510;** fax 0171/202-4131).

British Airways (☎ 0345/222-111), **Air France** (☎ 0181/742-6600), and **British Midland** (☎ 0181/897-4000).

Flying from England to France is often very expensive, even though the distance is short. That's why most Brits depend on a good travel agent to get them the lowest possible fares. Good values are offered by a number of companies, such as **Nouvelles Frontières,** 2–3 Woodstock St., London W1R 1HE (☎ 0171/629-7772). If you don't want to use a travel agent, an APEX ticket might be the way to trim costs. You must reserve these tickets in advance. However, this ticket offers a discount without the usual booking restrictions. You might also ask the airlines about a Eurobudget ticket, which has restrictions or length-of-stay requirements.

The newspapers are always full of classified ads touting "slashed" fares from London to other parts of the world. Another good source is *Time Out* magazine. London's *Evening Standard* maintains a daily travel section, and the Sunday editions of virtually every newspaper in Britain run many ads. Though competition is fierce, a well-recommended company that consolidates bulk ticket purchases and passes the savings on to you is **Trailfinders** (☎ 0171/937-5400 in London). It offers access to tickets on such carriers as British Airways, KLM, and SAS.

BY TRAIN

From the United Kingdom, most passengers arrive in Paris before going the rest of the way by train to Provence. There's excellent and fast service from Paris's Gare de Lyon to Marseille via Avignon. Passengers take the TGV (Train à Grande Vitesse). The TGV zips from Paris to Marseille in 5 hours, to Avignon in 4 hours, and to Nice in 7 hours. If you'd like to have your car transported, call the French rail office in London at ☎ 0171/803-3030 for more information.

Rail passes as well as individual train tickets in Europe are available at most travel agents or at **BritRail Travel International** (☎ 0171/928-5151), Victoria Station, London SW1B 1JY. You might also want to stop in at the **International Rail Centre,** Victoria Station, London SW1V 1JY (☎ 0171/834-7066).

In London, an especially convenient place to buy rail tickets to virtually anywhere is **Wasteels Ltd.,** opposite Platform 2 in Victoria Station, London SW1V 1JY (☎ 0171/834-6744). It provides railway-related services and information on the pros and cons of various types of fares and rail passes; its staff will probably spend more than the usual amount of time with you while planning your itinerary. Depending on circumstances, Wasteels sometimes charges a £5 fee, but for the information provided the fee might be worth it.

BY FERRY

There are a bewildering number of options for those who want to steam, or motor, their way to France across La Manche ("the sleeve," as the French call the Channel) from Britain. All these face stiff competition from the recently inaugurated Channel Tunnel (see below).

Service aboard ferryboats and hydrofoils operates day and night, in all seasons, with the exception of last-minute cancellations during particularly fierce storms. Many Channel crossings are carefully timed to coincide with the arrival/departure of major trains (especially those between London and Paris). Trains disgorge passengers and their luggage only a short walk from the piers. Most ferries carry cars, trucks, and massive amounts of freight, but some hydrofoils take passengers only. The major routes include at least 12 trips a day between Dover or Folkestone and Calais or Boulogne. Hovercraft and hydrofoils make the trip from Dover to Calais, the shortest distance across the Channel, in just 40 minutes during good weather, whereas the slower-moving ferries might take several hours, depending on weather conditions and tides. If you're bringing a car, it's important to make reservations, as space below decks is usually crowded. Timetables can vary depending on weather conditions and many other factors.

The most visible operator of ferryboats across the channel is **P&O Channel Lines** (☎ **800/677-8585** for reservations in the U.S. and Canada, or 01301/212-121 in England). It operates car and passenger ferries between Portsmouth, England, and Cherbourg, France (three departures a day; 4¼ hours each way during daylight hours, 7 hours each way at night); and between Portsmouth and Le Havre, France (three a day; 5½ hours each way). Most popular of all are the routes it operates between Dover and Calais, France (25 sailings a day; 75 minutes each way).

P&O's major competitor is **Stena Sealink** (☎ **800/677-8585** for reservations in the U.S. and Canada, or 01233/615-455 in England), which carries both passengers and vehicles on most of its routes. It offers conventional ferryboat service between Cherbourg and Southampton (one or two trips a day; 6 to 8 hours each way). Its conventional car-ferries between Calais and Dover are very popular; they depart 20 times a day in both directions and take 90 minutes to make the crossing. Typical one-way fares between France and England are £25 ($40) for adults, £22 ($35.20) for seniors, and £15 ($24) for children.

As stated above, the shortest and by far the most popular route across the Channel is between Calais and Dover. **Hoverspeed** operates at least 12 hovercraft crossings daily; the trip takes 35 minutes. It also runs a SeaCat (a catamaran propelled by jet engines) that takes slightly longer to make the crossing between Boulogne and Folkestone; the SeaCats depart about four times a day on the 55-minute voyage. For reservations and information, call Hoverspeed (☎ **800/677-8585** for reservations in the U.S. and Canada or 01304/240-241 in Britain). Typical one-way fares are £25 ($40) per person.

If you plan to transport a rental car between England and France, check in advance with the rental company about license and insurance requirements and additional drop-off charges. And be alert that many car-rental companies, for insurance reasons, forbid transport of one their vehicles over the water between England and France. Transport of a car each way begins at 650F ($130).

BY THE CHANNEL TUNNEL

Elizabeth II and the late President François Mitterrand officially opened the Channel Tunnel (Chunnel) in 1994, and the *Eurostar Express* began twice-daily passenger service between London and both Paris and Brussels. The $15-billion tunnel, one of the great engineering feats of all time, is the first link between Britain and the Continent since the Ice Age. The 31-mile journey between Great Britain and France takes 35 minutes, though the actual time spent in the Chunnel is only 19 minutes.

Rail Europe (☎ 800/94-CHUNNEL) sells tickets for the *Eurostar* direct train service between London and Paris or Brussels. A round-trip fare between London and Paris, for example, is $278 to $298 in first class and $150 to $278 in second. But you can cut costs to $140 with a second-class 15-day nonrefundable advance-purchase round-trip ticket. In Britain, make reservations for *Eurostar* at ☎ 0345/303-030; in Paris, call ☎ 01-33-31-58-03; and in the United States call ☎ 800/387-6782.

The Chunnel's *Le Shuttle* accommodates passenger cars, charter buses, taxis, and motorcycles under the English Channel from Folkestone, England, to Calais, France. It operates 24 hours a day year-round, running every 15 minutes during peak travel times and at least once an hour at night. You can buy tickets at the toll booth. With *Le Shuttle,* gone are weather-related delays, seasickness, and the need for advance reservations.

Before boarding *Le Shuttle,* motorists stop at a toll booth and pass through Immigration for both countries at one time. Then they drive onto a half-mile-long train and travel through an underground tunnel built beneath the seabed through a layer of impermeable chalk marl and sealed with a reinforced-concrete lining. During the ride, they stay in air-conditioned carriages, remain inside their cars, or step outside to stretch their legs. When the trip is completed, they simply drive off toward their destinations—in our case, to France. Travel time between the English and French highway system is about 1 hour. Once on French soil, Britain-based drivers must, obviously, begin driving on the right-hand side of the road.

Stores selling duty-free goods, restaurants, and service stations are available to travelers on both sides of the Channel. A bilingual staff is on hand to assist travelers at both the French and the British terminals.

10 Getting to the South of France from Paris

You can rent a car in Paris and drive to the south, but the best way to get there is either by plane or train.

BY PLANE

In 1995 the French domestic airline Air Inter, a subsidiary of Air France, was reorganized into the broader, more wide-ranging **Air Inter Europe,** with scheduled stopovers in some of the larger (non-French) cities of Europe. Today it flies in and out of both Orly and Charles de Gaulle airports, serving 30 cities in France, including Toulouse, Carcassonne, Montpellier, Toulon, Nice, Marseille, and Avignon. Non-stop flights between cities on the mainland of France usually require about an hour each.

If you're planning to see more of France than just the south, you can take advantage of the airline's network by investing in one of the **Air Inter Europe Passes,** all offering significant savings over the cost of individual tickets. The most popular is **Le France Pass,** allowing 7 days of unlimited travel to any of the airline's destinations in France, to be used within a period of 1 month, for a cost of $339 per person. The more expensive **Le France Europe Pass** sells for $459 and allows you to add two European segments on Air Inter Europe, one per day, within the 7-day validity of Le France Pass. If you're thinking of renting a car after your arrival at any of France's airports, consider spending $369 for **Le France Air-Car Pass**. It allows 2 days of unlimited air travel, plus the 7-day use of a Hertz Rent-a-Car during any 1-month period. You must arrange car reservations 24 hours in advance of whenever you want to pick up a vehicle at an airport.

Finally, those under 25 or any student under 27 should check out **Le France Youth and Student Pass.** It costs $219 and allows 5 days of unlimited air travel within any 2-month period. These passes are sold only in North America and are valid only for U.S. residents. Passes aren't refundable, replaceable, or transferable. Air travel days don't have to be consecutive. For information and purchase, call Air France at ☎ **800/237-2747.**

BY TRAIN

With some 50 cities in France, including Marseille and Nice, linked by the world's fastest trains, Paris is connected to many areas of the country by a trip of just a few hours. With 24,000 miles of track and about 3,000 stations, **SNCF (French National Railroads)** is fabled throughout the world for its on-time performance. You can travel first or second class by day as well as in couchette or sleeper by night. Many trains carry dining facilities, which range from cafeteria-style meals to formal dinners.

INFORMATION   If you plan much travel on European railroads, get the latest copy of the *Thomas Cook European Timetable of Railroads.* This comprehensive 500-plus-page book documents all Europe's mainline passenger rail services with detail and accuracy. It's available exclusively in North America from the **Forsyth Travel Library,** P.O. Box 480800, Kansas City, MO 64148 (☎ **800/367-7984**), at a cost of $27.95, plus $4.50 postage (priority airmail to the U.S. and $5 U.S. for shipments to Canada).

In the United States: For more information and to purchase rail passes (see below) before you leave, contact Rail Europe at 226–230 Westchester Ave., White Plains, NY 10604 (☎ **800/848-7245;** fax 914/682-3712).

In Canada: Rail Europe offices are at 2087 Dundas St. East, Suite 105, Mississauga, ON L4X 1M2 (☎ **800/361-7245** or 905/602-4195; fax 905/602-4198).

In London: SNCF maintains offices at French Railways, 179 Piccadilly, London W1V OBA (☎ **0171/803-3030;** fax 0171/491-9956).

In Paris: The SNCF administrative offices are at 10 place Budapest, 75436 Paris (☎ **01-42-85-60-00**), but for information about rail departures, call or visit the nearest rail station, where staffs are on hand to assist with ticket sales and inquiries. Paris railway stations are Gare de l'Est, Gare du Nord, Gare St-Lazare, Gare Montparnasse, Gare d'Austerlitz, and Gare de Lyon.

FRENCH RAIL PASSES   Working cooperatively with SNCF, Air Inter Europe, and Avis, Rail Europe offers three flexible cost-saving rail passes that can reduce travel costs considerably, especially if you're heading somewhere else in France either before or after you explore the south.

The **France Railpass** provides unlimited rail transport throughout France for 3 days within 1 month, costing $198 in first class and $160 in second. You can purchase up to 6 more days for an extra $30 per person per day. Costs are even more reasonable for two adults traveling together: $148.50 per person for first class and $120 for second. Children 4 to 11 travel for half price.

The **France Rail 'n Drive Pass,** available only in North America, combines good value on both rail travel and Avis car rentals and is best used in conjunction with arriving at a major rail depot, then striking out to explore the countryside by car. It includes the rail pass above, along with unlimited mileage on a car rental. Costs are lowest when two or more adults travel together. You can use it during 5 nonconsecutive days in 1 month, and it includes 3 days of travel on the train and 2 days' use of a rental car. If rental of the least expensive car is combined with first-class rail travel, the price is $189 per person; if rental of the least expensive car is combined with second-class travel, the price is $159 per person. Cars can be upgraded for a supplemental fee. The above prices apply to two people traveling together; solo travelers pay from $279 for first class and $239 for second.

The **France Fly, Rail, 'n Drive Pass** is an arrangement whereby air, rail, and car transport in France are combined into an all-encompassing discount purchase. You fly to any destination in metropolitan France on Air Inter Europe, the French domestic airline; then travel any 3 days by train and any 2 days by car—all in any month-long period. When two people travel together, each pays an all-inclusive $289 for first class and $259 for second. When a solo adult travels alone, the price rises to $379 for first class and $339 for second. For a fee, extra days can be added to any of these passes (whether it be by plane, train, or automobile).

EURAILPASSES   For years, many in-the-know travelers have been taking advantage of one of Europe's greatest travel bargains: the **Eurailpass,** which permits unlimited first-class rail travel in any country in Western Europe except the British Isles (good in Ireland). Passes are for periods as short as 15 days or as long as 3 months and are strictly nontransferable.

The pass is sold only in North America. A Eurailpass for 15 days is $522; it's $678 for 21 days, $838 for 1 month, $1,188 for 2 months, and $1,468 for 3 months. Children 3 and under travel free providing they don't occupy a seat (otherwise they're charged half fare); children 4 to 11 are charged half fare. If you're under 26, you can purchase a **Eurail Youthpass,** entitling you to unlimited second-class travel for 1 or 2 months, costing $598 and $798, respectively.

Seat reservations are required on some trains. Many of the trains have couchettes (sleeping cars), which cost extra. Obviously, the 2- or 3-month traveler gets the greatest economic advantages; the Eurailpass is ideal for such extensive trips. With the pass you can visit all of France's major sights, from Normandy to the Alps, then end your vacation in Norway, for example.

If you'll be traveling for 14 days to 1 month you have to estimate rail distance before determining if such a pass is to your benefit. To obtain full advantage of the ticket for 15 days or a month, you'd have to spend a great deal of time on the train. Eurailpass holders are entitled to considerable reductions on certain buses and ferries as well.

Travel agents in all towns and railway agents in such major cities as New York, Montréal, and Los Angeles sell all these tickets. A Eurailpass is available at the North American offices of CIT Travel Service, the French National Railroads, the German Federal Railroads, and the Swiss Federal Railways.

The **Eurail Flexipass** allows you to visit Europe with more flexibility. It's valid in first class and offers the same privileges as the Eurailpass. However, it provides a number of individual travel days that you can use over a much longer period of consecutive days. That makes it possible to stay in one city and yet not lose a single day of travel. There are two passes: 10 days of travel in 2 months for $616 and 15 days of travel in 2 months for $812.

With many of the same qualifications and restrictions as the previously described Flexipass is a **Eurail Youth Flexipass.** Sold only to travelers under 26, it allows 5 days of travel within 2 months for $255, 10 days of travel within 2 months for $438, and 15 days of travel within 2 months for $588.

11 Getting Around the South of France by Car

The most charming Provençal villages and best country hotels always seem to lie away from the main cities and train stations. You'll find that renting a car is usually the best way to travel once you get to the south of France, especially if you plan to explore in depth and not stick to the standard route along the coast.

Driving time in Europe is largely a matter of conjecture, urgency, and how much sightseeing you do along the way. The driving time from Marseille to Paris is a matter of national pride, and tall tales abound about how rapidly the French can do it. With the accelerator pressed to the floor, you might conceivably make it in 7 hours, but we always make a 2-day journey of it.

CAR RENTALS

Renting a car in France is easy. You'll need to present a passport, a valid driver's license, and a valid credit or charge card. (In lieu of that, unless you've made alternative arrangements with the rental company before your departure, you'll need to make a significant cash deposit.) You'll also have to meet the minimum age requirement of the company. (For their least expensive cars this is 21 at Hertz, 23 at Avis, and 25 at Budget. More expensive cars at any of the above-mentioned companies might require that you be at least 25.) It usually isn't obligatory, at least within France, but certain companies, especially the smaller ones, have at times asked for the presentation of an International Driver's License, even though this is becoming increasing superfluous in Western Europe.

Note: The best deal is usually a weekly rental with unlimited mileage. All car-rental bills in France are subject to a whopping 20.6% government tax, among the highest in Europe. And though the rental company won't usually mind if you drive your car across the French border—into, say, Germany, Switzerland, Italy, or Spain—it's often expressly forbidden to transport your car on any ferryboat, including the dozens that ply the waters of the Channel to England.

Unless it's already factored into the rental agreement, an optional collision-damage waiver (CDW) carries an extra charge of 80F to 95F ($16 to $19) per day for the least expensive cars. Buying this will usually eliminate all but 1,500F ($300) of your responsibility in the event of accidental damage to the car. Because most newcomers aren't familiar with local driving customs and conditions, we highly recommend that you buy the CDW, though certain credit/charge-card issuers will compensate you for any accident-related liability to a rented car if the imprint of their card appears on the original rental contract. At some of the companies the CDW won't protect you against the theft of a car, so if this is the case, ask about buying extra theft protection. This cost is around 37F ($7.40) extra per day.

At all four of the big car-rental companies, the least expensive car will probably be a Ford Fiesta, a Nissan Micra, a Renault Clio, a Peugeot 106, a VW Polo, a Fiat Punto, or an Opel Corsa, usually with manual transmission, no air-conditioning, and few frills. Depending on the company and the season, prices may range from $176 to $195 per week, with unlimited mileage (but not tax or CDW) included. Discounts are sometimes granted for rentals of 2 weeks or more. Automatic transmission is regarded as a luxury in Europe, so if you want it you'll have to pay dearly. All agencies allow you to prepay your rental in U.S. dollars, though the benefits of prepayment vary from case to case and company to company, depending on what's included as part of the proposed prepayment.

Budget (☎ 800/472-3325 in the U.S. and Canada) has numerous locations in southern France, including those in **Avignon** at the airport (☎ 04-90-27-94-95) and at 2 av. de Montclair-Gare (☎ 04-90-27-94-95); in **Marseille** at the airport (☎ 04-42-14-24-55), at 40 bd. de Plombières (☎ 04-91-64-40-03), and at Première Avenue No. 23 (☎ 04-42-10-03-10); in **Montpellier** at the airport (☎ 04-67-50-07-34) and at 4 rue J.-Ferry, Immeuble Le Regent (☎ 04-67-92-69-00); in **Nice** at the airport (☎ 04-93-21-36-50) and at 23 rue de Belgique, opposite the rail station (☎ 04-93-16-24-16); and in **Toulouse** at the airport (☎ 05-61-71-85-80) and at 49 rue Bayard (☎ 05-61-63-18-18). For rentals of more than 7 days, in most cases cars can be picked up in one French city and dropped off in another, but there are additional charges. Still, Budget's rates are among the most competitive, and its cars are well maintained.

Hertz (☎ 800/654-3001 in the U.S. and Canada) is also well represented in these same locations, with offices in **Avignon** at the airport (☎ 04-90-84-19-50) and at 4 bd. St-Michel (☎ 04-90-82-37-67); in **Marseille** at the airport (☎ 04-42-14-32-70) and at 16 bd. Charles-Nedeler (☎ 04-91-14-04-24); in **Montpellier** at De Frejorgnes (☎ 04-67-20-04-64) and at Parking des Gares (☎ 04-67-58-65-18); in **Nice** at the airport (☎ 04-93-21-36-72) and at 12 av. de Suède (☎ 04-93-87-11-87); and in **Toulouse** at the airport (☎ 05-61-30-00-26) and at 15 bis bd. Bon Repos (☎ 05-61-62-94-12). When making inquiries, be sure to ask about promotional discounts.

Avis (☎ 800/331-2112 in the U.S. and Canada) has offices in **Avignon** at the airport (☎ 04-90-87-17-75) and at 160 bis av. Pierre-Senmard (☎ 04-90-87-17-75); in **Marseille** at the airport (☎ 04-42-14-21-63) and at 267 bd. National (☎ 04-91-50-70-11); in **Montpellier** at the airport (☎ 04-67-20-14-95) and at 900 av. des Prés d'Arènes (☎ 04-67-92-51-92); in **Nice** at the airport (☎ 04-93-21-36-33) and at place Massena, 2 av. des Phocéens (☎ 04-93-80-63-52); and in **Toulouse** at the airport (☎ 05-61-30-04-69) and at the train station (☎ 05-61-63-71-71).

National (☎ 800/227-3876 in the U.S. and Canada) is represented in France by Europcar, with locations in **Avignon** at 27–29 av. St-Ruf (☎ 04-90-14-40-80) and at the train station, 2A av. Montclair (☎ 04-90-14-40-80); in **Marseille** at the airport (☎ 04-42-14-24-75), at the St-Charles train station, 7 bd. Maurice-Bourdet (☎ 04-91-90-07-84), and on avenue du Prado (☎ 04-91-17-53-00); in **Montpellier** at the airport (☎ 04-67-15-55-77) and at 6 rue Jules-Ferry (☎ 04-67-58-16-17); in **Nice** at the airport (☎ 04-93-21-42-53), at the Hôtel Ibis, 14 av. Thiers (☎ 04-93-88-64-04), and at 6 av. de Suède (☎ 04-93-88-64-04); and in **Toulouse** at the airport (☎ 05-61-30-02-30) and at 363 av. des Etats-Unis (☎ 05-61-70-73-40). You can rent a car on the spot at any of these offices, but lower rates are available by making advance reservations from North America.

GASOLINE

Known in France as *essence,* gas is extraordinarily expensive for those used to North American prices. All but the least expensive cars usually require an octane rating that the French classify as *essence super,* the most expensive variety. At press time, *essence super* sold for about 6.50F ($1.30) per liter, which works out to around 24.50F ($4.90) per U.S. gallon. (Certain smaller engines might get by on *essence ordinaire,* which costs a fraction less than *super,* but be warned that these are increasingly rare,

Museum Passes

Anyone who plans to visit a lot of the monuments of France should consider buying a **Laissez-Passer** at 280F ($56) per year. Available at the ticket office of any of the hundreds of monuments that participate in the program, it allows free entrance to any building, site, or ruin administered by the Caisses des Monuments Historiques. The list encompasses sites of major interest in Provence as well as some that are more esoteric.

You can also benefit from a cultural program offered by 13 cities with populations over 90,000. The **Culture/Ville** 3-day pass unlocks the door to various museums, monuments, and sights in the following cities: Nice, Marseille, Nîmes, Toulouse, Besançon, Dijon, Lille, Lyon, Metz, Nancy, Orléans, St-Etienne, and Bordeaux. The all-inclusive price of 50F ($10) features either a guided or an audio tour in each city and entrance to one museum or one monument in each city; ask about this at each city's tourist office. For more information, contact the French Government Tourist Office in the U.S. at ☎ **900/990-0040** (50¢ per minute) for the *Cities in France* brochure.

if they ever appear at all.) Depending on your car, you'll need either leaded *(avec plomb)* or unleaded *(sans plomb)*, which costs just a fraction (about 25 centimes per liter) less than the version with lead. Depending on the capacity of your tank, filling a medium-size car will cost between $45 and $65.

Beware of the mixture of gasoline and oil sold in certain rural communities called *mélange* or *gasoil;* this mixture is for very old two-cycle engines.

Note: Sometimes you can drive for miles in rural France without encountering a gas station, so don't let your tank get dangerously low.

DRIVING RULES

Everyone in the car, in both the front and the back seats, must wear seat belts. Children 11 and under must ride in the back seat. Drivers are supposed to yield to the car on their right, except where signs indicate otherwise, as at traffic circles. If you violate the speed limits, expect a big fine. Those limits are about 130 kilometers per hour (80 m.p.h.) on expressways, about 100 kilometers per hour (60 m.p.h.) on major national highways, and 90 kilometers per hour (56 m.p.h.) on small country roads. In towns, don't exceed 60 kilometers per hour (37 m.p.h.).

MAPS & ASSISTANCE

Before setting out on a tour of the south of France, pick up a good regional map. If you're visiting a town, ask at the local tourist office for a town plan, usually given away free.

For France as a whole, most motorists opt for the Michelin map 989. For regions, Michelin publishes a series of yellow maps that are quite good: Look for Languedoc-Roussillon (no. 240), Provence and the Côte d'Azur (no. 245), Rhône-Alpes (no. 244), or Vallée du Rhône (no. 246). Big travel-book stores in North America carry these maps, and they're commonly available in France (at lower prices). One useful feature of the Michelin map is its designations of alternative *routes de dégagement,* which let you skirt big cities and avoid traffic-clogged highways.

A breakdown is called *une panne* in France, and it's just as frustrating here as anywhere else. Call the police at ☎ **17** anywhere in France, and they'll put you in touch with the nearest garage. Most local garages have towing services. If your breakdown should occur on an expressway, find the nearest roadside emergency phone box, pick up the phone, and put a call through. You'll immediately be connected to the nearest breakdown service facility.

FAST FACTS: The South of France

Auto Club   Contact **Touring Club de France**, 11 allée Léon-Gambetta in Marseille (☎ **04-91-64-73-11**).

Business Hours   Business hours here are erratic, as befits a nation of individualists. Most **banks** are open Monday to Friday from 9:30am to 4:30pm. Many, particularly in smaller towns or villages, take a lunch break at varying times. Hours are usually posted on the door. Most **museums** close 1 day a week (often Tuesday), and they're generally closed on national holidays. Usual hours are 9:30am to 5pm. Some museums, particularly the smaller and less-staffed ones, close for lunch from noon to 2pm. Most French museums are open on Saturday; many are closed Sunday morning but open Sunday afternoon. Again, refer to the individual museum listings.

Generally, **offices** are open Monday to Friday from 9am to 5pm, but always call first. In Paris or other big French cities, **stores** are open from 9 or 9:30am (often 10am) to 6 or 7pm without a break for lunch. Some shops, particularly those operated by foreigners, open at 8am and close at 8 or 9pm. In some small stores the lunch break can last 3 hours, beginning at 1pm. This is more common in the south than in the north.

Customs   Customs restrictions differ for citizens of the European Union and for citizens of non-EU countries. Non-EU nationals can bring in duty-free 200 cigarettes or 100 cigarillos or 50 cigars or 250 grams of smoking tobacco. This amount is doubled if you live outside Europe. You can, as well, bring in 2 liters of wine and 1 liter of alcohol over 22 proof and 2 liters of wine 22 proof or under. In addition, you can bring in 60cc of perfume, a quarter liter of toilet water, 500 grams of coffee, and 200 grams of tea. Those 15 and over can bring in 300F ($60) of other goods; for those 14 and under the limit is 150F ($30).

Goods obtained with duty and tax paid for personal use within the EU don't require any further Customs duty, but there are set levels if a Customs official thinks you're bringing in more than needed for your personal use.

Items destined for personal use, including bicycles and sports equipment, already in use, whether or not contained in personal luggage, are admitted without formality providing the quantity or type of goods imported doesn't indicate the owner's intention to carry out a commercial transaction. They cannot be sold or given away in France and must be reexported.

Electricity   In general, expect 200 volts, 50 cycles, though you'll encounter 110 and 115 volts in some older establishments. Adapters are needed to fit sockets. Many hotels have two-pin (in some cases, three-pin) sockets for electric razors. It's best to ask your hotel concierge before plugging in any appliance.

Embassies/Consulates   All embassies are in Paris. The Embassy of **Australia** is at 4 rue Jean-Rey, 75015 Paris (☎ **01-45-59-33-00;** Métro: Bir-Hakeim), open Monday to Friday from 9am to 1pm and 2:30 to 5pm. The Embassy of **Canada** is at 35 av. Montaigne, 75008 Paris (☎ **01-44-43-29-00;** Métro: Franklin-D.-Roosevelt), open Monday to Friday from 9am to noon and 2 to 5pm; the Canadian Consulate is at the same address. The Embassy of the **United Kingdom** is at 35 rue du Faubourg St-Honoré, 75383 Paris CEDEX 08 (☎ **01-44-51-31-00;**

Métro: Concorde), open Monday to Friday from 9:30am to 1pm and 2:30 to 6pm; the U.K. consulate, 16 rue d'Anjou, 75008 Paris (☎ **01-44-51-31-00**), is open Monday to Friday from 9:30am to 12:30pm and 2:30 to 5pm. The Embassy of **New Zealand** is at 7 ter rue Léonard-de-Vinci, 75116 Paris (☎ **01-45-00-24-11;** Métro: Victor-Hugo), open Monday to Friday from 9am to 1pm and 2 to 5:30pm; summer hours are Monday to Thursday from 8:30am to 1pm and 2 to 5:30pm and Friday from 8:30am to 2pm.

The Embassy of the **United States** is at 2 av. Gabriel, 75008 Paris (☎ **01-43-12-22-22;** Métro: Concorde), open Monday to Friday from 9am to 6pm. Passports are issued at its consulate at 2 rue St-Florentin (☎ **01-43-12-22-22**; Métro: Concorde). Getting a passport replaced costs about $65. In addition to its embassy and consulate in Paris, the United States maintains the following consulates: 12 bd. Paul-Peytral, 13286 Marseille (☎ **04-91-54-92-00**); and 15 av. d'Alsace, 67082 Strasbourg (☎ **03-88-35-31-04**).

Emergencies   In an emergency while at a hotel, contact the front desk. Most staffs are trained in dealing with a crisis and will call the police, summon an ambulance, or do whatever is necessary. But if it's something like a stolen wallet, go to the police station in person. Otherwise, you can get help anywhere in France by calling ☎ **17** for the **police** or ☎ **18** for the **fire** department *(pompiers)*. For roadside emergencies, see "Getting Around France," earlier in this chapter.

Legal Aid   The French government advises foreigners to consult their embassy or consulate (see above) in case of a dire emergency, such as an arrest. Even if your consulate or embassy declines to offer financial or legal help, the staff can generally offer advice as to how you can obtain help locally. For example, it can furnish a list of attorneys who might represent you. Most arrests are for illegal possession of drugs, and the U.S. embassy and consular officials cannot interfere with the French judicial system. A consulate can only advise you of your rights.

Mail   Most post offices in France are open Monday to Friday from 8am to 7pm and Saturday from 8am to noon. Allow 5 to 8 days to send or receive mail from your home. Airmail letters to North America cost 4.30F (85¢) for 20 grams or 7.90F ($1.60) for 40 grams. Letters to the U.K. cost 2.80F (55¢) for up to 20 grams. An airmail postcard to North America or Europe (outside France) costs 4.30F (85¢).

You can exchange money at post offices. Many hotels sell stamps, as do local post offices and cafes displaying a red TABAC sign outside.

Medical Emergencies   If you're ill and need medicine, go to a *pharmacie* (drugstore). At night and on Sunday the local Commissariat de Police will tell you the location of the nearest drugstore that's open or the address of the nearest doctor on duty. The police will also summon an ambulance if you need to be rushed to a hospital. Seek assistance first at your hotel desk if language is a problem.

Newspapers/Magazines   Most major cities carry copies of the *International Herald Tribune, USA Today,* and usually a major London paper or two. Nearly all big-city newsstands also sell copies of *Time* and *Newsweek*.

The major French newspapers are *Le Monde, Le Figaro,* and *La Libération*. The major French newsmagazines are *L'Express, Le Point,* and *Le Nouvel Observateur*.

Police   Call ☎ **17** anywhere in France.

Rest Rooms   If you're in dire need, duck into a cafe or brasserie. It's customary to make some small purchase if you do so. France still has many "hole-in-the-ground" toilets, so be forewarned.

Number, Please: France's Country & Area Codes

The **international access code** when calling from the United States and Canada is **011**. The **country code** for France is **33**. All phone numbers in France require 10 digits, and this includes the **area code**. For example, the phone number for the Hôtel Négresco—04-93-16-64-00—contains the area code for southeastern France (04). If you were anywhere in France, to call the Négresco all you'd have to dial is this 10-digit number. When calling from outside France, dial the international access code for your country, the country code for France (33), and then the last nine digits of the number, dropping the 0 (zero) from the area code.

Safety   Those intending to visit the south of France, especially the Riviera, should exercise extreme caution—robberies and muggings here are commonplace. It's best to check your baggage into a hotel and then go sightseeing instead of leaving it unguarded in the trunk of a car, which can easily be broken into. Marseille is among the most dangerous cities.

Taxes   *Watch it:* You could get burned. As a member of the European Union, France routinely imposes a value-added tax (VAT) on many goods and services. The standard VAT on merchandise is 20.6%, including clothing, appliances, liquor, leather goods, shoes, furs, jewelry, perfumes, cameras, and even caviar. Refunds are made for the tax on certain goods and merchandise, but not on services. The minimum purchase is 1,200F ($240) in the same store for nationals or residents of countries outside the EU.

Telephone   You'll find public **phone booths** in cafes, restaurants, post offices, airports, and train stations and occasionally on the streets. Pay phones accept coins of $^1/_2$F, 1F, 2F, and 5F; the minimum charge is 1F (20¢). Pick up the receiver, insert the coin(s), and dial when you hear the tone, pushing the button when there's an answer.

The French also use a *télécarte,* a phone debit card, which you can purchase at rail stations, post offices, and other places. Sold in two versions, it allows you to use either 50 or 120 charge units (depending on the card) by inserting the card into the slot of most public phones. Depending on the type of card you buy, they cost 41F to 98F ($8.20 to $19.60).

If possible, avoid making calls from your hotel, as some French establishments double or triple the charges on you.

When you're calling **long distance** within France, pick up the receiver, wait for the dial tone, and then dial the 10-digit number of the person or place you're calling. To make an **international call** from France to anywhere in the world, dial 00 (double zero, the French international access code), wait for the dial tone, then dial the country code (1 for the United States and Canada), area or city code, and the local number you want to reach. To reach an **AT&T operator** from within France, for assistance in placing collect or credit-card calls back to North America or whatever, dial ☎ 00-CALL-ATT. For **information,** dial ☎ 12.

Time   The French equivalent of daylight saving time lasts from around April to September, which puts it 1 hour ahead of French winter time. Depending on the time of year, France is 6 or 7 hours ahead of U.S. eastern standard time.

Tipping   All bills, as required by law, are supposed to say *service compris,* which means that the tip has been included. Here are some general guidelines: For **hotel**

staff, tip 6F to 10F ($1.20 to $2) for every item of baggage the porter carries on arrival and departure and 10F ($2) per day for the chambermaid. You're not obligated to tip the concierge (hall porter), doorman, or anyone else—unless you use his or her services. In cafes, **waiter** service is usually included. For **porters,** there's no real need to tip extra after their bill is presented, unless they've performed some special service. Tip **taxi drivers** 10% to 15% of the amount on the meter. In theaters and restaurants, give **cloakroom attendants** at least 5F ($1) per item. Give **rest-room attendants** about 2F (40¢) in nightclubs and such places. Give **cinema and theater ushers** about 2F (40¢). Tip the **hairdresser** about 15%, and don't forget to tip the person who gives you a shampoo or a manicure 10F ($2). For **guides** for group visits to sights, 5F to 10F ($1 to $2) per person is a reasonable tip.

Languedoc-Roussillon & the Camargue

4

anguedoc, one of southern France's great old provinces, is a loosely defined area encompassing such cities as Nîmes, Toulouse, and Carcassonne. It's one of France's leading wine-producing areas and is fabled for its art treasures.

The coast of Languedoc—from Montpellier to the Spanish frontier—might be called France's "second Mediterranean," first place naturally going to the Côte d'Azur. A land of ancient cities and a generous sea, it's less spoiled than the Côte d'Azur, with an almost-continuous strip of sand stretching west from the Rhône and curving snakelike toward the Pyrénées. Back in the days of de Gaulle, the government began an ambitious project to develop the Languedoc-Roussillon coastline, and it has been a booming success, as the miles of sun-baking bodies in July and August testify.

Ancient Roussillon is a small region of greater Languedoc, forming the Pyrénées Orientales *département*. This is the French Catalonia, inspired more by Barcelona in neighboring Spain than by remote Paris. Over its long and colorful history it has known many rulers. Legally part of the French kingdom until 1258, it was surrendered to James I of Aragón. Until 1344 it was part of the ephemeral kingdom of Majorca, with Perpignan as the capital. By 1463 Roussillon was annexed to France again. Then Ferdinand of Aragón won it back, but by 1659 France had it again. In spite of local sentiment for reunion with the Catalans of Spain, France still firmly controls the land.

The Camargue is a marshy delta between two arms of the Rhône. South of Arles is cattle country. Strong wild black bulls are bred here for the arenas of Arles and Nîmes. The small white horses, amazingly graceful, were said to have been brought here by the Saracens. They're ridden by *gardiens,* French cowboys, who can usually be seen in wide-brimmed black hats. The whitewashed houses, plaited-straw roofs, pink flamingos that inhabit the muddy marshes, vast plains, endless stretches of sandbars—all this qualifies as Exotic France.

EXPLORING THE REGION BY CAR

Here's how to link together the best of the region if you rent a car.

Days 1–2 Begin in **Toulouse,** the ancient capital of Languedoc and France's fourth-largest city. On the second day here, consider a

Languedoc-Roussillon

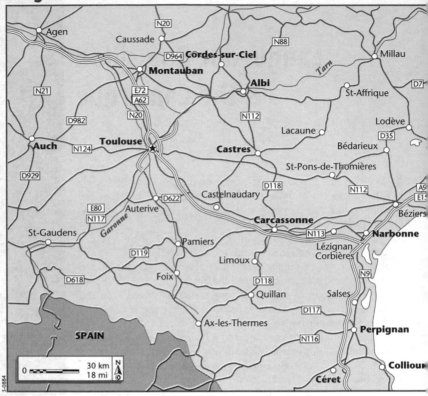

detour to **Auch,** 43 miles west along N124, for a meal at the **Hôtel de France.** If the idea of spending time in a major urban center like Toulouse doesn't appeal to you, consider spending only 1 night, skipping Auch, and proceeding with the rest of this tour.

Day 3   From Toulouse, drive northeast on N88 and D922 for 43 miles to **Cordes,** a medieval village perched on a rocky hilltop. After your visit, drive southeast on D600 to **Albi,** site of the fortified Eglise Ste-Cecilia and one of the bloodiest religious massacres in French history. Spend the night here.

Day 4   Drive south for 25 miles on N112 for a visit to the brooding medieval city of **Castres.** Then continue 40 miles south on D112 and D118 for a tour of one of the most spectacular fortified sites in Europe, **Carcassonne,** where you'll stay the night.

Day 5   The day's final destination is **Perpignan,** but rather than reaching it via high-speed superhighways, we prefer to drive south and then west along D118 and D117. Spend the afternoon exploring Perpignan, but retire early with the expectation of some complicated driving (and serious sunbathing) tomorrow.

Day 6   Your day's final destination is Collioure, but en route we recommend a mountain detour to the hamlet of **Céret.** (Reach Céret from Perpignan by driving south—toward Spain—along A9, then exiting after about 12 miles and driving west for 4 miles along D115.) Céret is well suited to a quiet hour or two in the sun, and you may decide to dine at **La Terrasse au Soleil,** route de Fontfrède, whose restaurant is a cost-conscious hideaway once favored by Salvador Dalí.

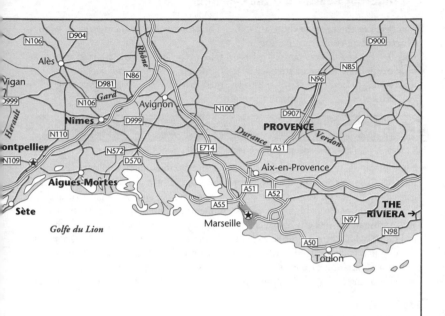

Mediterranean Sea

After your meal, drive east along D618 for 20 miles to the seaside hamlet of **Collioure.** Shaped like a half moon and flanked by a fortified château, it resembles St-Tropez before that town's tourist invasion. It was favored by artists during the Fauve period of early modern art. Spend the night here near what's the most charming village on the Côte Vermeille.

Day 7 This is your day to beach hop. Stop for a swim or a snack wherever the view inspires you, but keep moving with your final destination in mind: **Narbonne,** 50 miles north of Collioure. Even though A9 can get you there most efficiently, we suggest that you at least begin the day by driving north on the narrow coastal road, admiring the string of fast-developing beach resorts. If traffic is dense, you can detour inland 7 miles, then continue along A9. Spend the night in Narbonne.

Day 8 Now you can explore the **Camargue,** a grass-covered wetland. Your first destination is canal-sided **Sète,** 50 miles northeast of Narbonne. Drive along A9, then detour through Agde along N112. Follow N112 east to Sète, built on a network of canals like Venice. Its golden age was the 19th century, when it became the principal link to France's North African colonies; a ferry still departs daily for Algeria. Many visitors are fascinated by its architecture, a somewhat bizarre combination of Second Empire and art deco. Try to stop for a meal at the **Restaurant La Rotonde,** in Le Grand Hôtel, 17 quai de Tassigny (☎ **04-67-46-12-20**); closed for lunch on Saturday and from December 5 to January 5.

From Sète, drive on the coastal road off to the northeast. Your route will follow a string of connected barrier islands and lead you through wetlands favored by waterfowl to the heart of the Camargue. The crown jewel of the district is **Aigues-Mortes,** where you'll stay overnight.

Day 9　Backtrack westward 20 miles on D62 for a view of the ancient Roman town of **Montpellier.** Know in advance that despite the town's *charme méridionale,* traffic is going to be dense. Tour the town, then drive 31 miles northeast along A9 to visit **Nîmes,** where you'll spend the night.

1 Toulouse

438 miles SW of Paris, 152 miles SE of Bordeaux, 60 miles W of Carcassonne

The old capital of Languedoc and France's fourth-largest city, Toulouse (known as La Ville Rose) is cosmopolitan in flavor. The major city of the southwest, filled with gardens and squares, it's the gateway to the Pyrénées. Toulouse is an artistic and cultural center, but also a high-tech center, home to two huge aircraft makers—Airbus and Aérospatiale. The city also has 20 historic pipe organs, more than any other city in France, which lure people to the annual international organ festival. Also making the city tick is its extraordinarily high population of students: some 100,000 in all, out of a population of 600,000. It has had a stormy history, playing many roles— once it was the capital of the Visigoths and later the center of the comtes de Toulouse.

ESSENTIALS

GETTING THERE　The **Toulouse-Blagnac airport** lies in the city's northwestern suburbs, 7 miles from the center; call ☎ **05-61-42-44-00** for flight information. Some 9 trains per day arrive from Paris (trip time: 7 hr.), 8 from Bordeaux (trip time: 2¹/₄ hr.), and 11 from Marseille (trip time: 4¹/₂ hr.). For **rail information** and schedules, call ☎ **08-36-35-35-35.** The Canal du Midi links many of the region's cities with Toulouse by waterway.

VISITOR INFORMATION　The **Office de Tourisme** is in the Donjon du Capitole, rue Lafayette (☎ **05-61-11-02-22**).

SEEING THE TOP ATTRACTIONS

The city's major monument is the ✪ **Basilique St-Sernin,** 13 place St-Sernin (☎ **05-61-21-80-45**). Consecrated in 1096, this is the largest and finest Romanesque church extant in the Old World. One of its most outstanding features is the Porte Miègeville, opening onto the south aisle and decorated with 12th-century sculptures. The door opening into the south transept is the Porte des Comtes, its capitals depicting the story of Lazarus. Nearby are the tombs of the comtes de Toulouse. Entering by the main west door, you can see the double side aisles that give the church five naves, an unusual feature in Romanesque architecture. An upper cloister forms a passageway around the interior. Look for the Romanesque capitals surmounting the columns.

In the axis of the basilica, 11th-century bas-reliefs depict *Christ in His Majesty.* The ambulatory leads to the crypt (ask the custodian for permission to enter), containing the relics of 128 saints, plus a thorn said to be from the Crown of Thorns. In the ambulatory, the old baroque retables and shrine have been reset; the relics here are those of the Apostles and the first bishops of Toulouse. The church is open daily from 9am to noon and 2 to 6pm, although you are asked to refrain from purely touristic visits during Sunday-morning masses. Entrance to the church is free. You can visit the crypt Monday to Saturday from 9am to noon and 2 to 6pm and Sunday from noon to 6pm. Admission to the crypt is 10F ($2).

Toulouse

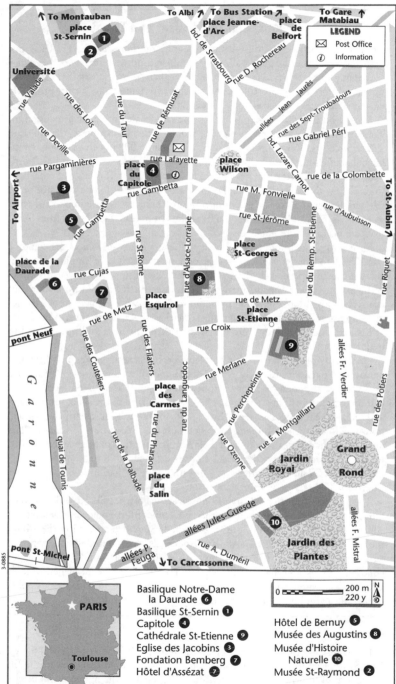

Toulouse-Lautrec: A Giant of a Talent

The painter Henri de Toulouse-Lautrec spent his most creative years in Paris, but his name still evokes the pink-walled city of Albi in southwestern France that clings tenaciously to his legacy. Never growing taller than 5 feet, he was famous for his unfettered portraits of prostitutes and cabaret entertainers and for his brilliantly vicious caricatures of belle époque pretentions.

Despite his physical shortcomings, no one can debate the titanic dimensions of Toulouse-Lautrec's art. In a span of less than 20 years he executed 737 canvases, 275 watercolors, 363 prints and posters, more than 5,000 drawings, some ceramics and stained-glass windows, and more than 300 artworks classified as "pornography." Many believe that he depicted his characters in a ruthless and cruel light to get even with the world for the way those around him treated him because of his size and deformities. Yet he was brilliant in his ability to capture images, whether real or imagined, and in his ability to free colors from reality (and lines from form) to create his caricature-like figures.

Born into a much-intermarried family of aristocrats whose ancestors could be traced back to Charlemagne, he was the only surviving child of his parents' union and the cousin of several children with epilepsy, dwarfism, neurological disorders, and alarming skeletal malformations. Toulouse-Lautrec grew into a short but relatively normal-looking young man, but his later years were marred by changes in his appearance that included violent toothaches, repeated fractures in the bones of his legs, and eventually a growth in the side of his nose and lips that led to frequent drooling.

Geneticists blame some of his problems on his genetic makeup and its propensity for pycnodysostosis (*pick*-no-dis-os-*to*-sis), a sometimes painful form of dwarfism attended by such complications as underdeveloped facial bones, incomplete closure of the "soft spots" between the plates of the skull, short fingers and toes, and easily decayed teeth. But despite the cogency of scientific reasoning, no one will ever know for sure why Toulouse-Lautrec suffered as he did: His descendents have repeatedly refused their permission either to be genetically tested for the disorder or to have the artist's corpse exhumed.

Ironically, Toulouse-Lautrec's 1901 death at age 36 had little to do with his dwarfism: The cause was acute alcoholism.

The family's **Château du Bosc,** also known as the Fortresse Berenger-Bosc, owned during his life by the artist's grandmother, is 29 miles from Toulouse, reached from Albi by N88 (☎ **05-65-69-20-83**). Built in 1180 and renovated in the 1400s, the château is midway between Albi and Rodez (also spelled Rodes) and is open to visitors daily from 9am to 7pm. Admission is 30F ($6) for adults, 15F ($3) for children 8 to 14, and free for children 7 and under. The present owner, Mlle de Céleran, is most gracious to those interested in Toulouse-Lautrec's life. It's polite to precede a visit here with a phone call, as visits must be guided.

Opposite St-Sernin is the **Musée St-Raymond,** place St-Sernin (☎ **05-61-22-21-85**), housed in a college reconstructed in 1523. It contains one of the finest collections of imperial busts outside Rome. Regrettably, the museum will be closed for renovations throughout most of the life of this edition.

Another important museum is the **Musée des Augustins,** 21 rue de Metz (☎ **05-61-22-21-82**). Originally conceived as a convent, its 14th-century cloisters contain the world's largest and most valuable collection of Romanesque capitals. The sculptures and carvings are magnificent, and there are some fine examples of early Christian sarcophagi. On the upper floors is a large painting collection, with works by Toulouse-Lautrec, Gérard, Delacroix, and Ingres. The museum also contains several portraits by Antoine Rivalz, a local artist of major talent. The museum is open Wednesday from 10am to 9pm and Thursday to Monday from 10am to 6pm. Admission is 12F ($2.40), free for children 11 and under.

The **Fondation Bemberg,** place d'Assézat, rue de Metz (☎ **05-61-12-06-89**), opened in 1995 and quickly became one of the city's most important museums. Housed in the Assézat mansion, a magnificent structure that's a sightseeing attraction in its own right (see below), the museum offers an overview of five centuries of European art. The nucleus of the collection represents the lifelong work of George Bemberg, collector extraordinaire, who donated 331 works. The largest bequest was 28 paintings by Pierre Bonnard, including his *Moulin Rouge*. Bemberg also donated works by Pissarro, Matisse *(Vue d'Antibes),* and Monet, plus the Fauves. The foundation also owns Canaletto's much-reproduced *Vue de Mestre.* The museum is open year-round: Tuesday, Wednesday, and Friday to Sunday from 10am to 6pm and Thursday from 10am to 9pm. Admission is 25F ($5).

The other major ecclesiastical building is the **Cathédrale St-Etienne,** place St-Etienne, at the eastern end of rue de Metz (☎ **05-61-52-03-82**). Because of the centuries required to build it (it was designed and constructed between the 11th and the 17th century) some critics scorn it for its mishmash of styles, yet it nonetheless conveys a solemn dignity. The rectangular bell tower is from the 16th century. It has a unique ogival nave to which a Gothic choir has been added. The cathedral is open daily from 7:30am to 7:30pm.

The Gothic brick **Eglise des Jacobins,** parvis des Jacobins, is in Old Toulouse, west of place du Capitole along rue Lakanal (☎ **05-61-11-39-52**). The convent, daring in its architecture, has been restored and forms the largest extant monastery complex in France. It's open daily throughout the year from 10am to 6pm. Entrance to most of the complex is free, but a visit to the cloisters is 10F ($2) per person. Small, charming, and dating mostly from the 18th century, the **Basilique Notre-Dame La Daurade** is at 7 quai de la Daurade (☎ **05-61-21-38-32**); its name derives from the gilding that covers some of its partially baroque exterior. It's open daily from 10am to noon and 2 to 6pm. Admission is free.

In civic architecture, the **Capitole,** place du Capitole (☎ **05-61-22-29-22**), is an outstanding achievement, and one of the most potent symbols of Toulouse itself. Built in 1753, it houses the **Hôtel de Ville** (city hall), plus the **Théâtre du Capitole** (☎ **05-61-22-80-22**), which is devoted exclusively to presentations of concerts, ballets, and operas. Renovated in 1996, it's outfitted in an Italian-inspired 18th-century style with shades of scarlet and gold. Admission, which usually includes a view of the theater, is free. The Capitole complex is open Monday to Friday from 9am to noon and 2 to 5pm and Saturday from 9am to noon.

Toulouse has a number of fine old mansions, most of them dating from the Renaissance, when Toulouse was one of the richest cities in Europe. The finest is the **Hôtel d'Assézat,** on rue de Metz. Built in 1555, with an unaltered 16th-century courtyard, it houses the Académie des Jeux-Floraux, which since 1323 has presented flowers made of wrought metal to poets. It's also the headquarters of the above-mentioned Fondation Bemberg.

After all that sightseeing, head for the oval **place Wilson,** a showcase 19th-century square sheltering fashionable cafes.

SHOPPING

The streets to attack during your shopping frenzy include **rue St-Rome** and **rue d'Alsace-Lorraine.** This town has a great shopping mall, **Centre Commercial St-Georges,** rue du Rempart St-Etienne, where you can fill your suitcases with all kinds of glittery loot. But for upscale clothing boutiques, head for **rue Croix-Baragnon** and **rue des Arts.** The pearly gates of antiques heaven can be found on **rue Fermat.** More downmarket antiques are sprawled out each Saturday and Sunday during the weekly **flea market** at the Basilique St-Sernin, the first Saturday and Sunday of each month in allée Jules-Guesde, and on the second Saturday of each month at place du Val d'Aran.

In addition, **Olivier Desforges,** 3 place St-Georges (☎ 05-61-12-07-00), sells the most exotic and luxurious linens, and **Le Jardin de Len,** 10 rue St-Pantaléon (☎ 05-61-22-14-22), offers everything imaginable connected with violets, from violet-scented perfume to silk scarves patterned with the dainty purple flower.

ACCOMMODATIONS

EXPENSIVE

✪ **Grand Hôtel de l'Opéra.** 1 place du Capitole, 31000 Toulouse. ☎ **05-61-21-82-66.** Fax 05-61-23-41-04. 40 rms, 9 suites. A/C TV TEL. 650F–900F ($130–$180) double; 980F ($196) suite. AE, DC, MC, V. Métro: Capitole.

The owners of this opulent hotel have won several prestigious awards for transforming a 17th-century building (once a convent) into a sophisticated new address. The public rooms contain early 19th-century antiques and Napoleonic-inspired tenting over the bars. Some guest rooms have urn-shaped balustrades overlooking formal squares, and all have high ceilings and modern amenities. Regrettably, in November 1996 the upper floors were damaged by a fire, prompting the owners to inaugurate a radical restoration to be completed sometime in 1998. At press time, 13 of the accommodations were finished, but look for a full complement of rooms, at rates about 25% higher than those noted above, during the lifetime of this edition. The hotel also runs the town's most prestigious restaurant (see "Dining," below), plus a brasserie.

Sofitel Toulouse Centre. 84 allée Jean-Jaurès, 31000 Toulouse. ☎ **05-61-10-23-10.** Fax 05-61-10-23-20. 103 rms, 16 suites. A/C MINIBAR TV TEL. 950F ($190) double; 1,700F ($340) suite. AE, DC, MC, V. Parking 60F ($12). Métro: Jean-Jaurès.

This 18-story hotel is the best in town, at least by many regular business travelers' standards (however, we still view the Grand Hôtel de l'Opéra, at least after it completes its renovations, as the choicest, most tranquil retreat). Adjacent to place Wilson, this Sofitel employs a charming bilingual staff and offers rooms for travelers with disabilities and suites outfitted for use either as mini-offices or as lodgings for families. The hotel has 24-hour room service, an in-house parking garage (much needed in this congested neighborhood), a bar, and a bustling brasserie.

MODERATE

Hôtel des Beaux-Arts. 1 place du pont-Neuf, 31000 Toulouse. ☎ **05-61-23-40-50.** Fax 05-61-22-02-27. 20 rms. A/C MINIBAR TV TEL. 450F–900F ($90–$180) double. AE, DC, MC, V. Parking 70F ($14).

Occupying a richly dignified pink-brick villa built 250 years ago on the banks of the Garonne, this is a charming hotel in the heart of town. Despite the historic facade, the well-equipped, soundproof rooms are modernly refined and comfortable. Breakfast is the only meal served; diners often head for the Brasserie des Beaux-Arts (see "Dining," below), in the same building but with an entrance around the corner.

INEXPENSIVE

Hôtel Raymond-IV. 16 rue Raymond-IV, 31000 Toulouse. ☎ **05-61-62-89-41.** Fax 05-61-61-38-01. 38 rms. MINIBAR TV TEL. 230F–380F ($46–$76) double. AE, DC, MC, V. Parking 25F ($5); free weekends. Métro: Jean-Jaurès or Capitole.

On a quiet street close to the town center and the train station, this antique building contains pleasantly decorated rooms, which are discounted on weekends. The location means that you're within walking distance of the historic quarter with its theaters, shops, and nightclubs. Although breakfast is the only meal served, the English-speaking staff will direct you to nearby restaurants.

DINING

EXPENSIVE

✪ **Les Jardins de l'Opéra.** In the Grand Hôtel de l'Opéra, 1 place du Capitole. ☎ **05-61-23-07-76.** Reservations required. Main courses 165F–280F ($33–$56); fixed-price lunch 200F ($40); fixed-price menus 295F–540F ($59–$108). AE, DC, MC, V. Mon–Sat noon–2pm and 8–10pm. Closed Jan 1–4 and Aug 3–26. Métro: Capitole. FRENCH.

The entrance to the city's best restaurant is in the 18th-century Florentine courtyard of the Grand Hôtel. The dining area is a series of intimate salons, several of which face a winter garden and a reflecting pool. You'll be greeted by the gracious Maryse Toulousy, whose husband, Dominique, prepares what critics have called the perfect combination of modern and old-fashioned French cuisine. The outstanding menu listings are likely to include rack of lamb in pepper sauce with fried and poached celeriac, lobster grilled over a wood fire with artichoke and marrow ragoût, stew of pigeon and foie gras with truffle bouillon and herb salad, and ravioli stuffed with foie gras and a distillation of truffles.

MODERATE

✪ **Brasserie des Beaux-Arts.** 1 quai de la Daurade. ☎ **05-61-21-12-12.** Reservations recommended. Main courses 65F–152F ($13–$30.40); fixed-price menus 112F–153F ($22.40–$30.60). AE, DC, MC, V. Daily noon–3:30pm and 7pm–1am. Métro: Esquirol. FRENCH.

This turn-of-the-century brasserie offers a pure and authentic art nouveau decor that's been enhanced because of its connection with the Jean Bucher chain. (They're the most successful directors of art nouveau French brasseries in the world, with at least a dozen similar places, some of which are classified as national historic monuments.) The carefully restored decor includes walnut paneling and many mirrors, and the cuisine emphasizes well-prepared fresh fish and seafood and all the predictable local dishes, such as cassoulet, magret of duckling, and confit of duckling. Try the foie gras or country-style sauerkraut, accompanied by the house riesling, served in an earthenware pitcher. During warm weather, eat on the terrace. A menu for 103F ($20.60) is available only after 10pm.

Chez Emile. 13 place St-Georges. ☎ **05-61-21-05-56.** Reservations recommended. Main courses 89F–148F ($17.80–$29.60); fixed-price menus 99F ($19.80) at lunch, 210F–235F ($42–$47) at dinner. AE, DC, MC, V. Tues–Sat noon–2pm and 7–10:30pm (also Mon 7–10:30pm in summer). Métro: Capitole or Esquirol. TOULOUSIEN.

In an old-fashioned house on one of the most beautiful squares of Toulouse, this restaurant offers the specialties of chef François Ferrier. In winter, meals are served one floor above street level in a cozy enclave overlooking the square; in summer, the venue moves to the street-level dining room and the flower-filled terrace. Menu choices include cassoulet toulousain, magret de canard (duck) traditional style, and parillade of grilled fish with a pungently aromatic cold sauce of sweet peppers and olive oil. The wine carte is filled with intriguing surprises.

NEARBY ACCOMMODATIONS & DINING

Hôtel de Diane. 3 route de St-Simon, 31100 St-Simon. ☎ **05-61-07-59-52.** Fax 05-61-86-38-94. 22 rms, 13 bungalows. MINIBAR TV TEL. 450F ($90) double; 510F ($102) bungalow. AE, DC, MC, V. Take D23 to exit 27, 5 miles east from Toulouse.

This hotel/restaurant surrounded by a 5-acre park is the most tranquil retreat near Toulouse. It occupies a turn-of-the-century villa with comfortable, not particularly opulent rooms that appeal to people who want to be away from the traffic and congestion of the inner city. The bungalow-style units are built side by side in a row facing the park, each with a kitchenette, a private terrace, and private parking. The rustic atmosphere befits this getaway, where there's a private pool and groves of pines and venerable hardwoods. The restaurant, Saint-Simon, offers a choice of meals in the garden or the Louis XV–style dining room. The fixed-price menus at 105F to 190F ($21 to $38) offer the best value. The restaurant serves lunch Monday to Friday and dinner Monday to Saturday until 9:30pm. In spite of the attentive service and gracious welcome, the food is somewhat uneven, sometimes delicious, other times less so. The bordeaux, however, is divine.

TOULOUSE AFTER DARK

Toulouse has theater, dance, and opera that's often on a par with that found in Paris. The best way to stay on top of the city's arts scene is to pick up a copy of *Toulouse Culture* from the Office de Tourisme.

The most notable theaters are the **Théâtre du Capitole,** place du Capitole (☎ **05-61-23-21-35**); the **Théâtre de la Digue,** 3 rue de la Digue (☎ **05-61-42-97-79**); and the **Halle aux Grains,** place Dupuy (☎ **05-61-63-18-65**). In addition to the theatrical performances that take place here, these venues serve as stages for world-class operas from October to May as well as classical and modern ballet and dance performances by local and international companies.

The liveliest squares to wander after dark are **place du Capitole, place St-Georges, place St-Pierre,** and just off **rue St-Rome** and **rue des Filatiers.**

For bars and pubs, check out the Latin flair of **La Tantina de Bourgos,** 27 rue de la Garonette (☎ **05-61-55-59-29**), which is always popular with the student scene, and the rowdier **Chez Tonton,** 16 place St-Pierre (☎ **05-61-21-86-54**), with its *après-match* frolicking atmosphere complete with the winning teams boozing it up. To keep the party going, try out the rock club **Le Bikini,** route de Lacroix-Falgarde (☎ **05-61-55-00-29**), with its occasional live concerts and endless supply of hot bods.

A couple of out-of-the-ordinary entertainment venues are the **Cave Poésie,** 71 rue du Taur (☎ **05-61-23-62-00**), where you can see a full range of one-acts, stand-up comics, poetry readings, small concerts, you name it; and the disco/restaurant **L'Ubu,** 16 rue St-Rome (☎ **05-61-23-26-75**), where the stars come out to eat, dance, and be seen.

Gays and lesbians come together at **L'Artcor,** 6 rue de Colombette (☎ **05-61-99-61-87**). With its loud yet somewhat tame atmosphere, it has made a name for itself by offering a different style of music, from disco to techno, each night. As you first enter **Le New Shanghai,** 12 rue de la Pomme (☎ **05-61-23-37-80**), you notice that this is a man's dance domain playing the latest in techno; then, venturing farther inside, you'll discover that it gives way to a darker, sexy cruise-bar environment with lots of hot men on the prowl. Plan on paying 50F to 80F ($10 to $16) to get in.

2 Auch

451 miles SW of Paris, 126 miles SE of Bordeaux, 40 miles W of Toulouse

On the west bank of the Gers, in the heart of the ancient Duchy of Gascony, of which it was the capital, the lively market town of Auch is divided into an upper and a lower quarter, connected by several flights of steps. In the old part of town the narrow streets are called *pousterles.* These streets center on **place Salinis,** from which there's a good view of the Pyrénées. Branching off from here, the **Escalier Monumental** leads down to the river, a descent of 232 steps.

On the north of the square is the **Cathédrale Ste-Marie,** on place de la Cathédrale (☎ 05-62-05-22-89). Built from the 15th to the 17th century, this is one of the handsomest Gothic churches in the south of France. It has 113 Renaissance choir stalls made of carved oak, and a custodian will let you in for 6F ($1.20). The stained-glass windows, also from the Renaissance, are impressive. Its 17th-century organ was one of the finest in the world at the time of Louis XIV. The cathedral is open daily from 8:30am to noon and 2 to 6pm (from 9:30am to noon and 2 to 7pm in winter).

Next to the cathedral stands an 18th-century **archbishop's palace** with a 14th-century bell tower, the **Tour d'Armagnac,** which was once a prison.

For the majority of shops and boutiques in this town, walk down **rue Dessoles** and **avenue de l'Alsace.** These are the streets where you'll find everything from confectionery shops to clothing stores. Also consider visiting the ✪ **Caves de l'Hôtel de France,** rue d'Etigny (☎ 05-62-61-71-71), for a bottle or two of armagnac. It has the best selection of this fire water, with more than 100 distilleries represented.

ESSENTIALS

GETTING THERE   Five to ten SNCF trains or buses per day run between Toulouse and Auch (trip time: 1¹/₂ hr.), at a one-way fare of 70F ($14). Six to 13 SNCF buses arrive in Auch daily from Agen. The trip takes 1¹/₂ hours and costs 58F ($11.60) one-way. For more **information and schedules,** call ☎ 08-36-35-35-35.

VISITOR INFORMATION   The **Office de Tourisme** is at 1 rue Dessoles (☎ 05-62-05-22-89).

ACCOMMODATIONS & DINING

✪ **Hôtel de France (Restaurant André-Daguin).** Place de la Libération, 32003 Auch CEDEX. ☎ **05-62-61-71-84.** Fax 05-62-61-71-81. 27 rms, 2 suites. MINIBAR TV TEL. 505F–975F ($101–$195) double; 1,500F–2,500F ($300–$500) suite. AE, DC, MC, V. Parking 35F ($7) in a garage.

Built around the much-modernized 16th-century core of an old inn, this hotel in the center of town offers comfortable, conservative rooms (14 air-conditioned) and one of the most famous restaurants in France. The cuisine is called "innovative within traditional boundaries." Menu choices include an assortment of preparations of foie gras from Gascony, brochette of oysters with foie gras, a duo of magrets de canard (duck) cooked in a rock-salt shell and served with a medley of vegetables, and stuffed pigeon roasted with spiced honey. The desserts include a platter of four chocolate dishes and café au café, a presentation of mousses and pastries unified by their coffee content. Over the years we've had some of our most memorable meals here, yet there have also been disappointments. The restaurant is open for lunch Tuesday to Sunday and for dinner Tuesday to Saturday; it's closed in January.

Le Relais de Gascogne. 5 av. de la Marne, 32000 Auch. ☎ **05-62-05-26-81.** Fax 05-62-63-30-22. 38 rms. A/C TV TEL. 280F–355F ($56–$71) double. MC, V. Closed Dec 25–Jan 10. Parking 33F ($6.60).

This hotel, the second choice in town, offers economical accommodations and meals. The rooms have been modernized and are comfortably furnished. The food is often quite good, especially the salad of duck breast, foie gras of duck, and hearty cassoulet. This place, though small, remains a stronghold of Gascon gastronomy. Fixed-price menus run 90F to 200F ($18 to $40).

3 Cordes-sur-Ciel

421 miles SW of Paris, 15 1/2 miles NW of Albi

This site is remarkable, like an eagle's nest on a hilltop, opening onto the Cérou valley. In days gone by, many celebrities, such as Jean-Paul Sartre and Albert Camus, have considered this town a favorite hideaway. The name Cordes is derived from the textile and leather industries that thrived here during the 13th and 14th centuries. It became a fortified Protestant refuge during the wars of religion.

In the 14th century, when the town's troubles eased, artisans working with linen and leather prospered. It also became known throughout France for its brilliantly colored silks. In the 15th century, however, plagues and religious massacres reduced the city to a minor role. A brief renaissance occurred in the 19th century, when automatic weaving machines were introduced.

Today Cordes is an arts-and-crafts city, and many of the ancient houses on the narrow streets contain artisans plying their skills—blacksmiths, enamelers, graphic artists, weavers, engravers, sculptors, and painters. You park outside, then go under an arch leading to the old town.

ESSENTIALS

GETTING THERE   If you're coming by train, you'll have to get off in nearby Vindrac and either rent a bicycle or take a taxi the remaining 2 miles to Cordes. For **rail information** and schedules, call ☎ **08-36-35-35-35.**

VISITOR INFORMATION   The **Office de Tourisme** is in the Maison Fonpeyrouse (☎ **05-63-56-00-52**).

SEEING THE TOP ATTRACTIONS

Often called "the city of a hundred Gothic arches," Cordes contains numerous **old houses** built of pink sandstone. Many of the doors and windows are fashioned of pointed (broken) arches that still retain their 13th- and 14th-century grace. Some of the best-preserved ones line **Grande-Rue,** also called **rue Droite.**

The **Musée d'Art et d'Histoire,** le Portail-Peint, is named after the archivist of the Tarn region who was also an avid historian of Cordes. In a medieval house whose foundations date from the Gallo-Roman era, it contains everyday artifacts of the textile industry of long ago, farming measures, samples of local embroidery, a reconstructed peasant home interior, and other medieval memorabilia. Official visiting hours are severely limited to several hours a week and only during the busiest seasons: For example, in July and August, it's open daily from 11am to noon and 3 to 6pm. April to June and in September and October it's officially open only on Sunday and public holidays from 11am to noon and 3 to 6pm. If you happen to arrive when the museum is closed, ask someone at the tourist office (see above) to accompany you for your visit (if they're not busy, they often will). Barring that, try to make an appointment for a visit later in the day. Admission is 10F ($2) for adults and 5F ($1) for children.

An even more visible monument, which uses the same system described for the monument listed above, is the **Maison du Grand-Fauconnier** (House of the Falcon Master), named for the falcons carved into the stonework of the wall. A grandly proportioned staircase in the building leads to the **Musée Yves-Brayer,** Grande-Rue (☎ **05-63-56-00-40**). Yves Brayer came to Cordes in 1940 and became one of its most ardent civic boosters. After watching Cordes fall gradually into decay, he renewed interest in its restoration. The museum contains minor artifacts relating to the town's history; the most interesting exhibits are rather fanciful scale models of the town itself. The museum is open daily from 11am to noon and 2:30 to 5:30pm, with extended hours, as determined by the tourist office, in July and August. Admission is 10F ($2) for adults and 2F (40¢) for children 11 and under.

The **Eglise St-Michel,** Grande-Rue, dates from the 13th century, but many alterations have been made since. The view from the top of the tower encompasses much of the surrounding area. Much of the lateral design of the side chapels probably comes from the cathedral at Albi. Before being shipped here, the organ (dating from 1830) was in Notre-Dame de Paris. Visiting hours are erratic. If the church is closed, ask at the *tabac* (tobacco shop) across from the front entrance or call the tourist office to make an appointment.

ACCOMMODATIONS & DINING

Hostellerie du Parc. Les Cabannes, 81170 Cordes. ☎ **05-63-56-02-59.** Fax 05-63-56-18-03. Reservations recommended. Main courses 75F–110F ($15–$22); fixed-price menus 130F–220F ($26–$44). AE, MC, V. Mon–Sat noon–2pm and 7–10pm, Sun noon–2pm. Closed Mon Nov–Mar. Take route de St-Antonin (D600) for about 1 mile west from the town center. FRENCH.

This century-old stone house offers generous meals in a wooded garden or paneled dining room. The specialties include homemade foie gras, duckling, poularde (chicken) occitane, rabbit with cabbage leaves, and calf's sweetbreads with morels.

The hotel offers 17 simply furnished rooms; a double costs 275F to 305F ($55 to $61). There's an outdoor pool, and lessons in French cuisine are offered by the chef.

✪ **Maison du Grand Ecuyer.** Rue Voltaire, 81170 Cordes. ☎ **05-63-53-79-50.** Fax 05-63-53-79-51. Reservations required. Main courses 150F–210F ($30–$42); fixed-price menus 170F–440F ($34–$88). AE, DC, MC, V. July–Aug, daily noon–2pm and 7–9:30pm; Easter–June and Sept–Oct 14, Tues 7–9:30pm, Wed–Sun noon–2pm and 7–9:30pm. Closed Oct 15–Easter. FRENCH.

The medieval monument that contains this restaurant is classified as a national historic treasure. In the 15th-century hunting lodge of Raymond VII, comte de Toulouse, it's perched near the top of the steep rock that's the site of the village of Cordes. But despite its glamour and undeniable charm, it remains intimate and unstuffy. Chef Yves Thuriès prepares platters that have made his restaurant an almost mandatory stop. Specialties include three confits of lobster, red mullet salad with fondue of vegetables, and noisette of lamb in orange sauce. The dessert selection is about the grandest and most overwhelming in this part of France. As a novelty, a 340F ($68) menu reproduces the meal served to then-President Mitterrand during a visit, a 360F ($72) menu duplicates the food offered Elizabeth II, and the grandest of all, the 440F ($88) menu presents a replica of what was dished up for the emperor of Japan.

The hotel contains 12 rooms and one suite, all with antiques and an undeniable sense of the Middle Ages blended discreetly with modern comforts. Doubles cost 450F to 850F ($90 to $170); the suite is 1,200F ($240). The most-desired room, honoring a former guest, Albert Camus, has a four-poster bed and a fireplace.

4 Albi

433 miles SW of Paris, 47 miles NE of Toulouse

The "red city" (for the color of the building brick) of Albi straddles both banks of the Tarn River and is dominated by its brooding 1282 **Cathédrale Ste-Cécile,** near place du Vigan, the medieval center (☎ 05-63-49-48-80). Fortified with ramparts and parapets and containing frescoes and paintings, it was built by local lord-bishop after a religious struggle with the comte de Toulouse (the crusade against the Cathars). You can view the exceptional 16th-century rood screen with a unique suit of polychromatic statues from the Old and New Testaments. The cathedral is open daily: June to August from 8:30am to 7pm and September to May from 8:30 to 11:30am and 2 to 5:30pm. Admission is 3F (60¢).

Opposite the north side of the cathedral is the **Palais de la Berbie** (Archbishop's Palace), another fortified structure dating from the late 13th century. Inside, the ✪ **Musée Toulouse-Lautrec** (☎ 05-63-49-48-70) contains the world's most important collection of that artist's paintings, more than 600 specimens. His family bequeathed the works remaining in his studio. Toulouse-Lautrec was born at Albi on November 24, 1864. Crippled in childhood, his legs permanently deformed, he lived in Paris most of his life and produced posters and sketches of characters in music halls and circuses. His satiric portraits of the turn-of-the-century demimonde were both amusing and affectionate. (For more on this genius, see the box "Toulouse-Lautrec: A Giant of a Talent," earlier in this chapter.) The museum also owns paintings by Degas, Bonnard, Matisse, Utrillo, and Rouault. It's open April to September, daily from 9am to noon and 2 to 6pm; October to March, Wednesday to Monday from 10am to noon and 2 to 5pm. Admission is 24F ($4.80) for adults and 10F ($2) for children.

Toulouse-Lautrec was born in the **Hôtel Bosc** in Albi; it's still a private home and cannot be toured, but there's a plaque on the wall of the building, on rue Toulouse-Lautrec (no number) in the historic town core.

ESSENTIALS

GETTING THERE   Fifteen trains per day link Toulouse with Albi (trip time: 1 hr.); the fare is 61F ($12.20) one-way. There's also a direct Paris–Albi night train. For **rail information** and schedules, call ☎ 08-36-35-35-35. Motorists from Paris can take R.N. 20 via Cahors and Caussade; from Bordeaux, take the autoroute des Deux Mers and exit at Montauban.

VISITOR INFORMATION   The **Office de Tourisme** is in the Palais de la Serbie, place Ste-Cécile (☎ 05-63-49-48-80).

ACCOMMODATIONS

Hostellerie St-Antoine. 17 rue St-Antoine, 81000 Albi. ☎ **05-63-54-04-04.** Fax 05-63-47-10-47. 37 rms, 7 suites. A/C TV TEL. 620F–880F ($124–$176) double; 1,080F ($216) suite. AE, DC, MC, V. Parking 30F ($6).

This 250-year-old hotel has been owned by the same family for five generations; today it's managed by Jacques and Jean-François Rieux. Their mother focused on Toulouse-Lautrec when designing the hotel, since her grandfather was a friend of the painter and was given a few of his paintings, sketches, and prints. Several are in the lounge, which opens onto a rear garden. The rooms have been delightfully decorated, with a sophisticated use of color, good reproductions, and occasional antiques. Even if you're not spending the night, consider dining here: The Rieux culinary tradition is revealed in their traditional yet creative cuisine, and everything tastes better washed down with Gaillac wines.

⭐ **La Réserve.** Rte. de Cordes à Fonvialane, 81000 Albi. ☎ **05-63-60-80-80.** Fax 05-63-47-63-60. 24 rms, 4 junior suites. MINIBAR TV TEL. 600F–1,000F ($120–$200) double; 1,050F–1,300F ($210–$260) suite. AE, DC, MC, V. Closed Nov–Apr. From the center of town, follow the signs to Carmaux-Rodez until you cross the Tarn, then follow the signs to Cordes; the hotel is adjacent to the main road leading to Cordes, 1¹/₄ miles from Albi.

This country-club villa on the outskirts of Albi is managed by the Rieux family, who also run the Hostellerie St-Antoine. It was built in the Mediterranean style, with tennis courts, a pool, and a fine garden in which you can dine. The rooms, well furnished and color coordinated, contain imaginative decorations (but avoid those rooms over the kitchen); the upper-story rooms have sun terraces and French doors. In the restaurant, specialties are *pâté de grives* (thrush), *carré d'agneau aux cèpes* (lamb with flap mushrooms), and filet of beef with béarnaise sauce. Even if you're not a guest, consider a visit. The wine carte is rich in bordeaux and the prices per bottle are reasonable.

Mercure. 41 bis rue Porta, 81000 Albi. ☎ **05-63-47-66-66.** Fax 05-63-46-18-40. 56 rms. MINIBAR TV TEL. 460F–530F ($92–$106) double. AE, DC, MC, V.

The modern Mercure is one of the best places to stay in Albi, though the atmosphere is impersonal when stacked up against La Réserve and the Hostellerie St-Antoine. It was built in an 18th-century mill on the edge of the Tarn River, and the facade and huge entryway were preserved. The rooms are well equipped, and all the baths have been recently renovated. The first-class restaurant serves superb meals—both regional and continental. Tables are set on the terrace in summer.

DINING

La Réserve (see "Accommodations," above) boasts a wonderful restaurant.

Jardin des Quatre Saisons. 19 bd. de Strasbourg. ☎ **05-63-60-77-76.** Reservations recommended. Fixed-price menus 135F–160F ($27–$32). AE, DC, MC, V. Tues–Sun 12:30–2pm and 7:30–10pm. FRENCH.

The best food in Albi is served by Georges Bermond, who believes that menus, like life, should change with the seasons—and that's how the restaurant got its name. The setting is a modern, deceptively simple pair of dining rooms where the lighting has been subtly arranged to make everyone look as attractive as possible. The service is always competent and polite. Menu items have been fine-tuned to an artful science and include delicious versions of a fricassée of snails garnished with strips of the famous hams produced in the nearby hamlet of Lacoune; ravioli stuffed with pulverized shrimp and served with a truffled cream sauce; and a gratinée of mussels in a compote of fish. Most delectable of all—an excuse for returning a second time to this restaurant—is a pot-au-feu of the sea that contains three or four species of fish garnished with a crayfish-flavored cream sauce. The wine carte is the finest in Albi.

5 Castres

452 miles SW of Paris, 26 miles S of Albi

Built on the bank of the Agout River, Castres is the point of origin of trips to the Sidobre, the mountains of Lacaune, and the Black Mountains. Today the wool industry, whose origins go back to the 14th century, has made Castres one of France's two most important wool-producing areas. The town was formerly a Roman military installation. A Benedictine monastery was founded here in the 9th century, and the town fell under the comtes d'Albi in the 10th century. During the wars of religion it was Protestant.

ESSENTIALS

GETTING THERE   From Toulouse, there are eight trains per day (trip time: 1 hr.), at a one-way fare of 72F ($14.40). From Albi (above), there are seven trains via St-Sulpice (trip time: 2 hr.), at 78F ($15.60) one-way. For **rail information** and schedules, call ☎ **08-36-35-35-35.**

VISITOR INFORMATION   The **Office de Tourisme** is at 3 rue Milhau-Ducommun (☎ **05-63-62-63-62**).

TOURING THE TOP ATTRACTIONS

The ✪ **Musée Goya,** in the Jardin de l'Evêché (☎ **05-63-71-59-28**), is in the town hall, an archbishop's palace designed by Mansart in 1669. Some of the spacious public rooms have ceilings supported by a frieze of the archbishops' coats-of-arms. The collection includes 16th-century tapestries and the works of Spanish painters from the 15th to the 20th century. Most notable, of course, are the paintings of Francisco Goya y Lucientes, all donated to the town in 1894 by Pierre Briguiboul, son of the Castres-born artist Marcel Briguiboul. *Les Caprices* is a study of figures created in 1799, after the illness that left Goya deaf. Filling much of an entire room, the work is composed of symbolic images of demons and monsters, a satire of Spanish society.

The museum is open in July and August, Monday to Saturday from 9am to noon and 2 to 6pm and Sunday from 10am to noon and 2 to 6pm; September to March, Tuesday to Saturday from 9am to noon and 2 to 5pm. Admission is 15F ($3) for adults and 8F ($1.60) for children.

Le Centre National et Musée Jean-Jaurès, 2 place Pélisson (☎ **05-63-72-01-01**), is dedicated to the workers' movements of the late 19th and early 20th centuries. It gathers printed material issued by various Socialist factions in France during this era. See, in particular, an issue of *L'Aurore* containing Zola's famous "*J'accuse*" article from the Dreyfus case. Paintings, sculptures, films, and slides round out the collection. The museum is open in July and August, Monday to Saturday from 9am to noon and 2 to 6pm and Sunday from 10am to noon and 2 to 6pm; September to June, Tuesday to Saturday from 9am to noon and 2 to 5pm. Admission is 10F ($2) for adults and 5F ($1) for children.

The town's most visible and important church is Castres's outstanding example of French baroque architecture. The architect Caillau began construction of the **Eglise St-Benoît,** place du 8-Mai-1945 (☎ **05-63-59-05-19**), in 1677, on the site of a 9th-century Benedictine abbey. The baroque structure was never completed according to its original plans. The painting at the church's far end, above the altar, was executed by Gabriel Briard in the 18th century. The church is open Monday to Saturday from 9am to noon and 2 to 6:30pm and Sunday from 2 to 4pm. Except for religious services, the church is closed to casual visitors on Sunday between October and May.

ACCOMMODATIONS

Grand Hôtel. 11 rue de la Libération, 81103 Castres CEDEX. ☎ **05-63-59-00-30.** Fax 05-63-59-03-50. 40 rms. MINIBAR TV TEL. 250F–280F ($50–$56) double. AE, DC, V. Closed Dec 20–Jan 10. Parking 30F ($6).

This traditional hotel, owned by three generations of the same family since it was built in 1860, is one of the best of the moderately priced places in town. Half its comfortably furnished rooms open onto the river. In spite of its name, the Grand is no longer the hotel of choice for Castres, a position it has lost to the Renaissance.

✪ **Hôtel Renaissance.** 17 rue Victor-Hugo, 81100 Castres. ☎ **05-63-59-30-42.** Fax 05-63-72-11-57. 16 rms, 4 suites. TV TEL. 340F–400F ($68–$80) double; 510F–610F ($102–$122) suite. AE, MC, V.

The Renaissance is the best hotel in Castres. It was built in the 17th century as the courthouse, then functioned as a colorful but run-down hotel throughout most of the 20th century—until 1993, when it was discreetly restored. Today you'll see a severely dignified building composed, depending on which part you look at, of *colombages*-style half-timbering, with a mixture of chiseled stone blocks and bricks. Some rooms have exposed timbers; all are clean and comfortable, evoking the crafts of yesteryear. Simple platters can be prepared if you wish to eat in your room, but a recently completed restaurant and bar, Le Montaigne, provides other options. Fixed-price menus are available for 75F to 125F ($15 to $25).

DINING

La Mandragore. 1 rue Malpas. ☎ **05-63-59-51-27.** Reservations recommended. Main courses 90F–130F ($18–$26); fixed-price menus 75F ($15) with wine, served at lunch and dinner; and 90F–240F ($18–$48). AE, MC, V. Mon 7–10pm, Tues–Sat noon–2pm and 7–10pm. LANGUEDOCIEN.

On an easily overlooked narrow street, this restaurant occupies a small section of one of the many wings of the medieval château-fort of Castres. The decor is consciously simple, perhaps as an appropriate foil for the stone walls and overhead beams. Sophie (in the dining room) and Jean-Claude (in the kitchen) Belaut prepare a regional cuisine that's among the best in town. Served with charm and tact, it might include lasagne of foie gras, roast pigeon stuffed with foie gras and served with gâteau of potatoes and flap mushrooms, monkfish flavored with basil and black olives, and grilled fresh fish.

6 Carcassonne

495 miles SW of Paris, 57 miles SE of Toulouse, 65 miles S of Albi

Evoking bold knights, fair damsels, and troubadours, the greatest fortress city of Europe rises against a background of the snow-capped Pyrénées. Floodlit at night, it captures fairy-tale magic, but back in its heyday in the Middle Ages, all wasn't so romantic. Shattering the peace and quiet were battering rams, grapnels, a mobile tower (inspired by the Trojan horse), catapults, flaming arrows, and the mangonel.

Today the city that was used as a backdrop for the 1991 movie *Robin Hood, Prince of Thieves,* is overrun with hordes of visitors and tacky gift shops. The elusive charm of Carcassone comes out in the evening, when thousands of day-trippers have departed and floodlights bathe the ancient monuments.

ESSENTIALS

GETTING THERE   Carcassonne is a major stop for trains between Toulouse and destinations south and east. Two dozen trains from Toulouse pass through daily (trip time: 50 min.), at a one-way fare of 72F ($14.40). There are 14 trains per day from Montpellier (trip time: 2 hr.), at 130F ($26) one-way, and 12 trains per day from Nîmes (trip time: 2¹/₂ hr.), at 135F ($27) one-way. For **rail information** and schedules, call ☎ **08-36-35-35-35.**

VISITOR INFORMATION   The **Office de Tourisme** is at 15 bd. Camille-Pelletan (☎ **04-68-10-24-30**) and in the medieval town at Porte Narbonnaise (☎ **04-68-10-24-36**).

A Countryside Drive

After a visit to the walled city of Carcassonne, take D118 north to the **Montagne Noire** (Black Mountains). These mountains—arid on the southern slopes but wooded and lush on the northern rim—mark the southeastern extension of the Massif Central. Towering over the region is the 3,700-foot Pic de Noire, around which is the **Parc Régional du Haut Languedoc,** a part of France studded with panoramic scenery and tranquil lakes. The area is crisscrossed with narrow unmarked roads leading to one scenic vista after another. It's easy to get lost—but if you have the time, that's part of the fun.

For more specific guidance, you can visit the town of **Mazamet,** 30 miles north of Carcassonne. Here the **Office de Tourisme,** rue des Casernes (☎ 05-63-61-27-07), can provide maps and outline some of the best trails for exploring. Mazamet also makes a good lunch stop. The most elegant choice for dining is **Le Métairie Neuve** (☎ 05-63-61-23-31), a hotel 1 mile from the center at Boul-du-Point-de-Larn (reached via D54). Here you'll find the area's best selection of regional dishes; the menu changes frequently based on what's seasonal. Meals range from 95F to 120F ($19 to $24). If you'd like to anchor in for a day, the hotel rents 14 rooms furnished in a traditional French style at 460F ($92) for a double.

After spending as much time as you have exploring the beauty of the park, continue northwest on N112 to **Castres,** built on the banks of the Agout River and visited chiefly because of its **Musée Goya,** whose collection spans half a century of the troubled artist's life. If you didn't spend much time in the park and make it all the way to Castres for lunch, you'll find a number of good restaurants. A favorite is **La Mandragore** (see "Dining" in the Castres section, earlier in this chapter). Other worthy choices are **Le Victoria,** 24 place du 8-Mai-1945 (☎ 05-63-59-14-68), where meals cost 95F to 220F ($19 to $44). A superb French cuisine is served, with regional products used whenever available.

From Castres, and if time is available, you can detour east on D622 to **Sidobre** to see its bizarre rock formations. The Agout and Durenque rivers have cut deep gorges into the earth, and the area is filled with giant granite quarries. These great boulders have been given names such as Rock of the Three Cheeses and Rock of the Goose.

Then head back to Castres, where you can follow N112 into **Albi,** a distance of 25 miles. Plan to spend the night in Albi, which has some highly rated hotels (see "Accommodations" in the Albi section, earlier in this chapter). This is the hometown of Toulouse-Lautrec, and you can visit the **Musée Toulouse-Lautrec** the next day and take in the brooding **Cathédrale Ste-Cécile.**

Drivers ideally try to time their arrival so that they reach Albi just as the sun is setting. The cathedral and the bridges spanning the Tarn River are made of brick, as are most of the town's buildings, earning Albi the title of "the red city" (nothing political). In the rosy glow of a setting sun, Albi often looks as if it's in flames, a spectacular sight.

EXPLORING THE TOWN

Carcassonne consists of two towns: the **Ville Basse** (Lower City) and the medieval **Cité.** The former has little interest, but the latter is among the major attractions in France, the goal of many a pilgrim. The fortifications consist of the inner and outer walls, a double line of **ramparts.** The inner rampart was built by the Visigoths in the

5th century. Clovis, king of the Franks, attacked in 506 but failed. The Saracens over-came the city in 728, until Pepin the Short (father of Charlemagne) drove them out in 752. During a long siege by Charlemagne, the populace of the walled city was starving and near surrender until Dame Carcas came up with an idea. According to legend, she gathered up the last remaining bit of grain, fed it to a sow, then tossed the pig over the ramparts. It's said to have burst, scattering the grain. The Franks concluded that Carcassonne must have unlimited food supplies and ended their siege.

Carcassone's walls were further fortified by the vicomtes de Trencavel in the 12th century and by Louis IX and Philip the Bold in the following century. However, by the mid–17th century its position as a strategic frontier fort was over and the ramparts were left to decay. In the 19th century the builders of the Lower Town began to remove the stone for use in new construction. But interest in the Middle Ages revived, and the government ordered Viollet-le-Duc (who restored Notre-Dame in Paris) to repair and, where necessary, rebuild the walls. Reconstruction continued until very recently.

Within the walls resides a small populace. The **Basilique St-Nazaire,** La Cité (☎ 04-68-25-27-65), dates from the 11th to the 14th century, containing some beautiful stained-glass windows and a pair of rose medallions. The nave is in the Romanesque style, but the choir and transept are Gothic. The organ, one of the oldest in southwestern France, is from the 16th century. The tomb of Bishop Radulph, from 1266, is well preserved. The cathedral is open daily: in July and August from 9am to 7pm and off-season from 9:30am to noon and 2 to 5:30pm. Mass is celebrated on Sunday at 11am. Admission is free.

SHOPPING

Carcassone, more so than other French cities, is really two distinct shopping towns in one—the walled medieval city and the modern lower city. In the modern city, the major streets for shopping are **rue Clemenceau** and **rue de Verdun,** particularly if you're in the market for clothing. The whole of the medieval city is chock full of tiny stores and boutiques selling mostly gift items like antiques and local arts and crafts. On the third Saturday of every month at the portail Jacobin, in the center of the modern town, a **flea market** sets up from 9am to noon.

Stores worth visiting are the **Caveau des Vins,** tour du Tréseau (☎ 04-68-25-29-38), where you'll find a wide selection of regional wines ranging from simple table wines to those awarded the distinction of Appellation d'Origine Controlée; **Antiquités "Le St-Georges,"** 36 rue Victor-Hugo (☎ 04-68-47-52-66), which specializes in antique scientific instruments and furniture from the 17th to the 19th century; and **Dominique Sarraute,** 15 rue Porte-d'Aude (☎ 04-68-72-42-90), for antique firearms.

ACCOMMODATIONS
IN THE CITÉ

✪ **Cité.** Place de l'Eglise, 11000 Carcassonne. ☎ **04-68-25-03-34.** Fax 04-68-71-50-15. 23 rms, 3 suites. A/C TV TEL. 1,050F–1,300F ($210–$260) double; 1,600F–1,900F ($320–$380) suite. AE, DC, MC, V. Parking 40F ($8).

Originally a palace for whatever bishop or well-placed prelate happened to be in con-trol at the time, this historically important site has thrived as the most desirable ho-tel in town since 1905. Massively and luxuriously renovated, it's built into the actual walls of the city, adjoining the cathedral. You enter into a long Gothic corridor/gallery leading to the lounge. Many rooms open onto the ramparts and a garden and feature antiques or reproductions. Modern equipment has been discreetly installed, as well as a heated pool. The hotel is renowned for its restaurant, La Barbacane, with its mock Gothic windows and golden fleurs-de-lis shield and lion motifs. Menu items focus on upscale versions of the region's cuisine and include sophisticated interpretations of magret and confit of duck, cassoulet, and cuisine du marché based on market-fresh seasonal ingredients. Fixed-price menus cost 250F ($50).

Hôtel des Remparts. 3–5 place du Grand-Puits, 11000 Carcassonne. ☎ **04-68-71-27-72.** Fax 04-68-72-73-26. 18 rms. TEL. 300F–330F ($60–$66) double. MC, V. Parking 20F ($4).

An abbey in the 12th century, this building at the edge of a stone square in the town center was converted into a charming hotel in 1983 after major repairs to the masonry and roof. The rooms contain no-frills furniture. The owners are most proud of the massive stone staircase that twists around itself. Make reservations at least 2 months ahead if you plan to stay here during summer.

AT THE ENTRANCE TO THE CITÉ

✪ Hôtel du Donjon. 2 rue du Comte-Roger, 11000 Carcassonne. ☎ **800/528-1234** in the U.S. and Canada, or 04-68-71-08-80. Fax 04-68-25-06-60. 36 rms, 2 suites. A/C MINIBAR TV TEL. 380F–490F ($76–$98) double; 750F ($150) suite. AE, DC, V. Parking 25F ($5).

This little hotel is big on charm and the best value in the moderate range. Built in the style of the old Cité, it has a honey-colored stone exterior with iron bars on the windows. The interior is a jewel, reflecting the sophistication of the owner, Christine Pujol. Elaborate Louis XIII–style furniture graces the reception lounges. A newer wing contains additional rooms in a medieval architectural style, and the older rooms have been renewed. Their furnishings are in a severe style. The hotel also runs a restaurant nearby, the Brasserie Le Donjon. In summer the garden is the perfect breakfast spot.

IN VILLE-BASSE

Hôtel du Pont-Vieux. 32 rue Trivalle, 11000 Carcassonne. ☎ **04-68-25-24-99.** Fax 04-68-47-62-71. 19 rms. TV TEL. 290F ($58) double; 360F ($72) triple; 400F ($80) quad. AE, DC, V. Closed Jan 15–31. Parking 30F ($6).

One of the best and most reasonably priced hotels in Carcassonne, this rustic boarding house lies at the foot of the medieval city. It has been completely restored without losing its provincial French charm. From the elegantly furnished lounge to the quiet reading room, it's cozy and inviting. The rooms have traditional furnishings and double-glazed windows to cut down on the noise. Each has a fully fitted bath, and maintenance is state of the art. An indoor garden provides a retreat from the crowds.

Hôtel Montségur. 27 allée d'Iéna, 11000 Carcassonne. ☎ **04-68-25-22-17.** Fax 04-68-47-13-22. 21 rms. A/C TV TEL. 490F ($98) double. AE, DC, V.

This stately old town house with a mansard roof and dormers has a front garden that's screened from the street by trees and a high wrought-iron fence. Didier and Isabelle Faugers have furnished the hotel with antiques, avoiding that institutional look. Modern amenities include an elevator. The rooms are cheaper than you'd imagine from the looks of the place. A continental breakfast is available, and the highly recommended Le Languedoc serves every dish with a certain flair, ranging from angler fish to a duck cassoulet fit for a banquet.

DINING

Au Jardin de la Tour. 11 rue Porte-d'Aude. ☎ **04-68-25-71-24.** Reservations recommended in summer. Main courses 45F–140F ($9–$28); fixed-price menus 75F ($15) at lunch without wine, 85F–150F ($17–$30) at dinner. MC, V. Daily noon–2pm and 8–10pm. Closed Mon Nov–Easter. FRENCH.

A culinary team labors to create an authentic Languedoc cuisine. This restaurant is in the oldest part of the Cité, at the end of a long corridor. Menu choices include a large selection of salads, stuffed chicken, onglet of beef with shallots, confit of duckling, and the inevitable cassoulet, everybody's favorite.

✪ **La Barbacane.** In the Hôtel de la Cité, place de l'Eglise. ☎ **04-68-25-03-34.** Reservations recommended. Main courses 175F–320F ($35–$64); fixed-price menus 280F–420F ($56–$84). AE, DC, MC, V. Tues–Sat noon–2pm and 7:30–9:30pm, Sun noon–2pm. Closed Jan. FRENCH.

Named after the medieval neighborhood (La Barbacane) in which it sits, this restaurant enjoys equal billing with the celebrated hotel that contains it. Its soothing-looking dining room, whose walls are upholstered in fabric with gold fleur-de-lis on a cerulean blue background, features the cuisine of the noted chef Christophe Turquier. Menu items are based on seasonal ingredients, with just enough zest. Examples are green ravioli perfumed with seiche (a species octopus) and its own ink, pavé of seawolf with stuffed calamari, saltwater crayfish with strips of Bayonne ham, a fraîcheur of Breton lobster with artichoke hearts and caviar, and organically fed free-range chicken stuffed with truffles. A particularly succulent dessert is beignets (deep-fried fritters) of pineapple with vanilla sauce.

Le Languedoc. 32 allée d'Iéna. ☎ **04-68-25-22-17.** Reservations recommended. Main courses 95F–140F ($19–$28); fixed-price menus 130F and 175F ($26 and $35); *menu carte* 225F–240F ($45–$48). AE, DC, V. Tues–Sat noon–2pm and 7:30–9:30pm, Sun noon–2pm. Closed Dec 20–Jan 20. FRENCH.

Lucien Faugeras has passed on his carving fork to his son Didier, also an excellent chef (the family owns the Hôtel Montségur as well). The dining room has a warm Languedoc atmosphere, the proper setting for their culinary repertoire, achieved by rough plaster walls, ceiling beams, an open brick fireplace, and provincial tablecloths. The specialty is cassoulet au confit de canard (the famous stew made with duck cooked in its own fat). The *pièce de résistance* is tournedos Rossini, with foie-gras truffles and madeira sauce. A smooth dessert is flambéed crêpes Languedoc. In summer you can dine on a pleasant patio or in the air-conditioned restaurant.

NEARBY ACCOMMODATIONS & DINING

✪ **Domaine d'Auriac.** Rte. St-Hilaire, 11000 Carcassonne. ☎ **04-68-25-72-22.** Fax 04-68-47-35-54. 28 rms. A/C MINIBAR TV TEL. 500F–1,500F ($100–$300) double. AE, DC, MC, V. Closed Feb 17–Mar 3 and Nov 17–Dec 8. Take D104 about 2 miles from Carcassonne.

The premier place for food and lodging is this moss-covered 19th-century manor house, boasting gardens with reflecting pools and flowered terraces. The uniquely decorated rooms in this Relais & Châteaux have a certain photo-magazine glamour; some are in an older building with high ceilings, whereas others have a more modern decor. Renovations are ongoing. Bernard Rigaudis sets a grand table in his lovely dining room. In summer, meals are served beside the pool on the terraces. Afterward you might work off lunch on the tennis courts or golf course. The menu changes about five or six times yearly but might include truffles and purple artichokes with essences of pears and olives. Meals cost 190F ($38) for the minimalist and 390F ($78) for the gourmand. The restaurant is open daily from 12:30 to 2pm and 7:30 to 9:15pm, and reservations are required.

CARCASSONNE AFTER DARK

The town's nightlife sparkles with real pizzazz during its major summer festivals. The whole month of July is devoted to the **Festival de Carcassonne,** when instrumental concerts, modern and classical dance, operas, and original theater shower the city.

Tickets range from 125F to 275F ($25 to $55) and can be purchased by calling ☎ **04-68-77-71-26.** For more information, contact the **Théâtre Municipal** at ☎ **04-68-25-33-13.** On the night of July 14, **Bastille Day,** one of the best fireworks spectacles in all of France lights up the skies over the medieval city. In the beginning of August, the unadulterated merriment and good times of the Middle Ages overtake the city during the **Cité en Scènes.** You can get more information by contacting the Office de Tourisme or **Carcassone Terre d'Histoire,** chemin de Serres (☎ **04-68-47-97-97).**

Aside from these festivals, Carcassonne nightlife is centered along **rue Omer-Sarraut** and **place Verdun.** The most popular bar in town, **Le Day Break,** 11 rue du Grand-Puits (☎ **04-68-25-52-58),** provides a fantastic space for its 20- and 30-something patrons to enjoy the weekly jazz performances by local groups. **Le Bulle,** 115 rue Barbacane (☎ **04-68-72-47-70),** explodes with techno and rock dance tunes that keep the energy pumping and the place hopping until 4am. The cover is 40F to 70F ($8 to $14).

7 Perpignan

562 miles SW of Paris, 229 miles NW of Marseille, 40 miles S of Narbonne

At Perpignan you may think you've crossed the border into Spain, for it was once Catalonia's second city, after Barcelona. Even earlier it was the capital of the kingdom of Majorca. But when the Roussillon—the French part of Catalonia—was finally partitioned off, Perpignan became French forever, authenticated by the Treaty of the Pyrénées in 1659. However, Catalán is still spoken here, especially among the country people.

Perpignan derives its name from the legend of Père Pinya, a plowman said to have followed the Têt River down the mountain to the site of the town today, where he cultivated the fertile soil while the river kept its promise to water the fields.

Today Perpignan is content to rest on its former glory, its residents—some 110,000 in all—enjoying the closeness of the Côte Catalane and the mountains to their north. The pace is decidedly relaxed. You'll even have time to smell the flowers that grow here in great abundance.

This is one of the sunniest places in France, but summer afternoons in July and August are a cauldron. That's when many of the locals take the 6-mile ride to the beach to cool off. There's a young scene here that brings vibrance to Perpignan, especially along the quays of the Basse River, site of impromptu nighttime concerts, beer drinking, and the devouring of endless tapas, a tradition inherited from nearby Barcelona.

July, though terribly hot, is the time for **Les Estivales,** which causes the city to explode with a medley of music, expositions, and theater. However, our favorite time for this area is during the grape harvest in September. If you visit at this time, you may want to drive through the Rivesaltes district bordering the city to the west and north. Temperatures have usually dropped by then.

ESSENTIALS

GETTING THERE   Four trains per day arrive from Paris (trip time: 6 to 10 hr.) and 15 trains from Marseille (trip time: 5 hr.). There are also 3 trains per day from Nice (trip time: 6 hr.). For **rail information** and schedules, call ☎ **08-36-35-35-35.** If they're already on the French Riviera, motorists can continue west along A9 to Perpignan.

VISITOR INFORMATION   The **Office Municipal du Tourisme** is beside the Palais des Congrès, place Armand-Lanoux (☎ **04-68-66-30-30**).

SEEING THE TOP ATTRACTIONS

Among the chief sights, the **Castillet,** place de Verdun (☎ **04-68-35-42-05**), is a machicolated and crenellated redbrick building that's a combination gateway and fortress from the 14th century. It houses the **Musée des Arts et Traditions Populaires Catalans** (also known as La Casa Païral), which contains exhibitions of Catalán regional artifacts and folkloric items, including typical dress. Admission is 25F ($5) for adults and 15F ($3) for students and children 17 and under. It's open Wednesday to Monday: mid-June to mid-September from 9:30am to 7pm and mid-September to mid-June from 9am to noon and 2 to 6pm. Part of the charm of the Castillet derives from its bulky-looking tower, which you can climb for a good view of the town.

The ✪ **Cathédrale St-Jean,** place Gambetta / rue de l'Horloge (☎ **04-68-51-33-72**), dates from the 14th and 15th centuries and has an admirable nave and interesting 17th-century retables. Leaving via the south door, you'll find on the left a chapel with the *Devout Christ,* a magnificent wood carving depicting Jesus contorted with pain and suffering—his head, crowned with thorns, drooping on his chest. The cathedral is open daily from 8am to noon and 3 to 6pm.

At the top of the town, the Spanish citadel encloses the **Palais des Rois de Majorque** (Palace of the Kings of Majorca), rue des Archers (☎ **04-68-34-48-29**). This structure from the 13th and 14th centuries, built around a court encircled by arcades, has been restored by the government. You can see the old throne room with its large fireplaces and a square tower with a double gallery; from the tower there's a fine view of the Pyrénées. A free guided tour—only in French—departs at intervals, if demand warrants it, of 30 minutes throughout the open hours. Entrance to the palace is 20F ($4) for adults, 10F ($2) for students, and free for children 7 and under. The palace is open daily: June to September from 10am to 6pm and October to May from 9am to 5pm.

For a major excursion of historic importance, drive 15$^1/_2$ miles north of the city center to the **Château de Salses** (☎ **04-68-38-60-13**), in the hamlet of Salses. Since the days of the Romans, this fort has guarded the main road linking Spain and France. Ferdinand of Aragón erected a fort here in 1497 hoping to protect the northern frontier of his kingdom. Even today, Salses marks the language-barrier point between Catalonia in Spain and Languedoc in France. This Spanish-style fort designed by Ferdinand is a curious example of an Iberian structure in France, but in the 17th century it was modified by Vauban to look more like a château. After many changes of ownership, Salses fell to the forces of Louis XIII in September 1642 and its Spanish garrison left forever. Less than two decades later Roussillon was incorporated into France. The site is open daily: July and August from 9:30am to 7pm; June and September from 9:30am to 6:30pm; April, May, and October from 9:30am to 12:30pm and 2 to 6pm; and November to March from 10am to noon and 2 to 5pm. Admission is 30F ($6).

SHOPPING

With its inviting storefronts and pedestrian streets, Perpignan is a good town for shopping. Catalán is the style indigenous to the area, and it's characterized by textiles, pottery, and furniture in strong geometric patterns and sturdy structures. For one of the best selections of Catalán articles, including pottery, furniture, carpets, and even antiques, visit the ✪ **Galerie Sant Vicens,** rue Sant-Vicens (☎ **04-68-50-02-18**).

ACCOMMODATIONS

Hôtel de la Loge. 1 rue des Fabriques-Nabot, 66000 Perpignan. ☎ **04-68-34-41-02.** Fax 04-68-34-25-13. 22 rms. MINIBAR TV TEL. 350F ($70) double. AE, DC, MC, V.

This beguiling little place dates from the 16th century but has been renovated to become a modern three-star hotel. It's located right in the heart of town, near not only the Loge de Mer, from which it takes its name, but also the Castillet. The cozy rooms are attractively furnished, and many are air-conditioned.

✪ La Villa Duflot. 109 av. Victor-Dalbiez, 66000 Perpignan. ☎ **04-68-56-67-67.** Fax 04-68-56-54-05. 24 rms. A/C TV TEL. 740F ($148) double. Half board 505F–605F ($101–$121) per person extra. AE, DC, V.

This is the area's greatest hotel, yet its prices are reasonable for the luxury offered. Tranquillity, style, and refinement reign supreme. When this hotel opened, one local mayor proclaimed, "Now we have some class in Perpignan." Located in a suburb, La Villa Duflot is a Mediterranean-style dwelling surrounded by a 3-acre park of pine, palm, and eucalyptus. The hotel has an appealing, almost family touch to it and isn't the least bit intimidating. You can sunbathe in the gardens surrounding the pool and order drinks at any hour at the outside bar. The guest rooms are situated around a patio planted with century-old olive trees. All are spacious and soundproof, with solid marble baths and art deco interiors. The chef is a whiz, and the cuisine is reason enough to stay here. Surely you'll agree after sampling his lasagne made with fresh duck liver and asparagus, grilled red mullet in anchovy butter, or (most definitely) roast lamb with a tapenade of eggplant and caviar.

Park Hotel. 18 bd. Jean-Bourrat, 66000 Perpignan. ☎ **04-68-35-14-14.** Fax 04-68-35-48-18. 67 rms. A/C MINIBAR TV TEL. 280F–480F ($56–$96) double. AE, DC, MC, V. Parking 40F ($8).

This four-story hotel faces the Jardins de la Ville, and its rooms are well furnished and soundproof. A first-class cuisine is served in the restaurant, Le Chapon Fin, which offers both à la carte choices and fixed-price menus. The food served here is among the finest in the area and uses prime regional produce to turn out post-nouvelle choices like roast sea scallops flavored with succulent sea urchin velouté, various lobster dishes, and penne with truffles. As an accompaniment, try one of the local wines—perhaps a Collioure or Côtes du Roussillon. The restaurant is open for lunch Monday to Saturday and for dinner Monday to Friday. The hotel also houses Le Bistrot du Park, a less expensive eatery specializing in seafood.

DINING

✪ Festin de Pierre. 7 rue du Théâtre. ☎ **04-68-51-28-74.** Reservations required. Main courses 120F–210F ($24–$42); fixed-price menus 100F ($20) at lunch only, otherwise 150F ($30). AE, MC, V. Tues noon–2pm, Thurs–Mon noon–2pm and 7–9:30pm. Closed 3 weeks in Feb. FRENCH.

This restaurant, named after a subtitle of the 18th-century play *Don Juan*, is housed in the 15th-century home of a former grand inquisitor for the Catholic church. It attracts a conservative and socially prestigious crowd who dine under no pretenses: The excellent cuisine is traditional—no frivolity. Since Allain Boivin became chef, the restaurant has received the Golden Palms award for best restaurant in the region—a hearty welcome, high cooking quality, and low prices. In a clublike atmosphere, you can enjoy offerings like red mullet cutlets with watercress salad, filet of turbot in champagne sauce, or filet of Charolais beef with morels. Veal kidneys in an aged sweet-wine sauce is especially noteworthy. It also has the best wine cellar in the region with more than 400 wines, from the prestigious Château Mouton Rothschild 1957 to the little but surprising regional wine.

L'Apero. 40 rue de la Fusterie. ☎ **04-68-51-21-14.** Reservations required. Main courses 70F–90F ($14–$18); fixed-price menu 72F ($14.40) Mon–Fri only. AE, DC, MC, V. Daily noon–2pm and 8–11pm. FRENCH.

Despite its changing ownership through the years, we've always found that this informal bistro serves the best-value menus in town. Many locals opt for a meal Monday to Friday, as its bargain menu of 72F ($14.40) is available only then. The setting is battered and very old (at least 200 years, the owners think). Menu items include filet of trout with sorrel, roast lamb with rosemary and garlic, tournedos in Roquefort sauce, codfish, and filet of sole.

PERPIGNAN AFTER DARK

The Spanish influence permeates this town, even at night. Head for **place de Verdun,** with its cafes and bars, and you may even discover some Catalán folk dancing to enliven the evening. For a traditional Catalán-style bar with a hip staff, visit **Le Festival,** 40 place Rigaud (☎ **04-68-34-31-60**), the new hot spot for tantalizing tapas and heady sangría. But the bars in the center of town, including the **Républic Café,** 2 place de la République (☎ **04-68-51-11-64**), can be stimulating alternatives with their vivacious student scene and live music. During summer, the nearby area of **Canet-Plage** has a more vibrant, mainstream nightlife of bars and dance clubs that front the beach.

8 Collioure

577 miles SW of Paris, 17 miles SE of Perpignan

You may recognize this port and its sailboats from the Fauve paintings of Lhote and Derain. It's said to resemble St-Tropez before it was spoiled, attracting, in days of yore, Matisse, Picasso, and Dalí. Collioure is the most authentically alluring port of Roussillon, a gem with a vivid Spanish and Catalán image and flavor. Some visitors believe it's the most charming village on the Côte Vermeille.

The two curving ports are separated from each other by the heavy masonry of the 13th-century **Château Royal,** place du 8-Mai-1945 (☎ **04-68-82-06-43**). The château, now a museum of painting and folkloric artifacts, is open daily: June to September from 10am to 6pm and October to May from 9am to 5pm; closed January 1, May 1, November 1, and December 25. Admission is 20F ($4) for adults and 10F ($2) for children. Also try to visit the **Musée Jean-Peské,** route de Port-Vendres (☎ **04-68-82-10-19**), with its collection of works by artists who migrated here to paint. It's open in July and August, daily from 10am to noon and 2 to 7pm; September to June, Wednesday to Monday from 10am to noon and 2 to 6pm. Admission is 12F ($2.40) for adults, 8F ($1.60) for children 12 to 16, and free for children 11 and under.

The town's sloping narrow streets, charming semifortified church, antique lighthouse, and eerily introverted culture make it worth an afternoon stopover. This is the ideal small-town antidote to the condo-choked Riviera.

ESSENTIALS

GETTING THERE Collioure is serviced by frequent train and bus connections, especially from Perpignan. For **rail information** and schedules, call ☎ **08-36-35-35-35.** Many visitors drive along the coastal road (R.N. 114) leading to the Spanish border.

VISITOR INFORMATION   The **Office de Tourisme** is on place du 18-Juin
(☎ **04-68-82-15-47**).

ACCOMMODATIONS

Les Caranques. Rte. de Port-Vendres, 66190 Collioure. ☎ **04-68-82-06-68.** Fax 04-68-82-
00-92. 16 rms. TEL. July–Sept (including half board), 320F ($64) per person double. Apr–June
and Oct 1–14 (without meals), 300F ($60) double. AE, MC, V. Closed Oct 15–Mar.

Constructed around the core of a private villa built after World War II and enlarged
in the 1960s, this hotel is well scrubbed, comfortably furnished, personalized, and
one of the best bargains in town. Set on the perimeter of Collioure, away from the
crush (and the charm) of the center, it features a terrace that opens onto a view of
the old port. The restaurant is for guests only, almost all of whom elect to stay on
the half-board plan.

✪ **Relais des Trois Mas et Restaurant La Balette.** Rte. de Port-Vendres, 66190 Collioure.
☎ **04-68-82-05-07.** Fax 04-68-82-38-08. 19 rms, 4 suites. A/C MINIBAR TV TEL. 665F–965F
($133–$193) double; 1,095F–1,945F ($219–$389) suite. MC, V. Closed Nov 15–Dec 15. Parking
78F ($15.60).

This is not only the town's premier hotel but also the restaurant of choice. The hotel honors the famous artists who've lived at Collioure in the decoration of its beautiful rooms, which lead to spacious baths with Jacuzzis. The rooms open onto views
of the water. Even if you aren't a guest, you may want to take a meal in the dining
room, with its vistas of the harbor. Christian Peyre is unchallenged as the lead chef
of town. His cooking is inventive—often simple but always refined. There's also an
outdoor heated pool.

DINING

Note that the **Restaurant La Balette** at the Relais des Trois Mas (see "Accommodations," above) is the best dining room in town.

La Pérouse. 6 rue de la République. ☎ **04-68-82-05-60.** Reservations recommended. Main
courses 75F–170F ($15–$34); fixed-price menus 95F–148F ($19–$29.60). AE, MC, V. Thurs–Tues
noon–2pm and 7–9:30pm. Closed Nov 11–Dec 27. FRENCH.

This restaurant occupies the whitewashed cellar of a building in the heart of town.
Small windows illuminate the enormous antique barrels and the bullfighting accessories in back, though some visitors prefer a seat on the glassed-in veranda instead.
The kitchens make few concessions to modern cuisine; instead, the food is prepared
with solid authenticity, following regional traditions. Menu items might include
salade catalane, grilled fish, panache of anchovies, spicy preparations of scallops, and
bouillabaisse. Dessert might be a simple but satisfying crème catalane.

9 Narbonne

525 miles SW of Paris, 38 miles E of Carcassonne, 58 miles S of Montpelier

Medieval Narbonne was a port to rival Marseille in Roman times, its "galleys laden
with riches." It was the first town outside Italy to be colonized by the Romans, but
the Mediterranean, now 5 miles away, left it high and dry. For that reason it's an intriguing place, steeped in antiquity.

After Lyon, Narbonne was the largest town in Gaul. Even today you can still see
evidence of the town's former wealth. Too far from the sea to be a beach town, it attracts history buffs and others aware of the memories of its glorious past. Some
50,000 Narbonnais live here, in what is really a sleepy backwater. However, many

Liberté, Egalité, Fraternité . . . Nudité

The municipality known as ✪ **Agde,** 25 miles northeast of Narbonne and 31 miles southwest of Montpellier, operates like every other *commune* in France, with one startling exception: Thanks to its flourishing nudist colony, there's a higher percentage of cheerfully naked adults here than virtually anywhere outside of tropical Africa or the Amazon rain forest. In the 1970s the community's founder/matriarch, Mlle Geneviève Oltha, promoted a simple pine grove beside the sea as the venue for a supportive and understanding (clothing optional) escape from the stresses of urban life. Within less than 25 years the site has burgeoned into the largest nudist colony in Europe, with a roster of about 100 midwinter residents and a midsummer population usually approaching 50,000.

Don't expect everyone in Agde to be nude, as the town's four major subdivisions (Cité d'Agde, Cap d'Agde, Grau d'Agde, and La Tamarissière) offer options for the clothed as well. However, in the clearly signposted and for the most part fenced-in **Quartier Naturist Cap d'Agde,** nudity is required on the beaches and stridently encouraged in the labyrinth of condos and time shares. Don't expect shyness, modesty, or anything other than big business with a new-age or age-old twist. Stores, restaurants, a burgeoning roster of shops (most selling everything except—you guessed it—clothing) are part of the setup. Those who arrive on foot at the compound's gate pay 15F ($3) entrance; motorists with as many passengers as can be crammed into their cars pay 60F ($12). The **Agde Office de Tourisme,** Espace Molière (☎ 04-67-94-29-68), long ago became accustomed to answering questions for the clothed, unclothed, and clothing indecisive who head for their various areas of interest.

Conveniently close to but not within the nudist zone are two museums. The **Musée Agathois,** rue de la Fraternité (☎ 04-67-94-82-51), is noted for the homage it pays to (clothed) cultural models of the city's 19th-century fishing traditions and the region's handcrafts. The **Musée Ethèbe,** Mas de la Clape (☎ 04-67-94-69-60), showcases the artifacts dredged up after marine explorations of the nearby sea bottom.

If you think your visit might be for only a day or two, consider renting a room in the nudist colony's only hotel, the **Hôtel Eve,** impasse Gaissan (B.P. 857), 34307 Cap d'Agde CEDEX (☎ 04-67-26-71-70), where 37 doubles, with TV and phone, rent for 410F to 610F ($82 to $122), depending on the season. Like virtually everything else in the nudist zone, it's open only between Easter and late September. If you want your holiday to be as back to basics as possible, head for one of the largest campgrounds (3,000 sites) along the Côte d'Azur, the **Centre Helio-Marin Oltra,** Quartier Naturiste, B.P. 884, 34307 Cap d'Agde CEDEX (☎ 04-67-01-06-36), where nothing other than your tent will separate your skin from mosquitoes and other insects. If you want to pretend you're a European and commit to a long-term apartment or condo rental lasting a week or more, contact **L'Agence Resid,** B.P. 857, 34307 Cap d'Agde (☎ 04-67-26-84-71).

If you're more embarrassed by your lack of language skills than by your delts, lats, abs, and other things, don't worry. A knowledge of French would be useful, and German and Dutch would come in handy too, as many of your compatriots will hail from northern Europe. But overall, English is the unifying lingo at this offbeat version of the United Nations.

locals are trying to make a go with their vineyards. *Caves* are open to visitors in the surrounding area (the tourist office will advise). If you want to go to the beach, you'll have to head to the nearby sands of **Gruisson-Plage** or **Narbonne-Plage.**

ESSENTIALS

GETTING THERE   Narbonne has rail, bus, and highway connections with other cities on the Mediterranean coast and with Toulouse. Rail travel is the most popular means of transport, with 14 trains per day arriving from Perpignan (trip time: 45 min.), 13 per day from Toulouse (trip time: 1¹/₂ hr.), and 12 per day from Montpellier (trip time: 55 min.). For **rail information** and schedules, call ☎ 08-36-35-35-35.

VISITOR INFORMATION   The **Office de Tourisme** is on place Roger-Salengro (☎ 04-68-65-15-60).

TOURING THE TOP ATTRACTIONS

Few other cities in France contain such a massive architectural block in their centers dating from the Middle Ages. Within it is a labyrinth of religious and civic buildings. Foremost among them is the ✪ **Cathédrale St-Just,** place de l'Hôtel-de-Ville, entrance on rue Gauthier (☎ 04-68-32-09-52). Its construction began in 1272 but it was never finished. Only the transept and a choir were completed; the choir is 130 feet high, built in the bold Gothic style of northern France. At each end of the transept are 194-foot towers from 1480. There's an impressive collection of Flemish tapestries. The cloisters are from the 14th and 15th centuries and connect the cathedral with the Archbishops' Palace. It's open daily: May to September from 10am to 6pm and October to April from 10am to noon and 2 to 6pm.

The cathedral is attached to the **Palais des Archevêques** (Archbishops' Palace, sometimes referred to as the Vieux-Palais), place de l'Hôtel-de-Ville (☎ 04-68-90-30-30). It was conceived as part fortress, part pleasure palace, with three military-style towers from the 13th and 14th centuries. The Old Palace on the right is from the 12th century and the so-called New Palace on the left is from the 14th. It's said that the old, arthritic, and sometimes very overweight archbishops used to be hauled up the interior's monumental Louis XIII–style stairs on mules.

Part of the complex is devoted to the neo-Gothic **Hôtel de Ville** (town hall), which was reconstructed by Viollet-le-Duc, a 19th-century architect involved with the refurbishment of such sites as the cathedral at Paris, between 1845 and 1850.

Today the once-private apartments of the former bishops contain three museums. A **global ticket** costs 25F ($5) for adults, 15F ($3) for students and youths 12 to 18, and free for children 11 and under. It entitles you to visit all three, plus the Musée Lapidaire (below), over a period of 3 days. But if time or your interest is limited, you can buy tickets to each museum individually for 10F ($2). Hours for all three are the same: May to September, daily from 9:30am to 12:15pm and 2 to 6pm; October to April, Wednesday to Monday from 10am to noon and 2 to 5pm. For more information, call ☎ 04-68-90-30-54.

The **Musée Archéologique** contains prehistoric artifacts, Bronze Age tools, 14th-century frescoes, and Greco-Roman amphorae. Several of the sarcophagi date from the 3rd century and some of the mosaics are of pagan origin. The **Musée d'Art et d'Histoire de Narbonne** is located three floors above street level in the archbishop's once-private apartments, the rooms in which Louis XII stayed during his siege of Perpignan. Their coffered ceilings are enhanced with panels depicting the nine Muses. A Roman mosaic floor and 17th-century portraits are on display. There's also a collection of antique porcelain, enamels, and a portrait bust of Louis XIV. In the

Horreum Romain, you'll find a labyrinth of underground passageways, similar to catacombs but with none of the burial functions, dug by the Gallo-Romans and their successors for storage of food and supplies during times of siege.

If you happen to visit between mid-June and mid-September, you might want to participate in one of the occasional hikes up the steep steps of the **Donjon Gilles-Aycelin,** place de l'Hôtel-de-Ville. Originally a watchtower and prison in the late 13th century, it has a lofty observation platform with a view of the cathedral, the surrounding plain, and the Pyrénées. Tours, at 30F ($6) for adults and 20F ($4) for students and children 11 to 18, must be arranged through the Hôtel de Ville (☎ **04-68-90-30-66**) and are much more likely to be welcomed in summer than in winter.

You can see Roman artifacts at the **Musée Lapidaire,** place Lamourguier (☎ **04-68-65-53-58**), in the 13th-century Eglise de Lamourguier. The broken sculptures, Roman inscriptions, and relics of medieval buildings make up one of the largest (and most important) such exhibits in France. Although it maintains regular hours only in July and August (daily from 9:30am to 12:15pm and 2 to 6pm), you can visit it as part of the global museum ticket described above; outside those dates, you can visit only after special arrangements are made with the tourist office.

A final site worth visiting is the early Gothic **Basilique St-Paul-Serge,** rue de l'Hôtel-Dieu (☎ **04-68-41-12-29**), which was built on the site of a 4th-century necropolis. It has an elegant choir with fine Renaissance wood carving and some ancient Christian sarcophagi. The chancel, from 1229, is admirable. The north door leads to the Paleo-Christian Cemetery, part of an early Christian burial ground. It's open daily from 10am to noon and 2 to 6pm.

ACCOMMODATIONS

Hôtel Languedoc. 22 bd. Gambetta, 11100 Narbonne. ☎ **04-68-65-14-74.** Fax 04-68-65-81-48. 38 rms, 2 suites. TEL. 250F–380F ($50–$76) double; 480F ($96) suite. AE, DC, MC, V. Parking 30F ($6).

This oft-modernized turn-of-the-century hotel is near the canal de la Rhône. It offers well-equipped rooms and a restaurant serving regional specialties. The hotel's wine bar, Le Bacchus, is open Monday to Saturday from 7:30pm to 2am. Specializing in the many esoteric vintages grown nearby, it sells wine by the glass and serves simple but flavorful accompaniments to those wines. Examples are grilled salmon with anchovy butter, tender lamb cooked with beans, sautéed chicken chasseur, fresh oysters, and marmites of fish.

La Résidence. 6 rue du 1er-Mai, 11100 Narbonne. ☎ **04-68-32-19-41.** Fax 04-68-65-51-82. 25 rms. A/C TV TEL. 320F–415F ($64–$83) double. AE, MC, V. Parking 40F ($8).

Our favorite hotel in Narbonne is near the Cathédrale St-Just. The 19th-century La Résidence, converted from the premises of a once-stately villa, is comfortable and decorated with antiques. It doesn't have a restaurant but offers breakfast and a gracious welcome.

DINING

Aux Trois Caves. 4 rue Benjamin-Cremieux. ☎ **04-68-65-28-60.** Reservations required. Main courses 100F–205F ($20–$41); fixed-price menus 99F–230F ($19.80–$46). AE, DC, V. Daily noon–2pm and 7:30–10:30pm. FRENCH.

This excellent restaurant occupies a trio of carefully restored, interconnected Romanesque cellars. (Two contain medieval but cozy-looking dining rooms; the third contains the kitchen.) The owners present a classic menu whose repertoire focuses on popular platters from the region. The place is known for its traditional cassoulet but

Les Gardiens of the Camargue

Steamy, sweaty, and flat as the plains of Nebraska, the marshy delta of the Rhône has been called a less fertile version of the delta of the Nile. The waterlogged flatlands encompassed by the river's main branches, the Grand and Petit Rhône, were scorned by conventional farmers throughout centuries of French history because of their high salt content and root-rotting murk.

However, the area was seen as a fit grazing ground for the local black-pelted longhorn cattle, so a breed of cowpokes and cowboys evolved on these surreal flatlands, whose traditions evoke Dodge City in the gaslight era, with primal hints of the ancient Celts. These French cowboys are known and revered by schoolchildren as *les gardiens,* tenders of the cattle that survive amid the flamingos, ticks, hawks, snakes, and mosquitoes of the hot, salty wetlands.

They tend to be short, dark, and wiry; fond of pastis and the region's strong red wines; and not overly communicative, especially to outsiders. They lack the romance associated with the wide open spaces of America's West, and many generations ago most of them grew accustomed to the monotonous terrain whose highest point might be a mound of debris left from a medieval salt flat.

Many *gardiens* converse with one another in a clipped telegraphic form of Provençal or at least a form of heavily accented French whose syntax would make Académie Française members shudder. Until the advent of other kinds of lodging (including motor homes and caravans, which have begun to appear in unprotected areas), French cowpokes usually lived in distinctively traditional, single-story *cabanes* with thatched roofs and without windows. Bull's horns were positioned above each building's entrance as a means of driving away evil spirits.

The traditions of *les gardiens* originated in the 1600s, when the local monasteries began to disintegrate and large tracts of cheap land were bought by private owners for the only thing the soil was really good for—raising bulls and sheep. In the old days most of the work of *les gardiens* involved herding and protecting animals on the muddy open range. Today they're more alert to the demands of modern tourism and have developed, rightfully or not, into living symbols of the antique traditions of the Camargue.

Their ally in the business of tending cattle is the Camargue horse, probably a descendant of Arabian stallions brought here by Moorish invaders after the collapse of the Roman Empire. Brown or black at birth, they develop a white coat, usually after their fourth year. Traditionally, they weren't sheltered in stables but left to fend for themselves during the stifling summers and bone-chilling winters.

The cattle are raised today in ways that haven't changed much in decades: They run semi-wild, each branded with a mark unique to the *manadier* (owner of a Provençal *mas*) who owns them. Even bullfighting is alive and well in the Camargue. These high-energy odes to high jinx and high testosterone are conducted in ways that aren't completely *espagnol.* Sometimes the bull is killed and sometimes it will

also prepares confit of duckling with garlic, filet mignon with mushrooms, platters of fresh sardines cooked in white wine, grilled turbot, and gratin of John Dory—and does so exceedingly well.

L'Alsace. 2 av. Pierre-Sémard. ☎ **04-68-65-10-24.** Reservations recommended. Main courses 90F–150F ($18–$30); fixed-price menus 98F–160F ($19.60–$32). AE, DC, MC, V. Mon noon–2:30pm, Wed–Sun noon–2:30pm and 7:30–10pm. FRENCH.

mangle a local youth during a bullring celebration. Most *gardiens* are too shrewd to participate in a head-on confrontation with a deliberately provoked bull, though there are likely to be at least one or two on horseback in or near the ring during the contest.

Many historians believe that the first real cowboys of North America were *gardiens* in the bayous of Louisiana, imported from the Camargue to tend the flocks of the New World. Today, expect to see fewer *gardiens* than in the past, but many reminders of their traditions remain in the form of felt-sided cowboy hats as well as commemorative saddles and boots whose style resembles that of cowherds on the faraway plains of Spain.

Don't arrive in French cowboy country expecting balmy comforts or even anything particularly romantic: Except for within a strip of land adjacent to the sea, hordes of mosquitoes and biting flies evoke the worst scourges of the Middle Ages. The sultry heat is debilitating and the relentlessly horizontal terrain is anything but inspiring, as anyone who has ever ridden a bike there will tell you.

But if riding a horse through France's hottest and most legendary wetlands is your passion, consider staying at one of two hotels that might remind you of Nevada dude ranches. At **L'Etrier Camarguais,** chemin bas des Launes, 13460 Les-Stes-Maries-de-la-Mer (☎ **04-90-97-81-14;** fax 04-90-97-88-11), you'll find 27 rooms (with TV and phone) costing 980F ($196) for a double, half board included. Built in the 1970s and set about 1 mile north of Les-Stes-Maries-de-la-Mer on a compound surrounded by marshland, it resembles a combination log cabin / terra-cotta–and–stone farmhouse. The bar is decorated with saddles from around the world, the staff is accommodating, and the comfortably unpretentious rooms are outfitted in the Provençal style.

Offering a Camargue holiday on a somewhat grander scale is **Mas de la Fouque,** route d'Aigues-Mortes, 13460 Les-Stes-Maries-de-la-Mer (☎ **04-90-97-81-02;** fax 04-90-97-96-84). About 2 miles west of Les-Stes-Maries-de-la-Mer (about 3¹/₂ miles by car because of the meandering roads), its rooms face southern views over the marshy Etang des Launes and a pool. Everything here is better accessorized, more comfortable, and a lot more appealing than at its less expensive competitor. The 14 rooms (with air-conditioning, TV, phone, and minibar) cost 2,120F ($424) for a double, half board included. The restaurant offers respite even for nonguests, with elegant fixed-price lunches and dinners for 235F ($47).

Most guests at these places wouldn't consider a stay without a *ballade* on horseback lasting from 2 hours to a full day. Their horseback excursions focus on the ecology and panoramas of the marshlands, not on architecture or history per se. With equipment included, the cost is 130F to 140F ($26 to $28) for 2 hours, 180F to 200 F ($36 to $40) for half a day, and 400F to 450F ($80 to $90) for a full-day excursion that includes lunch.

Across from the train station, this restaurant is the most reliable in Narbonne. The comfortable dining room is done in an English style, with wood paneling and a glass-enclosed patio. In spite of the restaurant's name, the cuisine isn't derived from Alsace-Lorraine in eastern France, but is more typical of the food of southwestern France, with a focus on seafood. The Sinfreus, who own the place, offer a fry of red mullet, a savory kettle of bourride, and magret of duck with flap mushrooms.

Especially delectable is this restaurant's expertise at baking entire fish, such as sea wolf, in a salt crust, a process that usually produces a delightfully pungent and flaky product.

10 Aigues-Mortes

466 miles SW of Paris, 39 miles NE of Sète, 25 miles E of Nîmes, 30 miles SW of Arles

South of Nîmes, you can explore much of the Camargue by car. The most reward-ing target is Aigues-Mortes, the city of the "dead waters." In the middle of dismal swamps and melancholy lagoons, Aigues-Mortes is France's most perfectly preserved walled town. Now 4 miles from the sea, it stands on four navigable canals. Louis IX and his crusaders once set forth from Aigues-Mortes, then a thriving port, the first in France on the Mediterranean. The walls, which still enclose the town, were con-structed between 1272 and 1300. The **Tour de Constance** (☎ **04-66-53-61-55**) is a model castle of the Middle Ages, its stones looking out on the marshes. At the top, which you can reach by elevator, a panoramic view unfolds. Admission is 28F ($5.60) for adults, 15F ($3) for youths, and free for children 11 and under. The monument is open daily: Easter to August from 9am to 7pm and off-season from 9:30am to noon and 2 to 5:30pm.

ESSENTIALS

GETTING THERE   Five trains per day connect Aigues-Mortes and Nîmes (trip time: 1 hr.), and four buses per day arrive from Nîmes (trip time: 55 min.). For more **information** and schedules, call ☎ **08-36-35-35-35.**

VISITOR INFORMATION   There's an **Office de Tourisme** at Porte de la Gardette (☎ **04-66-53-73-00**).

ACCOMMODATIONS

Note that the **Restaurant Les Arcades** (see "Dining," below) also rents rooms.

Hostellerie des Remparts. 6 place Anatole-France, 30220 Aigues-Mortes. ☎ **04-66-53-82-77.** Fax 04-66-53-73-77. 19 rms. TEL. 280F–455F ($56–$91) double. AE, DC, V.

Established about 300 years ago, this weather-worn inn lies at the foot of the Tour de Constance, adjacent to the medieval fortifications. Popular and often fully booked (especially in summer), it evokes the defensive atmosphere of the Middle Ages, al-beit with charm and a sense of nostalgia. The rooms with simple furniture are acces-sible via narrow stone staircases; 13 contain TVs. Breakfast is the only meal served.

✪ **Hôtel Les Templiers.** 23 rue de la République, 30220 Aigues-Mortes. ☎ **04-66-53-66-56.** Fax 04-66-53-69-61. 10 rms. A/C TV TEL. 400F–750F ($80–$150) double. AE, DC, V. Closed Nov–Mar 22.

A gem of peace and tranquillity, along with luxurious comfort, is found at the lead-ing inn of town. Protected by the ramparts built by St. Louis, king of France, this 17th-century residence has been tastefully converted to receive guests. Your stay in-cludes all the comforts of a private home. The guest rooms are decorated in a Provençal style, with color coordination and just enough decorative objects to lend a homelike aura. You can relax in the courtyard, where you can also enjoy breakfast. Arrangements can be made to take half board at the Le Maguelone restaurant across the street, costing 600F ($120) per person. The cookery is very regional, with fresh products from the surrounding area used effectively.

Hôtel St-Louis. 10 rue de l'Amiral-Courbet, 30220 Aigues-Mortes. ☎ **04-66-53-72-68.** Fax 04-66-53-75-92. 22 rms. MINIBAR TV TEL. 320F–490F ($64–$98) double. AE, DC, MC, V. Closed Jan–Mar. Parking 45F ($9).

This small inn near place St-Louis offers attractively furnished but somewhat basic rooms—nevertheless, it's one of the most desirable addresses in town. The restaurant serves good regional food as part of fixed-price menus that range from 98F to 195F ($19.60 to $39), with meals that solidify high ranking by local gastronomes.

DINING

Restaurant Les Arcades. 23 bd. Gambetta, 30220 Aigues-Mortes. ☎ **04-66-53-81-13.** Fax 04-66-53-75-46. Reservations recommended. Main courses 75F–165F ($15–$33); fixed-price menus 120F–189F ($24–$37.80). AE, DC, MC, V. Tues 7:30–9:30pm, Wed–Sun noon–2pm and 7:30–9:45pm (also open Mon night July–Aug). Closed 2 weeks in Feb and 2 weeks in Nov. FRENCH.

This restaurant has several formal sections with ancient beamed ceilings or intricately fitted stone vaults. Almost as old as the nearby fortifications, the place is especially charming on sultry days, when the thickness of the masonry keeps the interior cool. Good food is served at reasonable prices and is likely to include warm oysters, fish soup, roasted monkfish in red-wine sauce, lobster fricassée, grilled filet of bull from the Camargue, and grilled duckling.

The owner also rents 10 large, comfortable rooms upstairs, each with air-conditioning, TV, and phone. A double is 480F ($96), breakfast included.

11 Montpellier

471 miles SW of Paris, 100 miles NW of Marseille, 31 miles SW of Nîmes

The capital of Mediterranean (or Lower) Languedoc, this ancient university city is still renowned for its medical school, founded in the 13th century. Nostradamus qualified as a doctor here, and even Rabelais studied at the school. Petrarch came to Montpellier in 1317 and stayed for 7 years.

Today Montpellier is a bustling metropolis, one of southern France's fastest-growing cities thanks to an influx of new immigrants. Except for some dreary suburbs, the city has a handsomely laid out core, with tree-flanked promenades, broad avenues, and historic monuments. One quarter of the population today is students, giving the city a lively, animated aura. In recent years many high-tech corporations, including IBM, have settled in Montpellier.

ESSENTIALS

GETTING THERE   Some 20 trains per day arrive from Avignon (trip time: 1 hr.), 8 from Marseille (trip time: 1³/₄ hr.), 1 every 2 hours from Toulouse (trip time: 2 hr.), and 10 per day from Perpignan (trip time: 1¹/₂ hr.). Eight trains per day arrive from Paris, calling for a change in Lyon (trip time: 4¹/₂ hr.). For **rail information** and schedules, call ☎ 08-36-35-35-35. Two buses a day arrive from Nîmes (trip time: 1³/₄ hr.). For motorists, Montpellier lies off A9 heading west.

VISITOR INFORMATION   The **Office de Tourisme** is at 78 av. du Pirée (☎ 04-67-22-06-16).

EXPLORING THE TOWN

Paul Valéry met André Gide in the **Jardin des Plantes,** 163 rue Auguste-Broussonnet (☎ 04-67-63-43-22), and you might begin here, as it's the oldest such garden in France, from the 16th century. Reached from boulevard Henri-IV, this botanical garden, filled with exotic plants and a handful of greenhouses, was opened in 1593. Admission is free. It's open April to September, Tuesday to Sunday from 10am to 7pm; October to March, Monday to Friday from 10am to 5pm.

Nearby is the town's spiritual centerpiece, the **Cathédrale St-Pierre,** on place St-Pierre (☎ 04-67-66-04-12), founded in 1364. Once associated with a Benedictine monastery, the cathedral suffered badly in the religious wars. (After 1795 the monastery was occupied by the medical school.) Today it has a somewhat-bleak western front with two towers and a canopied porch. It's open daily from 8:30am to 6pm.

Called the Oxford of France because of its burgeoning academic community, Montpellier is a city of young people, as you'll notice if you sit at a cafe opening onto the heartbeat **place de la Comédie,** admiring the Théâtre, the 18th-century Fountain of the Three Graces, or whatever else amuses you. It's the living room of Montpellier, the ideal place to flirt, chat, people watch, cruise, or whatever.

The ✪ **Musée Fabre,** 39 bd. Bonne-Nouvelle (☎ 04-67-14-83-00), is one of France's great provincial art galleries, occupying the former Hôtel de Massilian, where Molière once played for a season. The origins of the collection were an exhibition of the Royal Academy that was sent to Montpellier by Napoléon in 1803. The most important works of the collection, however, were given by François Fabre, a Montpellier painter, in 1825. After Fabre's death, many other paintings from his collection were donated to the gallery. Several of these he painted himself, but the more important works were ones he had acquired—including Poussin's *Venus and Adonis* and Italian paintings like *The Mystical Marriage of Saint Catherine.* This generosity was followed by donations from other parties, notably Valedau, who in 1836 left his collection of Rubens, Gérard Dou, and Téniers. The museum is open Tuesday to Friday from 9am to 5:30pm and Saturday and Sunday from 9:30am to 5pm. Admission is 20F ($4) for adults and 10F ($2) for students and children 11 and under.

Before leaving town, take a stroll along the 17th-century **promenade du Peyrou,** a terraced park with views of the Cévennes and the Mediterranean. This is a broad esplanade constructed at the loftiest point of Montpellier. Opposite the entrance is an Arc de Triomphe, erected in 1691 to celebrate the victories of Louis XIV. In the center of the promenade is an equestrian statue of Louis XIV, and at the end, the **Château d'Eau,** a pavilion with Corinthian columns that serves as a monument to 18th-century classicism. Water is brought here by a conduit, nearly 9 miles long, and an aqueduct.

SHOPPING

Shopping expeditions should include strolls down **place de la Comédie,** with its ultramodern Polygone shopping center, and **rue Jean-Moulin.** This town has a plethora of name-brand boutiques and department stores. But for a traditional regional delicacy, visit **Au Gourmets,** 2 rue Clos-René (☎ 04-67-58-57-04), or **Pâtissier Schoeller,** 121 av. de l'Odève (☎ 04-67-75-71-55), for a plentiful supply of *grisettes de Montpellier* (licorice-and-honey candies) and *comédie de Montpellier* (melt-in-your-mouth almond paste candies).

ACCOMMODATIONS

Note that **Le Jardin des Sens** (see "Dining," below) also rents rooms.

EXPENSIVE

Sofitel Antigone. 1 rue Pertuisanes, 34000 Montpellier. ☎ **04-67-99-72-72.** Fax 04-67-65-17-50. 90 rms, 1 suite. A/C TV TEL. 725F–925F ($145–$185) double; 1,400F ($280) suite. AE, DC, MC, V. Parking 70F ($14).

In the heart of Montpellier, this hotel, built in 1991, is the favorite of the traveling businessperson. However, in summer it does quite a trade with visitors. It's particularly distinguished for its pool, which, along with a bar and breakfast room, occupies most of the top floor. The rooms are chain format but first class. The best accommodations are on a floor known as *Privilège*, where you get such extras as an all-marble bath. Some rooms are suitable for those with disabilities. It's a winning choice, with the most efficient staff in the city.

MODERATE

✪ **Hôtel du Parc.** 8 rue Achille-Bège, 34000 Montpellier. ☎ **04-67-41-16-49.** Fax 04-67-54-10-05. 19 rms. A/C TV TEL. 295F–390F ($59–$78) double. AE, V.

One of the town's more charming moderately priced hostelries, this hotel lies in the heart of the city near the Palais des Congrès. It was a Languedocian residence in the 18th century but has been turned into a hotel with a lot of grace notes and French provincial charm. The rooms have been carefully decorated, including several modern conveniences, such as minibars and air-conditioning, not always found in Montpellier hotels. A garden and flowering terrace offer you a venue for breakfast if you'd like to eat outside. Numerous restaurants surround the hotel.

Hôtel George-V. 42 av. St-Lazare, 34000 Montpellier. ☎ **04-67-72-35-91.** Fax 04-67-72-53-33. 39 rms. TV TEL. 360F–410F ($72–$82) double. AE, DC, V.

Located near a park on the northern edge of the city, this well-managed hotel offers traditionally furnished rooms. Some wear and tear shows, but it's a good value nevertheless. The bar is for guests only.

La Maison Blanche. 1796 av. de la Prompignane, 34000 Montpellier. ☎ **04-67-79-60-25.** Fax 04-67-79-53-39. 36 rms, 2 suites. A/C TV TEL. 440F ($88) double; 780F ($156) suite. AE, DC, MC, V. A 5-minute drive southeast of Montpellier's center: Take bd. d'Antigone east until you reach the intersection with av. de la Pompignane and head north until you come to the hotel, on your right.

Few other hotels in the south of France have worked so hard to emulate the ginger-bread and French Créole *Gone with the Wind* ambience of this hotel. Built around 1990, it's set in a clapboard motel whose balconies drip with ornate gingerbread and whose gardens are verdant and bordered with lattices. The rooms are stylishly furnished in rattan and wicker. Parts of the interior, especially the dining room, might remind you of Louis XIII France more than Old Louisiana, but overall the setting is as charming and unusual as anything else in town. The in-house restaurant, open daily for lunch and Tuesday to Saturday for dinner, serves fixed-price menus at 95F to 150F ($19 to $30).

INEXPENSIVE

Les Arceaux. 33–35 bd. des Arceaux, 34000 Montpellier. ☎ **04-67-92-03-03.** Fax 04-67-92-05-09. 18 rms. TV TEL. 285F–315F ($57–$63) double. AE, MC, V.

A hotel has stood at this prime location, right off the renowned promenade du Peyrou, since the turn of the century. The rooms are pleasantly but simply furnished, and a shaded terrace adjoins the hotel. Breakfast is the only meal served.

Ulysse. 338 av. de St-Maur, 34000 Montpellier. ☎ **04-67-02-02-30.** Fax 04-67-02-16-50. 27 rms. MINIBAR TV TEL. 340F ($68) double. AE, DC, V. From bd. d'Antigone, head north along av. Jean-Mermoz to rue de la Pépinière; continue right for a short distance, then take a sharp left at the first intersection, which leads to av. de St-Maur.

One of the city's better bargains, Ulysse delivers a lot for the price. There's a simplicity here, though the owners have worked hard—on a budget—to make the hotel as stylish as possible. Each room is unique in its composition of colors and decorations. The furnishings are made with an original wrought-iron design, functional but with a certain flair. Much in-room comfort is found here, including fully equipped baths and extra features like a minibar, unusual for a budget hotel. The housekeeping is first rate, even though the prices aren't.

DINING

La Réserve Rimbaud. 820 av. de St-Maur. ☎ **04-67-72-52-53.** Reservations recommended. Main courses 100F–150F ($20–$30); fixed-price menus 160F–380F ($32–$76). AE, DC, MC, V. Tues–Sat noon–2pm and 8–10pm, Sun noon–2pm. Closed Jan–Mar 20. Take N113 (av. de Nîmes) northeast toward Nîmes and follow it to the intersection with av. St-Lazare, then turn left; the restaurant is on the right. FRENCH.

The most memorable restaurant in town is in what was built as a bulky, rectangular manor house in 1835 by a prosperous local family, the Rimbauds. It offers only about 30 seats in a setting that might've been plucked from the early 1900s. Menu items—prepared and presented by English-speaking members of the Tarrit family—change with the season but are likely to include gigot de mer (a slab of monkfish with local herbs), warm foie gras with apples, fricassée of sole with baby vegetables, and a thin-crusted croustillant aux pommes served with English cream.

Note: If you announce your intention before the beginning of your meal, the staff will rent you one of their rowboats for 60F ($12) per hour, so you can float like a character in one of Renoir's paintings beside the river's verdant banks.

Le Chandelier. Immeuble La Coupole Antigone. ☎ **04-67-15-34-38.** Reservations required. Main courses 92F–205F ($18.40–$41); fixed-price menus 150F ($30) at lunch, 260F and 310F ($52 and $62) at dinner. AE, DC, MC, V. Mon 7:30–9:30pm, Tues–Sat noon–1:30pm and 7:30–9:30pm. FRENCH.

This is a modern showcase, a panoramic restaurant with large windows, for the cuisine of Gilbert Furland. He searches for "temptations of the palate," which means that you'll find some unusual flavor combinations, with ragoût of lobster his most delightful dish. His menu changes frequently but may include smoked-eel mousse with mint-flavored mussels, lamb sweetbreads with crayfish in vinaigrette sauce, veal kidneys in basil, and a mosaic of hare with foie gras.

✪ **Le Jardin des Sens.** 11 av. St-Lazare, , 34000 Montpellier. ☎ **04-67-79-63-38.** Reservations required. Main courses 160F–280F ($32–$56); fixed-price lunch (Mon–Fri) 190F ($38); fixed-price menu 340F–550F ($68–$110). AE, MC, V. Mon–Sat noon–2:30pm and 7–10pm. FRENCH.

If we could award more than one star, we'd grant two to this citadel of fine cuisine. The chefs—the biological twins Laurent and Jacques Pourcel—have taken Montpellier by storm. Michelin has awarded them two stars, thus bestowing its divine blessing. Postnouvelle reigns here. The rich bounty of Languedoc is served, but only after going through a process designed to enhance its natural flavor. The meals often seem flawless, so it's no wonder the restaurateurs of Montpellier are wishing these twins had settled in some other city. The cuisine could be almost anything, depending on where the chefs' imaginations roam. An appropriate starter might be bon-bons of foie gras with new potatoes. A tarte fine with tomatoes, roasted monkfish, and essence of thyme is memorable, as is a filet of pigeon stuffed with pistachios. A dessert specialty is a gratin of limes with slices of pineapple en confit.

The Jardin des Sens also rents 12 deluxe guest rooms and two suites, each designed in cutting-edge modernism by Bruno Borrione, a colleague of Philippe Starck. They cost 800F ($160) for a double and 1,600F to 2,200F ($320 to $440) for a suite.

✪ **L'Olivier.** 12 rue Aristide-Olivier. ☎ **04-67-92-86-28.** Reservations recommended. Main courses 68F–140F ($13.60–$28); fixed-price menus 160F–198F ($32–$39.60). AE, DC. Wed–Sun noon–1:30pm and 7:30–9:30pm. Closed Aug and holidays. FRENCH.

No restaurant, with the exception of Le Jardin des Sens, has improved more than this. Chef Michel Breton is making his name known in the restaurant guides to the south of France. The decor is something out of a 1950s boudoir, but you don't come here for background—you want to try Breton's "creative statements." Some dishes that might appear regularly are salmon with oysters, fricassée of lamb with thyme, warm monkfish terrine, and salad of lamb sweetbreads with extract of truffles. The welcome is warm-hearted and sincere.

MONTPELLIER AFTER DARK

After the sun sets, head for **place Jean-Jaurès, rue de Verdun,** and **rue des Ecoles Laïques,** or take a walk down **rue de la Loge** for its carnival atmosphere of talented jugglers, mimes, and musical artists.

Le Notes en Bulles, 19 rue des Ecoles Laïques (☎ 04-67-60-38-21), is a great bohemian way to ease into the evening. Here you can loosen up with the locals before continuing on to something a bit more serious, like **Rockstore,** 20 rue de Verdun (☎ 04-67-58-70-10), with its 1950s rock memorabilia and live concerts drawing lots of students. Then walk up a flight of stairs to its disco, which continuously pounds out techno and rock. The cover for the disco is 50F ($10).

An exotic cocktail bar is **Viva Brazil,** 7 rue de Verdun (☎ 04-67-58-63-33), where you chop your way through the lush rain-forest vegetation and friendly natives to reach the mirrored sanctuary of the dance floor. For the best jazz and blues in town, check out **JAM,** 100 rue Ferdinand-de-Lesseps (☎ 04-67-58-30-30). In a noisy, smoky, and even gritty space, its regular concerts attract jazz enthusiasts from miles around. Concert tickets average 50F ($10).

Gays and lesbians start out an evening of light-hearted antics at the predominantly male **THT,** 29 av. de Castelnau (☎ 04-67-79-96-17), where a huge dance party breaks out on Saturday night. If you're still wired toward midnight, head over to **Le Rome Club,** 77 Mas de Fugières à Mauguio, in the shopping center (☎ 04-67-22-22-70), with its two levels and gargantuan dance floor plastered with a good mix of gays and lesbians.

You can enjoy an evening of opera or orchestra at the **Corum,** esplanade de Charles-de-Gaulle (☎ 04-67-51-66-16). For complete ticket information and schedules, contact the **Opéra Comédie,** place de la Comédie (☎ 04-67-60-19-99). From the end of June to the beginning of July, an array of classical and modern dance performances cascade into town for the **Festival International Montpellier Danse.** Tickets sell for 35F to 260F ($7 to $52) and can be purchased through the Hôtel d'Assas, 6 rue de la Vieille Aiguillerie (☎ 04-67-60-91-91). Further information is available by calling ☎ 04-67-60-83-60. In late July, the **Festival de Radio France et de Montpellier** presents a variety of orchestral music, jazz, and opera. Tickets range from 50F to 150F ($10 to $30) and can be purchased by calling ☎ 04-67-02-02-01. Or call ☎ 04-67-61-66-81 for complete information.

12 Nîmes

440 miles S of Paris, 27 miles W of Avignon

Nîmes, the ancient Nemausus, is one of the finest places in the world for wandering among Roman relics. The city grew to prominence during the reign of Caesar Augustus (27 B.C.–A.D. 14). Today it possesses one of the best-preserved Roman amphitheaters in the world and a near-perfect Roman temple. The city of 135,000 is more like Provence than Languedoc, in which it lies. There's a touch of Pamplona (Spain) here in the festivals of the *corridas* (bullfights) at the arena. The

Spanish image is even stronger at night, when the bodegas fill, usually with students, drinking sangría and listening to the sounds of flamenco.

By 1860 the togas of Nîmes's citizenry had long given way to denim, the cloth de Nîmes. An Austrian immigrant, Leví-Strauss, started to export this heavy fabric to California for use as material for work pants for gold diggers in those boomtown years. The rest, as they say, is history.

ESSENTIALS

GETTING THERE Nîmes has bus and train service from the rest of France and is near several autoroutes. It lies on the main rail line between Marseille and Bordeaux. Six trains a day arrive from Paris, taking 4¹/₂ hours and costing 350F to 400F ($70 to $80). For **rail information** and schedules, call ☎ **08-36-35-35-35**.

VISITOR INFORMATION The **Office de Tourisme** is at 6 rue Auguste (☎ **04-66-67-29-11**).

EXPLORING THE TOWN

The pride of Nîmes is the ✪ **Maison Carré,** place de la Comédie (☎ **04-66-36-26-76**), built during the reign of Caesar Augustus. On a raised platform with tall Corinthian columns, it's one of the most beautiful, and certainly one of the best-preserved, Roman temples of Europe. It inspired the builders of La Madeleine in Paris as well as Thomas Jefferson. A changing roster of cultural and art exhibits is presented here, beneath an authentically preserved roof that the city of Nîmes repaired in 1996. It's open daily from 9am to noon and 2:30 to 6pm. Admission is free.

Across the square stands its modern-day twin, the **Carré d'Art,** a sophisticated research center and exhibition space that contains a library, a newspaper kiosk, and an art museum. Its understated design from 1993 was inspired by (but doesn't overpower) the ancient monument nearby. The most visible component here is the **Musée d'Art Contemporain** (☎ **04-66-76-35-35**), whose permanent expositions are often supplemented with temporary exhibits of contemporary art. It's open Tuesday to Sunday from 11am to 6pm, charging 24F ($4.80) for adults and 18F ($3.60) for students and children 14 and under. *Note:* The view from this modern building's terrace allows you to rise above the roaring traffic and presents a panorama of most of the ancient monuments and medieval churches of Nîmes.

The elliptically shaped ✪ **Amphithéâtre Romain,** place des Arènes (☎ **04-66-76-72-77**), a better-preserved twin to the one at Arles, is far more complete than the Colosseum of Rome. It's two stories high, each floor with 60 arches, and was built of huge stones painstakingly fitted together without mortar. One of the best preserved of the arenas from ancient times, it once held more than 20,000 spectators who came to see gladiatorial combats and wolf or boar hunts. Today it's used for everything from ballet recitals to bullfights and is open daily from 9am to noon and 2:30 to 6pm. Admission is 24F ($4.80) for adults and 18F ($3.60) for students and children 15 and under.

The **Jardin de la Fontaine,** at the end of quai de la Fontaine, was laid out in the 18th century, using the ruins of a Roman shrine as an ornamental centerpiece. It was planted with rows of chestnuts and elms, adorned with statuary and urns, and intersected by grottos and canals—making it one of the most beautiful gardens in France. Adjoining it is the ruined **Temple of Diana** and the remains of some Roman baths. Over the park, within a 10-minute walk north of the town center, rises **Mont Cavalier,** a low but rocky hill on top of which rises the sturdy bulk of the **Tour Magne,** the city's oldest Roman monument. You can climb it for 12F ($2.40) for adults and 10F ($2) for students and children 14 and under and will receive a panoramic view

Nîmes

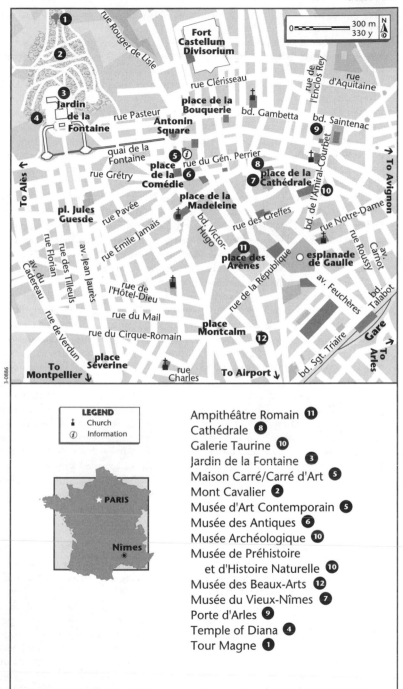

LEGEND
- ✝ Church
- ⓘ Information

Ampithéâtre Romain ⑪
Cathédrale ⑧
Galerie Taurine ⑩
Jardin de la Fontaine ③
Maison Carré/Carré d'Art ⑤
Mont Cavalier ②
Musée d'Art Contemporain ⑤
Musée des Antiques ⑥
Musée Archéologique ⑩
Musée de Préhistoire
  et d'Histoire Naturelle ⑩
Musée des Beaux-Arts ⑫
Musée du Vieux-Nîmes ⑦
Porte d'Arles ⑨
Temple of Diana ④
Tour Magne ①

over Nîmes and its environs. It's open daily: May to September from 9am to 6pm and October to April from 9am to 5pm.

Nîmes is home to a great number of museums. The largest and best respected, the **Musée des Beaux-Arts,** rue Cité-Foulc (☎ 04-66-67-38-21), contains French paintings and sculptures from the 17th to the 20th century as well as Flemish, Dutch, and Italian works from the 15th to the 18th century. Seek out in particular one of G. B. Moroni's masterpieces, *La Calomnie d'Apelle,* and a well-preserved Gallo-Roman mosaic. The museum is open Tuesday to Sunday from 11am to 6pm. Admission is 24F ($4.80) for adults and 18F ($3.60) for students and children 14 and under.

If time allows, visit the **Musée du Vieux-Nîmes,** place de la Cathédrale (☎ 04-66-36-00-64), housed in an episcopal palace from the 1700s. It's rich in antiques. The museum is open Tuesday to Sunday from 11am to 6pm, charging 24F ($4.80) for adults and 18F ($3.60) for children.

One of the city's busiest thoroughfares, boulevard de l'Amiral-Courbet, leads to the **Porte d'Arles**—the remains of a monumental gate built by the Romans during the reign of Augustus. Farther along, contained in the same stately building at 13 bis bd. l'Amiral-Courbet, are the **Musée de Préhistoire et d'Histoire Naturelle** (☎ 04-66-67-39-14), and the **Musée Archéologique** (☎ 04-66-67-25-57). Both are open Tuesday to Sunday from 11am to 6pm, and a fee of 24F ($4.80) for adults and 18F ($3.60) for children admits you to both museums.

Less popular is the **Galerie Taurine,** boulevard des Arènes (call the tourist office for data). Devoted to bullfighting and its memorabilia, it's open only erratically.

Interested in exploring the city's monuments and museums with zeal? Consider buying a *billet global,* sold at the ticket counter of any of the local museums and monuments. It provides access to all the above-mentioned cultural sites over a 3-day period, for an all-inclusive fee of 60F ($12) for adults and 30F ($6) for students and children 15 and under.

Outside the city, 14 miles to the northeast, the well-preserved, much-photographed **pont du Gard** spans the Gard River and was built without mortar; its huge stones have evolved into one of the region's most vivid reminders of the glory and technical competence of the ancient Romans. Consisting of three tiers of arches arranged into gracefully symmetrical patterns, it dates from about 19 B.C. Frédéric Mistral, the national poet of Provence and Languedoc, recorded a legend claiming that the devil constructed the bridge providing that he could claim the soul of the first person to go across. To visit it, take highway N86 from Nîmes to a point 2 miles from the village of Remoulins, where signs are prominently posted.

SHOPPING

Head to the center of town and **rue du Général-Perrier, rue des Marchands, rue du Chapître,** and the pedestrian streets of **rue de l'Aspic** and **rue de la Madeleine.** You'll find a Sunday-morning flea market beginning at 8am in the **Stade des Castières,** on boulevard Périphérique that encircles Nîmes.

To appease your sweet tooth, go to just about any pastry shop in town and ask for the regional almond-based cookies called *croquants villaret* and *caladons.* They're great for a burst of energy or for souvenirs. One of the best purchases you can make in Nîmes, especially if you're not continuing east into Provence, is a *santon.* These wood or clay figurines are sculpted into a cast of characters from Provençal country life and can be collected together to create a uniquely country-French nativity scene. For a selection of santons in various sizes, visit the **Boutique Provençale,** 10 place de la Maison Carré (☎ 04-66-67-81-71), or **Au Papillon Bleu,** 15 rue du Général-Perrier (☎ 04-66-67-48-58).

ACCOMMODATIONS
MODERATE
Atria Nîmes Centre. 5 bd. de Prague, 3000 Nîmes. ☎ **04-66-76-56-56.** Fax 04-66-76-56-59. 112 rms, 7 suites. A/C MINIBAR TV TEL. 520F ($104) double; 800F ($160) suite. AE, DC, MC, V.

Opened in mid-1995, this cost-conscious member of a nationwide chain occupies a desirable site in the heart of Nîmes, adjacent to the ancient arena. It was designed with six floors that wrap around a carefully landscaped inner courtyard, providing a garden setting. Each room contains a double bed, a single bed (which converts into a sofa), a well-equipped bath, and a wide writing desk. The hotel offers a bar and an attractive restaurant, Les Sept Collines, which is open daily for lunch and dinner.

Note: Nîmes contains an additional Novotel, which is older and more remotely located on the southern perimeter of town: the **Novotel Nîmes,** chemin de l'Hostellerie, boulevard Périphérique Sud, 30000 Nîmes (☎ **04-66-84-60-20**). Here 96 rooms sell at roughly equivalent rates, with the added advantage of having an on-site pool.

Imperator Concorde. Quai de la Fontaine, 30900 Nîmes. ☎ **04-66-21-90-30.** Fax 04-66-67-70-25. 62 rms, 3 suites. A/C MINIBAR TV TEL. 530F–680F ($106–$136) double; 850F–1,000F ($170–$200) suite. AE, DC, MC, V. Parking 70F ($14).

This leading hotel is near the Roman monuments, opposite the Jardin de la Fontaine. With a recent major renovation, it has been much improved. You can order lunch in the hotel's enticing rear gardens. The best rooms have Provençal pieces; others have been renewed in a traditional way to preserve their character.

INEXPENSIVE
New Hôtel La Baume. 21 rue Nationale, 30000 Nîmes. ☎ **04-66-76-28-42.** Fax 04-66-76-28-45. 34 rms. A/C MINIBAR TV TEL. 350F ($70) double. AE, DC, MC, V.

Our favorite nest in Nîmes was created in a 17th-century mansion. The designers were careful to preserve the original architectural heritage during its creation, and the result is a winning combination of modern and traditional. The 24 rooms are fitted with exceptional charm, worthy of a Venetian palace. They're equipped with thoughtful extras like hair dryers, and the plumbing is state of the art. The hotel restaurant is also worth a visit, turning out such dishes as fresh salmon flavored with anise and chicken saltimbocca with ham.

DINING
The dining room at the **New Hôtel La Baume** (see "Accommodations," above) is also a good dining choice.

✪ **Alexandre.** Rte. de l'Aéroport de Garons. ☎ **04-66-70-08-99.** Reservations required. Main courses 150F–190F ($30–$38); fixed-price menus 275F–410F ($55–$82). AE, MC, V. Tues–Sat noon–1:30pm and 7:30–9:30pm, Sun noon–1:30pm. Closed Feb. From the town center, take rue de la République southwest to av. Jean-Jaurès, then head south and follow the signs to the airport in the direction of Garons. FRENCH.

The most charming, amusing, and competent restaurant around is on the outskirts of Nîmes. In its verdant setting, you'll discover the elegant and rustic domain of Michel Kayser, an exceptional chef who adheres to classic tradition, with subtle improvements. He's assisted in the dining room by his charming wife, Monique. Menu items are designed to amuse as well as delight the palate: Examples are île flottante with truffles and velouté of cèpe mushrooms, roasted pigeon stuffed with purée of vegetables and liver of pigeon, and the region's most sophisticated version of an old country recipe, pieds et paquets. Especially appealing is the cheese trolley loaded with esoteric goat cheeses from the region and worthy cow cheeses from other parts of France. The dessert trolley is incredibly hard to resist.

Restaurant au Chapon Fin. 3 rue du Château-Fadaise. ☎ **04-66-67-34-73.** Reservations required. Main courses 79F–129F ($15.80–$25.80); fixed-price menus 72F ($14.40) at lunch, 120F ($24) at dinner. AE, MC, V. Mon–Fri noon–2pm and 7:30–10pm, Sat 7:30–10pm. Closed 2 weeks in Aug. FRENCH.

This tavern/restaurant, on a little square behind St-Paul's, is run by M. and Mme Grangier. It has beamed ceilings, small lamps, and a black-and-white stone floor. Madame Grangier is from Alsace, but don't scour the menu for many Alsatian specialties—it's more traditional and regional. From the à la carte menu you can order foie gras with truffles, coq au vin (chicken with wine), and entrecôte flambéed with morels. The proprietor makes his own confit d'oie (goose preserved in its own fat) from birds shipped in from Alsace.

Wine Bar Chez Michel. 11 place de la Couronne. ☎ **04-66-76-19-59.** Reservations not required. Main courses 55F–130F ($11–$26); fixed-price menus 77F ($15.40) at lunch, 80F–130F ($16–$26) at dinner. AE, DC, MC, V. Tues–Sat noon–2pm and 7pm–midnight. FRENCH.

This place is paneled with mahogany and has leather banquettes you might've found in a turn-of-the-century California saloon. An array of salads and platters is served, and at lunch you can order a quick menu, including an appetizer, a garnished main course, and two glasses of wine. Typical dishes are magret of duckling and contrefilet of steak with Roquefort sauce. You can now enjoy lunch on the terrace in the newly renovated courtyard. A restaurateur extraordinaire, Michel Hermet also makes his own wine. There are more than 300 other varieties of wine to choose from, by the glass or pitcher.

NIMES AFTER DARK

Once the warm weather hits, all sorts of activities take place at the arena, including concerts and theater under the stars. The Office de Tourisme has a complete listing of events and schedules, or you can contact the **Bureau de Location des Arènes,** 1 rue Alexandre-Ducros (☎ **04-66-67-28-02**). Concerts, theater, and operas are also performed at **Hall du Théâtre,** 1 place de la Calade (☎ **04-66-36-02-04**). All of Nîmes's central squares burst forth with music and dancing on Thursday nights during July and August as artists, musicians, and all kinds of revelers gather in celebration of **Marchés du Soir.** Other streets to explore for a healthy dose of good times are **impasse Porte-de-France** and **boulevard Victor-Hugo.**

If you like French soldiers, check out their favorite hangout, **Café Le Napoléon,** 46 bd. Victor-Hugo (☎ **04-66-67-20-23**). Popular with the intelligentsia is the **Haddock Café,** 13 rue de l'Agau (☎ **04-66-67-86-57**), with its weekly live rock concerts. But if you simply want to tank down some brew and have a rip-roaring good time, go to the **Queen's Beer,** 1 bis rue Jean-Reboul (☎ **04-66-67-81-10**).

All the town's jazz aficionados know that **Le Diagonal,** 41 bis rue Emile-Jamais (☎ **04-66-21-70-01**), hosts the area's best jazz and blues concerts. The flashy, sexy, and hip **La Comédie,** 28 rue Jean-Reboul (☎ **04-66-73-13-66**), is the hands-down best for dancing and attracts a pretty crowd of youthful danceaholics. A little less flashy, but a lot more fun, **Lulu,** 10 impasse de la Curaterie (☎ **04-66-36-28-20**), is the gay and lesbian stronghold in Nîmes. The cover at either of these dance clubs ranges between 50F and 70F ($10 and $14).

Provence: In the Footsteps of Cézanne & van Gogh

5

Provence has been called a bridge between the past and the present, where yesterday blends with today in a quiet, often melancholy way. Peter Mayle's best-selling *A Year in Provence* and *Toujours Provence* have played no small part in the burgeoning popularity this sunny corner of southern France has enjoyed during recent years.

The Greeks and Romans first filled the landscape with cities boasting Hellenic theaters, Roman baths, amphitheaters, and triumphal arches. These were followed in medieval times by Romanesque fortresses and Gothic cathedrals. In the 19th century Provence's light and landscapes attracted illustrious painters like Cézanne and van Gogh. Despite the changes over the years, the howling mistral will forever be heard through the broad-leaved plane trees.

Provence has its own language and its own customs. The region is bounded on the north by the Dauphine, on the west by the Rhône, on the east by the Alps, and on the south by the Mediterranean. We'll focus in the next two chapters on the part of Provence known as the glittering French Riviera or Côte d'Azur.

EXPLORING THE REGION BY CAR

Here's how to link together the best of the region if you rent a car:

Day 1   Beginning in **Orange,** tour the Roman ruins and the Musée Municipal, then drive south for 8 miles along A9 to **Châteauneuf-du-Pape** for a visit to the village's famous wineries and the Musée des Vieux Outils de Vignerons. Continue south for 8 miles along any of three highways marked AVIGNON. Spend the night in Avignon.

Day 2   This day is devoted to **Avignon,** where you can tour the Palais des Papes and walk among the sights of place du Palais, the Quartier de la Balance, and Old Avignon. Spend another night here.

Day 3   Head west, following A100 for 20 miles, past Remoulins to the pont du Gard; get on Rte. 981 going northwest for 12 miles to **Uzès,** the beautiful medieval town where you'll spend the day and night. Start your tour at Le Duché, then visit the town's 4th-century crypt and Cathédrale St-Théodorit, and end with a stroll through the assymetrical place aux Herbes.

Day 4   In the morning, drive southwest for 12 miles along Rte. 981 to the pont du Gard, then take Rte. 986 10 miles south to Beaucaire and drive 1 mile east on Rte. 999 to **Tarascon.** Spend the morning touring the Château du Roi René and admiring the art in the Eglise Ste-Marthe, then take Rte. 970 south for 2 miles, continuing south on A570 for 7^1/$_2$ miles to **Arles.** Spend the afternoon touring the Roman ruins, the museums, and the necropolis, then stay here overnight.

Day 5　Leave Arles along D17, driving north for 6^1/$_2$ miles to **Fontvieille.** The morning is a tribute to the author Alphonse Daudet. Begin by touring the Château de Montauban, a museum in his honor, and the Moulin de Daudet, the windmill that inspired his *Lettres de Mon Moulin.* Also view the Roman aqueducts. Then head 5 miles west on Rte. 17 to **Les Baux,** where you can contrast the buildings of the living village with the ruins of the ghost village. Drive on to **St-Rémy-de-Provence,** 6 miles north along the road marked ST-RÉMY, to spend the night.

Day 6　In the morning, tour St-Rémy's Roman monuments and Musée Archéologique, then walk the streets admiring its historic buildings. A 10-mile drive east along Rte. 99 brings you to **Cavaillon,** where you'll spend the afternoon and night. A tour of the town can include the vegetable markets, the reconstructed 1st-century A.D. Roman arch, the medieval Chapelle St-Jacques, the Musée Archéologique, and the 18th-century synagogue housing a small Jewish museum.

Day 7　Drive to **Gordes,** taking D2 north for 10 miles. Visit the 12th-century Château de Gordes, home to the Musée Didactique Vasarély; Frédérique Duran's Moulin des Bouillons, with its Museum of Stained Glass; and the mysterious Village des Bories or the isolated Cistercian Abbaye de Sénanque. Then take the route de Roussillon 10 miles east to **Roussillon,** where you can admire the scenic village and the Giants' Causeway, before continuing along the route de Bonnieux for 7 miles south to **Bonnieux.** Follow Rte. 36 for 7^1/$_2$ miles to the intersection with Rte. 943 and continue on that road 6 miles south, past the grave of Albert Camus, to Cadenet. Here transfer to Rte. 543 south and drive 10 miles to Lignane, where a 4-mile drive southeast on Rte. 7 will lead into **Aix-en-Provence,** your destination for the night. Here you can admire the countryside that inspired Cézanne and the buildings and shops of cours Mirabeau and Old Aix, as well as tour the Musée Granet.

Day 8　Continue your exploration of Aix and spend another night.

Day 9　Take A8 south for 17 miles to **Marseille,** where you can spend the day exploring the many sights, including its churches and museums. Stay here for the night.

Day 10　Drive to **Toulon,** taking A50 east for 42 miles. You can spend the night here after a day including stops at the Musée de l'Histoire Naturelle and the Musée de Toulon. Or you can boat to the **Iles d'Hyères** for an overnight stop.

Day 11　You'll need a full day if you want to explore the **Grand Canyon du Verdon.** The Verdon River, a tributary of the Durance, has cut Europe's biggest canyon into a limestone plateau. The canyon covers a distance of 13 miles east to west and is one of the most spectacular natural sights in France. Once you get there, for safety reasons it's best to go on guided hikes.

1 Orange

409 miles S of Paris, 34 miles NE of Nîmes, 75 miles NW of Marseille, 16 miles S of Avignon

Orange gets its name from the days when it was a dependency of the Dutch House of Orange-Nassau, not because it's set in a citrus belt. Actually, the last orange grove departed 2,000 years ago. The juice that flows in Orange today comes from its fabled vineyards, which turn out a Côtes du Rhône vintage, and many *caves* are spread throughout the district, some of which offer *dégustations* to paying customers. The tourist office (see "Essentials," below) will provide you with a list.

Provence

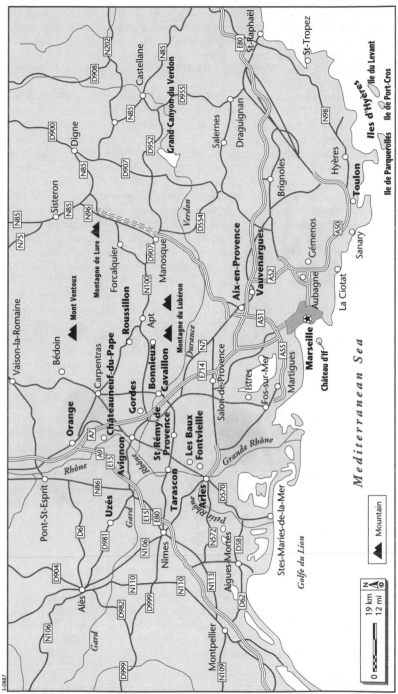

3-0887

117

Overlooking the Valley of the Rhône, today's Orange, with a somewhat sleepy population of about 30,000, tempts visitors with Europe's third-largest extant triumphal arch and best-preserved Roman theater. Louis XIV, who toyed with the idea of moving the theater to Versailles, said: "It is the finest wall in my kingdom." UNESCO has placed the arch on its World Cultural and Natural Heritage List in the hopes that it can be preserved "forever."

In the southern part of town, the ✪ **Théâtre Antique,** place des Frères-Mounet (☎ 04-90-51-17-60), dates from the days of Augustus. Built into the side of a hill, it once held 8,000 spectators in tiered seats divided into three sections based on class. Carefully restored, the nearly 350-foot-long and 125-foot-high theater is noted for its fine acoustics and is used today for outdoor entertainment. It's open daily: April to September from 9am to 6:30pm and October to March from 9am to noon and 1:30 to 5pm. Admission is 30F ($6) for adults and 25F ($5) for children.

To the west of the theater once stood one of the biggest temples in Gaul, which, with a gymnasium and the theater, formed one of the greatest buildings in the empire. Across the street on place des Frères-Mounet, the **Musée Municipal d'Orange,** place du Théâtre-Antique (☎ 04-90-51-18-24), displays fragments excavated in the area. Your ticket to the ancient theater will also admit you to this museum, which is open daily: April to September from 9:30am to 7pm and October to March from 9:30am to noon and 1:30 to 5:30pm.

Even older than the theater is the ✪ **Arc de Triomphe** on avenue de l'Arc-de-Triomphe. It has decayed, but its sculptural decorations and other elements are still fairly well preserved. Built to honor the conquering legions of Caesar, it rises 72 feet and is nearly 70 feet wide. Composed of a trio of arches held up by Corinthian columns, it was used as a dungeon for prisoners in the Middle Ages.

Before leaving Orange, head for the hilltop park, **Colline St-Eutrope,** for a view of the surrounding valley with its mulberry plantations.

ESSENTIALS

GETTING THERE   Orange sits on some of the major French north-south rail and highway arteries, making arrivals by train, bus, or car convenient. Some 20 trains per day arrive from Avignon (trip time: 17 min.), at a one-way fare of around 32F ($6.40). From Marseille there are 14 trains per day (trip time: 1¹/₂ hr.), at around 115F ($23) one-way. From Paris there are 14 trains per day (trip time: 4¹/₂ hr.) by TGV, which will require a transfer at either Valence or Avignon and ongoing transit by conventional train into Orange; a one-way fare is 380F ($76). For **rail information** and schedules, call ☎ 08-36-35-35-35.

VISITOR INFORMATION   The **Office de Tourisme** is on cours Aristide-Briand (☎ 04-90-34-70-88).

SPECIAL EVENTS   From mid-July to mid-August, a drama, dance, and music festival called **Les Chorégies d'Orange** takes place at the Théâtre Antique. For information or tickets, visit the permanent office on place Sylvain, adjacent to the antique theater, or call ☎ 04-90-34-15-52. Events for 1997 included *Tristan und Isolde* (presented in vocal and orchestral form but without costumes), *Turandot,* and *Lucia di Lammermoor*. Concert tickets range from 90F to 490F ($18 to $98); opera tickets, from 170F to 800F ($34 to $160).

ACCOMMODATIONS

Hôtel Louvre et Terminus. 89 av. Frédéric-Mistral, 84100 Orange. ☎ **04-90-34-10-08.** Fax 04-90-34-68-71. 32 rms, 2 suites. TV TEL. 280F–380F ($56–$76) double; 500F–650F ($100–$130) suite. AE, DC, MC, V. Parking 30F ($6) in garage.

Surrounded by a garden terrace, this conservatively decorated Logis de France offers good value in a much-renovated building begun around 1900. Some 12 rooms have minibars and 16 are air-conditioned. The pool enables those without air-conditioning to cool off via an alternative method. The hotel also has a simple but worthy restaurant, serving meals daily at both lunch and dinner.

Mercure Orange. 80 rte. de Caderousse, 84100 Orange. ☎ **04-90-34-24-10.** Fax 04-90-34-85-48. 99 rms. MINIBAR TV TEL. 470F–490F ($94–$98) double. AE, DC, MC, V. Drive half a mile west of Orange's center, following the directions to Caderousse.

This comfortable modern hotel lies about a mile west of the edge of the city, in a 20-year-old building whose wings curve around a landscaped courtyard. Its well-furnished rooms are arranged around a series of gardens, the largest of which contains a pool. Fixed-price menus are served in the poolside restaurant. This is your best bet for general overnight comfort far from the madding crowd. It was completely renovated in 1997.

DINING

Le Parvis. 3 cours Pourtoules. ☎ **04-90-34-82-00.** Reservations required. Main courses 55F–110F ($11–$22); fixed-price menus 98F–225F ($19.60–$45). AE, DC, MC, V. Tues–Sat noon–2:30pm and 7–9:30pm, Sun noon–2:30pm. Closed Nov 1–15. FRENCH.

Jean-Michel Berengier sets the best table in Orange, though the dining room is rather austere. He bases his cuisine not only on well-selected vegetables but also on the best ingredients from "mountain or sea." Try his escalope of braised sea bass with fennel or feuilleté of asparagus. A year-round can't-miss dish is the foie gras of the chef, which could be flavorfully followed by lamb whose preparation varies according to the season. (The staff prides itself on dozens of preparations.) The service is efficient and polite. A special children's menu is offered for 60F ($12).

NEARBY ACCOMMODATIONS & DINING

✪ Château de Rochegude. 26790 Rochegude. ☎ **04-75-97-21-10.** Fax 04-75-04-89-87. 25 rms, 4 suites. A/C MINIBAR TV TEL. 1,200F ($240) double; 1,800F–2,500F ($360–$500) suite. AE, DC, MC, V. Closed Jan–Feb. It lies 8 miles north of Orange; take D976, following the signs toward Gap and Rochegude.

This Relais & Châteaux stands on 25 acres of parkland. The stone castle is at the edge of a hill, surrounded by Rhône vineyards. Throughout its history this 12th-century turreted residence has been renovated by a series of distinguished owners, ranging from the pope to the dauphin. The current owners have made many 20th-century additions, but ancient touches still survive. Each room is done in a traditional Provençal style, with fabrics and furniture influenced by that region's 18th- and 19th-century traditions. The food and service are exceptional. You can enjoy meals surrounded by flowering plants in the stately dining room. There are also a barbecue by the pool and sunny terraces where refreshments are served. In the restaurant, fixed-price menus are 200F ($40) at weekday lunches; other menus (available at both lunch and dinner) are 220F to 490F ($44 to $98).

Hostellerie Le Beffroi. Rue de l'Evêché, 84110 Vaison-la-Romaine. ☎ **04-90-36-04-71.** Fax 04-90-36-24-78. 22 rms. MINIBAR TV TEL. 655F ($131) double. AE, DC, MC, V. Closed Feb 15–Mar 20 and Nov 10–Dec 20. Parking 40F ($8). From Orange, drive 21 miles northeast, following the signs to Vaison-la-Romaine. The hotel is in Vaison's medieval core (Cité Médiévale).

This charming 16th- and 17th-century hotel boasts ocher walls and original detailing on the exterior and flowered wallpaper, heavy ceiling beams, plaster detailing, and fireplaces in the rustic interior. The elegantly furnished rooms display 19th-century antiques. There's a garden with a view of the town where you can order meals

Driving Les Routes de la Lavande

As characteristic of Provence as heather is of the Yorkshire moors, lavender has played a major role here for hundreds of years. When part of the Roman Empire, Provence produced the flowers to scent the public baths. In the Middle Ages, quackery dictated that villages burn piles of the plant in the streets, the prevalent medical theory being that disease was spread by sense of smell. But it was during the Renaissance that the current industry took root, linked to the Médicis, who padded their wealth with a brisk trade in the distillation of the flower's essential oils. Today lavender production and distillation are more than just trades—they're a way of life for many families.

The heart of lavender production lies in Provençal fields stretching from the foothills of the Vercors mountains to the Verdon canyons and from Buech to the Luberon range. Plants grown and distilled in this area are sold under the Haute-Provence label, renowned for its quality. A drive through the region is most scenic just before the midsummer harvest, when the countryside takes on the purplish hue of lavender blossoms spread out in seemingly endless rows to the horizon—see the front cover of this guide. You can not only take in the sight and scent of the flowers but also tour the distilleries and farms. Some of these facilities are open only during summer, when the year's harvest is undergoing distillation. Those that are open all year sell the living plants, their essential oil, the dried flowers used in Provençal cooking, and derivative perfumes, honey, and herbal teas while also offering tours.

The lavender farms and distilleries are so numerous that you'd never be able to visit all of them, but a trip to **Nyons,** 26 miles northeast of Orange, and a few surrounding facilities will allow even the most avid connoisseurs to get their fill.

From Orange, take A7 northwest for $1^3/_4$ miles to Rte. 976 and drive northeast for 8 miles to St-Cécile-les-Vignes, where the road becomes Rte. 576. Continue northeast for $3^3/_4$ miles to Tulette, turn right onto Rte. 94, and go $13^1/_2$ miles northeast to Nyons. Stop at the **Office de Tourisme,** place Libération (☎ **04-75-26-10-35**), to pick up the brochure *Les Routes de la Lavande,* offering a brief explanation

under a giant fig tree; fixed-price menus are 145F to 185F ($29 to $37). For your convenience, the hotel, across from the chiseled fountain in the Haute-Ville sector, maintains a limited number of parking spaces.

The town itself is worth exploring, for it contains some fascinating reminders of its former Roman occupation, including Les Ruines Romaines, two areas that've been excavated—the Quartier Puymin and Quartier Villasse.

2 Châteauneuf-du-Pape

417 miles S of Paris, 12 miles N of Avignon, 8 miles S of Orange

Near Provence's north border, the **Château du Pape** was built as the Castelgandolfo, the country seat of the French popes of Avignon, during the 14th-century reign of Pope John XXII. Now in ruins, it overlooks the vast acres of vineyards that the popes planted, the start of a regional industry that today produces some of the world's best reds as well as an excellent white.

ESSENTIALS

GETTING THERE   There's no rail station in Châteauneuf, so train passengers must get off at Sorgues ($4^1/_2$ miles south) or Orange (8 miles north). For **rail**

and history of lavender production and a map of the region and its production facilities, with addresses, phone numbers, and hours.

On the outskirts of Nyons, start out at the **Jardin des Arômes (Garden of Scents),** promenade de la Digue (☎ **04-75-26-04-30**), with its collection of aromatic plants and lavenders; it's open around the clock throughout the year and charges no admission. To reach it from Nyons, follow the road signs pointing to Gap. After viewing and smelling the living plants at close proximity, go closer to town to **Bleu Provence,** 58 promenade de la Digue (☎ **04-75-26-10-42**), a traditional distillery of thyme and lavender that offers tours and a shop where you can buy the essential oils. It's open year-round, Monday to Saturday from 10am to noon and 2 to 6pm; admission is free to individuals but 10F ($2) per person for groups on a guided tour.

In St-Nazaire-le-Desert, northeast of Nyons, visit **Gérard Blache,** in the village center next to the Auberge du Desert (☎ **04-75-27-51-08**), a shop that sells all things lavender in July and August, daily from 10am to 7:30pm. From here, head southeast to Rosans, where the distillery of the **Cooperative des Producteurs de Lavande des Alpes (Lavender Cooperative of the Alps),** on D94 west of Rosans (☎ **04-92-66-60-30**), offers guided tours and sales of essential oils in July and August, daily from 10am to noon and 2 to 6pm. Southwest of here is Buis-les-Baronnies, where the **Shop Bernard Laget,** in the village center on place aux Herbes (☎ **04-75-28-12-01**), includes lavender products among its medicinal and aromatic plants; it's open Tuesday to Sunday from 9:30am to noon and 3:30 to 7pm. Finally, head southeast of Buis to Savoillan, where the **Ferme St-Agricole (St. Agricol Farm)** (☎ **04-75-28-86-57**) boasts botanical paths leading through an experimental garden, a species preservation garden, and a greenhouse. Its shop sells lavender products. The farm is open daily: June 15 to September 15 from 10:30am to 1pm and September 16 to June 14 from 10:30am to 1pm and 2 to 6pm. Admission is 20F ($4).

information, call ☎ **08-36-35-35-35.** There are about three buses a day into Châteauneuf from both towns. Buses from Sorgues originate in Avignon, making access from Avignon a possibility too. The tourist office (below) is the best source for schedules and information about bus access. Bus passengers are deposited and retrieved in place de la Bascule, behind Châteauneuf's post office.

VISITOR INFORMATION   The **Office de Tourisme** is at place du Portail (☎ **04-90-83-71-08**).

THE LURE OF WINE LORE

If you're absolutely fascinated by the town's wine-related lore, there are two major *associations de vignerons,* each representing a consortium of individually owned vineyards whose owners pool their marketing, advertising, and bottling programs. Open Monday to Friday from 8am to noon and 2 to 6pm, **Reflets,** 2 chemin du Bois de la Ville (☎ **04-90-83-71-07**), represents 6 vintners, and **Prestige et Tradition,** 3 rue de la République (☎ **04-90-83-72-29**), represents 12. They offer *dégustations* and sales.

Another useful source for wine and lore is **La Vinothèque**, 9 rue de la République (☎ **04-90-83-74-01**). A sales and marketing outlet for Mme Carre, matriarch of the Comtes d'Argelas vineyards, it's open for wine tasting and sales daily from 9am to

7pm. On the premises is **La Boutique de la Vinothèque,** where wine accessories (corkscrews, racks, decanters) are sold.

TASTING THE WINES

What makes the local wines distinctive is the blending of 13 varieties of grapes grown on vines surrounded by stones that reflect heat onto them during the day and keep them warm in the cool of night. As a result, the wines produced in the district's vineyards are among the most potent in France, with an alcohol content of at least 12^1/$_2$% and, in many instances, as high as 15%. The region played a central role in the initiation of the Appellation d'Origine Contrôlée, France's strict quality-control system. This was formed when the late Baron Le Roy de Boiseaumarie, the most distinguished of the local vintners, initiated geographical boundaries and minimum standards for the production of wines given the Châteauneuf-du-Pape label. This led to the filing of a lawsuit that in 1923 gave local producers exclusive rights to market their Côtes du Rhônes under that label, and thus paved the way for other regions to identify and protect their distinctive wines. You'll see a plaque devoted to his memory in the town's **place de la Renaissance.**

Few other towns in France devote as much time, energy, and civic pride to their wines. A map posted in the village square, **place du Portail** (but called **place de la Fontaine** by just about everyone), pinpoints 14 wineries open for touring and tasting. The best known is **Domaine de Mont-Redon,** on D68 about 3 miles north of the town center (☎ **04-90-83-72-75**). It offers sampling of recent vintages of red and white wines and sales of *eau-de-vie,* a clear grape liqueur produced in a limited batch of 2,000 bottles annually. A noteworthy competitor is **Clos des Papes,** avenue Le Bienheureux Pierre de Luxembourg, in the town center (☎ **04-90-83-70-13**), where unique humidified cellars produce what many connoisseurs consider the region's best wine.

The town's only museum devotes all its exhibition space to winemaking. The **Musée des Vieux Outils de Vignerons** of the **Caves du Père-Anselme,** avenue Le Bienheureux Pierre de Luxembourg (☎ **04-90-83-70-07**), contains the history and artifacts of local wine production, including a 16th-century wine press, 17th- and 18th-century plows, winemakers' tools, barrelmaking equipment, and a tasting cellar. It's open daily: mid-June to mid-September from 9am to 7pm and the rest of the year from 9am to noon and 2 to 6pm. Admission and tastings are free.

In early August the village hosts the annual **Fête de la Véraison,** a medieval fair. It includes tasting stalls set up by local winemakers, actors impersonating Provençaux troubadours, bear-baiters (who are much kinder to their animals than their medieval counterparts), falconers with their birds, lots of merchants selling locally made handcrafts, battered flea market kiosks, and food. Don't expect dancing—what you'll get is a festival where the antique fountain on place du Portail spurts out wine and vast amounts of that beverage are consumed. If you opt to attend, you can drink all the wine you want for the price of a *verre de la Véraison.* This souvenir glass, filled on demand at any vintner who participates, costs 16F ($3.20) and is sold at strategically positioned kiosks around town.

ACCOMMODATIONS

You might check with **La Mère Germaine** (see "Dining," below) to see if its guest rooms are now open.

✪ **Hostellerie du Château des Fines-Roches**. Rte. d'Avignon, 84230 Châteauneuf-du-Pape. ☎ **04-90-83-70-23.** Fax 04-90-83-78-42. 6 rms. A/C MINIBAR TV TEL. 750F–950F ($150–$190) double. AE, MC, V. From the center of town, drive 2 miles south, following the signs to Avignon.

This manor house was built late in the l9th century by local landowners who included dozens of architectural features inspired by the Middle Ages. Named for the smooth rocks *(fines roches)* found in the soil of the nearby vineyards, the château devotes its huge cellars to the storage of thousands of bottles of local wines and its upper floors to the lodgings and dining room of this charming hotel. The guest rooms were renovated in 1997 and include Provençal styling and many individual touches enhanced with a scattering of antiques.

A meal in the restaurant is highly recommended, with fixed-price menus at 210F to 340F ($42 to $68) and main courses at 95F to 150F ($19 to $30). Between mid-June and September it's closed only Monday at lunch; the rest of the year it's closed Sunday night and all day Monday. The menu items, carefully crafted and flavorful, include filets of red mullet prepared with aromatic herbs and garnished with its own liver marinated in vinaigrette, filet of bull from the Camargue marinated in a particular vintage *(syrah)* of strong red wine, and roast rack of local lamb with a gratin of eggplant and sheep's cheese. The wine list focuses on local vintages, particularly those from the village.

DINING

The **Hostellerie du Château des Fines-Roches** (see "Accommodations," above) is also a great dining choice.

La Mère Germaine. Place de la Fontaine, 84230 Châteauneuf-du-Pape. ☎ **04-90-83-70-72.** Fax 04-90-83-53-20. Reservations recommended. Main courses 80F–110F ($16–$22); fixed-price menus 185F–350F ($37–$70). AE, DC, MC, V. Thurs–Tues noon–2:30pm and 7–9:30pm. PROVENÇAL.

Named after the matriarch who opened it several generations ago, this restaurant enjoys such a wonderful panorama from its terrace that in good weather virtually everyone opts for a table there. Otherwise, you can dine in one of the two indoor rooms. A roster of Provençal dishes is featured, focusing on the bounty of the surrounding farms and fields. Menu items include zucchini flowers stuffed with mushrooms and drizzled with ratatouille juice, roasted rabbit stuffed with black-olive tapenade and fresh tomatoes, filet of turbot with *barigoule* (Provençal vinaigrette), and crispy rack of lamb scented with herbs from the surrounding *garrigue* (scrubland). Of special interest is the 350F ($70) *menu dégustation,* with each course accompanied by an appropriate wine or liqueur from Châteauneuf.

Though they probably won't be as sought after as a table at the restaurant, look for the availability of half a dozen guest rooms that were intended for a radical restoration and upgrade at press time.

3 Avignon

425 miles S of Paris, 50 miles NW of Aix-en-Provence, 66 miles NW of Marseille

In the 14th century Avignon was the capital of Christendom—the popes lived here during what the Romans called the Babylonian Captivity. The legacy left by that "court of splendor and magnificence" makes Avignon one of the most interesting and beautiful of Europe's cities of the Middle Ages.

Today this walled city of some 100,000 residents reaches its peak celebration time during the famous **Festival d'Avignon,** when bacchanalia reigns in the streets. Avignon at any time of the year remains a major stopover on the route from Paris to the Mediterranean. Lately, it has become increasingly known as a cultural center—and not just at festival time. Artists and painters in increasing numbers have been moving here, especially on rue des Teinturiers. Experimental theaters, painting galleries, and art cinemas have brought increasing diversity to the inner city. The popes are long gone, but life goes on exceedingly well.

ESSENTIALS

GETTING THERE   Avignon is a junction for bus routes throughout the region, and train service from other towns is frequent. The TGV trains from Paris arrive 21 times per day (trip time: 3¹/₂ hr.), and 12 trains per day arrive from Marseille (trip time: 1¹/₂ hr.). For **rail information** and schedules, call ☎ 08-36-35-35-35.

VISITOR INFORMATION   The **Office de Tourisme** is at 41 cours Jean-Jaurès (☎ 04-90-82-65-11).

EXPLORING THE TOWN

Even more famous than the papal residency is the ditty "*Sur le pont d'Avignon, l'on y danse, l'on y danse,*" echoing through every French nursery and around the world. Ironically, pont St-Bénézet was far too narrow for the *danse* of the rhyme. Spanning the Rhône and connecting Avignon with Villeneuve-lèz-Avignon, the bridge is now only a fragmented ruin, with only 4 of its original 22 arches still extant. According to legend, it was inspired by a vision a shepherd named Bénézet had while tending his flock. Actually, the bridge was built between 1117 and 1185 and suffered various disasters from then on. In 1669 half the bridge toppled into the river. On one of the piers is the two-story **Chapelle St-Nicolas**—one story in Romanesque style, the other in Gothic. The remains of the bridge are open daily from 9am to 6:30pm. Admission costs 15F ($3) for adults and 7F ($1.40) for students and seniors.

It's worth at least an hour to walk through the **Quartier de La Balance,** where the Gypsies lived in the 1800s. Over the years La Balance had grown seedy, but since the 1970s major renovations have taken place. Start at place du Palais, going along rue de La Balance. The main interest here is viewing the major restoration of the old town houses, with renewed elegant facades, many graced with mullioned windows. The district encompasses some of the ramparts that used to surround Avignon, once stretching for some 2³/₄ miles. Built in the 14th century by the popes, these ramparts were partially restored by Viollet-le-Duc in the 19th century. The most intriguing part is along rue du Rempart-du-Rhône, leading east to place Crillon. After a look, you can return to place de l'Horloge via rue St-Etienne.

Dominating Avignon from a hill is one of the most famous, and/or notorious, depending on your point of view, palaces in the Christian world, the ✪ **Palais des Papes,** place du Palais (☎ 04-90-27-50-74). Headquarters of a schismatic group of cardinals who came close to toppling the authority of the popes in Rome, this part fortress, part showplace is the monument most frequently associated with Avignon. You're shown through on a guided tour, usually lasting 50 minutes. The tour is somewhat monotonous, as most of the rooms have been stripped of their once-legendary finery. The exception is the **Chapelle St-Jean,** known for its beautiful frescoes attributed to the school of Matteo Giovanetti and painted between 1345 and 1348. These frescoes present scenes from the life of John the Baptist and John the Evangelist. More Giovanetti frescoes can be found above the Chapelle St-Jean in the **Chapelle St-Martial.** The frescoes depict the miracles of St. Martial, the patron saint of Limousin.

The **Grand Tinel** (banquet hall) is about 135 feet long and 30 feet wide, and the pope's table stood on the southern side. The pope's bedroom is on the first floor of the **Tour des Anges.** Its walls are entirely decorated in tempera with foliage on which birds and squirrels perch. Birdcages are painted in the recesses of the windows. In a

Palais des Papes

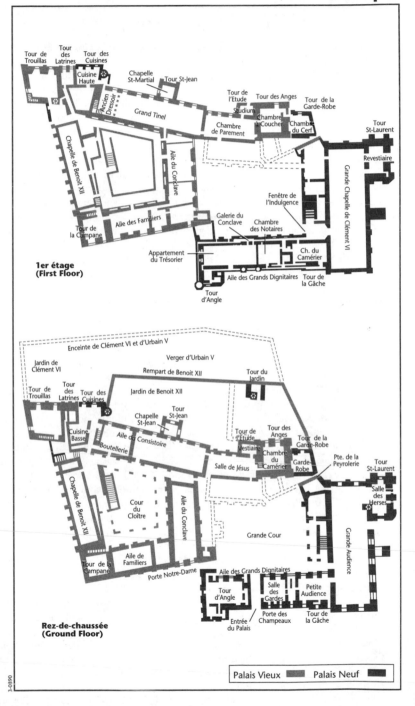

**1er étage
(First Floor)**

Tour de Trouillas
Tour des Latrines
Tour des Cuisines
Cuisine Haute
Chapelle St-Martial
Tour St-Jean
Ancien Dressoir
Grand Tinel
Tour de l'Etude
Studium
Tour des Anges
Tour de la Garde-Robe
Chambre à Coucher
Chambre du Cerf
Tour St-Laurent
Revestiaire
Chambre de Parement
Chapelle de Benoit XII
Aile du Conclave
Grande Chapelle de Clément VI
Fenêtre de l'Indulgence
Tour de la Campane
Aile des Familiers
Galerie du Conclave
Chambre des Notaires
Appartement du Trésorier
Ch. du Camérier
Aile des Grands Dignitaires
Tour de la Gâche
Tour d'Angle

**Rez-de-chaussée
(Ground Floor)**

Enceinte de Clément VI et d'Urbain V
Jardin de Clément VI
Verger d'Urbain V
Rempart de Benoit XII
Tour du Jardin
Tour de Trouillas
Tour des Latrines
Tour des Cuisines
Jardin de Benoit XII
Cuisine Basse
Chapelle St-Jean
Tour St-Jean
Aile du Consistoire
Boutellerie
Tour de l'Etude
Vestiaire
Tour des Anges
Tour de la Garde-Robe
Salle de Jésus
Chambre du Camérier
Garde-Robe
Pte. de la Peyrolerie
Tour St-Laurent
Salle des Herses
Chapelle de Benoit XII
Cour du Cloître
Aile du Conclave
Grande Cour
Grande Audience
Tour de la Campane
Aile de Familiers
Porte Notre-Dame
Aile des Grands Dignitaires
Tour d'Angle
Salle des Gardes
Petite Audience
Entrée du Palais
Porte des Champeaux
Tour de la Gâche

Palais Vieux ▓▓▓ Palais Neuf ████

3-0890

A Tale of Two Papal Cities

In 1309 a sick man named Pope Clement V, nearing the end of his life, arrived in Avignon. Lodged as a guest of the Dominicans, he died in the spring of 1314 and was succeeded by John XXII. The new pope, unlike the previous Roman popes, lived modestly in the Episcopal Palace. When Benedict XII took over, he enlarged and rebuilt the palace. Clement VI, who followed, built an even more elaborate extension called the New Palace. After Innocent VI and Urban V, Pope Gregory XI did no building. Inspired by Catherine of Siena, he wanted to return the papacy to Rome and succeeded. In all, seven popes reigned at Avignon. Under them, art and culture flourished, as did vice. Prostitutes blatantly went about peddling their wares in front of cardinals, rich merchants were robbed, and innocent pilgrims from the hinterlands were brutally tricked and swindled.

From 1378, during what's known as the Great Schism, one pope ruled in Avignon, another in Rome. The reign of the pope and the "antipope" continued, one following the other, until both rulers were dismissed by the 1417 election of Martin V. Rome continued to rule Avignon until it was joined to France at the time of the Revolution. The ramparts (still standing) around Avignon were built in the 14th century and are characterized by their machicolated battlements, turrets, and old gates.

---

secular vein, the **Studium (Stag Room)**—the study of Clement VI—was frescoed in 1343 with hunting scenes. Added under the same Clement, who had a taste for grandeur, the **Grande Audience** (Great Audience Hall) contains frescoes of the prophets, also attributed to Giovanetti and painted in 1352.

In July and August the palace is open daily from 10am to 6pm; the rest of the year it's open Wednesday to Monday from 9:30am to noon and 2 to 6:30pm. Admission is 35F ($7) for adults and 27F ($5.40) for students, children, and seniors. A 12F ($2.40) supplement is charged whenever a special exhibition on the region's art or culture is displayed. Guided tours in English depart whenever the staff feels there's a suitable demand, at schedules that vary widely with the seasons and the day of the week. They're priced at 45F ($9) for adults and 35F ($7) for children.

Near the palace is the 12th-century ✪ **Cathédrale Notre-Dame des Doms,** place du Palais (☎ 04-90-86-81-01), containing the Flamboyant Gothic tomb of some of the apostate popes. Crowning the top is a gilded statue of the Virgin from the 19th century. The cathedral's hours vary according to whatever religious ceremony is scheduled inside, but generally it's open daily from 11am to 6pm and admission is free. From the cathedral, enter the promenade du Rocher-des-Doms to stroll through its garden and enjoy the view across the Rhône to Villeneuve-lèz-Avignon.

The **Musée du Petit-Palais,** place du Palais (☎ 04-90-86-44-58), contains an important collection of paintings from the Italian schools from the 13th to the 16th century, including works from Florence, Venice, Siena, and Lombardy. In addition, salons display 15th-century paintings done in Avignon, and several galleries are devoted to Roman and Gothic sculptures. It's open in July and August, daily from 10:30am to 6pm; off-season, Wednesday to Monday from 9:30am to noon and 2 to 6pm. Admission is 30F ($6) for adults, 15F ($3) for students and youths 12 to 18, and free for children 11 and under.

The **Musée Calvet,** 65 rue Joseph-Vernet (☎ 04-90-86-33-84), is housed in an 18th-century mansion and displays fine and decorative arts collections. The fine-arts department features the works of Vernet, David, Corot, Manet, and Soutine, plus the most extensive collection of ancient silverware in provincial museums. Our favorite oil is by Brueghel the Younger, *Le Cortège nuptial* (The Bridal Procession). Look for a copy of Bosch's *Adoration of the Magi* as well. It's open Wednesday to Monday: June to September from 10am to 7pm and October to May from 10am to 1pm and 2 to 6pm. Admission is 30F ($6) for adults and 15F ($3) for children. Adjacent to the Calvet is the **Musée Requien,** 61 rue Joseph-Vernet (☎ 04-90-82-43-51), a very minor natural history museum focusing on local geology, botany, and zoology. Named after the Avignon-born naturalist Esprit Requien, it's open Tuesday to Saturday from 9am to noon and 2 to 6pm; admission is free.

The **Musée Louis-Vouland,** 17 rue Victor-Hugo (☎ 04-90-86-03-79), is devoted to 17th- and 18th-century fine arts. In a 19th-century mansion, opening onto a lovely garden, it displays Avignon's greatest treasure trove of lavish antiques and objets d'art, including Sèvres porcelain, the comtesse du Barry's tea set, great tapestries from Aubusson and Gobelins, Persian rugs, antique clocks, glittering chandeliers, and commodes to equal those at Versailles. Our favorites are the Louis XV inkpots with silver rats holding the lids. It's open Tuesday to Saturday: June to September from 10am to noon and 2 to 6pm and off-season from 2 to 6pm. Admission is 20F ($4) for adults and 10F ($2) for students.

The **Musée Lapidaire,** entered at 18 rue de la République (☎ 04-90-85-75-38), is in a 17th-century Jesuit church displaying an important collection of Gallo-Roman sculptures. It's open Wednesday to Monday from 10am to 1pm and 2 to 6pm. Admission is 10F ($2), free for children.

SEEING VILLENEUVE-LEZ-AVIGNON

The modern world is impinging on Avignon, but across the Rhône at Villeneuve-lèz-Avignon the Middle Ages slumber on. When the popes lived in exile at Avignon, wealthy cardinals built palaces *(livrées)* across the river. Many visitors prefer to stay or dine here rather than in Avignon (see our recommendations below).

However, even if you're staying at Avignon or just passing through, you'll want to visit Villeneuve, especially to see its Carthusian monastery, **Chartreuse du Val-de-Bénédiction,** 60 rue de la République (☎ 04-90-15-24-24). Inside France's largest charterhouse, built in 1352, you'll find a church, three cloisters, rows of cells that housed the medieval monks, and rooms depicting aspects of their daily lives. Part of the complex is devoted to a publicly and privately endowed workshop (the Centre National d'Ecritures et du Spectacle) for painters and writers who live in the monastic cells rent free for up to a year to pursue their craft. Exhibitions of photography and painting are presented throughout the year.

Pope Innocent VI (whose tomb you can view) founded this charterhouse, which became the country's most powerful. Inside one of the chapels, a remarkable *Coronation of the Virgin* by Enguerrand Charonton is enshrined; painted in 1453, the masterpiece contains a fringed bottom that's Bosch-like in its horror, representing the denizens of hell. The 12th-century graveyard cloister is lined with cells where the former fathers prayed and meditated. The charterhouse is open daily from 9am to 6:30pm. Admission is 30F ($6) for adults, 17F ($3.40) for children 12 to 17, and free for children 11 and under.

Crowning the town is the **Fort St-André,** Mont Andaon (☎ 04-90-25-45-35), founded in 1360 by Jean-le-Bon to serve as a symbol of might to the pontifical powers across the river. The Abbaye St-André, now privately owned, was installed in the 18th century. You can visit the formal garden encircling the mansion. The mood here is tranquil, with a rose-trellis colonnade, fountains, and flowers. It's open daily: April to October 9 from 10am to 12:30pm and 2 to 6pm and October 10 to March from 10am to noon and 2 to 7pm.

You can also visit the **Tour Philippe le Bel,** rue Montée-de-la-Tour (☎ **04-90-27-49-68**), constructed by Philippe the Fair in the 13th century, when Villeneuve became a French possession. The tower served as a gateway to the kingdom standing at the intersection of avenue Gabriel-Péri. If you're game and have the stamina, you can climb to the top for a panoramic view of Avignon and the Rhône Valley. The tower is open June 15 to September 15, daily from 10am to 12:30pm and 3 to 7pm; off-season, Tuesday to Sunday from 10am to noon and 2 to 5:30pm. Admission is 22F ($4.40) for adults, 14F ($2.80) for students, and 10F ($2) for children.

Last, visit the **Eglise Notre-Dame,** place Meissonier, founded in 1333 by Cardinal Arnaud de Via. Its proudest possession is a 14th-century ivory Virgin, one of the great French treasures. It's open Wednesday to Monday: April to September from 10am to 12:30pm and 3 to 7pm and October to March from 10am to noon and 2 to 5:30pm. Admission is free.

SHOPPING

Since the 1960s, **Antiquités Bourret,** 5 rue Linas (☎ **04-90-86-65-02**), has earned a reputation as a repository for 18th- and 19th-century Provençal antiques. ○ **Véronique Pichon,** place Crillon (☎ **04-90-85-89-00**), is the newest branch of a porcelain manufacturer whose colorful products have been a regional fixture since the 1700s. Manufactured in the nearby town of Uzès, the tableware, decorative urns, statues, and lamps are priced well enough to be shipped virtually anywhere.

The Avignon branch of **Les Olivades,** 28 rue des Marchants (☎ **04-90-86-13-42**), is one of the most visible of a chain of outlets associated in the States with Pierre Deux. Look for fabrics by the yard, bedcovers, slipcovers, draperies, and tablecloths. The fabrics, printed in a factory only 6 miles from Avignon, tend to feature intricate designs in colors inspired by 19th-century models or, to a somewhat lesser extent, Créole designs with butterflies, pineapples, bananas, and flowers.

The vision that launched ○ **Les Indiens de Nîmes,** 4 rue du College-de-Roure (☎ **04-90-86-32-05**), in the early 1980s involved the duplication of 18th- and 19th-century Provençal fabric patterns. They're sold by the meter as well as in clothing for men, women, and children. Also available are kitchenware and a selection of furniture inspired by origins from Provence and the steamy wetlands west of Marseille. The clothing at **Souleiado,** 5 rue Joseph-Vernet (☎ **04-90-86-47-67**), derives from a Provençal model, and even the Provençal name (meaning "first ray of sunshine after a storm") evokes a spirit on which the owners want to capitalize. Most, but not all, of the clothing is for women and comes in a wider choice than the garments (mostly shirts) for men. Fabrics are also sold by the meter.

ACCOMMODATIONS
VERY EXPENSIVE

○ **La Mirande.** 4 place Amirande, 84000 Avignon. ☎ **04-90-85-93-93.** Fax 04-90-86-26-85. 19 rms, 1 suite. A/C MINIBAR TV TEL. 1,700F–2,100F ($340–$420) double; 3,200F ($640) suite. AE, DC, V.

In the heart of Avignon, this restored 700-year-old town house is one of France's grand little luxuries, far better than anything else in town. Behind the Palais des

Avignon

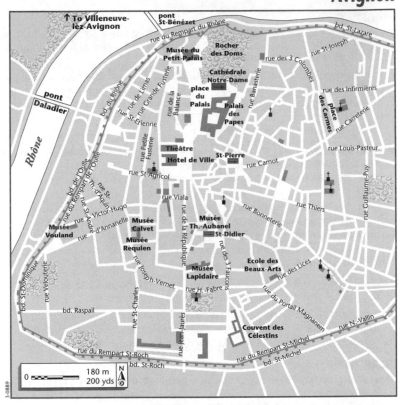

Papes, the hotel treats you to two centuries of decorative art—from the 1700s Salon Chinois to the Salon Rouge, its striped walls in Rothschild red. In 1987 the house was acquired by Achim and Hannelore Stein, who, with their son and daughter and a Paris decorator, transformed it into a citadel of opulence. The most sought-out room is no. 20, whose lavish decor opens directly onto the garden. But all the rooms are stunning, with huge bathtubs. The restaurant earns its one Michelin star and is among the finest in Avignon. Chef Alain Davi has a light, sophisticated touch, with fixed-price menus at 210F to 380F ($42 to $76). The restaurant is open every day for both lunch and dinner.

EXPENSIVE

✪ **Hôtel d'Europe.** 12 place Grillon, 84000 Avignon. ☎ **04-90-14-76-76.** Fax 04-90-85-43-66. 44 rms, 3 suites. A/C TV TEL. 620F–1,750F ($124–$350) double; 2,200F–2,500F ($440–$500) suite. AE, DC, MC, V. Parking 50F ($10).

The vine-covered Hôtel d'Europe has been in operation since 1799. You enter through a courtyard, where tables are set in the warmer months. The grand hall and salons boast tastefully arranged antiques and decorative elements. The good-size guest rooms have handsome decorations, period furnishings, and tile or marble baths. Three suites are perched on the roof with views of the Palais des Papes. In some twin-bedded rooms the beds are a bit narrow. Its restaurant, La Vieille Fontaine, is one of the best and most distinguished in Avignon. Meals are served in elegant dining rooms or a charming inner courtyard. The wine list is impressive but celestial in price.

MODERATE

Hôtel Bristol. 44 cours Jean-Jaurès, 84009 Avignon. ☎ **04-90-82-21-21.** Fax 04-90-86-22-72. 66 rms. TV TEL. 460F–520F ($92–$104) double. Rates include breakfast. AE, DC, MC, V. Closed Feb 15–Mar 9. Parking 45F ($9).

In the center of Avignon on one of the principal streets leading to the landmark place de l'Horloge and the Palais des Papes, the Bristol is one of the town's better bets. A traditional hotel, it offers comfortably furnished well-maintained rooms. Breakfast is the only meal served. Though it's not the most atmospheric place in Avignon, it offers good, solid value in an expensive city.

Mercure Palais-des-Papes. Quartier de la Balance, rue Ferruce, 84000 Avignon. ☎ **04-90-85-91-23.** Fax 04-90-85-32-40. 87 rms. A/C MINIBAR TV TEL. 525F–570F ($105–$114) double. Discounts available Fri–Sun on selected winter weekends. AE, DC, MC, V. Parking 40F–55F ($8–$11).

This chain hotel is a great choice, though nothing to equal the two previous hotels. Built in a discreetly contemporary three-story format in the early 1970s, it lies within the city walls, at the foot of the Palais des Papes. The rooms are well furnished but functional and without any particular style. There's a small bar but no restaurant, as breakfast is the only meal served.

Primotel Horloge. 1 rue Félicien-David, 84000 Avignon. ☎ **04-90-86-88-61.** Fax 04-90-82-17-32. 70 rms. A/C TV TEL. 455F–555F ($91–$111) double. AE, DC, MC, V.

In the heart of the city, overlooking place de l'Horloge near the Palais des Papes, this chain hotel is one of the best in its price category. The soundproof and well-furnished accommodations each come with a terrace. Breakfast is the only meal served.

INEXPENSIVE

Hôtel d'Angleterre. 29 bd. Raspail, 84000 Avignon. ☎ **04-90-86-34-31.** Fax 04-90-86-86-74. 40 rms, 35 with bath. TV TEL. 180F ($36) double without bath, 260F–370F ($52–$74) double with bath. MC, V. Closed Dec 22–Jan 15. Free parking.

In the heart of Avignon, this classical structure is the city's best budget hotel. The rooms are comfortably but basically furnished. Breakfast is the only meal served.

✪ **Hôtel Danieli.** 17 rue de la République, 84000 Avignon. ☎ **04-90-86-46-82.** Fax 04-90-27-09-24. 29 rms. TV TEL. 390F–435F ($78–$87) double. AE, DC, MC, V.

This hotel's Italian influence is clear in its arches, chiseled stone, tile floors, and baronial stone staircase. Built during the reign of Napoléon I, it's classified as a historic monument in its own right. Its small, informal public rooms are outfitted mostly in antiques acquired by the history-conscious owner. The guest rooms, however, have mostly painted bamboo furnishings. Unless special arrangements are made for a group (and this hotel accepts many), breakfast is the only meal served.

DINING

✪ **Brunel.** 46 rue de La Balance. ☎ **04-90-85-24-83.** Reservations required. Main courses 150F–170F ($30–$34); fixed-price menus 168F–300F ($33.60–$60). MC, V. Tues–Sat noon–1:30pm and 7:45–9:15pm. PROVENÇAL.

In the historic heart of Avignon, this is an elegant flower-filled restaurant with air-conditioning, managed by the Brunel family. It offers such specialties as warm pâté of duckling and breast of duckling with apples. The chef prepares a superb plate of ravioli stuffed with wild mushrooms served with roasted foie gras. The grilled John Dory is accompanied by artichoke hearts, and even the lowly pig's feet emerge with a sublime taste. The desserts are excellent and prepared fresh daily. Feel free to order house wines by the carafe.

✪ **Christian Etienne.** 10 rue Mons. ☎ **04-90-86-16-50.** Reservations recommended. Main courses 160F–200F ($32–$40); fixed-price menus 160F–480F ($32–$96). AE, DC, MC, V. July, daily noon–2:30pm and 8–10:30pm; the rest of the year, Mon–Fri noon–2:30pm and 8–10:30pm, Sat 8–10:30pm. FRENCH.

The stone house containing this restaurant was built in 1180, around the same time as the Palais des Papes (next door). The owner, Christian Etienne, is the star chef of Avignon, because he continues to explore the depths of his culinary repertoire. His dining room contains old ceiling and wall frescoes honoring the marriage of Anne de Bretagne to the French king in 1491. Several of the fixed-price menus present specific themes: The two 300F ($60) menus feature only tomatoes or vegetables, respectively; the 420F ($84) menu offers preparations of lobster; and the 480F ($96) menu relies on the chef's discretion *(menu confiance)* to come up with unique combinations. Note for strict vegetarians: The vegetable menus are among the most creative of their kind but aren't completely devoid of meat. They're flavored with small amounts of meat or fish or, sometimes, meat drippings. In summer, look for a vegetable menu where every course is based on ripe tomatoes; the main course is a mousse of lamb, eggplants, tomatoes, and herbs. A la carte specialties include filet of red snapper with a black-olive coulis, roast pigeon with a sauce of its own drippings enhanced with truffles, and a dessert specialty of fennel sorbet with saffron-flavored English cream sauce.

✪ **Hiély-Lucullus.** 5 rue de la République. ☎ **04-90-86-17-07.** Reservations required. Fixed-price menus 150F–320F ($30–$64). MC, V. Mon–Tues 7:30–9:45pm, Wed–Sun noon–1:30pm and 7:30–9:45pm. Closed June 17–30 and Mon in summer. FRENCH.

This Relais Gourmand used to reign supreme in Avignon before the arrival of Christian Etienne. It's still going strong and richly deserves its star, even if it's no longer as trendy as it was. The town's most fabled chef, Pierre Hiély, has retired, though he drops in occasionally to check on how his former sous chef, André Chaussy, is doing. He's doing just fine and is still offering those reasonably priced fixed-price menus (no à la carte). The same cuisine is featured, with occasional creative touches added. Try one of his special appetizers, like petite marmite du pêcheur, a savory fish soup ringed with black mussels. A main-dish specialty is pintadeau (young guinea hen) with peaches. The *pièce de résistance* is agneau des Alpilles grillé (grilled alpine lamb). Carafe wines include Tavel Rosé and Châteauneuf-du-Pape.

La Fourchette. 7 rue Racine. ☎ **04-90-85-20-93.** Fixed-price menus 100F–148F ($20–$29.60) at lunch, 148F ($29.60) at dinner. MC, V. Mon–Fri noon–2pm and 7:30–9:30pm. Closed Aug 5–29. FRENCH.

This bistro offers creative cooking at a moderate price. There are two dining rooms, one like a summer house with walls of glass, the other more like a tavern with oak beams. You might begin with fresh sardines flavored with citrus, ravioli filled with haddock, or a parfait of chicken livers with a spinach flan and a confiture of onions. For a main course we'd recommend the blanquette of monkfish with endives or daube of beef prepared in the local style with a gratin of macaroni.

Les Trois Clefs. 26 rue des Trois-Fauçons. ☎ **04-90-86-51-53.** Reservations required. Fixed-price menu 186F ($37.20). AE, DC, MC, V. Mon–Sat 12:15–1:30pm and 7:30–9:30pm. FRENCH.

Just behind the city ramparts and the Lapidary Museum, Les Trois Clefs is an intimate dining room with lacquered paneling, flowers, well-chosen fabrics, and good prices. The restaurant's dishes change according to the availability of ingredients at the markets. Laurent and Martine Mergnac's specialties might include hot foie gras of duckling in herb-flavored sauce, brioche of eggs with truffles, and suprême of guinea fowl with crayfish.

ACCOMMODATIONS & DINING IN VILLENEUVE-LEZ-AVIGNON

Hôtel de l'Atelier. 5 rue de la Foire, 30400 Villeneuve-lèz-Avignon. ☎ **04-90-25-01-84.** Fax 04-90-25-80-06. 19 rms. TV TEL. 220F–430F ($44–$86) double. AE, DC, MC, V. Parking 20F ($4) in nearby garage, free on street.

Villeneuve's budget offering is this 16th-century village house that has preserved much of its original style. Inside is a tiny duplex lounge with a large stone fireplace. Outside, a sun-filled rear garden, with potted orange and fig trees, provides fruit for breakfast. The immaculate accommodations are comfortable and informal, but a bit dowdy. In the old bourgeois dining room, a continental breakfast is the only meal served.

La Magnaneraie Hostellerie. 37 rue Camp-Bataille, 30400 Villeneuve-lèz-Avignon. ☎ **04-90-25-11-11.** Fax 04-90-25-46-37. 25 rms, 3 suites. A/C MINIBAR TV TEL. 500F–1,200F ($100–$240) double; 1,400F–1,800F ($280–$360) suite. AE, DC, MC, V.

One of the most charming accommodations in the region is on 2 acres of gardens under the direction of Gérard and Eliane Prayal. Tastefully renovated and enlarged with a new wing in the 1980s, the place is furnished with antiques and good reproductions. Many guests here arrive for only 1 night but remain for many days, to enjoy the good food, atmosphere, garden, tennis court, and landscaped pool. In 1993 the government rating of this inn was increased to four stars, mostly because of M. Prayal's excellent cuisine. His fixed-price menus range from 170F ($34) for a celebration of traditional Provençal recipes to 450F ($90) for a *menu dégustation*. Menu items may include zucchini flowers stuffed with mushroom-and-cream purée, feuilleté of foie gras and truffles, croustillant of red snapper with basil and olive oil, and rack of lamb with thyme. Dessert might be gratin of seasonal fruits with sabayon of lavender-flavored honey. Though the cuisine and ambience remain sublime, readers have lately noted a fall-off in the standards of service.

NEARBY ACCOMMODATIONS & DINING

✪ **Auberge de Cassagne.** 450 allée de Cassagne, rte. de Vèdene (D62), Le Pontet, 84130 Avignon. ☎ **04-90-31-04-18.** Fax 04-90-32-25-09. 24 rms, 3 suites. A/C MINIBAR TV TEL. 490F–1,180F ($98–$236) double; from 1,180F ($236) suite. AE, DC, MC, V. Parking 20F ($4). Take N7 and D62 for 4 miles northeast.

This could be your best bet for food and lodging in the Avignon area. The hotel, set in a park with a pool and a Jacuzzi, is an enchanting little Provençal inn with country-style rooms. The cuisine is exceptionally good, much of it in the style of Paul Bocuse. You can enjoy your meals in a rustically decorated dining room or at a table in the garden. The owner, Jean-Michel Gallon, features dishes like sea bass, turbot, and deviled lamb. The fixed-price meals, 230F to 460F ($46 to $92), are available to nonguests, and reservations are required.

✪ **Auberge de Noves.** 13550 Noves. ☎ **04-90-94-19-21.** Fax 04-90-94-47-76. 23 rms, 4 suites. A/C MINIBAR TV TEL. 1,470F–2,740F ($294–$548) double; from 2,175F ($435) suite. Rates include breakfast. AE, DC, MC, V. Follow Rte. 571 for 10 miles southeast.

The Auberge de Noves is an elegant Relais & Châteaux run by the Lalleman family, who offer modern and attractive rooms. In its own hilltop park, it's a cross between a Riviera villa and a 1920s Beverly Hills mansion. When M. and Mme Lalleman purchased the auberge in 1950, it was a religious retreat, which they transformed into one of the finest luxury country estates in Provence. The unique rooms are furnished with period pieces. Some have terraces, and most have exceptional views. During the day guests enjoy the tennis courts and pool.

The food is among the area's best, including herb-flavored filet d'agneau (lamb), chicken-liver mousse, superb sole, veal kidneys Printaneir, and rabbit in mustard sauce. From the first-class wine cellar come selections like Châteauneuf-du-Pape and Lirac. The restaurant doesn't serve lunch on Wednesday, and reservations are required. Fixed-price meals are 225F to 495F ($45 to $99).

AVIGNON AFTER DARK

Near the Palais des Papes is **Le Grand Café,** La Manutention (☎ 04-90-86-86-77), a restaurant/bar/cafe that might quickly become your favorite watering hole. The dancing staple is **Les Ambassadeurs,** 27 rue Bancasse (☎ 04-90-86-31-55), which is more animated than its more subdued competitor, **Piano Bar Le Blues,** 25 rue Carnot (☎ 04-90-85-79-71); the cover at both is 10F ($2). Near Le Blues is a restaurant, **Red Zone,** 27 rue Carnot (☎ 04-90-27-02-44), whose bar area is the site of live performances from whatever techno-punk band happens to be in town.

Winning the award for having the most unpronounceable name is **Le Woolloomoolloo** (it means "Black Kangaroo" in an Aboriginal dialect of Australia), 16 bis rue des Teinturiers (☎ 04-90-85-28-44). Here a bar and cafe complement a separate room devoted to the cuisine of France and West Africa. The perfect venue for slurping beer or cheap wine and watching university students listen to recorded punk rock and techno is **Club Z,** 58 rue de la Bonneterie (☎ 04-90-85-42-84). The best place for gays and lesbians is **L'Esclav,** 12 rue de Limas (☎ 04-90-85-14-91).

4 Uzès

424 miles S of Paris, 24 miles W of Avignon, 31¹/₂ miles NW of Arles

This village is famous for the long-standing House of Uzès, home of France's highest-ranking ducal family, who still live in Le Duché dominating the town. Uzès is the birthplace of the famed economist Charles Gide, and his brother Paul, a distinguished lawyer who fathered André Gide, recipient of the Nobel Prize for Literature in 1947. He recounted holidays spent here at his grandmother's home in *If It Die (Si le grain ne meurt).*

Jean Racine lived here in 1661, sent by his family to stay with an uncle, the vicar general of Uzès, in hopes that his dramatic ambitions might be dispelled. They weren't, and he went on to claim his place as one of France's great dramatists/poets. His experiences in Uzès weren't wasted, however, as they inspired *Les Plaideurs,* his only comedy. More recently, Uzès was the setting of Jean-Paul Rappeneau's version of *Cyrano de Bergerac,* in which Gérard Depardieu played the part of the soldier-poet.

In 1962 the village was named one of France's 500 *villes d'art* and has since taken good advantage of preservation funds set aside for restoration of its historic district. In this scenically beautiful village set on a limestone plateau that straddles the line between Provence and the Garrigues region, the designation has been viewed as a mixed blessing since many visitors, notably Parisians taking a break from city life, have discovered the charms of the village.

ESSENTIALS

GETTING THERE   There's no rail station in Uzès. Train passengers must get off at Avignon (a 45-minute bus ride) or Nîmes (a 35-minute bus ride). For **rail information** and schedules, call ☎ 08-36-35-35-35. There are about eight buses a day from both places. For information, contact the **Gare Routière d'Uzès,** avenue de la Libération (☎ 04-66-22-00-58).

VISITOR INFORMATION   The **Office de Tourisme** is on avenue de la Libération (☎ **04-66-22-68-88**).

SEEING THE SIGHTS

In the old part of town, every building is worth a moment or two of consideration. Foremost among the attractions is **Le Duché** (ducal palace), place du Duché (☎ **04-66-22-18-96**), in a massive conglomeration of styles, the result of nearly continuous expansion of the residence in direct correlation to the rising wealth and power of the duke and duchess. The Renaissance facade blends Doric, Ionic, and Corinthian elements. Easily seen from below is the **Tour de la Vicomté,** a 14th-century watchtower recognizable by its octagonal turret.

Large segments of the compound, most notably its sprawling annex, are occupied by the comte and comtesse de Crussol d'Uzès and cannot be visited. Parts that you can visit are the square 11th-century **Tour Bermonde,** which offers a sweeping view over the countryside from its elevated terrace, accessible by the spiral staircase winding up through the tower. The **11th-century cellar,** noted for its huge dimensions and vaulted ceilings, contains casks filled with fermenting wine from the surrounding vineyards. Tours of the site invariably end here, with a *dégustation* of the reds and rosés of the Cuvée Ducale. The cellars are accessible from the building's showcase apartments, which include a **dining room** with Louis XIII and Renaissance furnishings, a **great hall** done in the style of Louis XV, a large **library** that includes family memoirs, and the 15th-century **Chapelle Gothique,** which was at one time reserved for the exclusive use of the ducal family and their entourage. The complex is open daily: June to September from 10am to 6:30pm and October to May from 10am to noon and 2 to 6pm. Admission is 50F ($10) for adults, 35F ($7) for students and teens 12 to 16, 20F ($4) for children 7 to 11, and free for children 10 and under. Visits to the interior are usually part of a French-language tour, but you can follow the commentary in an English-language pamphlet. Tours are scheduled erratically, whenever enough people accumulate to justify the effort expended by the guide.

Adjacent to the palace, on place du Duché, and completely independent of its jurisdiction, stands one of Provence's oldest early Christian monuments: a **4th-century crypt.** Claustrophobic and visitable only through the auspices of the tourist office, it's a meeting place with walls niched to hold cult objects the new religion hadn't yet shed. Usually you must take a prearranged group tour, though between June 15 and September 15 it's open Monday and Friday at 10am and Wednesday at 4pm. Visits are 25F ($5) for adults and 15F ($3) for students and children 15 and under. These schedules change frequently, so confirm the hours with the tourist office.

A pleasant square for a stroll, the assymetrical **place aux Herbes** is defined by the medieval homes and sheltered walkways along its edges. The **Cathédrale St-Théodorit,** place de l'Evêché, still utilizes its original 17th-century organ, a remarkable instrument composed of 2,772 pipes. The cathedral charges no admission and is open daily from 9am to 6:30pm. If you're lucky enough to be here in late July, you can attend one of the organ concerts that highlight the **Nuits Musicales d'Uzès** festival. Adjacent is the circular six-story **Tour Fenestrelle.** Closed to the public, it's all that remains of the original 12th-century cathedral that was burnt by the Huguenots.

ACCOMMODATIONS

Hôtel d'Entraigues. 8 rue de la Calade, 30700 Uzès. ☎ **04-66-22-32-68.** Fax 04-66-22-57-01. 35 rms. MINIBAR TV TEL. 290F–525F ($58–$105) double. AE, DC, MC, V. Parking 50F ($10).

The core of this hotel was built in the 15th century as a manor house, then expanded into a compound with two separate buildings nestled in a Mediterranean garden adjacent to the cathedral. Much of it appears the way it did 300 years ago, though the room furnishings vary from comfortably old-fashioned to modern pieces with rattan and contemporary designs. The restaurant, Jardins de Castille, features open-air dining and fixed-price menus that begin at 100F ($20).

Hôtel Marie d'Agoult (Château d'Arpaillargues). Arpaillargues, 30700 Uzès. ☎ **04-66-22-14-48.** Fax 04-66-22-56-10. 27 rms, 2 suites. A/C TV TEL. 450F–800F ($90–$160) double; 800F–1,150F ($160–$230) suite. AE, MC, V. Closed Nov 4–Mar. Drive 2¹/₂ miles west of Uzès, following the signs to Andouze-Arpaillargues.

The foundations of this place are believed to date from a 3rd-century fortress, making it as old as the Gallo-Roman occupation of Provence. The combination of rough and chiseled stone you see today was set into place in the late 1600s and early 1700s and later was a site where silkworms were raised when this area was a silkmaking center. The hotel was named after a former occupant, Marie d'Agoult, the daughter of Franz Liszt and mother of the woman (Cosima) who eventually married Richard Wagner. All rooms except five (vaulted affairs, with exposed brick, on the ground floor) have air-conditioning, and each offers a sleepy and rather passive insight into a way of life of long ago.

DINING

If you'd like to dine in town, consider the Jardins de Castille, the restaurant of the **Hôtel d'Entraigues** (see "Accommodations," above). However, the area's best place to dine is in the hamlet of St-Maximin, 3¹/₂ miles southeast of Uzès. To reach it from Uzès, follow the signs to St-Maximin.

Auberge St-Maximin. Rue des Ecoles, St-Maximin. ☎ **04-66-22-26-41.** Reservations imperative. Main courses 80F–120F ($16–$24); fixed-price menus 150F ($30) at lunch Wed–Fri, and 150F–250F ($30–$50) anytime. AE, DC, MC, V. Wed–Sun noon–2:30pm and 7–9:30pm. Closed Nov 13–Mar 14. FRENCH/PROVENÇAL.

Close to the town hall of this agrarian village, the restaurant occupies the stone-sided premises of what was built in the 1700s as shelter for sheep and lambs. There's an outdoor terrace for dining in clement weather, but the heart and soul of the place lies beneath the narrow stone vaults of an interior that contains only seven tables. Menu items include snails with pine nuts and mushrooms in puff pastry, a pastillade of lamb with eggplant that's rendered more savory by its crispy roasted skin, and a filet of red mullet with crayfish tails and madeira sauce.

5 Tarascon

10 miles W of St-Rémy, 11 miles N of Arles, 15 miles E of Nîmes

On the banks of the Rhône, this former port is rich in lore if not much else. Legend has it that the earliest inhabitants were terrorized by a blood-thirsty dragon called the Tarasque, which devoured children and cattle. The town was saved by St. Martha, who landed in Provence with the St. Marys shortly after Jesus's resurrection. She called out to the Tarasque, made the sign of the cross, sprinkled holy water, and led it into town. The citizens of Tarascon promptly fell upon the Tarasque with all manner of weapons and killed it with a savage vengeance. St. Martha, seeing that her work was cut out for her, continued to live in the town and converted the pagans to Christianity.

Since the 1400s the **Fête de la Tarasque** has taken place on the final Sunday in June to commemorate this victory over the Tarasque. Young men parade down the streets of Tarascon operating a huge 18-foot puppet of the Tarasque. Happy, rowdy crowds line the route, celebrating the capture of the dreaded beast. Fringe elements of the festival extend to the several days surrounding the Tarasque parade and include arts events, bullfights, and dancing.

Another legend of sorts that Tarascon is famous for was created by Alphonse Daudet in the 19th century: the Taratin de Tarasque, a harmless and comical avenger along the lines of Don Quixote. Today the Taratin has become a cartoon that holds a special place in the hearts of all French children.

ESSENTIALS

GETTING THERE Tarascon is easily accessible by train, bus, and car. Seven daily trains leave Arles for Tarascon (trip time: 10 min.), averaging 15F ($3) one-way, and a dozen trains leave daily from Avignon for Tarascon (trip time: 10 min.), costing 20F ($4) one-way. Two buses per day depart the Gare Routière in Arles for the half-hour trip, costing 17F ($3.40) one-way, and three buses make the half-hour trip from Avignon, costing 22F ($4.40) one-way. For **rail information** and schedules, call **08-36-35-35-35.**

VISITOR INFORMATION The **Office de Tourism** is at 59 rue des Halles (☎ 04-90-91-03-52).

SEEING THE TOP ATTRACTIONS

Standing as a lone sentinel on the Rhône, the **Château de Tarascon,** boulevard du Roi-René (☎ 04-90-91-01-93), with its imposing stone walls and classical fairy-tale towers, was built in the 15th century by Provence's King René and his father, Louis II of Anjou. It served as a border defense between France and the proudly independent Provence. On its completion and after Louis's death, the castle was turned into a pleasure palace by René, who was addicted to festivities on the grandest of scales. He played host to artists, musicians, dancers, and all sorts of lavish parties. Alas, shortly after his death France annexed Provence and later converted the castle into a dreary prison. It remained a prison until 1926 and still contains graffiti and messages carved into the walls by the desperate prisoners. Today you can see the royal apartments, courtyard, garden, and old apothecary, as well as 10 tapestries from the 1600s, but you won't be treated to any of the fine trappings from René's day. The castle is open daily: April to September from 9am to 7pm and October to March from 9am to noon and 2 to 7pm. Admission is 32F ($6.40) for adults, 21F ($4.20) for youths 12 to 25, and free for children 11 and under.

Since St. Martha has played such a pivotal role in legend and history, try to see the **Collégiale Ste-Marthe,** across from the castle on boulevard du Roi-René (☎ 04-90-91-09-50). This church dates from the late 1100s and has been badly damaged by centuries of war and revolution. However, it still houses in the crypt a tomb that's said to be that of the famous saint herself. With the exception of masses, it's open daily from 8am to noon and 2 to 6pm. Admission is free.

For a whimsical break from the somber lore surrounding the town and its Tarasque, visit the **Maison de Tartarin,** 55 bis bd. Itam (☎ 04-90-91-05-08), a museum and shrine of sorts covering the life of Tartarin de Tarascon, the satirical character created in the 19th century by Alphonse Daudet in his *New Don Quixote.* Daudet angered residents in the beginning, as they felt that his Tartarin was an insulting slap in the face to the town and its citizens; however, when they saw how popular this fictional hero was becoming, they had a considerable change of opinion. The museum houses displays, models, and memorabilia illustrating the Tartarin and tracing its history to the present. The museum is open Monday to Saturday:

mid-April to September from 10am to noon and 2 to 7pm, and mid-March to mid-April and October to mid-December from 10am to noon and 1:30 to 5pm. Admission is 10F ($2) for adults, 5F ($1) for children 7 to 16, and free for children 6 and under.

For a glimpse into the history behind the popular hand-decorated fabrics known as *Souleiado,* take a tour of the **Musée Souleiado,** 39 rue Proudhon (☎ **04-90-91-08-80**). Souleiado is a Provençal word that means "sunbeam" and has come to describe these brightly colored calico fabrics decorated using designs carved from blocks of pear wood. The museum contains a display of more than 40,000 of these pear blocks, some more than 200 years old. You visit on a private tour arranged a minimum of 1 week in advance. The museum is open Monday to Friday from 8:30am to noon and 1:30 to 6pm. Tickets are 30F ($6) for adults and 15F ($3) for children 15 and under.

ACCOMMODATIONS

Hôtel des Echevins. 26 bd. Itam, 13150 Tarascon. ☎ **04-90-91-01-70.** Fax 04-90-43-50-44. 39 rms. TV TEL. 270F–295F ($54–$59) double. AE, MC, V. Closed late Nov to mid-Mar.

The subtle pink exterior of this private residence from the 17th century gives way to a refreshingly cool lobby with a mix of dark-wood period reproductions and antiques. A standout is the central stone staircase with its ornate black-and-gold wrought-iron banister. The rooms are average in both size and furnishings but provide a comfortable stay and views onto the surrounding houses. Some even offer glimpses of the château in the distance. In the decent restaurant with a terrace you can feast on traditional regional cuisine, like ratatouille and daube provençale.

Hôtel Les Mazets des Roches. Rte. de Fontvieille, 13150 Tarascon. ☎ **04-90-91-34-89.** Fax 04-90-43-53-29. 37 rms, 1 suite. AC TV TEL. 350F–700F ($70–$140) double, 640F–990F ($128–$198) double with half board; 850F ($170) suite, 1,140F ($228) suite with half board. AE, DC, MC, V. Closed Nov–Mar. Take D33 for 5 miles south of town, following the signs to Fontvieille.

This oasis of modern luxury is a country house set among 30 acres of countryside. The guest rooms are brought to life through a palette of earth tones and coordinating fabrics, light rattan furnishings, and a bounty of natural light streaming in through the windows. The public areas include a fully stocked bar and cheery sitting room. The impressive grounds give you plenty of opportunity to bask in the sun while playing on one of the two tennis courts or swimming in the immense pool. If a less athletic routine is more your style, simply sun yourself on the terrace by the pool or relax with a drink or light meal in the shade of the garden. The hotel boasts a restaurant of merit (open for lunch and dinner) offering a complete menu of Provençale specialties.

DINING

Aux Mille Pâtes. 4 rue Eugénie-Pellatan. ☎ **04-90-43-51-77.** Main courses 45F–80F ($9–$16); fixed-price menus 55F–110F ($11–$22). AE, MC, V. Mon–Thurs noon–2pm and 6:30pm–midnight, Sat–Sun 6:30pm–midnight. Closed last 2 weeks in Nov. ITALIAN.

At "The Place of 1,000 Pastas" you won't actually have quite that varied of a selection to choose from, but pasta reigns as the house specialty. You'd be treating yourself if you were to decide on a selection from its pasta menu, either something as simple as a fresh tomato-and-basil sauce or a more complex and filling red seafood sauce. The menu also features an array of meat dishes, like slices of veal and ham covered in rich cream sauce or a sizable beef filet with an aromatic Roquefort cheese sauce accompanied by a slice of fois gras. Don't expect fancy frills but do plan on having a good meal in a simple, colorful setting with lots of Souleiado-patterned fabrics. In warm months you can dine at the tables on the terrace of the Tarascon theater just in front of the restaurant.

6 Arles

450 miles S of Paris, 22 miles SW of Avignon, 55 miles NW of Marseille

Arles has been called "the soul of Provence," and art lovers, archaeologists, and historians are attracted to this town on the Rhône. Many of its scenes, painted so luminously by van Gogh in his declining years, remain to delight. The great Dutch painter left Paris for Arles in 1888, the same year he cut off part of his left ear. But he was to paint some of his most celebrated works in this Provençal town, including *Starry Night, The Bridge at Arles, Sunflowers,* and *L'Arlésienne.*

The Greeks are said to have founded Arles in the 6th century B.C. Julius Caesar established a Roman colony here in 46 B.C. Under Roman rule Arles prospered. Constantine the Great named it the second capital in his empire in 306, when it was known as "the little Rome of the Gauls." It wasn't until 1481 that Arles was incorporated into France.

Though Arles doesn't possess quite as much charm as Aix-en-Provence, it's still rewarding to visit, with first-rate museums, excellent restaurants, and summer festivals (like the early June international photography festival). The city today isn't quite as lovely as it was when Picasso came here, but it has enough antique charm of Provence to keep the appeal alive.

ESSENTIALS

GETTING THERE   Arles lies on the Paris–Marseille and the Bordeaux–St-Raphaël rail lines, so has frequent connections from most cities of France. Ten trains arrive daily from Avignon (trip time: 20 min.) and 10 per day from Marseille (trip time: 1 hr.). From Aix-en-Provence, 10 trains arrive per day (trip time: 1³/₄ hr.). For **rail information** and schedules, call ☎ **08-36-35-35-35.** There are about five buses per day from Aix-en-Provence (trip time: 1³/₄ hr.). For **bus information** and schedules, call ☎ **04-90-49-38-01.**

VISITOR INFORMATION   The **Office de Tourisme,** where you can buy a *billet global* (see below), is on the esplanade des Lices (☎ **04-90-18-41-20**).

SEEING THE TOP ATTRACTIONS

Go to the tourist office (see "Essentials," above), where you can purchase a *billet global,* the all-inclusive pass that admits you to the town's museums, Roman monuments, and all the major attractions, at a cost of 55F ($11) for adults and 35F ($7) for children.

The town is full of monuments from Roman times. The general vicinity of the old Roman forum is occupied by **place du Forum,** shaded by plane trees. Once the Café de Nuit, immortalized by van Gogh, stood on this square. You can see two columns in the Corinthian style and pediment fragments from a temple at the corner of the Hôtel Nord-Pinus. South of here is **place de la République,** the principal plaza, dominated by a 50-foot-tall blue porphyry obelisk. On the north is the impressive **Hôtel de Ville** (town hall) from 1673, built to Mansart's plans and surmounted by a Renaissance belfry.

On the east side of the square is the **Eglise St-Trophime** (☎ **04-90-96-07-38**), noted for its 12th-century portal, one of the finest achievements of the southern Romanesque style. In the pediment Christ is surrounded by the symbols of the

Arles

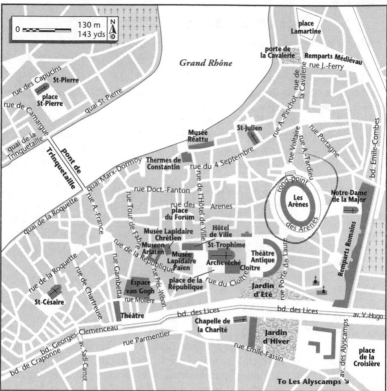

Evangelists. Frederick Barbarossa was crowned king of Arles on this site in 1178. The cloister, in both the Gothic and Romanesque styles, is noted for its medieval carvings. The church is open daily from 8am to 7pm and admission is free. The cloister is also open daily: June to September from 9am to 7pm and October to May from 9am to 7pm. The admission charge is 15F ($3) for adults and 9F ($1.80) for students and children.

The **Museon Arlaten** (☎ 04-90-96-08-23) is entered at 29 rue de la République—its name is written in Provençal style. It was founded by Frédéric Mistral, the Provençal poet and leader of a movement to establish modern Provençal as a literary language, using the money from his Nobel Prize for Literature in 1904. This is really a folklore museum, with regional costumes, portraits, furniture, dolls, a music salon, and one room devoted to mementos of Mistral. Among its curiosities is a letter (in French) from President Theodore Roosevelt to Mistral, bearing the letterhead of the Maison Blanche in Washington, D.C. Admission is 20F ($4) for adults and 10F ($2) for children. The museum is open April to October, daily from 9am to noon and 2 to 6:30pm; November to March, Tuesday to Sunday from 9am to noon and 2 to 5pm.

The city's two great classical monuments are the **Théâtre Antique,** rue du Cloître (☎ 04-90-96-93-30), and the Amphitheater (Les Arènes). The Roman theater, begun by Augustus in the 1st century, was mostly destroyed and only two Corinthian columns remain. The theater was where the *Venus of Arles* was discovered in 1651.

In Search of van Gogh's "Different Light"

What strikes me here is the transparency of the air.

—Vincent van Gogh

Before the impressionists found refuge in Provence, the district had already attracted many artists. During the pope's residency at Avignon, a flood of Italian artists frescoed the papal palace in a style worthy of St. Peter's, and even after their departure, Provençal monarchs like King René imported painters from Flanders and Burgundy to adorn his public buildings. This continued to the 18th and 19th centuries, as painters drew inspiration from the dazzling light of Provence, but it wasn't until the age of the impressionists that the role of Provence as an artistic catalyst became fully recognized.

The Dutch-born Vincent van Gogh (1853–90) moved to Arles in 1888 and spent 2 years migrating through the historic towns of Les Baux, St-Rémy, and Stes-Maries, recording through the filter of his neuroses dozens of impressionistic scenes now prized by museums everywhere. His search, he said, was for "a different light," which led to the generation of masterpieces like *Starry Night, Cypresses, Olive Trees,* and *Boats Along the Beach.*

Van Gogh wasn't alone in his pursuit of Provençal light: Gauguin joined him 8 months after his arrival, and soon thereafter engaged him in a violent quarrel, which reduced the Dutchman to a morbid depression that required his hospitalization in a local sanitarium. Within 2 years van Gogh returned to Paris, where he committed suicide in July 1890.

Things went somewhat better for Cézanne, who was familiar with the beauties of Provence thanks to his childhood in Aix-en-Provence. He infuriated his father, a prominent Provençal banker, by abandoning his studies to pursue painting. Later, his theories about line and color were publicized around the world. Although he migrated to Paris, he rarely set foot outside Provence from 1890 until his 1904 death. Some critics have asserted that Cézanne's later years were devoted to one obsession: recording the line, color, and texture of Montagne-St-Victoire, a rocky knoll a few hours' horse ride east of Aix. He painted it more than 60 times without ever grasping its essence the way he'd hoped. The bulk of the Provençal mountain, however, as well as the way shadows moved across its rocky planes, were decisive in affecting the cubists, whose work Cézanne directly influenced.

Take rue de la Calade from the city hall. Admission is 15F ($3) for adults and 9F ($1.80) for children.

Nearby, the **Amphitheater (Les Arènes),** rond-pont des Arènes (☎ 04-90-49-36-86), also built in the 1st century, seats almost 25,000 and still hosts bullfights in summer. The government warns you to visit the old monument at your own risk, as the stone steps are uneven and much of the masonry is worn down to the point where it might be a problem for older travelers or for those with disabilities. For a good view, you can climb the three towers that remain from medieval times, when the amphitheater was turned into a fortress. Both the theater and Les Arènes maintain the same hours as the above-mentioned Eglise St-Trophime. Admission to each of the three sites is 15F ($3) for adults and 9F ($1.80) for children.

Opened in 1995, the **Musée de l'Arles Antique,** Presqu'île du Cirque Romain (☎ 04-90-18-88-88), half a mile south of the town center, features one of the world's most famous collections of Roman Christian sarcophagi, plus a rich ensemble of sculptures, mosaics, and inscriptions from the Augustinian period to the 6th century A.D. Eleven detailed models show ancient monuments of the region as they existed in the past. The museum is open April to September, daily from 9am to 7pm; October to March, Wednesday to Monday from 10am to 6pm. Admission is 35F ($7) for adults, 25F ($5) for students, and free for children 13 and under.

The most memorable sight in Arles is **Les Alyscamps,** rue Pierre-Renaudel (☎ **04-90-49-36-87**), once a necropolis established by the Romans but converted into a Christian burial ground in the 4th century. As the latter it became a setting for legends in epic medieval poetry and was even mentioned in Dante's *Inferno.* Today it's lined with poplars as well as any remaining sarcophagi. Arlesiens escape here to enjoy a respite from the heat. It's open daily: June to September from 8:30am to 7pm, March to May and in October from 9am to 12:30pm and 2 to 7pm, and November to February from 9am to noon and 2 to 4:30pm. Admission is 15F ($3) for adults and 9F ($1.80) for children. Another ancient monument is the **Thermes de Constantín,** rue Dominique-Maisto (☎ **04-90-49-35-40**), near the banks of the Rhône. Today only the baths *(thermae)* remain of a once-grand imperial palace. Visiting hours are the same as at Les Alyscamps, and admission is 15F ($3) for adults and 9F ($1.80) for children.

Nearby, with an entrance at 10 rue du Grand-Prieuré, is the **Musée Réattu** (☎ **04-90-49-37-58**), with the collection of the local painter Jacques Réattu. The museum has been updated with more recent works, including etchings and drawings by Picasso. Other works are by Alechinsky, Dufy, and Zadkine. Note the Arras tapestries from the 16th century. It's open daily: April to September from 9am to 12:30pm and 2 to 7pm, in March from 10am to 12:30pm and 2 to 7pm, in October from 10am to 12:30pm and 2 to 6:30pm, and November to February from 10am to 12:30pm and 2 to 5:30pm. Admission is 20F ($4) for adults and 14F ($2.80) for children.

SHOPPING

In an isolated position 7¹/₂ miles north of Arles, ✪ **Les Olivades Factory Store,** chemin des Indienneurs, St-Etienne-du-Grès (☎ **04-90-49-19-19**), stands beside the road leading to Tarascon. Because of the wide array of art objects and fabrics inspired by the traditions of Provence, it's worth your while to make a trek out here. Fabrics, dresses, shirts for men and women, table linens, and fabric by the yard are all available at retail outlets of the Olivades chain throughout Provence, but here the selection is a bit cheaper and more diverse.

ACCOMMODATIONS

✪ **Hôtel Calendal.** 22 place du Docteur-Pomme, 13200 Arles. ☎ **04-90-96-11-89.** Fax 04-90-96-05-84. 27 rms. TEL. 250F–420F ($50–$84) double. AE, DC, MC, V. Bus: 4.

On a quiet square not far from the arena, the Calendal offers rooms that have Provençal decor and some antiques, most with views of the shaded garden. The limited menu includes omelets, soups, and small dishes at conservative prices, as well as homemade desserts and pastries. The Calendal has long been the bargain hunter's favorite in Arles, and the rooms have recently been redecorated.

Hôtel d'Arlatan. 26 rue du Sauvage, 13631 Arles. ☎ **04-90-93-56-66.** Fax 04-90-49-68-45. 33 rms, 7 suites. MINIBAR TV TEL. 450F–695F ($90–$139) double; 795F–1,350F ($159–$270) suite. AE, DC, MC, V. Parking 58F ($11.60).

In the former residence of the comtes d'Arlatan de Beaumont, near place du Forum, this hotel has been managed by the same family since 1920. It was built in the 15th century on the ruins of an old palace ordered by Constantine—in fact, there's still a wall from the 4th century. The rooms are furnished with authentic Provençal antiques, the walls covered with tapestries in the Louis XV and Louis XVI styles. Try to get a room overlooking the garden; 25 rooms are air-conditioned.

✪ **Hôtel Jules César et Restaurant Lou Marquês.** 7 bd. des Lices, 13200 Arles. ☎ **04-90-93-43-20.** Fax 04-90-93-33-47. 55 rms, 3 suites. MINIBAR TV TEL. 700F–1,250F ($140–$250) double; from 1,450F ($290) suite. AE, DC, MC, V. Closed Nov 2–Dec 23. Parking 60F ($12).

In the center of Arles, this 17th-century former Carmelite convent has been skillfully transformed into a stately country hotel, with the best restaurant in Arles. Though this is a noisy neighborhood, most rooms face the quiet, unspoiled cloister. The decoration is luxurious, with antique Provençal furnishings that the owner finds at auctions throughout the countryside. You wake to the scent of roses and the sounds of birds singing.

The restaurant, Lou Marquês, has tables outside on the front terrace. The food is extremely fresh. From the à la carte menu, we recommend bourride à la Provençale or Arles lamb. Fixed-price menus are 150F to 195F ($30 to $39), with à la carte dinners averaging 300F ($60).

Hôtel Le Cloître. 16 rue du Cloître, 13200 Arles. ☎ **04-90-96-29-50.** Fax 04-90-96-02-88. 30 rms. TEL. 210F–295F ($42–$59) double; 365F–395F ($73–$79) triple. AE, MC, V. Parking 30F ($6).

Between the ancient theater and the cloister, this hotel is a great value. Originally part of a 12th-century cloister, it still retains the Romanesque vaultings. The restored old house has a Provençal atmosphere, pleasant rooms, and a TV lounge, though 17 rooms have their own TVs. Parking is available nearby.

DINING

For a truly elegant meal, consider dining at the Restaurant Lou Marquês at the **Hôtel Jules César** (see "Accommodations," above).

Hostellerie des Arènes. 62 rue du Refuge. ☎ **04-90-96-13-05.** Reservations required. Main courses 45F–100F ($9–$20); fixed-price menus 75F–129F ($15–$25.80). MC, V. Wed–Mon noon–2pm and 7–9pm. Closed Jan 10–Feb 20. PROVENÇAL.

Close to the arena, the hostellerie offers Provençal meals whose well-prepared specialties include seafood in puff pastry, braised duckling laced with green peppercorns, brochette of mussels with tartar sauce, and veal marengo. In warm weather meals are served on the terrace. Chef Didier Pirouault prepares a natively enriched bouillabaisse. Inexpensive wines, by the carafe or the bottle, provide an added element to any meal.

La Côte d'Adam (Adam's Rib). 12 rue de la Liberté. ☎ **04-90-49-62-29.** Reservations required in summer. Main courses 65F–75F ($13–$15); fixed-price menus 70F–106F ($14–$21.20). AE, MC, V. Mon 7:15–9:30pm, Tues–Sun noon–2pm and 7:15–9:30pm. Closed Nov 15–30. PROVENÇAL.

In the historic center of town, this restaurant has a rustic interior with a beamed ceiling and a high carved-stone fireplace. It holds 40 and serves such dishes as aiguillettes of duck and John Dory with a confit of pear. Many dishes are imbued with fragrant olive oil. Between May and September the place is likely to be open daily.

Le Vaccarès. Place du Forum, 9 rue Favorin. ☎ **04-90-96-06-17.** Reservations required. Main courses 75F–155F ($15–$31); fixed-price menus 98F–280F ($19.60–$56). AE, MC, V. Tues–Sat noon–2pm and 7:30–9:30pm, Sun noon–2pm. Closed Jan 15–Feb 15 and all day Sun July–Aug. PROVENÇAL.

Le Vaccarès offers southern French elegance and the finest food in town, in a setting whose outdoor terrace (used during clement weather) opens onto the market of Arles.

Its staff uses unusual ingredients to create innovative Provençal dishes. Specialties are sauté of lamb with basil, mussels with fresh herbs, croquette of squid, sea-devil soup, steamed sea bass in an elegantly simple way, garnished only with olive oil, and émincé of beef with Châteauneuf. Its selection of wines is impressive (especially the Rhône Valley and Var).

ARLES AFTER DARK

Because of its relatively small population of around 50,000, Arles doesn't offer as rich a panoply of nightlife options as Aix-en-Provence, Avignon, Nice, or Marseille. The town's most appealing choice is the bar/cafe/music hall **Cargo de Nuit,** 7 av. Sadi-Carnot, route pour Barriol (☎ **04-90-49-55-99**). The cover charge of between 30F ($6) and 40F ($8) will provide a rich diet of recorded blues, salsa, reggae, and *cubano* music and access to a sprawling bar and a restaurant that does everything it can to break what might have become too constant a diet of southern French cooking.

Two good options farther from the city center, particularly for those in their 40s and 50s, are the very large **Le Krystal,** route de Pont-de-Crau (☎ **04-90-97-10-95**), about 6 miles south of Arles; and **La Camargue,** route des Stes-Maries-de-la-Mer, Quartier Moules (☎ **04-90-98-32-40**), about 12¹/₂ miles south of Arles. Both of these combine aspects of a country picnic, a cafe, a bar, and a dance hall into large indoor/outdoor venues where lots of the folk seem to have known one another for years.

7 Fontvieille

449 miles S of Paris, 6¹/₂ miles N of Arles, 18¹/₂ miles S of Avignon

This sleepy village is best known for the Moulin de Daudet, the windmill that inspired Alphonse Daudet to write his *Lettres de Mon Moulin,* a philosophical and anecdotal tract still popular in France. It's often required reading for foreign students of the French language. The book of short stories took as its theme the death of rural life in Provence, and the windmill, spared because of its association with the author, illustrates his point as it's the only one surviving for miles around. The upstairs illustrates the workings of the milling system, and the basement holds a museum dedicated to Daudet that includes photographs, letters, and documents. A patron of the young Proust, he died in 1897 at age 57, a victim of the venereal disease he contracted during his promiscuous life.

ESSENTIALS

GETTING THERE   As there's no train station in Fontvieille, rail passengers arrive at Avignon, 13¹/₂ miles away, which receives dozens of trains from virtually everywhere in Europe many times throughout the day. From Avignon, it's most convenient to rent a car. If that's not an option, consider one of the less frequent trains to Arles, 6¹/₂ miles away. Here, taxis line up at the train station, and one can carry you to Fontvieille for a one-way fare of around 150F ($30). For **rail information** and schedules, call ☎ **08-36-35-35-35.**

VISITOR INFORMATION   The **Office de Tourisme** is on place Honorat (☎ **04-90-54-67-49**).

PAYING HOMAGE TO DAUDET

The **Moulin de Daudet** (☎ **04-90-54-60-78**) is on D33, about half a mile south of the village center. It's clearly signposted from the center and makes a perfect destination for a pleasant stroll. It's open daily: June to September from 9am to noon and 2 to 7pm and February to May and October to December from 10am to noon and 2 to 5pm. The price of admission is 10F ($2), which includes free entrance to the exposition on the life of Daudet in the Château de Montauban (see below).

Less evocative, with much less of its interior open to sightseers, is the **Château de Montauban,** rue de Montauban (☎ **04-90-54-62-57**), where Daudet often stayed. In the town center, it was built around 1812 and devotes most of its interior to the headquarters of public-service organizations for the region. However, you can visit a room containing 46 illustrations on the life of Daudet, along with some of his memorabilia. The 10F ($2) admission includes permission to enter the Moulin de Daudet. The château is open only April to September, daily from 9am to noon and 2 to 6pm.

Standing in contrast to the Moulin de Daudet (just over a mile south of it on D33) are two **Roman aqueducts** whose waters long ago turned the wheels of 16 water mills. They stretch in a ruined, barely recognizable row that's signposted from the roadside—testimonials to the prosperity of Provence during the Roman occupation. Also of historic significance are the small **oratories** marking the town's four corners. Built of stone and terra-cotta roof tiles in 1721, they were conceived as miniature chapels, places of thanksgiving to commemorate the end of the plague.

ACCOMMODATIONS

Hostellerie St-Victor. Chemin des Fourques, 13990 Fontvieille. ☎ **04-90-54-66-00.** Fax 04-90-54-67-88. 11 rms, 1 suite. A/C MINIBAR TV TEL. 375F–625F ($75–$125) double; 995F ($199) suite. AE, DC, MC, V. From town, drive a third of a mile west, following the signs to Arles.

This stone farmhouse, a reproduction of a Provençal *mas,* makes a romantic inn. Its lounge boasts a large fireplace, a beamed ceiling, dark wood, and padded leather furniture; there's also a colonnaded terrace and a breakfast room overlooking landscaped shrubbery and flowers to the countryside beyond. Leading from the lobby to the second-floor guest rooms is a staircase flanked by a wide banister with ornate posts. The earth tones that prevail are offset by bright flowers blooming in pots and fresh flowers that appear in the rooms. The graciously large rooms are furnished with a mix of antiques. The hotel also features a bar and a pool with a flagstone terrace and several acres of orchards devoted to cherries and apricots.

✪ **Hôtel La Régalido**. Rue Frédéric-Mistral, 13990 Fontvieille. ☎ **04-90-54-60-22.** Fax 04-90-54-64-29. 13 rms, 2 junior suites. A/C TV TEL. 670F–1,140F ($134–$228) double; 1,540F ($308) suite. AE, MC, V. Closed Jan.

This stylish Relais & Châteaux occupies a converted 19th-century olive mill, surrounded by an abundance of fig and palm trees, magnolias, lavender, and roses. All these, combined with ivy climbing the exterior, seemingly swallow the inn in an impressive garden. Its plushly comfortable rooms are inspired by Old Provence. Some of the best cuisine in the region is served in the vaulted formal dining room (see "Dining," below).

Hôtel Val Majour. Route d'Arles, 13990 Fontvieille. ☎ **04-90-54-62-33.** Fax 04-90-54-61-67. 32 rms, 2 suites. TV TEL. 350F–400F ($70–$80) double; 550F ($110) suite. AE, MC, V. Closed Nov–Mar. From town, drive half a mile west, following the signs to Arles.

Impressions

All this beautiful Provençal landscape lives on light alone.

—Alphonse Daudet

Though it was built as recently as 1964, you might think this place is a lot older, thanks to the owners' attention to old-fashioned details. It occupies 5 acres with a pool, a tennis court, and verdant trees and flowering shrubs. A restaurant with a terrace is the site where the chef re-creates traditional Provençal cuisine; fixed-price menus run 100F to 140F ($20 to $28). The guest rooms are simple but comfortable, with a mix of contemporary and antique wooden furniture, balanced by floral fabrics, potted plants, and fresh flowers.

DINING

✪ **Auberge de la Régalido**. Rue Frédéric-Mistral. ☎ **04-90-54-60-22.** Reservations recommended. Fixed-price meals 165F–400F ($33–$80) at lunch, 260F–400F ($52–$80) at dinner. AE, MC, V. July–Sept, Wed–Sun 12:15–1:30pm; Oct–June, Tues–Sun 12:15–1:30pm and 7:30–9pm. FRENCH/PROVENÇAL.

A stroll through the garden, which some gardeners praise for its junglelike verdancy, is a wonderful preface to a meal at this Relais & Châteaux. Its vaulted dining room contains space for only 45 diners, who tend to move onto a small veranda on sultry days or nights. The menu items are the most carefully conceived in the region and include gratin of mussels with spinach, *papeton* (flan) of eggplant with herbs, sliced roast lamb in a casserole with bracing quantities of garlic, and seawolf stew infused with olive oil. Dessert might be moist chocolate cake.

8 Les Baux

444 miles S of Paris, 12 miles NE of Arles, 50 miles N of Marseille and the Mediterranean

Cardinal Richelieu called Les Baux a nesting place for eagles. In its lonely position high on a windswept plateau overlooking the southern Alpilles, Les Baux is a mere ghost of its former self. Once it was the citadel of the powerful *seigneurs* of Les Baux, who ruled with an iron fist and sent their conquering armies as far as Albania. The town is just 50 miles north of the Mediterranean, nestled in a valley surrounded by mysterious, shadowy rock formations. In medieval times troubadours from all over Europe came to this "court of love," where they recited Western Europe's earliest-known vernacular poetry. Eventually the notorious "Scourge of Provence" ruled Les Baux, sending his men throughout the land to kidnap people. If no one would pay ransom for one of his victims, the poor wretch was forced to walk a gangplank over the cliff's edge.

Fed up with the rebellions against Louis XIII in 1632, Richelieu commanded his armies to destroy Les Baux. Today the castle and ramparts are a mere shell, though you can see remains of great Renaissance mansions.

Accessed by D27 and D78 from Les Baux, the **Val d'Enfer** (Valley of Hell) is an irregular gorge that looks as inviting as the pictures of the hostile terrain of Mars flashed back to Earth. Centuries ago, caves in this gorge were inhabited by humans. Today the gorge is the source of many Provençal legends. Sprites, witches, and fairies are said to inhabit the caves.

ESSENTIALS

GETTING THERE   From Arles there are six buses daily from March to September, but only one bus per day from October to February (trip time: 30 min.). The fare is 27.50F ($5.50) one-way. For **bus information** and schedules, phone ☎ **04-90-49-38-01** in Arles.

VISITOR INFORMATION   The **Office de Tourisme** is on Ilôt Post Tenebras Lux (☎ **04-90-54-34-39**).

ACCOMMODATIONS

Note that **La Riboto de Taven** (see "Dining," below) has two rooms for rent.

VERY EXPENSIVE

✪ **L'Oustau de Beaumanière.** Les Baux, 13520 Maussane-les-Alpilles. ☎ **04-90-54-33-07.** Fax 04-90-54-40-46. 12 rms, 8 suites. A/C MINIBAR TV TEL. 1,250F–1,400F ($250–$280) double; 2,000F ($400) suite. AE, DC, MC, V. Closed Jan 3–Mar 10; Nov–Apr 1, both hotel and restaurant closed all day Wed and Thurs to 5pm.

This Relais & Châteaux is one of southern France's most legendary hotels. On the premises of a Provençal *mas* (farmhouse) bought in 1945 by the late Raymond Thuilier, it became a rendezvous for the glitterati in the 1950s and 1960s and continues today, in a less spectacular kind of glamour, under the founder's grandson, Jean-André Charial. The hotel consists of three stone houses, each draped in flowering vines, in the valley at the base of the rocky hill on which the fortified town rises. The plush guest rooms evoke the 16th and 17th centuries. In the stone-vaulted dining room, the chef serves specialties like "cappuccino" of crayfish with peppers and a rossini (stuffed with foie gras) of veal with fresh truffles. The award-winning gigot d'agneau (lamb) en croûte has become this place's trademark and is particularly succulent. For dessert, consider a soufflé of red fruits. Service is daily from noon to 3pm and 7:30pm to midnight, except between November 1 and early April, when both the hotel and its restaurant are closed all day Wednesday and Thursday at lunch. Reservations are essential.

MODERATE

Auberge de la Benvengudo. Vallon de l'Arcoule, rte. d'Arles, 13520 Les Baux. ☎ **04-90-54-32-54.** Fax 04-90-54-42-58. 17 rms, 3 suites. A/C TV TEL. 530F–700F ($106–$140) double; 800F–930F ($160–$186) suite. AE, MC, V. Closed Nov–Feb 1. Take RD78 for a mile southwest of Les Baux, following the signs to Arles.

This auberge is a tastefully converted 19th-century farmhouse surrounded by sculptured shrubbery, towering trees, and parasol pines. Extras include a pool, a tennis court, and an expansive terrace. An annex contains attractive modern rooms, some with antique four-poster beds, each with a terrace. The inn serves a delectable dinner cuisine, with menu items including filet of red mullet with concassé of tomatoes, grilled lamb chops with ratatouille, Mediterranean sole filet fried with rosemary, and osso buco Provençal. The 240F ($48) fixed-price menu changes daily and is now joined by an à la carte menu. It also serves lunch in the summer.

Mas d'Aigret. 13520 Les Baux. ☎ **04-90-54-33-54.** Fax 04-90-54-41-37. 14 rms, 1 suite. MINIBAR TV TEL. 500F–850F ($100–$170) double; 950F ($190) suite. AE, DC, MC, V.

Below the ruined fortress of Les Baux, this ancient but fully restored farmhouse offers spectacular terrace views over miles of Provence toward the Mediterranean. Tables are set among the pines, and its pool is floodlit at night. Your hosts are an Englishman, Pip Phillips, and his French wife, Chantal. The fully equipped guest rooms are attractive, with almost all boasting private balconies filled with flowers. Two of the larger rooms are partly built into natural rock and contain four-posters, one of which was made for Edward VII when he was Prince of Wales. The restaurant, carved out of rock, serves excellent regional and traditional dishes.

INEXPENSIVE

✪ **Hostellerie de la Reine-Jeanne.** Grand-Rue, 13520 Les Baux. ☎ **04-90-54-32-06.** Fax 04-90-54-32-33. 11 rms. TEL. 270F–340F ($54–$68) double. MC, V. Closed Nov 15–Feb 15 (open during the Christmas holidays).

This warm, immaculate inn is the best bargain in Les Baux. You enter through a typical provincial French bistro where you're welcomed by Alain Guilbard. All the rooms are comfortable, and three have their own terraces. Fixed-price menus are sumptuously prepared by chef Jean-Marc Hermann.

Hôtel Bautezar. Rue Frédéric-Mistral, 13520 Les Baux. ☎ **04-90-54-32-09.** Fax 04-90-54-51-49. 10 rms, 1 suite. TEL. 400F ($80) double; from 550F ($110) suite. MC, V. Closed Jan 4–Mar 15.

The entrance of this inn takes you down a few steps and into the large medieval vaulted dining room, where you'll find Provençal furnishings and cloth tapestries hanging from the white stone walls. At the end of the dining rooms is a terrace with a view of the Val d'Enfer. The food is good, with fixed-price menus that begin at 150F ($30) and represent good value. The well-maintained guest rooms are decorated in Louis XVI style.

DINING

Note that **L'Oustau de Beaumanière** (see "Accommodations," above) boasts an excellent dining room.

♣ **La Riboto de Taven.** Le Val d'Enfer, 13520 Les Baux. ☎ **04-90-54-34-23.** Fax 04-90-54-38-88. Reservations required. Main courses 140F–180F ($28–$36); fixed-price menus 200F ($40) at lunch, 300F–420F ($60–$84) at dinner. AE, DC, MC, V. Tues noon–2pm, Thurs–Mon noon–2pm and 7:30–10pm. Closed Jan 5–Mar 15. FRENCH.

This 1835 farmhouse outside the medieval section of town has been owned by two generations of the Novi family, of which Christine and Philippe Theme are the English-speaking daughter and son-in-law. In summer you can sit outdoors at the beautifully laid tables, one of which is a millstone. Menu items may include sea bass in olive oil, fricassée of mussels flavored with basil, and lamb en croûte with olives—plus homemade desserts. The cuisine is a personal statement of Jean-Pierre Novi, whose cookery is filled with brawny flavors and the heady perfumes of Provençal herbs.

It's also possible to rent two rooms so large they're like suites, each at 990F ($198), breakfast included.

9 St-Rémy-de-Provence

438 miles S of Paris, 16 miles NE of Arles, 12 miles S of Avignon, 8 miles N of Les Baux

Nostradamus, the famous French physician/astrologer, was born here in 1503. Though he has many fans today, he does have detractors, like those who denounce the astrologer and his more than 600 obscure verses as "psychotic." In 1922 Gertrude Stein and Alice B. Toklas found St-Rémy after "wandering around everywhere a bit," as Ms. Stein once wrote to Cocteau. But mainly St-Rémy is associated with van Gogh. He committed himself to an asylum here in 1889 after cutting off his left ear. Between moods of despair, he painted such works as *Olive Trees* and *Cypresses*.

Come here to sleepy St-Rémy today not only for its memories and sights but also for a preview of Provençal small-town living that you won't find in Aix or Avignon. It's a market town of considerable charm that draws the occasional visiting celebrity or even international royalty who sometimes like to "hide out" here away from the hordes.

ESSENTIALS

GETTING THERE   There are local **buses** from Avignon, taking 45 minutes and costing around 30F ($6) one-way. For **bus information** and schedules, call ☎ 04-90-82-07-35 in Avignon.

VISITOR INFORMATION   The **Office de Tourisme** is on place Jean-Jaurès (☎ 04-90-92-05-22).

SEEING THE TOP ATTRACTIONS

You can visit the cloisters of the asylum van Gogh made famous in his paintings at the 12th-century **Monastère de St-Paul-de-Mausolée,** avenue Edgar-le-Roy (☎ 04-90-92-77-00). Now a psychiatric hospital, the former monastery is east of D5, a short drive north of Glanum (see below). You can't visit the cell in which this genius was confined from 1889 to 1890, but it's still worth coming here to explore the Romanesque chapel and cloisters with their circular arches and columns, which have beautifully carved capitals. The cloisters are open daily: April to September from 9am to 6pm and October to March from 9am to 5pm. Admission is 10F ($2). On your way to the church you'll see a bust of van Gogh.

In the center of St-Rémy, the **Musée Archéologique,** in the Hôtel de Sade, rue du Parage (☎ 04-90-92-64-04), displays both sculptures and bronzes excavated at the ancient Roman excavations at nearby Glanum. It's open March 22 to September 30, Tuesday to Sunday from 10am to noon and 2 to 6pm; in October, Tuesday to Sunday from 10am to noon and 2 to 7pm. The rest of the year, it's open only by appointment, either at the number listed above or through the local tourist office. Entrance is 15F ($3) for adults, 12F ($2.40) for students and youths 12 to 17, and free for children 11 and under.

SEEING THE NEARBY ATTRACTIONS

A mile south of St-Rémy on D5 are the **Ruines de Glanum,** avenue Vincent-van-Gogh (☎ 04-90-92-23-79), a Gallo-Roman settlement that thrived during the final days of the Roman Empire. (To reach it from the town center, follow the signs to Les Antiques.) Its historic monuments include an Arc Municipal, a triumphal arch dating from the time of Julius Caesar, and a cenotaph called the Mausolée des Jules. Garlanded with sculptured fruits and flowers, the arch dates from 20 B.C. and is the oldest in Provence. The mausoleum was raised to honor the grandsons of Augustus and is the only extant monument of its type. In the area are entire streets and foundations of private residences from the 1st-century town. Some remains are from a Gallo-Greek town from the 2nd century B.C. Admission is 32F ($6.40) for adults, 21F ($4.20) for students and young adults 18 to 25, and 10F ($2) for children 17 and under. The excavations are open daily: April to September from 9am to 7pm and October to March from 9am to noon and 2 to 5pm.

ACCOMMODATIONS

Note that the **Bar/Hôtel/Restaurant des Arts** (see "Dining," below) also rents rooms.

✪ **Château de Roussan.** Rte. de Tarascon, 13210 St-Rémy-de-Provence. ☎ 04-90-92-11-63. Fax 04-90-92-50-59. 21 rms. TEL. 430F–600F ($86–$120) double. AE, MC, V.

Although there are other château hotels in the district that are more lavish and stylish, this one is more evocative of another time and place. This château's most famous resident, the Renaissance psychic Nostradamus, lived in a rustic outbuilding a few steps from the front door. Today you pass beneath an archway of 300-year-old trees leading to the neoclassical facade, which was constructed of softly colored local stone in 1701. As you wander around the grounds you'll be absorbed in the history, especially when you come on the baroque sculptures lining the basin, fed by a stream. The restaurant, open daily for lunch and dinner, serves fixed-price menus.

✪ **Hôtel Château des Alpilles.** Ancienne rte. du Grès, 13210 St-Rémy-de-Provence. ☎ **04-90-92-03-33.** Fax 04-90-92-45-17. 18 rms, 3 suites. MINIBAR TV TEL. 900F–1,080F ($180–$216) double; from 1,400F ($280) suite. AE, DC, MC, V. Closed Jan 5–Feb 17 and Nov 15–Dec 18.

When she converted this mansion in 1980, Françoise Bon wanted to create a "house for paying friends." When it was built in 1827 by the Pichot family, it housed Chateaubriand and a host of other luminaries. To reach it, you pass beneath the 300-year-old trees that surround the neoclassic exterior. The spacious rooms have combined the best of an antique framework with plush upholstery, rich carpeting, and vibrant colors. Each boasts whimsical accessories, like a pair of porcelain panthers flanking one of the carved mantels, and travertine-trimmed baths with large windows. Mme Bon has installed an elevator, though you may prefer to descend the massive stone staircase. In the garden the château has an outdoor pool, two tennis courts, a sauna, and a grill where you can order lunch in summer.

Les Antiques. 15 av. Pasteur, 13210 St-Rémy-de-Provence. ☎ **04-90-92-03-02.** Fax 04-90-92-50-40. 27 rms. MINIBAR TEL. 370F–600F ($74–$120) double. AE, DC, MC, V. Closed Oct 24–Apr 10.

This moderately priced stylish 19th-century villa is in a 7-acre park with a pool. It contains an elegant reception lounge, which opens onto several salons, and all furnishings are Napoléon III. Some of the accommodations are in a private modern pavilion, with direct access to the garden. The rooms are handsomely furnished, usually in pastels. In summer you're served breakfast (the only meal) in what used to be the Orangerie.

✪ **Vallon de Valrugues.** Chemin Canto-Cigalo, 13210 St-Rémy-de-Provence. ☎ **04-90-92-04-40.** Fax 04-90-92-44-01. 41 rms, 12 suites. MINIBAR TV TEL. 680F–1,380F ($136–$276) double; 1,680F–2,280F ($336–$456) suite. AE, DC, MC, V.

Surrounded by a park, this Mediterranean hotel has the best accommodations and restaurant in town. The owners, Françoise and Jean-Michel Gallon, offer beautifully furnished rooms and suites, all with built-in safes. The rooms have recently been enlarged and renovated, with marble baths added. The dining terrace alone may compete with the cuisine, which is winning praise for innovative light dishes. Facilities include a pool, tennis courts, a sauna and gym, and a horseback-riding ring with instructors (for which you pay extra).

DINING

Another great dining choice is the restaurant at **Vallon de Valrugues** (see "Accommodations," above).

✪ **Bar/Hôtel/Restaurant des Arts.** 32 bd. Victor-Hugo, 13210 St-Rémy-de-Provence. ☎ **04-90-92-08-50.** Reservations recommended. Main courses 70F–130F ($14–$26); fixed-price menus 110F–135F ($22–$27). AE, DC, MC, V. Wed–Mon noon–2pm and 7:30–9:30pm. Closed Feb and Nov 1–12. FRENCH.

This old-style cafe/restaurant evokes the earthy pleasures of *gitanes* and *pastis,* in many ways it hasn't changed a lot since the days of Albert Camus. The wait for dinner can be as long as 45 minutes, so you may want to spend some time in the bar, with its wooden tables, pine paneling, copper pots, and slightly faded decor. Don't expect cutting-edge cuisine or modern points of view, as everything about this place, including the accents of the all-Provençal staff, is immersed in the Midi of long ago. The menu lists specialties like rabbit terrine, pepper steak with champagne, tournedos with madeira and mushrooms, duckling in orange sauce, and three preparations of trout.

A Countryside Drive

This 40-mile drive northeast of Arles is filled with contorted limestone hills, the **Chaîne des Alpilles,** surrounded by olive and fruit orchards. Head south out of St-Rémy on D5, passing the Monastère St-Paul-de-Mausolée on the left and Les Antiques, two Roman monuments, on the right, before climbing into the hills. Take a left turn at **La Caume,** the highest of the bluffs at an elevation of 422 feet, where you can see the distant Parc Naturel Régional de Camargue and Mont Ventoux. After descending the far side of the slope, take a right on D27A to Les Baux, driving past the town to view the bleak **Val d'Enfer** (Valley of Hell). Then backtrack and continue south on D27/D78F until it deadends at D17.

A right turn takes you to **Fontvieille,** where you can pay tribute to the author Alphonse Daudet, whose *Lettres de Mon Moulin* were inspired by the Moulin de Daudet (windmill) here. To reach the windmill, take D33 (avenue des Moulins). Then go to the nearby Château de Montauban, which is now a museum in his honor. Continue south on D33 to D82 and turn left, stopping to walk along the road and view the ruins of the **Aqueducs de Barbegal** that supplied water between Arles and Eygalières when the area was part of the Roman Empire.

Backtrack to the main road and veer left on D78E to Paradou, where the road changes to D17. Keep driving straight, stopping if you wish in the village of **Maussane-les-Alpilles.** East of town, stay on the main road, which now becomes D78. Drive to Le Destet, where you'll make a left turn to head northeast on D24. A change of perspective now allows you to view La Caume, on the left, from a distance. Keep driving past the D25 intersection and turn right on D24B to reach the ancient village of **Eygalières,** with its medieval castle and church. Just beyond it, at the junction of D24B and D74A, take in the sweeping view from the Romanesque **Chapelle St-Sixte.** A left on D74A takes you north to D99, where another left provides you with a pleasant country drive back to St-Rémy.

If you want to spend the night, the hotel contains 15 rooms, a half dozen of which are in a nearby annex. The cheaper and more rustic ones are upstairs in the main building. Outfitted in Provençal style, many have ceiling beams and exposed timbers; 8 have full baths while the remainder have showers and sinks. Depending on the plumbing and the size of the room, doubles range from 290F to 370F ($58 to $74). You'll find it a very short walk east from the center of town.

Le Jardin de Frédéric. 8 bd. Gambetta. ☎ **04-90-92-27-76.** Reservations required. Main courses 95F–115F ($19–$23); fixed-price menus 135F–165F ($27–$33). MC, V. Thurs–Tues noon–2pm and 7:30–9:30pm. Closed Feb. FRENCH.

In a small villa close to the town center, this popular bistro is the best restaurant around. The family-run place offers rabbit with plums, duckling terrine, onion tart, and poached turbot with sorrel. It's almost the type of food you'd be served in a local Provençal home. In summer you can dine at tables in front of the house.

10 Cavaillon

436 miles SE of Paris, 17 miles SE of Avignon, 26 miles NE of Arles, 36$^{1}/_{2}$ miles NW of Aix-en-Provence

In the fertile Durance Valley, Cavaillon hosts France's largest vegetable market, the **Marché d'Intérêt National** (MIN), with more than 880,000 tons of vegetables annually shipped out of the gardens surrounding the town. Most famous is the *charentais,* better known as the melon de Cavaillon, a yellowish-green ribbed melon with sweet bright-orange flesh. The French have quite a taste for the melon—a fact best illustrated by an agreement between the author Alexandre Dumas *père* and the Cavaillon library. On November 15, 1864, Dumas agreed to donate the 194 volumes that constituted his writing to the local library in return for a lifetime yearly annuity of a dozen melons.

The area's thriving agriculture can be attributed to François I, who authorized the use of the Durance River for irrigation in 1537—thus the region's dry fields of grain gave way to the cornucopia of vegetables that still flood France's markets. Much earlier the town was a Roman trading center, and a reconstructed 1st-century A.D. **Roman arch** on place du Clos pays tribute to that epoch. A steep path behind the arch leads up the Colline St-Jacques to the medieval **Chapelle St-Jacques,** which offers a superb view of the farm valley, river, and distant mountains.

The **Musée Archéologique,** cours Gambetta, in the chapel of the Ancien Hôtel-Dieu (☎ 04-90-76-00-34), displays artifacts of previous settlements, including Neolithic and Roman objects, and screens films documenting the town's history. It's open Monday, Wednesday, and Sunday from 10am to noon and 2 to 5pm, with an admission charge of 20F ($4). The **Cathédrale Notre-Dame et St-Véran,** place Voltaire, dates to the 12th century, with 17th-century updates to the interior. It's in a state of disrepair but does hold minor paintings by Mignard and Parrocel.

In a nod to the tenacity of the pre-Revolution Jews, the 18th-century **synagogue,** rue Hébraïque, houses the **Musée Juif Comtadin** (☎ 04-90-76-00-34), a small museum of ritualistic objects that occupies a former bakery in the basement. However, the museum doesn't document the papal persecution of the once-sizable Jewish community, which was confined to a small ghetto surrounding the synagogue. Although small scaled, the synagogue's interior is quite beautiful—here a colony of Jews that never exceeded 200 attended services against a backdrop of Louis XV–style paneling and wrought-iron balustrades. In recent years restorers have exposed the synagogue's original colors: blue and yellow designs on a gray backdrop. The museum is open April to September, daily from 3 to 6pm; October to March, Monday to Saturday from 2 to 6pm. Admission is 20F ($4) for adults and 10F ($2) for students and children 17 and under.

ESSENTIALS

GETTING THERE   Cavaillon is connected to the other rail lines of the SNCF only via a spur line that goes into Avignon, and it operates only once (or at most twice) a day in either direction. Consequently, most railway passengers get off at Avignon, then take any of the taxis at the station, for a fee of around 140F ($28). About 10 buses a day depart from the train station at Avignon for the center of Cavaillon, charging around 19F ($3.80) per person each way. For **bus information,** call Halte Routière (☎ 04-90-78-32-39).

VISITOR INFORMATION   The **Office de Tourisme** is on place François-Tourel (☎ 04-90-71-32-01).

ACCOMMODATIONS

Hôtel du Parc. 183 place François-Tourel, 84300 Cavaillon. ☎ **04-90-71-57-78.** Fax 04-90-76-10-35. 40 rms. TV TEL. 250F ($50) double. DC, MC, V. Parking 24F ($4.80).

The town's most appealing hotel occupies a pair of buildings: one a private house built in the 18th century, the other a modern structure from the early 1980s. Both face a carefully landscaped courtyard with a fountain. Regardless of their location, the rooms are comfortable, done in a country-rustic theme. Breakfast is the only meal served (in clement weather it's presented in the courtyard), but the cheerful owners will direct you to a choice of eateries nearby. The Fin de Siècle (see "Dining," below) is very close to the hotel.

Hôtel Ibis. 175 av. du Pont, 84300 Cavaillon. ☎ **800/221-4542** in the U.S. and Canada, or 04-90-76-11-11. Fax 04-90-71-77-07. 35 rms. A/C TV TEL. 330F ($66) double. Half board 190F ($38) extra. AE, DC, MC, V.

This clean, well-maintained member of a nationwide French chain is a 10-minute walk south of the town center. Built in 1987, it's favored by European travelers in town to conduct business with the region's greengrocers, and thus is efficient and unpretentious. The rooms, scattered over two floors upstairs, and are blandly international and comfortable. The restaurant serves fixed-price menus at 55F to 75F ($11 to $15).

DINING

✪ **Alain Nicolet**. Route de Pertuis, Cheval Blanc. ☎ **04-90-78-01-56.** Reservations recommended. Main courses 145F–165F ($29–$33); fixed-price menus 150F–360F ($30–$72). AE, DC, MC, V. Tues–Sat noon–2pm and 7:30–9:30pm, Sun noon–2pm; also Sun–Mon 7:30–9:30pm July–Aug. Closed 1 week in Oct. From town, drive 2¹/₂ miles south, following the signs to Cheval Blanc. PROVENÇAL.

In an authentic replica of a stone-sided Provençal *mas*, this gourmet restaurant serves picture-perfect dishes made with the freshest seasonal ingredients. In summer, an olive-shaded terrace offers vistas that sweep out over olive groves, the surrounding countryside, and the Alpilles. There's a trio of dining rooms, each containing only four tables that are discreetly supervised by Mireille, the wife of owner/chef Alain Nicolet. Menu items include crayfish with spices and onion-and-tomato marmalade, lobster-stuffed zucchini flowers with basil-flavored cream sauce, and roast leg of lamb with its own juice and ratatouille. Dessert might be palette à la Nicolet, which is likely to include nougat glacé, a fondant of chocolate, a tulipe of strawberries, and a lemon or a chocolate tart. The cellars contain more than 300 vintages, mostly from Provence, at least 30% of which sell for under 150F ($30).

✪ **Prévot**. 353 av. de Verdun. ☎ **04-90-71-32-43.** Reservations recommended. Main courses 75F–150F ($15–$30); fixed-price menus 150F–320F ($30–$64) at lunch, 215F–320F ($43–$64) at dinner. AE, MC, DC, V. Tues–Sat noon–2pm and 7:15–9:30pm, Sun 12:30–3pm. PROVENÇAL.

This is Cavaillon's most sophisticated and endearing restaurant and has flourished since 1981 under the administration of Jean-Jacques Prévot and a well-trained staff. You'll dine in a 200-year-old building whose rooms contain so many references to melons and their cultivation that the municipal government often cites the decor as the town's unofficial "Museum of the Melon."

Menu items change with the season but usually include cured ham of wild boar, thinly sliced and served with slices of melon arranged into a daisy; two preparations of foie gras (one with fennel, the other with apples, cinnamon, and a confit of onions) arranged on the same platter; a soufflé of artichokes prepared with foie gras and barigoule sauce; a succulent tart layered with anchovies, tomato confit, and parmesan cheese; and a "trilogy" of scallops. Most controversial of all is a recipe that elevates the region's obsession with melons to heights that lesser chefs would never attempt: filet of red mullet baked with melon. According to the chef, the success of the dish depends entirely on knowing how to select a melon firm and ripe enough not to turn the dish into a fiasco. Selections from the cellar are usually excellent.

Restaurant Fin de Siècle. 46 place Clos. ☎ **04-90-71-12-27**. Reservations recommended. Fixed-price menus 89F–220F ($17.80–$44). AE, DC, MC, V. Tues noon–2pm, Thurs–Mon noon–2pm and 7–9:30pm. Closed Aug. FRENCH.

This restaurant is one floor above street level in a turn-of-the-century building near the heart of town, close to the Roman arch. On its ground floor is a place with virtually the same name (see below), so you're likely to hear a lot of emphasis on its role as a *restaurant gastronomique,* a name it deserves because of the cultivated finesse of most of the food it serves. You can order such Toulouse-derived dishes as cassoulet, confit of duckling, and magret of duckling with fruits; and such upscale Provençal plates as red mullet in puff pastry, goat-cheese mousse with thyme-flavored cream sauce, and a gâteau of eggplant with sweet-pepper/cream sauce. The dozen or so desserts include a succulent chocolate suprême served with a confit of oranges.

On the ground floor is the **Bar/Brasserie Fin de Siècle** (☎ **04-90-71-28-85**). Because of its sculpted and frescoed Napoléon III ceiling and because of the gruff compatibility of the Tallard family who run it, it's our favorie cafe in Cavaillon. It's open daily from 7am to 1am for coffee and drinks and serves generous platters at 49F to 55F ($9.80 to $11) Monday to Saturday from noon to 2pm; if you phone in advance and the staff isn't too busy, you can dine during the dinner hour as well. There's also a fixed-price lunch menu at 69F ($13.80). Menu items include two-fisted versions of spaghetti carbonara, roast guinea fowl with vegetables and french fries, brochettes of blood sausage, and sliced roast lamb. You might order one of those anise-flavored drinks, such as Ricard, elbow to elbow with some of the town's lorry drivers and greengrocers.

11 Gordes

443 miles SE of Paris, 22 miles E of Avignon, 10 miles NE of Cavaillon, 40 miles N of the Marseille airport

Gordes is a truly colorful village, whose twisted narrow cobblestone streets circle a rocky bluff above the Imergue valley. By the turn of the century it was suffering the attrition of many small agrarian-based villages, but then in one of life's many contradictions, the 12th-century village was saved by modern art. The cubist André Lhote discovered the hamlet in 1938 and renowned artists like Marc Chagall began visiting and summering here. The late Victor Vasarély, one of the founders of op art, became its most famous full-time resident.

ESSENTIALS

GETTING THERE   There's no rail station in Gordes. Train riders usually arrive at nearby Cavaillon (see above), then hire one of the taxis waiting at the railway station to carry them on into Gordes for around 150F ($30). For **rail information** and schedules, call ☎ **08-36-35-35-35**. There are no local buses. There's no driving in the village itself, but large parking lots are along its edge.

VISITOR INFORMATION   The **Office de Tourisme** is in the Salle des Gardes du Château (☎ **04-90-72-02-75**).

SEEING THE SIGHTS

Dominating the skyline, the **Château de Gordes** is a fortified 12th-century structure whose dramatic silhouette contributed to the town's nickname as the Acropolis of Provence. The château was really a fortress with round towers in each of its four corners. The crenellated roof is supported by the north walls. This is home to the **Musée Didactique Vasarély** (☎ **04-90-72-02-89**), where you can view the artist's famous geometric works along with visual studies and early works. Older works, untouched by the influence of surrealism, are on the third floor. In all, the château houses 1,500 paintings. It's open in July and August, daily from 10am to noon and 2 to 6pm; September to June, Wednesday to Monday from 10am to noon and 2 to 6pm. Admission is 25F ($5).

Five miles south of the village, surrounded by a rocky, arid landscape that supports only stunted olive trees and gnarled oaks (the Provençaux refer to this type of terrain as *la garrigue*) stands the **Moulin des Bouillons,** route de St-Pantaléon (☎ 04-90-72-22-11), an olive-oil mill so ancient it was mentioned in the 1st-century writings of Pliny the Elder. It's now owned by the stained-glass artist Frédérique Duran, and its interior boasts the original Roman floors and base of the press in combination with a 15th-century oak press and a surrounding 16th-century structure. In the garden is the **Musée du Vitrail** (Museum of Stained Glass), tracing the history of its manufacture. There's also an art gallery showing pieces by Duran and other artists. The complex is open February to October, daily from 10am to noon and 2 to 7pm; November to January, Saturday and Sunday from 10am to noon and 2 to 7pm. Admission to the mill and the museum is 10F ($2).

Cousin to the trullis of Italy are the reconstructed bories in the **Village des Bories,** Les Savournines (☎ 04-90-72-03-48), 2 miles southwest of town. These mysterious stone beehive structures are composed of thin layers of stone spiraled upward into a dome. The substantial buildings stand even though they were built with no mortar, surrounded by similarly constructed stone boundary walls. Their origin and use is a mystery—some sources claim they're Neolithic while others estimate that they're from the 18th century. Debates rage concerning their original function, but their form was probably developed by shepherds and goatherders as shelter for themselves and their flocks and were perhaps used as quarantine stations or primitive hospitals during onslaughts of the plague. To get here, take D15, veering right beyond a fork at D2. A sign marks another right turn toward the village, where you must park and walk for about 45 minutes to visit the site. The village is open February to mid-November, daily from 9am to dusk; mid-November to January, Saturday and Sunday from 10am to dusk. Admission is 30F ($6) for adults and 20F ($4) for children.

You can see further evidence of the devastation of the plagues in the hills above the village of **Cabrière,** 4 miles south of Gordes. Though you'll have to trek several miles into the hills to see them, the ruined vestiges of barriers known as **Le Mur de la Peste** are believed to have been built by the residents of Avignon, probably during the not particularly charitable tenure of the popes there, as fortifications against diseased refugees driven out of their homes by plagues. Don't expect great architecture if you try this—even locals have a hard time finding the site of these vestiges of yesteryear's health crises.

Founded in 1148, the **Abbaye de Sénanque,** a Cistercian monastery 2¹/₂ miles north of Gordes on D15/D177 (☎ 04-90-72-02-05), sits in isolation surrounded by lavender fields. It was abandoned during the Revolution, reopened in the 19th century, closed again in 1969, and reopened yet again (by the Cistercians) in 1988. The influential 20th-century writer and Catholic theologian Thomas Merton can be counted among those who found peace here. One of Provence's most beautiful medieval monuments, it's open Monday to Saturday from 10am to noon and 2 to 6pm and Sunday from 2 to 6pm. Admission is 20F ($4) for adults, 8F ($1.60) for children 6 to 18, and free for children 5 and under. Be aware that this is a working monastery, inhabited by monks, and not merely a tourist site. You can attend any of five masses per day, buy religious souvenirs and texts in the gift shop, and generally marvel at a medieval setting brought back to life.

ACCOMMODATIONS

Hôtel de la Gacholle. Route de Murs, 84220 Gordes. ☎ **04-90-72-01-36.** Fax 04-90-72-01-81. 12 rms. MINIBAR TV TEL. 420F–580F ($84–$116) double. Half board (required June 15–Aug) 990F–1,160F ($198–$232). MC, V. Closed Nov 16–Mar 14. From town, drive three-quarters of a mile northeast, following the only road with signs for Murs.

Built in the form of an earth-toned Provençal *mas*, this inn combines stone walls, wooden beams, a tiled roof, brick floors, and flagstone terraces into an intimate setting. It stands in a grove of holm oak, offering a great view over the Luberon valley from its pool and dining terrace. The guest rooms are cozy, comfortable, and designed for a maximum of peace and quiet.

The dining room's rough-hewn fireplace contrasts with the elegance of the linen, crystal, and china. It's open nightly for dinner from 7:30 to 9:30pm, but for lunch only on Saturday and Sunday from 12:30 to 2pm. The cuisine is sophisticated, featuring upscale adaptations of regional food. Examples are crust-covered red mullet studded with foie gras and two superb lamb platters (a galette of lamb with pistou and a white-bean mousse and a roast rack of lamb infused with thyme-flavored vinaigrette). Dessert might be a Provençal nougat glacée with strawberry sauce. Fixed-price menus are 165F to 260F ($33 to $52), with main courses at 85F to 120F ($17 to $24).

✪ **Hôtel La Bastide de Gordes**. Le Village, 84220 Gordes. ☎ **04-90-72-12-12.** Fax 04-90-72-05-20. 16 rms, 2 suites. A/C MINIBAR TV TEL. 520F–1,150F ($104–$230) double; 1,180F–1,380F ($236–$276) suite. AE, MC, V. Closed Nov 4–Mar 14.

This hotel occupies what was a 17th-century manor house that was enlarged after World War II to become the headquarters for the town's gendarmerie. In 1988 it was transformed into a tasteful four-star hotel in a building staggered progressively uphill, thanks to its position near the town summit. The decor of the public areas and guest rooms mixes contemporary, antique, and reproduction furnishings. Some rooms have views over the valley of the Luberon. The hotel doesn't have a restaurant but does feature an exercise room, a sauna, and a pool.

Hôtel La Mayanelle. 6 rue Combe, 84220 Gordes. ☎ **04-90-72-00-28.** Fax 04-90-72-06-99. 10 rms. TEL. 379F–506F ($75.80–$101.20) double. AE, DC, MC, V. Closed Dec 15–Feb 15 and the first weekend in Oct.

This 12th-century stone mansion is owned by Mme Mayard, who offers beautifully furnished guest rooms. The vaulted dining room contains high ceilings, an informal terrace with a weeping willow, an open stone staircase, arched windows, and flower planters. You'll be served such regional specialties as roast guinea fowl, duck with olives, lamb flavored with the herbs of Provence, grilled salmon, and homemade fruit tarts. If you visit for a meal only, fixed-price menus begin at 140F ($28). The small mansion, overlooking the rolling hills of Vaucluse, is closed for dining Tuesday and Wednesday lunch.

✪ **Hôtel Les Bories**. Route de l'Abbaye de Sénanque, 84220 Gordes. ☎ **04-90-72-00-51.** Fax 04-90-72-01-22. 17 rms, 1 suite. A/C MINIBAR TV TEL. 780F–1,630F ($156–$326) double; 1,530F–1,980F ($306–$396) suite. AE, DC, MC, V. Closed mid-Nov to mid-Feb. From town, drive 1¹⁄₂ miles north, following the signs to Abbaye de Sénanque or Venasque.

This is Gordes's best accommodation, a modern hotel clad in rough stone and built around the core of an old Provençal *mas*. It takes advantage of its hillside setting, offering vistas from the dining terrace, outdoor pool and terrace, glass-fronted lobby, and indoor pool. The garden ties into the valley with olive, holm oak, and lavender. The decor was inspired by high-tech Milanese design, with streamlined furniture, tile floors, and Oriental rugs in both the public spaces and the spacious guest rooms. The cozy dining room is in a nook rising into a craggy stone vault, and the matching fireplace is topped by a mantle of massive rugged beams. The sophisticated in-house restaurant is open daily except all day Monday and Tuesday at lunch: Fixed-price lunches are 180F to 390F ($36 to $78) and fixed-price dinners are 220F to 390F ($44 to $78).

DINING

The area's best cuisine is served at the **Hôtel Les Bories.** Also excellent are the restaurants at the **Hôtel de la Gacholle** and **Hôtel La Mayanelle.** See "Accommodations," above, for all three.

✪ **Comptoir de Victuailler**. Place du Château. ☎ **04-90-72-01-31.** Reservations required. Main courses 100F–220F ($20–$44); fixed-price lunch 175F ($35). DC, MC, V. July–Aug, Mon 12:30–2:30pm, Tues–Sun 12:30–2:30pm and 7–9:30pm; Apr–June, Sept–Nov 9, and Dec 21– Jan 9, Mon 7–9:30pm, Thurs–Tues 12:30–2:30pm and 7–9:30pm. Closed Jan 10–Mar and Nov 10–Dec 20. PROVENÇAL.

Our favorite restaurant in Gordes occupies a 200-year-old once-private home near the town's summit. It was opened in 1985 by its present owner, Jean-Michel Schmitt. The restaurant has only eight tables and—amazingly—only one chef, the good-natured Joelle Chaudet, who has virtually singlehandedly prepared all the meals from a cramped kitchen in back since the restaurant opened.

You'll dine in a setting like that of a generously stocked Provençal épicerie. Look for jars of olive oil and especially Côtes du Rhône wine, of which the owner is especially enamored. He knows most of the region's growers as well as their individual virtues. Menu items are classic and savory, like a rouelle of lamb that, according to the owners, must be made with new garlic; a best-selling codfish with sweet peppers; and a sophisticated recipe for roast guinea fowl with raspberries. Desserts may be a traditional recipe for chocolate cake or a more labor-intensive St-Honoré aux Trois Crèmes (puff pastry stuffed, frosted, and slathered with three cream-based sauces). The result is never "vulgar and heavy," in the words of the owner, but instead elicits rave reviews.

Le Mas Tourteron. Chemin de St-Blaise, Les Imberts. ☎ **04-90-72-00-16.** Fixed-price lunch 150F ($30) Tues–Sat, 180F ($36) Sun; fixed-price dinner 280F ($56). AE, MC, V. Tues–Sat noon– 2pm and 7:30–9:30pm, Sun noon–2pm. Closed Nov 15–Mar 1. Take D2 for 4 miles southwest of Gordes. PROVENÇAL.

On the outskirts of the village of Les Imberts, this restaurant occupies the 18th-century premises of what was a Provençal *mas* whose cherry trees and vines still produce worthy fruit. There's just one dining room, a sun-flooded, Provençal-inspired space, with additional seating that spills over into the verdant garden. Menu items are based on fresh ingredients and include cassolette of asparagus and herbs with a medley of other (strictly seasonal) ingredients, charlotte of lamb with Provençal herbs, and a tarte à l'envers (upside-down tart) of roast rabbit with black-olive tapenade.

12 Roussillon & Bonnieux

These villages lie so close to each other that you can visit both in a long morning or afternoon.

ROUSSILLON

28 miles E of Avignon, 6 miles E of Gordes

Color—17 shades of ocher, to be more precise—has proven to be this village's life-blood. From as far back as Roman times, the area's rich deposits of ocher have been valued. Beginning in the late 1700s Roussillon's ocher powders were shipped around the world from nearby Marseille. Though the mining industry has dried up, hordes of artists and visitors still flock here to marvel and be inspired by the gorgeous ranges of the vibrant warm tones. Roussillon also served as a giant laboratory of sorts for the famous American sociologist William Wylie, who packed up his family and moved to the village for a year, studying the complex life of work and fun, love and family feuds, and simple day-to-day existence. Later he published his studies in *A Village in the Vaucluse.*

ESSENTIALS

GETTING THERE   From Avignon, drive east on N7 to D973, then to D22. Finally, turn north on D149 and follow the signs to Roussillon. The trip takes about 45 minutes. There's no train or bus service.

VISITOR INFORMATION   The **Office de Tourisme** is on place de la Poste (☎ 04-90-05-60-25).

SEEING THE SIGHTS

Take time to explore the narrow, steep streets, soaking in the rusts, reds, and ochers of the stone used in the construction of the buildings and houses. In fact, the most magnificent sights you'll see are the vistas from a place called the **Castrum,** at the high point along rue de l'Eglise. Face north from this promontory and you'll gaze across the Vaucluse plateau and onto Mont Ventoux. If you turn south, you'll see the Coulon valley and the Grand Luberon. You can reach the old ocher quarries with their sunburned exposed rocks by taking a 40-minute scenic walk east of the village. Paths to the quarries start at the tourist office (see "Essentials," above). Another panorama is **Chaussée des Géants.** To view these huge red cliffs, take the path southeast of the tourist office. The walk is about 45 minutes and includes a great look back at Roussillon.

About 3 miles south of town on D149 is the **pont Julien.** Built more than 2,000 years ago, this three-arched Roman engineering feat of precisely hewn stone spans the Calavon River without the use of any mortar. It's thought to have been named in honor of the nearby Roman town of Apta Julia, known today as Apt.

ACCOMMODATIONS

Le Mas de Garrigon. Route de St-Saturnin d'Apt, 84220 Roussillon. ☎ **04-90-05-63-22.** Fax 04-90-05-70-01. 8 rms, 1 suite. MINIBAR TV TEL. 650F–830F ($130–$166) double; 900F–990F ($180–$198) suite. AE, DC, MC, V.

This sprawling country estate house has been transformed into an inviting inn with an authentic Provençal feel. The spotless guest rooms are spacious, with dark exposed beams, warm-colored walls, and beautiful contrasting fabrics. All have private south-facing terraces that look out onto the Luberon. There's a well-stocked library with comfortable armchairs, a sitting room with a large terra-cotta mantel and fireplace, and an intimate dining room with rustic antique furniture, where excellent meals are served. The grounds consist of an outdoor pool and patio surrounded by the shimmering greens and silvers of cedar, pine, aspen, almond, and olive trees.

Le Mas de la Tour. 84400 Gargas. ☎ **04-90-74-12-10.** Fax 04-90-04-83-67. 33 rms. TV TEL. 220F–480F ($44–$96) double. MC, V. Closed Oct–Mar. From Gargas, drive 2 miles south, following the signs to Apt.

The history of this *mas* on the outskirts of town dates back some 800 years. In 1985 it was completely renovated with all modern amenities added, including a large enticing pool. The rooms run the gamut from matchbox-size to palatial. The smaller ones have exterior entrances and are somewhat reminiscent of those found in simple motels; the larger ones have bathtubs and terraces. The common areas, with heavy exposed beams and stone walls, include a billiards room, a library, an English bar, and a restaurant where you can enjoy a good dinner for 125F to 180F ($25 to $36).

DINING

David. Place de la Poste. ☎ **04-90-05-60-13.** Reservations recommended. Main courses 95F–130F ($19–$26); fixed-price menus 129F–270F ($25.80–$54). MC, V. Tues–Sun noon–2pm and 7:30–9pm. Closed from the end of Nov to mid-Mar. PROVENÇAL.

The town's most popular restaurant, it creates a pleasurable experience with its airy dining area and panoramic views of the red cliffs and hills of the Vaucluse. The warmer months usher in dining *en plein air* on the flowered terrace. The talented chef/owner Jean David is a traditional restaurateur who takes pride in his vocation. He's been practicing his art since the 1950s and works alongside his wife, son, and daughter in this family-run place. Menu items include a rice casserole of scallops and spinach, grilled country lamb flank rubbed with rosemary and served with an assortment of seasonal vegetables, and a tender beef filet with dark morel sauce. The light homemade fruit sorbets are a perfect end to a satisfying meal.

Le Bistro de Roussillon. Place de la Mairie. ☎ **04-90-05-74-45.** Reservations recommended. Main courses 80F–130F ($16–$26); fixed-price menu 95F ($19). MC, V. Daily noon–2:30pm and 7–9pm. Closed Jan and mid-Nov to mid-Dec. PROVENÇAL.

Here's a place where the vibrancy of a fast-paced Paris bistro collides with relaxed Provençal *savoir-vivre*. T he result is the superlative ambience of hearty meals, intriguing chatter, and festive, friendly service. The bistro has one intimate dining room of wood and stone with its own fireplace for cooler weather and two terraces—one looking out onto a vista of valley and hills and the other facing the square. Menu items vary from light salads to regional fare like daube, a traditional beef-and-vegetable stew often served over pasta.

BONNIEUX

7 miles S of Roussillon, 28 miles N of Aix-en-Provence

This romantic hill town, nestled in the heart of the Petit Luberon, commands views of nearby Roussillon, the whole Coulon Valley, and the infamous **Château de Lacoste,** whose ruins bear testament to the life of its most disturbed owner, Donatien Alphonse François, comte de Sade (also known as the marquis de Sade), who lived there in the 1770s. The celebrated marquis (for whom sadism is named) lived a raucous and perverse life and was constantly being sent to prison. He died in a lunatic asylum. It's rumored that he committed cruelly sadistic acts against several of the local youths during his short stay here.

Strategically located between Spain and Italy, Bonnieux has had a bloody history of raids and battles since its beginnings in Roman times, when it stood closer to the valley floor. To better defend itself, the town was moved farther up the hill during the 1200s, when it also received sturdy ramparts and sentry towers. Bonnieux grew into a Catholic stronghold and often found itself surrounded by Protestants who were suspicious and jealous of its thriving economy. Since its streets were lined with mansion after mansion belonging to prominent bishops, allegations swirled that the town received particular "favors" to bolster its standing. Envy and zeal got the best of the Protestants and they eventually laid siege to the town, killing approximately 3,000 of the 4,000 inhabitants. Even though Bonnieux is the largest hill town in the area, its population never truly recovered and continues to hover around 1,500.

ESSENTIALS

GETTING THERE   From Roussillon, drive south along D149 directly to Bonnieux. The trip takes about 15 minutes. There's no train or bus service.

VISITOR INFORMATION   The **Office de Tourisme** is at 7 place Carnot (☎ **04-90-75-91-90**).

SEEING THE SIGHTS

You'll most likely want to work with gravity and not against it when exploring this steep village. Start at the summit with the **Vieille Eglise (Old Church)** and its cemetery. The grounds of stately cedars surrounding this Romanesque church, which dates from the 1100s, provide the best vantage point from which you can see the valley's hill towns. Farther down the incline is the **Musée de la Boulangerie,** 12 rue de la République (☎ **04-90-75-88-34**), dedicated to the authentic portrayal of the art of French breadmaking. Exhibits show all stages of the process, from planting and harvesting the grain to the final mixers and ovens that turn the flour, water, salt, and yeast mixture into warm, crusty loaves. The museum is open April to September, Wednesday to Monday from 10am to noon and 3 to 6:30pm; in October, Saturday and Sunday from 10am to noon and 3 to 6:30pm. Admission is 10F ($2) for adults and 5F ($1) for children 12 and under.

At the lower extreme of town is the **Eglise Neuve (New Church),** from the late 1800s. Many people find the architecture of this church to be less than inspiring. You don't visit for its architecture, however, but to admire the four beautiful panels from the Old Church. They date from the 1500s and are painted in the brightly colored German style to show the intensity of the Passion of Christ.

ACCOMMODATIONS

Au Relais de la Rivière. Off D943, 84480 Bonnieux. ☎ **04-90-04-47-00.** Fax 04-90-04-47-00. 9 rms, 3 suites. TV TEL. 550F–580F ($110–$116) double; 800F ($160) suite. MC, V. Closed Jan–Feb. From town, drive 4 miles southeast, following the signs to Lourmarin.

To relax in one of the most tranquil settings in Provence and soak up that special, surreal sunlight, come here. Artists and lovers seek out this remarkable 19th-century manor house enrobed by the Luberon hills and a mountain river. The intimate guest rooms are individually decorated with regional colors and look out over the river or the hills; the lounge blends together an eclectic collection of rustic Provençal antiques. Attention is lovingly paid to every detail: from the crackling fire on cooler evenings to the soft and uplifting chords of classical music wafting from room to room. Au Relais de la Rivière also has a superb restaurant with its own garden; it's open for lunch and dinner, with main courses for 110F to 160F ($22 to $32).

Hostellerie du Prieuré. Rue J.-B.-Aurard, 84480 Bonnieux. ☎ **04-90-75-80-78.** Fax 04-90-75-96-00. 10 rms. TEL. 498F–640F ($99.60–$128) double. MC, V. Closed mid-Nov to Feb.

Protected in the shadows of Bonnieux's medieval ramparts, this is an 18th-century abbey turned hotel. The medium-to-large rooms are individually furnished in a simple manner befitting the style of the building and overlook the hotel garden or the ramparts. You can breakfast near the large dining room's open hearth or in warmer weather on the flowered terrace. The restaurant serves lunch and dinner as well and offers a fixed-price menu for 198F ($39.60).

The Libertine Trail of the Marquis de Sade

By 1764 there were reports of trouble when the police alerted brothel madames to "refrain from providing the marquis with girls to go to any private chambers with him." Denounced and praised worldwide even today, Donatien Alphonse François, comte de Sade (1740–1814), was the world's greatest debauché. Of course, he's better known as the marquis de Sade. The term *sadism* was coined from his name, and this "freest spirit who ever was" led a life devoted to an unleashed libido. Sometimes this, and the fact that he recorded his controversial ideas for public consumption, led him to prison. To many, the marquis represented the peak of immorality, as flaunted during prolonged sexual orgies when he'd whip women—nevertheless, he was supposedly a "happily married man."

The marquis and his wife, the very plain but very wealthy Renée-Pélagie de Montreuil, hated Paris and court life and sought a secluded place in the country. The de Sades, along with their happy family of three, enjoyed the solitude of his château in Lacoste. His wife, who was totally devoted to him, apparently overlooked his "deviant behavior" and practices.

The marquis had grown up in the area around Lacoste, spending 6 years of his childhood with his uncle, the noted cleric/scholar Abbé de Sade (who also happened to be a libertine), at his castle at Saumane-de-Vaucluse, halfway between Lacoste and Mazan, where he had inherited another castle. (The marquis had been banished from home because of his violent temper and rages.) When the marquis returned to Paris to attend the prestigious Lycée Louis Le Grand, he discovered that flaggelation was the school's accepted form of punishment. He related to this on an erotic level, and this was the catalyst for his lifelong obsession with whipping and the explorations of the pain of pleasure and the pleasure of pain.

De Sade country really begins some 25 miles east of Avignon and not far from Ménerbes. The little village of Lacoste today is surmounted by the marquis's ancestral castle. Lacoste exists in a time pocket, its population about the same as it was back in the days of history's most articulate libertine.

A good way to orient yourself to the trail of the marquis de Sade is to have coffee in the town center at the **Café de Sade.** The château isn't in good shape—just a moat, a few walls, some ramparts, and a scattering of rooms that the revolutionary mobs of 1792 didn't destroy. More interesting is the panoramic view spread out before it. On a clear day, you can even see Bonnieux. It's said that this château inspired some of de Sade's most famous literary works, including *Justine* and the immortal and immoral *120 Days of Sodom*. As you stand here, it's easy to imagine the marquis's world of tortured damsels and debauched noblemen coming alive again in such a foreboding landscape.

Though he spent 1771 worrying about "garden, farmyard, cheeses, and firewood," in 1772 the marquis found himself deep in trouble. His manservant, Latour, had arranged for four girls to meet with the marquis. De Sade fed two some aniseed sweets, the sugar of which had been soaked with extract of Spanish fly. An orgy lasted throughout the morning, and that evening Latour procured another prostitute to

DINING

You can also consider dining at the two inns listed in "Accommodations," above.

Le Fournil. 5 place Carnot. ☎ **04-90-75-83-62.** Reservations recommended. Main courses 190F–220F ($38–$44); fixed-price menus 118F–165F ($23.60–$33). MC, V. Sept–June, Tues

whom he and de Sade gave the same sweets. Later some of the girls complained to the police that they'd been poisoned, and they accused Latour and de Sade of homosexual sodomy. The marquis fled but *in absentia* was found guilty of poisoning and sodomy, whose punishment was decapitation. Both de Sade and Latour were later executed in effigy at Aix-en-Provence.

The de Sade family was connected to yet another crenellated fortress from the Middle Ages; it had been a gift of the popes at Avignon. This is the one where the marquis spent years with his uncle, and it still stands in the hilltop village of Saumane-de-Vaucluse, to the west of Lacoste. The castle has been restored and you can visit. It's believed that the fictional Château de Silling, depicted in *The 120 Days of Sodom,* was based on this castle. This is where "all that the cruelest art and most refined barbarity could invent in the way of atrocity" was concealed for orgies and torture.

The days of the marquis in Provence came to an end in 1778. His mother-in-law, outraged at his behavior, had de Sade legally imprisoned for life with a *lettre de cachet.* While in prison, he wrote his novels and wasn't freed until 1790, following the onset of the Revolution. At this time his wife, who had previously adored him, abandoned him forever. Napoléon ordered that the marquis be placed in a mental institution on charges that he had written and published "immoral" books. In 1814 he died at age 74, leaving scores of unpublished manuscripts that weren't to see print for more than a century.

In time he won an adoring public and has been called "the most lucid hero in the history of thought." Sadists around the world now look to him as the father of their cult. Of course, he has his detractors and is still viewed in some quarters as an "abominable assemblage of all crimes and obscenities." In the 1990s de Sade entered the modern age: His admirers now maintain a host of Web sites on the Internet.

Foreigners attracted to the marquis's reputation have turned Lacoste into a lively place. An American art school was founded here in the 1970s, and, believe it or not, many locals are proud of their hometown boy. A small theater has been built in a stone quarry just below the château, and this **Théâtre de Lacoste** now draws some 1,600 patrons at a time, equaled in size in the region only by Avignon's outdoor theater. The marquis's long-cherished wish to make Lacoste into a mecca for thespians has come true. One recent production dramatized a fictional love affair between the marquis and St. Theresa of Avila.

In Lacoste, you can seek lodgings in the **Relais du Procurer,** rue Basse (☎ **04-90-75-82-28**), where a double rents for 585F ($117). The most popular bar/restaurant is the **Café de Sade,** in the center of town (☎ **04-90-75-82-29**); dinner costs 75F ($15), and you can accompany your meal with a local vintage, Cuvée du Divin Marquis.

The ghost of de Sade still lives on here, and you can almost hear him counseling young maidens and amiable debauchés to "spurn all those ridiculous precepts" taught them by their "imbecile parents."

7:30–9:30pm, Wed–Sun 12:15–2pm and 7:30–9:30pm; July–Aug, Tues–Sun 12:30–1:45pm and 7:30–9:30pm, Sat 7:30–9:30pm. Closed Jan to mid-Feb and mid-Nov to mid-Dec. PROVENÇAL.

Le Fournil sits in a peaceful square with a central trickling fountain—a place that bears witness to a former time. Your meal will be prepared by an inventive pair of chefs, Guy Malbec and Jean-Christophe Lèche, who've taken recipes of long standing and given them a new and livelier taste. The unique menu boasts a fine repertoire of satisfying dishes like monkfish filet, roasted with sweet garlic and served with a purée of potatoes and olive oil, and pan-sautéed hake with tender violet artichokes. The wine list contains 35 to 40 selections, mainly regional choices like Côtes du Rhône and Côte de Luberon.

13 Aix-en-Provence

469 miles S of Paris, 50 miles SE of Avignon, 20 miles N of Marseille, 109 miles W of Nice

Founded in 122 B.C. by a Roman general, Caius Sextius Calvinus, who named it Aquae Sextiae after himself, Aix (pronounced *ax*) was first a Roman military outpost and then a civilian colony, the administrative capital of a province of the later Roman Empire, the seat of an archbishop, and the official residence of the medieval comtes de Provence. After the union of Provence with France, Aix remained until the Revolution a judicial and administrative headquarters.

The celebrated son of this old capital city of Provence, Paul Cézanne, immortalized the countryside nearby. Just as he saw it, Montagne Ste-Victoire looms over the town today, though a string of high-rises has now cropped up on the landscape. The most charming center in all Provence, this faded university town was once a seat of aristocracy, its streets walked by counts and kings.

Today this city of some 150,000 is reasonably quiet in winter, but active and bustling when the summer hordes pour in. Many of the local population are international students. The Université d'Aix dates from 1413. Today Emile Zola's absinthe has given way to pastis in the many cafes scattered throughout the town. Summer is especially lively because of the frequent cultural events, ranging from opera to jazz, staged here from June to August. Increasingly, Aix is becoming a "bedroom community" for urbanites fleeing Marseille after 5pm.

ESSENTIALS

GETTING THERE   As a rail and highway junction, the city is easily accessible, with trains arriving hourly from Marseille, taking 40 minutes. For **rail information** and schedules, call ☎ **08-36-35-35-35**. Independent bus companies service Aix-en-Provence. **SATAP** (☎ **04-42-26-23-78** for schedule information) operates four buses a day to and from Avignon, taking 1¹/₂ hours.

VISITOR INFORMATION   The **Office de Tourisme** is at 2 place du Général-de-Gaulle (☎ **04-42-16-11-61**).

SPECIAL EVENTS   Aix is more closely geared to music and its performance than virtually any other city in the south of France, and it offers at least four midsummer festivals that showcase concerts, opera, and dance. They include the **Saison d'Aix** (June to August) that focuses on symphonic and chamber music and a well-attended **Jazz Festival** (June 28 to July 11) that brings in very cool musicians from virtually everywhere. For information on either of these, call the **Comité "Officielle" des Fêtes** (☎ **04-42-63-06-75**).

Also noteworthy is the **Festival International de Danse** (July 11 to 23), bringing in classical and modern dance troupes from throughout Europe and the world. For information, call ☎ **04-42-96-05-01**. At this writing, the **Festival d'Art Lyrique** was reduced to only a single concert in 1997, down from a much more impressive and comprehensive roster in years past. For information on this much-diminished, once world-class event (which may regain its strength and vision during the lifetime of this edition), call ☎ **04-42-17-34-00**.

Aix-en-Provence

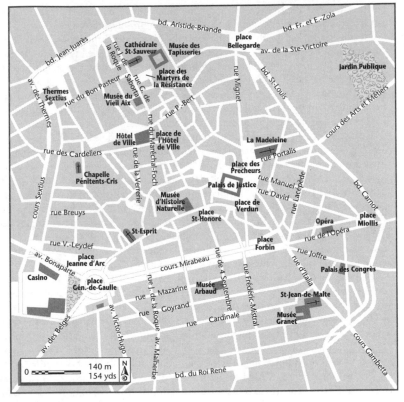

EXPLORING THE CITY

Aix's main street, ✪ **cours Mirabeau,** is one of Europe's most beautiful. Plane trees stretch their branches across the top to shade it from the hot Provençal sun like an umbrella, filtering the light into shadows that play on the rococo fountains below. On one side are shops and sidewalk cafes, on the other richly embellished sandstone *hôtels particuliers* (mansions) from the 17th and 18th centuries. Honoring Mirabeau, the revolutionary and statesman, the street begins at the 1860 landmark fountain on place de la Libération.

The **Cathédrale St-Sauveur,** place des Martyrs de la Résistance (☎ **04-42-23-45-65**), is dedicated to Christ under the title St-Sauveur (Holy Savior or Redeemer). Its Baptistery dates from the 4th and 5th centuries, but the architectural complex as a whole has seen many additions. It contains a brilliant Nicolas Froment triptych, *The Burning Bush,* from the 15th century. One side depicts the Virgin and Child; the other, Good King René and his second wife, Jeanne de Laval. It's open daily from 8:30am to 6pm. Masses are conducted every Sunday at 9am, 10:30am, and 7pm.

You might also visit the **Chapelle Penitents-Cris** (also known as the Chapelle des Bourras), 15 rue Lieutaud (☎ **04-42-26-26-72**), a 16th-century chapel honoring St. Joseph that was built on the ancient Roman Aurelian road linking Rome and Spain. The chapel was restored by Herbert Maza, founder and former president of the Institute for American Universities. It's open Monday to Friday from 9am to noon and 2 to 6pm. Guided visits, which are free except for a voluntary contribution for the upkeep of the premises, are only on Saturday from 2:30 to 4:30pm for most of the year and from 4:30 to 6pm in July and August.

Nearby in a former archbishop's palace is the **Musée des Tapisseries,** 28 place des Martyrs de la Résistance (☎ 04-42-23-09-91). Lining its gilded walls are three series of tapestries from the 17th and 18th centuries collected by the archbishops to decorate the palace: *The History of Don Quixote* by Natoire, *The Russian Games* by Leprince, and *The Grotesques* by Monnoyer. In addition, the museum exhibits rare furnishings from the 17th and 18th centuries. Charging 11F ($2.20) for admission, it's open daily from 10am to noon and 2 to 5:45pm.

Up rue Cardinale is the **Musée Granet,** place St-Jean-de-Malte (☎ 04-42-38-14-70), which owns eight paintings by Cézanne, none of them major, though a former director once claimed that the walls of this museum "would never be sullied by a Cézanne." The great painter had a famously antagonistic relationship with the people of Aix. Housed in the former center of the Knights of Malta, the fine-arts gallery contains works by van Dyck, van Loo, and Rigaud; portraits by Pierre and François Puget; and (the most interesting) a *Jupiter and Thetis* by Ingres. Ingres also did an 1807 portrait of the museum's namesake, François Marius Granet. Granet's own works abound. The museum is open Wednesday to Monday from 10am to noon and 2:30 to 6pm (closed January). Admission is 10F ($2).

Outside town, at 9 av. Paul-Cézanne, is the **Atelier de Cézanne** (☎ 04-42-21-06-53), the studio of the painter considered the major forerunner of cubism. Surrounded by a wall, the house was restored by American admirers. Repaired again in 1970, it remains much as Cézanne left it in 1906, "his coat hanging on the wall, his easel with an unfinished picture waiting for a touch of the master's brush," as Thomas R. Parker wrote. You can visit Wednesday to Monday from 10am to noon and 2:30 to 6pm. Admission is 15F ($3) for adults and 10F ($2) for children.

The best experience in Aix is to walk along the carefully signposted ✪ **route de Cézanne (D17),** which winds eastward through the Provençal countryside toward Ste-Victoire. From the east end of cours Mirabeau, take rue du Maréchal-Joffre across boulevard Carnot to boulevard des Poilus, which becomes avenue des Ecoles-Militaires and finally D17. The stretch between Aix and the hamlet of Le Tholonet is full of twists and turns where Cézanne often set up his easel to paint. It may be a longish hike (3 1/2 miles), but it's possible to do it leisurely by starting early in the morning. Le Tholonet has a cafe or two where you can refresh yourself while waiting for one of the frequent buses back to Aix.

SHOPPING

For the best selection of art objects and fabrics inspired by the traditions of Provence, head for **Les Olivades,** 15 rue Marius-Reinaud (☎ 04-42-38-33-66). It sells tasteful fabrics, shirts for both women and men, fashionable dresses, and table linens.

Opened a century ago, **Bechard,** 12 cours Mirabeau (☎ 04-42-26-06-78), is the most famous bakery in town. On the ground floor of a building on the main street, it takes its work so seriously that it refers to its underground kitchens as a *laboratoire* (laboratory). The pastries are truly delectable, in most cases made fresh every day.

Impressions

The privilege that this area give me: the freedom to stray away. This land becomes part of you. You see, from far away in Paris, I can still feel it.

—Paul Cézanne

Few boutiques other than **La Boutique du Pays d'Aix,** in the Office de Tourisme, 2 place du Général-de-Gaulle (☎ **04-42-16-11-61**), carry so many *santos* (carved figurines inspired by the Nativity of Jesus), locally woven textiles and carvings, and *calissons* (sugared confections made with almonds and a confit of melon).

Founded in 1934 on a busy boulevard about half a mile from the center of Aix, the showroom and factory of ✪ **Santons Fouque,** 65 cours Gambetta, route de Nice, RN7 (☎ **04-42-26-33-38**), stocks the largest assortment of *santos* in Aix. More than 1,800 figurines are cast in terra-cotta, finished by hand, then decorated with oil-based paint according to 18th-century models. Each of the trades practiced in medieval Provence is represented in the inventories, which include representations of grizzled but awestruck shoemakers, barrelmakers, coppersmiths and ironsmiths, and ropemakers, each poised to welcome the newborn Jesus. Depending on their size and complexity, figurines range from 40F to 5,300F ($8 to $1,600).

ACCOMMODATIONS
EXPENSIVE

Hôtel des Augustins. 3 rue de la Masse, 13100 Aix-en-Provence. ☎ **04-42-27-28-59.** Fax 04-42-26-74-87. 29 rms. 500F–1,200F ($100–$240) double. AE, DC, V. Parking 60F ($12).

Converted from the 12th-century Grands Augustins Convent, this hotel has been beautifully restored, with ribbed-vault ceilings, stained-glass windows, stone walls, terra-cotta floors, and Louis XIII furnishings. The reception desk is in a chapel, and oil paintings and watercolors decorate the public rooms. The spacious soundproof guest rooms—two with terraces—all have automatic alarm-call facilities. The hotel has a private garage on the other side of place de la Rotonde, where you can rent a space for your vehicle. This site won a place in history by sheltering an excommunicated Martin Luther on his return from Rome, but in 1892 the place was transformed from a church to a hotel.

Hôtel Pigonnet. 5 av. du Pigonnet, 13090 Aix-en-Provence. ☎ **04-42-59-02-90.** Fax 04-42-59-47-77. 49 rms, 1 suite. MINIBAR TV TEL. 750F–1,000F ($150–$200) double; from 1,250F ($250) suite. AE, DC, MC, V.

At the edge of town, this pink Provençal villa is surrounded by gardens. The hotel has antique and reproduction provincial furnishings in its rooms, 80% of which are air-conditioned. Breakfast is served under the colonnaded veranda overlooking the courtyard's reflecting pool. In summer, dinner is served outside or at the restaurant, which offers both a table d'hôte and an à la carte menu. There's also a pool.

✪ **Mercure Paul-Cézanne.** 40 av. Victor-Hugo, 13100 Aix-en-Provence. ☎ **04-42-26-34-73.** Fax 04-42-27-20-95. 54 rms, 1 suite. A/C MINIBAR TV TEL. 450F–555F ($90–$111) double; 660F–810F ($132–$162) suite. AE, DC, MC, V. Parking 50F ($10).

On a street of sycamores, this member of a nationwide chain is more plush and tasteful than you'd expect, thanks to its former owner, who poured a lot of time and money into it before selling it outright. It has a refined interior, though it has lost its former top position to the more stylish and tranquil Gallici. The lounge seems more like a private sitting room than a hotel lobby. Many of the rooms have mahogany Victorian furniture, Louis XVI chairs, marble-top chests, gilt mirrors, and oil paintings. All baths have hand-painted tiles. The small breakfast room opens onto a rear courtyard.

✪ **Villa Gallici.** Av. de la Violette (impasse des Grands Pins), 13100 Aix-en-Provence. ☎ **04-42-23-29-23.** Fax 04-42-96-30-45. 19 rms, 4 suites. A/C MINIBAR TV TEL. 950F–1,850F ($190–$370) double; 1,950F–2,950F ($390–$590) suite. AE, DC, MC, V.

This elegant inn is the most stylishly decorated hotel in Aix, created by a trio of architects and interior designers (Mssrs Dez, Montemarco, and Jouve). The original acclaim hailed it as "divinely over the top." Each room contains a private safe and an individualized decor of subtlety and charm, richly infused with the decorative traditions of Aix; some boast a private terrace or garden. The beds are hung with "waterfalls" of sprigged and striped cotton. The villa sits in a large enclosed garden in the heart of town, close to one of the best restaurants, Le Clos de la Violette (see "Dining," below). You can order meals from this restaurant to be served at lunchtime beside the pool. It also has its own in-house restaurant now, Gourmande d'Yvonne, but it still works together with La Violette. On the premises are a limited array of spa facilities as well.

MODERATE

Grand Hôtel Nègre Coste. 33 cours Mirabeau, 13100 Aix-en-Provence. ☎ **04-42-27-74-22.** Fax 04-42-26-80-93. 36 rms. A/C TV TEL. 350F–595F ($70–$119) double. AE, DC, V.

This hotel, a former 18th-century town house, is so popular with the dozens of musicians who flock to Aix for the summer music festivals that it's usually difficult to get a room at any price. Such popularity is understandable. Outside, flowers cascade from jardinières and windows are surrounded with 18th-century carvings. Inside, there's a wide staircase, marble portrait busts, and a Provençal armoire. The soundproof rooms contain interesting antiques. The higher floors overlook cours Mirabeau or the old city.

✪ **Hôtel Cardinal.** 22–24 rue Cardinale, 13100 Aix-en-Provence. ☎ **04-42-38-32-30.** Fax 04-42-26-39-05. 35 rms. TV TEL. 260F–390F ($52–$78) double. MC, V. Parking 60F ($12).

To many, the Cardinal is still the best address in town. Opposite the Musée Granet and St-Jean-de-Malte, it's distinguished by a lingering air of fragility and nostalgia. Everything is Provence provincial with a vengeance. The beautifully furnished old rooms are either in the main building or in the annex up the street. Some of the annex rooms have serviceable kitchens. M. F. K. Fisher, the author of *Two Towns in Provence,* lived nearby at no. 17 for many years.

Novotel Aix Point de l'Arc. Périphérique Sud, arc de Meyran, 13100 Aix-en-Provence. ☎ **800/221-4542** in the U.S., or 04-42-16-09-09. Fax 04-42-26-00-09. 80 rms. A/C MINIBAR TV TEL. 450F ($90) double. AE, DC, MC, V. Take the ring road 2 miles south of the town center (exit at Aix-Est 3 Sautets).

At the end of a labyrinthine but well-marked route, this clean member of a national chain offers large rooms. They've been designed for European business travelers or traveling families in summer, each with one single and one double bed and a fully accessorized bath. The hotel offers one of the most pleasant dining rooms in the suburbs, Côté Jardin, with big windows overlooking Rivière Arc de Méyran and an ivy-covered forest. There's an outdoor pool in the garden.

If this hotel is full, rooms are usually available at its twin, **Novotel Aix-Beaumanoir,** périphérique Sud, 13100 Aix-en-Provence (☎ **04-42-27-47-50;** fax 04-42-38-46-41). Set less than 500 yards away, it has its own outdoor pool, an in-house restaurant, and 102 rooms. Rooms and rates in both hotels are almost exactly the same.

Résidence Rotonde. 15 av. des Belges, 13100 Aix-en-Provence. ☎ **04-42-26-29-88.** Fax 04-42-38-66-98. 42 rms. MINIBAR TV TEL. 250F–380F ($50–$76) double. AE, DC, MC, V. Closed Dec–Jan 15.

A contemporary hotel in the town center, the Rotonde provides cheerful, streamlined accommodations. Occupying part of a residential building, it has an open spiral cantilevered staircase and molded-plastic and chrome furniture. The rooms have ornate wallpaper and Nordic-style beds. There's no restaurant, but breakfast is served.

INEXPENSIVE

Hôtel de France. 63 rue Espariat, 13100 Aix-en-Provence. ☎ **04-42-27-90-15.** Fax 04-42-26-11-47. 27 rms. MINIBAR TV TEL. 270F–340F ($54–$68) double. AE, MC, V.

At place des Augustins, around the corner from cours Mirabeau, this two-star 19th-century building has a glass-and-wrought-iron canopy and modernized yet simply furnished rooms. Those with streetside exposure tend to be noisy.

Hôtel La Caravelle. 29 bd. du Roi-René (at cours Mirabeau), 13100 Aix-en-Provence. ☎ **04-42-21-53-05.** Fax 04-42-96-55-46. 32 rms. TV TEL. 260F–390F ($52–$78) double. AE, DC, MC, V.

A 3-minute walk from the center is this conservatively furnished three-star hotel with a bas-relief of a three-masted caravelle on the beige stucco facade. The hotel is run by M. and Mme Henri Denis, who offer breakfast in the stone-floored lobby, part of their continuing tradition of warm hospitality. The majority of the rooms were restored in 1995; they have double-glazed windows to help muffle the noise.

NEARBY ACCOMMODATIONS & DINING
IN VAUVENARGUES

Named after the aristocratic Vauvenargues family, this town is the burial place of **Pablo Picasso.** It was here that the artist, who died at 91, painted his *Luncheon on the Grass* and did a red-and-black portrait of his wife, Jacqueline, who's also interred here. The Vauvenargues's turreted **château,** where Picasso lived from 1959 to 1961, has 14th-century ocher stone walls and 16th- and 17th-century additions. On top of the Louis XIII porch is the coat-of-arms of the Vauvenargues, who owned the château from 1790 to 1947. Later it was purchased by antiques dealers who sold all the furnishings; Picasso acquired it in 1958. You aren't allowed inside but can see some of the artist's sculptures in the castle park during the day.

Au Moulin de Provence. Rue des Maquisards, 13126 Vauvenargues. ☎ **04-42-66-02-22.** Fax 04-42-66-01-21. 12 rms. TEL. 250F–280F ($50–$56) double. MC, V. Closed Jan–Feb. Take D110 10 miles east of Aix.

Cozy and homelike, in the best tradition of a Provençal inn, this is Vauvenargues's only major hotel. The English-speaking host, Magdeleine Yemenidjian, welcomes her guests, most of whom were attracted here by the Picasso legacy. The rooms have balconies with views of Mont Ste-Victoire, the mountain range that inspired many artists, such as Cézanne. The inn serves a good meal for 90F ($18) and up.

IN MEYRARGUES

Château de Meyrargues. 13650 Meyrargues. ☎ **04-42-63-49-90.** Fax 04-42-63-49-92. 12 rms, 1 suite. TV TEL. 700F–1,300F ($140–$260) double; 2,000F ($400) suite. AE, MC, V. From Aix, take A51 for 10¹/₂ miles northeast, following the signs for Sisteron and Pertuis; get off at exit 14, then follow the signs to the château.

This 12th-century château is one of France's oldest fortified sites, having been a Celtic outpost in 600 B.C. Once the lords of Les Baux lived here, but now it's an award-winning holiday retreat. The entrance is imposing, with a reflecting pool and twin stone towers flanking a sweeping set of balustraded steps. From its terraces and rooms you can enjoy a panoramic view of the valley of the Durance. The spacious accommodations resemble rooms from Provençal châteaux, featuring canopied beds, local fabrics, and antiques.

Meals are served in one of two restaurants with a large chimney and a bar with a private terrace. The table d'hôte lunch and dinner begin at 250F ($50). The restaurant is closed Sunday night and Monday. There's also a pool with a solarium.

IN BEAURECUEIL

Mas de la Bertrande. 13100 Beaurecueil. ☎ **04-42-66-75-75.** Fax 04-42-66-82-01. 10 rms. MINIBAR TV TEL. 380F ($76) double. AE, DC, V. Closed Feb 15–Mar 15. From Aix, drive 6 miles southeast, following the signs to Trets.

This charming three-star hotel is set in what looks like a Cézanne canvas, at the foot of Montaigne Ste-Victoire. The former stable includes ceiling beams, a country fireplace, and plush furniture. The hotel has a very attentive staff.

The cuisine is one of the primary reasons for a stop here. The chef's innovative specialties are served on the terrace or in the dining room, both ringed with flowers. The cheese board has selections from all over France. Specialties are herb-flavored lamb, stuffed sole, bisque of mussels, foie gras of the region, and an excellent tarte Tatin. Fixed-price menus are 90F to 200F ($18 to $40). The restaurant is closed Sunday night and Monday.

DINING

EXPENSIVE

Le Clos de la Violette. 10 av. de la Violette. ☎ **04-42-23-30-71.** Reservations required. Main courses 185F–200F ($37–$40); fixed-price menus 230F–500F ($46–$100) at lunch, 370F–500F ($74–$100) at dinner. AE, V. Mon 7:30–9:30pm, Tues–Sat noon–1:30pm and 7:30–9:30pm. FRENCH.

In an elegant residential neighborhood, which most visitors reach by taxi, Le Clos de la Violette is a creative and innovative restaurant whose cuisine is usually a bit better than the attention span of its sometimes inexperienced staff. This imposing Provençal villa has an octagonal reception area and several modern dining rooms. Jean-Marc and Brigitte Banzo celebrate the bounty of Provence with a menu that changes every 2 months. It may include an upside-down tart of snails with parsley juice, a pissaladière of local fish, a slow-cooked version of lamb with brown sauce, and fricassée of sole with lobster. Filet of pigeon with foie gras is always appealing, as well as the sophisticated array of desserts.

MODERATE

Chez Maxime. 12 place Ramus. ☎ **04-42-26-28-51.** Reservations recommended. Main courses 80F–140F ($16–$28); fixed-price menus 75F–160F ($15–$32). MC, V. Mon 8–11pm, Tues–Sat noon–2pm and 8–11pm. Closed Jan 15–31. GRILLS/PROVENÇAL.

In the pedestrian zone, this likable restaurant reflects the skills and personality of its owner/namesake, Felix Maxime. There's a terrace on the sidewalk in front, plus a wood-trimmed stone interior where the most important element is the cuisine. The appetizer most redolent of the flavors of Provence is a *tian*—layers of eggplant, peppers, and Mediterranean herbs in a terra-cotta pot, infused with garlic, aromates, and olive oil, and baked until bubbly. Another superb beginning is rillettes (similar to a roughly textured pâté) of seawolf with a garlicky rouille mayonnaise. Specialties include as many as 19 kinds of grilled meat or fish, cooked over an oak-burning fire, and several preparations of lamb (M. Maxime, the resident chef, will dress your cut of meat adjacent to your table). The wine list features more than 530 vintages, many esoteric bottles from the region.

Restaurant de l'Abbaye des Cordeliers. 21 rue Lieutaud. ☎ **04-42-27-29-47.** Reservations required. Fixed-price menus 130F–185F ($26–$37). V. June–Sept, Tues 7:30–10:30pm,

Wed–Sat noon–1:30pm and 7:30–10:30pm; Oct–May, Tues–Sat noon–1:30pm and 7:30–10:30pm. Closed 3 weeks in Jan. FRENCH.

Nicole Cassone operates this excellent restaurant in an 11th-century cloister. You'll be impressed with the thick stone walls, stucco accents, high-timbered ceilings, and rows of copper pots. The chef specializes in various kinds of fresh fish, grilled or with sauce. You might also sample beef with morels and many other fine dishes, which vary according to the season and the produce markets. In both summer and winter 10 tables are placed on a veranda.

Trattoria Chez Antoine. 19 rue Mirabeau. ☎ **04-42-26-32-39.** Reservations recommended. Main courses 65F–135F ($13–$27). MC, V. Mon–Sat noon–2:30pm and 7:30pm–midnight. PROVENÇAL/ITALIAN.

In 1997 this popular trattoria moved into new quarters—an 18th-century town house a few steps from place Rotonde—and managed to lure most of its regulars along. These include Emanuel Ungaro and lots of film, fashion, and cinema types who mingle smoothly with old-time "Aixers." Despite the grandeur of the setting, the ambience is deliberately unpretentious, even jovial. Small pots of unctious purées (anchovy and basil) are placed at your table, along with crusty bread, even before a staff member takes your order. A simple wine, such as Côtes du Rhône, will go nicely with the kind of nearty Mediterranean food that's de rigueur. Examples are a memorable version of pastis, pasta Romano (flavored with calf's liver, flap mushrooms, and tomato sauce), filet of beef Rossini (stuffed with foie gras), osso buco (veal shank layered with salty ham), a selection of légumes farcies (such as eggplant and zucchini stuffed with minced meat and herbs), and at least half a dozen kinds of fresh fish.

INEXPENSIVE

✪ **Le Bistro Latin.** 18 rue de la Couronne. ☎ **04-42-38-22-38.** Reservations recommended. Fixed-price menus 75F ($15) at lunch, 99F–160F ($19.80–$32) at dinner. MC, V. Mon 7–10:30pm, Tues–Sat noon–2pm and 7–10:30pm. PROVENÇAL.

The best little bistro in Aix-en-Provence (for the price) is run by Bruno Ungaro and his partner, Gilles Holtz, who pride themselves on their fixed-price menus. They offer two intimate dining rooms, a street-level room and another in the cellar, decorated in Greco-Latin style. The staff is young and enthusiastic, and Provençal music plays in the background. Try the chartreuse of mussels, one of the meat dishes with spinach-and-saffron/cream sauce, or crêpe of hare with basil sauce. We've enjoyed the classic cuisine on all our visits, particularly the scampi risotto.

They've opened a second restaurant, **Amphitryon** (☎ **04-42-26-54-10**), in the center of the old town about 100 yards away; it concentrates on reasonably priced Provençal fare.

AIX AFTER DARK

Aix's role as a university town, and its status as one of Provence's largest towns (after Marseille and Nice), almost guarantees an animated roster of nightlife options.

Rockers head for **Le Mistral,** 3 rue Frédéric-Mistral (☎ **04-42-38-16-49**), where techno and house music blare long and loud. Its slightly more subdued competitor, **Le Richelme,** 24 rue de la Verrerie (☎ **04-42-23-49-29**), plays the same music but sometimes dips into 1970s and 1980s disco. Nearby is a woodsy-looking English pub that plays rock videos, **Bugsy,** 25 rue de la Verrerie (☎ **04-42-38-25-22**), where the good times are punctuated with bouts at billiard tables.

Less competitive and favored by those over 30 is the **Scat Club,** 11 rue de la Verrerie (☎ **04-42-23-00-23**), where a live pianist and a live jazz trio provide music to drink to. (Where did this relatively wholesome club gets its controversial name? From the popular French dance, of course.) Its most similar rival is **Hot Brass,** chemin de la Pleine des Vergueiers (☎ **04-42-21-05-57**), attracting lots of off-duty photographers, artists, actors, and literary types who appreciate the drinks and bouts of live music. Both these places boast two floors, each with its own bar, and live acts that include healthy doses of rhythm and blues.

If you're a university student or want to act like one, head for the **Jungle Café,** 4 bd. Carnot (☎ **04-42-21-47-44**), where live music enhances an everyday preoccupation with dating and mating. The town's most animated gay disco is **La Chimère,** Quartier des Plâtriers, route d'Avignon (☎ **04-42-23-36-28**); located about 1¼ miles north of Aix, it's big, loud, raucous, and very cruisy.

14 Marseille

479 miles S of Paris, 116 miles SW of Nice, 19 miles S of Aix-en-Provence

Bustling Marseille, with more than a million inhabitants, is the second-largest city in France (its population surpassed that of Lyon in the early 1990s) and France's premier port. A crossroads of world traffic—Dumas called it "the meeting place of the entire world"—the city is ancient, founded by Greeks from the city of Phocaea, near present-day Izmir, Turkey, in the 6th century B.C. The city is a place of unique sounds, smells, and sights. It has seen wars and much destruction, but trade has always been its raison d'être.

Perhaps its most common association is with the national anthem of France, "La Marseillaise." During the Revolution, 500 volunteers marched to Paris, singing this rousing song along the way. The rest is history.

Although in many respects Marseille is big and sprawling, dirty and slumlike in many places, there's much elegance and charm here as well. The Vieux Port, the old harbor, is especially colorful, somehow compensating for the dreary industrial dockland nearby. Marseille has always symbolized danger and intrigue, and that reputation is somewhat justified. It's also the goal of literally thousands of North and sub-Saharan Africans, creating a lively medley of races and creeds.

Marseille today actually occupies twice the amount of land space as Paris, and its age-old problems remain, including drugs, smuggling, corruption (often at the highest levels), the Mafia, and racial tension. Unemployment, as always, is on the rise. But in lieu of all these difficulties, it's a bustling, always-fascinating city unlike any other in France.

ESSENTIALS

GETTING THERE   The Marseille **airport** (☎ 04-42-14-14-14), 18 miles north of the center, receives international flights from all over Europe. From the airport, blue-and-white minivans *(navettes)* make the trip from a point in front of the arrivals hall to Marseille's St-Charles rail station, near the Vieux Port, at intervals, for a one-way fee of 44F ($8.80) per person. The minivans run daily from 6:20am to 10:50pm.

Marseille has train connections from hundreds of European cities, with especially good connections to and from Italy. The city is also the terminus for the TGV bullet train, which departs daily from Paris's Gare de Lyon (trip time: 4¾ hr.). Local trains leave Paris almost every hour, making a number of stops before reaching Marseille. For **rail information** and schedules call ☎ 08-36-35-35-35.

VISITOR INFORMATION   The **Office de Tourisme** is at 4 La Canebière (☎ 04-91-13-89-00).

Marseille

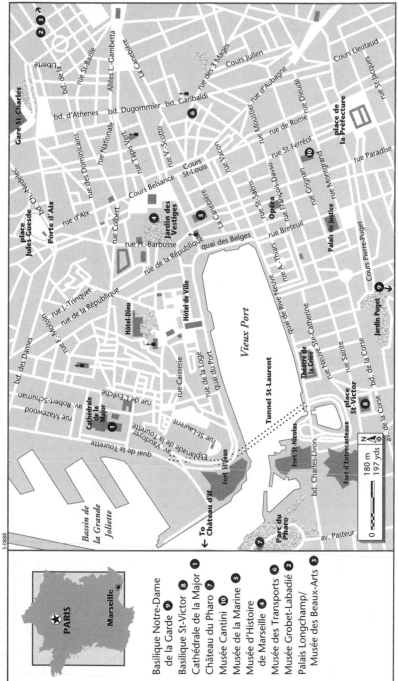

Basilique Notre-Dame de la Garde ⑨
Basilique St-Victor ⑧
Cathédrale de la Major ①
Château du Pharo ⑦
Musée Cantini ⑩
Musée de la Marine ⑤
Musée d'Histoire de Marseille ④
Musée des Transports ⑥
Musée Grobet-Labadié ②
Palais Longchamp/ Musée des Beaux-Arts ③

171

Exploring the Massif des Calanques

You can visit the Massif des Calanques, a wild and rugged terrain, from either Marseille or Cassis, as this craggy coastline lies between the two ports, directly south of Marseille and to the west of Cassis. With its highest peak at 1,850 feet, the Calanques stretch for some 12¹/₂ miles of dazzling limestone whiteness. This is one of France's great natural beauty areas.

Exactly what is a calanque? The word comes from the Provençal *cala,* meaning steep slopes. Nature has cut steep coastal valleys into solid rock, creating rivers. Most of these gorges extend less than a mile inland from the Mediterranean. They're similar to fjords, but fjords are created by glaciers, not by the raging sea. These needle-like rocks and cliff faces overhanging the sea attract rock climbers and deep-sea divers.

In July and August the **Société des Excursionnistes Marseillais,** 16 rue de la Rotonde (☎ 04-91-84-75-52), conducts free walking tours of the Calanques twice a week. Call for information, as the days of these walking tours can vary depending on weather. However, this outfit conducts boat trips daily in summer, leaving from quai des Belges in Marseille and costing 100F ($20) round-trip.

The highlight of the Calanques is **Sormiou,** with its beach, seafood eateries, and small harbor. Sormiou is separated from another small but enchanting settlement at **Morgiou,** which has tiny creeks for swimming, by **Cap Morgiou,** which offers a panoramic belvedere with splendid views of both the Calanques and the eastern side of the massif.

EXPLORING THE CITY

Many visitors never bother to visit the museums, preferring to absorb the unique spirit of the city as reflected on its busy streets and at its sidewalk cafes, particularly those along the main street, **La Canebière.** Known as "can of beer" to World War II GIs, it's the spine and soul of Marseille, but the seediest main street in France. Lined with hotels, shops, and restaurants, the street is filled with sailors of every nation and a wide range of foreigners, especially Algerians. In fact, some 100,000 North Africans live in the city and its tenement suburbs, often in souklike conditions. La Canebière winds down to the **Vieux Port,** dominated by the massive neoclassical forts of St-Jean and St-Nicholas. The port is filled with fishing craft and yachts and ringed with seafood restaurants.

Motorists can continue along to the **corniche Président-J.-F.-Kennedy,** a promenade running for about 3 miles along the sea. You pass villas and gardens along the way and have a good view of the Mediterranean. To the north, the **Port Moderne,** the "gateway to the East," is man-made. Its construction began in 1844, and a century later the Germans destroyed it. Motorboat trips are conducted along the docks.

SEEING THE TOP ATTRACTIONS

One of the most scenic oases here is the **Palais Longchamp,** on place Bernex, with its spectacular fountain and colonnade, built during the Second Empire. Housed in a northern wing of the palace is the **Musée des Beaux-Arts** (☎ 04-91-62-21-17), displaying a vast array of paintings, both foreign and domestic, from the 16th to the 19th century. They include works by Corot, Millet, Ingres, David, and Rubens. Some 80 sculptures and objets d'art were bequeathed to the museum as well, and particularly interesting is a gallery of Pierre Puget sculpture. One salon is devoted to Honoré

Daumier, born in Marseille in 1808. The museum is open Tuesday to Sunday: June 15 to September 15 from 11am to 7pm and the rest of the year from 10am to 5pm. Admission is 10F ($2), free for children and seniors.

Nearby is the **Musée Grobet-Labadié,** 140 bd. Longchamp (☎ **04-91-62-21-82**), containing a private collection that was bequeathed to the city in 1919. It possesses exquisite Louis XV and Louis XVI furniture, as well as an outstanding collection of medieval Burgundian and Provençal sculpture. Other exhibits are 17th-century Gobelins tapestries; 15th- to 19th-century German, Italian, French, and Flemish paintings; and 16th- and 17th-century Italian and French faïence. At press time it was closed for renovations, but will almost certainly be open in time for your visit in 1998. Admission will probably be 15F ($3) for adults, free for children. Call the tourist office or the number above for more information.

At the **Musée Cantini,** 19 rue Grignan (☎ **04-91-54-77-75**), the temporary exhibitions of contemporary art are often as good as the permanent collection. This museum is devoted to modern art, with masterpieces by Derain, Marquet, Ernst, Masson, Balthus, and others. It also owns a selection of important young international artists. The museum is open Tuesday to Sunday: June to September from 11am to 6pm and October to May from 10am to 5pm. Admission is 10F ($2), free for seniors and children 10 and under.

The **Musée d'Histoire de Marseille,** Centre Bourse, square Belsunce (☎ **04-91-90-42-22**), is unusual. You're allowed to wander through an archaeological garden where excavations are still going on, as scholars attempt to learn more about the ancient town of Massalia, founded by Greek sailors. Of course, many of the exhibits, such as old coins and fragments of pottery, only suggest their former glory. To help you more fully realize the era, you're aided by audiovisual exhibits, and the museum has a free exhibition room. A medieval quarter of potters has been discovered and the Louis XIV town is open to the public. You can also see what's left of a Roman wreck that was excavated from the site. The museum is open Monday to Saturday from noon to 7pm. Admission is 10F ($2) for adults and 5F ($1) for children.

For a city as ancient as Marseille, antique ecclesiastical monuments are few, thanks in part to the waves of building that have always reflected this city's role as a major commercial nerve center. One of the most noteworthy of these, however, is the semifortified **Basilique St-Victor,** place St-Victor (☎ **04-91-33-25-86**), built above a crypt from the 5th century, when the church and abbey were founded by St. Cassianus. You can visit the crypt, which also reflects work done in the 10th and 11th centuries, daily from 8am to 7pm. Admission to the crypt is 10F ($2). You reach it by going west along quai de Rive-Neuve (near the Gare du Vieux-Port).

The **Cathédrale de la Major,** place de la Major (☎ **04-94-92-28-91**), was one of the largest built in Europe in the 19th century, some 450 feet long. Its interior is adorned with mosaic floors and red-and-white marble banners, and the exterior is in a bastardized Romanesque-Byzantine style. The domes and cupolas may remind you of Istanbul. This vast pile has almost swallowed its 12th-century Romanesque predecesor (originally a baptistery) built on the ruins of a Temple of

Impressions

Everyone in Marseille seemed most dishonest. They all tried to swindle me, mostly with complete success.

—Evelyn Waugh

Diana. From mid-June to mid-September, the cathedral is open Tuesday to Saturday from 9 to 6:30pm and Sunday and Monday from 9am to noon. The rest of the year, it's open Tuesday to Sunday from 9am to noon and 2:30 to 5:30pm. Admission is free.

The landmark **Basilique Notre-Dame-de-la-Garde,** rue Fort-du-Sanctuaire (☎ 04-91-13-40-80), crowns a limestone rock overlooking the southern side of the Vieux Port. It was built in the Romanesque-Byzantine style popular in the 19th century and topped by a 30-foot gilded statue of the Virgin. Visitors come here not so much for the church as for the view—best seen at sunset—from its terrace. Spread out before you are the city, the islands, and the sea. It's open daily: mid-June to mid-September from 7am to 8pm and the rest of the year from 7am to 7pm.

Another vantage point for those seeking a panoramic view is the **Parc du Pharo,** a promontory facing the entrance to the Vieux Port. You stand on a terrace overlooking the Château du Pharo, built by Napoléon III for his Eugénie. You can clearly see Fort St-Jean and the old and new cathedrals.

BOATING TO CHÂTEAU D'IF

From quai des Belges at the Vieux Port you can take one of the motorboats on a 20-minute ride to Château d'If for 45F ($9) round-trip. Boats leave about every 15 minutes. Contact the **Groupement des Armateurs Côtiers;** its office on quai des Belges (☎ 04-91-55-50-09) is open daily from 7am to 7pm. Depending on the season, boats depart at intervals of between 60 and 90 minutes.

On the sparsely vegetated island of **Château d'If** (☎ 04-91-59-02-30), François I built a fortress to defend Marseille and its port. The site later housed a state prison; carvings by Huguenot prisoners can still be seen inside some of the cells. Alexandre Dumas used the château as a setting for *The Count of Monte Cristo,* though the adventure never took place. Its most famous association—with the legendary Man in the Iron Mask—is also apocryphal. The château is open Tuesday to Sunday: April to September from 9am to 7pm and October to March from 9am to 1pm and 2 to 5:30pm. Admittance to the island costs 25F ($5) for adults and 15F ($3) for children.

SHOPPING

Only Paris and Lyon can compete with Marseille in the breadth and diversity of merchandise. Your best bet is a trip to the **Vieux Port** and the streets surrounding it for a view of the folkloric things that literally pop out of the boutiques. Many are loaded with souvenirs like crèche-style *santons* (carved wooden figurines of saints appropriate for display at Christmas). But the best place for acquiring these artifacts is just above the Vieux Port, behind the Théâtre National de la Criée. At **Ateliers Marcel Carbonel,** 47 rue Neuve-Ste-Catherine (☎ 04-91-54-26-58), more than 600 Nativity-related figures, available in half a dozen sizes, sell at prices beginning at 50F ($10).

At **Amandine,** 69 bd. Eugène-Pierre (☎ 04-91-47-00-83), every theatrical agent in Marseille has benefited from the way chocolate syrup can be "photo-reproduced" onto delicious layer cakes in virtually any flavor you specify in advance. If you don't happen to have your scrapbook with you for something important to duplicate, you'll find a roster of artfully rich cakes, emblazoned with scenes of the Vieux Port or whatever. With a traditional inventory of pastries and chocolates is **Puyricard,** 25 rue Francis-Davso (☎ 04-91-54-26-25), with another location at 155 rue Jean-Mermoz (☎ 04-91-77-94-11). The treats available here include chocolates stuffed either with almond paste *(pâté d'amande)* or *confits de fruits,* along with a type of biscuit *(une Marseillotte).*

Checking Out a Tycoon's Private Island

Many people dream of living on a Mediterranean island. Paul Ricard had that dream too, except that in 1950 he actually bought one. The 17-acre ✪ **Ile de Bendor** can be reached from the port of Bandol, 31 miles from Marseille and 12¹/₂ miles from Toulon.

Paul Ricard is the Provence-born scion of a family known for the distillation of the region's most ethnic and evocative drink, anise-flavored Ricard—it's a translucent yellow until the addition of water turns it milky. When this liquor mogul purchased the island, it was nothing more than a sun-blasted rock.

Before Ricard's arrival, life was rough for the hearty souls who tried to survive here. Colonies of fishers were ravaged by Saracen pirates as early as 1259. During the 1600s the miscreant son of the duc de La Cadière was exiled here for murky reasons somehow tied in with the politics of Henry IV. After his political ambitions were foiled, he was accused of leading ships to wreck off the island's rocky shore so that he and his men could scavenge the cargo. He caused the ships to go aground by not placing torches along the most dangerous areas, as he was supposed to do.

Today ferries from Bandol make the 7-minute transit to the island at 30-minute intervals from 6:45am to midnight (to 2am in July and August), charging 25F ($5) per person round-trip. The only vehicles allowed on the island are those carrying building materials or whatever is needed to keep the island supplied with food, drink, and so on. Parking areas scattered along the port will hold your car for around 15F ($3).

Everything on the island (the ferries, the two hotels, the restaurants, the piers, the beaches, and the panoramic walkway flanking the water's edge) belongs to **Société Paul-Ricard** (☎ 04-94-29-44-34). The decorative theme, which extends even to the daily fruit-and-vegetable market, is that of a Provençal village. The focus is on affordable holiday fun.

The mailing address for the company is on another nearby island, Société Paul-Ricard, Ile de Embiez, 83140 Le Brusc.

At the **Hôtel Delos** (☎ 04-94-32-22-23), the 55 doubles rent for 480F to 950F ($96 to $190), depending on the season. At the more activities-oriented **Club Hôtel Soukana** (☎ 04-94-25-06-06), occupants of the 50 rooms participate in club activities and social mixers as if at a Club Med; half board included, doubles are 450F to 650F ($90 to $130) per person. Two of the island's most appealing restaurants are **Le Lilot Café** (☎ 04-94-32-46-05) and **Le Grand Large** (☎ 04-94-29-81-94), both amply stocked with (what else?) Ricard, a roster of other drinks, and food for daily lunch and dinner.

Also on the island is a **Musée des Vins,** where 8,000 bottles of wine from 52 nations are exhibited in a kind of oenophilic stateliness. It's open Thursday to Tuesday from 10am to noon and 2 to 6pm; entrance is free. There's also a commercial **Galerie de Art** and a worthwhile sandy beach. The island is open throughout the year.

Since medieval times, Marseille has thrived on the legend of Les Trois Maries—three saints named Mary, including everyone's favorite ex-sinner, Mary Magdalene. Assisted by awakened-from-the-dead St. Lazarus, they reportedly came ashore at a point near Marseille to Christianize ancient Provence. In commemoration of their voyage, small boat-shaped cookies *(les navettes)* flavored with secret ingredients that include tons of orange zest, orange-flower water, and sugar, are forever associated with Marseille. They're sold throughout the city, most notably at **Le Four des Navettes,** 136 rue Sainte (☎ 04-91-33-32-12). Opened in 1791, it sells the boat-shaped cookies for 40F ($8) per dozen and does very little else except perpetuate the city's most cherished (and dubious) medieval myth and ferociously guard the secret of how the pastries are made.

Two of the city's most sophisticated emporiums for food are **Traiteur Blanc,** 19 av. du Prado (☎ 04-91-79-21-09), where you can acquire many of the ingredients for a picnic, and its long-time rival, **Benette,** 7 place Notre-Dame-du-Mont (☎ 04-91-48-66-23), selling a slightly different roster of the same types of food. The city's best repository of the staggering numbers of cheese that confused even the ultimate francophile, Charles de Gaulle, is **La Fromagerie des Alpes,** place Notre-Dame-du-Mont (☎ 04-91-47-06-23).

The sunlight of Provence has always been cited by artists for its luminosity, and so Marseille has a handful of well-respected art galleries. The most internationally minded of the lot is **Galerie Cargo,** 55 rue Grignan (☎ 04-91-54-84-84), where paintings executed by a wide inventory of medium- to top-echelon artists from virtually everywhere (including California and New York) are exhibited and sold. Its most powerful competitor is **Galerie Roger-Pailhas,** 61 cours Julien (☎ 04-91-42-18-01). Antiques from around Provence are sold at **Galerie Wulfram-Puget,** 39 rue de Lodi (☎ 04-91-92-06-00), and **Antiquités François-Décamp,** 302 rue Paradis (☎ 04-91-81-18-00).

For hats, at **Felio,** 4 place Gabriel-Péri (☎ 04-91-90-32-67), you'll find large-brimmed numbers that would've thrilled ladies of the belle époque or something for a stylish wedding that might've been inspired in the 1920s by Lanvin. There's a selection of *casquettes Marseillaises* (developed for men as protection from the *soleil du Midi*) and berets that begin at 150F ($30).

All the souvenir shops along the pedestrian **rue St-Féréol,** running perpendicular to La Canebière, sell folkloric replicas of handcrafts from Old Provence, including the cream-colored or pale-green bars of the city's local soap, savon de Marseille. Infused with a healthy dollop of olive oil, it's known for its kindness to skin dried out by the sun and mistral. A large selection of the stuff is available at **La Savonnerie du Sérail,** 66 rue Jules-Marlet (☎ 04-91-37-17-59).

Looking for something that approximates, with a Provençal accent, the aura of a sun-flooded mall in California? Head for the most talked-about real-estate development in the city's recent history, **L'Escale Borély,** avenue Mendès-France. Within a 25-minute transit (take the Métro to rond-point du Prado, then transfer to bus no. 19) south of Marseille, it incorporates shops, cafes, bars, and restaurants. Note the newest fad from your seat on a terrace as you sip pastis: in-line skating. For more on L'Escale Borély, see "Marseille After Dark," below.

ACCOMMODATIONS
VERY EXPENSIVE
✪ **Résidence Le Petit Nice.** Corniche Président-J.-F.-Kennedy/Anse-de-Maldormé, 13007 Marseille. ☎ **04-91-59-25-92.** Fax 04-91-59-28-08. 17 rms, 2 suites. A/C MINIBAR TV TEL. 1,500F–1,900F ($300–$380) double; 2,900F–3,900F ($580–$780) suite. AE, DC, MC, V. Parking 100F ($20) in garage. Métro: Vieux-Port.

The best in Marseille, the Résidence opened in 1917, when the Passédat family joined two suburban villas. The narrow approach will take you past what looks like a row of private villas, in a secluded area below the street paralleling the beach. The guest rooms are in the main building or an annex. The restaurant is beautiful, with a view of the

Marseille shore and the rocky islands off its coast. In summer, dinner is served in the garden facing the sea. It's run by Jean-Paul Passédat and Gerald, his son, whose imaginative culinary successes include Breton lobster with thyme, vinaigrette of rascasse (hogfish), and sea devil with saffron and garlic. They run the finest restaurant in Marseille, a city where dinner often means a bowl of fish soup or a plate of couscous. The restaurant is open daily from April 18 to October; off-season it's closed for lunch on Saturday and all day Sunday. There's also a seawater pool and a solarium.

EXPENSIVE

Sofitel Marseille Vieux-Port. 36 bd. Charles-Livon, 13007 Marseille. ☎ **04-91-15-59-00.** Fax 04-91-15-59-50. 127 rms, 3 suites. A/C MINIBAR TV TEL. 750F–1,050F ($150–$210) double; 1,950F–2,600F ($390–$520) suite. AE, DC, MC, V. Parking 65F ($13). Métro: Vieux-Port.

This seven-story Sofitel looms above the massive embankments. Though having none of the charm, grace, or atmosphere of the above hotel, it's the choice address among the city's chain hotels, where you get good value. The rooms may look out on the boulevard traffic or on one of the best panoramic views of the port of Old Marseille. They're fairly generous in size, up-to-date, comfortable, and recently furnished in a Provence style. In 1987 its owner, the Accor hotel giant, turned over 93 rooms to a new three-star Novotel (below). Today two entrances, staffs, and dining/drinking facilities exist in the same building. There are also a pool, an elegant bar, and Les Trois Forts, a restaurant with views of the harbor and its defenses. Meals are served daily from noon to 2pm and 7 to 10:30pm.

MODERATE

Hôtel Concorde–Palm Beach. 2 promenade de la Plage, 13008 Marseille. ☎ **04-91-16-19-00.** Fax 04-91-16-19-39. 145 rms. A/C MINIBAR TV TEL. 550F ($110) double. AE, DC, MC, V. Parking 43F ($8.60). From the town center, take corniche J.-F.-Kennedy for 1 1/2 miles east, following the signs DIRECTION PLAGES.

Popular with commercial travelers, this is a modern hotel complex and seaside resort. The interior is a tasteful blend of big windows, soothing colors, expansive terraces, and well-chosen accessories. On the premises are an outdoor pool, a solarium, and international-style guest rooms, the best of which have balconies opening onto the sea. Meals in the grill room, Les Voiliers, are 100F ($20); a more elegant meal at La Réserve is 178F ($35.60).

Novotel Vieux-Port. 36 bd. Charles-Livon, 13007 Marseille. ☎ **04-91-59-22-22.** Fax 04-91-31-15-48. 90 rms. A/C TV TEL. 520F–610F ($104–$122) double. AE, DC, MC, V. Parking 40F ($8). Métro: Vieux-Port.

As mentioned for the Sofitel, above, this Novotel was created in 1987. In typical Novotel format, you don't receive the services offered at the Sofitel, but if that doesn't bother you, this is one of the best and most reasonably priced hotels in town. Each room contains a double and a single bed (which serves, thanks to bolster cushions, as a couch) and a desk; some, however, look a little tired. Those with views of the Old Port tend to fill up first. The lattice-decorated restaurant serves good basic meals, daily from 6am to midnight.

INEXPENSIVE

La Résidence du Vieux-Port. 18 quai du Port, 13001 Marseille. ☎ **04-91-91-91-22.** Fax 04-91-56-60-88. 52 rms, 1 suite. A/C MINIBAR TV TEL. 510F ($102) double; 1,050F ($210) suite. AE, DC, MC, V. Métro: Vieux-Port.

Old-fashioned, with a touch of raffish charm and an unbeatable location directly beside a harbor that was valued by the ancient Phoenicians, this eight-story hotel contains a cafe and a breakfast room on the second floor; a bar is behind the lobby. The guest rooms have loggia-style terraces opening onto the port; they're simple but serviceable thanks to a restoration completed in 1997. The conscientious staff tends to guests appropriately.

New Hôtel Vieux-Port. 3 bis rue Reine-Elisabeth, 13001 Marseille. ☎ **04-91-90-51-42.** Fax 04-91-90-76-24. 47 rms. A/C MINIBAR TV TEL. 390F ($78) double. AE, DC, MC, V. Parking 60F ($12) nearby. Métro: Vieux-Port.

Near the port, this stylish hotel is a good value, particularly since its complete renovation in 1995. The attractively furnished rooms with views of the port are priced the same as the rest but must be reserved long in advance. Breakfast is the only meal served.

DINING
EXPENSIVE

Au Pescadou. 19 place Castellane. ☎ **04-91-78-36-01.** Reservations recommended. Main courses 90F–120F ($18–$24); fixed-price menus 158F–198F ($31.60–$39.60). AE, DC, MC, V. Mon–Sat noon–2pm and 7–11pm, Sun noon–2pm. Closed July–Aug. Métro: Castellane. SEAFOOD.

Maintained by three multilingual sons of the original owner, Barthélémy Mennella, this is one of Marseille's finest seafood restaurants. Don't expect elaborate scraping and bowing—the venue is rough-edged but civil. Beside a busy traffic circle downtown, it overlooks a fountain, an obelisk, and a sidewalk display of fresh oysters. For an appetizer, try almond-stuffed mussels or "hors d'oeuvres of the fisherman." Main-dish specialties are bouillabaisse, gigot de lotte (monkfish stewed in cream sauce with fresh vegetables), and scallops cooked with morels.

Next to the main restaurant and under the same management are two informal newcomers, with rapid service and lower prices. In **Le Coin Bistrot,** straightforward and flavorful platters are served to a mostly youthful crowd for 100F to 120F ($20 to $24). **La Brasserie,** the least formal of all, serves platters of nonfish dishes, with menu items like blanquettes of veal, steak à la pizzaiola, and pastas, costing 40F to 65F ($8 to $13) for the *plat du jour.*

Michel-Brasserie des Catalans. 6 rue des Catalans. ☎ **04-91-52-64-22.** Reservations recommended. Main courses 180F–200F ($36–$40). AE, DC, MC, V. Daily noon–2pm and 7:30–10pm. Bus: 81 or 83. SEAFOOD.

Despite the fact that it's decorated with shellacked lobsters and starfish, this restaurant serves the finest bouillabaisse in Marseille. Just beyond the Parc du Pharo, next to the Old Port, it's one of the best old-time restaurants in town, emphasizing the taste of the seafood rather than using fancy sauces. In addition to the bouillabaisse, it offers a good bourride (fish stew with aïoli sauce). The waiter comes around and shows you an array of fresh fish from which you make your selection.

MODERATE

Brasserie Vieux-Port New-York. 33 quai des Belges. ☎ **04-91-33-91-79.** Reservations recommended at lunch. Main courses 50F–150F ($10–$30); fixed-price menu 145F ($29); bouillabaisse 245F ($49). DC, MC, V. Brasserie, daily noon–2:30pm and 7:30–11:30pm; bar and cafe, daily 6:30am–3:30am. Métro: Vieux-Port. FRENCH/PROVENÇAL.

This time-honored brasserie sits on one of the quays overlooking the city's ancient harbor. Many locals consider it their favorite cafe, taking advantage of its dawn-to-dusk hours for a glass of midmorning wine, afternoon coffee, pastis, or whatever. Amid a congenially battered art deco interior, you can enjoy a farci du jour (stuffed vegetable of the day, tomatoes, peppers, or onions, usually served as part of a main course), grilled fish (monkfish is especially flavorful), côte de boeuf with marrow sauce, fish soup or a succulent version of bouillabaisse, and a wide array of grilled meats. Also available are pizzas and salads. If you opt to dine on the terrace, service will be more perfunctory than if you select a table inside. Wines focus on the vintages of Provence.

✪ **Les Arcenaulx.** 25 cours Etienne-d'Orves. ☎ **04-91-59-80-30.** Reservations recommended. Main courses 65F–100F ($13–$20); fixed-price menus 135F–280F ($27–$56). AE, DC, MC, V. Mon–Sat noon–2:30pm and 8–11:30pm. Métro: Vieux-Port. PROVENÇAL.

These bulky stone premises were built by the navies of Louis XIV as part of warehouses. Close to the water near the Vieux Port, they contain this restaurant as well as two bookstores (one for French classics, one for modern titles), all directed by the hardworking and charming sisters, Simone and Jeanne Laffitte. Look for authentic and hearty Provençal cuisine with a Marseillais accent in dishes that include a baudroie (kettle of seasonal fish) à la Raimu—named for a popular 20th-century actor, it's equivalent to bouillabaisse. Equally tempting are artichokes barigoule (loaded with aromatic spices and olive oil), a charlotte of crabs, and a worthy assortment of petites légumes farcies (slit-open Provençal vegetables stuffed with chopped meat and herbs).

Les Echevins. 44 rue Sainte. ☎ **04-91-33-08-08.** Reservations recommended. Main courses 82F–170F ($16.40–$34); fixed-price menus 160F–300F ($32–$60). AE, DC, MC, V. Mon–Fri noon–2:30pm and 7:30–11:30pm, Sat 7:30–11:30pm. Métro: Vieux-Port. PROVENÇAL/ SOUTHWESTERN FRENCH.

On the opposite side of the same building that contains the previously recommended Les Arcenaulx, this restaurant occupies what was built as a dorm for the prisoners who were forced to row the ornamental barges of Louis XIV during his rare inspections of Marseille's harbor facilities. Today the setting contains crystal chandeliers, plush carpets, an enviable collection of antiques, and massive rocks and thick beams. You'll get a lot for your money, as the Moréni family insist on using fresh ingredients prepared at the last possible minute and charge relatively reasonable prices. Inspiration for menu items (cassoulet, magret of duckling, and foie gras) derive from either the southwest of France or from Provence, specifically Marseille. Provençal dishes include a succulent version of baked seawolf that's prepared as simply as possible—just with herbs and olive oil. There's also roast codfish with aïoli and a succulent version of baudroie (a simpler version of bouillabaisse).

INEXPENSIVE

Chez Angèle. 50 rue Caisserie. ☎ **04-91-90-63-35.** Reservations recommended. Pizzas, pastas, and salads 42F–90F ($8.40–$18); fixed-price menu 95F ($19). MC, V. Mon–Sat noon–2:30pm and 7–11pm. Closed July 20–Aug 20. Métro: Vieux-Port. PROVENÇAL/PIZZA.

A local friend guided us here, and though most of Marseille's cheap eating places aren't recommendable, this one is worthwhile if you're watching your francs. Small and unpretentious, with a raffish kind of amiability from the owner (whose name is Francis, not Angèle), it defines itself as a pizzeria-restaurant, with a menu that's much more comprehensive than the average pizzeria's. You can get pizza (the versions with pistou, fresh seafood, or cèpe mushrooms are among the best) or well-prepared ravioli, tagliatelle, osso buco, and grilled versions of shrimp, squid, and daurade Provençal style. If you're looking for something really ethnic, ask for Francis's version of *pieds et paquets,* a country recipe savored by locals that includes equal portions of grilled sheep's foot and sheep's intestines stuffed with garlic-flavored breadcrumbs, herbs, and chopped vegetables. Note that this place lies on the route between Marseille and Aix.

NEARBY ACCOMMODATIONS & DINING

Relais de la Magdeleine. Route d'Aix, 13420 Gemenos. ☎ **04-42-32-20-16.** Fax 04-42-32-02-26. 23 rms, 1 suite. TV TEL. 610F–870F ($122–$174) double; 1,040F–1,260F ($208–$252) suite. MC, V. Closed Dec–Mar 15. Head east of Marseille for 15 miles along A50.

In a stone-sided country mansion built in the early 18th century, at the foot of the Ste-Baume mountain range, this hotel is surrounded by large homes, open fields, and woodlands, near the venerated spot where, according to medieval legend, Mary Magdalene is believed to have died. Built of gray stone, with an upscale decor loaded with antiques and worthy reproductions, the inn has pleasant architectural details, like a carving of St. Roch, with his dog, above the entrance. The guest rooms are individually furnished, each in a different decorative motif that includes Directoire, Provençal, and some of the Louis styles. The relais also serves good meals at lunch and dinner every day. Fixed-price menus cost 250F ($50), though at lunch Monday to Friday there's also a menu at 160F ($32). Specialties include lamb cooked with Provençal herbs and filet of sole Beau Manoir. A good-size pool is on the premises, and tennis courts, a golf course, and the beach are nearby.

MARSEILLE AFTER DARK

You can get an amusing (and relatively harmless) exposure to the town's saltiness during a walk around the **Vieux Port,** where a medley of cafes and restaurants angle their sightlines for the best possible view of the harbor. Select any of them that strikes your fancy (or just park yourself by the waterfront for a view of the passing parade). But for a sure bet, head for the bar area of the previously recommended **Brasserie Vieux-Port New-York,** 33 quai des Belges (☎ 04-91-33-91-79). Joining you are likely to be a wide roster of Marseille's arts community, who are more interested in chatting with friends than in dining on the well-presented cuisine.

A modern-day equivalent of the Vieux Port is a 20-minute Métro ride away: **Escale Borély,** avenue Mendès-France, is a waterfront development south of the town center. About a dozen cafes as well as restaurants of every possible ilk present a wide choice of cuisines, views of in-line skaters on the promenade in front, and the potential for dialogues with friendly strangers. An especially worthwhile place here is **L'Assiette Marine** (☎ 04-91-71-04-04), a seafood restaurant with a separate bar area where fresh oysters, clams, and chilled lobster might accompany your drink.

Unless the air-conditioning is very powerful, Marseille's dance clubs produce a lot of sweat. The best of them is the **Café de la Plage,** in the above-mentioned Escale Borély (☎ 04-91-71-21-76), where a 35-and-under crowd dance in an environment that's safer and healthier than many of its competitors'. Closer to the Vieux Port, you can dance and drink at the **Metal Café,** 20 rue Fortia (☎ 04-91-54-03-03), where 20- to 50-year-olds listen to music that's been recently released in London and Los Angeles, or the nearby **Trolley Bus,** 24 quai de Rive-Neuve (☎ 04-91-54-30-45). Trolley Bus is best known for its techno, house, punk rock, and retro music, but the arts community especially appreciates it for the dramatic readings and philosophical debates held the first Tuesday of every month. (Call ahead for the highly flexible and oft-changing schedules.) Also very appealing, if only because people here seem to have more fun than at the usual run-of-the-mill pastis dive, is **Pêle-Mêle,** 8 place aux Huiles (☎ 04-91-54-85-26), a many-faceted bar/disco/cafe and host of occasional live music.

If you miss free-form modern jazz and don't mind taking your chances in the less-than-completely-savory neighborhood adjacent to the city's rail station (La Gare St-Charles—a taxi here and back is recommended), consider dropping into **La Cave à Jazz,** rue Bernard-du-Bois (☎ 04-91-39-28-28). If you're a single male looking for opposite-sex strangers who are no strangers to the art of entertaining foreign men, here are two disco/pickup bars: **The Bunny Club,** 2 rue Corneille (☎ 04-91-54-09-20), and **Le Victoria Club,** 3 rue Pythéas (☎ 04-91-54-15-17).

Gay and hopeful? **L'Enigme (Le Kempson),** 22 rue Beauvau (☎ 04-91-33-79-20), is the kind of bar where over-40 gay males might appreciate the jokes and randiness more than 20-somethings. It has the ambience of a French-speaking British pub where 98% of the crowd happens to be gay, male, and into either denim or leather. The youth-conscious **New Can Can,** 3–5 rue Sénac (☎ 04-91-48-59-76), is an enormous venue that's everybody's favorite place for dancing till dawn. Looking for an appropriate debut for your evening at Can Can that's just a short walk away? Head for the best *bar aux travesties* in town, **L'Eden,** 7 rue Curiol (☎ 04-91-47-30-06). Here lesbians and gays mingle freely in what's the most whimsical and playful gay environment in town. Don't be surprised at the many crossdressers, of every possible ilk, who feel more than at home here.

15 Toulon

519 miles S of Paris, 79 miles SW of Cannes, 42 miles E of Marseille

This fortress and modern town is the principal naval base of France: the headquarters of the Mediterranean fleet, with hundreds of sailors wandering the streets. A beautiful harbor, it's surrounded by hills and crowned by forts. The place is protected on the east by a large breakwater and on the west by the great peninsula of Cap Sicié. Separated by the breakwater, the outer roads are known as the **Grande Rade** and the inner roads the **Petite Rade.** On the outskirts is a winter resort colony. Although not as dangerous or as intriguing as Marseille, Toulon also has a large Arab population from North Africa. Note that there's racial tension here, worsened by the closing of the shipbuilding yards.

Park your vehicle underground at place de la Liberté, then go along boulevard des Strasbourg, turning right onto rue Berthelot. This will take you into the **pedestrian zone** in the core of the old city. This area is filled with shops, hotels, restaurants, and cobblestone streets but can be dangerous at night. The best beach, **Plage du Mourillon,** is 1 1/4 miles east of the heart of town.

ESSENTIALS

GETTING THERE   Trains arrive from Marseille about every 30 minutes (trip time: 1 hr.). If you're on the Riviera, frequent trains arrive from Nice (trip time: 2 hr.) and from Cannes (trip time: 80 min.). For **rail information** and schedules, call ☎ 08-36-35-35-35. Three buses per day arrive from Aix-en-Provence (trip time: 75 min.). For **bus information** and schedules, call ☎ 04-93-85-66-61 or 04-94-93-11-39.

VISITOR INFORMATION   The **Office de Tourisme** is on place des Riaux (☎ 04-94-18-53-00).

EXPLORING THE TOWN

In **Vieux Toulon,** between the harbor and boulevard des Strasbourg (the main axis of town), are many remains of the port's former days. Visit the **Poissonerie,** the typical covered market, bustling in the morning with fishmongers and buyers. Another colorful market, the **Marché,** spills over onto the narrow streets around cours Lafayette. Also in Old Toulon is the **Cathédrale Ste-Marie-Majeure** (St. Mary Major), built in the Romanesque style in the 11th and 12th centuries, then much expanded in the 17th. Its badly lit nave is Gothic, and the belfry and facade are from the 18th century. It's open daily from 9am to 5pm.

In contrast to the cathedral, tall modern buildings line quai Stalingrad, opening onto **Vieille d'Arse.** On place Puget, look for the *atlantes* (caryatids), figures of men used as columns. These interesting figures support a balcony at the Hôtel de Ville (city hall) and are also included in the facade of the naval museum.

The **Musée de la Marine,** place du Ingénieur-Général-Monsenergue (☎ 04-94-02-02-01), contains many figureheads and ship models. It's open daily: in July and August from 9:30am to noon and 3 to 7pm and September to June from 9:30am to noon and 2 to 6pm. Admission is 25F ($5) for adults and 19F ($3.80) for students. The **Musée de Toulon,** 113 bd. du Général-Maréchal-Leclerc (☎ 04-94-93-15-54), contains works from the 16th century to the present. There's a particularly good collection of Provençal and Italian paintings, as well as religious works. The latest acquisitions include New Realism pieces and minimalist art. It's open daily from 1 to 6pm; admission is free.

Once you've covered the top attractions, we suggest taking a drive, an hour or two before sunset, along the **corniche du Mont-Faron.** It's a scenic boulevard along the lower slopes of Mont Faron, providing views of the busy port, the town, the cliffs, and, in the distance, the Mediterranean.

Earlier in the day, consider boarding a funicular near the Altéa La Tour Blanche Hôtel. This *téléphérique* (cable car) operates daily from 9 to 11:45am and 2:15 to 6:30pm, costing 40F ($8) for adults and 25F ($5) for children round-trip. Once you get to the top, enjoy the view and then visit the **Memorial du Débarquement en Provence,** Mont Faron (☎ 04-94-88-08-09), which, among other exhibits, documents the Allied landings in Provence in 1944. It's open in summer, daily from 9:30 to 11:45am and 2:30 to 5:45pm; in winter, Tuesday to Sunday from 9:30 to 11:30am and 2:30 to 5:45pm. Admission is 25F ($5) for adults, 8F ($1.60) for children 5 to 12, and free for children 4 and under.

ACCOMMODATIONS

Hôtel La Corniche. 1 littoral Frédéric-Mistral (at Le Mourillon), 83000 Toulon. ☎ **04-94-41-35-12.** Fax 04-94-41-24-58. 19 rms, 4 suites. A/C MINIBAR TV TEL. 350F–450F ($70–$90) double; 400F–550F ($80–$110) suite. AE, DC, MC, V. Parking 40F ($8). Bus: 3, 13, or 23.

An attractive hotel with an interior garden, La Corniche offers a pleasant staff, two restaurants, and comfortable accommodations. Those opening onto the front have sea views and loggias and are more expensive. Room decoration is in the Provençal style. Ironically, the more formal of the two restaurants is referred to as the Bistro and features a trio of pine trees growing upward through the roof and a large bay window overlooking the port. The simpler restaurant is the cramped but cozy Rôtisserie. Both emphasize fish among their offerings. A fairly good but limited wine list complements the food, which is perfectly adequate but not something to savor. You'll find this place near the town's beaches, in the neighborhood known as Le Mourillon, a 15-minute walk from the congested commercial center of Toulon.

New Hôtel Tour Blanche. Bd. de l'Amiral-Vence, 83200 Toulon. ☎ **04-94-24-41-57.** Fax 04-94-22-42-25. 91 rms. A/C MINIBAR TV TEL. 380F–435F ($76–$87) double. AE, DC, MC, V. Bus: 40. From the town center, follow the signs to the Mont Faron téléphérique and you'll pass the hotel en route.

With excellent modernized accommodations, attractive gardens with terraces, and a pool, this seven-story hotel is the best in Toulon. It lies in the rocky hills about 2 miles north of the center of town, a position that contributes to sweeping views from even the lower floors out over the town to the port facilities and the sea. Many rooms have balconies, and each is comfortably and simply outfitted in an

The Unknown Masterpiece of Edith Wharton

Though the world is familiar with Edith Wharton's masterful novel *The Age of Innocence,* as well as her other major works *(The House of Mirth, Ethan Frome),* many of her fans are unaware that she created another masterpiece 11 miles east of Toulon in the Riviera resort of Hyères, dating from the 18th century.

Here the wealthy American novelist purchased a villa, ✪ **La Solitude,** which had first been rented by another writer, Robert Louis Stevenson, who had penned *A Children's Garden of Verse* here. Instead of renting La Solitude, Miss Wharton purchased it and on 28 terraced acres created gardens with the help of workers imported for the task. She even shipped in plants from all over the world to create this botanical fantasy.

Though allegedly not as spectacular as they were in Wharton's day, her gardens today are called **Parc Ste-Claire** and lie along the appropriately named avenue Edith-Wharton. You can visit them daily from 8am to 7pm, and admission is free. As you explore these terraces, you'll be following the footsteps of the avant-garde of yesterday, including "those Surrealist scandals," Buñuel and Dalí, even Man Ray and André Gide. Giacometti and Jean Cocteau also showed up here.

Hyères was once particularly popular with the British before they discovered Nice and Cannes. Its broad avenues shaded with date palms evoke the lazy belle époque. Hyères has changed so little from its heyday that many French film directors have used it as locations for period pieces, including Jean-Luc Godard *(Pierrot le fou)* and François Truffaut, who shot his last film here, *Vivement dimanche,* released as *Confidentially Yours* in the States.

Try to arrive early to attend a bustling morning market around place Massillon in the Vieille Ville (Old Town).

If you're in Hyères for lunch, head for the **Jardin de Bacchus,** 32 av. Gambetta (☎ **04-94-65-77-63**), the best choice. Here Jean-Claude Santioni offers a rich, traditional cuisine with a strong Provençal touch. Lunch and dinner are 140F to 300F ($28 to $60). There's no meal service Sunday night and Monday in winter.

international modern style. The restaurant, Les Terrasses, offers a panoramic view and food and wine whose selection is inspired by the culinary traditions of Provence and the Midi.

DINING

✪ **La Chamade.** 25 rue Denfert-Rochereau. ☎ **04-94-92-28-58.** Reservations recommended. Fixed-price menu 175F ($35). AE, MC, V. Mon–Fri noon–2:30pm and 7–9:30pm, Sat 7–9:30pm. Closed Aug 1–25. Bus: 1 or 21. FRENCH.

In the town center, in a relatively nondescript building whose thick walls hint at its age, this restaurant simplified its culinary format in 1996 by offering only one option—a 175F ($35) fixed-price menu that includes an oft-changing choice of three appetizers, three main courses, and three desserts. You'll be seated in a labyrinth of several small, appealingly modern dining rooms and be offered the carefully cultivated cuisine of Francis Bonneau, former disciple of some of the grandest restaurants of Paris and Brittany. Menu items change with the seasons and the availability of ingredients but might include stuffed and deep-fried zucchini blossoms, filet of sea bass with basil-flavored butter sauce, and roast whitefish garnished with ham and risotto with local herbs. Desserts often include a craqueline of dates served with gentian, a herb that flourishes on Provence's arid hillsides, or frozen custard garnished with local strawberries marinated in red wine.

TOULON AFTER DARK

Options in the town center are **Le Cocotier,** 330 av. Claret (☎ **04-94-92-78-76**), a disco for those 20 to 45. There's also one of the Azure Coast's best-known gay discos, **Boy's Paradise,** 1 bd. Pierre-Toesca (☎ **04-94-09-35-90**), where the gay crowd includes lots of French sailors—and to a lesser degree, women.

Adjacent to the port are **Bar La Lampa,** Port de Toulon (☎ **04-94-03-06-09**), where a roster of Spain-inspired tapas and bouts of live music accompany your bottles of beer and scotch; and **Bar à Thym,** 32 bd. Cuneo (☎ **04-94-03-23-13**), a less formal hangout where everybody seems to drink beer and listen to the live concerts by local rock bands. For jazz, try **Le Sax Génération,** Centre Commercial Grand Ciel, chemin des Plantades (☎ **04-94-75-19-00**), where live jazz ranges from Dixieland to modern fusion.

But if you feel claustrophobic in a town noted for its heavy industry and want more resorty outlets, you might be happy at Hyère, about 16 miles east of Toulon, where there's an upscale disco, **Le Fou du Roy,** in the Casino des Palmiers (☎ **04-94-12-80-80**). It attracts a more animated crowd than the nearby casino games. About 9 miles west of Toulon, in the small port town of Sanary, is a disco appealing to dancers under age 30: **Mai-Tai,** route de Bandol (☎ **04-94-74-23-92**).

16 Iles d'Hyères

24 miles ESE of Toulon, 74 miles SW of Cannes

Off the Riviera in the Mediterranean is a little group of islands enclosing the southern boundary of the Hyères anchorage. During the Renaissance they were called the Iles d'Or, from a golden glow sometimes given off by the rocks in the sunlight. The tranquil but increasingly touristed islands today give no reflection of the periods of attacks by pirates and Turkish galleys, British fleet activity, and the landing of Allied troops during World War II.

Don't expect the grand bourgeoisie of yesteryear if you opt to sojourn on these sun-baked Mediterranean islands, as the day of mass tourism has arrived, with some of the tackiness that goes with it. Fortunately, because cars are forbidden on all three of the archipelago's major islands (except for delivery and repair services), they cannot be transported on any of the ferryboats. Expect a summer holiday spirit that's equivalent to a Gallic version of Nantucket, and thousands of midsummer day-trippers who sometimes arrive, often skimpily clad, and often with their children, for a day of sun, sand, and people watching.

Which island is the most appealing? Ile des Porquerolles is the most beautiful. Thinking of heading to Le Levant? Be warned that only 25% of that strategic island is accessible to visitors, as three-quarters of the land mass there belongs to the French army, which uses it frequently for the test blasts of missiles. Consequently, you may want to steer clear of it.

ESSENTIALS

GETTING THERE Though ferryboats head for the Ile de Porquerolles from at least three points along the Côte d'Azur, by far the most frequent, most convenient, and shortest trip from the French mainland is from the peninsula of Gien (the harbor of La Tour Fondue), a 20-mile drive east of Toulon. Depending on the season, there are 4 to 20 departures a day for a crossing that takes only 15 minutes. Round-trip fares are 78F ($15.60) per person. For information, call the **Transports Maritimes et Terrestres du Littoral Varois,** La Tour Fondue, 83400 Giens (☎ 04-94-58-21-81). The next-best option involves longer, less convenient ferryboat rides from Toulon. Even worse are the infrequent boats (usually only twice a day, and only during July and August) from the French mainland ports of Le Lavandou and Cavalaire. For information on rides from the ports of Toulon, Le Lavandou, and Cavalaire, call **Trans-Med 2000,** quai Stalingrad, Toulon (☎ 04-94-92-96-82).

The most popular maritime route to Ile de Port-Cros is the 35-minute crossing from Le Lavandou, departing 3 to 10 times daily, depending on the season. For information, call the **Compagnie Maritime des Vedettes "Iles d'Or,"** 15 quai Gabriele-Peri, 83980 Le Lavandou (☎ 04-94-71-01-02). Round-trip fares are 120F ($24) for adults and 78F ($15.60) for children 4 to 12. The same company also offers less convenient, longer, and more tedious crossings to Ile de Port-Cros, usually in midsummer only, from the mainland port of Cavalaire. The same boats, for no additional fee, will drop you off at the mostly military installations at Le Levant after depositing the bulk of their passengers at Ile de Port-Cros.

VISITOR INFORMATION   Other than temporary, summer-only kiosks, without phones, that distribute brochures and advice near the ferry docks of Porquerolles and Port-Cros, there are no tourist bureaus on the islands. Consequently, the mainland tourist offices in Toulon and Hyères try to fill in the gaps. Contact the **Office de Tourisme,** Rotonde J.-Salusse, avenue de Belgique, Hyères (☎ 04-94-65-18-55), or the **Office de Tourisme,** place des Riaux, Toulon (☎ 04-94-18-53-00).

ILE DE PORQUEROLLES

This is the largest and westernmost of the Iles d'Hyères. It has a rugged south coast, whereas the north strand is made up of sandy beaches bordered by heather, scented myrtles, and pine trees. The island is about 5 miles long and 1 1/4 miles wide and is 3 miles from the mainland.

The population is only 400, and the island is said to receive 275 days of sunshine annually. It's a land of rocky capes, pine forests twisted by the mistral, sun-drenched vineyards, and pale ocher houses. The "hot spots," if there are any, are the cafes around place d'Armes where everybody gathers.

The island has had a violent history of raids, attacks, and occupation by everybody from the Dutch, English, and Turks to the Spaniards. Ten forts, some in ruins, testify to a violent past. The most ancient is Fort Ste-Agathe, built in 1531 by François I. In time it was a penal colony and a retirement center for soldiers of the colonial wars.

The French government in 1971 purchased the largest hunk of the island and turned it into a national park and botanical garden. The best beaches are along the north coast facing mainland France.

ACCOMMODATIONS & DINING

Le Relais de la Poste. Place d'Armes, 83540 Porquerolles. ☎ 04-94-58-30-26. Fax 04-94-58-33-57. 30 rms. TEL. 496F–716F ($99.20–$143.20) double. Rates include continental breakfast. No credit cards. Closed late Sept to Easter.

On a small square in the heart of the island's main settlement, this pleasant little hotel offers Provençal-style rooms with loggias. The oldest hotel on the island, it opened "sometime in the 19th century" and is today managed by the good-natured sixth generation of its founding family. The hotel has a billiard table and a crêperie that sells only sugared snack-style dessert crêpes that provide quick bursts of energy but nothing particularly nutritious. It also maintains a kiosk that'll rent bicycles for 40F ($8) per day.

✪ **Mas du Langoustier.** 83400 Porquerolles. ☎ **04-94-58-30-09.** Fax 04-94-58-36-02. 50 rms. TV TEL. 945F–1,271F ($189–$254.20) double. Rates include half board. AE, DC, MC, V. Closed Oct 15–Apr 25.

In a large park on the island's western tip, this is a tranquil resort hotel—actually an old Provençal *mas* (farmhouse)—with tennis courts and a view of a lovely pine-ringed bay. Employees greet guests in a covered wagon by the jetty. Should you visit only for a meal, prices begin at 320F ($64). The menu is the finest in the islands, mainly seafood in a light nouvelle style. Try the loup (sea bass) with Noilly Prat in puff pastry or tender kid with dried tomatoes roasted in casserole. The house wine is an agreeable rosé. You can drink and dine on the terraces.

ILE DE PORT-CROS

Lush subtropical vegetation reminiscent of a Caribbean island makes this a green paradise, 3 miles long and 1¼ miles wide. No cars are allowed on the island.

The most mountainous of the archipelago, Port-Cros has been a French national park since 1963. Although a fire in 1892 devastated the island, it has bounced back with pine forests and ilexes. Bird-watchers in France flock here to observe nearly 100 different species. Many trails are marked on the island, mainly for day-trippers. The most walked and the most scenic is *sentier botanique.* More adventurous and athletic visitors take the 6-mile *circuit historique* (you'll need a packed lunch for this one). Divers follow a 300-yard trail from Plage de la Palud to the islet of Rascas. A plastic guide sheet identifies the underwater flora. Thousands of pleasure craft call here annually, which does little to help the fragile environent of the island.

ACCOMMODATIONS & DINING

✪ **Le Manoir.** 83400 Ile de Port-Cros. ☎ **04-94-05-90-53.** Fax 04-94-05-90-89. 23 rms. TEL. 1,460F–2,100F ($292–$420) double. Rates include half board. DC, MC, V. Closed Oct–May 8.

This 18th-century colonial-style mansion, set in a park where there's a large pool, is the best place to stay on the island. The terrace overlooks the bay of Port-Cros, shaded by bamboo, eucalyptus, and oleander. Chef Sylvain Chaduteau serves lobster-and-fish terrine, several seasoned meats, and fresh local fish with baby vegetables, as well as regional goat cheese and velvety mousses. The Buffets charge 250F ($50) for a fixed-price menu, and dinner is served daily from 8 to 9:30pm.

17 Grand Canyon du Verdon

Trigance: 45 miles S of Digne-les-Baines, 12½ miles W of Castellane; 27 miles NW of Draguignan, 53 miles E of Manosque La-Palud-sur-Verdon: 40 miles S of Digne-les-Baines, 15½ miles W of Castellane, 37 miles NW of Draguignan, 41 miles E of Manosque

Over the centuries the Verdon River, a tributary of the Durance, has cut Europe's biggest canyon into the limestone plateau surrounding it. The canyon runs from pont de Soleils to Lac Ste-Croix, a distance of 13 miles east to west. The upper section of the gorge, to the east, is between 700 and 5,350 feet wide, and the lower section narrows to between 20 and 350 feet. All along its length, the cliffs rise and fall, with the distance from the plateau at the top to the depths of the gorge varying from 875 feet at one point to 2,500 feet at another.

Vertiginous roads wind along both rims of the canyon, giving you the opportunity to pull over at any of several scenic belvederes. Among the best of these is the

Balcon de la Mescla, the first stop traveling west from Trigance on the canyon's south side, where the sheer cliffs drop 900 feet to the river. A short distance away is **Falaise de Cavaliers** (Horseman's Cliff), dropping 1,075 feet and signaling the beginning of the **Corniche Sublime,** where the gorge plunges to depths of 1,425 feet along a stretch running west to Aiguines. In between these scenic stops, you can actually drive across the canyon on the dramatic **pont de l'Artuby,** a single-arched 400-foot-long span 2,125 feet above the river.

Ancient villages cling to rocky outcroppings along the two rim roads, offering information and accommodations to the area's visitors. At **Aiguines,** a private castle dominates the skyline, flanked by four turrets and covered in polished variegated tiles. On Route 19, $5^{1}/_{2}$ miles north of the canyon on its western end, sits **Moustiers-Ste-Marie,** a medieval village of potters selling their wares—but beware, prices here are celestial, especially in July and August when tourist dollars are easy to come by.

ESSENTIALS

GETTING THERE   From the Riviera, follow A85 for 52 miles northwest from Cannes to Castellane, then take Rte. 952 west to the intersection with Rte. 955 and proceed along 955 south to Trigance, about $12^{1}/_{2}$ miles. From here, continue south to Rte. 71, 2 miles distant, and take a left to travel west along the southern edge of the canyon. At Les-Salles-sur-Verdon, on the banks of Lac St-Croix, turn right on D957 and drive north, crossing the Verdon where it flows into Lac St-Croix, then just south of Moustiers-Ste-Marie turn right again on Rte. 952 to trace the north side of the canyon back to the east.

VISITOR INFORMATION   Information about accommodations, activities, and events is available from the **Verdon Accueil,** 83630 Aiguines (☎ 04-94-70-21-64) or rue Nationale, 04120 Castellane (☎ 04-92-83-67-36); the **Office de Tourisme d'Castellane,** 04120 Castellane (☎ 04-92-83-61-14); or the **Office de Tourisme d'Esparron,** 04800 Esparron (☎ 04-92-77-15-45).

EXPLORING THE CANYON

Activities available in the canyon include guided hikes from the **Bureau des Guides,** 04120 La-Palud-sur-Verdon (☎ 04-92-77-30-50), and the **Office de Tourisme d'Esparron,** 04800 Esparron (☎ 04-92-77-15-45); canoeing and kayaking, through the **Aqua Vivae Est,** La Piscine, 04120 Castellane (☎ 04-92-83-75-74), and the **Club Nautique,** 04800 Esparron (☎ 04-92-77-15-25); and rafting trips conducted by **Acti Raft,** 04120 Castellane (☎ 04-92-83-76-64), and **Aqua Verdon,** 04120 Castellane (☎ 04-92-83-72-75).

A deservedly popular walk in the area is a **2-hour round-trip trek** launched at the parking lot at Samson Corridor. The route is clearly marked as it bends its way to a tunnel after Point Sublime. Continue your trek to a footbridge spanning the Baou River. After crossing it, go straight ahead through another two tunnels until you reach a belvedere with a panoramic sweep of the Trescaïre Chaos. For the tunnels, carry along a flashlight.

A more strenuous **6- to 8-hour walk** starts at the Chalet de la Maline on the Crest Road and goes for about $9^{1}/_{2}$ miles to Point Sublime. The footpath is marked with arrows. Again, you'll need a flashlight, but this trek is so long that food and water are also recommended. Before heading out, you can call ☎ 04-92-83-68-06 or 04-92-83-65-38 for a taxi company that'll pick you up at a designated time when you reach Point Sublime.

ACCOMMODATIONS

Auberge Point-Sublime. 04120 Point Sublime, Rougon. ☎ **04-92-83-60-35.** 12 rms. TEL. 263F–283F ($52.60–$56.60) double. MC, V. Closed Nov 3–Mar. From Castellane, drive 12 miles north toward Moustiers-Ste-Marie; it's beside the road on the distant outskirts of Rougon.

This hotel offers simple, unpretentious rooms, each with a congenially battered roster of old-fashioned but not antique furniture. You do get views over the gorge and a location that's a convenient 1¼ miles south of the Couloir Samson, the point where many trekkers exit from hikes up and down the bottom of the nearby gorge. The restaurant serves all-Provençal fixed-price meals at 80F to 105F ($16 to $21). Specialties are civets of both rabbit and lamb, a truffle-studded omelet, and crayfish with truffles.

✪ **Château de Trigance**. 83840 Trigance, Var. ☎ **04-94-76-91-18.** Fax 04-94-85-68-99. 8 rms, 2 suites. TV TEL. 600F–900F ($120–$180) double; 900F ($180) suite. AE, MC, V. Closed Nov 12–Mar 22.

This is the district's best hotel, rising on a rocky spur above a hamlet of fewer than 120 full-time inhabitants; it occupies the core of a 9th- and 10th-century fortress. There's no room for a garden, but views extend from virtually every window out over the Provençal plain. The rooms contain strong hints of their medieval origins, baldaquin-style beds, and modern amenities that were added in 1969. At that time a team of entrepreneurs took an abandoned ruin and rebuilt it into the Relais & Châteaux you see today.

An unusual aspect is the dining room, originally used to store weapons. Notice the vaulted ceiling that was, in accordance with the era's techniques, built without groins or a central key. A wooden form was built and carefully chiseled stones laid into position on top. When complete, the form was burnt away and the vaulting remained—somewhat precariously until it was shored up with additional mortar. Nonguests are welcomed for full meals served daily from 12:30 to 2pm and 7 to 9pm. Fixed-price lunches are 150F to 280F ($30 to $56); fixed-price dinners run 210F to 280F ($42 to $56); à la carte main courses go for 135F to 154F ($27 to $30.80). The fare is intensely cultivated: a "trilogy" of foie gras that includes versions with truffles, with sweetbreads, and marinated in red Maurès wine; a tarte fine of scallops with sesame sauce, a leek fondue, and saffron-flavored endive; and roast leg of lamb en surprise, with a "spaghetti" of zucchini and cream of garlic confit.

Hôtel du Grand Canyon. Falaise des Cavaliers, 83630 Aiguines. ☎ **04-94-76-91-31.** Fax 04-94-76-92-29. 15 rms. TV TEL. 700F–780F ($140–$156) double. Rates include half board. AE, DC, MC, V. Closed Oct–Apr.

This is the most charming, most desirable, and most interesting hotel along the south bank of the Verdon canyon. It's on a rocky outcropping above the precipice, vertiginously close to the edge, and exists only because of the foresight of the grandfather of the present owner. In 1946, on holiday in Provence from his home in the foggy northern French province of Pas de Calais, he fell in love with the site, opened a brasserie, and secured permission to build a hotel here. In 1982 his charming grandson, Georges Fortini, erected the artfully positioned two-story hotel you see today. The rooms are simple but comfortable, with light-grained wood and off-white walls. Set on a 10-acre tract on the Corniche Sublime, it features a glassed-in restaurant overlooking a 1,075-foot drop to the canyon bottom. Meals are served daily from 11:30am to 9:30pm, with fixed-price menus at 95F to 140F ($19 to $28).

Hôtel Les Gorges du Verdon. 04120 La-Palud-sur-Verdon. ☎ **04-92-77-38-26.** Fax 04-92-77-35-00. 27 rms. TV TEL. 700F–870F ($140–$174) double. Rates include half board. AE, MC, V. Closed mid-Oct to mid-Apr.

Grand Canyon du Verdon

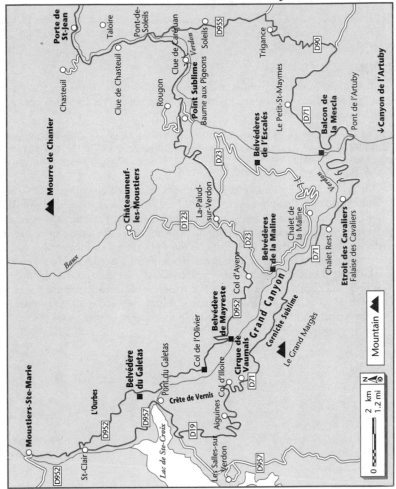

This hotel was inspired by an earth-toned Provençal *mas*. It's in the heart of La-Palud-sur-Verdon (pop. 250, alt. 3,000 ft.), about 4 miles west of the canyon edge. Though you won't be able to see the canyon from the windows of this place, views over the rugged countryside stretch out on virtually every side. The rooms aren't plush or even particularly cozy, designed as they were for budget-conscious nature enthusiasts who often spend their days driving and trekking. The severity of each is softened by the presence of a private terrace. Virtually everyone opts for half board (obligatory in midsummer).

Hôtel Le Vieil Amandier. 83840 Trigance, Var. ☎ **04-94-76-92-92.** Fax 04-94-85-68-65. 12 rms. TEL. 260F–320F ($52–$64) double. MC, V. Closed Nov 12–Apr 5.

At the edge of town, this hotel offers clean, uncomplicated guest rooms and a dining room with straightforward but thoughtfully prepared cuisine. Half the rooms face the pool and get southern light; the remainder are just as comfortable but without views. The largest is the rustic and woodsy no. 6; nos. 3 and 4 are more Provençal, and the others are blandly international. About half contain TVs. Your hosts are

Cécile and Bernard Clap (Bernard is the hamlet's mayor). They maintain a pleasant, unpretentious restaurant where fixed-price lunch and dinner at 100F to 280F ($20 to $56) are served daily.

DINING

Many of the inns recommended under "Accommodations," above, are also the finest places to dine—notably the **Château de Trigance** (for the absolutely best, albeit most expensive, cuisine).

✪ **Les Santons**. Place de l'Eglise, 04360 Moustiers-Ste-Marie, Alpes-de-Haut-Provence. ☎ **04-92-74-66-48.** Reservations recommended. Main courses 130F–170F ($26–$34); fixed-price menus 220F–300F ($44–$60). AE, DC, MC, V. Mon noon-2pm, Wed–Sun noon–2pm and 7:30–9:30pm. Closed Dec–Jan. FRENCH/PROVENÇAL.

One of the region's most charming restaurants occupies a stone-sided 12th-century house adjacent to the village church. You'll find a cozy dining room filled with 19th-century paintings and antique pottery, reminders of Old Provence, and fewer than 20 seats. A terrace, lined with flowering plants, doubles the seating space but only during clement weather. Claude Fichot is the sophisticated chef who makes as much use as possible of fresh local ingredients. These include truffles and honey, both of which might be used for roast turbot with truffles, homemade noodles studded with truffles and chunks of foie gras, chicken roasted with lavender-scented honey and Provençal spices, and Sisteron lamb roasted with honey and spices and served with a herb-scented ratatouille and gratin dauphinoise (potatoes with grated cheese).

The Western Riviera: From St-Tropez to Cannes to Cap d'Antibes

6

The western part of the Côte d'Azur begins at glittering St-Tropez and ends at the even more elegant Cap d'Antibes. In between are mostly middle-class resort towns, like St-Raphaël, scattered along a coast that also features the wild and desolate landscape of the Massif de l'Estérel.

At the doorstep of St-Tropez, Port Grimaud contrasts with the antiquity of many communities, for it's a well-to-do pseudo fishing village that sprang up out of a swamp, fully developed, just three decades ago. Ste-Maxime and Fréjus offer some of the area's best budget accommodations, having been taken over by French families in search of a holiday getaway on the once-exclusive coast.

The area does, of course, embrace Cannes, the most famous resort in the region because of the glitz and glamour surrounding its film festival, which overflows into the upscale La Napoule-Plage, home of the Clews Museum.

Inland, the terrain climbs away from the coast to the hillside communities of Grasse, with its perfume distilleries, and Mougins, a charming old village and culinary center that makes for a romantic retreat. Food also lures gastronomes to Golfe-Juan, which features one of the region's best restaurants, Chez Tétou, a stop for a rich bowl of bouillabaisse.

Nightlife is the focus of neighboring Juan-les-Pins, attracting spirited adventurers to its all-night jazz clubs and discos. Nearby Vaullaris hosts Galerie Madoura, a pottery firm with exclusive rights to reproduce Picasso's earthenware designs. Antibes also profits from its association with Picasso by containing the museum dedicated to his life and work. This largely middle-class resort gives way to Cap d'Antibes, the peninsular resort that's as tony today as when F. Scott Fitzgerald used it as the setting for *Tender Is the Night*.

EXPLORING THE REGION BY CAR

Here's how to link together the best of the region if you rent a car:
Day 1 Begin at **St-Tropez,** where you can try to find your own bronzed god or goddess sunning or swimming in the surf that was famous even before Bardot made *And God Created Woman*. Take a room for the night, then enjoy a day on the beach and in the shops before spending an evening in the clubs.

The French Riviera

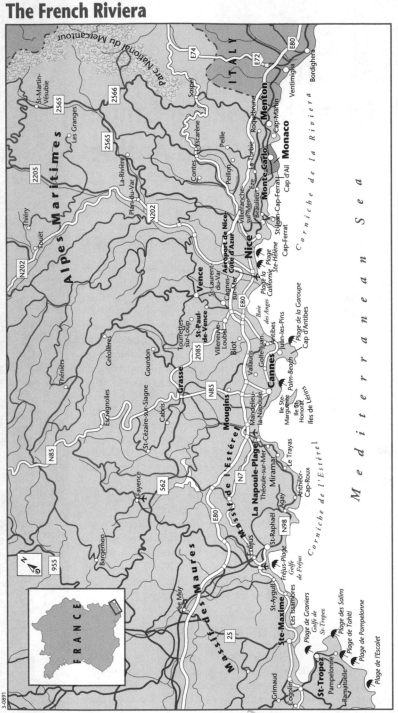

Day 2   Keep your hotel room in St-Tropez and make a day excursion. Drive 4 miles west, taking Rte. 98A to La Foux, then transfer to Rte. 98 and head northeast for the last half mile to arrive in **Port Grimaud,** the urban architect François Spoerry's vision of a coastal village. Stay on Rte. 98 headed northeast for another 4 miles to reach **Ste-Maxime,** which, like so many of the smaller resorts, is mainly about the beach. Return to St-Tropez for the night.

Day 3   Head northeast on Rte. 98 again, bypassing Port Grimaud and Ste-Maxime, then drive another 12^1/$_2$ miles to spend the morning in **Fréjus,** with its Roman ruins. From here, go 2 miles east on Rte. 98 to reach the beach at **St-Raphaël.** You can choose accommodations in whichever of the two resorts you like best.

Day 4   Drive northeast on Rte. 98 along the edge of the **Massif de l'Estérel** on your way to La Napoule-Plage, 18^1/$_2$ miles distant. You might turn inland along the way to view the surrounding landscape from the vantage point of Mont Vinaigre, 1,962 feet above sea level; Pic du Cap Roux, 1,438 feet above sea level; or Pic de l'Ours, 1,627 feet above the sea. You may also wish to see the panoramic view offered from St-Honorat's **Grotte de la Ste-Baume** or gaze into the depths of the **Gorge du Mal-Infernet.** Continue onward to **La Napoule-Plage,** which functions as a satellite community of Cannes, balancing that resort with its relatively low-key lifestyle. Overnight here.

Day 5   In the morning, follow Rte. 98 as it bends eastward around the Gulf of Napoule, driving 5 miles into **Cannes,** where you can stroll along the region's most famous beach, try your luck in the casinos, or expose yourself to a nightlife that's more sophisticated than any other offered along this stretch of coast. This is a day unto itself, so plan to stay at least a night.

Day 6   Briefly turning inland, follow Rte. 85 north for 10 miles to **Grasse,** with its perfume distilleries, then backtrack 6 miles along Rte. 85 to **Mougins,** an old stone village that contrasts with the modernity of much of the coast. For a change of pace, spend the night at this gastronomic citadel.

Day 7   Backtrack 4 miles into Cannes, then head northeast on Rte. 7, driving 3 miles into a cluster of communities that contrast middle-class values with the lifestyles of the rich and famous. Begin with **Golfe-Juan,** a middle ground to the exotica of Cannes or Cap d'Antibes. You may wish to take lunch here, dining on superb bouillabaisse, then continue on to **Vallauris,** standing at Golfe-Juan's inland edge. Here you'll definitely want to see Picasso's pottery. From Vallauris, get on Rte. 7 and follow the coastal road for 2 miles to **Juan-les-Pins,** on the Antibes peninsula, the primarily middle-class resort that sits in the midst of the grandeur that's the Côte d'Azur. Overnight here.

Day 8   On the same small peninsula lies **Cap d'Antibes,** an exclusive resort that contrasts with Juan-les-Pins. It borders **Antibes,** with its Picasso museum, a major attraction among the options offered during this excursion. Spend your final night here.

1 St-Tropez

543 miles S of Paris, 47 miles SW of Cannes

Sun-kissed lasciviousness is rampant in this carnival town, but the true Tropezian resents the fact that the port has such a bad reputation. "We can be classy too," one native has insisted. Creative people in the lively arts along with ordinary folk create a volatile mixture. One observer said that St-Tropez "has replaced Naples for those who accept the principle of dying after seeing it. It's a unique fate for a place to have made its reputation on the certainty of happiness."

Impressions

It was the happy mixture of old and young, wealthy and class. A person with no money could live like a millionaire and a millionaire could have fun living like a bohemian.
—Roger Vadim on St-Tropez

St-Tropez—this palimpsest of nostalgia—was greatly popularized by Brigitte Bardot in *And God Created Woman,* but it has been known for a long time. Colette lived here for many years. Even the late diarist Anaïs Nin, confidante of Henry Miller, posed for a little cheesecake on the beach here in 1939 in a Dorothy Lamour–style bathing suit. Earlier, St-Tropez was known to Signac, Matisse, and Bonnard, and even Maupassant before he died of syphilis.

Artists, composers, novelists, and the film colony are attracted to St-Tropez in summer. Trailing them is a line of humanity unmatched anywhere else on the Riviera for sheer flamboyance. Some of the most fashionable yachts bringing the chicest people anchor here in summer, disappearing long before the dreaded mistral of winter.

In 1995 Bardot pronounced St-Trop dead—"squatted by a lot of no-goods, drugheads, and villains." She swore she'd never go back, at least in summer. But 1997 saw her return, as headlines in France flashed the news that St-Tropez was "hot once again." Not only Bardot but other celebrities have been showing up, including Oprah Winfrey, Don Johnson, Quincy Jones, Barbra Streisand, Jack Nicholson, Robert DeNiro, and even Elton and Sly (not together!).

ESSENTIALS

GETTING THERE   The nearest rail station is in St-Raphaël, a neighboring resort; at the Vieux Port, four or five boats per day leave the **Gare Maritime de St-Raphaël,** rue Pierre-Auble (☎ **04-94-95-17-46**), for St-Tropez (trip time: 50 min.), costing 50F ($10) each way. Some 15 Sodetrav buses per day, leaving from the **Gare Routière** in St-Raphaël (☎ **04-94-95-24-82**), go to St-Tropez, taking 1^1/$_2$ to 2^1/$_4$ hours, depending on the bus and the traffic density, which during midsummer is usually horrendous. A one-way ticket costs 55F ($11). Buses run directly to St-Tropez from Toulon and Hyères.

If you drive, you'll have to squeeze your car into impossibly small parking spaces wherever you can find them. One large parking lot lies just south of place des Lices / place du XVe-Corps, several blocks inland from the port.

VISITOR INFORMATION   The **Office de Tourisme** is on quai Jean-Jaurès (☎ **04-94-97-45-21**).

VISITING THE TOP ATTRACTIONS

Near the harbor is the **Musée de l'Annonciade (Musée St-Tropez),** on place Grammont (☎ **04-94-97-04-01**), installed in the former chapel of the Annonciade. As a legacy from the artists who loved St-Tropez, the museum shelters one of the finest modern art collections on the Riviera. Many of the artists, including Paul Signac, depicted the port of St-Tropez. Opened in 1955, the collection includes such works as Van Dongen's yellow-faced *Women of the Balustrade* and paintings and sculpture by Bonnard, Matisse, Braque, Dufy, Utrillo, Seurat, Derain, and Maillol. The museum is open Wednesday to Monday: June to September from 10am to noon and 3 to 7pm and October and December to May from 10am to noon and 2 to 6pm (closed November). Admission is 30F ($6) for adults and 15F ($3) for children.

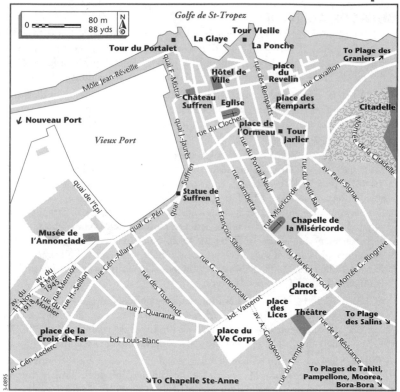

The **Château Suffren** is east from the port at the top end of quai Jean-Jaurès. Now home to occasional art exhibits, it was built in 980 by Comte Guillaume I of Provence.

Near the junction of quai Suffren and quai Jean-Jaurès stands the bronze **statue de Suffren,** paying tribute to Vice-Admiral Pierre André de Suffren. This St-Tropez hometown boy became one of the greatest sailors of 18th-century France, though he's largely forgotten today. And in the Vieille Ville, one of the most interesting streets is **rue de la Misércorde.** At the corner of rue Gambetta is the **Chapelle de la Misércorde,** with a blue, green, and gold tile roof.

A DAY AT THE BEACH

The hottest Riviera beaches are at St-Tropez. The best for families are those closest to the center, including the amusingly named **Plage de la Bouillabaisse** and **Plage des Graniers.** The more daring are the 6-mile sandy cresents at **Plage des Salins** and **Plage de Pampellone,** beginning some 2 miles from the town center and best reached by bike (below) if you're not driving. Called "notoriously decadent," ✪ **Plage de Tahiti** occupies the north end of the 3½-mile-long Pampellone, lined with concessions, cafes, and restaurants. It's a strip of golden sand that has long been favored by exhibitionists wearing next to nothing or truly nothing and crusing one another shamelessly. If you ever wanted to go topless or bottomless or wear a truly daring bikini, this is the place to do it. *Vive la France!*

OUTDOOR ACTIVITIES

BICYCLING   The largest outfitter for bikes and motorscooters is **Louis Mas,** 5 rue Josef-Quaranta (☎ **04-94-97-00-60**). It requires a deposit of 1,000F ($200), payable with American Express, MasterCard, or Visa, plus 48F ($9.60) per hour for a bike and 190F to 275F ($38 to $55) per hour for a motor scooter, depending on its size.

BOATING   The well-recommended **Suncap Company,** 15 quai de Suffren (☎ **04-94-97-11-23**), rents boats from 18 feet to 40 feet. The smallest can be rented to qualified sailors without a captain, but the larger ones come with a captain at the helm. Prices per day begin at 3,000F ($600).

GOLF   The nearest golf course, at the edge of Ste-Maxime, across the bay from St-Tropez, is the **Golf Club de Beauvallon,** boulevard des Collines (☎ **04-94-96-16-98**), a popular 18-hole course. Known for a terrain that allows you to walk rather than rent a cart, it charges 280F to 320F ($56 to $64) for 18 holes.

Sprawling over a rocky, vertiginous landscape that requires a golf cart and a lot of physical labor is the Don Harradine–designed **Golf de Ste-Maxime-Plaza,** route du Débarquement, Ste-Maxime (☎ **04-94-49-26-60**). Built in 1991 with the four-star Plaza de Ste-Maxime, it welcomes nonguests; phone to reserve tee-off times. Greens fees for 18 holes are 280F ($56) per person; rental of a cart for two golfers and their equipment is 125F ($25) per 18 holes.

SCUBA DIVING   Head for **Les Plongeurs du Golfe,** Nouveau Port de St-Tropez (☎ **04-94-56-81-27**). Its boat, *L'Idéal,* offers first-timers a one-on-one *baptême,* teaching the rudiments of scuba for 200F ($40). Experienced divers pay 235F ($47) for a one-tank dive, all equipment included. Reservations are needed.

TENNIS   Anyone who phones in advance can use the eight courts (both artificial grass and "Quick," a form of concrete) at the **Tennis-Club de St-Tropez,** route des Plages, in St-Tropez's industrial zone of St-Claude (☎ **04-94-97-80-76**), about half a mile from the resort's center. Open throughout the year, the courts rent for 100F ($20) per hour to 5pm and 120F ($24) per hour after 5pm.

SHOPPING

Though better stocked than the norm, **Choses,** quai Jean-Jaurès (☎ **04-94-97-03-44**), is a women's clothing store typical of the hundreds of middle-bracket, whimsically nonchalant shops that thrive along the Riviera. Its specialty is clingy and often provocative T-shirt dresses. **Galeries Tropéziennes,** 56 rue Gambetta (☎ **04-94-97-02-21**), crowds hundreds of unusual gift items—some worthwhile, some rather silly—and textiles into its rambling showrooms near place des Lices. The inspiration is Mediterranean, breezy and sophisticated.

In a resort that's increasingly loaded with purveyors of suntan lotion, touristy souvenirs, and T-shirts, **Jacqueline Thienot,** 12 rue Georges-Clemenceau (☎ **04-94-97-05-70**), maintains an inventory of Provençal antiques that's prized by dealers from as far away as Paris. The three-room shop is in a late 18th-century building that shows the 18th- and 19th-century antiques to their best advantage. Also sold are antique examples of Provençal wrought iron and rustic farm and homemaker's implements.

ACCOMMODATIONS
VERY EXPENSIVE

✪ **Hôtel Byblos.** Av. Paul-Signac, 83990 St-Tropez. ☎ **04-94-56-68-00.** Fax 04-94-56-68-01. 47 rms, 55 suites, 10 duplex suites. A/C MINIBAR TV TEL. 1,450F–2,950F ($290–$590) double; 2,700F–4,250F ($540–$850) suite; 4,300F–5,900F ($860–$1,180) duplex suite. AE, DC, MC, V. Closed Oct 15–Easter. Parking 140F ($28) in garage.

The builder said he created "an anti-hotel, a place like home." That's true if your home resembles a palace in Beirut with salons decorated with Phoenician gold statues from 3000 B.C. On a hill above the harbor, this deluxe complex has intimate patios and courtyards and seductive retreats filled with antiques and rare decorative objects, including polychrome carved woodwork on the walls, marquetry floors, and a Persian-rug ceiling. Every room is unique. In one, for example, there's a fireplace on a raised hearth, paneled blue-and-gold doors, and a bed recessed on a dais. Le Hameau contains 10 duplex suites built around a small courtyard with an outdoor spa. Some rooms have balconies overlooking an inner courtyard; others open onto a terrace of flowers.

Dining/Entertainment: You can dine by the pool at Les Arcades, enjoying Provençal food, or try an Italian restaurant offering an antipasta buffet, many pasta courses, and other typical fare from France's neighbor. Later in the evening you can dance on a circular floor surrounded by bas-relief columns in the hotel's nightclub, Caves du Roy. There are also two bars.

Services: Room service (24 hours), same-day laundry/valet, beauty salon.

Facilities: "High-fashion" pool, sauna.

✪ **Résidence de la Pinède.** Plage de la Bouillabaisse, 83990 St-Tropez. ☎ **04-94-55-91-00.** Fax 04-94-97-73-64. 36 rms, 7 suites. A/C MINIBAR TV TEL. 1,265F–4,290F ($253–$858) double; 2,310F–7,480F ($462–$1,496) suite. AE, DC, MC, V. Closed mid-Oct to Mar.

This four-star luxury hotel was built in the 1950s around a rustic stone-sided tower once used to store olives. Jean-Claude and Nicole Delion own this seaside Relais & Châteaux. The airy, spacious rooms are decorated in pastels; they open onto balconies or terraces with a view over the bay of St-Tropez. Stylishly offhanded, with a staff that seems constantly overburdened, the hotel is St-Tropez's only rival for the Byblos. It welcomes many North American and non-French guests and, though as luxurious as the Byblos, receives a more serious and staid clientele.

Dining/Entertainment: Excellent food, especially seafood, is served in the dining room or on the terrace under the pine trees. In the past, mainly residents of the hotel dined here. However, the cuisine of Hervé Quesnel, who worked at the deluxe Crillon in Paris, has drawn Tropezians anxious to sample his refined cooking with a Provençal flavor.

Services: Room service (24 hours), same-day laundry/valet.

Facilities: Kidney-shaped pool, beach.

EXPENSIVE

Hôtel La Mandarine. Rte. de Tahiti, 83990 St-Tropez. ☎ **04-94-97-06-66.** Fax 04-94-97-33-67. 38 rms, 4 suites. A/C MINIBAR TV TEL. 930F–1,160F ($186–$232) double; from 1,470F ($294) suite. Rates include continental breakfast. AE, DC, MC, V. Closed Oct 15–Mar 15. Take the road leading to Plage de Tahiti; it's just off the road, half a mile southeast of the center.

One of the area's finest hotels, La Mandarine is built in the Provençal style with strong angles, thick stucco walls, a tile roof, and patios. The rooms in the complex are luxuriously furnished and open onto one or more terraces. Some of the suites offer as many as three terraces. You definitely get glamour here. The restaurant specializes in *cuisine moderne* using fish and shellfish. There's also a heated pool and a private beach.

Hôtel Le Yaca. 1 bd. d'Aumale, 83900 St-Tropez. ☎ **04-94-97-11-79.** Fax 04-94-97-58-50. 20 rms, 2 suites. A/C TV TEL. 900F–2,500F ($180–$500) double; from 2,900F ($580) suite. AE, DC, MC, V. Closed Oct 6–Easter. Parking 130F ($26).

Built in 1722 off a narrow street in the old part of town, this was the first hotel in St-Tropez. Colette lived here in 1927, and before that it was the home of pre-impressionists like Paul Signac. The high-ceilinged reception area boasts a view of an inner courtyard filled with flowers. Many of the rooms also have views of this courtyard. Some are on the upper floor, with handmade terra-cotta floor tiles and massive ceiling timbers. There's a pool.

Hôtel Résidence des Lices. 135 av. Augustin-Grangeon, 83900 St-Tropez. ☎ **04-94-97-28-28.** 41 rms. A/C TV TEL. 400F–1,600F ($80–$320) double. AE, MC, V. Closed Jan 4–Easter and Nov 11–Dec 23.

One consistently reliable bet for lodgings in St-Tropez is this modern hotel in its own small garden close to place des Lices. The tastefully furnished rooms are tranquil, overlooking either the pool or the garden; their rates vary widely according to their view, the season, and their size. Breakfast is the only meal served, though afternoon snacks are provided beside the pool. It isn't associated in any way with the also-recommended Bistro des Lices.

✪ La Bastide de St-Tropez. Rte. des Carles, 83990 St-Tropez. ☎ **04-94-97-58-16.** Fax 04-94-97-21-71. 20 rms, 6 suites. A/C MINIBAR TV TEL. 980F–1,900F ($196–$380) double; 1,400F–3,500F ($280–$700) suite. AE, DC, MC, V. Closed Jan.

Near the landmark place des Lices, this tile-roofed replica of a Provençal manor house looks deliberately severe, but the interior is far more opulent. It contains a monumental staircase leading from a sun-filled living room to the upper floors. The guest rooms are named according to their unique decor, including "Rose of Bengal," "Fuschia," and "Tangerine Dawn." Each has a terrace or private garden, and some have Jacuzzis. Several, however, are quite small. The hotel is noted for its restaurant, L'Olivier, which receives a star from Michelin.

MODERATE

Hôtel Ermitage. Av. Paul-Signac, 83990 St-Tropez. ☎ **04-94-97-52-33.** Fax 04-94-97-10-43. 26 rms. TEL. 590F–990F ($118–$198) double. AE, DC, MC, V.

Attractively isolated amid the rocky heights of St-Tropez, this hotel was built in the 19th century as a private villa. Today its red-tile roof and green shutters shelter a plush hideaway. A walled garden is illuminated at night, and a cozy corner bar near a wood-burning fireplace takes the chill off blustery evenings. The guest rooms are pleasantly but simply furnished, and the staff can be charming. Breakfast is the only meal served.

Hôtel La Ponche. 3 rue des Remparts, 83990 St-Tropez. ☎ **04-94-97-02-53.** Fax 04-94-97-78-61. 18 rms. A/C MINIBAR TV TEL. 500F–2,200F ($100–$440) double. AE, MC, V. Closed Nov–Mar 15.

Overlooking the old fishing port, this has long been a cherished address, run by the same family for more than half a century. The hotel is filled with the original, airy paintings of Jacques Cordier, which adds to the elegant atmosphere. Each room has been newly redecorated and is well equipped, opening onto views of the sea. The hotel restaurant is big on Provençal charm and cuisine, and a sophisticated crowd can be found on its terrace almost any night in fair weather.

Hôtel La Tartane. Rte. des Salins, 83990 St-Tropez. ☎ **04-94-97-21-23.** Fax 04-94-97-09-16. 14 rms. A/C MINIBAR TV TEL. 650F–900F ($130–$180) double. AE, DC, V. Closed Oct 15–Easter.

This small-scale hotel is midway between the center of St-Tropez and the Plage des Salins, about a 3-minute drive from each. There's a stone-rimmed pool set into the garden, attractively furnished public rooms with terra-cotta floors, and an attentive management that works hard to keep everything pulled together. The guest rooms are well-furnished bungalows centered around the pool. Breakfasts are elaborate and attractive, lunch is offered between 1 and 3pm, and dinner is 7:30 to 9:30pm. Bouillabaisse and fresh fish from the Mediterranean are the specialties, and in addition to the à la carte dishes, there's a fixed-price menu at 120F ($24).

Hôtel Le Levant. Rte. des Salins, 83990 St-Tropez. ☎ **04-94-97-33-33.** Fax 04-94-97-76-13. 28 rms. MINIBAR TV TEL. 395F–850F ($79–$170) double. AE, DC, MC, V. Closed mid-Oct to Mar 15.

On the road leading from the old town of St-Tropez to the beach at Les Salins, this hotel is behind a screen of cypresses and palmettos. It was designed like a low-slung Provençal *mas*, with thick stucco walls and a tile roof. The rooms, in Provençal motifs, have big windows and white walls as well as private entrances overlooking the garden and its pool.

Hôtel Lou Cagnard. Av. Paul-Roussel, rte. de Ramatuelle, 83990 St-Tropez. ☎ **04-94-97-04-24.** Fax 04-94-97-09-44. 19 rms. TEL. 300F–500F ($60–$100) double. MC, V. Closed Nov 4–Dec 20.

This pleasant roadside inn, with a tile roof and green shutters, has quiet rooms in the rear overlooking the garden. M. and Mme Yvon have recently taken over and improved the hotel considerably, for it's fresher and more inviting than ever. They extend a warm welcome to their international guests. Most rooms are at the low end of the price scale. Continental breakfast is available. Of all the hotels in the center, Michelin gives this one the lowest rating, but at least it made the list—and it's a bargain in pricey St-Trop.

DINING

The restaurant at the **Résidence de la Pinède** (see "Accommodations," above) serves wonderful Provençal dishes.

EXPENSIVE

✪ **Bistrot des Lices.** 3 place des Lices. ☎ **04-94-97-29-00.** Reservations required in summer. Main courses 110F–235F ($22–$47); fixed-price menus 140F–525F ($28–$105) at lunch, 295F–525F ($59–$105) at dinner. AE, MC, V. Daily noon–2pm and 7:30–10:15pm (to midnight July–Aug). Closed Jan–Feb and all day Wed and Sun night in winter. FRENCH.

Don't let the "bistrot" in the name fool you. This is a first-class restaurant, with the most celebrated cuisine in St-Tropez, a glamorous clientele, and an amused and bemused staff. There's a glass-enclosed outdoor cafe, plus a piano bar/cafe in the outer room. In summer, tables are placed in the rear garden. Chef Laurent Tarridec, known for his creative use of local produce in its prime, features a menu filled with Provençal flavor. Aïoli, the garlicky mayonnaise of Provence, is delectable with certain fresh fish courses, like John Dory with fresh fennel and dried tomatoes. The classic vegetable medley, ratatouille, appears with oven-roasted turbot, and risotto might be flavored with snails and essence of fresh parsley. Young rabbit or roast veal is sometimes offered with fresh herbs and tomatoes. For a superb dessert, try the *gourmandise de chocolat très noir* (a medley of chocolate desserts). Some of the finest wines of Provence, many of them reasonably priced, appear on the menu.

✪ **L'Echalotte.** 35 rue Allard. ☎ **04-94-54-83-26.** Reservations recommended in summer. Main courses 80F–160F ($16–$32); fixed-price menus 98F–150F ($19.60–$30). AE, MC, V. Thurs 8–11:30pm, Fri–Wed 12:30–2pm and 8–11:30pm. Closed Nov 15–Dec 15. FRENCH.

This charming restaurant, with a tiny garden and simple but clean dining room and tables that, weather permitting, extend onto a veranda, serves consistently good food for moderate prices. Because of demand, the tables may be difficult to get, especially in peak summer weeks. The cuisine is solidly bourgeois, including grilled veal kidneys, crayfish with drawn-butter sauce, filet of turbot with truffles, and some of the classic dishes of southwestern France, like three preparations of foie gras and magret of duckling. The menu includes several species of fish, like sea bass and daurade royale, which can be cooked in a salt crust.

Les Mouscardins. 1 rue Portalet. ☎ **04-94-97-01-53.** Reservations required. Main courses 100F–300F ($20–$60); fixed-price menus 128F–198F ($25.60–$39.60). AE, MC, V. Daily noon–2:30pm and 7:30–11:30pm. Closed 2 weeks in Nov, and for lunch mid-Nov to mid-Mar. FRENCH.

At the end of St-Tropez's harbor, this restaurant has won awards for culinary perfection. The dining room is in formal Provençal style with an adjoining sunroom under a canopy. The menu includes classic Mediterranean dishes, and as an appetizer we recommend moules (mussels) marinières. The two celebrated fish stews of the Côte d'Azur are offered: bourride provençale and bouillabaisse. The fish dishes are excellent, particularly the loup (sea bass). The dessert specialties are soufflés made with Grand Marnier or Cointreau.

MODERATE

Le Girelier. Quai Jean-Jaurès. ☎ **04-94-97-03-87.** Main courses 150F–250F ($30–$50); fixed-price menu 160F ($32). AE, DC, MC, V. Daily noon–2:30pm and 7–11:30pm. Closed Jan to mid-Feb and Nov 11–Dec 15. PROVENÇAL.

The Rouets own this portside restaurant whose blue-and-white color scheme has become its own kind of trademark. Filled with rattan furniture and boasting a large glassed-in veranda, it serves well-prepared grilled fish in many versions, as well as bouillabaisse, served only for two. Also available is brochette of monkfish, a kettle of mussels, and *pipérade* (a Basque omelet with pimentoes, garlic, and tomatoes).

INEXPENSIVE

Chez Maggi. 7 rue Sibille. ☎ **04-94-97-16-12.** Reservations recommended. Fixed-price menu with wine 130F ($26). MC, V. Daily 8pm–3am. Closed Nov–Mar. PROVENÇAL/ITALIAN.

Across from Chez Nano (below), this restaurant retained the name it was given by two women during its earlier incarnation as a lesbian bar. Since its acquisition by the present owners, it has emerged as St-Tropez's most flamboyant gay restaurant/bar. At least half its floor space is devoted to a very busy bar, where patrons tend to range from 25 to 35 and whose turf extends out onto the pavement in front. There are no tables and chairs in front. Consequently, cruising at Chez Maggi, in the words of loyal patrons, is *très crazee* and seems to extend for blocks in every direction.

Meals are served in an adjoining dining room. Menu items include chicken salad with ginger, goat-cheese salad, *petits farcis provençaux* (local vegetables stuffed with minced meat and herbs), brochettes of sea bass with lemon sauce, and a well-recommended chicken curry with coconut milk, capers, and cucumbers.

Chez Nano. Place de la Mairie. ☎ **04-94-97-01-66.** Reservations recommended. Main courses 100F–400F ($20–$80). AE, MC, V. May–Sept, daily 1–3pm and 8pm–midnight; Oct–Apr, Wed–Mon 1–3pm and 8pm–midnight. Closed Jan–Feb. FRENCH.

This restaurant/bar has been a stylish fixture on the St-Tropez scene since it was founded by Nano (an omnipresent celebrity who seems to know every show-biz personality in France) many ages ago. The cozy bar is outfitted with varnished wooden panels, oil paintings, and photos of Nano welcoming the stylish and famous (Elton John, George Michaels, Michael Bolton); the crowd is heavily gay and fashionable. Glasses of champagne are 65F ($13) and served to an animated crowd that seems to remain in place every night from 7pm to 6am the next morning. (Like the restaurant, the bar is closed Tuesday off-season.)

Adjacent to the bar is a restaurant of about 35 tables, giving you lots of opportunities for table gazing. Menu items are consciously gastronomic and artful, like lobster salad, an adventurous tartare of salmon and lobster that's advisable only for the strong and the brave, tournedos Rossini, grilled jumbo shrimp, and fricassée of scallops. Except for one or two costly seafood dishes, most prices are quite reasonable.

✪ **Le Bar à Vin.** 13 rue des Feniers. ☎ **04-94-97-46-10.** Reservations recommended. Main courses 80F–97F ($16–$19.40); fixed-price menu 100F ($20). MC, V. May–Sept, daily 7pm–1am; Oct–Apr, Thurs–Tues 7pm–1am. Closed Jan. FRENCH/PROVENÇAL.

This appealing and reasonably priced bistro is close to place des Lices. In summer the guests tend to be Europeans in their 20s and 30s on holiday. The crowd is mixed, though heavily gay male. Things are calmer in winter, when the diners are usually locals. Managed by a bilingual entrepreneur named Jean-Jacques (nicknamed Bill), it boasts paneled walls and a red-tile floor by the ceramic artist Alain Vagh. The menu items are designed to accompany a small but choice selection of wines, at 20F to 25F ($4 to $5) per glass. Specialties reek with Provençal and Mediterranean flavors, like sardines en escabèche (grilled sardines marinated in olive oil, herbs, and vinegar and served cold), gratin of eggplant with goat's cheese, and grilled beefsteak and veal.

ST-TROPEZ AFTER DARK

On the lobby level of the Hôtel Byblos, **Les Caves du Roi,** avenue Paul-Signac (☎ **04-94-58-68-00**), is the most self-consciously chic nightclub in St-Tropez. It's the kind of place where, if Aristotle Onassis were still alive and roving, he'd camp out with a cellular phone for late-night trysts. Entrance is free, but drink prices begin at 140F ($28).

Le Papagayo, in the Résidence du Nouveau-Port, rue Gambetta (☎ **04-94-97-07-56**), is one of the largest nightclubs in town, with two floors, three bars, and lots of attractive women and men from throughout the Mediterranean eager to pursue their bait. The decor was inspired by the psychedelic 1960s. Entrance is 90F ($18) and includes the first drink.

Le Pigeonnier, 13 rue de la Ponche (☎ **04-94-97-36-85**), rocks, rolls, and welcomes a crowd that's 80% to 85% gay, male, and 20 to 50. Most of the socializing revolves around the long and narrow bar, where menfolk from all over Europe seem to enjoy chitchatting. There's also a dance floor. Entrance is 70F ($14) and includes your first drink.

Located below the Hôtel Sube, the **Café de Paris,** sur le Port (☎ **04-94-97-00-56**), is one of the most consistently popular hangouts. An attempt has been made to glorify a utilitarian room with turn-of-the-century globe lights, an occasional 19th-century bronze, masses of artificial flowers, and a long zinc bar. The crowd is irreverent and animated. Busy even in winter, after the yachting crowd departs, it's open daily.

The reporter Leslie Maitland once described the kind of crowd attracted to the **Café Sénéquier,** sur le Port (☎ **04-94-97-00-90**), at cocktail hour: "What else can one do but gawk at a tall, well-dressed young woman who appears *comme il faut* at Sénéquier's with a large white rat perched upon her shoulder, with which she occasionally exchanges little kisses, while casually chatting with her friends?"

For a gay hotspot, check out the action at the bar of **Chez Maggi** or cruise over to **Chez Nano** or **Le Bar à Vin** (see "Dining," above).

2 Port Grimaud

4 miles W of St-Tropez, 17 miles S of Fréjus

Inspired by both Europe's ancient fishing villages and the wealthy dockside neighborhoods of St. Petersburg, Fla., this 247-acre marine village was created in a former swamp by the urban architect François Spoerry. Contractors broke ground in 1966, utilizing 4 miles of 13-foot-deep canals to drain the wetlands, and now 2,500 Provençal-style homes (including that of Joan Collins) line the fingerlike extensions of a 7¹/₂-mile basin capable of docking 3,000 boats. Sitting on an island of its own, the hamlet's **Eglise St-François-d'Assise** features stained glass by Victor Vasarély and a great view from its bell tower.

Port Grimaud was hailed as a great success upon opening, one journalist calling the community "the most magnificent fake since Disneyland." In this miniature Provençal version of Venice, there are no roads or cars, and it's exceptionally clean and quiet, as mandated by the governing residents' association. However, it's an actual working village—as illustrated by the main square, lined with shops, cafes, banks, a post office, and a church. One point of interest: **Denise Spoerry Decoration,** 1 rue de Ponant (☎ **04-94-56-16-63**), is an interior-decor shop owned by the wife of the village's creator, François Spoerry; it sells lamps and other items designed by the couple and their backup team. If you plan to eat or shop in Port Grimaud, be warned: This isn't a cheap town, and disproportionate prices reflect its status as a man-made tourist center.

A mile and a half inland, at a southeastern edge of the Massif des Maures, the authentically ancient village of **Grimaud** offers counterpoints to its fraudulent namesake. Steep, narrow alleys run between restored Gothic homes that sit in shadows cast by the ruins of a multitowered **feudal castle,** once the stronghold of the Grimaldi family and a small army of Knights Templar. Their legacy is still evident, and you can follow the rue des Templiers to view the **Maison des Templiers,** which isn't open to the public, and the neighboring 12th-century **Eglise St-Michel.**

ESSENTIALS

GETTING THERE   The nearest train station is in St-Raphaël, a 30-minute drive east. Taxis line up at St-Raphaël's station to carry passengers to Port Grimaud. The fare is about 225F ($45) each way. There are also about six daily buses running from St-Raphaël to Port Grimaud. For **information on bus service** to Port Grimaud and throughout the region, call Sodetrav (☎ **04-94-97-88-51**). By car from St-Tropez, drive 3 miles west on A98 to Rte. 98, then drive 1 mile north to the Port Grimaud exit. From Fréjus, follow Rte. 98 south to the exit.

VISITOR INFORMATION   You can get additional information about accommodations and attractions in the **Offices de Tourisme** at **St-Tropez,** quai Jean-Jaurès (☎ **04-94-97-45-21**); **Grimaud,** boulevard des Aliziers (☎ **04-94-43-26-98**); **Ste-Maxime,** promenade Simon-Lorière (☎ **04-94-96-19-24**); and **Fréjus,** rue Jean-Jaurès (☎ **04-94-17-19-19**).

ACCOMMODATIONS

Hôtel Giraglia. Place du 14-Juin, 83310 Port Grimaud, Var. ☎ **04-94-56-31-33.** Fax 04-94-56-33-77. 43 rms, 6 suites. A/C MINIBAR TV TEL. 665F–1,665F ($133–$333) double; 1,515F–2,065F ($303–$413) suite. Half board 160F ($32) per person extra. AE, DC, MC, V. Closed Oct–Apr 21.

Sitting on an extended dock between a canal and the beach, this hotel has the air of a rural Provençal inn (though it's fully modern). The illusion is carried over into rooms decorated in the styles of various bygone eras. The hotel surrounds a pool and features a sandy private beach. The restaurant, Amphitrite, serves creative variations of traditional Provençal cuisine, with fixed-price menus at 135F to 250F ($27 to $50). The hotel overlooks the bay of St-Tropez and in summer allows dining on the pool terrace.

DINING

You can also consider the dining possibilities offered at the **Hôtel Giraglia** (see "Accommodations," above).

La Table du Mareyeur. 10–11 place des Artisans. ☎ **04-94-56-06-77.** Reservations recommended. Main courses 100F–145F ($20–$29); fixed-price menus 150F ($30) at lunch (with wine and coffee), 250F ($50) at dinner (without wine or coffee). AE, DC, MC, V. Daily noon–3:30pm and 7pm–midnight. SEAFOOD.

This is one of the resort's most engaging seafood restaurants. Near the resort's entrance, with a marine theme that includes varnished wood and polished copper, it offers terrace seating overlooking a flotilla of deep-sea fishing craft and yachts. Scotland-born Ewan Scutcher is the hardworking master of ceremonies. The seafood is fresh and flavorful and includes bouillabaisse perked up with lobster and crayfish as well as lobster prepared in half a dozen ways, including salads, chowders, as part of a flavorful tagliatelle, and even in a fricassée with cream-based port-wine sauce. There's also filet of beef flambéed with peppercorns, chicken, and sautéed foie gras served with a glass of sweet Muscat wine.

La Tartane. 8 rue de l'Octogone. ☎ **04-94-56-38-32.** Reservations recommended. Main courses 60F–225F ($12–$45); fixed-price menus 150F–210F ($30–$42). Daily noon–3pm and 7–11pm. Closed mid-Nov to Mar. FRENCH/SEAFOOD.

Across from the village church, this restaurant has a terrace that opens onto a view of boats and yachts and a nautical theme. The lobsters and shellfish are kept in a bubbling aquarium, a focal point near the entrance. Consequently, you'll find lots of fresh shellfish, artfully arranged on oversize platters, lobsters galore, and fresh grilled fish; other choices include Bresse chicken in champagne, filet of beef with green peppercorns, tournedos Rossini (beef layered with foie gras), and a flavorful beef cooked with marrow sauce.

3 Ste-Maxime

15 miles SW of St-Raphaël, 38 miles SW of Cannes

Ste-Maxime is just across the gulf from glitzy St-Tropez, but its atmosphere is much more sedate. Young families are the major vacationers here, though an occasional refugee from across the water will come over to escape the see-and-be-seen crowd. The town is surrounded by the red cliffs of the Massif des Maures, protecting it from harsh weather. A 16th-century fort, built by the monks of Lérins (who also named the port), houses a museum. However, the wide sand stretches and the cafe-lined promenades lure travelers to spend their days basking in the sun. More active vacationers may want to try windsurfing or waterskiing in the calm waters or even golfing (see "Outdoor Activities" under St-Tropez). The best thing about Ste-Maxime is the price—though the town isn't as in vogue as St-Tropez, it's fun and affordable.

ESSENTIALS

GETTING THERE   There's no train service to Ste-Maxime. If you're coming from St-Raphaël, call **Sodetrav** buses (☎ 04-94-53-78-46). Buses also travel to Ste-Maxime from St-Tropez. Boats take passengers from St-Tropez to Ste-Maxime from July to September. The trip takes about 20 minutes and costs 60F ($12)—only slightly more than bus fare for a much more pleasant ride. **Transports Maritimes MMG,** quai L.-Condroyer (☎ **04-94-96-51-00**), provides the service.

GETTING AROUND   At 13 rue Magali, **Rent Bike** (☎ **04-94-43-98-07**) rents bikes and mopeds with which you can explore the town and the countryside. Mountain bikes are 80F ($16) per day, with a 1,500F ($300) deposit; mopeds are 90F ($18), with a 2,500F ($500) deposit.

VISITOR INFORMATION   The **Office de Tourisme** is on promenade Simon-Lorière (☎ **04-94-96-19-24**).

SEEING THE SIGHTS

The beaches are the main attraction here—Ste-Maxime has four (see below)—but if you want to explore the city, start with the 16th-century **Tour Carrée des Dames** (Dames Tower) at place des Aliziers. It was originally a defensive structure; later it housed the Ste-Maxime courts. Today it's home to the **Musée des Traditions Locales** (☎ **04-94-96-70-30**), with exhibits on the area's history and traditions. The museum is open Wednesday to Monday: April to October from 10am to noon and 3 to 6pm and November to March from 3 to 6pm only. Admission is 15F ($3) for adults and 5F ($1) for children. Facing the tower is the **Eglise Ste-Maxime,** with a green marble altar from the former Carthusian monastery of La Verne in the Massif des Maures. The choir stalls date from the 15th century.

St-Maxime hosts various markets, including a daily **flower-and-food market** on rue Fernand-Bessy. Vendors tend their stands Monday to Saturday from 6am to 1pm and 4:30 to 8pm. On Thursday a **crafts market** is held on and around place du Marché; on Friday vendors sell a variety of knickknacks on place Jean-Mermoz. In the pedestrian streets of the old town, an **arts-and-crafts fair** takes place daily in summer from 4 to 11pm.

Outside town are several worthy sights. About 6 miles north on the road to Muy is the **Musée du Phonagraphe et de la Musique Méchanique** (☎ **04-94-26-50-52**). This extensive display of audio equipment (such as one of Edison's original "talking machines" and an audiovisual pathegraphe used to teach foreign language in 1913) is the result of one woman's 40-year obsession. Sometimes she gives personal tours. The museum is open Easter to September only, Wednesday to Sunday from 10am to noon and 2:30 to 6pm. Admission is 25F ($5).

If you're more of a nature lover than a technology buff, you may prefer to head to the little town of **Sémaphore.** Follow the signs along boulevard Bellevue for 1 mile north of town to have a panoramic view of the mountains and oceans from an altitude of 400 feet. There are also many hiking trails that wind along the coast or into the mountains. The tourist office has maps, or you can head for the **Sentier du Littoral,** a trail that meanders along the coast toward St-Tropez and has access to the sea at almost all points along the way.

A DAY AT THE BEACH

At least four worthy beaches are nearby. Two beaches lie an easy walk from the town's commercial core. Across the road from the casino is **Plage du Casino,** which we propose that you avoid because of the fumes from the nearby roadway, the narrow sands, and the hordes of sunbathers. A better bet is **Plage de la Croisette,** a wider, nominally less congested expanse that's a 2-minute walk west of Plage du Casino. The most appealing of the three is **Plage de la Nartelle** and the adjacent **Plage des Eléphants,** broad expanses of clean, fine-textured light beige sand about 1$^{1}/_{4}$ miles west of town. (To reach them, follow signs along the coastal road pointing to St-Tropez.) There you can rent a mattress from any of several concessionaires for around 70F ($14) and gaze out on all kinds of bodies cavorting or sunning.

ACCOMMODATIONS

Although hotels are less expensive here than in the neighboring towns, you may find that you're required to pay for half board in July and August and that most places are closed in winter. May, June, and September are the best times to find a good deal.

MODERATE

Hôtel La Belle Aurore. 4 bd. Jean-Moulin, 83120 Ste-Maxime. ☎ **04-94-96-02-45.** Fax 04-94-96-63-87. 17 rms. TV TEL. 600F–1,900F ($120–$380) double. AE, CB, DC, MC, V. Closed Jan 7–Feb, Oct 11–24, and Nov 16–Dec 20.

La Belle Aurore is on its own private beach. It's without argument the finest address in Ste-Maxime; if it has a serious challenger at all, it's Les Santolines (see below). The large terrace dining area is the perfect place to enjoy a meal from the restaurant. Though the well-furnished guest rooms aren't air-conditioned, each has a terrace overlooking the sea; the breezes keep the temperature inside comfortable.

Hôtel La Croisette. 2 bd. des Romarins, 83120 Ste-Maxime. ☎ **04-94-96-17-75.** Fax 04-94-96-52-40. 17 rms. MINIBAR TV TEL. 390F–980F ($78–$196) double. AE, CB, MC, V. Closed Nov–Feb.

This hotel is charming, surrounded by its own lush garden. In the pleasant outdoor dining area the chef presents flavorful dishes prepared with fresh ingredients. The room rates vary according to what kind of view you prefer; those with a balcony and sea view are most expensive; those that open onto the garden, the least. Maintenance here is high, and the hotel has an intimate aura.

Hôtel Les Santolines. Quartier de la Croisette, 83120 Ste-Maxime. ☎ **04-94-96-31-34.** Fax 04-94-49-22-12. 13 rms. TV TEL. 650F–800F ($130–$160) double. CB, MC, V. Closed Jan 6–Mar 3.

This is a good choice for those who want remove themselves from the madding crowds. Les Santolines is 10 minutes from the busy center area but still close to the beach. The building is arranged around a grassy courtyard that includes a pool and the town's most inviting *jardin fleuri*. The rooms are comfortable and private; most have balconies. The hotel also has private tennis courts.

INEXPENSIVE

Hôtel de la Poste. 7 bd. Frédéric-Mistral, 83120 Ste-Maxime. ☎ **04-94-96-18-33.** Fax 04-94-96-41-68. 24 rms. TEL. 290F–590F ($58–$118) double. AE, CB, DC, MC, V. Closed Oct 11–May 6.

This modern hotel's location in the town center, convenient to the beach and shopping, makes up for what it lacks in personality. The exterior is uninviting, but the inside is cool and comfortable, with a quiet lounge and a simple bar. The guest rooms aren't style setters, but they're clean, well maintained, and comfortably furnished. There's a pool, and the staff will be happy to help you decide how to spend your day. There's no restaurant in the hotel, but you're not far from a wide selection of restaurants.

Hôtel Le Chardon Bleu. 20 rue de Verdun, 83120 Ste-Maxime. ☎ **04-94-96-02-08.** Fax 04-94-43-90-89. 25 rms. A/C TV TEL. 356F–526F ($71.20–$105.20) double. AE, MC, V.

Situated 100 yards from the beach, Le Chardon Bleu is also close to the pedestrian streets and the casino. The hotel has a garden where you can enjoy a meal while taking in the aroma of the flowers. The well-maintained rooms are comfortable and inviting, though the furnishings are only standard; all have small balconies.

Hôtel Muzelle-Montfleuri. 4 av. Montfleuri, 83120 Ste-Maxime. ☎ **04-94-96-19-57.** Fax 04-94-49-25-07. 31 rms. TV TEL. 290F–570F ($58–$114) double. CB, MC. Closed Oct 14–Mar 26.

This hotel is on a hillside in a quiet residential neighborhood, from which it provides a superb view of the Gulf of St-Tropez. The large guest rooms are comfortably furnished; some have balconies. The hotel restaurant serves "family cooking" Provençal style in a pleasant garden. There's also a pool.

DINING

Le Gruppi. Av. Charles-de-Gaulle. ☎ **04-94-96-03-61.** Reservations recommended. Main courses 85F–230F ($17–$46); fixed-price menus 98F–208F ($19.60–$41.60). AE, MC, V. Apr–Sept, daily noon–2:30pm and 7–10pm; Oct–Mar, Tues noon–2:30pm, Thurs–Mon noon–2:30pm and 7–10pm. Closed 2 weeks in Dec. FRENCH/PROVENÇAL.

Earthy and amusing, this restaurant has thrived on the promenade adjacent to the sea since the 1960s, when it was opened by members of the family that maintains it today, the Lindermanns. Bay windows illuminate dining rooms on two floors; bright green and salmon, they boast rattan furnishings and varnished hardwoods. The savory bouillabaisse goes for 230F ($46) per person, less than at many competitors. Other menu items are seafood platters; herbed and roasted lamb from Sisteron; and veal, chicken, and all the vegetarian bounty of Provence. If you opt for fish, a staff member will carry a basket filled with the best of the day's catch for your inspection and advise you on their respective merits.

Restaurant Sans Souci. 58 rue Paul-Bert. ☎ **04-94-96-18-26.** Reservations recommended. Main courses 68F–98F ($13.60–$19.60); fixed-price menus 96F–136F ($19.20–$27.20). MC, V. May–Sept, daily noon–2pm and 7–10:30pm; Feb–Mar and Oct, Tues–Sun noon–2pm and 7–10:30pm. Closed Nov–Jan. FRENCH/PROVENÇAL.

The fun you're likely to have here derives from the confidence the owners have, thanks to a successful venture begun in 1953 by the Italian-born grandfather of the present proprietor. It occupies a turn-of-the-century building adjacent to the village church and features a Provençe-inspired decor with ceiling beams and old-time accessories. Menu items prepared by the good-humored owner, Philippe Sibilia, are concocted from fresh ingredients and years of practice. Examples are pan-fried Provençal veal, seawolf with fennel, octopus salad, filet of hake with basil, and one of our favorite dishes anywhere, noisettes of lamb with a tapenade of olives that's enhanced with pulverized anchovies and a hint of fresh cream.

4 Fréjus

2 miles W of St-Raphaël, 9 miles NE of St-Tropez

Fréjus was founded by Julius Caesar in 49 B.C. as Forum Julii; under Augustus's rule it became a key naval base. The warships with which Augustus defeated Antony and Cleopatra were built here prior to the battle at Actium in 31 B.C. By the Middle Ages, however, the port had declined; it began to silt up from disuse and was eventually filled in by its new owner, who bought it after the Revolution. The port now lies more than 2 miles inland.

This area is known today as the **Vieille Ville** (old town) and still boasts remnants from Roman times, including parts of an arena and a theater. There's also an interesting section called the **Cité Episcopale,** located at the heart of the Vieille Ville and dating to medieval times; the baptistry is one of France's oldest ecclesiastical buildings. Fréjus has expanded back toward the water in more recent times. The beach area, **Fréjus Plage,** tends to blend into St-Raphaël (discussed later in this chapter). The two towns are often considered a single holiday destination, though serious beachgoers often opt to stay in St-Raphaël, where the hotels are closer to the water and cheaper. History buffs and the fair-skinned should probably choose a hotel in Fréjus, where they can enjoy the festive atmosphere but escape the crowds.

ESSENTIALS

GETTING THERE   Fréjus has a small **train station** on rue Martin-Bidoure (☎ 04-94-82-16-92). No matter where you're traveling from in France, you'll probably end up at the larger station in St-Raphaël. From there, several trains per day make the short trip to Fréjus. If you're headed for the beach, it's a shorter walk (about 15 minutes) from the St-Raphaël station than from the Fréjus station.

For travel from St-Raphaël to Fréjus, bus service is much more frequent and convenient than the train. **Estérel** (☎ 04-94-53-78-46) runs between the two towns every 30 minutes. The cost is 6.50F ($1.30) for a one-way ticket. Buses arrive at the Fréjus **Gare Routière** (☎ 04-93-99-50-50), at the east end of the town center at place Paul-Vernet. **Sodetrav** buses (☎ 04-94-53-78-46) en route to St-Tropez from St-Raphaël stop along the coast in Fréjus.

GETTING AROUND   You can rent mopeds at **Location 2 Roues,** 83 Le Méditerranée–Nouveau Port (☎ 04-94-52-03-16). Prices range from 150F to 300F ($30 to $60). Credit-card deposits are required. **Holiday Bikes,** 93 av. de Provence (☎ 04-94-52-30-65), rents the pedal-powered version of two-wheeled transportation. Expect to pay 50F to 100F ($10 to $20), plus a security deposit.

The easiest way to get an overview of Fréjus's charms is on the municipally funded blue-and-white **Trains du Soleil**. Electrically powered and rubber wheeled, they operate hourly between 2:20 and 6:20pm Tuesday to Saturday (daily in July and August) on a circuit that passes the town's rich assortment of ancient and medieval monuments. They cost 25F ($5) for adults, 15F ($3) for children 10 to 15, and 10F ($2) for children 2 to 9. Tours begin at the indicated departure point in place Paul-Vernet, near La Mairie and across from the tourist office.

VISITOR INFORMATION   The **Office de Tourisme** is at 325 rue Jean-Jaurès (☎ 04-94-51-83-83).

EXPLORING THE TOWN

Jaded travelers may say that the Roman ruins are unspectacular, but they're worth seeing—if only to get a better idea of the extent of the settlement of Forum Julii. Because the ruins are scattered around the Vieille Ville, it may take a full day to view them all if you try to guide yourself; hop on one of the town's tourist trains (see "Essentials," above) to get a less time-consuming look.

The best preserved of the ruins is the **Amphithéâtre,** rue Henri-Vadon (☎ 04-94-51-34-31), which during Roman times held up to 10,000 spectators. Today it's used as a venue for rock concerts and the city's two annual *corridas* (bullfights), where, as in Spain, the bull dies at the end. Ask the tourist office for dates and details. The upper levels of the galleries have been reconstructed with the same greenish stone that was used to create the original building. The amphitheater is open Wednesday to Monday: April to September from 9:30am to noon and 2 to 6:30pm and October to March from 9am to noon and 2 to 4:30pm. Admission is free.

North of town on avenue du Théâtre-Romain, the **Théâtre Romain,** not to be confused with the amphitheater, has been largely destroyed. However, one wall and a few of the lower sections remain and are used as a backdrop for occasional summer concerts. The site is open 24 hours, and visits, which aren't monitored, are free. Northwest of the theater you can see a few soaring arches as they follow the road leading to Cannes. These are the remaining pieces of the 25-mile-long **aqueduct** that once brought fresh water to Fréjus's water tower.

The town's most frequently visited site is its fortified cathedral close, **Cité Episcopale,** rue de Fleury (☎ 04-94-51-26-30), in the heart of the Vieille Ville. At its center is the **Cathédrale St-Léonce,** completed in the 16th century after many generations of laborers had worked on it since Gothic times. Its most striking features are from the Renaissance—ornately carved walnut doors depicting scenes from the Virgin's life and tableaux inspired by Saracen invasions. The 5th-century **baptistry,** somehow saved from numerous invasions, is one of the oldest in France. Octagonal like many paleo-Christian baptistries, it features eight black granite columns with white capitals. Most interesting are the two doors, which are different sizes. Catechumens would enter by the smaller of the two; inside, a bishop would wash their feet and baptize them in the center pool. The baptized would then leave through the larger door; this signified their enlarged spiritual stature.

The most beautiful of all the structures in the Episcopal quarter is the 12th-century **cloister.** The colonnade's two slender marble pillars are typical of the Provençal style. Inside, the wooden ceiling is divided into 1,200 small panels, most of which were decorated with animals, portraits, and grotesques by 15th-century artists. A bell tower rises above the cloister, its steeple covered with colored tiles. In the building is the **Musée Archéologique,** which features a collection of Roman finds from the area. Roman sculptures dominate, but the small Greek vases that Romans used during their travels are some of the most attractive pieces. Be sure to see the two-headed bust of Hermes; since its discovery in 1970, it has come to be the town's symbol.

Admission to the Cité Episcopale, including entrance to the Archaeological Museum and each of the religious sites in its confines, is 25F ($5) for adults and 15F ($3) for students under 25 and children. Included in the price is an (optional) guided tour of the cloister and baptistry. These tours are conducted during the open hours: April to September, Sunday to Tuesday from 9am to 7pm; October to March, 9am to noon and 2 to 7pm.

Another famous religious sight in Fréjus is the small round **Chapelle Cocteau,** avenue Nicola (☎ 04-94-40-76-30). Designed by the legendary artist, film director, dilettante, social gadfly, and *prince des poètes* Jean Cocteau, it was built and decorated between 1961 and 1965. It's noteworthy for its octagonal design and low-slung, small-windowed format; the shape might remind you of an African thatch-covered hut. Most of the frescoes were executed by Cocteau himself, though the work was completed, because of his ill health and eventual death, by an artist that towns-people have referred to ever since as M. Dermit. The chapel is open Wednesday to Monday: April to September from 2 to 6pm and October to March from 2 to 5pm. Admission is free.

Two art galleries may be worth visiting. The more important is the **Centre d' Art Contemporain,** 4 miles north of Fréjus's historic core beside A8, in the Zone Industrielle du Capitou. At press time it was closed for renovations, with a reopening expected sometime in 1998. Call the tourist office for more information. Devoted to a frequently changing roster of temporary exhibits of painting, sculpture, and photography is the gallery in the neoclassical **Villa Aurélienne,** avenue du Général-d'Armée-Calliès (☎ 04-94-53-11-30). It's open Tuesday to Sunday from 2 to 6pm. The 47-acre park surrounding the villa hosts festivals and shows through-out the year; most notable are the **Fête des Plantes** (a yearly flower fesival) and an every-other-year festival called **Art Tendence Sud,** a 4-day art show stressing the works of artists from the southern tier of France. It's next scheduled for May 1998, at dates to be announced.

Just outside Fréjus are two interesting structures that reflect the unusual cultural medley of France's early 20th-century empire. The **Pagode Hong-Hien** (☎ 04-94-53-25-29), still used as a Buddhist temple, is about 1 ¼ miles northeast on R.N. 7 (one of the roads leading from Fréjus to Cannes). Built in 1919 by soldiers conscripted from France's colony of Indochina as a shrine to their comrades who fell in the trenches of eastern France in World War I, it's open daily from 9am to noon and 3 to 6:30pm; admission is 5F ($1).

Built in 1930 as a mosque by Muslim soldiers conscripted from the French colony of Mali, the **Mosquée Soudanaise** is off D4 leading to Bagnols. The building is modeled after the Grand Mosque in Djenne, Mali, but is more garish than majestic. Because of its position in what was at the time a military base, it's controlled today by the French Ministry of Defense and off-limits to casual visitors. From the highway you can see its purple-red exterior, which has been compared to a fortress with minarets.

Also in the area is the **Parc Zoologique**, Le Capitou (☎ 04-94-40-70-65), off A8 about 3 ½ miles north of the center of Fréjus, not far from the Mosquée Soudanaise. The safari park is home to more than 250 species of animals and is open daily: May to September from 9:30am to 6pm and October to April from 10am to 5pm. Admission is 55F ($11) for adults, 35F ($7) for children 3 to 10, and free for children 2 and under.

ACCOMMODATIONS

Hôtel L'Aréna. 145 rue du Général-de-Gaulle, 83615 Fréjus. ☎ **04-94-17-09-40.** Fax 04-94-52-01-52. 22 rms. A/C MINIBAR TV TEL. 290F–450F ($58–$90) double. AE, V. Closed Nov.

This hotel in the center of the Vieille Ville used to be a bank. Beautifully restored in bright tropical colors, L'Aréna is the perfect beachtown retreat. Each of the small but comfortable rooms opens onto a garden and pool area where tropical plants give the air a sweet smell. The sunny dining room is a pleasant place to stop for well-prepared seafood. The staff is friendly, and the hotel is a good value for the area.

DINING

Les Potiers. 135 rue des Potiers. ☎ **04-94-51-33-74.** Reservations required. Main courses 80F–98F ($16–$19.60); fixed-price menus 120F–165F ($24–$33). MC, V. Wed–Mon noon–2pm and 7–9:30pm. FRENCH/PROVENÇAL.

One of the town's smallest and most charming restaurants is midway between the town hall and the ancient arena. Staffed only by chef Hubert Guillard and his wife, Jeanne, it occupies a century-old stone house that contains only 15 seats. Menu items change with the seasons but usually include a salad of red mullet (the fish is fried in olive oil, drenched in sherry vinegar, and garnished with wild greens); filet of lamb marinated in thyme, olive oil, and garlic and served with a sauce miroir concocted from cream of Cassis and red Bandol wine; and filet of seawolf with a rosemary-cream sauce. For dessert, how about a thin slice of apple tart with cinnamon-flavored ice cream?

5 St-Raphaël

2 miles E of Fréjus, 27 miles SW of Cannes

Between the red lava peaks of the Massif de l'Estérel and the densely forested hills of the Massif des Maures, St-Raphaël was first popular during Roman times, when rich families came to the large resort here. Barbaric hordes and Saracen invasions characterized the Middle Ages; it wasn't until 1799, when a proud Napoléon landed at the small harbor beach on his return from Egypt, that the city once again drew attention.

Fifteen years later that same spot in the harbor was the point of embarkation for the fallen emperor's journey to exile on Elba. In 1864 Alphonse Karr, a journalist and ex-editor of *Le Figaro,* helped reintroduce St-Raphaël as a resort. Dumas, Maupassant, and Berlioz came here from Paris on his recommendation. Gounod took his friend's advice and also came; he composed *Romeo et Juliet* here in 1866. Unfortunately, most of the belle époque villas and grand hotels were destroyed during World War II when St-Raphaël served as a key landing point for Allied soldiers.

Today some of the mansions have been rebuilt and others have been replaced by modern resorts and buildings. The city boasts the wide beaches, good restaurants and hotels, and coastal ambience of other Côte d'Azur resorts—at a fraction of the price. This is why St-Raphaël, one of the richest towns on the coast, draws more families than couture-clad Parisians.

ESSENTIALS

GETTING THERE   St-Raphaël is the western terminus of the Metrazur rail line that runs along the coast; the Gare St-Raphaël–Valescure is the main station on the Marseille–Ventigmilia line. Nine trains a day make the trip between Paris and St-Raphaël for 453F ($90.60) one-way. Trains from Lyon, Dijon, and Marseille are almost as frequent, costing 267F ($53.40), 349F ($69.80), and 111F ($22.20), respectively. Trains arrive from Cannes and Nice approximately every 30 minutes. The 25-minute ride from Cannes is 35F ($7) one-way; the 1-hour ride from Nice goes for 58F ($11.60). The TGV bullet train from Paris also stops here. For **rail information** and schedules, call ☎ 08-36-35-35-35.

The bus station is behind the train station and provides both local and regional service. Several lines operate from here; among these, **Estérel** (☎ 04-94-53-78-46) is the direct link from Fréjus. Buses run about every 30 minutes; the fare is 6.50F ($1.30) one-way. From St-Tropez, take a **Sodetrav** bus (☎ 04-94-95-24-82). The ride will take about 1¹/₂ hours and cost 45F ($9). **Forum Cars** (☎ 04-94-95-16-71) provides service between Nice and St-Raphaël eight times daily. The scenic trip takes a little more than an hour; the fare is 32.50F ($6.50).

Les Bateaux Bleus (☎ 04-94-95-17-46) provides service from St-Tropez for 100F ($20) round-trip. Ferries also make the 45-minute journey from the Red Rock Cliffs; the round-trip fare is 50F ($10).

GETTING AROUND   Normally, **taxis** line up at the bus station; if you can't find one, call ☎ 04-94-95-04-25. You can also rent bikes and scooters from **Patrick Moto,** 260 av. du Général-Léclerc (☎ 04-94-53-65-99). Bikes rent for 50F ($10), with an 800F ($160) deposit; mountain bikes rent for 90F ($18), with a 2,000F ($400) deposit; and scooters go for 180F ($36), with a 5,000F ($1,000) deposit. MasterCard and Visa can be used for the deposit.

VISITOR INFORMATION   The **Office de Tourisme** faces the train station on rue Waldeck-Rousseau (☎ 04-94-19-52-52).

SEEING THE SIGHTS

St-Raphaël is divided in half by railroad tracks. The historically interesting Vieille Ville (old city) lies inland from the tracks. Here you'll find St-Raphaël's only intact ancient structure, the **Eglise des Templiers,** place de la Vieille Eglise, Quartier des

Templiers (☎ **04-94-82-15-00**). The 12th-century church is the third to stand on this site; two Carolingian churches underneath the current structure have been revealed during digs. A Templar watchtower sits atop one of the chapels, and at one time men stared out over the sea searching for ships that might pose a threat. The church served as a fortress and refuge in case of pirate attack. In the courtyard are fragments of a Roman aqueduct that once brought water from Fréjus. Regrettably, at press time the church was closed because of an archaeological dig going on beneath its floors, with a completion anticipated for 1998 or 1999.

In the meantime, your religious yearnings will have to be satisfied by St-Raphaël's other major church, **Notre-Dame-de-la-Victoire,** rue Félix-Martin (☎ **04-94-82-15-00**). Completed in 1887, it functions as the town's most visible religious structure, an ostentatious monument to the gilded age commerce that helped finance its construction.

Near the Eglise des Templiers, the **Musée d'Archéologie Sous-Marine** (Museum of Underwater Archaeology), rue des Templiers (☎ **04-94-19-25-75**), displays amphorae, ships' anchors, ancient diving equipment, and other interesting items recovered from the ocean's depths. At one time rumors circulated about a "lost city" off the coast of St-Raphaël. Jacques Cousteau came to investigate; instead of a sunken city, he discovered a Roman ship that had sunk while carrying a full load of building supplies. The museum is open mid-June to mid-September, Wednesday to Monday from 10am to 2pm and 2 to 6pm; mid-September to mid-June, Monday to Saturday from 10am to noon and 2 to 5pm. Admission is 25F ($5) for adults and 15F ($3) for students and children 17 and under.

You'll also find **flower and fruit markets** in the old city. Stall owners open every morning. On the second Saturday of each month, vendors selling a variety of odds and ends also emerge. If you want a glimpse of the Provençal wholesomeness of the town, check out the **Marché Alimentaire de St-Raphaël,** where carloads of produce, fish, meat, wines, and cheeses are sold. Daily from 8am to around 1:30pm, it's held simultaneously at two sites—place Victor-Hugo and place de la République—a 5-minute walk apart.

The seafront's broad **promenades,** dotted with statues dedicated to Félix Martin (a 19th-century mayor and tireless promoter of the resort) and Alphonse Karr (a 19th-century artist and local luminary), wind between the beaches and hotels. Near the old port, a **pyramid** commemorating Napoléon's return to France from Egypt stands on avenue du Commandant-Guillbaud.

A DAY AT THE BEACH

Of course, most visitors come here to have fun on the beaches. The best ones (some rock, some sand) are between the Vieux Port and Santa Lucia; stands rent equipment for water sports on each beach.

The closest to the town center is the **Plage du Veillat,** a long stretch of sand that's the most crowded and family friendly. Within a 5-minute walk east from the town center is **Plage Beau Rivage,** whose name is misleading because it's covered with a smooth and even coating of light-gray pebbles that might cut into you if you lie down without a towel. History buffs will enjoy a 4¹/₂-mile excursion east of town to the **Plage du Débarquement,** a partly pebble and partly sand stretch that was hurled into world headlines on August 15, 1945, when it was the site of the Mediterranean answer to the D-Day invasion. From here, Allied forces overran the southern tier of occupied France, bringing World War II to a more rapid conclusion. Today expect relatively uncrowded conditions, except during the midsummer crush.

A Drive in the Hills

This drive is only 35 miles but it's across hilly, rough terrain, so allow about 3 hours, plus extra time to get out for walks and views and perhaps a *pique-nique.* The roads aren't always surfaced, but the views are always dramatic.

Leave St-Raphaël on N98. Follow this route, the Estérel cliff road, as far as **Agay,** a little resort bordering a deep anchorage. The red porphyry slopes of Rastel d'Agay overlook a bay where Greeks and Romans traded centuries ago. After leaving Agay, follow the Valescure road, keeping right toward **Pic de l'Ours** (Ours Peak). After crossing the Agay River, follow the signposts to Ours Peak. The road leads around the north side of St-Pilon and Cap Roux. Eventually the route comes to the Evêque Pass and then the Lentisques Pass, where only one-way traffic is permitted. At **Pic d'Aurelle,** one of the great panoramas on the Riviera unfolds at an elevation of 1,060 feet. The road continues from the Lentisques Pass to the Notre-Dame Pass, one of the most scenic rides in the Estérel.

At **Notre-Dame** another panoramia unfolds, extending all the way to Cannes. Hairpin bends in the road lead to the summit of Pic de l'Ours at 1,627 feet. One of France's greatest views, a sweeping panorama of the coast, is the star here. Back at Notre-Dame Pass, continue for 3 miles, taking in the peaks of Petites Grues and Grosses Grues, until you come to the pass at **Cadière,** where you can stop for more views. At the next pass, Trois Termes, turn left and continue along a bad road to the **Suvières Pass.** The vegetation of cork oaks and evergreens is tough in this rugged terrain.

At Suvières, continue left in the direction of the Mistral Pass, where you connect with a tarred road. Keep left, moving toward the **Belle-Barbe Pass.** Here you can park and take a break, walking along a signposted trail that leads to a beauty spot, the lake of **Ecureuil.** Back at the Belle-Barbe Pass, continue left. At a lodge housing forest rangers, take a right and follow the signs back to St-Raphaël, going by way of Velescure. Passing vineyards, orchards, and eucalyptus trees, you reach **Velescure,** a pocket of posh surrounded by the villas of the wealthy. It has one of the finest climates in the south of France. After a look around, continue along D37 back to St-Raphaël.

St-Raphaël's answer to the decadence of nearby St-Tropez is most visible in the municipality's official nude beach, the **Plage de St-Ayguls,** 6 miles west of the town center. Surrounded by thick screens of reeds that thrive along the marshy seafront, it's a short, clearly signposted walk from heart of the simple fishing village of St-Ayguls.

ACCOMMODATIONS

There are plenty of places to stay in St-Raphaël, but during summer even the less-than-desirable places fill up fast. Reserve well in advance.

Hôtel Bleu Marine. Noveau Port Santa Lucia, 83700 St-Raphaël. ☎ **04-94-95-31-31.** Fax 04-94-95-31-31. 100 rms. A/C MINIBAR TV. 480F–760F ($96–$152) double. AE, DC, V.

This three-star hotel overlooking the harbor at Santa Lucia provides comfortable accommodations in a setting that's a bit removed from the crowded beaches. All the well-furnished rooms have private balconies and come with hair dryers and safes. The restaurant boasts well-prepared regional food, which can be served on a sunny terrace that looks down on the sailboats and yachts. The hotel also has an outdoor pool and a fitness room.

Hôtel Continental. 100 promenade du Président-René-Coty, 83700 St-Raphaël. ☎ **04-94-83-87-87.** Fax 04-94-19-20-24. 44 rms. A/C MINIBAR TV. 370F–990F ($74–$198) double. AE, V. Parking 40F ($8).

The Continental is a good choice for a beach vacation. It has modern facilities and comfortably furnished accommodations; some rooms have balconies that look out over the promenade and the sea. The restaurant serves regional specialties and reasonably priced *plats du jours.* You can be sure that your car is secure in the basement garage.

Hôtel Excelsior. 193 promenade du Président-René-Coty, 83700 St-Raphaël. ☎ **04-94-95-02-42.** Fax 04-94-95-33-82. 40 rms. A/C MINIBAR TV TEL. 490F–755F ($98–$151) double. AE, DC, V.

This hotel, on the beachfront promenade, is a charming family-run place and is the best address at St-Raphaël. The guest rooms are comfortably appointed; most have views of the ocean. A sand beach is directly across the street. The restaurant, with its pretty outdoor eating area, is a popular choice.

DINING

L'Arbousier. 6 av. de Valescure. ☎ **04-94-95-25-00.** Reservations recommended. Main courses 90F–160F ($18–$32); fixed-price menus 140F–310F ($28–$62) at lunch, 180F–310F ($36–$62) at dinner. AE, DC, MC, V. Thurs–Tues noon–2:30pm and 7:30–10:30pm. Closed 2 weeks at Christmas. FRENCH/PROVENÇAL.

Adjacent to the Eglise des Templiers, this well-managed restaurant serves a cuisine whose ingredients are based mostly on seasonal, locally available ingredients. You'll appreciate the rich, sunny, and sometimes earthy textures produced by chef Philippe Troncy. Menu items might include a parmentier of duckling layered in a casserole with mashed potatoes, a fondue of onions, and fiery Szechuan peppers; crayfish with marjoram from the chef's garden; and chapon (a Mediterranean Sea fish) with green-olive confit. In midsummer the desserts will probably include a refreshing salad of red Provençal fruit with a sorbet infused with Italian mascarpone cheese and fresh basil.

Restaurant Pastorel. 54 rue de la Liberté. ☎ **04-94-95-02-36.** Reservations recommended. Fixed-price menus 160F–195F ($32–$39). AE, MC, V. Tues–Sat noon–2pm and 7pm–1am, Sun noon–2pm. FRENCH.

Across from the town hall, this restaurant has thrived since 1922, when it was founded by the mother (Mme. Pastorel) of the present owner, Charles Floccia. Virtually everyone in town has dined here or is familiar with the place, and most remember enjoying the signature dish, a succulent pot of stewed fish flavored with garlic and a medley of vegetables. In either of two dining rooms or on an outdoor terrace, you can enjoy traditional Provençal recipes for such dishes as bourride (a close approximation of the bouillabaisse served in Marseille), marinated sardines, rack of lamb with Provençal herbs, and a medley of stuffed baby vegetables.

ST-RAPHAEL AFTER DARK

Because this is a family vacation spot, the after-dark scene is a little sparse. Of course, there's the **Grand Casino,** square de Grand (☎ **04-94-95-10-59**), with slot machines and gambling, plus a nightly dance party in summer featuring an upbeat orchestra. The slot machines are open daily from 11am to 4am; gambling begins at 8pm, and the dance club opens at 10pm. In summer the entire place stays open to 4am.

La Réserve, promenade du Président-René-Coty (☎ 04-94-95-02-02), is a popular disco with a sometimes punkish crowd between 16 and 25. Catering to a somewhat older (but not too much older) crowd is **Disco L'Embassy,** boulevard Félix-Martin (☎ 04-94-95-02-19). Be warned, however, that drinks at these places, and at other discos at this resort, aren't cheap: Your first will cost around 80F ($16); thereafter, drinks are usually 50F ($10). A calmer atmosphere pervades at the **Madison Club** (☎ 04-94-95-10-59), the piano bar that's part of the casino. It's open to 4am in summer. A worthwhile competitor is **Le Kilt,** rue Jules-Barbier (☎ 04-94-95-29-20).

The **Competition Internationale de Jazz de New Orleans** is held during 3 days in July. Check with the tourist office for exact dates. Musicians from around the world gather on the promenades to display their talent. In August, the **Fête de Pêcheurs** is a fisher's festival with traditional food, music, and dancing at the port.

6 Massif de l'Estérel

2 miles NE of Fréjus, 5 miles SE of Cannes

Stretching for 24 miles of coast from La Napoule to St-Raphaël, this mass of twisted red volcanic rock is a surreal landscape through which to hike and linger over dramatic panoramas. Forest fires have devastated all but a small section of cork oak, adding a barrenness to an already otherwordly place. One colorful real character from the region's trove of stories is the 19th-century highwayman Gaspard de Besse, who hid in the region's many caves and terrorized local travelers until at age 25 he was hanged, then decapitated, by military authorities in the main square at Aix-en-Provence.

Following the path of the ancient Roman Aurelian Way, N7 traces the area's northern edge, running through the Estérel Gap between Fréjus and Cannes. To get to the massif's summit, **Mont Vinaigre** (elevation 1,962 ft.), turn right at the Testannier crossroads 7 miles northeast of Fréjus. A parking area allows you to leave your car and make the final 15 minutes of the ascent on foot, climbing to the observation deck of a watchtower for a view stretching from the Alps to the Massif des Maures. At La Napoule, turn around to follow the southwesterly trail of N98 back to Fréjus.

This route offers the massif's most stunning vistas, first turning inland just beyond Le Trayas at **Pointe de l'Observatoire,** where you can ascend to the **Grotte de la Ste-Baume** for the views that inspired the medieval hermit St. Honorat, who once dwelt in the cave. Farther along N98, at **Pointe de Baumette,** is a memorial to the French writer/aviator Antoine de St-Exupéry. At **Agay,** turn inland again to reach the rocky **Gorge du Mal-Infernet,** a twisted rut in the earth, offering a contrast to the surrounding peaks with their overview of the region. Continuing along this inland route leads you to **Pic du Cap-Roux,** at 1,438 feet, and **Pic de l'Ours,** at 1,627 feet, both offering sweeping views of land and sea.

ESSENTIALS

GETTING THERE   Both of the area's twisted boundary roads run from Cannes to Fréjus, with N7 tracing the northern boundary and the southerly N98 following a route along the coast.

VISITOR INFORMATION   You can get additional information on sights, routes, and accommodations at the **Offices de Tourisme** in **St-Raphaël,** rue Waldeck-Rousseau (☎ 04-94-19-52-52); **Fréjus,** 325 rue Jean-Jaurès (☎ 04-94-17-51-83-83); **Les-Adrets-de-l'Estérel,** place de la Mairie (☎ 04-94-40-93-57); and **Agay,** boulevard de la Plage (☎ 04-94-82-01-85).

ACCOMMODATIONS

Note that the **Auberge des Adrets** (see "Dining," below) also rents rooms.

Hôtel Le Chrystalin. Place de l'Eglise, chemin des Philippons, 83600 Les-Adrets-de-l'Estérel, Var. ☎ **04-94-40-97-56.** Fax 04-94-40-94-66. 11 rms, 3 suites. TV TEL. 430F–650F ($86–$130) double; 750F ($150) suite for up to four. DC, MC, V. Closed Nov–Feb.

Adjacent to the village church of a town with fewer than 1,000 full-time residents, this is a three-star hotel. The rooms are outfitted in a simple but cozy Provençal style, unfrilly and basic but comfortable. Your hosts are Hervé Pandelle and his charming mother, Christiane, who work hard at maintaining a family-style dining room that attracts its share of locals. Dinner is the only meal served, nightly from 7:30 to 9pm, with traditional fixed-price menus at 100F to 150F ($20 to $30).

DINING

Auberge des Adrets. R.N. 7, 83600 Fréjus. ☎ **04-94-40-36-24.** Fax 04-94-40-34-06. Main courses 120F–180F ($24–$36); fixed-price menu 138F ($27.60). MC, V. Tues–Sat noon–2pm and 7:30–10pm, Sun noon–2pm (open daily July–Aug). Closed Nov. PROVENÇAL/FRENCH.

Despite an official mailing address that places this medieval inn in Fréjus, 11 miles away, it lies only 1 1/2 miles east of Les-Adrets-de-l'Estérel. Records of its existence go back to 824, when troubadours sang and horses rested here after treks across a landscape that's still rougher and more arid than other points nearby. In 1653 the site was designated a Relais de Poste, where travelers and their horses could find lodging. Today it focuses on upscale versions of Provence's rural dishes, as interpreted by Cosima de Megvinet and her partner, Virginia-born Alan Cuny. They preside over an antiques-filled dining room that spills out onto a large terrace overlooking arid landscapes and the faraway Baie de Cannes. Menu items are likely to include warm foie gras sautéed with roughly textured bread, magret of duckling roasted with a honey-flavored sesame sauce, and aromatic rack of lamb with an olive tapenade. Dessert might be a croustillant of pineapple with a confit of lemon and English cream.

The hotel offers five carefully decorated rooms, each with TV, phone, some kind of ornate (usually baldaquin) bed, and views over a garden. Depending on the season, doubles are 450F to 650F ($90 to $130).

7 La Napoule-Plage

560 miles S of Paris, 5 miles W of Cannes

This secluded resort is on the sandy beaches of the Golfe de la Napoule. In 1919 the once-obscure fishing village was a paradise for the eccentric sculptor Henry Clews and his wife, Marie, an architect. Fleeing America's "charlatans," whom he believed had profited from World War I, this New York banker's son emphasized the fairy-tale qualities of his new home. His house is now the **Musée Henry-Clews**—an inscription over the entrance reads ONCE UPON A TIME.

The ✪ **Château de la Napoule,** boulevard Henry-Clews (☎ 04-93-49-95-05), was rebuilt from the ruins of a medieval château. Clews covered the capitals and lintels with his own grotesque menagerie—scorpions, pelicans, gnomes, monkeys, lizards—the revelations of a tortured mind. Women, feminism, and old age are recurring themes in the sculptor's work, as exemplified by the distorted suffragette depicted in his *Cat Woman*. The artist was preoccupied with old age in both men and women and admired chivalry and dignity in man as represented by Don Quixote—to whom he likened himself. Clews died in Switzerland in 1937, and his body was

Following La Route Napoléon

On March 1, 1815, having escaped from a Senate-imposed exile on Elba that began in April 1814, Napoléon, accompanied by a small band of followers, landed at Golfe-Juan. The deposed emperor was intent on marching northward to reclaim the throne he'd first seized in 1799, though he hadn't officially proclaimed himself emperor until 1804.

Though the details of his journey have been obscured by time, two versions of a local legend about one of his first mainland encounters hint at a return that was amazingly anticlimactic. The first claims that shortly after landing at Golfe-Juan, Napoléon and his military escort were waylaid by highwaymen unimpressed by his credentials. The other twists the story around, claiming that Napoléon's men, attempting to build a supply of money and arms, waylaid the coach of the prince de Monaco, whose principality, stripped of its independence during the Revolution, had just been restored by Louis XVIII. When the prince told Napoléon that he was on his way to reclaim his throne, the exiled emperor stated that they were in the same business and bid his men to let the coach pass unhindered.

Napoléon's return was far from triumphant. He was met by sullen rejection at the garrison in Antibes where he planned to spend the night. This lack of enthusiasm was echoed throughout the region, the result of a series of international blunders, still fresh in the minds of the citizenry, that had isolated France from the rest of Europe and alienated Napoléon from his bourgeois followers. On being denied a bed at Antibes, he moved on to Cannes for the night. His cool reception didn't dampen his desire to reclaim the throne, but it was a key factor in his determining that travel north should be along rough mule paths carved through the hinterlands, avoiding large population centers. It was a sound plan, and by March 19 he was back in the Tuileries in Paris. But there was little time to savor the victory, as he lost the Battle of Waterloo only 100 days later. He was finally and

returned to La Napoule for burial. Marie Clews later opened the château to the public as a testimonial to the inspiration of her husband. At press time, the only option for visiting this site was through guided French-language tours that are conducted throughout the year Wednesday to Monday at 3 and 4pm. They cost 25F ($5) for adults and 20F ($4) for children. Look for an expansion of this sometime during the lifetime of this edition, as well as a renewed emphasis on the "artists in residency" program that Clews and his wife envisioned.

ESSENTIALS

GETTING THERE   La Mandelieu Napoule-Plage lies on the bus and train routes between Cannes and St-Raphaël. For **information and schedules,** call ☎ 08-36-35-35-35.

VISITOR INFORMATION   The **Office de Tourisme** is at 274 bd. Henry-Clews (☎ 04-93-49-95-31).

ACCOMMODATIONS

✪ **Ermitage du Riou.** Bd. Henry-Clews, 06210 La Napoule. ☎ **04-93-49-95-56.** Fax 04-92-97-69-05. 42 rms, 1 suite. A/C MINIBAR TV TEL. 980F–1,550F ($196–$310) double; from 1,900F ($380) suite. AE, DC, V.

absolutely banished to the island of St. Helena, where he died a broken man on May 5, 1821.

In the 1930s the French government decided to recognize Napoléon's positive influence on internal affairs—despite his monumental international gaffes—by building Rte. 85, **La Route Napoléon,** to roughly trace the steps of their exiled emperor in search of a throne. It stretches from Golfe-Juan to Grenoble, but the most scenic stretch is in Provence, between Grasse and Digne-les-Bains. The route is well marked with commemorative plaques sporting an eagle in flight, though the "action" documented south of Grenoble revolves around simple stops made for food and sleep along the way.

After embarking from Cannes on the morning of March 2, the group passed through Grasse and halted just beyond St-Vallier-de-Thiey, spending the night. The **Office de Tourisme** here, at place du Tour (☎ **04-93-42-78-00**), can provide you with a detailed account of the trek, a map of the three campsites where Napoléon and his men slept, and another map indicating where the road deviates from Napoléon's actual route, now maintained as a hiking trail where you can follow in his footsteps. The office is open Monday to Friday from 9am to noon and 2:30 to 5:30pm and Saturday from 10am to noon.

From this point to our end destination at **Digne-les-Baines,** the route touches only a handful of small settlements, the most notable of which is Castellane and the village of Barrème, where an encampment was set up on the night of March 3. The next day the group stopped for lunch in Digne-les-Bains before leaving the region to continue north toward the showdown at Grenoble. Although the relais where he dined is long gone, you can stop at **Bourgogne,** 3 av. Verdun (☎ **04-92-31-00-19**), our choice for dining in the town, where a good meal will cost 90F to 250F ($18 to $50).

This old Provençal house, the most tranquil choice at the resort, was turned into a seaside hotel in 1952. It borders the Riou River and the Cannes-Mandelieu international golf club. The rooms are furnished in Provençal style with genuine furniture and ancient paintings. The most expensive rooms have private safes. Views are of either the sea or the golf course. The restaurant, boasting a wood ceiling with beams, features seafood, with meals beginning at 175F ($35). There's also a pool, solarium, garden, and sauna.

✪ **La Calanque.** Bd. Henry-Clews, 06210 La Napoule. ☎ **04-93-49-95-11.** Fax 04-93-49-67-44. 17 rms, 11 with bath. TEL. 440F–480F ($88–$96) double without bath, 600F–630F ($120–$126) double with bath. Rates include half board. MC, V. Closed Nov–Mar.

The foundations of this charming hotel date from the Roman Empire, when an aristocrat built a villa here. The present hotel, run by the same family that's been in place since 1942, looks like a hacienda, with salmon-colored stucco walls and shutters. Register in the bar in the rear (through the dining room). The hotel's simple restaurant spills onto a terrace and offers some of the cheapest fixed-price meals in La Napoule, at 95F to 135F ($19 to $27). Nonguests are welcome.

Royal Hôtel Casino. 605 av. du Général-de-Gaulle, 06212 Mandelieu La Napoule. ☎ **04-92-97-70-06.** Fax 04-92-97-70-49. 185 rms, 25 suites. A/C MINIBAR TV TEL. 690F–1,620F ($138–$324) double; from 2,500F ($500) suite. AE, DC, MC, V. Parking 60F ($12).

This Las Vegas–style hotel is on the beach near a man-made harbor, about 5 miles from Cannes. It was the first French hotel to include a casino and the last (just before the building codes changed) to be allowed to have a casino directly on the beach. The hotel has one of the most contemporary designs on the Côte d'Azur, and a balance sheet that was enhanced in the mid-1990s when it was bought by the Accor group and added to its upscale Sofitel chain (once again, as the only Sofitel in the world with its own casino). The interior is dramatically contemporary, with plush touches, warm shades, and lots of marble. Most of the attractive modern rooms are angled toward a view of the sea. Those facing the street are likely to be noisy in spite of soundproofing. Le Féréol is recommended under "Dining," below. An informal cafe (Le Poker) serves both Tex-Mex and specialties of Provence, and a nightclub offers live music. The casino (open daily from 8pm to 4am) offers blackjack, craps, and roulette. Facilties include a pool, tennis courts, a sauna, a private beach, and a 27-hole golf course.

DINING

Note that the restaurant in **La Calanque** (see "Accommodations," above) is open to nonguests.

Brocherie II. Au Port. ☎ **04-93-49-80-73.** Reservations recommended. Main courses 120F–150F ($24–$30); fixed-price menu 190F ($38). AE, V. July–Sept, daily noon–2pm and 7:30–10:30pm; Oct–June, Wed–Mon noon–2pm and 7:30–10:30pm. Closed Jan 5–Feb 5. FRENCH.

The shoreline design gives the impression of dining on a floating houseboat, and the entrance is across a gangplank flanked by flaming torches. The interior is brass and mahogany with a nautical theme. Specialties are bouillabaisse, grilled turbot, brochette of lamb, and (very expensive) lobster from a bubbling tank. The cookery is solid and reliable, with an emphasis on the freshest of ingredients.

Le Féréol. In the Royal Hôtel Casino, 605 av. du Général-de-Gaulle. ☎ **04-92-97-70-00.** Reservations recommended. Main courses 95F–170F ($19–$34); buffet lunch (June–Sept only) 210F ($42); fixed-price dinner 260F ($52). AE, DC, MC, V. Daily noon–2:30pm (to 3:30pm July–Aug) and 7:30–10:30pm (to 11pm July–Aug). FRENCH.

This well-designed restaurant services most of the culinary needs of the largest hotel (and the only casino) in town. Outfitted in a nautical style that includes some of the seagoing accessories of an upscale yacht, it offers one of the most impressive lunch buffets in the neighborhood. At night the place is candlelit and more elegant, and the view through bay windows over the pool is more soothing. Menu items include foie gras, scampi tails fried with ginger, zucchini flowers with mousseline of lobster, mignon of veal with Parma ham and tarragon sauce, sole braised with shrimp, and an émincé of duckling baked under puff pastry with cèpe mushrooms. The dessert buffet lays out a wide array of sophisticated pastries, some light and fruity summer dishes, others designed as irresistable temptations for chocoholics.

L'Oasis. Rue Honoré-Carle. ☎ **04-93-49-95-52.** Reservations required. Main courses 180F–280F ($36–$56); fixed-price lunch (with wine) 275F ($55); fixed-price lunch or dinner (without wine) 290F–650F ($58–$130). AE, DC, MC, V. Daily noon–1:30pm and 8–10pm. Closed Sun night and all day Mon, Sept–Easter. FRENCH.

At the entrance near the harbor of La Napoule, in a 40-year-old house with a lovely garden and an unusual re-creation of a mock-medieval cloister, this restaurant became world famous under the tutelage of the now-retired Louis Outhier. Today chef Stéphane Raimbault prepares the most sophisticated cuisine in La Napoule. Presumably, Raimbault has learned everything Outhier had to teach him and charts his own culinary course. Because Raimbault cooked in Japan for 9 years, many of his dishes are of the "East Meets West" variety. In summer meals are served in the shade of the plane trees in the garden. Menu specialties may be taboulette of crayfish with tamarind juice, warm foie gras of duckling with verdure de blettes (a Provençal vegetable similar to spinach), turbot en meunière with beets and capers, filet of pork with sage oil, and John Dory roasted with herbs in the traditional style. The wine cellar houses one of the finest collections of Provençal wines anywhere. Regrettably, there can be rocky moments here thanks to a staff that's a lot less helpful than they could be.

8 Cannes

562 miles S of Paris, 101 miles E of Marseille, 16 miles SW of Nice

When Coco Chanel went here and got a suntan, returning to Paris bronzed, she startled the milk-white ladies of society. However, they quickly began copying her. Today the bronzed bodies—in nearly nonexistent swimsuits—that line the sandy beaches of this chic resort continue the late fashion designer's example.

Cannes is at its most frenzied during the **International Film Festival** at the Palais des Festivals on promenade de la Croisette. The festival celebrates its 51st anniversary in 1998. Held in either April or May, it attracts not only film stars but also those with similar aspirations, as well as seemingly every photographer in the world. On the seafront boulevards, flashbulbs pop as the stars and wannabes emerge and pose and pose and pose. For wannabes (particularly female), *outrageous* is the key word. The festival's stellar activities are closed to most visitors, who are forced to line up in front of the Palais des Festivals. Known as "the bunker," this concrete structure is the venue for premières that draw some 5,000 spectators. With paparazzi shouting ("Bruce, Demi, over here!") and shooting away and a guard of gendarmes holding back the fans, the guests parade along the red carpet into the building, perhaps stopping for a moment or two to strike a pose and chat with a journalist. *C'est la Cannes!*

International regattas, galas, *concours d'élégance,* and even a Mimosa Festival in February—something's always happening at Cannes, except in November, traditionally a dead month.

ESSENTIALS

GETTING THERE   Cannes is connected to each of the Mediterranean resorts, Paris, and the rest of France by rail and bus lines. Cannes lies on the major coastal rail line along the Riviera, with trains arriving frequently throughout the day. From Antibes to Cannes by train takes only 15 minutes, or 35 minutes from Nice. The TGV from Paris going via Marseille also services Cannes. (Transit from Paris to Cannes via TGV takes only about 3 breathless hours.) For **rail information** and schedules, call ☎ 08-36-35-35-35. Buses pick up passengers at the Nice airport every 40 minutes during the day, delivering them to Cannes at the **Gare Routière,** place de la Gare (☎ 04-93-39-18-71). Service to Cannes is also available from Antibes at the rate of one bus every half an hour. The international airport at Nice lies a 20-minute drive northeast.

VISITOR INFORMATION   The **Office de Tourisme** is in the Palais des Festivals, boulevard de la Croisette (☎ 04-93-39-24-53).

SPECIAL EVENTS   The world-famous **International Film Festival** is held in April or May.

Cannes

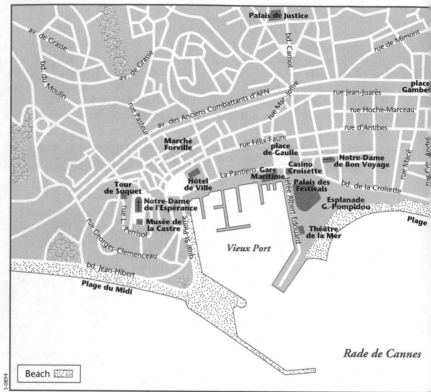

Map labels:
Palais de Justice
bd. Carnot
av. de Grasse
rue de Mimont
bd. du Moulin
av. de Grasse
place Gambel
rue Jean-Juarès
rue Pasteur
av. des Anciens Combattants d'AFN
rue Hoche-Marceau
rue Mar.-Joffre
rue d'Antibes
rue Félix-Faure
place de-Gaulle
Marché Forville
rue Macé
rue Cdt André
Notre-Dame de Bon Voyage
La Pantiero
Casino Croisette
Tour de Suquet
Hôtel de Ville
Gare Maritime
Palais des Festivals
bd. de la Croisette
Notre-Dame de l'Espérance
Esplanade G.-Pompidou
jetée Albert-Édouard
Musée de la Castre
rue Perrisol
rue St-Pierre
Théâtre de la Mer
Plage
rue Georges-Clemenceau
Vieux Port
bd. Jean-Hibert
Plage du Midi
Rade de Cannes
Beach
3-0894

TOURING THE TOP ATTRACTIONS

Some 16 miles southwest of Nice, Cannes is sheltered by hills. For many it consists of only one street, **promenade de la Croisette** (or just **La Croisette**), curving along the coast and split by islands of palms and flowers. It's said that the Prince of Wales (before he became Edward VII) contributed to its original cost. But he was a Johnny-come-lately to Cannes. Setting out for Nice in 1834, Lord Brougham, a lord chancellor of England, was turned away because of an outbreak of cholera. He landed at Cannes and liked it so much that he decided to build a villa here. Returning every winter until his death in 1868, he proselytized it in London, drawing a long line of British visitors. In the 1890s Cannes became popular with Russian grand dukes (it's said that more caviar was consumed here than in all of Moscow). One French writer claimed that when the Russians returned as refugees in the 1920s, they were given the garbage-collection franchise.

A port of call for cruise liners, the seafront of Cannes is lined with hotels, apartment houses, and chic boutiques. Many of the bigger hotels, some dating from the 19th century, claim part of the beaches for the private use of their guests. But there are also public areas. Above the harbor, the old town of Cannes sits on Suquet Hill, where you'll see a 14th-century tower, the **Tour de Suquet,** which the English dubbed the Lord's Tower.

Nearby is the **Musée de la Castre,** in the Château de la Castre, Le Suquet (☎ **04-93-38-55-26**), containing paintings, sculpture, examples of decorative arts,

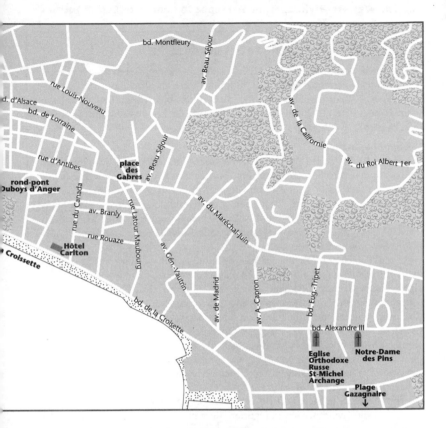

and a section on ethnography. The latter includes relics and objects from everywhere from the Pacific islands to Southeast Asia, including both Peruvian and Mayan pottery. There's also a gallery devoted to relics of ancient Mediterranean civilizations, from the Greeks to the Romans, from the Cypriots to the Egyptians. Five rooms are devoted to 19th-century paintings. The museum is open Wednesday to Monday: April to June from 10am to noon and 2 to 6pm, July to September from 10am to noon and 3 to 7pm, and October to March from 10am to noon and 2 to 5pm. Admission is 10F ($2), free for students and children.

Though nobody plans a trip to Cannes to see churches, the city does contain four worthy examples. The largest and most prominent is **Notre-Dame de Bon Voyage,** square Mérimée (☎ **04-93-39-16-22**), near the Palais des Festivals; it was built in a *faux* Gothic style in the late 19th century. **Notre-Dame des Pins,** 24 bd. Alexandre-III (☎ **04-93-39-16-22**), is a serviceable but not overwhelmingly interesting building from the 1920s. The most historic church, **Notre-Dame de l'Espérance,** place de la Castre (☎ **04-93-39-17-49**), was built between 1521 and 1627 and combines both Gothic and Renaissance elements. The town's most unusual church is the **Eglise Orthodoxe Russe St-Michel Archange,** 36–40 bd. Alexandre-III (☎ **04-93-43-00-28**), built in 1894 through the efforts of Alexandra Skripytzine, a Russian in exile; it's capped with a cerulean-blue onion dome and a gilded triple cross. Be warned that it's usually locked, except for services on Saturday at 5pm and Sunday between 9:30am and noon.

Ferrying to the Iles de Lérins

Across the bay from Cannes, the Lérins Islands are the most interesting excursion from the port. Ferryboats depart at 30-minute intervals throughout the day, beginning at 7:30am and lasting until 30 minutes before sundown, from the **Compagnies Estérel-Chanteclair,** Gare Maritime des Iles, 06400 Cannes (☎ **04-93-39-11-82**). Round-trip passage is 50F ($10) per person.

Ile Ste-Marguerite

The first island is named after St. Honorat's sister, Ste. Marguerite, who lived here with a group of nuns in the 5th century. Today this is a youth center whose members (when they aren't sailing and diving) are dedicated to the restoration of the fort. From the dock where the boat lands, you can stroll along the island (signs point the way) to the **Fort de l'Ile,** built by Spanish troops from 1635 to 1637. Below is the 1st-century B.C. Roman town where the unlucky man immortalized in *The Man in the Iron Mask* was imprisoned.

One of French history's most perplexing mysteries is the identity of the man who wore the *masque du fer,* a prisoner of Louis XIV who arrived at Ste-Marguerite in 1698. Dumas fanned the legend that he was a brother of Louis XIV, and it has even been suggested that the prisoner and a mysterious woman had a son who went to Corsica and "founded" the Bonaparte family. However, the most common theory is that the prisoner was a servant of the superintendent, Fouquet, named Eustache Dauger. At any rate, he died in the Bastille in Paris in 1703.

You can visit his cell at Ste-Marguerite, in which every visitor seemingly has written his or her name. As you stand listening to the sound of the sea, you realize what a forlorn outpost this was.

The **Musée de la Mer,** Fort Royal (☎ **04-93-43-18-17**), traces the history of the island, displaying artifacts of Ligurian, Roman, and Arab civilizations, plus the remains discovered by excavations. These include paintings, mosaics, and ceramics. It's open June to September, daily from 10:30am to 12:15pm and 2:15 to 6:30pm; the rest of the year, it closes between 4:30 and 5:30pm, depending on sundown. Admission is 10F ($2) for adults, free for children and students.

Ile St-Honorat

Only a mile long, Ile St-Honorat is even lonelier. St. Honorat founded a monastery here in the 5th century. Since the 1860s the Cistercians have owned the ecclesiastical complex, consisting of both an old fortified monastery and a contemporary one. You can spend the day wandering through the pine forests on the west side of the island—the other part is reserved for silent prayer.

A DAY AT THE BEACH

Beachgoing in Cannes is more concerned with exhibitionism and voyeurism than with actual swimming, which in some cases might be considered gauche. Here's a rundown on the resort's most user-friendly beaches:

✪ **Plage de la Croisette** extends between the Vieux Port and the Port Canto. Though the beaches along this billion-dollar stretch of sand aren't in the strictest sense private, they're *payante,* meaning that you must pay between 90F and 100F ($18 and $20). You don't need to be a guest of the Noga Hilton, Martinez, Carlton, or Majestic to use the beaches associated with those hotels, though if you are, you'll usually get a reduction of around 50%. Each of the respective beaches is separated from its neighbors by a wooden barricade that stops several feet from the sea, allowing easy transit from one to another.

Why should you pay a fee at all? Well, it includes a full day's use of a mattress, a chaise longue (the seafront isn't particularly sandy or even soft, covered as it is with pebbles and dark-gray shingle), and a parasol, as well as easy access to freshwater showers and kiosks selling beverages. Many of them include outdoor restaurants where no one minds if you appear in swimsuits.

For nostalgia's sake, our preferred beach is the one associated with the Carlton—it was the first beach we ever attended, as teenagers, in Cannes. The relative merits of each of the 20 or so beaches along La Croisette varies daily depending on the crowd. And since every beach here is insouciant about topless bathing and absolutely adamant in outlawing bottomless sea- or sunbathing, you're likely to find the same forms of décolletage along the entire strip.

Looking for a free public beach where you'll have to survive without rentable chaises or parasols? Head for the **Plage du Midi,** sometimes called **Midi Plage,** just west of the Vieux Port (☎ **04-93-39-92-74**), or **Plage Gazagnaire,** just east of the Port Canto (no phone). Here you'll find greater numbers of families with children and lots of caravan-type vehicles parked nearby.

OUTDOOR ACTIVITIES

BICYCLING & MOTOR-SCOOTERING   Despite the roaring traffic, the flat landscapes between Cannes and such satellite resorts as La Napoule are well suited for riding a bike or motor scooter. **Cannes Location Deux Roues,** 11 rue Hélène-Vagliano (☎ **04-93-39-46-15**), across from the Gray-d'Albion, rents pedal bikes for 62F ($12.40) per day and requires a 1,000F ($200) deposit (payable with American Express, MasterCard, or Visa). Motor scooters rent for 165F to 200F ($33 to $40) per day and require a deposit of 4,000F to 10,000F ($800 to $2,000) per day, depending on their value. None of the motor scooters rented here requires a driver's license or special permit.

BOATING   In an annex of the Hôtel Latitude, **New Boat,** rue de la Laiterie (☎ **04-93-93-12-34**), is in Mandelieu, 4 miles west of Cannes. With a good reputation and a hardworking staff, it maintains a flotilla of powerboats and small yachts, ranging from 12 to 45 feet long. They rent, usually with a staff included for navigation and safety, from 3,500F ($700) per day.

GOLF   One of the region's most challenging and interesting courses, **Country-Club de Cannes-Mougins,** 175 rte. d'Antibes, Mougins (☎ **04-93-75-79-13**), 4 miles north of Cannes, was a 1976 reconfiguration by Dye & Ellis of an under-accessorized course laid out in the 1920s. Noted for the olive trees and cypresses that adorn a relatively flat terrain, it has many water traps and a deceptively tricky layout loaded with technical challenges. It has a par of 72 and a much-envied role, since 1981, as host to the Cannes-Mougins Open, an important stop on the PGA European Tour. The course is open to anyone with proof of his or her handicap willing to pay greens fees of 340F to 380F ($68 to $76), depending on the day of the week. An electric golf cart rents for 280F ($56), and golf clubs can be rented for 150F ($30) per set. Reservations are recommended.

SWIMMING   Most of the larger hotels in Cannes have their own pools. In addition, the **Complexe Sportif Montfleury,** 23 av. Beauséjour (☎ **04-93-38-75-78**), boasts a large modern pool that's about 100 feet long. Anyone who pays the entrance fee of 22F ($4.40) can spend the entire day lounging beside it.

TENNIS   Its 10 tennis courts are one of the highlights of the **Complexe Sportif Montfleury,** 23 av. Beauséjour (☎ **04-93-38-75-78**). You'll find 8 hard-surfaced courts, at 70F ($14) per hour, and 2 clay-surfaced courts, at 90F ($18) per hour.

SHOPPING

Cannes competes more successfully than many of its neighbors in a highly commercial blend of resort-style leisure, luxury glamour, and media glitz. So you're likely to find branch outlets of virtually every stylish Paris retailer.

There's every big-name designer you can think of (Saint Laurent, Rykiel, Hermès) as well as big-name designers you've never heard of (Claude Bonucci, Durrani)—but, more important, there are real-people shops, resale shops for gently worn star-studded castoffs, two flea markets for fun junk, and a fruit, flower, and vegetable market.

ANTIQUES & *BROCANTE*   In the Casino Croisette (also called the Palm Beach Casino) on La Croisette, Cannes hosts one of France's most prestigious **antiques salons,** conducted biannually during week-long periods in mid-July and late December or early January. Its organizers absolutely refuse to include low- or even middle-bracket merchandise. This is serious—not for the gilt-free crowd—with lots of 18th- and early 19th-century stuff that might've appealed to the mistresses of various kings and emperors. Admission is 50F ($10) per person. A bevy of satellite services is available at this event, like crating and freighting and flying whatever you buy to wherever you want it sent. For dates and information, call or write the **Association des Antiquaires de Cannes,** 13 rue d'Oran, 06400 Cannes (☎ **04-93-38-13-64**).

Looking for top-notch antiques dealers whose merchandise will wow you? Two of the city's most noteworthy dealers are **Hubert Herpin,** 20 rue Macé (☎ **04-93-39-56-18**), and **Marc Franc,** 142 rue d'Antibes (☎ **04-93-43-86-43**). You'll find a wide selection of bronze and marble statues, marquetry, and 18th- and 19th-century furniture.

Admittedly, things are a lot less elevated at Canne's two regular flea markets. Casual, dusty, and to an increasing degree filled with the castaways of various estate sales, the **Marché Forville,** conducted in the Marché Forville neighborhood, near the Palais des Festivals, is a battered stucco structure with a roof and a few arches but no sides. It usually functions as the fruit-and-vegetable market that supplies the raw materials for dozens of grand restaurants. But Monday is *brocante* day, when the market fills with offhanded, sometimes strident antiques dealers selling everything from grandmère's dishes to bone-handled carving knives.

Every Saturday, a somewhat disorganized and invariably busy **flea market** is held outdoors, along the edges of the allée de la Liberté, across from the Palais des Festivals. Exact hours depend on the whims of whatever dealer happens to feel compelled to haul in a cache of merchandise, but they usually begin around 8am and run out of steam by around 4:30pm. Note that the vendors at the two flea markets may or may not be the same.

CHOCOLATE & JELLIED FRUITS   There are several famous chocolatiers in Cannes—try **Maiffret,** 31 rue d'Antibes (☎ **04-93-39-08-29**)—but the real local specialty is *fruits confits* (jellied fruits, also called crystallized fruits), which became the rage in the 1880s. Maiffret sells these as well, especially in summer, when the chocolates tend to melt. Pâtés and confits of fruit, some of which decorate cakes and tarts, are also sold as desirable confections. Look for the Provençal national confection, *calissons,* crafted from almonds, a confit of melon, and sugar. A block away is **Chez Bruno,** 50 rue d'Antibes (☎ 04-93-39-26-63). Opened in 1929 and maintained today by a matriarchal descendent of its founder, the shop is famous throughout Provence for *fruits confits* as well as its recipe for glazed chestnuts *(marrons glacés)*, made fresh daily.

DEPARTMENT STORES   Near the train station in the heart of Cannes, **Galeries Lafayette** has a small branch at 6 rue du Maréchal-Foch (☎ 04-93-39-27-55). It's noted for the self-consciously upscale fashion available in carefully arranged interiors. You'll save some francs and get an insight into the layout of a French-speaking five-and-dime by checking out its downscale sibling, **Monoprix,** across the street at no. 9 (☎ 04-93-39-35-01). Monoprix contains a grocery store as well.

DESIGNER SHOPS   Most of the big names in designer fashion, for both men and women, line **promenade de la Croisette,** known as **La Croisette,** the main drag facing the sea. These stores are all in a row, stretching from the Hôtel Carlton almost to the Palais des Festivals, with the best names closest to the high-rise **Gray-d'Albion,** 17 La Croisette (☎ 04-92-99-79-79), which is both a mall and a hotel (how convenient). The stores in the Gray-d'Albion mall include **Hermès** and **Souleiado.** The mall is broken into two parts, so you go outdoors from the first part of the building and then enter again for the second part. It serves as the shopper's secret cutaway from the primary expensive shopping street, La Croisette, to the less expensive shopping street, **rue d'Antibes.**

You'll find a few more designer shops inside the posh hotels lining La Croisette: **Alexandra,** rond-point d'Angers (☎ 04-93-38-41-29), is the fanciest boutique in town for a mixture of designers and for the kind of service demanded by stars and local ladies who lunch. In the words of the owners, "*pour la ville, le soir, et les cérémonies.*" Here you'll find garments by Mori, Givenchy, Rochas, Lacroix, and Montana. Find it by ducking around to the back end of the Noga Hilton.

FOOD   A charmingly old-fashioned shop, **Cannolive,** 16–20 rue Vénizelos (☎ 04-93-39-08-19), is owned by the Raynaud family, who founded the place in 1880. It sells Provençal olives and their by-products—purées *(tapenades)* that connoisseurs refer to as "Provençal caviar," black "olives de Nice," and green "olives de Provence," as well as three grades of olive oil from several regional producers. Oils and food products are dispensed from no. 16, but gift items (fabrics, porcelain, and Provençal souvenirs) are sold next door.

MARKETS   At the edge of the Quartier Suquet, the **Marché Forville** is the town's primary fruit, flower, and vegetable market. On Monday it's a *brocante* market. See "Antiques & *Brocante*," above.

PERFUME   The best shop is **Bouteille,** 59 rue d'Antibes (☎ 04-93-39-05-16), but it's also the most expensive. Its prices are high because it stocks more brands, has a wider selection, gives away many more free samples, and presents you with a tote bag. A selection of other perfume shops dots rue d'Antibes. Any may feature your favorite fragrance in a promotional deal (they rotate the deals). If you hit it right, you'll save money at **Starlett,** 18 rue d'Antibes (☎ 04-93-39-23-77).

ACCOMMODATIONS
VERY EXPENSIVE

✪ **Hôtel Carlton Intercontinental.** 58 bd. de la Croisette, 06400 Cannes. ☎ **800/ 327-0200** in the U.S., or 04-93-06-40-06. Fax 04-93-06-40-25. 326 rms, 28 suites. A/C MINIBAR TV TEL. 1,250F–3,800F ($250–$760) double; from 3,910F ($782) suite. AE, DC, MC, V. Parking 160F ($32).

Cynics say that one of the most amusing sights in Cannes is the view from under the vaguely art deco grand gate of the Carlton. Here you'll see vehicles of every description pulling up to drop off huge amounts of baggage and vast numbers of oh-so-fashionable (and sometimes not-so-fashionable) guests. It's the epitome of luxury and has become such a part of the city's heartbeat that to ignore it would be to miss the resort's spirit. The twin gray domes at either end of the facade are often the first things recognized by starlets planning their grand entrances, grand exits, and grand scenes in the hotel's public and private rooms.

Shortly after it was built in 1912, the Carlton attracted the most prominent members of Europe's *haut monde,* including royalty. They were followed decades later by battalions of the most important screen stars. Today the hotel is more democratic, hosting lots of conventions and motor-coach tour groups; however, in summer (especially during the film festival) the public rooms still are filled with all the voyeuristic and exhibitionistic fervor that seems so much a part of the Riviera. The guest rooms were renovated in 1990. Double-glazing, big combination baths with hair dryers, and luxurious appointments are standard. The most spacious rooms are in the west wing, and many of the upper-floor rooms open onto balconies fronting the sea.

Dining/Entertainment: The hotel contains five restaurants. The one offering the most intensely cultivated cuisine is La Belle Otéro, on the seventh floor, followed by the elegant but less spectacular Restaurant du Casino and Restaurant de la Côte, which was renovated in 1997. A ground-floor Brasserie doles out less expensive fare, and at the waterfront Restaurant de la Plage, virtually everyone seems to arrive in *maillots de bain.*

Facilities: Private beach, health club with spa facilities, glass-roofed indoor pool.

Hôtel Majestic. 14 bd. de la Croisette, 06400 Cannes. ☎ **04-92-98-77-00.** Fax 04-93-38-97-90. 239 rms, 23 suites. A/C MINIBAR TV TEL. 1,950F–4,100F ($390–$820) double; from 4,100F ($820) suite. AE, DC, MC, V. Parking 130F ($26).

At the west end of La Croisette, the Majestic has stood for glamour since 1926 and, like the Carlton, is a favorite with celebs during the annual film festival. Constructed around an overscale front patio with a pool, the hotel opens directly onto the esplanade and the sea. Inside, the setting is one of marble, clusters of crystal chandeliers, tapestries, seasoned antiques and reproductions, salons with Oriental carpets, Louis XV silk furniture, and potted palms. The guest rooms are furnished with antiques and reproductions, offset by Oriental rugs and marble tables.

Dining/Entertainment: There's a classic haute cuisine restaurant and a grill with tables placed around the pool. There's also a restaurant and bar on the beach.

Services: Room service (24 hours), same-day laundry/valet service, hairdresser.

Facilities: Pool.

✪ **Hôtel Martinez.** 73 bd. de la Croisette, 06400 Cannes. ☎ **04-92-98-73-00.** Fax 04-93-39-67-82. 418 rms, 12 suites. A/C MINIBAR TV TEL. 1,650F–3,360F ($330–$672) double; from 3,600F ($720) suite. AE, DC, MC, V. Parking 100F ($20).

When this landmark art deco hotel was built in the 1930s, it rivaled any other hotel along the coast in sheer size alone. Over the years, however, it has fallen into disrepair and closed and reopened several times. But in 1982 the Concorde chain returned the hotel and its restaurants to their former luster, and today it competes with the Carlton and Noga Hilton. Despite its grandeur, the hotel is a little too convention-oriented for our tastes, but the rooms remain in good shape. The aim of the decor was a Roaring Twenties style, and all units boast private safes, marble baths, wood furnishings, tasteful carpets, and pastel fabrics.

Dining/Entertainment: La Palme d'Or, among the finest restaurants in Cannes, is recommended under "Dining," below. The poolside restaurant, L'Orangerie, serves light, low-calorie meals in a decor of azure and white lattices.

Services: Room service (24 hours), same-day laundry/valet.

Facilities: Private beach, waterskiing school, cabanas, octagonal pool, seven tennis courts.

✪ **Noga Hilton Cannes.** 50 bd. de la Croisette, 06414 Cannes. ☎ **800-445-8667** in the U.S., or 04-92-99-70-00. Fax 04-92-99-70-11. 196 rms, 33 suites. A/C MINIBAR TV TEL. 990F–3,390F ($198–$678) double; from 1,950F ($390) suite. AE, DC, MC, V.

The owners were able to procure one of Cannes's most sought-after building sites, the lot occupied by the old (since demolished) Palais des Festivals. Finished in 1992, the Hilton was the first major palace hotel to open in Cannes since the 1930s. This six-story deluxe place, with massive amounts of exposed glass, boasts a contemporary design mimicking the best aspects of its older twin, the lakefront Noga Hilton in Geneva. You register in a soaring lobby sheathed with a semitranslucent white marble. The guest rooms are stylish, containing impeccable soundproofing and all the electronic accessories you'll ever need. Since all rooms are equivalent, the difference in rates is determined by your room's exposure (or lack thereof) to the sea.

Dining/Entertainment: The most expensive dining venue is La Scala, a smart restaurant with its own piano bar one floor above lobby level. It specializes in the cuisines of the Riviera—both French and Italian. Less grand is the Brasserie Le Grand Bleu. La Plage is an informal lunch restaurant on the beach. There is also a casino and an 825-seat theater for cabarets and conventions.

Services: Room service (24 hours), baby-sitting.

Facilities: Health club with sauna, 20 tennis courts, outdoor pool, shopping arcade with about 30 boutiques, waterfront pier for mooring yachts, business center, access to nearby golf course.

EXPENSIVE

Grand Hôtel. 45 bd. de la Croisette, 06400 Cannes. ☎ **04-93-38-15-45.** Fax 04-93-68-97-45. 76 rms, 2 junior suites. A/C MINIBAR TV TEL. 660F–1,580F ($132–$316) double; 1,580F–2,600F ($316–$520) suite. AE, MC, V. Closed Nov–Dec 14. Parking 30F ($6).

This hotel is graced with a garden with tall date palms and a lawn sweeping down to the waterfront esplanade. A recently renovated structure of glass and marble, it's part of a complex of adjoining apartment-house wings and encircling boutiques. Eleven floors of rooms (with wall-to-wall picture windows) open onto tile terraces. Vibrant colors are used throughout: sea blue, olive, sunburst red, and banana. The baths are lined with colored checkerboard tiles, with matching towels and rows of decorative bottles. Those rooms with sea views are the most expensive.

Hôtel Gray-d'Albion. 38 rue des Serbes, 06400 Cannes. ☎ **04-92-99-79-79.** Fax 04-93-99-26-10. 172 rms, 14 suites. A/C MINIBAR TV TEL. 600F–700F ($120–$140) double; from 2,600F ($520) suite. AE, DC, MC, V.

The smallest of the major hotels here isn't on La Croisette, but this building contains pastel-colored rooms, each outfitted with all the luxury a modern hotel can offer—some critics consider the Gray-d'Albion among France's most luxurious hotels. Groups form a large part of its clientele, but it also caters to the individual guest. Rooms on the eighth and ninth floors have views of the Mediterranean. Dining selections include Le Royal Gray, one of the best in Cannes (see "Dining," below); a beach-club restaurant; and a brasserie that features special dishes from Lebanon.

Novotel Montfleury. 25 av. Beauséjour, 06400 Cannes. ☎ **800/221-4542** in the U.S. and Canada, or 04-93-68-91-50. Fax 04-93-38-37-08. 180 rms, 1 suite. A/C MINIBAR TV TEL. 550F–800F ($110–$160) double; from 1,500F ($300) suite. AE, DC, MC, V. From Cannes, follow the signs to Montfleury or the blue-and-white signs to the Novotel.

Though this hotel seems distant from the crush of Cannes, it's actually only a short, but winding, drive away. The modern palace is set in a 10-acre park that it shares with a sports complex. The magnificent curved pool has a sliding roof and is surrounded by palms. Other facilities are tennis courts (many lit for night play), a volleyball court, a sauna, massage facilities, and a gymnasium, plus two restaurants. The comfortable guest rooms are stylishly filled with all the modern conveniences.

MODERATE

Hôtel Canberra. 120 rue d'Antibes, 06400 Cannes. ☎ **04-93-38-20-70.** Fax 04-92-98-03-47. 45 rms. A/C MINIBAR TV TEL. 492F–722F ($98.40–$144.40) double. AE, DC, MC, V. Parking 42F ($8.40).

This hotel has a marvelous location between the deluxe Carlton and the Palais des Festivals but seems little known. However, it's often booked during the festival by independent producers hoping to hit the big time. The rooms are well maintained, a blend of traditional and modern; those with southern exposure are sunnier and cost more. Breakfast is the only meal served, and limited parking is available by the hotel's small garden.

Hôtel Le Fouquet's. 2 rond-point Duboys-d'Angers, 06400 Cannes. ☎ **04-93-38-75-81.** Fax 04-92-98-03-39. 10 rms. A/C MINIBAR TV TEL. 590F–790F ($118–$158) double. AE, DC, MC, V. Closed Nov 30–Mar. Parking 50F ($10).

This is an intimate low-rise hotel drawing a discreet clientele, often from Paris, who'd never think of patronizing the grand palace hotels, even if they could afford them. Very "Riviera French" in design and decor, it's several blocks from the beach, behind the Noga Hilton. Each of the attractive, airy rooms is decorated in bold colors, containing a loggia, a dressing room, and a hair dryer. Most rooms are spacious. There's no restaurant.

Hôtel Splendid. Allée de la Liberté (4 and 6 rue Félix-Faure), 06400 Cannes. ☎ **04-93-99-53-11.** Fax 04-93-99-55-02. 62 rms, 2 suites. A/C TV TEL. 690F–970F ($138–$194) double; from 1,300F ($260) suite. Rates include continental breakfast. AE, DC, MC, V.

This is a good, conservative hotel—a favorite of academicians, politicians, actors, and musicians. Opened in 1871, it's one of the oldest hotels at the resort. An ornate white building with sinuous wrought-iron accents, the Splendid looks out onto the sea, the old port, and a park. The rooms boast antique furniture, paintings, and videos; 40 of them have kitchenettes. The more expensive rooms have sea views.

Hôtel Victoria. Rond-point Duboys-d'Angers, 06400 Cannes. ☎ **04-93-99-36-36.** Fax 04-93-38-03-91. 25 rms. A/C MINIBAR TV TEL. 410F–1,250F ($82–$250) double. AE, DC, MC, V. Closed Nov–Dec. Parking 60F ($10.80).

A stylish modern hotel in the heart of Cannes, the Victoria offers accommodations with period reproductions and refrigerators. Nearly half the rooms have balconies overlooking the small park and the hotel pool. Bedspreads of silk and padded headboards evoke a boudoir quality. The accommodations facing the park cost a little more but are well worth it. The best rooms have terraces. After a day on the beach, guests congregate in the paneled bar and sink comfortably into the couches and armchairs.

INEXPENSIVE

Hôtel Athénée. 6 rue Lecerf, 06400 Cannes. ☎ **04-93-38-69-54.** Fax 04-92-98-68-30. 15 rms. A/C MINIBAR TV TEL. 450F ($81) double. AE, DC, MC, V.

On a quiet business street about 4 blocks from the seafront, this small hotel occupies the first floor of a modern apartment building. The owner, M. Belvisi, who lives on the premises, offers comfortable, unpretentious rooms that are clean and relatively affordable. Breakfast is the only meal served, though three neighborhood bistros offer inexpensive fixed-price meals to guests: 50F ($10) at lunch and 100F ($20) at dinner. They offer good value in an otherwise relatively expensive neighborhood.

✪ **Hôtel de France.** 85 rue d'Antibes, 06400 Cannes. ☎ **04-93-06-54-54.** Fax 04-93-68-53-43. 34 rms. A/C TV TEL. 350F–450F ($70–$90) double. AE, DC, MC, V. Parking 30F ($6). Closed Nov 15–Dec 1.

This centrally located hotel is 2 blocks from the sea. The rooms are functional but well maintained and reasonably comfortable. This hotel is viewed, even by the Michelin inspectors, as one of the best of the affordable hotels of Cannes. Except for July and August, when it charges its highest prices, it maintains the 350F ($70) double rate the rest of the year. You can sunbathe on the rooftop.

Hôtel de Provence. 9 rue Molière, 06400 Cannes. ☎ **04-93-38-44-35.** Fax 04-93-39-63-14. 30 rms. A/C MINIBAR TV TEL. 300F–450F ($60–$90) double. AE, MC, V. Parking 35F ($7).

Built in the 1930s and renovated into its present comfortable but uncluttered format in 1992, this hotel is small scale and unpretentious—a distinct contrast to the intensely stylish larger hotels with which it competes. Most of the rooms have private balconies, and many overlook the carefully tended shrubs and palms of the hotel's walled garden. In warm weather, breakfast is served under the vines and flowers of an arbor.

Hôtel Le Florian. 8 rue du Commandant-André, 06400 Cannes. ☎ **04-93-39-24-82.** Fax 04-92-99-18-30. 20 rms. A/C TV TEL. 200F–350F ($40–$70) double. AE, MC, V. Parking 45F ($9) in a nearby public facility.

This hotel is on a busy but narrow commercial street that leads directly into La Croisette, less than 100 yards from the beach and the Palais des Festivals. Built about a century ago, it has been maintained by three generations of the Giordano family since the 1950s. In 1992 many (much-needed) improvements were made to the physical setting. The effect is basic but adequate, and even comfortable. You'll get the sense that the strong and not particularly subtle doorman is keeping a careful eye on things. Breakfast is the only meal served.

Hôtel Les Charmettes. 47 rue de Grasse, 06400 Cannes. ☎ **04-93-39-17-13.** Fax 04-93-68-08-41. 15 rms. TV TEL. 260F–350F ($52–$70) double. AE, DC, MC, V.

This is a modern somewhat boxy hotel near the center of Cannes, with a laissez-faire attitude about who checks in and with whom. As they say at the reception desk, "What else would you expect in France, the world's centerpiece of human rights?" The hotel enjoys one of the most liberal images in a very liberal town and welcomes many gays and lesbians. Each soundproofed room is individually decorated in a tasteful style. Breakfast is the only meal served, though you can get drinks in the lobby. Be warned that the hotel doesn't have any parking facilities.

Hôtel Mondial. 77 rue d'Antibes and 1 rue Teïsseire, 06400 Cannes. ☎ **04-93-68-70-00.** Fax 04-93-99-39-11. 56 rms. A/C TV TEL. 550F–770F ($110–$154) double. AE, DC, MC, V.

This is a modern hotel on a commercial street, with stores on its lower floor. The hotel is about a 3-minute walk from the beach; three-quarters of its rooms have views of the water, and the others overlook the mountains and a street. The soft Devonshire-cream facade has a few small balconies. The attractive rooms are the draw here, with matching fabric on the beds and draperies and sliding mirror doors for wardrobes.

Hôtel Toboso. 7 allée des Olivers (bd. Montfleury), 06400 Cannes. ☎ **04-93-38-20-05.** Fax 04-93-68-09-32. 12 rms. A/C MINIBAR TV TEL. 250F–700F ($50–$140) double. AE, DC, MC, V.

Adjacent to the largest sports center in Cannes, this former private villa has been transformed into a small, homey hotel. (In a romantic outburst, the former owner named it after the city in Spain where Cervantes's Don Quixote is said to have met Dulcinea.) The main lounge—formerly the family salon—has a concert piano. Dancers from the neighboring Rosella Hightower School often frequent the place. Most of the personalized rooms have windows facing the gardens, and some have terraces and kitchens. There's a pool in the garden.

Hôtel Villa de l'Olivier. 5 rue des Tambourinaires, 06400 Cannes. ☎ **04-93-39-53-28.** Fax 04-93-39-55-85. 24 rms. TV TEL. 495F–715F ($99–$143) double. Extra bed 120F–150F ($24–$30). AE, DC, V. Free parking.

In a verdant compound whose palms, figs, and shrubs shield it from the commercial neighborhood surrounding it, this hotel grew from what was a private villa around 1900. Because of its beige stucco walls and terra-cotta roof, it evokes a Provençal farmhouse. The rooms open onto views of the free-form pool or the sea and are thoughtfully decorated. Beaches and the diversions of La Croisette are within a 15-minute walk. Breakfast is the only meal served. Your hosts, the Schildknecht family, do everything they can to make your sojourn in their home comfortable.

Le St-Yves. 49 bd. d'Alsace, 06400 Cannes. ☎ **04-93-38-65-29.** Fax 04-93-68-50-67. 10 rms, 2 suites. TV TEL. 350F–450F ($70–$90) double; 650F ($130) suite. DC.

Set back from the busy coastal boulevard by a garden and a grove of palm trees, this villa is a historic monument. The English-speaking Marylene Camplo owns the villa, part of which she has converted into private apartments you can rent by the week or the month. However, she has kept some rooms to rent for short periods. The rooms differ in size and are pleasantly furnished, mainly with odds and ends accumulated over the years. Breakfast includes fresh croissants, country butter, and rich jam.

DINING
EXPENSIVE

✪ **La Palme d'Or.** In the Hôtel Martinez, 73 bd. de la Croisette. ☎ **04-92-98-74-14.** Reservations required. Main courses 180F–480F ($36–$96); fixed-price menus 295F ($59, Mon–Sat lunch only) and 350F–580F ($70–$116). AE, DC, MC, V. Wed–Sun 12:30–2pm and 7:30–10:30pm (also Tues 7:30–10:30pm mid-June to mid-Sept). Closed Nov 20–Dec 20. FRENCH.

When this hotel was renovated by the Taittinger family (of champagne fame), one of their primary concerns was to establish a restaurant that could rival the tough competition in Cannes. And they've succeeded. The result is this light-wood-paneled, art deco marvel with bay windows, a winter garden theme, and outdoor and enclosed terraces overlooking the pool, the sea, and La Croisette. Your experience will be artfully handled by Vincent Rouard, maître d'hôtel, and the Alsatian-born chef Christian Willer. Menu items change with the seasons but are likely to include warm foie gras with fondue of rhubarb; filets of fried red mullet with a beignet of potatoes, zucchini, and an olive-cream sauce; or a medley of crayfish, clams, and squid marinated in peppered citrus sauce. A modernized version of a Niçois staple includes three parts of a rabbit with rosemary sauce, fresh vegetables, and chickpea rosettes. The most appealing dessert is wild strawberries from nearby Carros, with a Grand

Marnier–flavored nage and a "cream sauce of frozen milk." The service is sensitive, sophisticated, and worldly, without being stiff.

Le Royal Gray. In the Hôtel Gray-d'Albion, 38 rue des Serbes. ☎ **04-92-99-79-60.** Reservations required. Main courses 130F–190F ($26–$38); fixed-price menus 190F–280F ($38–$56). AE, DC, MC, V. Daily noon–2pm and 8–10:30pm. FRENCH.

This restaurant manages to be both cozy and grand, replete with leather chairs, late 19th-century colors of brown and bordeaux, and warm lighting. Michel Bigot's cuisine is subtle and sometimes surprisingly simple, not aiming for the cutting-edge cerebrality of the place's more innovative competitors. Examples are terrines of foie gras, open-faced lobster ravioli, smoked salmon with a "bouquet" of shrimp and sweet-and-sour quenelles, fricassée of lobster with creamy tarragon sauce, and filets of sole either grilled or meunière style. Especially appealing is a duet of lobster and crayfish with truffle-studded risotto. Service is first-class.

MODERATE

Gaston-Gastounette. 7 quai St-Pierre. ☎ **04-93-39-49-44.** Reservations required. Main courses 125F–200F ($25–$40); fixed-price menus 168F ($33.60) at lunch, 199F ($39.80) at dinner. AE, DC, MC, V. Daily noon–2pm and 7–11pm. Closed Dec 1–20. FRENCH.

This is the best restaurant for views of the marina. Located in the old port, it has a stucco exterior with oak moldings and big windows and a sidewalk terrace surrounded by flowers. Inside you'll be served bouillabaisse, breast of duckling in garlic-cream sauce, grilled sea bass with herbs, stuffed mussels, pot-au-feu de la mer (a stew of seafood), and such fish platters as turbot and sole. Sorbet, after all that savory Mediterranean food, is appropriate for dessert.

✪ La Mère Besson. 13 rue des Frères-Pradignac. ☎ **04-93-39-59-24.** Reservations required. Main courses 75F–140F ($15–$28); fixed-price menus 145F–170F ($29–$34) at dinner. AE, DC, MC, V. Mon 7:30–10:30pm, Tues–Fri 12:15–2pm and 7:30–10:30pm, Sat 7:30–10:30pm (open Sun in summer). FRENCH.

The culinary traditions of the late Mère Besson, who opened her restaurant in the 1930s, are carried on in one of Cannes's favorite places. All the specialties are prepared with respect for Provençal traditions and skill, especially some dishes that are served up in great steaming portions. Most delectable is estouffade provençal (beef braised with red wine and rich stock flavored with garlic, onions, herbs, and mushrooms). You can also sample an old-fashioned platter with codfish, fresh vegetables, and dollops of the famous garlic mayonnaise (aïoli) that Provence produces by the tubful. Other specialties are fish soup and, whenever the chef feels inspired, lou piech, a Niçois name for veal brisket stuffed with white-stemmed vegetables, peas, ham, eggs, rice, grated cheese, and herbs. The meat is cooked in salted water with vinegar, carrots, and onions, like a stockpot, then served with thick tomato coulis.

Le Festival. 55 bd. de la Croisette. ☎ **04-93-38-04-81.** Reservations required. Main courses 150F–300F ($30–$60); fixed-price menus 95F–195F ($19–$39). AE, DC, V. Daily 11:30am–3pm and 7:30–10pm. Closed Nov 15–Dec 10 and Mon Oct–Mar. FRENCH.

Screen idols and sex symbols flood the front terrace of this place during the film festival. Almost every chair is emblazoned with the name of movie stars (who may or may not have graced it with their bottoms), and tables here are among the most sought-after entity in town. You can choose from the Restaurant or the less formal Grill Room. Meals in the Restaurant may include bourride provençale, soupe des poissons (fish soup) with rouille, simply grilled fresh fish (perhaps with aïoli), bouillabaisse with lobster, pepper steak, and sea bass flambéed with fennel. Items in the Grill are more in the style of an elegant brasserie, served a bit more rapidly and without as much fuss. An appropriate finish in either section might be a smoothly textured peach Melba, invented by Escoffier.

Le Relais des Semailles. 9 rue St-Antoine. ☎ **04-93-39-22-32.** Reservations required. Main courses 140F–200F ($28–$40); fixed-price menus 155F–280F ($31–$56). AE, DC, MC, V. Daily 7–11:30pm. FRENCH.

This long-enduring favorite is reason enough to visit Le Suquet, Canne's old town. The casual atmosphere is complemented by the food, based on available local ingredients. Stuffed pigeon is a typical dish, and the vegetables are always beautifully prepared. Try, if featured, their foie gras lasagne—sublime. The grilled sea bass is perfectly fresh and aromatically seasoned with herbs. Depending on what looked good at the market that day, the chef might be inspired to, say, whip up a rabbit salad with tarragon jus. The setting is intimate, offering casual dining out on the terrace or in air-conditioned comfort.

INEXPENSIVE

Au Bec Fin. 12 rue du 24-Août. ☎ **04-93-38-35-86.** Reservations required. Main courses 45F–50F ($9–$10); fixed-price menus 88F–108F ($17.60–$21.60). AE, DC, MC, V. Mon–Fri noon–2:30pm and 7–10pm, Sat noon–2:30pm. Closed Dec 15–Jan 15. FRENCH.

On a street halfway between the train station and the beach, this 1880s bistro has little decor but offers especially good meals. Sometimes red carnations are brought in from the fields to brighten the tables. A typical meal might include salade niçoise, the house specialty; then caneton (duckling) with cèpes (flap mushrooms); and finally a choice of cheese and dessert.

Le Caveau 30. 45 rue Félix-Faure. ☎ **04-93-39-06-33.** Reservations required. Main courses 110F–180F ($22–$36); fixed-price menus 114F–165F ($22.80–$33). AE, DC, MC, V. Daily noon–2pm and 7–11pm. FRENCH/SEAFOOD.

This restaurant, specializing in fine cuisine, emphasizes seafood. Begin with a seafood platter and follow with one of the chef's classic dishes, pot-au-feu "from the sea" or shellfish paella. Bouillabaisse is the classic dish to order, but you may prefer a filet au poivre (pepper steak) or even fresh pasta. The 1930s decor, the air-conditioning, and the terrace all make dining a pleasant experience.

Le Marais. 9 rue du Suquet. ☎ **04-93-38-39-19.** Reservations recommended. Main courses 80F–130F ($16–$26); fixed-price menu 125F ($25). MC, V. Tues–Sun 7:30–11pm. FRENCH.

This is the most successful gay restaurant in Cannes, with a crowd of mostly gay men dining as couples or groups, sometimes with their entourages from the worlds of fashion and entertainment. The setting is a warm and appealing mix of Parisian and Provençal, with paneled walls and a bustling terrace that in its way is one of the most sought-after outdoor venues in town. Menu items are conservative and not particularly experimental, like ravioli of duck meat, a mixed fish platter, and jumbo shrimp fried with garlic.

✪ Le Monaco. 15 rue du 24-Août. ☎ **04-93-38-37-76.** Reservations required. Main courses 50F–90F ($10–$18); fixed-price menus 88F–110F ($17.60–$22). MC, V. Mon–Sat noon–2pm and 7–10:30pm. Closed Nov 10–Dec 10. FRENCH/ITALIAN.

This workingperson's favorite eatery, crowded but always cheap, is conveniently near the train station. The likable ambience features closely placed tables, clean napery, and a staff dressed in bistro-inspired uniforms. Menu choices include osso buco with sauerkraut, spaghetti bolognese, paella, couscous, roast rabbit with mustard sauce, mussels, trout with almonds, and minestrone with basil. Another specialty is grilled sardines, which many restaurants won't serve anymore, considering them too messy and old-fashioned.

Villa Dionysos. 7 rue Marceau. ☎ **04-93-38-79-73.** Reservations required. Main courses 80F–160F ($16–$32); fixed-price menu 130F ($26). AE, V. Mar–Oct, daily 12:30–2pm and 7:30–11pm; Nov–Feb, Mon 12:30–2pm, Tues–Sat 7:30–1pm. FRENCH/PROVENÇAL.

This former private home is a few paces from rue d'Antibes. The flowering terrace has painted columns; the interior is decorated with trompe l'oeil and ornate plaster ceilings. You can dine very well here. The menu isn't terribly long but is well chosen, based on the freshest ingredients. Menus change with the season, but typical dishes are filet of duck with peaches, roast hare with herbs, filet of fresh mackerel with beurre blanc, and even pig's feet with green cabbage. This is also a good place to visit for a drink, as it contains a big wooden bar that's quite beautiful. After dinner there's either live or recorded music—mellow tunes, nothing too noisy.

CANNES AFTER DARK

On the eighth floor (seventh in France) of the Hôtel Carlton Intercontinental, 58 bd. de la Croisette, is **Le Carlton Casino Club** (☎ **04-93-68-00-33**). Considerably smaller than its major competitor (the Casino Croisette), its modern decor nonetheless draws many devotees. Jackets are required for men, and a passport or government-issued identity card is required for admission. It's open daily from 7:30pm to 4am. Admission is 70F ($14).

The largest and most legendary casino in Cannes is the **Casino Croisette,** in the Palais des Festivals, 1 jetée Albert-Edouard, near promenade de la Croisette (☎ **04-93-38-12-11**). Within its glittering confines you'll find all the gaming tables you'd expect—open daily from 5pm to 4 or 5am—and one of the best nightclubs in town, **Jimmy's de Régine** (☎ **04-93-68-00-07**). Jimmy's is open Wednesday to Sunday from 11pm to dawn. You must present your passport to enter the gambling room. Admission is 100F ($20) and includes a drink.

Jane's is in the cellar of the Hôtel Gray-d'Albion, 38 rue des Serbes (☎ **04-92-99-79-79**). This is a stylish and appealing nightclub with an undercurrent of coy permissiveness. The crowd is well dressed (often with the men wearing jackets and ties) and from a wide gamut of ages. The cover is 50F to 100F ($10 to $20), depending on business, and on some slow nights women enter free.

Gays and lesbians should check out the action in **Le Vogue,** open Tuesday to Sunday to 2:30am. Another bar/disco that lures the gay crowd is **3 Cloches,** 6 rue Vidal (☎ **04-93-68-32-92**), charging 70F ($14) including the first drink. The bar opens at 11pm, and the disco gets rocking at midnight. Attracting an older gay crowd, **Zanzi-Bar,** La Pantiéro, opposite Vieux Port, charges a 50F to 100F ($10 to $20) cover.

9 Grasse

563 miles S of Paris, 11 miles N of Cannes, 6 miles NW of Mougins, 14 miles NW of Antibes

Grasse, a 20-minute drive from Cannes, is the most fragrant town on the Riviera, though it looks tacky modern. Surrounded by jasmine and roses, it has been the capital of the perfume industry since the 19th century. It was once a famous resort, attracting such royalty as Queen Victoria and Princess Pauline Borghese, Napoléon's lascivious sister.

Today some three-quarters of the world's essences are produced here from foliage that includes violets, daffodils, wild lavender, and jasmine. It takes 10,000 flowers to produce 2.2 pounds of jasmine petals. Another statistic: Almost a ton of petals is needed to distill 1^{1}/$_{2}$ quarts of essence. These figures are important to keep in mind when looking at that high price tag on a bottle of perfume.

ESSENTIALS

GETTING THERE   Some 21 buses per day pull in from Cannes (trip time: 45 min.), at a one-way fare of 19.50F ($3.90), and 30 per day from Nice (trip time: 1^{1}/$_{2}$ hr.), at 36F ($7.20) one-way. For **bus information,** call ☎ **04-93-85-61-81** in Nice or ☎ **04-93-39-18-71** in Cannes.

VISITOR INFORMATION   The **Office de Tourisme** is in the Palais des Congrès on place du Cours (☎ **04-93-36-66-66**).

SEEING THE TOP ATTRACTIONS

One of the best-known perfume factories is the **Parfumerie Fragonard,** 20 bd. Fragonard (☎ **04-93-36-44-65**), named after the 18th-century French painter. This factory has the best villa, the best museum, and the best tour. An English-speaking guide will show you how "the soul of the flower" is extracted. After the tour, you can explore the museum of perfumery, which displays bottles and vases that trace the industry back to ancient times. It's open in summer, daily (including holidays) from 9am to 6:30pm; off-season, Monday to Saturday from 9am to 12:30pm and 2 to 6pm. Of course, if you're shopping for perfume and want to skip the tour, that's okay with these factories.

Nearby is the **Villa Fragonard,** 23 bd. Fragonard (☎ **04-93-40-32-64**), whose collection includes the paintings of Jean-Honoré Fragonard; his sister-in-law, Marguerite Gérard; his son, Alexandre; and his grandson, Théophile. Fragonard was born in Grasse in 1732. The grand staircase was decorated by Alexandre. It's open Wednesday to Sunday from 10am to noon and 2 to 5pm. Admission is 20F ($4) for adults and 10F ($2) for children.

The **Musée d'Art et d'Histoire de Provence,** 2 rue Mirabeau (☎ **04-93-36-01-61**), is in the Hôtel de Clapiers-Cabris, built in 1771 by Louise de Mirabeau, the marquise de Cabris and sister of Mirabeau. The collection includes paintings, four-poster beds, marquetry, ceramics, brasses, kitchenware, pottery, urns, and even archaeological finds. It's open June to September, daily from 10am to 12:30pm and 1:30 to 7pm; October and December to May, Wednesday to Sunday from 10am to noon and 2 to 5pm; closed November. Admission is 20F ($4) for adults, 10F ($2) for children 8 to 16, and free for children 7 and under.

Another popular place is the **Parfumerie Molinard,** 60 bd. Victor-Hugo (☎ **04-93-36-01-62**). The firm is well known in the United States and its products are sold at Saks, Neiman Marcus, and Bloomingdale's. In the factory you can witness the extraction of the essence of the flowers, and the process of converting flowers into essential oils is explained in detail. You'll discover why turning flowers into perfume has been called a "work of art" and can admire a collection of antique perfume-bottle labels as well as see a rare collection of perfume *flacons* (bottles) by Baccarat and Lalique. It's open daily: May to September from 9am to 6:30pm and October to April from 9am to noon and 2 to 6pm. Entrance is free.

ACCOMMODATIONS

Hôtel Les Arômes. 115 rte. de Cannes, 06130 Grasse. ☎ **04-93-70-42-01.** 7 rms. TV TEL. 350F ($70) double. Rates include breakfast. AE, MC, V.

Although Les Arômes is near a noisy highway between Grasse and Cannes, it's private and calm thanks to the surrounding wall and gravel-covered courtyard. Half a mile south of the center of Grasse, this modern building was designed in the 1950s in a Provençal style, with beige stone, pink stucco, and terra-cotta tiles. The dining room, with three large arched windows overlooking the courtyard, is open daily except Saturday lunch from noon to 2pm and 7:30 to 9:30pm; nonguests are welcome. Fixed-price menus are 80F to 140F ($16 to $28). Don't expect high style or spit-and-polish glamour, as this place is deliberately laid-back and informal.

Hôtel Panorama. 2 place du Cours, 06130 Grasse. ☎ **04-93-36-80-80.** Fax 04-93-36-92-04. 36 rms. MINIBAR TV TEL. 275F–420F ($55–$84) double. AE, MC, V. Parking 25F ($5).

In the commercial core of Grasse, this hotel has a facade in a sienna hue that its owners call "Garibaldi red." The more expensive rooms have balconies, southern exposures, and views of the sea; 20 have air-conditioning. The furnishings are basic and simple. There's no bar or restaurant, but food is brought to your room on request, and the staff is cooperative and hardworking.

DINING

Note that the dining room at the **Hôtel Les Arômes** (see "Accommodations," above) is open to nonguests.

✪ **La Bastide St-Antoine (Restaurant Chibois).** 48 av. Henri-Dunant. ☎ **04-93-09-16-48.** Reservations recommended. Main courses 170F–280F ($34–$56); fixed-price menus 210F ($42) (Mon–Sat lunch) and 380F–550F ($76–$110). AE, MC, V. Daily noon–2pm and 8–10:30pm. FRENCH/PROVENÇAL.

The fame that this restaurant has attracted since it opened in 1996 is viewed with amazement and envy by every restaurateur in France. It occupies a 200-year-old Provençal farmhouse surrounded by 7 acres of stately trees and verdant shrubberies. The aspect that intrigued the French press was Jacques Chibois, formerly employed in the dining room of Cannes's Hôtel Gray-d'Albion; his elevation to superstar came in 1997 through awards lavished on him by the controversial Gault-Millau group.

With a hardworking team directed by the maître d'hôtel Herve Domenge, the restaurant serves a sophisticated array of dishes that aren't as much composed as they are "harmonized," at least according to Domenge. To begin, you might try a salad of scallops with pasta flavored with fresh herbs, a salad of red snapper with a parsley salad and Provençal vegetables and olive oil, or a slice of braised foie gras with a "pyramid" of artichokes and a dollop of terrine of foie gras. Main courses to look for are roast rack of lamb with brochettes of rosemary and basil juice, veal kidneys with an émincé of purple artichokes and risotto, and an exotic recipe for veal chops cooked in laurel leaves and flavored with sherry and a pain perdu of eggplant and dried flap mushrooms. Dessert might be sliced apples in puff pastry with a caramel sauce or frozen rhubarb flavored with oranges, wild strawberries, and rhubarb sorbet.

Restaurant Amphitryon. 16 bd. Victor-Hugo. ☎ **04-93-36-58-73.** Reservations recommended. Main courses 95F–160F ($19–$32); fixed-price menus 116F–244F ($23.20–$48.80). AE, DC, MC, V. Mon–Sat noon–1:30pm and 7:30–9:30pm. Closed Aug 15–Sept 15 and Dec 23–31. FRENCH.

Many of the buildings that line this street, including the premises of this restaurant, functioned as stables in the 19th century. Today, amid fabric-covered walls and soothing grays and off-whites, you can enjoy the flavorful cuisine of Michel André. The food is inspired by southwestern France, with plenty of foie gras and duckling, as well as lamb roasted with thyme and a ragoût of fish in red wine that in recent years has become one of the chef's most popular dishes. Also recommendable are the Mediterranean fish soup with Provençal rouille and virtually any of the autumn dishes enhanced with seasonal fresh mushrooms.

10 Mougins

561 miles S of Paris, 7 miles S of Grasse, 5 miles N of Cannes

This once-fortified town on the crest of a hill provides an alternative for those who want to be near the excitement of Cannes but not in the midst of it. Picasso and other artists appreciated the rugged, sun-drenched hills covered with gnarled olive trees. The artist arrived in 1936, and in time was followed by Jean Cocteau, Paul Eluard, and Man Ray. Picasso decided to move here permanently, choosing as his refuge an ideal site overlooking the Bay of Cannes, near the Chapelle Notre-Dame de Vie, which Winston Churchill once painted. Here Picasso continued to work and spend the latter part of his life with his wife, Jacqueline. Fernard Léger, René Clair, Isadora Duncan, and even Christian Dior have lived at Mougins.

Mougins is the perfect haven for those who feel that the Riviera is overrun, spoiled, and overbuilt. It preserves the quiet life very close to the international resort, and gentle streams flow in the little valleys. The wealthy come from Cannes to golf here. Though Mougins looks serene and tranquil, it's actually part of the industrial park of Sophia Antipolis, a technological center where more than 1,000 national and international companies have offices.

ESSENTIALS

GETTING THERE   There's limited daily **bus** service from Cannes. The bus from Cannes to Grasse stops a mile from Mougins. Call ☎ **04-93-39-18-71** for information and schedules.

VISITOR INFORMATION   The **Syndicat d'Initiative** (tourist office) is at 15 av. Jean-Charles-Mallet (☎ **04-93-75-87-67**).

SEEING THE SIGHTS

For a preview of the history of the area, the **Musée Municipal,** place du Village (☎ **04-92-92-50-42**), is in the Sant Bernardin Chapel, built in 1618. It's open Monday to Friday from 8:30am to noon and 2:30 to 6pm (closed November), charging no admission.

An even bigger attraction is the **Musée de l'Automobiliste,** Aire des Bréguières (☎ **04-93-69-27-80**), ranked seventh in the list of cultural sights for the Côte d'Azur. Founded in 1984 by Adrien Maeght, this ultramodern concrete-and-glass structure rises out of a green clearing. It houses temporary exhibitions but also owns one of Europe's most magnificent collections of original and prestigious automobiles—more than 100 vehicles from 1894 until the present. It's open daily from 10am to 7pm (closed November 15 to December 15), charging 40F ($8) for adults and 25F ($5) for children 11 and under.

You can also visit the **Chapelle Notre-Dame de Vie,** a mile southeast of Mougins, where Picasso spent the last 12 years of his life next to the chapel that Churchill painted. It was a priory from the 12th century that was rebuilt in 1646. It was an old custom at one time to bring stillborn babies here to have them baptized.

ACCOMMODATIONS

Note that **Le Moulin de Mougins** (see "Dining," below) offers charming rooms and suites.

Manoir de l'Etang. Aux Bois de Font-Merle, allée du Manoir, 06250 Mougins. ☎ **04-93-90-01-07.** Fax 04-92-92-20-70. 14 rms, 2 apts. TV TEL. 600F–900F ($120–$180) double; 1,300F–1,500F ($260–$300) apt. AE, V. Closed Feb and mid-Nov to mid-Dec.

In the midst of olive trees and cypresses, this is one of the choice places to stay on the Riviera, housed in a 19th-century Provençal building. It boasts all the romantic extras associated with some Riviera properties, including "love goddess" statuary in the garden and candlelit dinners around a pool, but it charges reasonable rates. The rooms are bright and modern—you'll feel almost as if you're staying in a private home, which this place virtually is. Some rooms are extremely spacious. In winter, meals are served around a wood-burning fireplace. The chef bases his menu on the freshest ingredients available in any season, with fixed-price menus for 145F to 190F ($29 to $38).

Mas Candille. Bd. Rebuffel, 06250 Mougins. ☎ **04-93-90-00-85.** Fax 04-92-92-85-56. 23 rms, 1 suite. A/C TEL. 680F–1,180F ($136–$236) double; from 1,800F ($360) suite. AE, DC, MC, V. Closed Nov 4–Mar 14.

This 200-year-old Provençal farmhouse was skillfully converted. The public rooms contain many 19th-century furnishings, and some open onto the gardens. The renovated guest rooms are cozy and tranquil, with traditional Provençal furnishings. The family managers are always willing to provide you with whatever you need to make your room more comfortable.

The dining room has elegant stone detailing and a massive fireplace with a timbered mantelpiece. The food is exceptional, with menus costing 185F to 250F ($37 to $50). Typical dishes are soupe de poissons (fish), stuffed zucchini flowers, and braised sweetbreads with mushrooms. Fresh salads and light meals are available throughout the day. In good weather lunch is served on the terrace; dinner is served on the terrace in summer only.

DINING

L'Amandier de Mougins Café-Restaurant. Place du Commandant-Lamy. ☎ **04-93-90-00-91.** Reservations recommended. Main courses 70F–100F ($14–$20). AE, DC, MC, V. Daily noon–2:15pm and 8–10pm. NIÇOIS/PROVENÇAL.

The illustrious founder of this relatively inexpensive bistro is the world-famous Roger Vergé, whose much more expensive Moulin de Mougins is described below. Conceived as a mass-market satellite to its exclusive neighbor, this restaurant serves relatively simple platters in an airy stone house. The specialties are usually based on traditional recipes and may include tuna and swordfish carpaccio, tagliatelle with truffle-cream sauce, magret of duckling, or veal kidneys with fricassée of mushrooms.

Le Feu Follet. Place de la Mairie. ☎ **04-93-90-15-78.** Reservations required. Main courses 130F–145F ($26–$29); fixed-price menu 158F ($31.60). AE, MC, V. Tues–Sat noon–2pm and 7:30–10pm, Sun noon–2pm. FRENCH.

Beside the square in the old village, this restaurant has two roughly plastered rooms that always seem cramped and overcrowded, but the quality of the cuisine (and the affordable prices) make it a worthy choice. Only top-quality ingredients, the best in the market, go into the cooking. One longtime habitué, describing the Provençal vegetables served here, claimed they were "filled with the sun." Fancy sauces and overpreparation of dishes are never a factor, and the fresh herbs of Provence are used effectively. Typical dishes are fish soup with rouille, ravioli with foie gras and morels, magret of duckling with tarragon, and veal kidneys in a mustard sauce.

✪ Le Moulin de Mougins. Notre-Dame de Vie, 06250 Mougins. ☎ **04-93-75-78-24.** Fax 04-93-90-18-55. Reservations required. Main courses 180F–400F ($36–$80); fixed-price menus 305F–740F ($61–$148) at lunch, 615F–740F ($123–$148) at dinner. AE, DC, MC, V. Tues–Sun noon–2:15pm and 8–10pm. Closed Feb 12–Mar 12. FRENCH.

This place, 4 miles north of Cannes, is either among France's top 20 restaurants or an overpublicized place that's in serious decline, depending on which critic you read. Michelin now gives it only one star.

A 10-foot-wide stone oil vat, with a wooden turnscrew and a grinding wheel, is near the entrance. This is the kingdom of Roger Vergé, the maître cuisinier de France. His specialties include filets de rougets (red mullet) with artichokes; noisettes d'agneau (lamb) de Sisteron with an eggplant cake in thyme-flavored sauce and poupeton (zucchini flowers) stuffed with a mixture of truffles and pulverized mushrooms, served with truffle-flavored butter sauce; fricassée of lobster with sweet wine, cream sauce, and sweet peppers; and pepper steak "à la Mathurin," with grapes, pepper, and brandy. Dessert might be a lemon soufflé. His forté is fish from the Mediterranean, bought fresh each morning. Monsieur Vergé offers a lot of fantastic, even historic wines but also has a good selection of local vintages.

The old mill offers four beautiful suites and three rooms, with air-conditioning, minibars, TVs, phones, and fax machines. The rooms are decorated with French antiques. These rent for 800F to 1,300F ($160 to $260).

✪ **Le Relais à Mougins.** Place de la Mairie. ☎ **04-93-90-03-47.** Reservations recommended. Fixed-price menus 80F–125F ($16–$25) at lunch, 150F–375F ($30–$75) at dinner. MC, V. Tues–Sat noon–2:15pm and 7:30–10:30pm, Sun noon–2:15pm. FRENCH.

This is one of the village's best restaurants, attracting celebrities from both sides of the Atlantic. It's housed in a beautifully proportioned Provençal building, with a black-and-white marble floor and a vaulted ceiling. Photographs of Picasso are part of the decor. The restaurant fronts one of Provence's most perfect village squares, with three graceful fountains and flowering shrubs. Many diners prefer the outdoor terrace with a canopy. The owner, André Surmain, who founded Lutèce in New York, has had a colorful, adventurous life. Born in Cairo, he was a member of the French Resistance and of the OSS in the U.S. Army. His menu embraces light and creative dishes, though he's most proud of his *menu dégustation.* Specialties are salade oasis (lobster, apples, and endive), saddle of baby lamb en chemise (boned and served in thin pancakes with fresh tarragon), and Bresse pigeon en croûte (baked in a thin potato crust).

11 Golfe-Juan & Vallauris

Golfe-Juan: 567 miles S of Paris, 4 miles E of CannesVallauris: 565 miles S of Paris, 4 miles E of Cannes

Napoléon and 800 men landed at Golfe-Juan in 1815 to begin his Hundred Days. Protected by hills, Golfe-Juan, beside the coast, was also the favored port for the American navy, though it's primarily a family resort known for its beaches. It contains one notable restaurant: Chez Tétou. The 1¼-mile-long R.N. 135 leads inland from Golfe-Juan to Vallauris. Once merely a stopover along the Riviera, Vallauris (noted for its pottery) owes its reputation to Picasso, who "discovered" it. The master came to Vallauris after World War II and occupied a villa known as "The Woman from Wales."

ESSENTIALS

GETTING THERE   Buses travel to both Vallauris and Golfe-Juan from Cannes, and other **buses** connect the two towns. In Cannes call ☎ **04-93-39-18-71** for information and schedules.

VISITOR INFORMATION   There's an **Office de Tourisme** at 84 av. de la Liberté in Golfe-Juan (☎ **04-93-63-73-12**) and another on square 8-Mai in Vallauris (☎ **04-93-63-82-58**).

SEEING THE TOP ATTRACTIONS

Because of its position beside the sea, Golfe-Juan developed long ago into a warm-weather resort, and landlocked Vallauris depends on the sale of tourist items and ceramics—many the color of rich burgundy—for part of its livelihood. Merchants selling the colorful wares line both sides of avenue Georges-Clemenceau, which begins at a point adjacent to the Musée Picasso and slopes downhill and southward to the edge of town. Frankly, at least some of the pieces displayed in these shops are in poor taste, though in recent years the almost-universal emphasis on the traditional deep-red color has been replaced with a wider variety geared to modern tastes.

Picasso's **Homme et Mouton** (Man and Sheep) is the outdoor statue where Aly Kahn and Rita Hayworth were married. The council of Vallauris had intended to ensconce this statue in a museum, but Picasso insisted that it remain on the square "where the children could climb over it and the dogs water it unhindered."

At place de la Libération stands a chapel of rough stone shaped like a Quonset hut. It's the focal point of a three-in-one sightseeing highlight, the **Musée Magnelli / Musée de la Céramique/Musée National Picasso La Guerre et La Paix** (☎ **04-93-64-16-05**). The museum grew from the site of a chapel that Picasso decorated with two paintings: *La Paix* (Peace) and *La Guerre* (War). The paintings offer contrasting images of love and peace on the one hand and violence and conflict on the other. In 1970, a house painter gained illegal entrance to the museum one night and substituted one of his own designs, after whitewashing a portion of the original. When the aging master inspected the damage, he said, "Not bad at all." In July 1996, the site was enhanced with a permanent exposition devoted to the works of the Florentine-born Alberto Magnelli, a pioneer of abstract art whose first successes were acclaimed in 1915, and who died in 1971, 2 years before Picasso. A third section showcases ceramics, both traditional and innovative, from potters throughout the region. All three sections are open Wednesday to Monday from 10am to noon and 2 to 6pm. Admission is 17F ($3.40) for adults, 8.50F ($1.70) for students, and free for children 15 and under.

A DAY AT THE BEACH

The town's twin strips of beach are **Plages du Soleil** (east of the Vieux Port and the newer Port Camille-Rayon) and **Plages du Midi** (west of those two). Each stretches half a mile and is free, with the exception of small areas administered by concessions that rent mattresses and chaises and offer access to kiosks dispensing snacks and cold drinks. Regardless of which concession you select (on Plage du Midi they sport names like **Au Vieux Rocher, Palma Beach,** and **Corail Plage;** on Plage du Soleil, **Plage Nounou** and **Plage Tétou**), you'll pay around 70F ($14) for a day's use of a mattress. Plage Tétou is associated with the upscale Chez Tétou (see "Dining," below). If you don't want to rent a mattress, you can cavort unhindered anywhere along the sands, moving freely from one area to another. Golfe-Juan indulges bathers who remove their bikini tops, but in theory forbids nude sunbathing.

SHOPPING

One shop that rises far above its neighbors is the **Galerie Madoura,** avenue des Anciens-Combattants-d'Afrique-du-Nord in Vallauris (☎ **04-93-64-66-39**); it's the only shop licensed to sell Picasso reproductions. The master knew and admired the work of the Ramie family, who founded Madoura, open Monday to Friday from 10am to 12:30pm and 2:30 to 7pm (to 6pm October to March). Some of the reproductions are limited to 25 to 500 copies.

Other galleries to seek out are **Galerie 52,** 52 av. Georges-Clemenceau (☎ 04-93-63-10-12); **Galerie Jean Marais,** avenue des Martyrs-de-la-Résistance (☎ 04-93-63-85-74); and **Galerie Sassi-Milici,** 65 bis av. Georges-Clemenceau (☎ 04-93-64-65-71), displaying works by contemporary artists.

Market day at Vallauris takes place Monday to Saturday in the morning at **place de l'Homme au Mouton,** with its flower stalls and local produce. For a souvenir, you may want to visit a farming cooperative, **Cooperative Nérolium,** 12 av. Georges-Clemenceau (☎ 04-93-64-27-54), and purchase some locally made perfumes direct from the producers. Another outlet is **Parfumerie Bouis,** 50 av. Georges-Clemenceau (☎ 04-93-64-38-27).

DINING

✪ **Chez Tétou.** Av. des Frères-Roustand, sur la Plage, Golfe-Juan. ☎ **04-93-63-71-16.** Reservations required. Fixed-price menus 500F–700F ($100–$140); bouillabaisse 400F–480F ($80–$96). No credit cards. Daily noon–2:30pm and 8–10pm. Closed Nov–Apr. SEAFOOD.

In its own amusing way, this is one of the Côte d'Azur's most famous restaurants, capitalizing richly on the glittering *beau monde* who frequented it during the 1950s and 1960s. Retaining its Provençal earthiness despite its incredibly high prices, it has thrived in a white-sided beach cottage for more than 65 years. It still serves a bouillabaisse often remembered years later by diners. Other items on the deliberately limited menu are grilled sea bass with tomatoes provençal, sole meunière, and several preparations of lobster—the most famous of which is grilled and served with lemon-butter sauce, fresh parsley, and a bed of Basmati rice. The list of appetizers is limited to platters of charcuterie (cold cuts) or several almost-perfect slices of fresh melon, as most diners order the house specialty, bouillabaisse. Your dessert might be a special powdered croissant with grandmother's jams (winter) or a homemade raspberry and strawberry tart (summer).

12 Juan-les-Pins

567 miles S of Paris, 6 miles S of Cannes

This suburb of Antibes is a resort that was developed in the 1920s by Frank Jay Gould. At that time people flocked to "John of the Pines" to escape the "crassness" of nearby Cannes. In the 1930s Juan-les-Pins drew a chic crowd during winter. Today it attracts young Europeans from many economic backgrounds, in pursuit of sex, sun, and sea in that order.

Juan-les-Pins is often called a honky-tonk town or the "Coney Island of the Riviera," but anyone who calls it that hasn't seen Coney Island in a long time. One newspaper writer called it "a pop-art Monte Carlo, with burlesque shows and nude beaches"—a description much too provocative for such a middle-class resort. Another newspaper writer said that Juan-les-Pins is "for the young and noisy." Even F. Scott Fitzgerald decried it as a "constant carnival." If he could see it now, he'd know that he was a prophet.

ESSENTIALS

GETTING THERE   Juan-les-Pins is connected by train and bus to most other Mediterranean coastal resorts, especially Nice, from which frequent trains arrive throughout the day (trip time: 30 min.). For **rail information** and schedules, call ☎ 08-36-35-35-35. There are also buses that arrive from Nice and its airport at 40-minute intervals throughout the day.

VISITOR INFORMATION   The **Office de Tourisme** is at 51 bd. Charles-Guillaumont (☎ 04-92-90-53-05).

A DAY AT THE BEACH

Part of the success of Juan-les-Pins as a beach resort is the fact that its beaches actually have sand. **Plage de Juan-les-Pins** is the town's most central beach. Its subdivisions, all public, include **Plage de la Salis** and **Plage de la Garoupe.** Many
people opt to tote their own blankets, chairs, and picnic hampers, but if you're
interested in renting a chaise with a mattress, go to the concessions operated by each
of the major beachfront hotels, even if you're not a guest; they cost between 60F and
70F ($12 and $14). The chicest of the lot is the area maintained by the Hôtel des
Belles-Rives. Competitors more or less in the same category are **La Jetée** and **La Voile
Blanche,** both opposite the tourist information office. Topless sunbathing is permitted, but total nudity isn't.

OUTDOOR ACTIVITIES

If you're interested in **scuba diving,** check with your hotel concierge or one of these
companies: the **Spondyle Club,** 62 av. des Pins-du-Cap (☎ **04-93-61-45-45**); **Club
de la Mer,** Port Gallice (☎ **04-93-61-26-07**); or **EPAJ,** embarcadère Courbet
(☎ **04-93-67-52-59**). **Waterskiing** is available at virtually every beach in Juan-les-
Pins, including one outfit that's more or less permanently located on the beach of the
Hôtel des Belles-Rives. Ask any beach attendant or bartender, and he or she will guide
you to the waterskiing representatives who station themselves on the sands. The cost
for a 10-minute session is about 150F ($30).

ACCOMMODATIONS

Note that the **Auberge de l'Estérel** (see "Dining," below) also rents rooms.

EXPENSIVE

Belles-Rives. 33 bd. Baudoin, 06160 Juan-les-Pins. ☎ **04-93-61-02-79.** Fax 04-93-67-43-51.
41 rms, 4 suites. A/C MINIBAR TV TEL. 990F–2,450F ($198–$490) double; 3,240F–4,400F
($648–$880) suite. Half board 390F ($78) per person extra. AE, MC, V. Closed Oct–Mar.

This is one of the Riviera's fabled addresses, on a par with the equally famous Juana,
though the Juana boasts a somewhat superior cuisine. Once it was a holiday villa
occupied by Zelda and F. Scott Fitzgerald, so it was the scene of many a drunken
brawl. In the following years it hosted the illustrious, like the duke and duchess of
Windsor, Josephine Baker, and even Edith Piaf. A certain 1930s aura still lingers.
A major restoration was concluded in 1990, with subsequent, less comprehensive
upgrades made at 2-year intervals since. Double-glazing and a new air-conditioning
system help a lot. The lower terraces are devoted to garden dining rooms and a
waterside aquatic club with a snack bar/lounge and a jetty extending into the water.
Dinners are served in a romantic setting on the terrace with a panoramic bay view;
lunches are stylish but somewhat less formal and offered in a setting overlooking the
beach. Also on the premises are a private beach and a landing dock.

✪ **Hôtel Juana.** La Pinède, av. Gallice, 06160 Juan-les-Pins. ☎ **04-93-61-08-70.** Fax 04-93-
61-76-60. 45 rms, 5 suites. A/C TV TEL. 850F–2,050F ($170–$410) double; 1,600F–3,500F
($320–$700) suite. MC, V. Closed Nov–Mar.

This balconied art deco four-star hotel, owned by the Barache family since 1931, is
separated from the sea by the park of pines that gave Juan-les-Pins its name and that
was so beloved by F. Scott Fitzgerald. The hotel has a private swimming club where
you can rent a "parasol and pad" on the sandy beach at reduced rates. Nearby is a
park with umbrella tables and shady palms. The hotel is constantly being refurbished,
as reflected in the attractive rooms, with mahogany pieces, well-chosen fabrics, tasteful
carpets, and large baths in marble or tile imported from Italy. The rooms also have
such extras as safes and (in some) balconies. We discuss La Terrasse restaurant

under "Dining," below. There's a bar in the poolhouse. Also on the premises are a private beach club and a heated marble outdoor pool with a solarium.

MODERATE

Hôtel des Mimosas. Rue Pauline, 06160 Juan-les-Pins. ☎ **04-93-61-04-16.** Fax 04-9.2-93-06-46. 36 rms. MINIBAR TEL. 470F–650F ($94–$130) double. AE, MC, V. Closed Sept 30–Apr 26. From the town center, drive a quarter mile west, following N7 toward Cannes.

This elegant 1870s-style villa sprawls in a tropical garden on a hilltop. Michel and Raymonde Sauret redesigned the interior with the help of an architect who trained in the United States. The decor is a mix of high-tech and Italian-style comfort, with antique and modern furniture. There's a bar but no restaurant. The rooms have balconies. A pool is set, California style, amid huge palm trees. The hotel is fully booked in summer, so reserve far in advance.

Hôtel Le Pré Catelan. 22 av. des Palmiers, 06160 Juan-les-Pins. ☎ **04-93-61-05-11.** Fax 04-93-67-83-11. 18 rms. TEL. 400F–600F ($80–$120) double. AE, DC, MC, V.

In a residential area near the town park, this circa-1900 Provençal villa has a garden with rock terraces, towering palms, lemon and orange trees, large pots of pink geraniums, trimmed hedges, and outdoor furniture. The atmosphere is casual, the setting uncomplicated and unstuffy. The more expensive rooms have terraces, and the furnishings are durable and rather basic. Despite the setting in the heart of town, the garden here manages to provide a sense of isolation. No meals are served other than breakfast, as the place closed its faltering restaurant in 1996.

INEXPENSIVE

Hôtel Cecil. Rue Jonnard, 06160 Juan-les-Pins. ☎ **04-93-61-05-12.** Fax 04-93-67-09-14. 21 rms. TV TEL. 220F–380F ($44–$76) double. MC, V. Closed Oct 15–Jan 1. Parking 50F ($10).

Located 50 yards from the beach, this well-kept hotel is one of the best bargains in Juan-les-Pins. The owner/chef Michel Courtois provides a courteous welcome and good meals beginning at 80F ($16). The rooms are well worn yet clean. In summer you can dine on a patio.

Hôtel Le Passy. 15 av. Louis-Gallet, 06160 Juan-les-Pins. ☎ **04-93-61-11-09.** Fax 04-93-67-91-78. 35 rms. TV TEL. 240F–340F ($48–$68) double. AE, DC, MC, V. Parking 25F ($5).

Centrally located, Le Passy opens onto a wide flagstone terrace. The other side faces the sea and coastal boulevard. The furnishings are Nordic modern, and the newer rooms have little balconies. Those that overlook the sea carry the higher price tag. In high-priced Juan-les-Pins, this is considered one of the more affordable choices, even though it's a bit sterile.

DINING

La Romana. 21 av. Dautheville. ☎ **04-93-61-05-66.** Pizzas 35F–55F ($7–$11); main-course salads and platters 50F–100F ($10–$20). MC, V. Daily 9:30am–11:30pm (to 2:30am June–Sept). Closed mid-Nov to mid-Feb. FRENCH/INTERNATIONAL.

Behind the town's casino, this is an aggressively unpretentious restaurant that successfully caters its trade to the thousands of budget-conscious holiday makers who flood the town every season. Don't expect grande cuisine, as the venue is too simple, too informal. What you'll get—amid a generic 1930s-style decor accented with touches of wrought iron—is pizzas, meal-sized salads, fried fish and fried scampi, grilled steaks with french fries, and *plats du jour* whose composition changes every day.

✪ **La Terrasse.** In the Hôtel Juana, La Pinède, av. Gallice. ☎ **04-93-61-20-37.** Reservations required. Main courses 260F–350F ($52–$70); fixed-price menus 270F ($54) at lunch, 410F–630F ($82–$126) at dinner. AE, MC, V. July–Aug, daily 12:30–2pm and 7:30–10:30pm;

Apr–June and Sept–Oct, Thurs–Tues 12:30–2pm and 7:30–10:30pm. Closed Nov–Mar. FRENCH/ MEDITERRANEAN.

Bill Cosby loves this gourmet restaurant so much that he's been known to fly chef Christian Morisset and his Dalí mustache to New York to prepare dinner for him. Morisset, who trained with Vergé and Lenôtre, cooks with a light, precise, and creative hand. His cuisine is the best in Juan-les-Pins. The setting is lively and sophisticated, with a conservatively modern decor overlooking the verdant garden, and a glassed-in terrace whose roof opens for midsummer ventilation and a view of the stars. Scampi-stuffed ravioli, roast turbot with crusty mashed potatoes studded with Périgord truffles, and pink roasted crayfish with risotto and asparagus are examples of a flavorful, satisfying cuisine that's invariably delectable. We have to mention the crunchily fresh roster of "baby vegetables," for eating baby vegetables is what distinguishes the rich from the rest of us, according to the late Truman Capote.

✪ **Le Bijou.** Bd. Charles-Guillaumont. ☎ **04-93-61-36-07.** Reservations recommended. Main courses 150F–190F ($30–$38); fixed-price menus 165F–280F ($33–$56); shellfish platters 270F ($54); bouillabaisse 300F ($60). AE, DC, MC, V. Daily noon–2:30pm and 7:30–10:30pm (to 11:30pm June to mid-Sept). FRENCH/PROVENÇAL.

This upscale brasserie has flourished beside the seafront promenade for almost 80 years. The marine-style decor includes lots of varnished wood and bouquets of blue and white flowers in a mostly blue-and-white interior. Windows overlook a private beach whose sands are much less crowded than those of the public beaches nearby. Menu items are succulent, sophisticated, and less expensive than you'd expect. Examples are a version of bouillabaisse that might make you clamor for more, platters of grilled sardines, steamed mussels with sauce poulette (frothy cream sauce with herbs and butter), grilled John Dory with a vinaigrette enriched with a tapenade of olives and fresh basil, and a supersized plateau des coquillages et fruits de mer (shellfish). Don't confuse this informally elegant place with its beachfront terrace, open only from April to September every day from noon to 4pm. Here a lunch buffet—served to diners in swimsuits, which are strictly forbidden in the main restaurant several paces uphill—is 70F ($14) per person.

Le Perroquet. Av. Georges-Gallice. ☎ **04-93-61-02-20.** Reservations recommended. Main courses 80F–165F ($16–$33); fixed-price menus 138F–168F ($27.60–$33.60). MC, V. Daily noon–2pm and 7–10:30pm. Closed Nov–Dec 20. PROVENÇAL.

The cuisine is well presented and prepared, and the restaurant's ambience is carefully synchronized to the casual and carnival-like aura that permeates this seafront resort in summer. You'll dine across from the resort's central Parc de la Pinède, in a setting surrounded by depictions of every imaginable form of parakeet, the restaurant's namesake. Look for savory versions of fish that's at its best when it's grilled simply, with olive oil and basil, and served with lemons. A worthwhile appetizer is the assortiment provençale, which includes tapanade of olives, marinated peppers, grilled sardines, and stuffed and grilled vegetables. Steaks might be served with green peppercorns or béarnaise sauce, and desserts include three types of pastries on the same platter.

JUAN-LES-PINS AFTER DARK

The town offers some of the best nightlife on the Riviera, and the action reaches its frenzied height during the annual jazz festival. The **Festival International de Jazz** descends at the end of July, attracting stellar jazz masters and their devoted fans. Tickets range from 110F to 200F ($22 to $40) and can be purchased at the Office de Tourisme (see "Essentials," above).

For starters, visit the **Eden Casino,** boulevard Baudoin in the heart of Juan-les-Pins (☎ 04-92-93-71-71), and try your luck at the roulette wheel or at one of the slot machines. Or for a more tropical experience, head to **Le Pam Pam,** route Wilson (☎ 04-93-61-11-05), where you can sip rum drinks in an exotic ambience created and celebrated by live reggae, Brazilian, and African performances of music and dance.

If you prefer some high-energy reveling, check out the town's many discos, the best of which are **Whisky à Gogo,** boulevard de la Pinède (☎ 04-93-61-26-40), with its young trendsetters and pounding rock beat; the **Wak-Up Club,** avenue Dauthe-ville (☎ 04-93-67-78-87), where everyone bumps and grinds to a stellar house rock mix while surrounded by huge lunar landscape murals; the richly dramatic **Le Bureau,** avenue Georges-Gallice (☎ 04-93-67-22-74), keeping the fast and frenzied beat going with anything from Latin salsa to disco; and **Voom Voom,** 1 bd. de la Pinède (☎ 04-93-61-18-71), which boasts an action-packed dance floor and hip DJs spinning the latest from the international music scene. The cover charge at these clubs is a stiff 100F ($20).

For a more relaxed evening, go to the British pub **Le Ten's Bar,** 25 av. du Dr.-Hochet (☎ 04-93-67-20-67), where you'll find 56 brands of beer and a sociable crowd of young and old merrymakers. You could even choose the tranquil piano bar **Le Cambridge,** 25 rue du Dr.-Hochet (☎ 04-93-67-49-89), with its older, more sophisticated crowd, or **Le Madison,** 1 av. Alexandre-III (☎ 04-93-67-83-80), with the town's best jazz and blues.

13　Antibes & Cap d'Antibes

567 miles S of Paris, 13 miles SW of Nice, 7 miles NE of Cannes

On the other side of the Baie des Anges (Bay of Angels), across from Nice, is the port of Antibes. This old Mediterranean town has a quiet charm unique on the Côte d'Azur. Its little harbor is filled with fishing boats and pleasure yachts, and in recent years it has emerged as a new "hot spot." The marketplaces are full of flowers, mostly roses and carnations. If you're in Antibes in the evening, you can watch fishers playing the popular Riviera game of *boule.*

Spiritually, Antibes is totally divorced from Cap d'Antibes, a peninsula studded with the villas and pools of the super-rich. In *Tender Is the Night,* F. Scott Fitzgerald described it as a place where "old villas rotted like water lilies among the massed pines." Photos of film and rock stars lounging at the Eden Roc have appeared in countless magazines.

ESSENTIALS

GETTING THERE　Trains from Cannes arrive every 30 minutes (trip time: 10 min.), at a one-way fare of 16F ($3.20), and trains from Nice arrive every 30 minutes (trip time: 18 min.), at 22F ($4.40) one-way. For **rail information** and schedules, call ☎ 08-36-35-35-35.

VISITOR INFORMATION　The **Office de Tourisme** is at 11 place du Général-de-Gaulle (☎ 04-92-90-53-00).

TOURING THE TOP ATTRACTIONS

On the ramparts above the port is the Château Grimaldi, place du Château, which contains the **Musée Picasso** (☎ 04-92-90-54-20 for recorded message, or 04-92-90-54-26 for an attendant). Once the home of the princes of Antibes of the Grimaldi family, who ruled the city from 1385 to 1608, today it houses one of the world's greatest Picasso collections. Picasso came to the small town after his bitter war years in Paris and stayed in a small hotel at Golfe-Juan until the museum director at Antibes invited him to work and live at the museum. Picasso then spent 1946 painting here. When he departed, he gave the museum all the work he'd done— 24 paintings, 80 pieces of ceramics, 44 drawings, 32 lithographs, 11 oils on paper, 2 sculptures, and 5 tapestries. In addition, there's a gallery of contemporary art exhibits—Léger, Miró, Ernst, and Calder, among others, though be warned in advance that some of the works by those other artists might be in storage at the time of your visit, based on whatever temporary exhibition is being displayed.

The museum is open Tuesday to Sunday: July to September from 10 to 11:50am and 2 to 5:50pm and October to June from 10 to 11:50am and 2 to 4:50pm. Admission is 30F ($6) for adults, 15F ($3) for students and those 15 to 24 and over 60, and free for children 14 and under.

Anyone interested in the meteoric career of Napoléon Bonaparte, and in the methods of waging war before the advent of electricity and electronics, should be intrigued by the **Musée Naval et Napoléonien,** Batterie du Grillon, boulevard J.-F.-Kennedy (☎ 04-93-61-45-32). In a stone-sided fort and tower that was built in stages between the 17th and 18th century, it contains an interesting collection of Napoleonic memorabilia, naval models, paintings, and mementos, many of which were donated to the museum by at least two world-class collectors. A toy soldier collection depicts various uniforms, including one used by Napoléon in the Marengo campaign. A wall painting on wood shows Napoléon's entrance into Grenoble; another tableau shows him disembarking at Golfe-Juan on March 1, 1815. In contrast to Canova's Greek-god image of Napoléon, a miniature pendant by Barrault reveals the Corsican general as he really looked, with pudgy cheeks and a receding hairline. In the rear rotunda is one of the many hats worn by the emperor. You can climb to the top of the tower for a view of the coast that's worth the admission price.

The museum is open Monday to Friday from 9:30am to noon and 2:15 to 6pm and Saturday from 9:30am to noon. Admission is 20F ($4) for adults, 10F ($2) for students, and free for children 14 and under.

ACCOMMODATIONS
VERY EXPENSIVE

✪ **Hôtel du Cap–Eden Roc.** Bd. J.-F.-Kennedy, 06160 Cap d'Antibes. ☎ **04-93-61-39-01.** Fax 04-93-67-76-04. 130 rms, 10 suites. A/C TEL. 2,050F–2,600F ($410–$520) double; from 4,800F ($960) suite. No credit cards. Closed mid-Oct to mid-Apr. Bus: A2.

Legendary for the glamour of both its setting and its clientele, this Second Empire hotel, opened in 1870, is surrounded by 22 splendid acres of gardens. It's like a great country estate, with spacious public rooms, marble fireplaces, scenic paneling, chandeliers, and richly upholstered armchairs. Some guest rooms and suites have regal period furnishings. Know in advance that this is not a place to go slumming, as some visitors consider its cachet as one of the most elevated anywhere. Even though the guests snoozing by the pool—which was blasted out of the cliffside at enormous expense and as such is one of the most famous of the Azure Coast—might appear artfully undraped during daylight hours, evenings here are intensely upscale, with lots of emphasis on clothing and style. The staff is well rehearsed, but regardless of how important you are, they can always claim they've dealt with bigger and more famous names. The world-famous Pavillon Eden Roc, near a rock garden apart from the hotel, has a panoramic Mediterranean view. Venetian chandeliers, Louis XV chairs, and elegant draperies add to the drama. Lunch is served on an outer terrace, under umbrellas and an arbor. Dinner specialties include bouillabaisse, lobster Thermidor, and sea bass with fennel.

MODERATE

Auberge de la Gardiole. Chemin de la Garoupe, 06160 Cap d'Antibes. ☎ 04-93-61-35-03. Fax 04-93-67-61-87. 21 rms. MINIBAR TV TEL. 370F–450F ($74–$90) per person. Rates include half board. AE, DC, MC, V. Closed Nov–Feb. Bus: A2.

Monsieur and Mme Courtot run this country inn with a delightful personal touch. The large villa, surrounded by gardens, is in an area of private estates. The charming rooms, on the upper floors of the inn and in the little buildings in the garden, contain personal safes; 15 are air-conditioned. The owners buy the food and supervise its preparation; the cuisine is French/Provençal with fixed-price menus at 90F to 120F ($18 to $24). The cheerful dining room has a fireplace and hanging pots and pans, and in good weather you can dine under a wisteria-covered trellis.

Hôtel Beau Site. 141 bd. J.-F.-Kennedy, 06600 Cap d'Antibes. ☎ 04-93-61-53-43. Fax 04-93-67-78-16. 30 rms. TV TEL. 360F–650F ($72–$130) double. AE, DC, MC, V. Bus: A2.

This white stucco villa with a tile roof and heavy shutters is surrounded by eucalyptus trees, pines, and palms. Located off the main road, a 7-minute walk from the beach, it has a low wall of flower urns and wrought-iron gates. The interior is like a country inn, with oak beams and antiques. The guest rooms are comfortable and well maintained.

Hôtel Royal. Bd. du Maréchal-Leclerc, 06600 Antibes. ☎ 04-93-34-03-09. Fax 04-93-34-23-31. 38 rms. TEL. 385F–480F ($77–$96) double. Rates include half board. AE, DC, MC, V. Closed Nov 5–Dec 26. Parking 35F ($7). Bus: A2.

Built 85 years ago, this is the oldest hotel in Antibes. Former guests include Bing Crosby and Graham Greene. The Royal has its own private beach, a cafe terrace in front, two restaurants, and an English bar just off the lobby. Even if you're not a guest at the hotel, you can enjoy a meal at Le Dauphin (open April to October, daily from noon to 2:30pm and 7 to 10pm). Fixed-price menus run 98F to 158F ($19.60 to $31.60). The most expensive menu is a seafood specialty.

Manoir Castel Garoupe Axa. 959 bd. de la Garoupe, 06160 Cap d'Antibes. ☎ 04-93-61-36-51. Fax 04-93-67-74-88. 27 apts. MINIBAR TV TEL. 660F–955F ($132–$191) apt for two. Rates include continental breakfast. MC, V. Closed Nov 15–Mar 7. Bus: A2.

We highly recommend this Mediterranean villa, on a private lane in the center of the cape, because it offers spacious rooms tastefully furnished; some are equipped with a kitchenette. The hotel has a tile roof, private balconies, arches, shuttered windows, and a tranquil garden. Facilities include a freshwater pool and a tennis court.

INEXPENSIVE

Le Cameo. Place Nationale, 06600 Antibes. ☎ 04-93-34-24-17. 8 rms, 3 with shower only, 5 with bath. TEL. 220F ($44) double with shower only, 280F ($56) double with bath. Rates include breakfast. DC, MC, V. Closed Jan–Feb. Bus: A2.

On a historic square, this 19th-century Provençal villa is the best-known inn in the center of town. The rooms are old-fashioned and admittedly not for everyone, perhaps typical of the place where Picasso might have stayed when he first hit town. Locals gather every afternoon and evening in the bar, often taking a meal in the adjacent home-style dining room. Amid bouquets of flowers and crowded tables, you'll enjoy local fish, stuffed mussels, bouillabaisse, and fried scampi. The restaurant is open daily, and the staff provides a more direct exposure to Provençal values than at larger, less personalized hotels.

DINING

La Bonne Auberge. Quartier de Brague, rte. N7. ☎ **04-93-33-36-65.** Reservations required. Fixed-price menu 195F ($39). MC, V. Tues–Sun noon–2pm and 7–10pm. Closed mid-Nov to mid-Dec. Take the coastal highway (N7) 2¹/₂ miles from Antibes. FRENCH.

For many years following its 1975 opening this was one of the most famous restaurants on the French Riviera. In 1992, in the wake of the death of its famous founder, Jo Rostang, his culinary heir, Philippe Rostang, wisely limited its scope and transformed it into a worthwhile but less ambitious restaurant. The fixed-price menu offers a wide selection. Choices vary but may include a Basque-inspired pipérade with poached eggs, savory swordfish tart, chicken with vinegar and garlic, and perch-pike dumplings Jo Rostang. Dessert might be an enchanting peach soufflé.

Les Vieux Murs. Promenade de l'avenue de l'Amiral-de-Grasse. ☎ **04-93-34-06-73.** Reservations recommended. Main courses 100F–200F ($20–$40); fixed-price menu 200F ($40). AE, MC, V. Daily noon–2pm and 7:30–10pm. Closed Mon Oct–Apr. Bus: A2. FRENCH/SEAFOOD.

This charming Provençal tavern occupies a room inside the 17th-century ramparts that used to fortify the old seaport. Close to the Picasso Museum (see above), the space contains soaring stone vaults and a simple decor painted for the most part in white. There's also a glassed-in front terrace that offers a pleasant view of the water. Menu specialties are a warm salad of mullet, sophisticated arrays of crudités that reflect the bounty of the local harvest, artichoke hearts with a confit of tomatoes, and fresh filets of such fish as daurade, hogfish, sole, salmon, and red mullet, prepared dozens of ways. Especially appealing is the roast chapon, a local seafish, with a simple but ultra-fresh fricassée of fresh vegetables and olive oil. Suzanne and Georges Romano often have more hungry diners than tables, so try to book early. Their fixed-price menu is one of the best values on the coast.

✪ **Restaurant de Bacon.** Bd. de Bacon. ☎ **04-93-61-50-02.** Reservations required. Fixed-price menus 250F–400F ($50–$80). AE, DC, MC, V. Tues–Sun 12:30–2pm and 8–10pm (open Mon dinner July–Aug). Closed Nov–Jan.

Set among ultra-expensive residences, this restaurant on a rocky peninsula has a panoramic coast view. Bouillabaisse aficionados claim that Bacon offers the best version in France. This fish stew, conceived centuries ago as a simple fisher's supper, is now one of the world's great dishes. In its deluxe version, saltwater crayfish float atop the savory brew; we prefer the simple version—a waiter adds the finishing touches at your table. If bouillabaisse isn't to your liking, try fish soup with the traditional garlic-laden rouille sauce, fish terrine, sea bass, John Dory, or something from an exotic collection of fish unknown in North America. These include sar, pageot, and denti, prepared in several ways. Many visitors are confused by the way fish dishes are priced by the gram: A guideline is that light lunches cost around 250F to 400F ($50 to $80); substantial dinners go for 550F to 800F ($110 to $160).

7

The Eastern Riviera: From Biot to Monaco to Menton

At Biot, the Riviera continues east through a string of upscale resorts that embody the glamour of the Côte d'Azur, several of which have been home to some of the 20th century's great writers and artists. Biot is no exception, with its museum dedicated to the art and life of long-time resident Fernand Léger. Set back from the coast, nearby Villeneuve-Loubet pays tribute to art in another genre, the haute cuisine of Auguste Escoffier, the greatest chef ever to man a kitchen in a nation with a rich culinary heritage.

Farther into the foothills, many artisans live and work in Tourrettes-sur-Loup, where they sell their wares in small shops. Nearby Vence boasts Matisse's Chapelle du Rosaire, an entire chapel adorned by the masterful painter in his twilight years. The great artist is represented side by side with his contemporaries in St-Paul-de-Vence's Fondation Maeght, a museum as modern as the art it houses.

Along the coast, Cagnes-sur-Mer continues the region's list of who's who among 20th-century artists—it was once home to Simone de Beauvoir, and it contains Les Collettes, Renoir's final home. Nice, the Riviera's capital and largest city, is one of the few budget-oriented resorts on the coast, making it a good base from which to explore the region. It features no less than five worthy museums and is filled with architecture noteworthy for its design and residents, who have included Matisse, Stendhal, Nietzsche, Sand, and Flaubert.

East of Nice is Villefranche-sur-Mer, a fishing village and naval port where small houses climb the hillside; these were once the residences of notables like Huxley, Mansfield, and Cocteau. If you can't afford to stay at the ultra-chic St-Jean-Cap-Ferrat, you can at least sample the lifestyle at the Musée Ile-de-France, former home of a Rothschild heir, Baronne Ephrussi. Beaulieu is another pocket of posh, featuring a replica of an ancient Greek residence. Eze attracts with its garden of exotic plants, and the Roman ruins at La Turbie ensure a never-ending stream of visitors. Peillon offers a place to stay in a scenic foothill village, seated 1,000 feet above the nearby shore.

The tiny principality of Monaco is awash with rumors of royal romance and indiscretion, glamorous nightlife, and gambling. Just inland, northeast of Monaco, Roquebrune is a tranquil medieval mountain village. Cap-Martin is another posh spot, associated with the rich and famous ever since Empress Eugénie wintered here in the

19th century. And sleepy Menton, 5 miles east of Monaco, is more Italianate than French as it stands right at the border with Italy at the far eastern extremity of the Côte d'Azur.

EXPLORING THE REGION BY CAR

Here's how to link together the best of the region if you rent a car:

Day 1   Start at the Musée National Fernand-Léger in **Biot,** 5 miles north of Antibes off A8. Then drive north on A8 for 3 miles and turn west on Route 2085, going another mile to **Villeneuve-Loubet,** where you can visit a museum dedicated to the memorabilia of Escoffier, France's greatest chef. From here, backtrack to A8 and take the first exit, no. 48 at Cagnes-sur-Mer, following Rte. 36 for 5¹/₂ miles to Vence; then turn west on Rte. 2210, driving 3 miles to **Tourrettes-sur-Loup,** where artisans sell their crafts. Backtrack and stop for the night in **St-Paul-de-Vence,** a lovely village of 16th-century homes occupied by great artists in the 1920s. The highlight is the Fondation Maeght's impressive collection of contemporary art.

Day 2   Start the day in **Vence,** spending the morning in Matisse's masterful Chapelle du Rosaire, then backtrack to **Cagnes-sur-Mer** for a visit to the Musée d'Art Moderne Méditerranéen and Renoir's Les Collettes. Spend the night here.

Day 3   Get on A7 and drive 8 miles northeast to **Nice,** where you'll spend the day and night. Visit the museums and architectural sights, then stroll along the coast of this former home of Matisse, Nietzsche, Flaubert, and Hugo.

Day 4   A little over 4 miles northeast of Nice on A7, small houses climb the hillside in **Villefranche-sur-Mer,** which was once home to Huxley, Mansfield, and Cocteau. Unwind here, spending the day and night in this scenic port.

Day 5   Two miles south of Villefranche-sur-Mer on the peninsula they share, **St-Jean-Cap-Ferrat** is an area of luxurious living, which is well illustrated in the Musée Ile-de-France, once home of Baronne Ephrussi. Spend a day and night here enjoying the coast.

Day 6–7   Still traveling on A7, head toward Monaco, 10 miles northeast, stopping along the way in **Beaulieu** at the replicated ancient Greek residence. Then admire the layout and architecture of the medieval hilltop towns **Eze** and **La Turbie.** From La Turbie, take D2204 inland to D21 and go 3 miles to **Peillon,** an unspoiled village 1,000 feet above the coast, where the architecture is the attraction. Backtrack and drive into **Monaco,** spending 2 nights so that you'll have time to visit the palace, museums, shops, beach, casinos, and nightclubs.

Day 8   Continue north on Rte. 7 for 5 miles to the mountain village of **Roquebrune** and its seaside companion community at **Cap-Martin.** Just 3¹/₂ miles farther along, **Menton** is your final stop. Be sure to include visits to the Musée Jean-Cocteau and Musée des Beaux-Arts.

1 Biot

570 miles S of Paris, 6 miles E of Cagnes-sur-Mer, 4 miles NW of Antibes

Biot has been famous for its pottery ever since merchants began to ship earthenware jars to Phoenicia and destinations throughout the Mediterranean. Biot was first settled by Gallo-Romans and has had a long war-torn history. Somehow the potters still manage to work at their ancient craft. Biot is also the place Fernand Léger chose to paint until the day he died. The greatest collection of his work is on display at a museum here.

ESSENTIALS

GETTING THERE   Biot's train station is 2 miles east of the town center. There's frequent service from Nice and Antibes. For **rail information** and schedules, call ☎ 08-36-35-35-35. The bus from Antibes is even more convenient than the train. For **bus information** and schedules, call ☎ 04-93-34-37-60 in Antibes.

VISITOR INFORMATION   The **Office de Tourisme** is on place de la Chapelle (☎ 04-93-65-05-85).

SEEING THE TOP ATTRACTIONS

The most popular attraction is the ✪ **Musée National Fernand-Léger,** chemin du Val-de-Pome (☎ 04-92-91-50-30), opened in 1960 on the eastern edge of town, beside the road leading to Biot's train station. The collection was assembled by his widow, Nadia Léger, who donated its contents to the French government after the artist's death. The stone-and-marble facade is enhanced by Léger's mosaic-and-ceramic mural. On the grounds is a polychrome ceramic sculpture, *Le Jardin d'enfant.* Inside are two floors of geometrical forms in pure flat colors. The collection includes gouaches, paintings, ceramics, tapestries, and sculptures—showing the development of the artist from 1905 until his death. His paintings abound in cranes, acrobats, scaffolding, railroad signals, buxom nudes, casings, and crankshafts. From his first cubist paintings, Léger was dubbed a "Tubist." The most unusual work depicts a Léger *Mona Lisa (La Giaconde aux Clés)* contemplating a set of keys, a wide-mouthed fish dangling at an angle over her head.

The museum is open Wednesday to Monday from 10am to 12:30pm and 2 to 6pm (to 5:30pm in winter). Admission is 30F ($6) for adults, 20F ($4) for young adults 18 to 24 and seniors over 60, and free for children 17 and under. Guided tours can be arranged upon request by calling ☎ 04-92-91-50-20.

If you have time, you might explore the village. Begin at the much-photographed **place des Arcades,** where you can see the 16th-century gates and the remains of the town's former ramparts. The **Eglise de Biot,** place des Arcades (☎ 04-93-65-00-85), dates from the 15th century, when it was built by Italian immigrants who arrived to resettle the town after its population was decimated by the black death. The church is known for two stunning 15th-century retables: the red-and-gold *Retable du Rosaire* by Ludovico Bréa and the recently restored *Christ aux Plaies* by Canavesio.

You can also visit the **Musée d'Histoire Locale et de Céramique Biotoise,** place de la Chapelle (☎ 04-93-65-11-79), which over the years has assembled the best work of local glass-blowing artists, potters, ceramists, painters, and silver- and goldsmiths. It's open Thursday to Sunday from 2:30 to 6:30pm, charging 5F ($1) admission.

At **Verreries de Biot** (see "Shopping," below), you can visit the Galerie International du Verre, where beautifully displayed glass works are for sale, often at exorbitant prices. Even if you don't buy, you can stop to look at these one-of-a-kind collector pieces. You can also visit the **Galerie Jean-Claude Novaro** (also known as **Galerie de la Patrimoine**), place des Arcades (☎ 04-93-65-60-23). Its namesake is known as the Picasso of glass artists. His works are pretty and colorful, though sometimes lacking the diversity and intellectual flair of works by some of the artists displayed at the Galerie International du Verre. Most of his glass art, except for some exhibition pieces, is for sale.

SHOPPING

In the late 1940s glassmakers created a bubble-flecked glass known as *verre rustique.* It comes in brilliant colors like cobalt and emerald and is displayed in many store windows on the main shopping street, **rue St-Sebastien.** The town also is known for its carnations and roses, sold on the arcaded square known as **place des Arcades.** Flowers also are flown to the capitals of northern Europe.

The best place to watch the glassblowers and buy glass, aside from the shops along rue St-Sebastien, is the ✪ **Verrerie de Biot,** 5 chemin des Combes (☎ **04-93-65-05-85**), at the edge of town. Prices are about the same as in town. Hours are Monday to Saturday from 9am to 6:30pm. You can also visit the showroom on Sunday from 10:30am to 1pm and 2:30 to 6:30pm.

A final shopping option is **La Poterie Provençale,** 1689 rte. de la Mer (☎ **04-93-65-63-30**). Nearly adjacent to the Musée Fernand-Léger, about 2 miles southeast of town, it's one of the last potteries in Provence to specialize in the tall amphoralike containers known as *jarres.* (The place defines itself as *une jarrière* because of its emphasis on the containers.)

DINING

✪ **Les Terraillers.** 11 rte. du Chemin-Neuf. ☎ **04-93-65-01-59.** Reservations required, as far in advance as possible. Main courses 170F–190F ($34–$38); fixed-price menus 180F–360F ($36–$72) at lunch, 250F–360F ($50–$72) at dinner. AE, MC, V. Thurs–Tues noon–2pm and 7–10pm. Closed lunchtime July–Aug and 2 weeks Oct–Nov. Take rte. du Chemin-Neuf, following the signs to Antibes. MEDITERRANEAN.

Stone-sided and deeply evocative of Provence, this restaurant is about half a mile south of Biot, in what was built in the 1500s as a studio for the production of clay pots and ceramics. Today, under the guidance of chef Claude Jacques, it functions as a well-respected restaurant. The menu may include terrine of foie gras with armagnac, seawolf roasted in a salt crust, ravioli stuffed with foie gras and essence of morels, and saddle of rabbit with wild mushrooms. There are those who say his cookery could use a bit of simplification, but that didn't prevent Michelin and us from awarding him a star.

2 Villeneuve-Loubet

568 miles SE of Paris, 10 miles W of Nice, 6 miles N of Antibes, 13 miles N of Cannes, 14 miles E of Grasse

This small fishing village dominated by a 12th-century castle was where François I and Charles V came to make peace in 1538 after their disputes over the duchies of Burgundy and Milan. However, it's much better known as the birthplace of Auguste Escoffier, "the king of chefs and the chef of kings."

The house where he was born in 1846 has been made into the **Musée de l'Art Culinaire,** 3 rue Escoffier (☎ **04-93-73-93-79**). Inside is a 19th-century Provençal kitchen complete with every utensil imaginable—many of which Escoffier invented. Displayed throughout is a collection of several thousand menus describing dishes that would make cardiologists and their patients run for their lives. There are also some elaborate sugar sculptures, such as one in the shape of a Japanese pagoda. Of course, Escoffier's most famous creations are featured; a signed photo of opera singer Nellie Melba graces one wall, thanking the chef for naming his peach dessert for her. This culinary center was created in 1956 by Joseph Donon, Escoffier's former apprentice. Escoffier's career began in 1859 at the age of 13, and he became the world-famous chef of the Savoy in London in the 1890s. He worked until he retired from London's Carlton in 1920 and died in 1935 at Monte Carlo, at the age of 89. The museum is open Tuesday to Sunday from 2 to 6pm (to 7pm June to August; closed November). Admission is 10F ($2) for adults and 7.50F ($1.50) for students and children.

Villeneuve-Loubet-Plage is home to the **Marina Baie des Anges,** at the center of the beachfront. This grouping of four concrete ziggurats built by André Minanfoy in the 1970s caused an uproar among locals, who cried that they marred the beautiful coast. The buildings remain, however, and are referred to by some as the most fascinating and amazing properties on the Riviera. Whether you like the architecture or not, the marina is the place to go for water sports. There are 600 slips for docking boats, a public pool, and facilities for sailing, waterskiing, windsurfing, and deep-sea fishing.

ESSENTIALS

GETTING THERE   The nearest train stations are in Antibes ($3^3/_4$ miles away) and Nice ($7^1/_2$ miles away). From either of those places, buses run at 20-minute intervals along R.N. 7 and stop in both parts of Villeneuve-Loubet. Transit from Nice is 17F ($3.40) each way; from Antibes, 9F ($1.80). Other buses make less frequent transits from the Nice airport.

VISITOR INFORMATION   The **Office de Tourisme** is on place de Verdun (☎ 04-93-20-20-09). In Villeneuve-Loubet-Plage there's an office on place de l'Hôtel-de-Ville (☎ 04-93-20-49-14).

ACCOMMODATIONS

Rooms are also available at **La Franc Comtoise** (see "Dining," below).

Hamotel. Hameau du Soleil, rte. de la Colle-sur-Loup, 06270 Villeneuve-Loubet. ☎ 04-93-20-86-60. Fax 04-93-73-33-94. 30 rms. MINIBAR TV TEL. 350F ($70) double. AE, DC, MC, V.

About two-thirds of a mile from the center of Villeneuve-Loubet, this hotel was inspired by a sprawling Provençal *mas,* complete with a tiled roof and a boxy earth-toned exterior. Rated three stars by the local municipality, it's a simple affair, with modern rooms and a setting amid unpretentious private homes on the outskirts of the village. There's a pool on the premises, the focal point of much of the social life; the staff is quite likable. Breakfast is the only meal served.

DINING

La Franc Comtoise. Grange Rimade, rte. de la Colle-St-Paul, 06270 Villeneuve-Loubet. ☎ 04-93-20-97-58. Fax 04-92-02-74-76. Reservations not required. Main courses 55F–100F ($11–$20); fixed-price menus 120F–150F ($24–$30); bouillabaisse 300F ($60). MC, V. Daily noon–1:15pm and 7:30–8:30pm. PROVENÇAL.

This is the dining room of a hotel about half a mile from town, beside the highway leading to St-Paul-de-Vence. Its only drawback is the narrow range of hours, but if you don't mind that, you'll find some surprisingly well-prepared food. Menu items include a wonderful version of bouillabaisse, authentic paella, a Niçois version of daube (stew) of beef, and Niçois-style daurade. The hotel contains 30 unpretentious and very clean rooms, each with TV and phone; a double is 400F ($80) without meals and 620F ($124) per person with half board and wine. A pool is adjacent to the hotel, and guests can use the parking garage for free.

3 Tourrettes-sur-Loup

577 miles SE of Paris, 18 miles W of Nice, 4 miles W of Vence, 13 miles NE of Grasse

Often called the City of Violets because of the small purple flowers that are cultivated in abundance beneath the olive trees, Tourrettes-sur-Loup sits atop a sheer cliff overlooking the Loup valley. Though the violets are big business for the town (they're sent to the perfume factories in Grasse, made into candy, and celebrated during a festival held each March), you'll probably find the many shops lining the streets much more interesting. These small businesses are often owned by artisans who sell their own art—most notably hand-woven fabrics and unique pottery. Even if you're not interested in buying, walking through the old town is worth the trip up the hill.

The unusual city was built so that the walls of the outermost buildings form a rampart; three towers rising above the village give it its name. A rocky horseshoe-shaped path leads from the main square then loops back again; follow it for a pleasant tour of the medieval village. Along the way, you'll pass the **Chapelle St-Jean,** with naïve frescoes that tell biblical stories while weaving in the traditions of local life. Also in the village is a 15th-century **church** that has paintings by the school of Brea and a 1st-century **pagan shrine** in honor of the Roman god Mercury.

ESSENTIALS

GETTING THERE   The nearest rail junction is at Cagnes-sur-Mer, from which buses run about every 45 minutes to Vence. In Vence, you'll have to change to another bus (about six a day) that makes the 10-minute continuation on to Tourrettes-sur-Loup. Overall, factoring in the transfer in Vence, it takes about an hour to travel by bus from Cagnes to Tourrettes. It's more convenient to take a taxi from Cagnes (they line up at the train station) to Tourrettes for around 120F ($24) each way.

VISITOR INFORMATION   The **Office de Tourisme** is at 2 rte. de Vence (☎ 04-93-24-18-93).

SHOPPING

Tourrettes-sur-Loup boasts more crafts studios than any other town its size in Provence. The two best products coming out of here are violets and handcrafts. Nearly 30 artisans, including a handful of noted ones from as far away as Paris, have set up their studios and outlets, often in stone-sided buildings facing the town's main street, **Grand'Rue.** The best way to sample their offerings is to wander and window shop (the town's small size makes this feasible). Here's a list of recommendable artisans:

You'll find jewelry, in designs ranging from old-fashioned to contemporary, at **La Paësine,** 14 Grand'Rue (☎ 04-93-24-14-55). Original clothing for men, women, and children, some of it printed with creative patterns, is available at the **Atelier Arachnée,** 8 Grand'Rue (☎ 04-93-24-11-42). Ceramics crafted from local clay in patterns inspired by the many civilizations that have pillaged or prospered in Provence is sold at **Poterie Tournesol,** 7 Grand'Rue (☎ 04-93-59-35-62). **Marie L'Amoureux Fonderie d'Art,** 73 Grand'Rue (☎ 04-93-24-11-74), sells very unusual bronzes, some authorized by well-known masters of the modernist movement. For a view of canvases by painters inspired by the colors and traditions of Provence, head for the **Galerie Gil Franco,** 1 cours du Château (☎ 04-93-59-24-64).

Looking for a pick-me-up after a day of shopping? Head for one of the region's best candy shops, **Confiserie des Gorges du Loup,** rue Principale (☎ 04-93-59-32-91), where age-old techniques are used to layer fresh fruit with sugar. The result is an ultra-chewy, ultra-sweet confection that gradually melts as it explodes flavor into your mouth. It wreaks havoc with dentures and diabetics, but for those who can handle it, the taste has been called "angelic." Sample chocolate-covered orange peel, rose-petal jam, and sugar-permeated sliced apricots, tangerines, plums, cherries, and grapes. Even the local violets are transformed into edible, albeit sugary, treats.

ACCOMMODATIONS

Auberge Belles Terrasses. 1315 rte. de Vence, 06140 Tourrettes-sur-Loup. ☎ **04-93-59-30-03.** Fax 04-93-59-31-27. 15 rms. TEL. 280F–330F ($56–$66) double. MC, V. From town, drive about half a mile, following the signs toward Vence.

This hotel was built on a site whose views encompass the faraway peninsula of Antibes and the sea beyond. Its boxy shape and terra-cotta roof were inspired by an architect's fantasy of an old Provençal manor house, and it was named after the terraces that are angled for maximum exposure to the view. The rooms are simple, traditional, and comfortable but not particularly stimulating. Much of the allure of this place is its restaurant, where fixed-price menus are 90F to 150F ($18 to $30). Menu items include civet of roast suckling pig, young hen with freshwater crayfish, roast wild hare with mustard sauce, Provençal frogs' legs with garlic-and-butter sauce, and assorted game dishes. The restaurant is closed every Monday to nonguests.

Résidence des Chevaliers. Rte. du Caire, 06140 Tourrettes-sur-Loup. ☎ **04-93-59-31-97.** Fax 04-93-59-27-97. 12 rms. TEL. 420F–700F ($84–$140) double. MC, V. Closed Nov–Mar.

About 500 yards from the village's periphery, this place was built around 1900 as a *bastide Provençal* (manor house), and because the furnishings are relatively simple and the lines severe, the inn evokes a monastery. It has functioned as a hotel since the 1960s, when a pool was installed in the garden. Breakfast is the only meal served. The site has a low-key allure and a degree of very simple comfort.

DINING

The **Auberge Belles Terrasses** (see "Accommodations," above) is also recommended for its cuisine, except on Monday when it's closed to nonguests.

Le Petit Manoir. 21 Grande'Rue, Tourrettes-sur-Loup. ☎ **04-93-24-19-19.** Reservations recommended. Main courses 60F–160F ($12–$32); fixed-price menus 94F–245F ($18.80–$49). AE, MC, V. Mon–Tues and Thurs–Sat noon–1:45pm and 7:30–10pm, Wed 7:30–10pm, Sun noon–1:45pm. Closed Nov 15–Dec 15 and 2 weeks in Feb. FRENCH.

There are only about 25 seats in the simple dining room of this 17th-century building in an all-pedestrian zone in the heart of town, and the cuisine is based on traditional French recipes with an occasional modern twist. Your hosts are the Taburet family, a soft-spoken pair whose shyness might surpise you. The food is flavorful and appetizing and includes old-fashioned staples like cured ham braised with herbs, foie gras of duckling with lavender-scented honey, and roast rack of rabbit stuffed with basil.

4 St-Paul-de-Vence

575 miles S of Paris, 14 miles E of Grasse, 17 miles E of Cannes, 19 miles N of Nice

Of all the perched villages of the Riviera, St-Paul-de-Vence is the best known. It was popularized in the 1920s when many noted artists lived here, occupying the 16th-century houses flanking the narrow cobblestone streets. The feudal hamlet grew up on a bastion of rock, almost blending into it. Its ramparts (allow about 30 minutes to circle them) overlook a peaceful setting of flowers and olive and orange trees. They remain somewhat as they were when they were constructed from 1537 to 1547 by François I. From the ramparts to the north you can look out on Baou de St-Jeannet, a sphinx-shaped rock that was painted into the landscape of Poussin's *Polyphème*.

ESSENTIALS

GETTING THERE   Some 20 buses per day leave from Nice's Gare Routière, taking 55 minutes and costing 19.50F ($3.90) one-way. For **bus information** and schedules, call ☎ **04-93-85-61-81.**

VISITOR INFORMATION   The **Office de Tourisme** is at Maison Tour, rue Grande (☎ **04-93-32-60-27**).

EXPLORING THE TOWN

The pedestrians-only **rue Grande** is the most interesting street, running the entire length of St-Paul. Most of the stone houses along it are from the 16th and 17th centuries, many still bearing the coats-of-arms placed here by the original builders. Today most of the houses are antiques shops, art-and-craft galleries, and souvenir and gift shops; some are still artists' studios.

The village's chief sight is **La Collégiale de la Conversion de St-Paul,** constructed in the 12th and 13th centuries though much altered over the years. The Romanesque choir is the oldest part, containing some remarkable stalls carved in walnut in the 17th century. The bell tower was built in 1740, but the vaulting was reconstructed in the 1600s. Although the facade today isn't alluring, the church is filled with art, notably a painting of Ste-Cathérine d'Alexandrie, attributed to Tintoretto and hanging to the left as you enter. The Trésor de l'Eglise is one of the most beautiful in the Alpes-Maritimes, with a spectacular ciborium. Look also for a low relief of the Martyrdom of St-Clément on the last altar on the right. In the baptismal chapter is a 15th-century alabaster Madonna.

Near the church is the **Musée d'Histoire de St-Paul,** place de Castre (☎ **04-93-32-53-09**), a minor museum in a 16th-century village house. It was restored and refurnished in a 1500s style, with many artifacts illustrating the history of the village. It's open daily from 10am to 7pm (to 5:30pm in winter). Admission is 5F ($1).

SEEING THE TOP ATTRACTION

The most important attraction of St-Paul-de-Vence lies outside the walls at the ✪ **Fondation Maeght** (☎ **04-93-32-81-63**), one of the most modern art museums in Europe. On a hill in pine-studded woods, the Maeght Foundation is like a Shangri-la. Not only is the architecture avant-garde, but also the building houses one of the finest collections of contemporary art along the Riviera. Nature and the creations of men and women blend harmoniously in this unique achievement of the architect José Luís Sert. Its white concrete arcs give the impression of a giant pagoda.

A stark Calder rises like some futuristic monster on the grassy lawns. In a courtyard, the elongated bronze works of Giacometti form a surrealistic garden, creating a hallucinatory mood. Sculpture is also displayed inside, but it's at its best in a natural setting of surrounding terraces and gardens. The museum is built on several levels, its many glass walls providing an indoor-outdoor vista. The foundation, a gift "to the people" from Aimé and Marguerite Maeght, also provides a showcase for new talent. Exhibitions are always changing. Everywhere you look, you see 20th-century art: mosaics by Chagall and Braque, Miró ceramics in the "labyrinth," and Ubac and Braque stained glass in the chapel. Bonnard, Kandinsky, Léger, Matisse, Barbara Hepworth, and many other artists are well represented.

There are a library (open only to scholars and only by appointment), a cinema, and a cafeteria here. In one showroom you can buy original lithographs by artists like Chagall and Giacometti and limited-edition prints. Admission is 40F ($8) for adults, 30F ($6) for students and youths 10 to 18, and free for children 9 and under. A 5F ($1) supplement is charged during some special exhibits. It's open daily: July to September from 10am to 7pm and October to June from 10am to 12:30pm and 2:30 to 6pm.

ACCOMMODATIONS

La Colombe d'Or also rents deluxe rooms (see "Dining," below).

VERY EXPENSIVE

Le Mas d'Artigny. Rte. de la Colle et des Hauts de St-Paul, 06570 St-Paul-de-Vence. ☎ **04-93-32-84-54.** Fax 04-93-32-95-36. 54 rms, 29 suites. A/C MINIBAR TV TEL. 640F–1,800F ($128–$360) double; 1,760F–6,000F ($352–$1,200) suite. MC, V. Parking 60F ($12) in a garage. From the town center, follow the signs west about 1¹/₄ miles.

This hotel, one of the Riviera's grandest, evokes a sprawling Provençal homestead set in an acre of pine forests. In the lobby is a constantly changing exhibition of art. Each of the comfortably large rooms has its own terrace or balcony, and private suites with a private pool are on a slope below the blue-tile pool, with hedges for privacy. For such an elegant Relais & Châteaux, the restaurant is a bit lackluster in decor and has a staff that isn't always too alert, but it does have great views of the garden. Chef Francis Scordel regales you with his flavors of Provence, everything tasting as if it were ripened in the sun. Only quality ingredients are used to shape this harmonious and rarely complicated cuisine. The wine cellar deserves a star for its vintage collection, but watch those prices!

EXPENSIVE

☼ Hôtel Le St-Paul. 86 rue Grande, 06570 St-Paul-de-Vence. ☎ **04-93-32-65-25.** Fax 04-93-32-52-94. 15 rms, 3 suites. A/C MINIBAR TV TEL. 850F–1,500F ($170–$300) double; 1,150F–2,200F ($230–$440) suite. Half board 390F ($78) per person extra. AE, DC, MC, V.

Converted from a 16th-century Renaissance residence and retaining many original features, this four-star Relais & Châteaux is in the heart of the medieval village. The rooms, decorated in a sophisticated Provençal style, have safe-deposit boxes, satellite TVs, and many extras. One woman wrote us that while sitting on the balcony of Room 30 she understood why Renoir, Léger, Matisse, and even Picasso were inspired by Provence. Many rooms enjoy a view of the valley with the Mediterranean in the distance. The restaurant has a flower-bedecked terrace sheltered by the 16th-century ramparts as well as a superb dining room with vaulted ceilings. Menus may include locally inspired dishes like cream of salt cod with a thin slice of grilled pancetta, risotto of crayfish and broadbeans, roast veal chop with morels and barley, and a delightful crème brûlée with a hint of rosemary.

MODERATE

Auberge Le Hameau. 528 rte. de la Colle (D107), 06570 St-Paul-de-Vence. ☎ **04-93-32-80-24.** Fax 04-93-32-55-75. 16 rms, 3 suites. A/C MINIBAR TEL. 400F–620F ($80–$124) double; from 720F ($144) suite. MC, V. Closed Jan 7–Feb 15 and Nov 16–Dec 22. From the town, take D107 about a quarter mile, following the signs toward Colle.

This romantic Mediterranean villa is on a hilltop on the outskirts of St-Paul-de-Vence, on the road to Colle at Hauts-de-St-Paul. You get a remarkable view of the surrounding hills and valleys, and most of the comfortable whitewashed rooms overlook a vineyard. There's also a sunny terrace with fruit trees, flowers, and a pool.

Les Orangers. Chemin des Fumerates, rte. de la Colle (D107), 06570 St-Paul-de-Vence. ☎ **04-93-32-80-95.** Fax 04-93-32-00-32. 7 rms, 2 suites. TEL. 590F–680F ($118–$136) double; 790F ($158) suite. Rates include breakfast. MC, V. From the town center, follow the signs to Cagnes-sur-Mer for half a mile south.

Monsieur Franklin has created a beautiful "living oasis" in his villa. The scents of roses, oranges, and lemons waft through the air. The main lounge is impeccably decorated with original oils and furnished in a provincial style. Expect to be treated like a guest in a private home. The rooms, with antiques and Oriental carpets, have panoramic views. On the sun terrace are banana trees and climbing geraniums.

INEXPENSIVE

Comfort Hotel. Quartier des Fumerates, 06570 St-Paul-de-Vence. ☎ **04-93-32-94-24.** Fax 04-93-32-91-07. 19 rms. TV TEL. 350F–450F ($70–$90) double. AE, MC, V. From the town center, go downhill toward the main thoroughfare, heading west for half a mile and following the signs toward Cagnes-sur-Mer.

This complex of low-slung, tile-roofed town houses is at the end of a steep driveway. While reclining in a chair by a pool, you can survey the countryside. Each comfortably furnished room has its own small salon, balcony, or terrace. The restaurant serves a fixed-price menu at 115F ($23).

Les Bastides St-Paul. 880 rte. des Blaquières (rte. Cagnes–Vence), 06570 St-Paul-de-Vence. ☎ **04-92-02-08-07.** Fax 04-93-20-50-41. 17 rms. MINIBAR TV TEL. 400F–650F ($80–$130) double; 620F ($124) triple. AE, DC, MC, V. From the town center, follow the signs toward Cagnes-sur-Mer for 1 mile south.

This hotel is in the hills outside town, a mile south of St-Paul and 2 1/2 miles south of Vence. Divided into three buildings, it offers clean and comfortably carpeted rooms, each accented with regional artifacts and a terrace and garden. On the premises is a pool shaped like a cloverleaf, a cozy breakfast area, and a sensitive management staff headed by the long-time hoteliers Marie José and Maurice Giraudet. Breakfast is served anytime you want it.

DINING

La Colombe d'Or. 1 place du Général-de-Gaulle, 06570 St-Paul-de-Vence. ☎ **04-93-32-80-02.** Fax 04-93-32-77-78. Reservations required. Main courses 120F–180F ($24–$36). AE, DC, MC, V. Daily noon–2:30pm and 7–10:30pm. Closed Nov–Dec 15. FRENCH.

"The Golden Dove" has for decades been St-Paul's most celebrated restaurant, famous for its remarkable art collection: You can dine amid Mirós, Picassos, Klees, Dufys, Utrillos, and Calders. In fair weather everyone tries for a seat on the terrace—to soak up the view. Note that you won't find cutting-edge cuisine or wildly exotic experiments. You may begin with smoked salmon or foie gras from Landes if you've recently won at the casino. Otherwise, you can count on a soup made with the fresh seasonal vegetables. The best fish dishes are poached sea bass with mousseline sauce and seawolf baked with fennel. Tender beef comes with gratin dauphinois (potatoes), or you may prefer lamb from Sisteron. A classic finish to any meal is a soufflé flambé au Grand-Marnier.

The guest rooms (16 doubles, 10 suites) in this three-star hotel contain French antiques and fabrics and accessories inspired by the traditions of Provence. They're scattered among three areas: the original 16th-century stone house, a more recent wing that stretches into the garden adjacent to the pool, and an even more modern annex, built in the 1950s and upgraded several times since. Some have exposed stone and heavy ceiling beams; all are very comfortable and clean, with air-conditioning, minibars, TVs, and phones. Prices are 1,300F ($260) for a double and 1,500F ($300) for a suite.

5 Vence

575 miles S of Paris, 19 miles N of Cannes, 15 miles NW of Nice

Travel up into the hills northwest of Nice—across country studded with cypresses, olive trees, and pines, where bright flowers, especially carnations, roses, and oleanders, grow in profusion—and Vence comes into view. Outside the town, along boulevard Paul-André, two olive presses carry on with their age-old duties. But the charm lies in the **Vieille Ville (Old Town).** Visitors invariably have themselves photographed on place du Peyra in front of the urn-shaped **Vieille Fontaine (Old Fountain),** a background shot in several motion pictures. The 15th-century square tower is also a curiosity.

If you're wearing the right kind of shoes, the narrow, steep streets of the Old Town are worth exploring. Dating from the 10th century, the **cathedral** on place Godeau is unremarkable except for some 15th-century Gothic choir stalls. But if it's the right day of the week, most visitors quickly pass through the narrow gates of this once-fortified walled town to where the sun shines more brightly.

It was a beautiful golden autumn along the Côte d'Azur. The great Henri Matisse was 77, and after a turbulent introspective time he set out to design and decorate his masterpiece—"the culmination of a whole life dedicated to the search for truth," as he said. Just outside Vence, Matisse created the **Chapelle du Rosaire,** avenue Henri-Matisse (☎ **04-93-58-03-26**), for the Dominican nuns of Monteils. (Part of his action was a gesture of thanks for Sister Jacques-Marie, a member of the order who nursed him back to health after a debilitating illness.) From the front you might find it unremarkable and pass it by—until you spot a 40-foot crescent-adorned cross rising from a blue-tile roof.

Matisse wrote: "What I have done in the chapel is to create a religious space . . . in an enclosed area of very reduced proportions and to give it, solely by the play of colors and lines, the dimensions of infinity." The light picks up the subtle coloring in the simply rendered leaf forms and abstract patterns: sapphire blue, aquamarine, and lemon yellow. In black-and-white ceramics, St. Dominic is depicted in only a few lines. The most remarkable design is in the black-and-white tile Stations of the Cross, with Matisse's self-styled "tormented and passionate" figures. The bishop of Nice came to bless the chapel in the late spring of 1951 when the artist's work was completed. Matisse died 3 years later.

Unless special arrangements are made, the chapel is open only on Tuesday and Thursday from 10 to 11:30am and 2:30 to 5:30pm. Admission is 10F ($2); contributions to the maintenance of the chapel are welcomed. The price of admission includes entrance to **L'Espace Matisse,** a gallery devoted to the documentation of the way Matisse handled the design and construction of the chapel during its construction (1949–51). It also contains lithographs and religious artifacts that concerned Matisse in one way or another.

ESSENTIALS

GETTING THERE   Frequent **buses** (no. 400 or 410) from Nice take 1 hour and cost 21F ($4.20) one-way. Call ☎ **04-93-58-37-60** for schedules.

VISITOR INFORMATION   The **Office de Tourisme** is on place Grand-Jardin (☎ **04-93-58-06-38**).

ACCOMMODATIONS
VERY EXPENSIVE
✪ **Le Château du Domaine St-Martin.** Rte. de Coursegoules, 06140 Vence. ☎ **04-93-58-02-02.** Fax 04-93-24-08-91. 25 rms, 10 suites. A/C MINIBAR TV TEL. 2,800F–3,000F ($560–$600) double; 3,500F–5,000F ($700–$1,000) suite. AE, DC, MC, V. Closed Oct–Apr. From the town center, follow the signs toward Coursegoules and Col-de-Vence for 1 mile north.

This château, in a 35-acre park, was built in 1936 on the grounds where the Golden Goat treasure was reputedly buried. A complex of tile-roofed villas with suites was built in the terraced gardens. You can walk through the gardens on winding paths lined with tall cypresses, past the ruined chapel and olive trees. The guest rooms are

Exploring the Gorges du Loup

After paying your respects to Matisse at the Chapelle du Rosaire in Vence, you can take D2210 through some of the Riviera's most luxuriant countryside. The 4-mile-long **Gorges du Loup** isn't as dramatic as the Grand Canyon du Verdon (see chapter 5) but still features a scenic 8-mile drive that loops along the eastern and western edges. This drive showcases waterfalls, most notably the **Cascades des Demoiselles,** with its partially fossilized plantlife, and the 130-foot **Cascade de Courmes.** There are also jagged glacial holes best exemplified by the **Saut du Loup** at the valley's northeastern end.

Gourdon, the only village along the gorge's western rim, with a year-round population of only 59 and a summer population that's much larger, functions as a tourist trap. If you stop here, ignore the souvenir shops and visit the immense 13th-century **Château de Gourdon** (☎ 04-93-09-68-02). It houses two museums: The **Musée Historique** features a Rembrandt self-portrait, Marie Antoinette's writing desk, and an assortment of armor, arms, and torture instruments, and the **Musée de Peinture Naïve** offers a small Rousseau portrait among other works. The magnificent 17th-century formal garden is graced with topiaries often photographed by gardening magazines. The museums are open June to September, daily from 11am to 1pm and 2 to 7pm; October to May, Wednesday to Monday from 2 to 5pm. A combined ticket to the garden and the museums is 20F ($4). Tickets to one or the other aren't available.

On the southeastern edge of the gorge, at **Pont-du-Loup,** go to **La Confiserie des Gorges du Loup,** rue Principale (☎ 04-93-59-32-91), where you can sample sweets while watching the confectioners sugarcoat tangerines or chocolate-dip orange peels. Less than a mile farther south, the 15th-century **Gothic church** at **Le Bar-sur-Loup** features the morbid *Danse Macabre,* a 15th-century painting of fallen and dancing humans whose souls are being wrested away by black demons, then weighed by St. Michael before being tossed into the pits of Hell. Speculation links the anonymous work of art to the plague.

After taking in this sober vision, backtrack to Pont-du-Loup and travel 5 miles east to **Tourrettes-sur-Loup,** where you can find accommodations in an unspoiled medieval village on a rocky bluff high above a violet-filled valley (see earlier in this chapter). The residents are mainly artisans selling engravings, jewelry, cloth, pottery, paintings, and other handcrafted goods; the village features three towers inside a defensive wall of connected houses.

If you're coming from Cannes, take A85 for 13 miles northwest to Grasse, then travel east for 3³/₄ miles on Rte. 2085, where you'll turn north at Magagnosc, following D3 for 5 miles north to Gourdon, at the edge of the gorge. To come from Nice, take E80 for 2 miles west to Rte. 2085, then drive 16 miles west to Magagnosc, to follow the same path north to Gourdon. Once in Gourdon, you can continue north on D3 to follow along the western rim of the gorge, and after 4 miles turn right onto D6 to return south along its eastern lip, turning east on D2210 at Pont-du-Loup for a 5-mile drive to the accommodations of Tourrettes-sur-Loup, or continue on to Vence, another 2 miles along, where you can turn south on Rte. 36 for a 5¹/₂-mile drive back to the coast.

For information, contact the **Office de Tourisme,** 22 cours Henri-Cresp, 06130 Grasse (☎ 04-93-36-66-66); place Grand-Jardin, 06140 Vence (☎ 04-93-58-06-38); or route de Vence, 06140 Tourrettes-sur-Loup (☎ 04-93-24-18-93).

furnished in elegant taste. The restaurant has a view of the coast and offers superb French cuisine. In summer, many guests prefer the poolside grill.

MODERATE

Le Floréal. Av. Rhin-et-Danube, 06140 Vence. ☎ **04-93-58-64-40.** Fax 04-93-58-79-69. 43 rms. A/C TV TEL. 350F–470F ($70–$94) double. AE MC, V. Free parking.

On the road to Grasse is this pleasant, comfortable hotel with a view of the mountains and a refreshing lack of pretension. Many of the well-furnished rooms look out on the large pool in the well-kept garden, where orange trees and mimosa add fragrance to the breezes. The hotel has air-conditioned lounges, a restaurant (Le Patio), and a bar.

INEXPENSIVE

Auberge des Seigneurs (Inn of the Noblemen). Place du Friene, 06140 Vence. ☎ **04-93-58-04-24.** Fax 04-93-24-08-01. 8 rms. TEL. 334F–364F ($66.80–$72.80) double. AE, DC, MC, V. Closed Nov 15–Mar 15.

This 400-year-old stone hotel gives you a taste of Old Provence. Inside is a long wooden dining table, in view of an open fireplace with a row of hanging copper pots and pans. The cuisine of François I is served in an antique atmosphere with wooden casks of flowers and an open spit for roasting and grilling. Fascinating decorative objects and antiques are everywhere.

The guest rooms are well maintained and comfortable, though management gives priority to the running of the restaurant here instead, as that generates far more revenue.

Hôtel La Roseraie. Av. Henri-Giraud, rte. de Coursegoules, 06140 Vence. ☎ **04-93-58-02-20.** Fax 04-93-58-99-31. 12 rms. TV TEL. 390F–550F ($78–$110) double. AE, MC, V. From the town center, drive for less than a quarter mile, following the signs toward Col-de-Vence.

This 19th-century manor house is on the road to Col-de-Vence. The belle époque architecture is framed by a tropical landscape of trees, including kumquat, banana, orange, and a giant magnolia and cedar. Some of the newer rooms are spacious, with a private garden and terrace. Maurice and Josette Ganier have a reputation for good food and hospitality.

DINING

The **Auberge des Seigneurs** (see "Accommodations," above) is an excellent place to dine at reasonable prices.

La Farigoule. 15 rue Henri-Isnard. ☎ **04-93-58-01-27.** Reservations recommended. Fixed-price menus 120F–150F ($24–$30). No credit cards. Sat 7–10pm, Sun–Thurs 12:30–2pm and 7–10pm (also open for lunch on Sat in summer). Closed Nov 10–Dec 15. PROVENÇAL.

In summer you can enjoy regional cuisine in the garden under a rose arbor. Chef Georgette Gastaud grills much of the food over an open fire. A long line forms on Sunday afternoon. The least expensive fixed-price menu may include fish soup, trout meunière, a vegetable, and cheese or dessert—service and drinks are extra. The most expensive fixed-price menu is far more enticing and may include asparagus vinaigrette, mussels marinara, a tender rabbit with seasonal vegetables, cheese, and dessert—drinks and service extra. There's no à la carte.

6 Cagnes-sur-Mer

570 miles S of Paris, 13 miles NE of Cannes

Cagnes-sur-Mer, like the Roman god Janus, has two faces. Perched on a hill in the "hinterlands" of Nice, **Le Haut-de-Cagnes** is one of the most charming spots on the Riviera. Naomi Barry of the *New York Times* wrote that it "crowns the top of a blue-cypressed hill like a village in an Italian Renaissance painting." At the foot of the hill is an old fishing port and rapidly developing beach resort called **Cros-de-Cagnes,** between Nice and Antibes.

For years Le Haut-de-Cagnes attracted the French literati, including Simone de Beauvoir, who wrote *Les Mandarins* here. A colony of painters also settled here; Renoir said the village was "the place where I want to paint until the last day of my life." Today the racecourse is one of the finest in France.

ESSENTIALS

GETTING THERE   Buses from Nice and Cannes stop at Cagnes-Ville and at Béal / Les Collettes, within walking distance of Cros-de-Cagne. For **bus information,** call ☎ **04-93-39-18-71** in Cannes or ☎ **04-93-85-61-81** in Nice. The climb from Cagnes-Ville to Le Haut-de-Cagnes is very strenuous, so there's a minibus running about every 30 minutes from place du Général-de-Gaulle in the center of Cagnes-Ville to Le Haut-de-Cagnes.

VISITOR INFORMATION   The **Office de Tourisme** is at 6 bd. du Maréchal-Juin, Cagnes-Ville (☎ **04-93-20-61-64**).

SPECIAL EVENTS   The **International Festival of Painting** is presented by the Musée d'Art Moderne Méditerranéen from November 22 to January 20 in the Château-Musée, 7 place Grimaldi; 40 nations participate. For information, call ☎ **04-93-20-87-29.**

SEEING THE TOP ATTRACTIONS

The orange groves and fields of carnations of the upper village provide a beautiful setting for the narrow cobblestone streets and 17th- and 18th-century homes. Drive your car to the top, where you can enjoy the view from **place du Château** and have lunch or a drink at a sidewalk cafe.

While in Le Haut-de-Cagnes, visit the **fortress** on place Grimaldi. It was built in 1301 by Rainier Grimaldi I, a lord of Monaco and a French admiral (see the portrait inside). Charts reveal how the defenses were organized. In the early 17th century the dank castle was converted into a more gracious Louis XIII château.

The château contains two interconnected museums, the **Musée de l'Olivier** (Museum of the Olive Tree) and the **Musée d'Art Moderne Méditerranéen** (Museum of Modern Mediterranean Art), 7 place Grimaldi (☎ **04-93-20-85-57**). The ethnographic museum shows the steps in cultivating and processing the olive. The modern art gallery displays works by Kisling, Carzou, Dufy, Cocteau, and Seyssaud, among others, with temporary exhibitions. In one salon is an interesting trompe-l'oeil fresco, *La Chute de Phaeton.* From the tower you get a panoramic view of the Côte d'Azur. The museums are open Wednesday to Monday: April to September from 10:30am to 12:30pm and 1:30 to 6pm and October 1 to 14 and November 16 to June 14 from 10am to noon and 2 to 5pm; closed October 15 to November 15. Admission to both museums is 10F ($2) for adults and 10F ($2) for students. The International Festival of Painting (see "Essentials," above) takes place here.

A DAY AT THE BEACH

Cros-de-Cagnes is known for 2¹/₄ miles of seafront evenly covered with light-gray pebbles (the French refer to it as *galet*) that've been worn smooth by centuries of wave action. These beaches are collectively identified as the **Plages de Cros-de-Cagnes.** The expanse is punctuated by five concessions that rent beach mattresses and chaises for around 85F ($17). The best, or at least the most centrally located, are **Tiercé**

Plage (☎ 04-93-20-02-09), Le Cigalon (☎ 04-93-07-74-82), and La Gougouline (☎ 04-93-31-08-72). As usual, toplessness is accepted but full nudity isn't.

A NEARBY ATTRACTION

Les Collettes, 19 chemin des Collettes (☎ 04-93-20-61-07), has been restored to what it looked like when Renoir lived here from 1908 until his death in 1919. He continued to sculpt here, even though he was crippled by arthritis and had to be helped in and out of a wheelchair. He also continued to paint, with a brush tied to his hand and with the help of assistants. One of his last paintings, *Rest After Bathing,* can be seen in the Louvre.

The house was built in 1907 in an olive and orange grove. There's a bust of Mme Renoir in the entrance room. You can explore the drawing room and dining room on your own before going up to the artist's bedroom. In his atelier are his wheelchair, easel, and brushes. From the terrace of Mme Renoir's bedroom is a stunning view of Cap d'Antibes and Le Haut-de-Cagnes. Although Renoir is best remembered for his paintings, it was in Cagnes that he began experimenting with sculpture. The museum has 20 portrait busts and portrait medallions, most of which depict his wife and children. The curators say they represent the largest collection of Renoir sculpture in the world. On a wall hangs a photograph of one of Renoir's sons, Pierre, as he appeared in the 1932 film *Madame Bovary.* The house is open May to October 14, daily from 10:30am to 12:30pm and 1:30 to 6pm; the rest of the year, Wednesday to Monday from 10am to noon and 2 to 5pm. Ticket sales end 30 minutes before the lunch and evening closing hour. Admission is 20F ($4) for adults and 10F ($2) for children.

ACCOMMODATIONS

IN CAGNES-SUR-MER

Hôtel Le Chantilly. Chemin de la Minoerie, 06800 Cagnes-sur-Mer. ☎ **04-93-20-25-50.** Fax 04-92-02-82-63. 20 rms. MINIBAR TV TEL. 300F ($60) double. V. Closed Oct 15–Dec 15.

This is the best bargain for those who prefer to stay at a hotel near the beach instead of an inn in the hills. It won't win any architectural awards, but the owners have landscaped the property and made the interior as homelike and inviting as possible, using Oriental rugs and potted plants, including dwarf palms, as grace notes. In fair weather you can enjoy breakfast, the only meal served, on an outdoor terrace. The rooms, for the most part, are small but cozily furnished and well kept, often opening onto balconies. The owners, Monique and Jean-Claude Barran, will direct you to nearby restaurants.

IN LE HAUT-DE-CAGNES

Note that **Le Grimaldi** (see "Dining," below) also rents rooms.

✪ **Le Cagnard.** Rue du Pontis-Long, Le Haut-de-Cagnes, 06800 Cagnes-sur-Mer. ☎ **04-93-20-73-21.** Fax 04-93-22-06-39. 18 rms, 10 suites. MINIBAR TV TEL. 800F–950F ($160–$190) double; 950F–1,500F ($190–$300) suite. AE, DC, MC, V.

Several village houses have been joined to form this handsome hostelry owned by Félix Barel. The dining room is covered with frescoes, and there's a vine-draped terrace. The rooms and salons are furnished with family antiques, such as provincial chests, armoires, and Louis XV chairs. Each room has its own style: some are duplexes; others have terraces and views of the countryside. The cuisine of chef Jean-Yves Johany is reason enough to make the trip here. Fresh ingredients are used in the delectable dishes placed on one of the finest tables set in Provence. This talented chef features Sisteron lamb (carré d'agneau) spit-roasted with Provençal herbs for two, as well as tender côte de boeuf. The *pièce de résistance* dessert is the extravagant mousseline of ice cream.

IN CROS-DE-CAGNES

Hôtel Le Minaret. Av. Serre, 06800 Cros-de-Cagnes. ☎ **04-93-20-16-52.** Fax 04-92-13-05-56. 20 rms. TV TEL. 200F–300F ($40–$60) double. MC, V.

This two-star hotel has a courtyard with tables in the front and a hardworking staff. It once sported a decorative minaret in the Provençal style; though it was removed in a restoration, the name has remained. Fifty yards from the beach, Le Minaret also has a shaded garden filled with mimosa, orange trees, and palms. Some rooms offer terraces or balconies; all have kitchenettes. There's a bar on the premises, but no restaurant. Several dining places are within walking distance.

DINING
IN LE HAUT-DE-CAGNES

Josy-Jo. 8 place du Planastel. ☎ **04-93-20-68-76.** Reservations required. Main courses 140F–180F ($28–$36). AE, MC, V. Mon–Fri noon–2pm and 7:30–10pm, Sat 7:30–10pm. Closed Aug 1–15. FRENCH.

Sheltered behind a 200-year-old facade covered with vines and flowers, this restaurant on the main road to the château used to be the home and studio of Modigliani and Soutine, when they borrowed it from a friend during their hungriest years. Today it belongs to the cheerful Bandecchi family, who have lined the dining room with art. Their cuisine is simple, fresh, and excellent, featuring grilled meats and a roster of fish. You can enjoy brochette of gigot of lamb with kidneys, four succulent varieties of steak, calves' liver, a homemade terrine of foie gras of duckling, and an array of salads.

Le Grimaldi. 6 place du Château. ☎ **04-93-20-60-24.** Reservations recommended. Main courses 55F–130F ($11–$26); fixed-price menus 75F–180F ($15–$36). AE, DC, MC, V. Daily noon–3pm and 7:30–11pm. Closed Jan 15–Feb 15. FRENCH.

Here you can dine under bright umbrellas on the town's main square or in a dining room whose walls were built during the Middle Ages. Run by the same hardworking family since 1963, the restaurant serves specialties like salade niçoise, lapin (rabbit) chasseur, a savory version of bouillabaisse, mussels provençal, and trout with almonds.

The hotel also offers six simply furnished rooms, usually with original roughly hewn ceiling beams, a wash basin, and a bidet. The price is 200F ($40) for a single or double, plus 50F ($10) for overnight parking.

✪ **Restaurant des Peintres.** 71 montée de la Bourgade. ☎ **04-93-20-83-08.** Reservations required. Main courses 110F–160F ($22–$32); fixed-price menus 190F–310F ($38–$62). AE, DC, V. Mon 7:30–10:30pm, Tues noon–2pm, Thurs–Sun noon–2pm and 7:30–10:30pm. Closed Dec 1–20. FRENCH.

About half a mile north of the town center, on the rocky hillside above the center of Cagnes, this 200-year-old building contains an undeniable sense of Provençal authenticity, and Philippe Guerin presents a well-choreographed cuisine. Menu items include foie gras, vegetarian risotto, filets of fried red mullet with eggplant caviar, and stuffed pigeon en cocotte.

IN CROS-DE-CAGNES

✪ **Loulou (La Réserve).** 91 bd. de la Plage. ☎ **04-93-31-00-17.** Reservations recommended. Main courses 140F–325F ($28–$65); fixed-price menu 200F ($40). AE, MC, V. Mon–Fri noon–2:30pm and 7–9:45pm, Sat 7–9:45pm. Closed for lunch July 14–Aug 15. FRENCH.

Run by the Campo family, whose brothers perform various functions inside, this place is named for a famous long-departed chef and sits across from the sea. The place is known as one of the few restaurants that specialize in line-caught (as opposed to net-caught) fish, which Eric Campo prepares with gusto and flair. Specialties are rockfish soup (in season); aiguillettes of duckling with herbs; baby squid served as simply as possible, with just a drizzling of olive oil and balsamic vinegar; and a selection of grilled meats. Though many of the French gastronomic guides continue to ignore this talented chef, Michelin has bestowed a star, of which Campo is rightly proud. Everything is solid and reliable, yet he also knows how to be inventive in bringing out the inherent flavor in every dish. In front is a glassed-in veranda perfect for people watching.

7 Nice

577 miles S of Paris, 20 miles NE of Cannes

The Victorian upper class and tsarist aristocrats loved Nice in the 19th century, but it's solidly middle class today, far less glamorous and less expensive than Cannes. In fact, of all the major resorts of France, from Deauville to Biarritz to Cannes, Nice is the least expensive. It's also the best excursion center on the Riviera, especially if you're dependent on public transportation. For example, you can go to San Remo, "the queen of the Italian Riviera," and return to Nice by nightfall. From the Nice airport, the second largest in France, you can travel by bus along the entire coast to resorts like Juan-les-Pins and Cannes.

Nice is the capital of the Riviera, the largest city between Genoa and Marseille. It's also one of the most ancient, having been founded by the Greeks, who called it "Nike," or Victory. Because of its brilliant sunshine and relaxed living, artists and writers have been attracted to Nice for years. Among them were Dumas, Nietzsche, Apollinaire, Flaubert, Hugo, Sand, Stendhal, Chateaubriand, and Mistral. Henri Matisse, who made his home in Nice, said, "Though the light is intense, it's also soft and tender." The city has, on the average, 300 days of sunshine a year.

ESSENTIALS

GETTING THERE   Visitors who arrive at **Aéroport Nice–Côte d'Azur** (☎ 04-93-21-30-30) can take an airport bus departing every 20 minutes to the Station Centrale in the city center. Buses run from 6am to 10:30pm and cost 8F ($1.60). For 25F ($5) you can take a *navette* (airport shuttle) that goes several times a day between the airport and the train station. A taxi ride into the city center will cost at least 180F ($36).

Trains arrive at **Gare Nice-Ville,** avenue Thiers (☎ 08-36-35-35-35). From here you can take frequent trains to Cannes, Monaco, and Antibes, among other destinations. An information office at the station is open Monday to Saturday from 8am to 6:30pm and Sunday from 8am to noon and 2 to 5:30pm. If you face a delay, you can take showers at the station and eat at the cafeteria. The *navette* travels several times a day from the train station to the airport for 25F ($5).

VISITOR INFORMATION   The **Office de Tourisme** is at 5 promenade des Anglais (☎ 04-92-14-48-00), near place Masséna. This office will make you a hotel reservation; the fee depends on the classification of the hotel.

GETTING AROUND   Most local buses in Nice form connections with one another at the **Station Centrale,** 10 av. Félix-Faure (☎ 04-93-16-52-10), in the vicinity of place Masséna. Take bus no. 2 or 12 to the beach for 8F ($1.60). To save

Nice

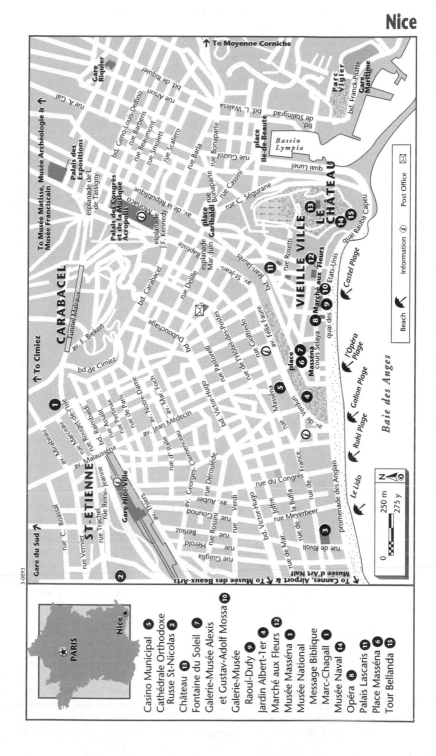

money, purchase a *carnet* of 10 tickets for 68F ($13.60), available at the tourist office (see above). Buses making the trek between Nice and other parts of France and Europe depart from the Intercars Terminal, **Gare Routière,** 5 bd. Jean-Jaurès (☎ 04-93-80-08-70).

You can rent bicycles and mopeds at **Nicea Rent,** 9 av. Thiers (☎ 04-93-82-42-71), near the Station Centrale. March to October, it's open daily from 9am to noon and 2 to 6pm (closed Sunday November to April). The cost begins at 120F ($24) per day, plus a 1,500F ($300) deposit. Credit cards are accepted.

SPECIAL EVENTS   At certain times Nice is caught up in frenzied carnival activities. The **Nice Carnaval** draws visitors from all over Europe and North America to this ancient spectacle. The Mardi Gras of the Riviera begins sometime in February, usually 12 days before Shrove Tuesday, celebrating the return of spring with parades, floats *(corsi),* masked balls *(veglioni),* confetti, and battles in which young women toss flowers—and only the most wicked throw rotten eggs instead of carnations. Climaxing the event is a fireworks display on Shrove Tuesday, lighting up the Baie des Anges (Bay of Angels). King Carnival goes up in flames on his pyre but rises from the ashes the following spring.

Also important is the **Nice Festival du Jazz,** from July 11 to 20, where a roster of jazz artists perform in the ancient Arène de Cimiez. For information and tickets, contact the Comité des Fêtes, Mairie (town hall) de Nice, 5 rue de l'Hôtel-de-Ville, 06000 Nice (☎ 04-93-13-20-00).

EXPLORING THE CITY

In 1822 the orange crop at Nice was bad and the workers faced a lean time. So the English residents put them to work building the **promenade des Anglais,** which remains a wide boulevard fronting the bay and, split by "islands" of palms and flowers, stretches for about 4 miles. Fronting the beach are rows of grand cafes, the Musée Masséna, villas, and hotels—some good, others decaying.

Crossing this boulevard in the briefest of bikinis or thongs are some of the world's most attractive bronzed bodies. They're heading for the beach—"on the rocks," as it's called here. Tough on tender feet, the beach is shingled (covered with pebbles), one of the least attractive (and least publicized) aspects of the cosmopolitan resort city. Many bathhouses provide mattresses for a charge.

In the east, the promenade becomes **quai des Etats-Unis,** the original boulevard, lined with some of the best restaurants in Nice, each specializing in bouillabaisse. Rising sharply on a rock is the site known as **Le Château,** the spot where the ducs de Savoie built their castle, which was torn down in 1706. Don't expect sights of the Middle Ages: all that remains is two or three stones—even the foundations have disappeared in the wake of Louis XIV's deliberate destruction of what was viewed at the time as a bulwark of Provençal resistance to his regime. The steep hill has been turned into a garden of pines and exotic flowers. To reach the panoramic site, you can take an elevator; actually, many prefer to take the elevator up, then walk down. The park is open daily from 8am to 7:30pm.

At the north end of Le Château is the famous old **graveyard** of Nice, visited primarily for its lavishly sculpted monuments that form their own enduring art statement. It's the largest one in France and the fourth largest in Europe. To reach it, you can take a small canopied **Train Touristique de Nice** (☎ 04-93-18-81-58), which departs from the Jardin Albert-1er. Rolling on rubber wheels, it makes a 40-minute sightseeing transit past many of Nice's most heralded sites—like place Masséna, promenade des Anglais, and quai des Etats-Unis. It operates daily: April to October from 10am to 6pm and November to March from 10am to 5pm. The price is 30F ($6) per person.

In the Tour Bellanda is the **Musée Naval** (Naval Museum), Parc du Château (☎ 04-93-80-47-61), sitting on "The Rock." The tower stands on a precariously perched belvedere overlooking the beach, the bay, the old town, and even the terraces of some of the nearby villas. Of the museum's old battle prints, one depicts the exploits of Caterina Segurana, the Joan of Arc of the Niçois. During the 1543 siege by Barbarossa, she ran along the ramparts, raising her skirt to show her shapely bottom to the Turks as a sign of contempt, though the soldiers were reported to have been more excited than insulted. The museum is open June to September, Wednesday to Sunday from 10am to noon and 2 to 7pm (to 5pm off-season). Admission is 15F ($3) for adults and 9F ($1.80) for students and children.

Continuing east from "The Rock" you reach **the harbor,** where the restaurants are even cheaper and the bouillabaisse is just as good. While sitting here lingering over an apéritif at a sidewalk cafe, you can watch the boats depart for Corsica (perhaps take one yourself). The port was excavated between 1750 and 1830. Since then an outer harbor—protected by two jetties—has also been created.

The "authentic" Niçois live in **Vieille Ville,** the old town, beginning at the foot of "The Rock" and stretching out from place Masséna. Sheltered by sienna-tiled roofs, many of the Italianate facades suggest 17th-century Genoese palaces. The old town is a maze of narrow streets, teeming with local life and studded with the least expensive restaurants in Nice. Buy an onion pizza *(la pissaladière)* from one of the local vendors. Many of the old buildings are painted a faded Roman gold, and their banners are multicolored laundry flapping in the sea breezes.

While here, try to visit the **Marché aux Fleurs,** the flower market at cours Saleya. The vendors start setting up their stalls Tuesday to Sunday at noon, then conduct the serious business of adorning the interiors of homes and businesses with bouquets until sometime between 2 and 4pm, depending on the vendor. A flamboyant array of carnations, violets, jonquils, roses, and birds of paradise is hauled in by vans or trucks, then displayed in the greatest regularly scheduled market in town.

Nice's commercial centerpiece is **place Masséna,** with pink buildings in the 17th-century Genoese style and the **Fontaine du Soleil** (Fountain of the Sun) by Janoit, from 1956. Stretching from the main square to the promenade is the **Jardin Albert-1er,** with an open-air terrace and a Triton Fountain. With palms and exotic flowers, it's the most relaxing oasis at the resort.

THE TOP MUSEUMS

There's a higher density of museums in Nice than in many comparable French cities. If you decide to forgo the pleasures of the pebbly beach and devote your time to visiting some of the best-repected museums in the south of France, you can buy a **Carte Passe-Musée** from the local tourist office for 120F ($24) for adults and 60F ($12) for students and children. It'll allow you visits to up to 15 of the city's museums, over an unlimited time period.

The partner of the Galerie-Musée Raoul-Dufy (below), the **Galerie-Musée Alexis et Gustav-Adolf Mossa,** 59 quai des Etats-Unis (☎ 04-93-62-37-11), was inaugurated in 1990. Here you can admire the dynamic lines of a veritable family dynasty of Nice-born artists. Among them is Alexis Mossa, famous for local landscapes and scenes of the Nice carnival. He's one of the early symbolist painters, a representative of a movement that brought a definitive end to the romantic movement of the late 19th century and a harbinger of surrealism. Also here are the works of Alexis's son,

Gustav-Adolf Mossa, who continued his father's work. One series of works executed between 1903 and 1919 gracefully serves as a precursor to surrealism. The museum is open Tuesday to Saturday from 10am to noon and 2 to 6pm and Sunday from 2 to 6pm. Admission is 15F ($3). Take bus no. 8.

La Galerie des Ponchettes, inaugurated in 1950 by Matisse, became, in 1990, the **Galerie-Musée Raoul-Dufy,** 77 quai des Etats-Unis (☎ 04-93-62-31-24), in an annex of the Musée des Beaux-Arts (below). It presents one of the most beautiful collections by the Havrais artist (that means he came from Le Havre), who lived from 1877 to 1953. Most of the collection was bequeathed to the museum by his widow. The extremely diversified works include 28 oils, 15 watercolors, 88 drawings, three ceramics, a tapestry, and 15 proposals for fabric designs commissioned by the legendary couturier Paul Poiret. In its new setting, Dufy is immortalized, facing the waters of the Baie des Anges, which his works helped immortalize. The museum is open Tuesday to Saturday from 10am to noon and 2 to 6pm and Sunday from 3 to 6pm. Admission is 15F ($3) for adults and 9F ($1.80) for children, or 25F ($5) for adults and 15F ($3) for children to both museums. Take bus no. 8.

The ✪ **Musée des Beaux-Arts,** 33 av. des Baumettes (☎ 04-93-15-28-28), is housed in the former residence of the Ukrainian Princess Kotchubey. Its construction began in 1878 and was completed by a later owner, the American James Thompson. It has an important gallery devoted to the masters of the Second Empire and belle époque, with an extensive collection of the 19th-century French experts. The gallery of sculptures includes works by J. B. Carpeaux, Rude, and Rodin. Note the important collection by a dynasty of painters, the Dutch Vanloo family. One of its best-known members, Carle Vanloo, born in Nice in 1705, was Louis XV's premier *peintre.* A fine collection of 19th- and 20th-century art is displayed, including works by Ziem, Raffaelli, Boudin, Renoir, Monet, Guillaumin, and Sisley. The museum is open Tuesday to Sunday from 10am to noon and 2 to 6pm. Admission is 25F ($5) for adults and 15F ($3) for children and includes entry to the Galerie-Musée Raoul-Dufy (above). Take bus no. 9, 12, 22, 23, or 38.

The **Musée International d'Art Naïf Anatole-Jakovsky** (Museum of Naïve Art), avenue Val-Marie (☎ 04-93-71-78-33), is housed in the beautifully restored Château Ste-Hélène in the Fabron district. The collection was once owned by the namesake of the museum, for years one of the world's leading art critics. His 600 drawings and canvases were turned over to the institution and made accessible to the public. Artists from more than two dozen countries are represented here—from primitive painting to contemporary 20th-century works. The museum is open Wednesday to Monday from 10am to noon and 2 to 6pm. Admission is 25F ($5) for adults, 15F ($3) for students and seniors, and free for children 17 and under. Take bus no. 9, 10, or 12; the walk from the bus stop takes 10 minutes.

The fabulous villa housing the **Musée d'Art et d'Histoire Palais Masséna,** 65 rue de France (☎ 04-93-88-11-34), was built in 1900 in the style of the First Empire as a residence for Victor Masséna, the prince of Essling and grandson of Napoléon's marshal. The city of Nice has converted the villa, next door to the Hôtel Négresco, into a museum of local history and decorative art. A remarkable First Empire drawing room furnished in the opulent taste of that era, with mahogany-veneer pieces and ormolu mounts, is on the ground floor. Of course there's the representation of Napoléon as a Roman Caesar and a bust by Canova of Maréchal Masséna. The large first-floor gallery exhibits a collection of Niçois primitives and also has a display of 14th- and 15th-century painters, as well as a collection of 16th- to 19th-century masterpieces of plates and jewelry decorated with enamel

(Limoges). There are art galleries devoted to the history of Nice and the memories of Masséna and Garibaldi. Yet another gallery is reserved for a display of views of Nice during the 18th and 19th centuries. The museum is open Tuesday to Sunday from 10am to noon and 2 to 6pm. Admission is 25F ($5) for adults and 15F ($3) for children; it's free for everyone one Sunday per month. Take bus no. 3, 7, 8, 9, 10, 12, 14, or 22.

MORE ATTRACTIONS

Ordered built by none other than Tsar Nicholas II, the ✪ **Cathédrale Orthodoxe Russe St-Nicolas à Nice,** avenue Nicolas-II off boulevard du Tzaréwitch (☎ 04-93-96-88-02), is the most beautiful religious edifice of the Orthodoxy outside Russia and is the perfect expression of Russian religious art abroad. It dates from the belle époque, when some of the Romanovs and their entourage turned the Riviera into a stamping ground. Everyone from grand dukes to ballerinas walked the promenade. The cathedral is richly ornamented and decorated with lots of icons. You'll easily spot the building from afar because of its collection of ornate onion-shaped domes. Church services are held on Sunday morning. The cathedral is open daily: June to September from 9am to noon and 2:30 to 6pm and October to May from 9:30am to noon and 2:30 to 5pm. Admission is 12F ($2.40). From the central rail station, head west along avenue Thiers to boulevard Gambetta; then go north to avenue Nicolas-II.

The baroque **Palais Lascaris,** 15 rue Droite (☎ 04-93-62-05-54), in the city's historic core, is intimately linked to the Lascaris-Vintimille family, whose recorded history predates the year 1261. Built in the 17th century, it contains elaborately detailed ornaments. An intensive restoration undertaken by the city of Nice in 1946 brought back its original beauty, and the palace is now classified a historic monument. The most elaborate floor is the *étage noble,* retaining many of its 18th-century panels and plaster embellishments. A circa-1738 pharmacy, complete with many of the original Delftware accessories, is on the premises. The museum maintains the same hours and prices as the Musée d'Art et d'Histoire Palais Masséna (see above). Every Wednesday between 2 and 4pm it focuses special attention on children of any age: various craftspeople are imported to show the details of how they accomplish their art forms through live demonstrations. Take bus no. 1, 2, 3, 5, 6, 14, 16, or 17.

Nice is the home of an independent museum founded/maintained by a retired airline pilot and Vietnam veteran, Eric Huitric, who has appeared frequently on French TV promoting his unusual attraction. The **Musée des Trains Miniatures,** boulevard de l'Impératrice-Eugénie (☎ 04-93-97-41-40), is 2 miles west of the town center, beside the road leading to the airport. It contains one of the world's most comprehensive collections of miniature trains, plus an impressive number of accessories made in France, Germany, Denmark, and the United States between 1910 and the present. Its eight complete track layouts represent all the major railway guages of Europe and North America. In 1996 the museum attracted more than 28,000 visitors, making it the 23rd most frequently visited museum along the Côte d'Azur. It's open daily: April to September from 9:30am to 7pm and October to May from 9:30am to 5pm. Admission is 35F ($7) for adults and 20F ($4) for children. Don't be confused by the fact that this museum lies in an outdoor museum that at press time was closed and bankrupt. Formerly known as the Parc des Miniatures, its Disney-esque theme used to celebrate the architectural diversity of Nice and its region. Today the weather-beaten premises are closed to the public, with the exception of the Musée des Trains Miniatures, which is separately (and privately) owned.

Two Countryside Drives

From Nice to Mont Chauve

This scenic 33-mile tour circles through the much-eroded rocky foothills north of Nice, where vertiginous cliffs add to the drama. Leave Nice by heading north on avenue du Ray. Take a sharp right on avenue de Gairaut, marked with signs to get you to D14, heading toward Aspremont. Pass under the motorway (about 1¼ miles), then follow the D14 signs, first bearing right and then turning left. The first sight, after four switchbacks just north of town, is the **Cascade de Gairaut** (Gairaut waterfall), to your left, where the water of the Vesubie Canal makes two descents into a basin that supplies water to Nice.

The next 3 miles includes views to the left of Nice and Cap d'Antibes before climbing to **Aspremont,** where the panorama expands to include the Baous, the Var Valley, and the Alps. Aspremont is known for its Gothic church and the ruins of a hilltop castle from whose terrace you have a commanding view of the villages and hills. Leave on D719, which follows the Aspremont Pass between two hills to **Tourrette-Levens.** The sights here include an 18th-century church and a partially restored castle from which you can enjoy another great view.

Leave by turning left onto D19, the new name for D719 south of town, and drive down into the Gabre Valley. On the right you'll pass the **Gorges du Gabres** (Gabre Gorge), with its sheer walls of limestone, and will shortly come to an intersection with D114, where you'll bear right toward **Falicon,** with its buildings clustered on a rocky outcropping in the midst of olive groves. In the village, the Bellevue Inn pays tribute to the author Jules Romains and offers a splendid view from its terrace. Continue along D114, turning left out of the village. At the Chapelle St-Sebastien, turn right onto D214, a narrow curving road that ends at the foot of **Mount Chauve.** A half-hour hike will take you to the summit, where an abandoned fort overlooks the Alps, the Nice foothills, and the coast.

NEARBY ATTRACTIONS IN CIMIEZ

In the once-aristocratic hilltop quarter of **Cimiez,** Queen Victoria wintered at the Hôtel Excelsior and brought half the English court with her. Founded by the Romans, who called it Cemenelum, Cimiez was the capital of the Maritime Alps province. To reach this suburb, take bus no. 15 or 17 from place Masséna. Recent excavations have uncovered the ruins of a Roman town, and you can wander among the diggings. The arena was big enough to hold at least 5,000 spectators, who watched contests between gladiators and wild beasts shipped in from Africa.

The **Monastère de Cimiez** (Cimiez Convent), place du Monastère (☎ 04-93-81-40-04), embraces a church that owns three of the most important works from the primitive painting school of Nice by the Bréa brothers. See the carved and gilded wooden main altarpiece. In a restored part of the convent where some Franciscan friars still live, the **Musée Franciscain** is decorated with 17th-century frescoes. Some 350 documents and works of art from the 15th to the 18th century are displayed, and a monk's cell has been re-created in all its severe simplicity. See also the 17th-century chapel. In the gardens you can get a panoramic view of Nice and the Baie des Anges. Matisse and Dufy are buried in the cemetery. The museum is open Monday to Saturday from 10am to noon and 3 to 6pm; the church is open daily from 8am to 12:30pm and 2 to 7pm. Entrance to both the church and its museum are free.

Backtrack past Falicon and make a sharp right on D19, heading toward Nice. On the way, you'll see the **Benedictine Abbaye St-Pontius,** dating from the reign of Charlemagne and rebuilt early in the 18th century, recognizable looming above the horizon with its Genoese bell tower and tall baroque facade. Its elliptical floor plan includes a semicircular choir loft and side chapels, the latter separated from the main sanctuary by immense columns. After viewing the abbey, continue south on D19 for about 2¹/₂ miles to return to Nice.

From Nice to Levens

Levens is an attractive residential town guarding the Vallée de la Vésubie. Fifteen miles from Nice on D19, it's at an altitude of 1,800 feet. Here you'll find some of the most beautiful spots in the mountains. We recommend taking a trip to **Saut des Français** (Frenchmen's Leap), at the exit from the village of Duranus. In 1793 French Republican soldiers were tossed over this belvedere by guerrilla bands from Nice, called Barbets. The fall—without a parachute—was some 1,200 feet down to the Vésubie. Fifteen miles farther, **La Madone d'Utelle,** at 3,900 feet, offers a panoramic view of the Maritime Alps.

If you want to overnight here, try the **Hôtel Malaussena,** 9 place de la République, Levens, 06670 St-Martin-du-Var (☎ **04-93-79-70-06;** fax 04-93-79-85-89). This centrally located hotel offers 14 clean, comfortable rooms, some with first-rate plumbing. Though the inn is fairly simple, the welcome is first-class. The rates are 180F to 230F ($36 to $46) for a double (American Express and MasterCard accepted). The food is excellent but not recommended for dieters, and two fixed-price menus are offered. Dinner is served at 7:30pm. The restaurant is closed to nonguests, except in July and August when the public is welcome, with reservations. The hotel is closed in November and December.

The **Musée Matisse,** in the Villa des Arènes-de-Cimiez, 164 av. des Arènes-de-Cimiez (☎ **04-93-81-08-08**), honors the great artist who spent the last years of his life in Nice; he died here in 1954. Seeing his nude sketches today, you'll wonder how early critics could've denounced them as "the female animal in all her shame and horror." The museum has several permanent collections, most painted in Nice and many donated by Matisse and his heirs. These include *Nude in an Armchair with a Green Plant* (1937), *Nymph in the Forest* (1935/1942), and a chronologically arranged series of paintings from 1890 to 1919. The most famous of these is *Portrait of Madame Matisse* (1905), usually displayed near another portrait of the artist's wife, by Marquet, painted in 1900. There's also an ensemble of drawings and designs *(Flowers and Fruits)* he prepared as practice sketches for the Matisse Chapel at Vence. The most famous are *The Créole Dancer* (1951), *Blue Nude IV* (1952), and around 50 dance-related sketches he did between 1930 and 1931. Admission fees and hours are the same as those for the Musée d'Art et d'Histoire Palais Masséna (see above).

In the hills of Cimiez above Nice, the **Musée National Message Biblique Marc-Chagall,** avenue du Dr.-Ménard (☎ **04-93-53-87-20**), is devoted to Marc Chagall's treatment of biblical themes. The handsome museum is surrounded by shallow pools and a garden planted with thyme, lavender, and olive trees. Born in Russia in 1887, Chagall became a French citizen in 1937. The artist and his wife donated the works—the most important collection of Chagall ever assembled—to the French state in 1966 and 1972. Displayed are 450 of his oils, gouaches, drawings, pastels, lithographs, sculptures, and ceramics; a mosaic; three stained-glass windows; and a tapestry. A splendid concert room was especially decorated by Chagall with brilliantly hued stained-glass windows. Temporary exhibitions are organized each summer about great periods and artists of all times. Special **lectures** in the rooms are available in both French and English (call ☎ **04-92-91-50-20** for an appointment). The museum is open Wednesday to Monday: July to September from 10am to 6pm and October to June from 10am to 5pm. Admission is 30F ($6) for adults, 20F ($4) for young adults 18 to 24, and free for children 17 and under. Fees may be higher for special exhibits.

OUTDOOR ACTIVITIES

GOLF   The oldest golf course on the Riviera is about 10 miles from Nice: **Golf Bastide du Roi** (also known as the Golf de Biot), avenue Jules-Grec, Biot (☎ **04-93-65-08-48**). Open daily throughout the year, this is a flat, not particularly challenging sea-fronting course. (Regrettably, it's necessary to cross over a highway midway through the course to complete the full 18 holes.) Tee-off times are 8am to 6pm, with the understanding that players then continue their rounds as long as the daylight allows. Reservations aren't necessary, though on weekends you should probably expect a delay. Greens fees are 200F ($40) for 18 holes, and clubs can be rented for 50F ($10). No carts are available.

HORSEBACK RIDING   The only equestrian venue in the area, the **Club Hippique de Nice,** 368 rte. de Grenoble (☎ **04-93-13-13-16**), contains about 40 horses, 13 of which are available for rentals. About 3 miles from Nice, near the airport, it's hemmed in on virtually every side by busy roads and highways and conducts all its activities in a series of riding rinks. Riding sessions should be reserved in advance, last about an hour, and cost 65F ($13).

SCUBA DIVING   The best-respected outfit is the **Centre International de Plongée de Nice,** 2 ruelle des Moulins (☎ **04-93-55-59-50**). Adjacent to the city's old port, midway between quai des Docks and boulevard Stalingrad, it's maintained by the Champagne-born Raymond Lefevre, whose dive boat, *René-Madeleine,* is an amalgam of the names of his parents. A *baptême* (initiatory dive for first-timers) costs 180F ($36) and a one-tank dive for experienced divers, with all equipment included, is 200F ($40).

TENNIS   The oldest tennis club in Nice is the **Nice Lawn Tennis Club,** Parc Impérial, 5 av. Suzanne-Lenglen (☎ **04-93-96-17-70**), near the train station. It's open daily from 8:30am to 9pm and charges 120F ($24) per person for 2 noncontiguous hours of court time, or a reduced rate of 250F ($50) per person for unlimited access to the courts for 1 week. The club contains a cooperative staff, a loyal clientele, 13 clay courts, and 6 hard-surfaced courts. Reservations should be made the evening before.

SHOPPING

You might want to begin with a stroll through the streets and alleys of Nice's historic core. The densest concentrations of boutiques are along **rue Masséna, place Magenta,** and **rue Paradis,** as well as on the streets funneling into and around them. Examples are **Gigi,** 7 rue de la Liberté (☎ **04-93-87-81-78**); **Carroll,** 9 rue de la Liberté (☎ **04-93-16-15-25**); and **Trabaud,** 10 rue de la Liberté (☎ **04-93-87-53-96**). Timeless and endlessly alluring, despite the passage of time, are the products of **Yves Saint Laurent,** 4 av. de Suède (☎ **04-93-87-70-79**).

Since 1925, **Allées de la Côte d'Azur,** 1 rue St-François-de-Paul (☎ 04-93-85-87-30), has sold food products inspired by the bounty of Provence. Near La Mairie (town hall) in the old town, it specializes in anything concocted from a fig, like fig sausages, fig loafs, fresh figs, and fig liqueur. Equally tempting are tinned or glass-encased tapenades concocted from pulverized black olives, various types of basil and herbs from the foothills of the Alps, perfumes, dried lavender, and gift items carved from olivewood.

Opened in 1949 by Joseph Fuchs, the grandfather of the present English-speaking owners, the **Confiserie du Vieux-Nice,** 14 quai Papacino (☎ 04-93-45-43-50), is near the Old Port. The specialty here is glazed fruits crystallized in sugar or artfully arranged into chocolates. Look for exotic jams (rose-petal preserves or mandarin marmalade) and the free recipe leaflet as well as candied violets, verbena leaves, and rosebuds. Prices run from 15F ($3) to 600F ($120), for a large gift basket.

Façonnable, 7–9 rue Paradis (☎ 04-93-87-88-80), is the site that sparked the creation of what is today several hundred Façonnable menswear stores around the world. This is one of the largest Façonnable stores in the world, with a wide range of men's suits, raincoats, overcoats, sportswear, and jeans. The look is youthful and conservatively stylish, for relatively slim (French) bodies.

If you're thinking of indulging in a Provençale *pique-nique,* **Nicola Alziari,** 14 rue St-François-de-Paule (☎ 04-93-85-77-98), will provide everything you'll need: from olives, anchovies, and pistous to aïolis and tapenades. It's one of Nice's oldest purveyors of olive oil, with a house brand that comes in two strengths—a light version that aficionados claim is vaguely perfumed with Provence and a stronger version suited to the earthy flavors and robust ingredients of a Provençal winter. Also look for a range of objects crafted from olive wood.

Other shopping recommendations are **La Couquetou,** 8 rue St-François-de-Paule (☎ 04-93-80-90-30), selling *santos,* the traditional Provençal figurines. The best selection of Provençal fabrics is found at **Les Olivades,** 7 rue de la Boucherie (☎ 04-93-85-85-19). There are several stores specializing in arts and crafts, including decorative items in wood, silk, and leather. The best is **Atelier Contre-Jour,** 3 rue du Pont-Vieux (☎ 04-93-80-20-50).

Nice is also known for its colorful street markets. The flower market, **Marché aux Fleurs,** cours Saleya, is open from 6am to 5:30pm except Monday and Sunday afternoon. The main Nice flea market, **Marché à la Brocante,** also at cours Saleya, takes place every Monday from 8am to 5pm. There's another flea market on the port, **Les Puces de Nice,** place Robilante, open Tuesday to Saturday from 10am to 6pm.

ACCOMMODATIONS
VERY EXPENSIVE

✪ **Hôtel Négresco.** 37 promenade des Anglais, 06007 Nice CEDEX. ☎ **04-93-16-64-00.** Fax 04-93-88-35-68. 132 rms, 18 suites. A/C MINIBAR TV TEL. 1,300F–2,350F ($260–$470) double; from 3,950F ($790) suite. AE, DC, MC, V. Parking 160F ($32) in the garage. Bus: 9, 10, or 11.

The Négresco is one of the Riviera's many super-glamorous hotels, though those pockets of posh in Beaulieu and St-Jean-Cap-Ferrat are even more regal and better sited for tranquillity, as the Négresco stands in the heart of noisy Nice. Jeanne Augier has taken over the place and has triumphed. This Victorian wedding-cake hotel is named after its founder, Henry Négresco, a Romanian who died franc-less in Paris in 1920. It was built on the seafront, in the French château style, with a mansard roof and domed tower; its interior design was inspired by the country's châteaux and the decorators scoured Europe to gather antiques, tapestries, paintings, and art. Some guest rooms have personality themes: The Louis XIV chamber has a green-velvet bed under a brocaded rose canopy. The Chambre Impératrice Joséphine 1810 regally re-creates an Empire bedroom, with a huge rosewood swan bed set in a fleur-de-lis–draped recess. The Napoléon III room has swagged walls and a half-crowned canopy in pink, with a leopard-skin carpet. The most expensive rooms with balconies face the Mediterranean. (Be sure to note the occasional jarring notes, like clear plastic toilet seats flecked with glitter.) The staff wears 18th-century costumes. Reasonably priced meals are served in La Rotonde, but the featured restaurant—one of the Riviera's greatest—is Chantecler (see "Dining," below).

✪ **Palais Maeterlinck.** Basse Corniche, 06300 Nice. ☎ **04-92-00-72-00.** Fax 04-92-04-18-10. 22 rms, 6 suites. A/C MINIBAR TV TEL. 1,450F–2,800F ($290–$560) double; 2,500F–4,500F ($500–$900) suite. AE, DC, MC, V. Closed Jan 5 to mid-Mar. Drive 4 miles east of Nice along the Basse Corniche.

On 9 landscaped acres east of Nice, this deluxe hotel—"the jewel of the Côte d'Azur"—occupies a fin-de-siècle villa that was inhabited between the world wars by the Belgian-born writer Maurice Maeterlinck, winner of the Nobel Prize for Literature. Many visitors find the setting sumptuous, though, frankly, the service and experience of the staff are simply not as elevated as at similarly priced palace hotels. Calmer and more tranquil than the hotels in more central positions, it enjoys the added allure of verdant terraces and a large outdoor pool, set amid banana trees, gnarled olive trees, and soaring cypresses. A funicular will carry you down to the rock-strewn beach and nearby marina. Each of the elegant guest rooms is outfitted in a different monochromatic color scheme and neoclassical Florentine styling, with a terrace opening onto views of such chic enclaves as Cap d'Antibes and Cap-Ferrat. Two restaurants (Le Gastronomique and the less formal Mélisande) offer excellent French and international cuisine, with Provençal specialties.

EXPENSIVE

Hôtel Beau Rivage. 24 rue St-François-de-Paule, 06300 Nice. ☎ **04-93-80-80-70.** Fax 04-93-80-55-77. 98 rms, 10 junior suites. A/C MINIBAR TV TEL. 850F–1,000F ($170–$200) double; 1,800F ($360) suite. AE, DC, MC, V. Bus: 1, 2, 5, or 12.

This hotel is famous for having housed both Matisse and Chekhov during its heyday around the turn of the century. It was radically renovated in the early 1980s, and today the interior has a bland but tasteful modern decor and a staff that seems to make a point of appearing overworked regardless of how few guests might be in residence. The soundproof rooms are vaguely art deco and rather small, with contemporary baths. For dining, Le Relais Beau Rivage is relatively formal and very appealing. Its specialties are meats and fish prepared on a large grill. Between May and September, tables are set on a terrace.

Hôtel Elysée Palace. 59 promenade des Anglais, 06000 Nice. ☎ **04-93-86-06-06.** Fax 04-93-44-50-40. 121 rms, 22 suites. A/C MINIBAR TV TEL. 1,190F–1,300F ($238–$260) double; from 1,450 ($290) suite. AE, DC, MC, V. Parking 75F ($15). Bus: 9, 10, or 12.

This hotel, with a rooftop pool, was built in 1989 on the site of a demolished 19th-century hotel with the same name. Views sweep out from most of its rooms over the sea. The room decor is conservative and contemporary, and the amenities are typical. The hotel has its own private beach a short walk from its premises. The well-managed restaurant, Le Caprice, serves French cuisine.

Hôtel Méridien. 1 promenade des Anglais, 06000 Nice. ☎ **04-93-82-25-25.** Fax 04-93-16-08-90. 304 rms, 10 suites. A/C MINIBAR TV TEL. 1,250F–1,650F ($250–$330) double; from 2,850F ($570) suite. Discounts of around 15% during selected dates Oct–Apr. AE, DC, MC, V. Bus: 8, 9, 10, or 12.

One of Nice's largest hotels, this one rises five floors above the junction of the promenade des Anglais and a small formal park, the Jardin Albert-1er. Built in the 1960s by Air France in an angular design with lots of shiny metal and glass, it was later acquired by Britain's Forte group and is the target of many organized tours from Britain and northern Europe. Two escalators carry you up through a soaring, impersonal atrium to the reception area. The guest rooms are comfortable, modern, and standardized, many with sea views. There's a piano bar, two indoor/outdoor restaurants, and a formal dining room, L'Habit Blanc. On the roof are a pool and sun deck.

Hôtel Splendid-Sofitel. 50 bd. Victor-Hugo, 06048 Nice. ☎ **800/221-4542** in the U.S. and Canada, or 04-93-16-41-00. Fax 04-93-87-02-46. 116 rms, 14 suites. A/C MINIBAR TV TEL. 690F–890F ($138–$178) double; from 1,090F ($218) suite. AE, DC, MC, V. Parking 80F ($16). Bus: 9 or 10.

This is one of Nice's best modern hotels, on the corner of a wide boulevard lined with shade trees, 4 blocks from the beach. Built on the site of the circa-1881 Hôtel Splendid, it was heralded as a new era in French hotels. Frequent renovations have kept the place fresh. The rooms usually have terraces or balconies, and several floors are reserved for nonsmokers. Le Concerto features classic French cooking, with a three-course lunch or dinner at 145F ($29). Adjacent to the rooftop pool, the Topsail Bar offers a salad buffet and views over the city and sea. Facilities include an open-air solar-heated pool and a wading pool for kids.

Radisson SAS Hotel. 223 promenade des Anglais, 06200 Nice. ☎ **04-93-37-17-17.** Fax 04-93-71-21-71. 321 rms, 12 suites. A/C MINIBAR TV TEL. 900F–1,280F ($180–$256) double; 1,800F–6,000F ($360–$1,200) suite. AE, DC, MC, V. Parking 100F ($20). Bus: 9, 10, or 11.

Alongside the major beachside thoroughfare, this streamlined contemporary hotel is one of the most alluring palaces in town, yet nowhere near as grand or as pretentious as the Négresco or the Maeterlinck. In 1997 its administration was taken over by the Radisson SAS group as the first representative of that deluxe chain in France. A discreet portico leads into the sun-flooded lobby. Most of the attractive guest rooms open onto promenade des Anglais, with balconies fronting the sea; they're filled with amenities. You can enjoy a drink at the Blues Bar in the lobby. Les Mosaïques Restaurant offers a Mediterranean cuisine and Lebanese specialties. Spa facilities, a beauty farm, and a health club are open year-round, and between June and September one of the most sumptuous lunch buffets in Nice is served beside the pool on the panoramic terrace.

Westminster Concorde. 27 promenade des Anglais, 06000 Nice. ☎ **04-93-88-29-44.** Fax 04-93-82-45-35. 105 rms, 15 junior suites. A/C MINIBAR TV TEL. 700F–950F ($140–$190) double; from 1,250F ($250) junior suite. AE, DC, MC, V. Parking 100F ($20). Bus: 9, 10, or 11.

This 1880 hotel stands prominently along the famous promenade. Its elaborate facade was restored in 1986 to its former grandeur, and many renovations were made, including the installation of air-conditioning. The contemporary rooms are comfortable and have soundproof windows; a few open onto balconies. The dining and drinking facilities include plant-ringed terraces with a view of the water and a simple in-house restaurant.

MODERATE

Grand Hôtel Aston. 12 av. Félix-Faure, 06000 Nice. ☎ **04-92-17-53-00.** Fax 04-93-80-40-02. 156 rms. 600F–1,100F ($120–$220) double. AE, DC, MC, V. Parking 90F ($18).

One of the most alluring in its price bracket, this elegantly detailed 19th-century hotel has been radically renovated. Most rooms overlook the splashing fountains of place et éspace Masséna, a few blocks from the water. The rooftop garden offers dance music and a bar on summer evenings and has a panoramic coastline view.

Hôtel Busby. 36–38 rue du Maréchal-Joffre, 06000 Nice. ☎ **04-93-88-19-41.** Fax 04-93-87-73-53. 80 rms. A/C TV TEL. 500F–700F ($100–$140) double. AE, DC, MC, V. Closed Nov 15–Dec 20. Bus: 9, 10, 12, or 22.

This place should please you if you want a nostalgic hotel whose faded grandeur dates from around 1910. (The owners, the Busby family, refer to its ornate facade as *style Garibaldi* and have retained the balconies and the shutters at the tall windows.) Totally renovated, the guest rooms are dignified yet colorful, and some contain pairs of mahogany twin beds and white-and-gold wardrobes. There's a cozy bar on the premises; however, faced with stiff competition from neighboring places, the hotel's restaurant closed in 1997.

Hôtel Excelsior. 19 av. Durante, 06000 Nice. ☎ **04-93-88-18-05.** Fax 04-93-88-38-69. 45 rms. TV TEL. 420F–490F ($84–$98) double. Rates include breakfast. AE, MC, V.

Its ornate corbels and chiseled stone pediments—evidence of its original function as a private villa in the 1880s—rise grandly a few steps from the railway station. Inside you'll find a pleasantly modern decor with comfortably upholstered armchairs. There's a reflecting pool in the large lobby, a larger one (with fish) in the rear garden, and high-ceilinged and cozy guest rooms. The beach is a 20-minute walk from the hotel through the residential and commercial center of Nice.

✪ **Hôtel Gounod.** 3 rue Gounod, 06000 Nice. ☎ **04-93-88-26-20.** Fax 04-93-88-23-84. 42 rms, 6 suites. A/C MINIBAR TV TEL. 400F–590F ($80–$118) double; 500F–790F ($100–$158) suite. AE, DC, MC, V. Parking 55F ($11). Closed Nov 20–Dec 20. Bus: 8.

This is our favorite three-star hotel in Nice, built around 1910 in a neighborhood where the street names honor composers. The Gounod *(un petit Négresco)* boasts ornate balconies, a domed roof, and an elaborate canopy of wrought iron and glass. The attractive lobby and adjoining lounge are festive and stylish, with old prints, copper pots with flowers, and antiques. The high-ceilinged guest rooms are quiet and usually overlook the gardens of private homes on both sides. There are few amenities, but you have free unlimited use of the facilities at the Splendid-Sofitel next door, especially the pool, cafe-bar, and heated Jacuzzi.

Hôtel Victoria. 33 bd. Victor-Hugo, 06000 Nice. ☎ **800/528-1234** in the U.S., or 04-93-88-39-60. Fax 04-93-88-39-60. 39 rms. MINIBAR TV TEL. 470F–650F ($94–$130) double. Rates include breakfast. AE, DC, MC, V. Parking 60F ($12). Bus: 8.

A Best Western about 5 blocks from the seafront, this hotel faces one of the main boulevards of downtown Nice. It was built around 1920 and retains its elegantly restrained beaux-arts facade, wide French windows, and shutters that are sometimes used to block off the traffic noise. The soundproof rooms are outfitted stylishly with modern furnishings. The best aspects of the place are the quiet rear garden and the reception area and salon that open onto a view of a lawn studded with trees.

Hôtel West-End. 31 promenade des Anglais, 06000 Nice. ☎ **800/528-1234** in the U.S., or 04-92-14-44-00. Fax 04-93-88-79-91. 130 rms, 3 suites. A/C MINIBAR TV TEL. 650F–1,350F ($130–$270) double; 1,500F–1,600F ($300–$320) suite. AE, DC, MC, V. Parking 80F ($16). Bus: 8.

Few other hotels in Nice cater to the nostalgia a British traveler might feel for London and its traditions. A belle époque monument whose flowering terrace overlooks the sea, this Best Western is named after London's theater district. Though the ornate facade and the stately lobby were retained in honor of the original construction,

Nice Accommodations & Dining

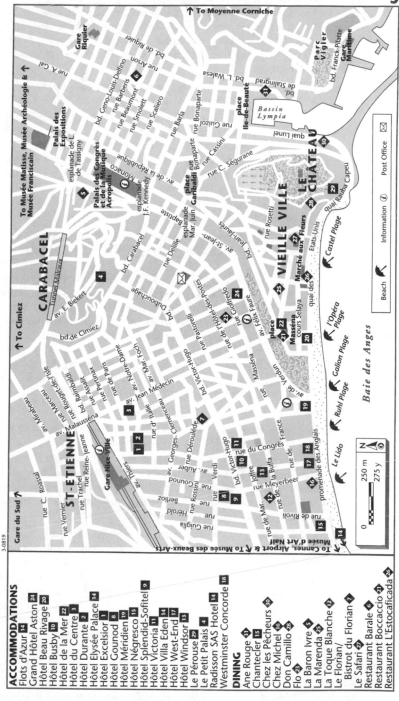

To Moyenne Corniche

ACCOMMODATIONS
Flots d'Azur **11**
Grand Hôtel Aston **24**
Hôtel Beau Rivage **20**
Hôtel Busby **10**
Hôtel de la Mer **22**
Hôtel du Centre **3**
Hôtel Durante **2**
Hôtel Elysée Palace **1**
Hôtel Excelsior **1**
Hôtel Gounod **8**
Hôtel Méridien **19**
Hôtel Négresco **15**
Hôtel Splendid-Sofitel **9**
Hôtel Victoria **11**
Hôtel Villa Eden **14**
Hôtel West-End **17**
Hôtel Windsor **13**
Le Pérouse **29**
Le Petit Palais **4**
Radisson SAS Hotel **14**
Westminster Concorde **18**

DINING
Ane Rouge **31**
Chantecler **15**
Chez les Pêcheurs **40**
Chez Michel **16**
Don Camillo **28**
Flo **23**
La Baron Ivre **5**
La Marenda **25**
La Toque Blanche **42**
Le Florian/ **7**
Bistrot du Florian
Le Safari **27**
Restaurant Barale **6**
Restaurant Boccaccio **21**
Restaurant L'Estocaficada **26**

CARABACEL

ST-ETIENNE

VIEILLE VILLE

LE CHÂTEAU

Baie des Anges

To Cannes, Airport & To Musée des Beaux-Arts
Musée d'Art Naïf

Beach · Information *i* · Post Office ⊠

0   250 m
0   275 y

3-0819

277

the guest rooms were streamlined during several modernizations, yet are comfortable and well furnished. Most offer sea views. You can enjoy drinks on the terrace near a restaurant serving French and international cuisine. There's also a private beach. Because of the hotel's relatively large size, the staff can often appear a bit overworked, but overall it's a worthy choice.

✪ **Hôtel Windsor.** 11 rue Dalpozzo, 06000 Nice. ☎ **04-93-88-59-35.** Fax 04-93-88-94-57. 60 rms. A/C MINIBAR TV TEL. 400F–670F ($80–$134) double. AE, DC, MC, V. Bus: 8.

This stone-sided hotel was built as a private villa in the 1880s and designed by Gustave-Alexandre Eiffel (before he created that Paris tower). It takes pride in a kind of exoticism that's more pronounced and more whimsical than any of its competitors'. The Windsor has a charming multinational staff, most of whom speak English. Each room contains a mural by one of about half a dozen early or late 20th-century artists; none overlooks the sea, though the ocean and the beach are a short block away. On the premises are a small pool, a drawing room with a fireplace, a rooftop fitness center, and even a meditation room.

La Pérouse. 11 quai Rauba-Capéu, 06300 Nice. ☎ **04-93-62-34-63.** Fax 04-93-62-59-41. 63 rms, 3 suites. A/C MINIBAR TV TEL. 670F–890F ($134–$178) double; 1,640F ($328) suite. AE, DC, MC, V. Parking 60F ($12).

Once a prison, La Pérouse has been reconstructed and is now a unique Riviera hotel. Set on a cliff, it overlooks the sea and is entered through a lower-level lobby, where an elevator takes you up to the gardens and a pool. There's no hotel in Nice with a better view over both the old city and the Baie des Anges. Many people stay here just for the view alone. In fact, La Pérouse is built right into the gardens of an ancient château-fort. Inside, the hotel is like an old Provençal home, with low ceilings, white walls, and antiques. Most of the lovely rooms have loggias overlooking the bay. The restaurant, with a different menu every day, specializes in a Niçois cuisine and is open only for dinner in summer (in winter, guests rely on room service).

INEXPENSIVE

Flots d'Azur. 101 promenade des Anglais, 06000 Nice. ☎ **04-93-86-51-25.** Fax 04-93-97-22-07. 21 rms. A/C TEL. 250F–500F ($50–$100) double. MC, V. Bus: 8.

This three-story villa-hotel is next to the sea, a short walk from the more elaborate and costlier promenade hotels. While the rooms vary in size and decor, all have good views and sea breezes, and 12 contain TVs and minibars. Double-glazed windows were recently added to cut down on the noise. There's a small sitting room and sun terrace in front, where a continental breakfast is served.

Hôtel de la Mer. 4 place Masséna, 06000 Nice. ☎ **04-93-92-09-10.** Fax 04-93-85-00-64. 12 rms. MINIBAR TV TEL. 250F–380F ($50–$76) double. AE, MC, V. Parking 70F ($14) in a nearby covered garage. Bus: 1, 5, or 12.

In the center of Old Nice, this place was built around 1910, transformed into a hotel in 1947, and renovated in 1993. Despite that, it manages to keep its prices low. Ms. Feri Forouzan, the owner, welcomes you with personalized charm. Most guest rooms are of good size and have such items as a minibar and TV, not often found in inexpensive Nice hotels. From the hotel it's a 2-minute walk to promenade des Anglais and the seafront. Breakfast will be served in one of the public salons or your room.

Hôtel du Centre. 2 rue de Suisse, 06000 Nice. ☎ **04-93-88-83-85.** 28 rms, 20 with bath. TV TEL. 180F–200F ($36–$40) double without bath, 240F–320F ($48–$64) double with bath. AE, DC, MC, V. Parking 10F ($2). Bus: 23.

Near the train station, this simple but clean hotel was built in 1947 and today welcomes guests that many Nice sources estimate at about 100% gay. The simple, clean, uncomplicated rooms are very close to the attractions and charms of downtown Nice with its bars. The staff is well versed in the many diversions the city can provide, a useful source of inside information for whatever you might be seeking.

Hôtel Durante. 16 av. Durante, 06000 Nice. ☎ **04-93-88-84-40.** Fax 04-93-87-77-76. 26 rms. TV TEL. 350F–390F ($70–$78) double. MC, V. Closed Nov 15–Feb 15.

A comfortable and much-modified building dating from around the turn of the century, this hotel is very popular with producers, actors, and directors during the nearby Cannes Film Festival. Many rooms face a quiet courtyard, and all have a kitchenette and refrigerator. The owner, Mme Dufaure de Citres, dispenses both charm and information about local cinematic events. There's also a private garden.

Hôtel Magnan. Square du Général-Ferrié, 06200 Nice. ☎ **04-93-86-76-00.** Fax 04-93-44-48-31. 25 rms. TV TEL. 280F–360F ($56–$72) double. AE, MC, V. Parking 35F ($7). Bus: 12, 23, or 24.

This well-run modern hotel was built around 1945 and renovated frequently during its long and busy life. It's a 10-minute bus ride from the heart of town but only a minute or so from promenade des Anglais and the bay. Many of the simply furnished rooms have balconies facing the sea, and some contain minibars. The owner, Daniel Thérouin, occupies the apartment on the top floor, guaranteeing a closely supervised set-up. Breakfast can be served in your room.

✪ **Hôtel Villa Eden.** 99 bis promenade des Anglais, 06000 Nice. ☎ **04-93-86-53-70.** Fax 04-93-97-67-97. 15 rms. A/C TV TEL. 200F–390F ($40–$78) double. AE, DC, MC, V. Bus: 3, 9, 10, 22, 23, or 24 from the center, or 12 from the train station.

In 1925 an exiled Russian countess built this art deco villa on the seafront, surrounded it with a wall, and planted a tiny garden. The pastel-pink villa still remains, despite the construction of much-taller modern buildings on both sides. You can enjoy the ivy and roses in the garden and stay in old-fashioned partly modernized rooms whose sizes vary greatly. The owner maintains a wry sense of humor and greets you at breakfast, the only meal served.

Le Petit Palais. 10 av. Emile-Bieckert, 06000 Nice. ☎ **04-93-62-19-11.** Fax 04-93-62-53-60. 25 rms. TV TEL. 430F–780F ($86–$156) double. AE, DC, V. Parking 50F ($10).

This whimsical hotel occupies a mansion built around 1890; in the 1970s it was the home of the actor/writer Sacha Guitry, a name that's instantly recognized in millions of French households. It lies about a 10-minute drive from the city center in the Carabacel residential district. Much of its architectural grace remains, as evoked by the art deco/Italianate furnishings and Florentine moldings and friezes. The preferred rooms, and the most expensive, have balconies for sea views during the day and sunset watching at dusk. You can order light food from room service until midnight, and breakfast is served in a small but pretty salon.

DINING
VERY EXPENSIVE

✪ **Chantecler.** In the Hôtel Négresco, 37 promenade des Anglais. ☎ **04-93-16-64-00.** Reservations required. Main courses 100F–330F ($20–$66); fixed-price menus 205F–250F ($41–$50) at lunch, 395F–560F ($79–$112) at dinner. AE, DC, MC, V. Daily 12:30–2:30pm and 7:30–10:30pm. Closed mid-Nov to mid-Dec. Bus: 9, 10, or 11. FRENCH.

This is Nice's most prestigious restaurant. In 1989 a massive redecoration sheathed its walls with panels removed from a château in Puilly-Fussé, a Regency-style salon was installed for before- or after-dinner drinks, and a collection of 16th-century paintings, executed on leather backgrounds in the Belgian town of Malines, was imported. A much-respected chef, Alain Llorca, revised the menu to include the most sophisticated and creative dishes in Nice. They change almost weekly but usually include fresh asparagus with Parmesan cheese, black truffles, and a sabayon of black truffles; filet of turbot with a purée of broad beans, sun-dried tomatoes, and fresh asparagus; roast suckling lamb with beignets of vegetables and ricotta-stuffed ravioli; and a melt-in-your-mouth fantasy of marbled hot chocolate drenched in an almond-flavored cream sauce. Gourmands take note: The most expensive fixed-price dinner menu includes a well-orchestrated banquet followed by three separate desserts.

EXPENSIVE

Restaurant Barale. 39 rue Beaumont. ☎ **04-93-89-17-94.** Reservations imperative. Fixed-price menu 250F ($50). Dinner Tues–Sat by special request only, often between 7:30 and 8:30pm. Bus: 8. PROVENÇAL.

Don't expect to simply show up here: Advance reservations are demanded. The doyenne is Hélène Barale, a venerable survivor of more than 80 years of watching (her parents) or participating (in her own kitchens) in the preparations of the culinary specialties of Provence. Nothing here is innovative: The pissaladière and sauté de veau aux champignons (veal with mushrooms) are prepared exactly the way they were when Mme Barale was a girl. Even if the food is occasionally scorched or reheated (which some locals suspect it occasionally might be), the evocative dining room lined with copper pots, the wood-fired oven, and the old-fashioned Provençal accent and allure of Mme Barale herself add to what might be a memorable cultural experience.

MODERATE

Ane Rouge. 7 quai des Deux-Emmanuels. ☎ **04-93-89-49-63.** Reservations required. Main courses 95F–138F ($19–$27.60); fixed-price menus 148F–248F ($29.60–$49.60); bouillabaisse 265F ($53). AE, MC, V. Thurs–Tues noon–2pm and 7:30–10:30pm. Closed 2 weeks in Jan. Bus: 30. PROVENÇAL.

Facing the old port and occupying an antique building whose owners have carefully retained its ceiling beams and stone walls, this is one of the city's best-known seafood restaurants. In one of the pair of modern dining rooms noteworthy for their coziness, you can enjoy traditional and time-tested specialties like bouillabaisse; bourrides; filet of John Dory with roulades of stuffed lettuce leaves; mussels stuffed with chopped parsley, breadcrumbs, and herbs; and salmon in wine sauce with spinach. Service is correct and commendable.

Chez les Pêcheurs. 18 quai des Docks. ☎ **04-93-89-59-61.** Reservations recommended. Main courses 90F–140F ($18–$28); fixed-price menu 155F ($31); bouillabaisse 430F ($86) for two. AE, MC, V. May–Oct, Thurs 7–10pm, Fri–Tues noon–2pm and 7–10pm; mid-Dec to Apr, Tues noon–2pm, Thurs–Mon noon–2pm and 7–10pm. Closed Nov to mid-Dec. Bus: 1, 2, or 7. FRENCH.

This likable, well-managed tavern is directly on the old harbor at the end of a long string of less desirable restaurants, with a view of the city's ruined castle and the rows of sailboats and fishing craft bobbing at anchor. The decor is inspired by the interior of a yacht, complete with touches of polished brass and varnished hardwood. You can enjoy bouillabaisse (more reasonably priced here than at some nearby competitors), bourride, grilled lobster, or sea bass flavored with tarragon. Some of the best dishes are also the simplest, including carefully grilled fish seasoned with herbs, olive oil, and lemon.

Chez Michel (Le Grand Pavois). 11 rue Meyerbeer. ☎ **04-93-88-77-42.** Reservations required. Main courses 125F–160F ($25–$32); bouillabaisse 320F–365F ($64–$73); fixed-price menus 185F–295F ($37–$59). AE, DC, MC, V. Daily noon–2:30pm and 7–11pm. Bus: 8. SEAFOOD.

Chez Michel is nestled under an art deco apartment building near the water. One of the partners, Jacques Marquise, is from Golfe-Juan, where for 25 years he managed the famous fish restaurant Chez Tétou. At Golfe-Juan, M. Marquise became celebrated for his bouillabaisse, which he now prepares here. Other delectable specialties are baked sea bass in white wine, herbs, and lemon sauce and grilled flambé lobster. The wine list has a number of reasonably priced bottles.

Don Camillo. 5 rue des Ponchettes. ☎ **04-93-85-67-95.** Reservations recommended. Main courses 150F–165F ($30–$33); fixed-price menus 200F–320F ($40–$64). AE, MC, V. Mon 8–9:30pm, Tues–Sat noon–1:30pm and 8–9:30pm. Bus: 8. PROVENÇAL.

Named in the 1950s after its founder, a Niçois patriot named Camille who preferred the Italian version of his name, this nine-table restaurant promises (and delivers) some of Nice's most authentic versions of Provençal food. The dining room is adorned with the modern paintings of the Niçois painter Laurent Gerbert, and Franck Cerutti, assisted by his wife, Véronique, applies the gilded training he learned during stints at some of the grandest restaurants of the Côte d'Azur. Staples of the menu are fava beans, Swiss chard, goat cheese, stockfish, cuttlefish, and a medley of herbs produced on the region's dry hillsides. Every dish bears the mark of a master chef who's almost guaranteed to become much better known among Provence's gastronomes. At the end of your meal, do your best to sample the selections from the cheese tray. Each derives from a small local farm, with goodly numbers fermented from sheep's or goat's milk.

✪ La Marenda. 4 rue Terrasse. No phone. Reservations required. Fixed-price menus 150F–210F ($30–$42). No credit cards. Mon–Fri noon–2:30pm and 7–9:30pm. Closed Aug 4–18, Dec 24–Jan 4, and Feb 16–22. Bus: 8. NIÇOIS.

Since there's no phone, you have to go by this place twice: once to make a reservation and once to dine. However, it's worth the extra effort, as this is the best bistro in Nice. Forsaking his two-star chef crown at the renowned Chantecler (above), Dominique Le Stanc opened up this tiny bistro serving a sublime cuisine. "A no-star hole in the wall," the press screamed. But that's what Le Stanc wanted. Born in Alsace, his heart and soul belong to the Mediterranean, the land of black truffles, seasonal wild morels, fat sea bass, and plump asparagus. His food is rightly called a lullaby of gastronomic unity, with texture, crunch, richness, and balance. "I've known my days of glory in the gastronomic world. Now I'm doing family cooking, which is what I always like to eat." Le Stanc never knows what he's going to serve until he goes to the market. Look for his specials on a chalkboard. Perhaps you'll find stuffed cabbage, fried zucchini flowers, or oxtail flavored with fresh oranges. Lamb from the Sisteron is cooked until it practically falls from the bone. Raw artichokes are paired with a salad of mâche. Service is discreet and personable. We wish we could dine here every day.

La Toque Blanche. 40 rue de la Buffa. ☎ **04-93-88-38-18.** Reservations not required. Main courses 65F–145F ($13–$29); fixed-price menus 145F–290F ($29–$58). MC, V. Tues–Sat 12:30–2pm and 7:30–9:30pm, Sun 12:30–2pm. Bus: 8. FRENCH.

La Toque Blanche has only about a dozen tables amid its winter-garden decor. The owners, Denise and Alain Sandelion, pay particular attention to their shopping and buy only very fresh ingredients. The cuisine is skillfully prepared—try the sea bass roasted with citrus juice, sautéed sweetbreads with crayfish, or salmon prepared with fresh shrimp. The fixed-price menus are a particularly good value.

Le Florian / Bistrot du Florian. 22 rue Alphonse-Karr. ☎ **04-93-88-86-60.** Reservations recommended. Main courses 79F–135F ($15.80–$27); fixed-price menu 155F ($31). AE, MC, V. Mon–Fri noon–2pm and 7–10:30pm, Sat 7–10:30pm. Closed 1 month in midsummer (dates uncertain). Bus: 9, 10, or 12. FRENCH.

This pair of art deco restaurants occupies the ground floor of a turn-of-the-century apartment building. Amid mahogany paneling and a vivid sense of the 1930s, chef Claude Gillon prepares such dishes as shellfish-stuffed ravioli with lobster bouillon and cream sauce, oxtail with foie-gras sauce, stuffed pigs' feet, suckling lamb with lima beans, and Challons duckling with red-wine sauce. Each item we've tried has been profoundly flavorful. Though the owners maintain that there's a fundamental difference between the gregarious Bistrot du Florian and its more dignified neighbor, Le Florian (where the chairs are somewhat more comfortable), there's absolutely no difference in prices, hours, or menus.

Restaurant Boccaccio. 7 rue Masséna. ☎ **04-93-87-71-76.** Reservations recommended. Main courses 85F–210F ($17–$42); fixed-price menu 200F ($40); bouillabaise 210F ($42) per person. AE, DC, MC, V. Daily noon–2:30pm and 7–11pm. Bus: 4, 5, or 22. MEDITERRANEAN.

Adjacent to place Masséna, in a pedestrian zone that enhances the desirability of its streetfront terrace, this restaurant boasts worthy cuisine and a devoted local following. Bouillabaisse is reasonably priced here, and the range of fresh fish (grilled with lemon-butter or baked in a salt crust) is broad and well prepared. The paella might remind you of Spain, and desserts like cappuccino tiramisù and crêpes Suzettes round off meals nicely. There's a large dining room upstairs, inspired by the interior of a yacht, if the outdoor terrace doesn't appeal to you.

INEXPENSIVE

Flo. 2–4 rue Sacha-Guitry. ☎ **04-93-13-38-38.** Reservations recommended. Main courses 80F–100F ($16–$20); fixed-price menus 106F ($21.20) at lunch, 153F ($30.60) all day, and 106F ($21.20) after 10pm. AE, DC, MC, V. Daily noon–3pm and 7pm–12:30am. Bus: 1, 2, or 5. FRENCH.

In 1991 a France-based restaurant chain (the Jean-Paul Bucher group) noted for its skill at restoring historic brasseries bought the premises of a faded turn-of-the-century restaurant near place Masséna and injected it with new life. Its high ceilings covered with their original frescoes, the place is brisk, stylish, reasonably priced, and fun. Menu items include an array of grilled fish, *choucroute* (sauerkraut) Alsatian style, steak with brandied pepper sauce, and fresh oysters and shellfish. Flo isn't associated with Le Florian (above), with which it competes and with which it's frequently confused.

La Baron Ivre. 6 rue Maraldi. ☎ **04-93-89-52-12.** Reservations recommended. Main courses 70F–110F ($14–$22); fixed-price menu 100F ($20). DC, MC, V. Daily 7:30pm–midnight. Closed Wed Oct–Mar. Bus: 2. GERMAN/FRENCH.

Behind Nice's enormous exhibition center, this is a highly reputable restaurant whose clientele happens to be about 80% gay. It has survived changes in management and some rough initial moments, when the only gay member of the trio who managed the place fell in love and moved back to Germany, leaving Baron Recum and his tactful wife in charge of a mostly French, mostly gay crowd. The result is a cosmopolitan and attractively indulgent blend of Teutonic and Gallic food and ethics that's one of the most appealing on the Riviera. Menu items are affordably priced, flavorful, and served in generous portions. They include filets of beef with peppercorns, magret of duckling with honey sauce, and such German specialties as rouladen of beef, goulasch soup, schnitzels in cream sauce, and (in winter) Berliner leber (Berlin-style calf's liver).

There are more than 40 vintages of wine in stock, and the original paintings decorating the place are for sale.

⭘ **Le Safari.** 1 cours Saleya. ☎ **04-93-80-18-44.** Reservations recommended. Main courses 60F–135F ($12–$27); fixed-price menu 150F ($30). AE, DC, MC, V. Daily noon–2:30pm and 7–11:30pm. Bus: 1. PROVENÇAL/NIÇOIS.

The decor couldn't be simpler: a black ceiling, white walls, and an old-fashioned terra-cotta floor. The youthful staff is relaxed, sometimes in jeans, and always alert to the waves of fashion. Look for mobs here, many of whom prefer the outdoor terrace overlooking the Marché aux Fleurs and all of whom appreciate the earthy, reasonably priced meals that appear in generous portions. Menu items include a pungent bagna cauda, where vegetables are immersed in a sizzling brew of hot oil and anchovy paste; grilled peppers bathed in olive oil; daube (stew) of beef; fresh pasta with basil; an omelet with blettes (tough but flavorful greens); and the unfortunately named *merda de can* (dogshit), which, as a gnocchi stuffed with spinach, is a lot more appetizing than it sounds.

Restaurant L'Estocaficada. 2 rue de l'Hôtel-de-Ville. ☎ **04-93-80-21-64.** Reservations recommended. Main courses 50F–95F ($10–$19); fixed-price menus 58F–78F ($11.60–$15.60); pizzas 30F–45F ($6–$9). AE, MC, V. Tues–Sun noon–2pm and 7–10pm. Bus: 1, 2, or 5. NIÇOIS.

Estocaficada is the Provençal word for stockfish, the ugliest fish in Europe. You can see one for yourself—there might be a dried-out, balloon-shaped version on display in the cozy dining room. Brigitte Autier is the owner/chef, and her busy kitchens are visible from everywhere in the dining room. Descended from a matriarchal line (since 1958) of mother-daughter teams who have managed this place, she's devoted to the preservation of recipes prepared by her Niçois grandmother. Examples are gnocchis, beignets, several types of farcies (tomatoes, peppers, or onions stuffed with herbed fillings), grilled sardines, or bouillabaisse served as a main course or in a mini-version. As a concession to popular demand, the place also serves pizzas and pastas.

NICE AFTER DARK

Nice has some of the most active nightlife along the Riviera, with evenings usually beginning at a cafe. You can pick up a copy of *La Semaine des Spectacles,* available at kiosks around town, that outlines the week's diversions.

The major cultural center along the Riviera is the **Opéra de Nice,** 4 rue St-François-de-Paule (☎ **04-92-17-40-44**), with a busy season in winter. A full repertoire is presented, with special emphasis on serious, often large-scale operas. In one season you might see *La Bohème, Tristan und Isolde,* Verdi's *Don Carlo,* Massenet's *Thaïs,* and *Carmen,* as well as a *saison symphonique,* dominated by the Orchestre Philharmonique de Nice. The opera hall is also the major venue for concerts and recitals. The box office is open Monday to Friday from 10am to 6pm and Saturday from 11am to 5pm. Tickets cost from 40F ($8) for a high-altitude, low-visibility seat to 320F ($64) for front-and-center seats.

Near the Hotel Ambassador, **L'Ambassade,** 18 rue des Congrès (☎ **04-93-88-88-87**), was deliberately designed in a mock-Gothic style that includes the wrought-iron accents you'd expect to find in a château, two bars, and a dance floor. At least 90% of its clients are straight, or at least profess to be, and come in all physical types and age ranges. The cover is 80F ($16), including the first drink. **Piano Bar Louis XV / Disco Inferno,** 10 rue Cité-du-Parc (☎ **04-93-80-49-84**), is a double-tiered nightclub with a piano bar in its 200-year-old vaulted cellar and a modern disco on its street level. There's a cover of 80F ($16), including the first drink.

Le Cabaret du Casino Roule (La Madonette), in the Casino Roule, 1 promenade des Anglais (☎ 04-93-87-95-87), is Nice's answer to the cabaret glitter that appears in more ostentatious forms in Monte Carlo and Las Vegas. It includes just enough flesh to titillate; lots of spangles, feathers, and sequins; a medley of cross-cultural jokes and nostalgia for the good old days of French *chanson;* and an acrobat or juggler. The cover of 90F ($18) includes the first drink; women are admitted free Sunday to Thursday. Shows are presented on Friday and Saturday at 10pm.

Le Relais American Bar, in the Hotel Négresco, 37 promenade des Anglais (☎ 04-93-16-64-00), is the most beautiful bar in Nice, filled with white columns, an oxblood-red ceiling, Oriental carpets, English paneling, Italianate chairs, and tapestries. It was once a haunt of the actress Lillie Langtry. With its piano music and white-jacketed waiters, the bar still attracts a chic crowd.

Near the Hôtel Négresco and promenade des Anglais, **Le Blue Boy,** 9 rue Spinetta (☎ 04-93-44-68-24), is the oldest gay disco on the Riviera. With two bars and two floors, it's a vital nocturnal stopover for passengers aboard the dozens of all-gay cruises (most of which are administered from Holland) that make regular calls at Nice and such nearby ports as Villefranche. The cover is 50F ($10) on Saturday, 30F ($6) other days.

8 Villefranche-sur-Mer

581 miles S of Paris, 4 miles E of Nice

According to legend, Hercules opened his arms and Villefranche was born. It sits on a big blue bay that looks like a gigantic bowl, large enough to attract U.S. Sixth Fleet cruisers and destroyers. Quietly slumbering otherwise, Villefranche takes on the appearance of an exciting Mediterranean port when the fleet's in. Four miles from Nice, it's the first town you reach along the Lower Corniche.

Once popular with such writers as Katherine Mansfield and Aldous Huxley, it's still a haven for artists, many of whom take over the little houses—reached by narrow alleyways—that climb the hillside. Two of the more recent arrivals who've bought homes in the area are Tina Turner and Bono. **Rue Obscure** is vaulted, one of the strangest streets in France (to get to it, take rue de l'Eglise). In spirit it belongs more to a North African casbah. People live in tiny houses on this street, protected from the elements. Occasionally, however, there's an open space, allowing for a tiny courtyard.

One artist who came to Villefranche left a memorial: Jean Cocteau, the legendary painter, writer, filmmaker, and well-respected dilettante, spent a year (1956–57) painting frescoes on the 14th-century walls of the Romanesque **Chapelle St-Pierre,** quai de la Douane/rue des Marinières (☎ 04-93-76-90-70). He eventually presented it to "the fishermen of Villefranche in homage to the Prince of Apostles, the patron of fishermen." One panel pays homage to the gypsies of the Stes-Maries-de-la-Mer. In the apse is a depiction of the miracle of St. Peter walking on the water, not knowing that he's supported by an angel. On the left side of the narthex Cocteau honored Villefranche's young women in their regional costumes. The chapel, which charges 12F ($2.40) admission, is open Tuesday to Sunday: July to September from 10am to noon and 4 to 8:30pm, April to June from 9:30am to noon and 3 to 7pm, and October to March from 9:30am to noon and 2 to 5pm (closed mid-November to mid-December).

ESSENTIALS

GETTING THERE   Trains arrive from most towns on the Côte d'Azur, especially Nice (every 30 min.), but most visitors drive via the Corniche Inférieure (Lower Corniche). For more **rail information** and schedules, call ☎ 08-36-35-35-35.

VISITOR INFORMATION   The **Office de Tourisme** is on Jardin François-Binon (☎ **04-93-01-73-68**).

ACCOMMODATIONS

Hôtel Versailles. Av. Princesse-Grace-de-Monaco, 06230 Villefranche-sur-Mer. ☎ **04-93-01-89-56.** Fax 04-93-01-97-48. 46 rms, 3 suites. A/C MINIBAR TV TEL. 400F–600F ($80–$120) double; 500F–800F ($100–$160) suite. Rates include breakfast. AE, DC, MC, V. Free parking. Closed late Nov to Dec.

Several blocks from the harbor and outside the main part of town, this three-story hotel gives you a perspective of the entire coast. The hotel offers comfortably furnished rooms and suites (suitable for up to three) with big windows and panoramas. Guests congregate on the roof terrace, where they can order breakfast or lunch under an umbrella. The hotel's pool has a terrace and is surrounded by palms and bright flowers.

Hôtel Welcome. 1 quai Courbet, 06230 Villefranche-sur-Mer. ☎ **04-93-76-76-93.** Fax 04-93-01-88-81. 32 rms. A/C MINIBAR TV TEL. 490F–930F ($98–$186) double. Rates include breakfast. Half board 150F ($30) per person extra. AE, DC, MC, V. Closed Nov 15–Dec 20.

Involving you instantly in Mediterranean port life, the Welcome was a favorite of Jean Cocteau, who'd probably still check in if he were to return from the dead, as it's the best hotel at the port. In this six-floor villa hotel, with shutters and balconies, everything has recently been modernized. Try for a fifth-floor room overlooking the water. Once Pope Paul III embarked from this site with Charles V, but nowadays the departures are more casual—usually for fishing expeditions. The sidewalk cafe is the focal point of town life. The lounge and the restaurant, St-Pierre, have open fireplaces and fruitwood furniture.

DINING

La Campanette. 2 rue du Baron-de-Brès. ☎ **04-93-01-79-98.** Main courses 65F–95F ($13–$19); fixed-price menus 80F–140F ($16–$28). AE, MC, V. Daily 7–9:30pm. Closed Sun late Sept to Easter. FRENCH/SPANISH.

Near the Eglise St-Michel, this old-fashioned bistro with belle époque decoration is one of the most affordable places in town. Though most of its dishes are French, it occasionally offers Spanish-style paella and even zarzuela of seafood, similar to bouillabaisse. Other dishes likely to please are mussels in pastry with chicory and fish ravioli in shellfish sauce. The cookery is solid and reliable, using very fresh ingredients.

La Mère Germaine. Quai Courbet. ☎ **04-93-01-71-39.** Reservations recommended. Main courses 140F–460F ($28–$92); fixed-price menu 195F ($39). AE, MC, V. Daily noon–2:30pm and 7–10:30pm. Closed Nov 20–Dec 20. FRENCH/SEAFOOD.

Plan to relax here over lunch while watching fishers repair their nets, as this is the very best of a string of restaurants on the port. The cuisine is prepared by the grandson (the likable Thierry Blouin) of the matriarch, mère Germaine, who opened the place in the 1930s. It's popular with U.S. Navy officers, who've discovered the bouillabaisse made with tasty morsels of freshly caught fish and mixed in a cauldron with savory spices. We recommend the grilled loup (sea bass) with fennel, salade niçoise, sole Tante Marie (stuffed with mushroom purée), and beef filet with three peppers. The perfectly roasted carré d'agneau (lamb) is for two.

✪ **La Trinquette.** Port de la Darse. ☎ **04-93-01-71-41.** Reservations recommended. Main courses 50F–140F ($10–$28); bouillabaisse 220F ($44); fixed-price menus 99F–180F ($19.80–$36). No credit cards. Thurs–Tues noon–2:15pm and 7:30–10pm. Closed Dec–Jan. PROVENÇAL/SEAFOOD.

Charming and traditional, in a pre-Napoleonic building that rises a few steps from the harborfront, this restaurant prides itself on its fish. These are hauled out of a backroom, on platters, for anyone skeptical enough to ask to see the actual fish before it's cooked. You can choose from among 15 to 20 kinds, prepared any way you specify, with a wide variety of well-flavored sauces. Bouillabaisse is an enduring favorite that's much cheaper here than at many other places. There's even a roasted version of chapon de mer, served with a Provençal sauce. How do the hardworking owners, Paul and Monique Osiel, recommend their John Dory? Roasted in as simple and fresh a means as possible, served only with a hint of beurre blanc. Alternatives for this or any of the other offerings include aïoli, the region's garlic-enriched mayonnaise.

9 St-Jean-Cap-Ferrat

583 miles S of Paris, 6 miles E of Nice

This has been called "Paradise Found." Of all the oases along the Côte d'Azur, no place has the snob appeal of Cap-Ferrat. It's a 9-mile promontory sprinkled with luxurious villas, outlined by sheltered bays, beaches, and coves. The vegetation is lush. In the port of St-Jean, the harbor accommodates yachts and fishing boats.

ESSENTIALS

GETTING THERE   Most visitors drive or take the hourly bus or a taxi from the rail station at nearby Beaulieu. There's also bus service from Nice. For **bus information** and schedules, call ☎ **04-93-85-61-81.**

VISITOR INFORMATION   The **Office de Tourisme** is on avenue Denis-Séméria (☎ **04-93-01-02-21**).

SEEING THE TOP ATTRACTIONS

The Italianate ✪ **Musée Ile-de-France,** avenue Denis-Séméria (☎ **04-93-01-33-09**), affords you a chance to visit one of the Côte d'Azur's most legendary villas, built by Baronne Ephrussi. Born a Rothschild, she married a Hungarian banker and friend of her father, M. Ephrussi, about whom even the curator of the museum says that very little is known. She died in 1934, leaving the stately building and its magnificent gardens to the Institut de France on behalf of the Académie des Beaux-Arts. The wealth of her collection is preserved: 18th-century furniture; Tiepolo ceilings; Savonnerie carpets; screens and panels from the Far East; tapestries from Gobelins, Aubusson, and Beauvais; original drawings by Fragonard; canvases by Boucher; rare Sèvres porcelain; and more. Covering 12 acres, the gardens contain fragments of statuary from churches, monasteries, and torn-down palaces. One entire section is planted with cacti.

The museum and its gardens are open daily: July and August from 10am to 7pm (to 6pm the rest of the year). Admission is 45F ($9) for adults, 33F ($6.60) for those 9 to 24, and free for children 8 and under.

Though there are few **public paths** to enjoy the scenery, the most scenic goes from Plage de Paloma to Pointe St-Hospice. At the point a panoramic view of the Riviera landscape unfolds.

You can also spend time wandering around **St-Jean,** a colorful fishing village with bars, bistros, and simple inns. The **beaches,** though popular, aren't really good ones, as they're shingly. The best and most luxurious one belongs to the Grand Hôtel du Cap-Ferrat (see "Accommodations," below) but is open to anyone willing to pay

100F ($20) to rent equipment. Since you don't want to lie on the shingles, a member of the hotel staff will rent mattresses to you as well as umbrellas.

Everyone tries to visit the **Villa Mauresque,** avenue Somerset-Maugham, but it's closed to the public. Near the cape, it's where Maugham spent his final years, almost begging for death. Often tourists tried to visit him and he'd loudly proclaim that he wasn't one of the local sights. One man did manage to crash through the gate. When he encountered the author, Maugham snarled, "What do you think I am, a monkey in a cage?"

Once the property of Leopold II, king of Belgium, the **Villa Les Cèdres** lies directly west of the port of St-Jean. Although the villa is in private hands and can't be visited, you can go to the nearby **Parc Zoologique,** boulevard du Général-de-Gaulle, northwest of the peninsula (☎ 04-93-76-04-98). It's open daily: April to October from 9:30am to 7pm, to 5:30pm in winter. Admission is 25F ($5). This private zoo is set in the basin of a now-drained lake and was Leopold's private domain. You'll find a wide variety of reptiles, birds, and animals in outdoor cages. Six times a day there's a chimps' tea party, which explains Maugham's remark.

ACCOMMODATIONS
VERY EXPENSIVE

✪ **Grand Hôtel du Cap-Ferrat.** Bd. du Général-de-Gaulle, 06230 St-Jean-Cap-Ferrat. ☎ **04-93-76-50-50.** Fax 04-93-76-04-52. 57 rms, 13 suites. A/C MINIBAR TV TEL. 1,100F–5,500F ($220–$1,100) double; 2,600F–11,000F ($520–$2,200) suite. AE, DC, MC, V.

One of the best features of this turn-of-the-century palace is its location—at the tip of the peninsula in the midst of a 14-acre garden of semitropical trees and manicured lawns. It has been the retreat of the international elite since 1908, and it occupies the same celestial status as the Réserve and Métropole in Beaulieu. Its cuisine even equals the Métropole's. Parts of the exterior have open loggias and big arched windows, and you can enjoy the views from the elaborately flowering terrace over the sea. The guest rooms are conservatively modern, with dressing rooms, and rates include admission to the pool, Club Dauphin. The beach is accessible via funicular from the main building. The hotel is open year-round.

Dining/Entertainment: The hotel's indoor/outdoor restaurant serves *cuisine du marché,* which might include salad of warm foie gras and chanterelle mushrooms, nage of crayfish and lobster, or breast of duckling with honey and cider vinegar. The dining room is one of the last of the great belle époque palaces on the Côte d'Azur. The meals and service are flawless but come at a very high price. The American-style bar opens onto the garden.

Services: Room service (24 hours), same-day laundry.

Facilities: Olympic-size heated pool, tennis courts, hotel bicycles.

✪ **La Voile d'Or.** 31 av. Jean-Mermoz, St-Jean-Cap-Ferrat, 06230 Villefranche-sur-Mer. ☎ **04-93-01-13-13.** Fax 04-93-76-11-17. 45 rms, 4 suites. A/C MINIBAR TV TEL. 700F–1,700F ($140–$340) double; 900F–2,900F ($180–$580) suite. Rates include continental breakfast. No credit cards. Closed Nov–Mar 12.

The "Golden Sail" is a brilliant tour de force offering intimate luxury in a converted villa. As a deluxe hotel it's absolutely equal to the Grand Hôtel, though its cuisine isn't quite as superb. An antiques collector turned hôtelier, Jean R. Lorenzi owns this hotel at the edge of the little fishing port and yacht harbor, with a panoramic view of the coast. The guest rooms, the lounges, and the restaurant open onto terraces. The rooms are individually decorated with hand-painted reproductions, carved gilt headboards, baroque paneled doors, parquet floors, antique clocks, and paintings.

Dining/Entertainment: Guests gather on the canopied outer terrace for lunch and in the evening dine in a stately room with Spanish armchairs and white wrought-iron chandeliers. The sophisticated menu offers regional specialties and international dishes, as well as classic French cuisine. The drawing room is richly decorated. Most intimate is a little bar, with Wedgwood-blue paneling and antique mirroring.

Facilities: Two pools, private beach.

MODERATE

Hôtel Brise Marine. Av. Jean-Mermoz, St-Jean-Cap-Ferrat, 06230 Villefranche-sur-Mer. ☎ **04-93-76-04-36.** Fax 04-93-76-11-49. 16 rms. A/C TV TEL. 670F–730F ($134–$146) double. AE, MC, V. Closed Nov–Jan.

This circa-1878 villa with a front and rear terrace is on a hillside. A long rose arbor, beds of subtropical flowers, palms, and pines provide an attractive setting. The atmosphere is casual and informal, and the rooms are comfortably but simply furnished. You can have breakfast either in the beamed lounge or under the rose trellis. The little corner bar is for afternoon drinks.

✪ **Hôtel Clair Logis.** 12 av. Centrale, 06230 St-Jean-Cap-Ferrat. ☎ **04-93-76-04-57.** Fax 04-93-76-11-85. 18 rms. TEL. 370F–680F ($74–$136) double. AE, DC, MC, V. Closed Jan–Feb and Nov–Dec 15.

A rare find here, this hotel occupies what was a 19th-century villa surrounded by 2 acres of semitropical gardens. The pleasant rooms are scattered over three buildings in the confines of the garden. The hotel's most famous guest was de Gaulle, who lived in a room called Strelitzias (Bird of Paradise) during many of his retreats from Paris. Each room is named after a flower. The most romantic and spacious accommodations are in the main building; the rooms in the annex are the most modern but have the least character.

Hôtel Panoramic. 3 av. Albert-1er, 06230 St-Jean-Cap-Ferrat. ☎ **04-93-76-00-37.** Fax 93-76-15-89. 20 rms. TV TEL. 615F–715F ($123–$143) double. AE, DC, MC, V. Closed Nov 4–Dec 20.

This hotel was built in 1958 with a red-tile roof and much style and glamour. It's one of the most affordable choices in a pricey part of the Côte. You'll reach the hotel by passing over a raised bridge lined with colorful pansies. The well-furnished rooms have a sweeping view of the water and the forest leading down to it. Breakfast is the only meal served.

Les Tourterelles. 9 av. Denis-Séméria, 06230 St-Jean-Cap-Ferrat. ☎ **04-93-76-06-32.** Fax 04-93-76-06-48. 17 apts. TV TEL. July–Sept, 535F–666F ($107–$133.20) apt; Oct–June, 413F–663F ($82.60–$132.60) apt. Minimum 1-week stay. No credit cards.

At this small hillside apartment house you can live economically and independent of a hotel staff. It's surrounded by a garden and reached via a lane with roses and geraniums. Guests gather to sunbathe in the garden and swim in the pool. The living space will amaze you: a private sun terrace, a living room, a dining area, a twin-bedded room, a tile bath, and a fully equipped kitchen. Each apartment is named after a painter and contains reproductions of the artist's work—Rousseau, Utrillo, Gauguin, Degas. Most apartments accommodate one to three; the rates remain the same, varying only according to the time of year. No food is served.

DINING

✪ **Le Provençal.** 2 av. Denis-Séméria. ☎ **04-93-76-03-97.** Reservations required. Fixed-price menus 190F–490F ($38–$98). AE, MC, V. Mid-May to mid-Oct, Wed 7:30–9:30pm; Thurs–Mon noon–2:30pm and 7:30–9:30pm; Mar to mid-May, daily noon–2:30pm and 7:30–9:30pm. Closed mid-Oct to Mar. FRENCH.

With the possible exception of the Grand Hôtel's dining room, this is the grandest restaurant of this very grand resort. Near the top of the resort's highest peak, it has the most panoramic view, with sightlines that sweep, on good days, as far away as Menton and the Italian border. Many of the menu items are credited directly to the inspiration of "the Provençal" in the kitchens, which in this case is the well-trained Jean-Jacques Jouteux. No stranger to the fine art of catering to an upscale clientele, he's assisted by an alert and attractively bemused staff. Menu items include marinated artichoke hearts presented beside half a lobster, a tarte fine of potatoes with deliberately undercooked foie gras, rack of lamb with local herbs and tarragon sauce, and crayfish asparagus and black-olive tapenade. The best way to appreciate the desserts is to order the house sampler, "les cinq desserts du Provençal"—a potpourri of five petits desserts that usually includes macaroons with chocolate and crème brûlée. With the passage of years here, the cooking seems more inspired than ever.

Le Sloop. Au Nouveau Port. ☎ **04-93-01-48-63.** Reservations recommended. Main courses 110F–300F ($22–$60); fixed-price menu 155F ($31). AE, MC, V. June–Sept, Wed 7–9:30pm, Thurs–Tues noon–2:30pm and 7–9:30pm; Oct–Nov 15 and Dec 15–May, Thurs–Tues noon–2:30pm and 7–9:30pm. Closed Nov 15–Dec 15. FRENCH.

This is the most popular and most reasonably priced bistro in this very expensive area. Outfitted in blue and white inside and out, it sits directly at the edge of the port, overlooking the yachts in the harbor. The best of regional produce is handled deftly by the chefs, who present dishes like salmon tartare with baby onions; warm salad of red mullet; salad composed of fresh mozzarella, avocados, and lobster; John Dory with fresh pasta and basil; turbot with lobster sauce and calamari; and filet of veal with basil sauce. The regional wines are reasonably priced.

10 Beaulieu

583 miles S of Paris, 6 miles E of Nice, 7 miles W of Monte Carlo

Protected from the cold north winds blowing down from the Alps, Beaulieu-sur-Mer is often referred to as "La Petite Afrique" (Little Africa). Like Menton, it has the mildest climate along the Côte d'Azur and is especially popular with wintering wealthy. Originally, English visitors staked it out, after an English industrialist founded a hotel here between the rock-studded slopes and the sea. Beaulieu is graced with lush vegetation, including oranges, lemons, and bananas, as well as palms.

ESSENTIALS
GETTING THERE   Train service connects Beaulieu with Nice, Monaco, and the rest of the Côte d'Azur. For **rail information** and schedules, call ☎ **08-36-35-35-35.** Most visitors drive from Nice via the Moyenne Corniche or the coastal highway.

VISITOR INFORMATION   The **Office de Tourisme** is on place Georges-Clemenceau (☎ **04-93-01-02-21**).

SEEING THE TOP ATTRACTIONS
The ✪ **Villa Kérylos,** rue Gustave-Eiffel (☎ **04-93-01-01-44**), is a replica of an ancient Greek residence, painstakingly designed and built by the archaeologist Theodore Reinach. Inside, the cabinets are filled with a collection of Greek figurines and ceramics. But most interesting is the reconstructed Greek furniture, much of which would be fashionable today. One curious mosaic depicts the slaying of the minotaur and provides its own labyrinth (if you try to trace the path, expect to stay for weeks). It's open daily from 10:30am to 12:30pm and 2 to 6pm (to 5pm from

October to March). Admission is 35F ($7) for adults and 20F ($4) for children and seniors.

The **Casino de Beaulieu,** avenue Fernand-Dunan (☎ 04-93-76-48-00), built in the art nouveau style in 1903, was revitalized with new management in 1997. Open every night from 8pm to dawn, it charges 70F ($14) admission, requests that men wear jackets and ties into the gaming rooms, and maintains a bar and disco in a separate area. At this writing there were no slot machines.

The town boasts an important church, the late 19th-century **Eglise de Sacré-Coeur,** a quasi-Byzantine, quasi-Gothic mishmash at 13 bd. du Maréchal-Leclerc (☎ 04-93-01-18-24). With the same address and phone is the 12th-century Romanesque chapel of **Santa Maria de Olivo,** used mostly for temporary exhibits of painting, sculpture, and civic lore.

As you walk along the seafront promenade, you can see many stately belle époque villas that evoke the days when Beaulieu was the very height of fashion. Although you can't go inside, you'll see signs indicating **Villa Namouna,** which once belonged to Gordon Bennett, the owner of the *New York Herald,* who sent Stanley to find Livingstone, and **Villa Léonine,** former home of the marquess of Salisbury.

For a memorable **2-hour walk,** start directly north of boulevard Edouard-VII, where a path leads up the Riviera escarpment to Sentier du Plateau St-Michel. A belvedere here offers panoramic views from Cap d'Ail to the Estérel. A **1-hour alternative** is the stroll along promenade Maurice-Rouvier. The promenade runs parallel to the water, stretching from Beaulieu to St-Jean. On one side you'll see the most elegant of mansions set in well-landscaped gardens; on the other you'll get views of the distant Riviera landscape and the peninsular point of St-Hospice.

A DAY AT THE BEACH

Don't expect soft sands. Some seasons might have more sands than others, depending on tides and storms, but usually the surfaces are covered with light-gray gravel whose texture is finer than at beaches at other resorts nearby. The longer of the town's two beaches is **Petite Afrique,** adjacent to the yacht basin; the shorter is **Baie des Fourmis,** beneath the casino. Both are free public beaches. If you want to rent a mattress for the day and have easy access to a beachfront kiosk selling snacks and drinks, the two most visible purveyors of comfort on the sands are on Petite Afrique: **Africa Plage** (☎ 04-93-01-11-00) and **Beaulieu Plage** (☎ 04-93-01-14-36). Mattresses rent for 80F ($16).

ACCOMMODATIONS
VERY EXPENSIVE

✪ **La Réserve de Beaulieu.** 5 bd. du Maréchal-Leclerc, 06310 Beaulieu-sur-Mer. ☎ **04-93-01-00-01.** Fax 04-93-01-28-99. 27 rms, 10 suites. A/C MINIBAR TV TEL. 1,800F–4,000F ($360–$800) double; 3,150F–5,700F ($630–$1,140) suite. AE, DC, MC, V. Closed Nov–Mar.

One of the Riviera's most famous hotels, this pink-and-white fin-de-siècle palace is on the Mediterranean. Here you can sit having an apéritif watching the sun set over the Riviera while a pianist treats you to Mozart. A number of the public lounges open onto a courtyard with bamboo chairs, grass borders, and urns of flowers. The social life centers around the main drawing room, much like the grand living room of a country estate. The hotel has been rebuilt in stages, so the rooms range widely in size and design; however, all are deluxe and individually decorated, with a beautiful view of either the mountains or the sea.

Dining/Entertainment: The dining room has a coved frescoed ceiling, parquet floors, crystal chandeliers, and picture windows facing the Mediterranean.

Specialties are sea bass with thin slices of potatoes in savory tomato sauce, sea bream stuffed with local vegetables, and roast rack of lamb.

Facilities: Private harbor for yachts, submarine fishing gear, sauna, thalassotherapy, seawater pool.

✪ Le Métropole. 15 bd. du Maréchal-Leclerc, 06310 Beaulieu-sur-Mer. ☎ **04-93-01-00-08.** Fax 04-93-01-18-51. 46 rms, 3 suites. A/C MINIBAR TV TEL. 1,800F–3,900F ($360–$780) double; 3,400F–6,300F ($680–$1,260) suite. Rates include half board. AE, MC, V. Closed Oct 20–Dec 20.

This Italianate villa offers some of the most luxurious accommodations along the Côte d'Azur and as a hotel is on equal rank with the fabled Réserve. It's classified as a Relais & Châteaux and set on 2 acres of grounds that's discreetly shut off from the traffic of the resort. Here you'll enter a world of polished French elegance, with lots of balconies opening onto sea views. The marble, Oriental carpets, and polite staff members set a pervasive grace note. The guest rooms are furnished in tasteful fabrics and flowery wallpapers. The baths are elegantly spacious, most often tiled, and have double sinks.

Dining/Entertainment: Though the in-house restaurant lost a star from the Michelin judges in 1997, the food is nonetheless superb. The restaurant has a seaside terrace/bar, which elegantly retreats inside when the weather turns chilly.

Services: Room service (24 hours).

Facilities: Concrete jetty for sunning, heated pool; tennis and golf nearby.

EXPENSIVE

Hôtel Carlton. 7 av. Edith-Cavell, 06310 Beaulieu-sur-Mer. ☎ **04-93-01-14-70.** Fax 04-93-01-29-62. 33 rms. A/C TV TEL. 750F–980F ($150–$196) double. AE, DC, MC, V. Closed mid-Oct to mid-Apr.

This contemporary four-star hotel rises from a desirable position within 200 yards of the beach and a 3-minute walk from the public tennis courts. Immaculate and painted a rosy tone of beige, it's a solid, reliable, and oft-recommended choice. The restaurant is open daily for lunch and dinner but closed when the hotel closes. The rooms are sunny, conservatively modern, and tasteful.

Don't confuse this hotel with the less expensive, less desirable **Hôtel Carlton Résidence,** avenue Albert-1er (☎ **04-93-01-06-02**). The 30 simple rooms (with phone) are available here only when the main hotel deems that business will justify the cost of its opening. That tends to be only from late June to early September, but at press time the joint management hadn't yet solidified their plans. The rates are 300F to 700F ($60 to $140) for a double.

MODERATE

Hôtel Frisia. Bd. Eugène-Gauthier, 06310 Beaulieu-sur-Mer. ☎ **04-93-01-01-04.** Fax 04-93-01-31-92. 32 rms. A/C MINIBAR TV TEL. 350F–690F ($70–$138) double. AE, V. Closed Feb 16–23 and Dec 16–30.

In 1994 this hotel was renovated and a bath was installed in each room. In 1996 all the rooms were provided with air-conditioning as well. The Frisia's rooms, decorated in a modern style, most often open onto views of the harbor, with sea-view rooms the most expensive. English is spoken, and the American ownership makes foreign guests feel especially welcome. The hotel has a sunny garden and inviting lounges. Breakfast is the only meal served, but many reasonably priced dining places are nearby.

INEXPENSIVE

Hôtel Le Havre Bleu. 29 bd. du Maréchal-Joffre, 06310 Beaulieu-sur-Mer. ☎ **04-93-01-01-40.** Fax 04-93-01-29-92. 22 rms. TEL. 270F–310F ($54–$62) double. AE, DC, MC, V.

This has one of the prettiest facades of any inexpensive hotel in town. Housed in what used to be a private Victorian villa, the hotel has a front garden dotted with flowering urns and arched ornate windows. The comfortable guest rooms are impeccable and functional. Breakfast is the only meal served.

Hôtel Marcellin. 18 av. Albert-1er, 06310 Beaulieu-sur-Mer. ☎ **04-93-01-01-69.** Fax 04-93-01-37-43. 21 rms, 15 with bath; 1 suite. TEL. 160F–180F ($32–$36) double without bath, 250F–300F ($50–$60) double with bath; 500F–700F ($100–$140) suite. MC, V. Closed Nov–Dec 15.

A good budget selection in an otherwise high-priced resort, the turn-of-the-century Marcellin rents restored rooms with homelike amenities, each with a southern exposure. It has been run by the same family since 1938. The hotel stands amid the town's congestion, near its western periphery, a 5-minute walk to the beach. Its only breathing space consists of a small outdoor terrace. Despite that, it's a pleasant, well-maintained place to stay. The government has given the Marcellin a well-deserved two stars. Breakfast is the only meal served, but many restaurants are nearby.

DINING

The African Queen. Port de Plaisance. ☎ **04-93-01-10-85.** Reservations recommended. Main courses 78F–150F ($15.60–$30); pizzas 48F–62F ($9.60–$12.40). MC, V. Daily noon–11:30pm. INTERNATIONAL.

Named by its movie-loving founders after the Hollywood classic, this hip and popular restaurant is filled with posters of Hepburn and Bogie and has a jungle-inspired decor. Much influenced by U.S. restaurants (its sophisticated maître d' lived in Miami for 6 years), it has welcomed stars like Jack Nicholson, Raymond Burr, Robert Wagner, and Diana Ross during their appearances at the nearby Cannes Film Festival. Menu specialties are a *dégustation de bouillabaisse,* African curry of lamb or beef and served like a rijstaffel with about a dozen condiments, or any of an array of steaks, fish, or shellfish. Less expensive are the seven or eight kinds of pizza, which even visiting Italians claim are very good. No one will mind if you stop in for only a strawberry daiquiri or piña colada. The check is presented in a videocassette case labeled as—what else?—*The African Queen.*

La Pignatelle. 10 rue de Quincenet. ☎ **04-93-01-03-37.** Reservations recommended. Main courses 55F–130F ($11–$26); fixed-price menus 80F–170F ($16–$34). AE, MC, V. Thurs–Tues 12:15–1:30pm and 7:15–9:30pm. Closed mid-Nov to mid-Dec. FRENCH.

Even in this super-expensive resort, you can find an excellent and affordable Provençal bistro. After all, the locals have to eat somewhere and not all visitors, of course, can afford the higher-priced palaces. Despite its relatively low prices, La Pignatelle prides itself on the fact that all the products that go into its robust cuisine are fresh. As a result, it's usually crowded. Specialties are salade niçoise, a succulent version of soupe de poissons where someone has labored to remove the bones, cassolette of mussels, monkfish steak garnished only with olive oil and herbs, scampi provençal, tripe niçoise, scallops, and a "petite friture du pays" that incorporates very small fish with Provençal traditions that are many hundreds of years old.

11 Eze & La Turbie

585 miles S of Paris, 7 miles NE of Nice

The hamlets of Eze and La Turbie, though 4 miles apart, have so many similarities that most of France's tourist officials speak of them as if they're one. Both boast fortified feudal cores high in the hills overlooking the Provençal coast, and both were built during the early Middle Ages to stave off raids from corsairs who wanted to capture harem slaves and laborers. Clinging to the rocky hillsides around these hamlets are upscale villas, many of which were built since the 1950s by retirees from colder climes. Closely linked, culturally and fiscally, to nearby Monaco, Eze and La Turbie have full-time populations of fewer than 3,000, and the medieval cores of both contain art galleries, boutiques, and artisans' shops that have been restored.

Eze is accessible via the Moyenne (Middle) Corniche, La Turbie via the Grande (Upper) Corniche. Signs are positioned along the coastal road indicating the direction motorists should take to reach either of the hamlets.

The leading attraction in Eze is the **jardin Exotique,** boulevard du Jardin-Exotique (☎ **04-93-41-10-30**), a lushly landscaped showcase of exotic plants set in Eze-Village, at the pinnacle of the town's highest hill. Entrance is 12F ($2.40), free for children 11 and under. It can be visited daily at hours that correspond to the setting of the sun: in July and August, it's open from 8:30am to 8pm; the rest of the year, it opens between 8:30 and 9am and closes between 5 and 7:30pm, depending on the time of the sunset.

La Turbie boasts a ruined monument erected by the ancient Roman emperor Augustus in 6 B.C., the **Trophée des Alps (Trophy of the Alps).** (Many locals call it La Trophée d'Auguste.) It rises near a rock formation known as La Tête de Chien, at the highest point along the Grand Corniche, 1,500 feet above sea level. The monument, restored with funds donated by Edward Tuck, was erected by the Roman Senate to celebrate the subjugation of the people of the French Alps by the Roman armies. A short distance from the monument is the **Musée du Trophée des Alps,** rue Albert-1er, La Turbie (☎ **04-93-41-10-11**), a minimuseum containing finds from archaeological digs nearby and information about the monument's restoration. It's open daily: April to June from 9am to 6pm, July to September from 9am to 7pm, and October to March from 9:30am to 5pm. Entrance is 25F ($5) for adults, 15F ($3) for students and youths 12 to 25, and free for children 11 and under. Closed January 1, May 1, November 1, and December 25.

ESSENTIALS

GETTING THERE   Eze (also known as Eze-Village) is most easily reached by car via the Moyenne (Middle) Corniche road.

VISITOR INFORMATION   The **Office de Tourisme** is on place du Général-de-Gaulle, Eze-Village (☎ **04-93-41-26-00**).

ACCOMMODATIONS & DINING

Auberge Eric Rivot. 44 av. de la Liberté, 06360 Eze-Bord-de-Mer. ☎ **04-93-01-51-46.** Fax 04-93-01-58-40. 10 rms. TV TEL. 280F ($56) double. Half board 280F ($56) per person extra. AE, DC, MC, V. Closed mid-Nov to Dec 1.

This straw-yellow stucco villa is a few steps from the Basse Corniche. It has a quiet rear terrace, and the interior is filled with rattan chairs, exposed brick, and lots of brass. The simply furnished doubles draw mainly a summer crowd, though the inn is open most of the year. Half board is a good deal here—the meals are satisfying, with wine included.

✪ **Hostellerie du Château de la Chèvre d'Or.** Rue du Barri, 06360 Eze-Village. ☎ **04-92-10-66-66.** Fax 04-93-41-06-72. 30 rms, 8 suites. A/C TV TEL. 1,600F–3,600F ($320–$720) double; 2,900F–3,600F ($580–$720) suite. AE, MC, DC, V. Closed late Nov to Mar 1.

This is a miniature village retreat built in the 1920s in neo-Gothic style, but without a beach. On the side of a stone village off the Moyenne Corniche, this Relais & Châteaux is a complex of village houses, all with views of the coastline. The owner has had the interior of the "Golden Goat" flawlessly decorated to maintain its old character while adding modern comfort. Even if you don't stop in for a meal or a room, try to visit for a drink in the lounge, which has a panoramic view.

Le Grill du Château is a traditional restaurant where you can enjoy grilled fish and meat. Other choices are Chez Justin, for informal meals, and La Chèvre d'Or, known for its *menu dégustation* at 560F ($112).

Le Cap Estel. 06380 Eze-Bord-de-Mer. ☎ **04-93-01-50-44.** Fax 04-93-01-55-20. 31 rms, 9 suites. A/C MINIBAR TV TEL. 2,310F–2,960F ($462–$592) double; from 2,540F ($508) suite. MC, V. Parking 50F ($10). Closed Oct 26–Mar.

At one of the most dramatic points along the Côte between Nice and Monte Carlo, this hotel is on a rocky promontory jutting into the sea. Two miles east of Beaulieu, reached along the Lower Corniche, this is a successful reincarnation of a turn-of-the-century villa built for a princess. Below the coast road, Le Cap Estel is on 5 acres of terraced, landscaped gardens. A heated indoor pool projects out over the waves like the bow of a ship. Exotic birds are kept in cages, mauve petunias add color, and the reflection pool has a spray fountain and is lit by colored lights at night. Because of the hotel's location, all the rooms overlook the sea, and each is near a terrace. You can dine inside, on an open-air terrace, or at umbrella-shaded tables under the trees. Occasional barbecues and chicken-on-the-spit dinners are featured.

12 Peillon

12 miles NW of Nice

This fortified medieval town is the most spectacular "perched village" along the Côte d'Azur. At 1,000 feet above the sea, it's also unspoiled, unlike so many other perched villages, which are filled with day-trippers and souvenir shops.

The main interest is the semifortified architecture of the town itself. You can visit the simple parish church, the **Eglise St-Sauveur,** built in a country-baroque style in the early 1700s, near the village's highest point, and the 15th-century **Chapelle des Pénitents Blancs,** on place Auguste-Arnuls. The parish church is always open, but local authorities don't encourage interior visits of the chapel, unless tours, usually for art historians, are prearranged several weeks in advance through the town hall (☎ 04-93-79-91-04). Instead, most of the interior is visible through an iron gate. If you plunk 2F (40¢) into a machine near the gate, lights will illuminate the interior's noteworthy frescoes. Painted in 1491 by Jean Cannavesio, they represent eight stages of the passion of Christ.

Each of the town's narrow streets, some of which are enclosed with vaulting and accented with potted geraniums and strands of ivy, radiates outward from the town's "foyer," **place Auguste-Arnuls,** which is shaded by rows of plantain trees centered around a fountain that has splashed water from its basin since 1800.

If you're in the mood for walking, consider a 2-hour, 7¹/₂-mile northward hike across the dry and rocky landscapes of eastern Provence to Peillon's remote twin, **Peille,** a smaller version of what you'll find in Peillon.

ESSENTIALS

GETTING THERE   Few other towns in Provence are as easy to reach by car and as inconvenient to reach by public transportation. Peillon is an easy 20-minute drive (depending on traffic) northeast from Nice, reached by taking D2204 to D21.

Only two trains a day stop near Peillon, at the train station of St-Techle, an antiquated, rarely used station along an antique-looking train spur connecting Nice with a town across the border in Italy, Coni. For **rail information** and schedules, call

☎ 08-36-35-35-35. You'll find lots of dilapidated local color at the railway station of St-Techle (which is partially abandoned and in great decline). Know in advance that there are no taxis waiting in line. There's also no bus service to carry you on to Peillon. Most backpackers continue into Peillon by hitchhiking.

The Santa Azur bus line operates four buses that make the transit from Nice every day, with multiple stops en route and transit time of around 25 minutes each way. Don't expect it to be convenient, as you'll be dropped off about 2 miles from Peillon's center, at a tiny crossroads known as Le Moulin. Many hardy souls opt to continue on to the center by foot, as there's no other regularly scheduled transport into Peillon and taxis aren't available. For **bus information,** call ☎ 04-93-85-61-81.

VISITOR INFORMATION   The **Syndicat d'Initiative** (tourist office) is in the village center (☎ 04-93-79-92-04).

ACCOMMODATIONS & DINING

The only hotel and restaurant in town is a magnet in its own right for urban escapists who want a view of the Provence of long ago.

✪ **Auberge de la Madone.** 06440 Peillon. ☎ **04-93-79-91-17.** Fax 04-93-79-99-36. 17 rms, 3 suites. TEL. 450F–650F ($90–$130) double; 800F ($160) suite. DC, MC, V. Closed Jan 7–24; restaurant closed Wed.

This hotel, with its well-recommended restaurant, has thrived here since the 1930s, when it was installed in a stone-sided complex of buildings whose oldest sections dated from the 12th century. Evocative of a sprawling *mas provençal* (Provençal farmhouse), it's capped with terra-cotta tiles and draped with a small version of the hangling gardens of Babylon. The auberge is on the opposite side of place Auguste-Arnuls from the rest of the village and boasts a wide terrace offering one of the best views of the town's vertical and very angular architecture. The guest rooms are comfortable and rustic, each outfitted with Provençal themes and fabrics. The hotel plans an annex within a 5-minute walk, with seven additional rooms. Expect accommodations much simpler than those in the main building, many without baths, and rates of between 180F and 320F ($36 and $64) per night, depending on the plumbing and views.

The hotel restaurant is by far the most formal in town, serving lunch and dinner daily except Wednesday and during the annual closing noted above. Menu items are based on cuisine that developed in this pocket of Provence over the centuries and include unusual dishes like *tourton des pénitents,* a salty tart enriched with 17 herbs, almonds, eggs, and cream; suckling lamb with garlic-enriched mashed potatoes and a tapenade of olives; farm-raised guinea fowl with a confit of pears; and a pot au feu, a savory kettle of seafood served with aïoli.

13 Monaco

593 miles S of Paris, 11 miles E of Nice

The outspoken Katharine Hepburn once called Monaco "a pimple on the chin of the south of France." She wasn't referring to the principality's lack of beauty but rather to the preposterous idea of having a little country, a feudal anomaly, taking up some of the choicest coastline along the Riviera. Hemmed in by France on three sides and facing the Mediterranean, tiny Monaco staunchly maintains its independence. Even Charles de Gaulle couldn't force Prince Rainier to do away with his tax-free policy. As almost everybody in an overburdened world knows by now, the Monégasques do not pay taxes. Nearly all their country's revenue comes from tourism and gambling.

Monaco—or rather its capital of Monte Carlo—has for a century been a symbol of glamour. Its legend was further enhanced by the 1956 marriage of the man who was at that time the world's most eligible bachelor, Prince Rainier III, to the American actress Grace Kelly. She had met the prince when she was in Cannes for the film festival to promote the Hitchcock movie she made with Cary Grant, *To Catch a Thief*; a journalist friend had arranged a *Paris Match* photo shoot with the prince—and the rest is history. A daughter, Caroline, was born to the royal couple in 1957; a son, Albert, in 1958; and a second daughter, Stephanie, in 1965. The Monégasques welcomed the birth of Caroline, but went wild at the birth of Albert, a male heir. According to a 1918 treaty, Monaco would become an autonomous state under French protection should the ruling dynasty become extinct. However, the fact that Albert is still a bachelor has the entire principality concerned.

Though not always happy in her role, Princesse Grace soon won the respect and adoration of her people. In 1982 a sports car she was driving, with her daughter Stephanie as a passenger (not as the driver, as was viciously rumored), plunged over a cliff, killing Grace but only injuring Stephanie. The Monégasques still mourn her death.

Monaco became a property of the Grimaldi clan, a Genoese family, as early as 1297. With shifting loyalties, it has maintained something resembling independence ever since. In a fit of impatience the French annexed it in 1793, but the ruling family recovered it in 1814; however, the prince at the time couldn't bear to tear himself away from the pleasures of Paris for "dreary old Monaco."

ESSENTIALS

GETTING THERE   Monaco has rail, bus, and highway connections from other coastal cities, especially Nice. Trains arrive every 30 minutes from Cannes, Nice, Menton, and Antibes. For more **rail information** and schedules, call ☎ 08-36-35-35-35. There are no border formalities for anyone entering Monaco from mainland France.

VISITOR INFORMATION   The **Direction du Tourisme** office is at 2A bd. des Moulins (☎ 92-16-61-16).

SPECIAL EVENTS   Some of the most-watched **car-racing events** in Europe are held every February (Le Rallye) and May (the Grand Prix). Mid-April witnesses one of the Riviera's most famous **tennis tournaments,** and there's always lots of emphasis on the duration of the hold the Grimaldis have exerted over Monaco since the Middle Ages. (In 1998 they will celebrate the 701st year of their reign.)

EXPLORING THE PRINCIPALITY

The second-smallest state in Europe (Vatican City is the tiniest), Monaco consists of four parts: The old town, **Monaco-Ville,** on a promontory, "The Rock," 200 feet high, is the seat of the royal palace and the government building, as well as the Oceanographic Museum. To the west of the bay, **La Condamine,** the home of the Monégasques, is at the foot of the old town, forming its harbor and port sector. Up from the port (walking is steep in Monaco) is **Monte Carlo,** once the playground of European royalty and still the center for wintering wealthy, the setting for the casino and its gardens and the deluxe hotels. The fourth part, **Fontvieille,** is a neat industrial suburb.

Ironically, **Monte-Carlo Beach,** at the far frontier, is on French soil. It attracts a chic crowd, including movie stars in the skantiest bikinis and thongs. The resort has a freshwater pool, an artificial beach, and a sea-bathing establishment.

No one used to go to Monaco in summer, but now that has totally changed—in fact, July and August tend to be so crowded it's hard to get a room. Further, with the decline of royalty and multimillionaires, Monaco is developing a broader base of

Number, Please: Monaco's Telephone System

On June 21, 1996, Monaco's phone system underwent drastic changes. It's now considered a separate entity from France by the phone company, so Monégasques pay high long-distance rates for calls to such adjacent locales as Nice. It's a blow to Monégasque businesses, which will now have to pay more for the privilege of operating tax-free within a few minutes' drive of the French border.

If you're calling Monaco from within France, dial 00 (the new international access code for all international long-distance calls placed from mainland France), followed by Monaco's new country code, 377, and then the eight-digit local phone number. (Don't dial the 33 code; this is the country code for France and no longer applies to Monaco.) To call Monaco from the North America, dial the international access code, 011, followed by the country code, 377, plus the local eight-digit Monaco number.

If you're calling France from within Monaco, dial 00 (the international access code), 33 (the country code for France), 4 (the area code, without the zero), and the eight-digit number.

To call locally within Monaco, dial all eight digits of the phone number.

tourism (you can stay here moderately—but it's misleading to suggest that you can stay cheaply). The Monégasques very frankly court the affluent visitor. And at the casinos here you can also lose your shirt. "Suicide Terrace" at the casino, though not used as frequently as in the old days, is still a real temptation to many who have foolishly gambled away family fortunes.

Life still focuses around the **Monte Carlo Casino,** which has been the subject of countless legends and the setting for many films (remember poor Lucy Ricardo and the chip she found lying on the casino floor?). High drama is played to the fullest here. Depending on the era, you might've seen Mata Hari shooting a tsarist colonel with a jewel-encrusted revolver when he tried to slip his hand inside her bra to discover her secrets—military, not mammary. The late King Farouk, known as "The Swine," used to devour as many as 8 roast guinea hens and 50 oysters before losing thousands at the table. *Chacun à son goût.* Richard Burton presented Elizabeth Taylor with the obscenely huge Koh-i-noor diamond here.

SEEING THE TOP ATTRACTIONS

During summer, most visitors—many over from Nice for the day—want to see the Italianate home of Monaco's royal family, the ✪ **Palais du Prince,** dominating the principality from "The Rock." When touring Les Grands Appartements du Palais, place du Palais (☎ 93-25-18-31), you're shown the Throne Room and allowed to see some of the art collection, including works by Brueghel and Holbein, as well as Princesse Grace's stunning state portrait. The palace was built in the 13th century and part dates from the Renaissance. You're also shown the chamber where England's George III died. The ideal time to arrive is 11:55am to watch the 10-minute Relève de la Garde (changing of the guard). The palace is open June to September, daily from 9:30am to 6:30pm; and in October, daily from 10am to 5pm. It's closed between November and May. Admission is 30F ($6) for adults, 15F ($3) for children 8 to 14, and free for children 7 and under.

In a wing of the palace, the **Musée du Palais du Prince** (Souvenirs Napoléoniens et Collection d'Archives), place du Palais (☎ 93-25-18-31), contains a collection of mementos of Napoléon and Monaco itself. When the royal residence is closed, this museum is the only part of the palace the public can visit. It's open June to September, daily from 9:30am to 6:30pm; October to November 11, daily from 10am to 5pm; and December 17 to May, Tuesday to Sunday from 10:30am to 12:30pm and 2 to 5pm. It's closed from November 12 to December 16. Admission is 20F ($4) for adults and 10F ($2) for children.

The **Jardin Exotique,** boulevard du Jardin-Exotique (☎ 93-30-33-65), was built on the side of a rock and is known for its cactus collection. The gardens were begun by Prince Albert I, who was a naturalist and a scientist. He spotted some succulents growing in the palace gardens, and knowing that these plants were normally found only in Central America or Africa, he created the garden from them. You can also explore the grottoes here, as well as the **Musée d'Anthropologie Préhistorique** (☎ 93-15-80-06). The view of the principality is splendid. The museum is open daily: June to September from 9am to 7pm and October to May from 9am to 6pm. Admission is 40F ($8) for adults, 18F ($3.60) for children 6 to 18, and free for children 5 and under.

The **Musée de l'Océanographie,** avenue St-Martin (☎ 93-15-36-00), was founded in 1910 by Albert I, great-grandfather of the present prince. In the main rotunda is a statue of Albert in his favorite costume—that of a sea captain. Displayed are specimens he collected during 30 years of expeditions aboard his oceanographic ships. The aquarium—one of the finest in Europe—contains more than 90 tanks.

Prince Albert's collection is exhibited in the zoology room. Some of the exotic creatures here were unknown before he captured them. You'll see models of the oceanographic ships aboard which he directed his scientific cruises from 1885 to 1914. Albert's last cruises were on board the *Hirondelle II.* The most important part of its laboratory has been preserved and reconstituted as closely as possible. The cupboards contain all the equipment and documentation necessary for a scientific expedition. Skeletons of specimens are on the main floor, including a giant whale that drifted ashore at Pietra Ligure in 1896—it's believed to be the same one the prince harpooned earlier that year. The skeleton is remarkable for its healed fractures sustained when a vessel struck the animal as it was drifting asleep on the surface. An exhibition devoted to the discovery of the ocean is in the physical-oceanography room on the first floor. In addition, underwater movies are shown continuously in the lecture room.

The Oceanography Museum is open daily: in July and August from 9am to 8pm, April to June and in September from 9am to 7pm, in March and October from 9:30am to 7pm, and November to February from 10am to 6pm. Admission is 60F ($12) for adults, 30F ($6) for children 6 to 18, and free for children 5 and under.

In the **Collection des Voitures Anciennes de S.A.S. le Prince de Monaco,** Les Terrasses de Fontvieille (☎ 92-05-28-56), Prince Rainier III has opened a showcase of his private collection of more than 100 exquisitely restored vintage autos, including the 1956 Rolls-Royce Silver Cloud that carried the prince and his princess on their wedding day. It was given to the royal couple by Monaco shopkeepers as a wedding

Impressions

Real Hell, the cleanest, most polished place I've ever seen.

—Katherine Mansfield on Monaco

Monaco

↑ To Grande Corniche
BEAUSOLEIL

↑ To Menton

av. de Villaini

des Moulins

av. P. Doumer

FRANCE
MONACO

bd. Princesse- Charlotte

MONTE
CARLO

MONEGHETTI

bd. du Jardin-Exotique

bd. de Belgique

Rainier-III

Costa

la

pl. du
Casino ⑦

⑨

bd. Larvotto

av. Princesse-Grace

⑧ Plage
de
Larvotto

To Nice ↑

Parc
Princesse
Antoinette

Grimaldi

bd. Albert-1er

av. de

av. d'Ostende

quai des Etats-Unis

Stade Nautique
Rainier-III

Port de Monaco

rue

LA
CONDAMINE

Station
bd. Charles-III

① ②

Jardin
Exotique

pl. du
Canton

bd.

③

av. de la Porte-Neuve

quai Antoine-1er

MONACO-
VILLE

pl. du
Palais

⑤

Héliport
FONTVIEILLE

④

av. St-Martin

⑥

Jardins
St-Martin

LEGEND	
✝	Church
✉	Post Office
ⓘ	Information

0 ———— 300m
330y

N

3-0892

PARIS

Monaco •

Cathedral ⑤
Collection des Voitures Anciennes du Prince ④
Jardin Exotique ①
Monte Carlo Casino ⑦
Musée d'Anthropologie Préhistorique ②
Musée National ⑨
Musée de l'Océanographie ⑥
Palais du Prince/Musée du Palais ③
Sun Casino ⑧

present. A 1952 Austin Taxi on display was once used as the royal "family car." Other exhibits are a Woodie, a 1937 Ford station wagon once used by Prince Louis II when on hunting trips, and a 1925 Bugatti 35B, winner of the Monaco Grand Prix in 1929. Other oustanding autos are a 1903 De Dion Bouton and a 1986 Lamborghini Countach. The museum is open daily from 10am to 6pm (closed in November). Admission is 30F ($6) for adults, 15F ($3) for students and children 8 to 14, and free for children 7 and under.

The **Musée National de Monaco,** 17 av. Princesse-Grace (☎ **93-30-91-26**), features "automatons and dolls of yesterday," along with sculptures in the rose garden. In a villa designed by Charles Garnier (architect of Paris's Opéra Garnier), this museum houses one of the world's greatest collections of mechanical toys and dolls. See especially the 18th-century Neapolitan crèche, which contains some 200 figures. This collection, assembled by Mme de Galea, was presented to the principality in 1972; it stemmed from the 18th- and 19th-century trend of displaying new fashions on doll models. The museum is open daily: Easter to September from 10am to 6:30pm and

October to Easter from 10am to 12:15pm and 2:30 to 6:30pm. Admission is 26F ($5.20) for adults, 15F ($3) for children 6 to 14, and free for children 5 and under.

A DAY AT THE BEACH

Just outside the border, on French (not Monacan) soil, the ✪ **Monte-Carlo Beach** adjoins the Monte-Carlo Beach Hotel, 22 av. Princesse-Grace (☎ 04-93-28-66-66). Permeated with intricate social rituals that might not be immediately visible to first-timers, the beach club has thrived for years as an integral part of Monaco's social life. You'll find a beach whose sand is replenished at regular intervals, two large pools (one for children), beach cabanas, a restaurant, a cafe, a bar, and memories of Princess Grace, who used to come here in flowery swimsuits, greeting her friends and subjects with humor and style. As the Celsius reading lowers in late August, expect the beach to close for the winter. The admission is 100F ($20). As usual, topless is acceptable but bottomless isn't.

Monaco, in its role as the quintessential kingdom by the sea, also offers sea bathing at its most popular beach, the **Plage de Larvetto,** off avenue Princesse-Grace (☎ 93-30-63-84). There's no charge for bathing on this strip of beach, whose sands are frequently replenished with sand hauled in by barge. The beach is open to public access at all hours.

OUTDOOR ACTIVITIES

GOLF The **Monte Carlo Golf Club,** route N7, La Turbie (☎ 04-93-41-09-11), on French soil, is a par-72 golf course with ample amounts of prestige, scenic panoramas, and local history. Certain perks (including use of electric golf buggies) are reserved for members. Before they're allowed to play, nonmembers will be asked to show proof of membership in another golf club and provide evidence of their handicap ratings. Greens fees for 18 holes are 350F ($70) Monday to Friday and 450F ($90) Saturday and Sunday. Clubs can be rented for 120F ($24). The course is open daily from 8am to sunset.

SPA TREATMENTS In 1908 the Société des Bains de Mer launched a seawater (thalassotherapy) spa in Monte Carlo. It was inaugurated by Prince Albert I himself. However, in World War II it was bombed and reopened only in 1996. **Les Thermes Marins de Monte-Carlo,** 2 av. de Monte-Carlo (☎ 04-92-16-40-40), is one of the largest spas in Europe. Spread over four floors are a gigantic pool, a Turkish haman, a diet restaurant, a juice bar, two tanning booths, a fitness center, a beauty center, and private treatment rooms.

SWIMMING Of course, you can try the beaches mentioned above. But if you're looking for a pool instead, you might want to try these two. Built to overlook the yacht-clogged harbor, the stupendous **Stade Nautique Rainier-III,** quai Albert-1er, at La Condamine (☎ 93-15-28-75), a pool frequented by Monégasques, was a gift from the prince to his loyal subjects. It's open in July and August, daily from 9am to midnight; and March to June and September to November, daily from 9am to 6pm (closed December to February). Admission is 25F ($5).

If your visit doesn't correspond to the warm-weather months, you can still go swimming indoors. A pool open year-round, the **Piscine du Prince Héréditaire Albert,** lies in the Stade Louis II, at 7 av. de Castellane (☎ 92-05-42-13). It's open Monday, Tuesday, Thursday, and Friday from 7:30am to 2:30pm; Saturday from 2 to 6pm; and Sunday from 9am to 1pm. Admission is 15F ($3).

TENNIS & SQUASH The **Monte Carlo Country Club,** in France on avenue Princesse-Grace, Roquebrune–St-Roman (☎ 04-93-41-30-15), includes 23 tennis courts (21 clay and 2 concrete). But if that isn't enough, you'll also find a cornucopia of other warm-weather distractions. Payment of the 215F ($43) entrance fee will provide access to a restaurant, a health club with Jacuzzi and sauna, a putting green, a beach, squash courts, and the well-maintained tennis courts. Plan to spend at least half a day, ending a round of tennis with use of any of the other facilities. It's open daily from 8am to 8 or 9pm, depending on the season.

SHOPPING

Rising costs and an increase in crime have changed women's tastes in jewelry, perhaps forever. **Bijoux Cascio,** in Les Galeries du Métropole, 207 av. des Spélugues (☎ 93-50-17-57), sells only imitation gemstones. They're rather shamelessly copied from the real McCoys sold by Cartier and Van Cleef & Arpels. Made in Italy of gold-plated silver, the fake jewelry costs between 200F and 2,000F ($40 and $400) per piece, many thousands of francs less than what you might've paid for the authentic gems.

The **Boutique du Rocher,** 1 av. de la Madone (☎ 93-30-91-17), is the largest of two roughly equivalent boutiques opened in 1966 by Princesse Grace as the official retail outlets of her charitable foundation. The organization merchandizes Monégasque and Provençal handcrafts. A short walk from place du Casino, the shop sells carved frames for pictures or mirrors; housewares; gift items crafted from porcelain, textiles, and wood; toys; and dolls. On the premises are workshops where local artisans produce the goods you'll find for sale.

Old River, 17 bd. des Moulins (☎ 93-50-33-85), is a menswear store aiming at a solid middle-bracket man who simply wants to dress appropriately and look good. You can pick up a swimsuit, shorts, slacks, a blazer, and a pair of socks to replace the ones you ruined by too many walking tours, at prices that won't require that you remortgage your house.

You don't have to be Princesse Caroline to be able to afford to shop in Monaco, especially now that **FNAC** (☎ 93-10-91-91), a member of the big French chain that sells records, CDs, tapes, and books, has opened in the heart of town at the **Centre Commercial Le Métropole,** in the Jardins du Casino, alongside the Hôtel Métropole and across from the casino.

If you insist on ultra-fancy stores, you'll find them cheek by jowl with the Hôtel de Paris and the casino and lining the streets leading to the Hôtel Hermitage or across from the gardens at the minimall Park Palace. Look for the Belgian handbag maker deluxe, **Delvaux,** in the Park Palace, 27 av. de la Costa (☎ 93-25-11-80); **D. Porthault,** the luxury French linen maker, at 26 av. de la Costa (☎ 93-50-16-28); **Chanel,** on place de la Casino at allée Serge-Diaghilev (☎ 93-50-55-55); and **Harel,** the fanciest shoemaker in town, at the Galerie du Sporting (☎ 92-16-15-30). Allée Serge-Diaghilev is just that, an alley, but a very tony one filled with designer shops.

However, to get a better perspective on upper-middle-class shopping, visit the **Centre Commercial,** 17 av. des Spélugues. It has a few specialty shops worth visiting (especially if you aren't going into France). Check out **Geneviève Lethu** (☎ 93-50-09-41) for colorful and country tabletop design or **Manufacture de Monaco** (☎ 93-50-64-63) for glorious bone china and elegant tabletop design. If the prices send you to bed, two doors away is a branch of the chic but often affordable French linen house **Yves Delorme** (☎ 93-50-08-70). The **Marché Royal** (☎ 93-15-05-04) is a tiny gourmet grocery store down a set of curving stairs hidden in the side entrance of the mall; here you can buy gifts or stock up for *le picque-nique* or for your day trips. This market is open Monday to Saturday from 9am to 8pm.

The Shaky House of Grimaldi

Monaco, according to a famous quote from Somerset Maugham, is defined as 370 sunny acres peopled with shady characters. Tax free, thanks to the provisions of a 1918 treaty whose clauses included the insistence that the kingdom maintain an ongoing stream of male heirs to retain its independence from France, the principality is the oddest fiscal and social anomaly in Europe, a curious blend of Las Vegas hype and aristocratic glitter whose luster has been sorely tarnished since the demise of Princesse Grace ("a snow-covered volcano," according to Alfred Hitchcock).

Ah, those young Grimaldis—Albert, Stephanie, and Caroline. Beneficiaries of an empire based on medieval precedent, gambling, and showmanship, they're descended from Genoese merchants on their father's side and a curious blend of Philadelphia conservatism and Hollywood flash on their mother's. Before the advent of Prince Charles and Princess Di, they were the product of the most unhappy royal marriage in Europe. The only difference is that Rainier and Grace didn't discuss their squabbles and extramarital affairs in the media.

The marriage of the world's most eligible bachelor and the Hollywood golden goddess dominated headlines around the world in April 1956. However, omens were ripe for marital disaster. All six of Grace's bridesmaids ended at least one of their marriages in divorce, and the much photographed and endlessly embarrassing mother of the bride frequently managed to confuse Monaco and Morocco as the site of her famous daughter's love nest.

Like Grace and Rainier themselves, the marriage did not age gracefully. Rainier's snide public assessments of his celebrity wife's accomplishments showed an unpleasant rivalry: Even though the Monégasques had reacted in horror when, a few years into the marriage, Grace contemplated returning to Hollywood to star in Hitchcock's *Marnie* (she backed out because of the furor), they soon embraced her again and her many cultural projects, like the establishment of the Monaco Arts Festival and the Princesse Grace Foundation.

"How can I bring up my daughters not to have an affair with a married man," Grace once asked, "when I was having affairs with married men all the time?" Clark Gable, Ray Milland, and William Holden come to mind. The admired and envied fairy-tale princess was, beneath it all, a lonely and frustrated woman with a strong sense of loyalty to her friends, a gift for promoting her kingdom by the sea, an obsession with appearances, and a predilection for romances with younger men as she matured. When she was young, the men had been older. But as she reached middle age, the men became younger. For example, she was 46 (in 1976) when she met one of her long-standing lovers, the 30-year-old film director Robert Dornhelm. Even after the *Marnie* furor, Grace still talked of returning to Hollywood, but nothing ever came of it. However, she and Dornhelm once went so far as to option Gore Vidal's *A Search for the King.*

The children of this ill-fated union, obviously, have rebelled against the strictures imposed on them by their less-than-noble parents. More at home in the watering holes of big-city Paris, far from the claustrophobia and judgments of their concrete wonderland, they each replace one another at frequent intervals as the one most likely to shock the multinational residents of their tax-free domain.

The most obvious in her disaffection is Stephanie, whose tantrums as a 13-year-old were duly noted by scads of journalists and whose sexual insouciance has contributed, according to local wits, to the ill health of her not particularly serene father. Her affairs have included the sons of both Jean-Paul Belmondo and Alain Delon, children of second-generation fame *à la française*. For a time she even left Monaco and moved to Los Angeles, where she tried to build a show-business career. Promising beginnings in Stephanie's fertile roster of career options included an ill-conceived stint as a model. Many of her commitments were stymied by last-minute maneuvering from the Grimaldi fortress. These ambitions have mostly collapsed, as did her attempt to become a pop singer. In 1995 Stephanie married a former palace guard, Alain Ducruet, by whom she had borne two children; however, in 1996 she divorced him because he had been caught cavorting naked with Miss Bare Breasts of Belgium. She still makes public appearances and lives around the corner from her father and brother.

Everyone in his prospective kingdom constantly urges 40-year-old Albert to take a bride. He has publicly denied rumors of homosexuality and has cavorted with an assortment of famous faces, from Brooke Shields to Donna Rice to Claudia Schiffer. As a local commentator has said, "It's one thing for him to marry a bimbo; it's another to marry someone like his mother." At the moment (subject to change at any minute) Albert continues to play the field, finding no replacement to fill the shoes of Princesse Grace.

Caroline, mother of three, has done her royal part and would if she could, according to observers, force a power struggle with Albert for the right of succession. Her first husband, the much older businessman/*boulevardier* Philippe Junot, was the sort of man every mother hopes her daughter will *not* marry—which is probably why Caroline did. After she announced that she was divorcing the womanizing Junot, the Vatican was called in to annul the marriage (which it *finally* did in 1992). Within a year of her mother's death, Caroline met and fell deeply in love with the 27-year-old Stefano Casiraghi, son of an Italian industrialist. Caroline was 4 months pregnant when they married in 1984, and she and Stefano had two more children (who remained "illegitimate" until 3 years after their father's death). In 1989 Stefano died in a speedboating accident and Caroline went into severe mourning, chopping off her hair and withdrawing from her duties. Eventually she and her children moved to France, and she has now begun to return to her position as "First Lady of Monaco." In 1996 *People* magazine cruelly put on its cover a photo, snapped without her awareness by paparazzi, of a bald Princess Caroline. Her hair loss has been blamed on a dermatological problem but remains a mystery to palace watchers.

On May 31, 1997, the prince and his family marked the 700th anniversary of Grimaldi rule when 6,600 Monégasques showed up for an open-air ceremony at place du Palais. With all their troubles and scandals, the clan has come a long way since January 8, 1297. That's when a political refugee from Genoa, Francesco Grimaldi, accompanied by some cronies in monks' clothing, persuaded the defenders of the local castle to give them shelter. Once they had penetrated the defenses, they ripped off their hoods and took the castle by force. The Principality of Monaco was born, and it's been in Grimaldi hands ever since.

One Monégasque summed up the Grimaldi situation well: "I go to church every morning to pray for the Prince and his family. I pray God will keep them safe and sane. Because that is my security. Without the Grimaldis, we would be merely hors d'oeuvres for France."

For real-people shopping, stroll **rue Grimaldi,** the principality's most commercially minded street, near the fruit, flower, and food market (below) and **boulevard des Moulins,** closer to the casino, where glamorous boutiques specialize in international chicness. There's also an all-pedestrian thoroughfare with shops less forbiddingly chic than those along boulevard des Moulins: **rue Princesse-Caroline** is loaded with bakeries, flower shops, and the closest thing you'll find to funkiness in Monaco. Also check out the **Formule 1** shop, 15 rue Grimaldi (☎ 93-15-92-44), where everything from racing helmets to specialty keychains and T-shirts celebrates the roar of high-octane—and outside the racetrack, utterly impractical—racing machines.

Should you be looking for the heart and soul of the real Monaco, get away from the glitz and head to place des Armes for the **fruit, flower, and food market** held daily from 9am to noon; it has an indoor and an outdoor market complete with a fountain, cafes, and hand-painted vegetable tiles set beneath your feet. While the outdoor market packs up promptly at noon, some dealers at the indoor market stay open to 2pm. If you prefer bric-a-brac, there's a small but very funky (especially for Monaco) flea market, **Les Puces de Fontvieille,** held Saturday from 9am to 6pm at the Espace Fontvieille, a panoramic open-air site near the heliport in Monaco's Fontvieille district.

ACCOMMODATIONS
VERY EXPENSIVE

✪ **Hôtel de Paris.** Place du Casino, 98000 Monaco. ☎ **92-16-30-00.** Fax 93-16-38-50. 160 rms, 40 suites. A/C MINIBAR TV TEL. 2,000F–3,100F ($400–$620) double; from 5,700F ($1,140) suite. AE, DC, MC, V. Parking 130F ($26).

On the resort's ornate main plaza, opposite the casino, this is one of the world's most famous hotels and most spectacular beaux-arts monuments. Linked with the sybaritic, high-spending image of Monte Carlo, it's the principality's choice address, more famous and legendary even than the Hermitage. At least two dozen movie companies have used its lobby as a background. The ornate facade has marble pillars, and the impressive lounge has an art nouveau rose window at the peak of the dome. The hotel is furnished with a dazzling decor that includes marble pillars, statues, crystal chandeliers, sumptuous carpets, Louis XVI chairs, and a wall-size fin-de-siècle mural. The guest rooms are fashionable and, in many cases, sumptuous. Unlike most hotels, the rooms opening onto the sea aren't as spacious as those in the rear.

Dining/Entertainment: The evening usually begins in the bar. The hotel's most famous dining options are Le Louis XV and Le Grill (see "Dining," below). Both restaurants benefit from a collection of rare fine wines kept in a dungeon chiseled out of the rock. The less formal Restaurant Côté Jardin offers a daily lunch buffet whose rich roster of food is inspired by the culinary traditions of the Mediterranean specialties.

Facilities: Thermes Marins spa, directly connected to both the Hôtel de Paris and the Hôtel Hermitage, offers complete cures of thalassotherapy under medical supervision, (including "antismoking," "anticellulite thighs," and "postnatal" cures); a large indoor pool; two saunas; fitness center; beauty center.

✪ **Hôtel Hermitage.** Square Beaumarchais, 98005 Monaco CEDEX. ☎ **92-16-40-00.** Fax 92-16-38-52. 231 rms, 16 suites. A/C MINIBAR TV TEL. 1,550F–2,900F ($310–$580) double; from 4,300F ($860) suite. AE, DC, MC, V. Parking 120F ($24).

Picture yourself sitting in a wicker armchair, being served drinks under an ornate stained-glass dome with an encircling wrought-iron balcony. You can do this at the clifftop Hermitage, with its "wedding cake" facade. The "palace" was the creation of

Jean Marquet (who created marquetry). Large brass beds anchor every room, wherein decoratively framed doors open onto balconies. You have a choice of rooms in the Prince wing, where accommodations are more traditionally old-fashioned, or in the more modern Costa or Excelsior wing, with a choice of either contemporary or period furnishings. The most expensive rooms open onto the water. High-season rates are charged during Christmas, New Year's, Easter, and July and August. The stylish dining room has Corinthian columns and chandeliers and serves a refined modern cuisine. The Bar Terrasse is a chic rendezvous that at night is a piano bar.

EXPENSIVE

Hôtel Mirabeau. 1 av. Princesse-Grace, 98000 Monaco. ☎ **92-16-65-65.** Fax 93-50-84-85. 93 rms, 10 suites. A/C MINIBAR TV TEL. 1,300F–2,400F ($260–$480) double; 2,100F–6,000F ($420–$1,200) suite. AE, DC, MC, V. Parking 120F ($24).

Only the five lowest floors of this 30-story skyscraper are devoted to a hotel—the remainder house upscale private apartments. Set in the heart of Monte Carlo, next to the casino, and known for its well-recommended La Coupole restaurant (which earned a Michelin star), it's a sophisticated hybrid with many functions. Each of the rooms boasts conservatively modern, rather elegant furnishings, and many contain terraces with a romantic view overlooking the pool and Mediterranean seascape. La Coupole is highly praised for its inventive yet classical cooking (closed August). Between May and September, the poolside Café Mirabeau provides an attractive setting for relaxed breakfasts, casual buffet lunches, and upscale dinners.

Le Métropole Palace. 4 av. de la Madone, 98000 Monaco. ☎ **93-15-15-15.** Fax 93-25-24-44. 98 rms, 30 suites. A/C MINIBAR TV TEL. 1,450F–1,800F ($290–$360) double; from 2,000F ($400) suite. AE, DC, MC, V. Parking 120F ($24).

In the heart of Monaco, this hotel was rebuilt on the site of the original Métropole, on Monte Carlo's "golden square." The hotel is superb in every way and has an array of handsomely furnished and beautifully decorated rooms. Each includes a radio, hypoallergenic pillows, a hair dryer, and a full line of toiletries. The upscale Le Jardin serves splendid French and international cuisine. Services include 24-hour room service, same-day and overnight laundry, valet service, and baby-sitting. There's also a heated seawater pool.

Loews Monte-Carlo. 12 av. des Spélugues, 98007 Monaco CEDEX. ☎ **93-50-65-00.** Fax 93-30-01-57. 600 rms, 35 suites. A/C MINIBAR TV TEL. 1,350F–1,500F ($270–$300) double; from 3,500F ($700) suite. AE, DC, MC, V. Parking 100F ($20).

The Loews is in the heart of Monte Carlo, below the terraces that support the famous casino, on one of the most valuable pieces of real estate along the Côte d'Azur. Architecturally daring when it was completed in 1975 (some of its foundations were sunk directly into the seabed, and some of the principality's busiest highways roar beneath it) the resort is now viewed as an integral and much-appreciated enhancement of Monégasque life. It contains Monaco's highest concentration of restaurants, bars, and nightclubs—it's somewhat like Las Vegas with a Gallic accent. Many celebrities have been attracted here, including Walter Cronkite and Peter Ustinov. Even Prince Albert and Princess Stephanie show up for regular workouts in the seventh-floor health club. The guest rooms in this entertainment extravaganza are tastefully furnished and comfortable and have sweeping views. The cavernous Sun Casino, with its slot-machine "annex" on the seventh floor, has all any gambler could ask for.

Dining/Entertainment: The drinking facilities include a sunny Tahitian lobby bar with a view of the water and the more intimate Jockey Club. L'Argentin serves

South American–style grilled meats and succulent fish. The nautical Café de la Mer is open for breakfast. Near the rooftop, Le Pistou re-creates the flavors of Provence. Guests also enjoy the regular cabaret.

Facilities: Tennis, golf, deep-sea fishing, sailing, and scuba diving are some of the sports that can be arranged at the Monte Carlo Country Club and Monte Carlo Yacht Club.

Monte-Carlo Beach Hotel. Av. Princesse-Grace, Monte-Carlo Beach, 06190 Roquebrune/Cap-Martin. ☎ **04-93-28-66-66.** Fax 04-93-78-14-18. 44 rms. A/C MINIBAR TV TEL. 1,800F–2,500F ($360–$500) double. AE, DC, MC, V. Parking 140F ($28). Closed Oct 31–Apr 1.

Despite its name, this hotel is in France, not Monaco. Built in 1928, it was known for years as the "Old Beach Hotel" until the Société des Bains de Mer decided that that was too unglamorous a title for such a luxury retreat. Tons of money later, it emerged with a new name and vastly improved rooms and facilities. The most pampered guest always asks for the most beautiful accommodation in the house, the spacious circular unit above the lobby. Eva Peron stayed here in 1947 during her infamous Rainbow Tour of Europe, and Princess Grace came here almost every day in summer to paddle around the pool, a rendezvous for the rich and beautiful. Though Roquebrune/Cap-Martin is its postal address in France, the hotel is located not there but at the border of Monaco.

MODERATE

Hôtel Alexandra. 33 bd. Princesse-Charlotte, 98000 Monaco. ☎ **93-50-63-13.** Fax 92-16-06-48. 56 rms. A/C TV TEL. 600F–850F ($120–$170) double. AE, DC, MC, V. Parking 45F ($9).

This hotel is in the center of the business district, on a busy and often-noisy street corner. Its comfortably furnished guest rooms don't generate much excitement, but they're reliable and respectable. The Alexandra knows it can't compete with the giants of Monaco and doesn't even try. But it attracts those who'd like to visit the principality without spending a fortune.

Hôtel Balmoral. 12 av. de la Costa, 98006 Monaco. ☎ **93-50-62-37.** Fax 04-93-15-08-69. 77 rms, 2 suites. MINIBAR TV TEL. 650F–850F ($130–$170) double; 1,000F–1,500F ($200–$300) suite. AE, DC, MC, V. Parking 40F ($8).

This hotel was built in 1898 by the grandfather of the present owner, Jacques Ferreyrolles. On a cliff halfway between the casino and the Palais du Prince, it boasts eight floors of rooms and lounges with sea views. The rooms, 50 of which are air-conditioned, are like the public rooms—homelike, immaculate, and quiet. The Balmoral is so inviting that guests often extend their stays.

Hôtel du Louvre. 16 bd. des Moulins, 98000 Monaco. ☎ **93-50-65-25.** Fax 04-93-30-23-68. 34 rms. A/C MINIBAR TV TEL. 730F–830F ($146–$166) double. AE, DC, MC, V. Parking 40F ($8).

Built like a traditional century-old mansion, this hotel is filled with antique furniture. The guest rooms are comfortable, carpeted, and unique. Expect to pay higher prices for rooms facing the sea. Breakfast is the only meal served.

INEXPENSIVE

Hôtel Cosmopolite. 4 rue de la Turbie, 98000 Monaco. ☎ **93-30-16-95.** Fax 93-30-23-05. 24 rms, none with toilet, all with sink, some with shower. 200F ($40) double without shower or toilet, 310F ($62) with shower but without toilet. No credit cards. Free parking on street.

When it was built in the 1930s, this hotel was sited in the then-fashionable neighborhood a few steps downhill from the railway station. Today it's an appealingly dowdy art deco monument with three floors, no elevator, and comfortable but anonymous-looking rooms. Madame Gay Angèle, the English-speaking owner, is proud of her "Old Monaco" establishment. Her more expensive rooms have showers, but the cheapest way to stay here is to request a room without a shower— there are adequate facilities in the hallway.

Hôtel de France. 6 rue de la Turbie, 98000 Monaco. ☎ **93-30-24-64.** Fax 92-16-13-34. 26 rms. TEL. 380F ($76) double; 450F ($90) triple. V. Parking 40F ($8).

Not all Monégasques are rich, as a stroll along this street will convince you. Here you'll find some of the cheapest living and eating places in the high-priced principality. This 19th-century hotel, 3 minutes from the rail station, has modest furnishings but is clean and comfortable.

DINING
VERY EXPENSIVE
Le Grill de l'Hôtel de Paris. In the Hôtel de Paris, place du Casino. ☎ **92-16-29-66.** Reservations required. Main courses 265F–680F ($53–$136). AE, DC, MC, V. Daily noon–2:30pm and 8–10:30pm. Closed Jan 6–31 and at lunch in summer. FRENCH.

In the flood of publicity awarded to this hotel's street-level restaurant, Le Louis XV (below), it's been easy to overlook this equally elegant contender on the rooftop. The view alone is worth the expense, with the turrets of the fabled casino on one side and the yacht-clogged harbor of Old Monaco on the other. The decor is gracefully modern, the ambience somewhat less intense than that in the self-consciously cutting-edge Ducasse citadel downstairs. Despite that, the place is undeniably elegant, with a two-fisted approach to cuisine that includes a succulent list of every imaginable sort of grilled fish (seawolf, monkfish, sole, salmon, mullet, cod, or turbot) and meat such as Charolais beef and lamb from the foothills of the nearby Alps. In fair weather and in summer, the ceiling opens to reveal the starry sky. The fine cuisine is backed up by one of the Riviera's finest wine lists, with some 20,000 bottles; the wine cellar is carved out of the rock below. Service is faultless but never intimidating or offputting.

✪ **Le Louis XV.** In the Hôtel de Paris, place du Casino. ☎ **92-16-30-01.** Reservations recommended. Jacket and tie required for men. Main courses 300F–400F ($60–$80); fixed-price menus 780F–890F ($156–$178). AE, DC, MC, V. July–Aug, Wed 8–10pm, Thurs–Mon noon–2pm and 8–10pm; Sept–June, Thurs–Mon noon–2pm and 8–10pm. Closed Feb 17–Mar 4 and Dec 1–30. FRENCH/ITALIAN.

On the lobby level of the five-star Hôtel de Paris, the two-star Louis XV offers what one critic called "down-home Riviera cooking within a Fabergé egg." Despite the place's regal trappings (or as a reaction against them?), the culinary star chef/namesake Alain Ducasse creates a refined but not overly adorned cuisine, which is served by the finest staff in Monaco. Everything is light, attuned to the seasons, with an intelligent and modern interpretation of both Provençal and northern Italian dishes. The service is superb. Ducasse is now dividing his time between this glittering enclave and his new restaurant in Paris.

EXPENSIVE
Café de Paris. Place du Casino. ☎ **92-16-20-20.** Main courses 50F–160F ($10–$32). AE, DC, MC, V. Daily 8am–4am. INTERNATIONAL.

Frankly, we've always found this place cramped, glittery, and relatively devoid of charm, but it provides one of the best front-row seats in town to observe the continuing carnival that is Monte Carlo. Set across from the casino and the Hôtel de Paris, it's owned by the Société des Bains de Mer and was completely rebuilt in the late 1980s, when a reproduction belle époque–style brasserie was created. Come here for an ongoing jangle of about a hundred slot machines, English-style or continental breakfasts, and brasserie-style meals that begin at noon and are served continuously throughout the afternoon until very late in the evening. The premises also contains the Monte Carlo branch of Le Drugstore, that trendsetting and somewhat claustrophobic temple to impulse buying that seems to have changed little since the concept made its debut in Paris in the 1970s.

L'Argentin. In the Loews Monte-Carlo, 12 av. des Spélugues. ☎ **93-50-65-00.** Reservations recommended. Main courses 170F–220F ($34–$44); fixed-price menu 365F ($73). AE, DC, MC, V. Daily 7:30pm–4am. STEAKS/GRILLS.

Conceived with panache by the developers of one of the brassiest hotels on the Riviera, L'Argentin is a generous, stylishly international restaurant. It's one of the largest restaurants in town, banked with windows facing the sea, and has the most impressive grill set-up. Uniformed chefs tend three blazing fires, from which diners are protected by a thick sheet of glass. The decor was inspired by the Argentinian pampas and has gaucho accessories, like cowskin-draped banquettes. The restaurant remains open, albeit with a limited menu, from 1 to 4am, mimicking the hours of the roulette wheels in the hotel's nearby casino. All the beef served here is imported from the American Midwest; menu choices include a mixed grill called parillada Argentine, Mexican-style flank steak, many kinds of grilled fish, and a perennial favorite, standing rib of American beef grilled over a wood-burning fire.

Rampoldi. 3 av. des Spélugues. ☎ **93-30-70-65.** Reservations required. Main courses 130F–280F ($26–$56). AE, MC, V. Daily 12:15–2:30pm and 7:30–11:30pm. FRENCH/ITALIAN.

One of the leading independent restaurants, Rampoldi serves some of the finest cuisine in Monte Carlo. Its spirit is more Italian than French, though classic meats of both countries are served in an agreeable setting at the edge of the Casino Gardens. First, try the soupe de poissons (fish soup), a house specialty. The fish dishes are universally good, including sole prepared in two ways and grilled sea bass with fennel (for two). All the meat dishes are well prepared, including veal kidneys in madeira sauce. A spectacular finish is the crêpes Suzette.

INEXPENSIVE

Le Texan. 4 rue Suffren-Reymond. ☎ **93-30-34-54.** Reservations recommended. Main courses 69F–100F ($13.80–$20). AE, DC, MC, V. Mon–Thurs noon–2:30pm and 7–10:30pm, Fri noon–2:30pm and 7–11:30pm, Sat 7–11:30pm. TEX-MEX.

These Tex-Mex specialties have entertained even the most discriminating French taste buds. There's a handful of outdoor tables, a long bar, a roughly plastered dining room draped with the flag of the Lone Star State, and a scattering of Mexican artifacts. You'll find Le Texan on a sloping residential street leading down to the old harbor—a world away from the glittering casinos and nightlife of the upper reaches. Menu items include T-bone steak, barbecued ribs, pizzas, nachos, tacos, a Dallasburger (with guacamole), and the best margaritas in town.

Pizzeria Monégasque. 4 rue Terrazzani. ☎ **93-30-16-38.** Pizzas 40F–60F ($8–$12); main courses 90F–105F ($18–$21); fixed-price menu 130F ($26). AE, MC, V. Sun–Thurs noon–2:30pm and 7:30–11pm, Fri–Sat noon–2:30pm and 7:30–midnight. Closed Dec 25–Jan 1. FRENCH/ITALIAN.

This *pizzeria de luxe* offers four dining rooms, an outdoor terrace, and an ambience that, at its best, might seem like the cost-conscious melting pot of Monte Carlo. Almost anyone might arrive—in a limousine or on a bicycle, in all kinds of garb that might quickly convince you that Monaco is actually a rather small and gossipy town. The owner has grown accustomed to seeing all the follies and vanities of this town pass through his door; he serves pizzas, fish, and grilled meats to whomever shows up. Specialties are magret du canard (duckling), grilled steaks, carpaccio, and beef tartare. Of the 10 kinds of pizza, the most popular are pizza Terrazzini (it includes cheese and pistou) and the "special" version that's served with Tunisian-style *merguez*.

Stars 'n Bars. 6 quai Antoine-1er. ☎ **93-50-95-95.** Reservations recommended. Dinner salads and platters 70F–140F ($14–$28); sandwiches 50F–65F ($10–$13). AE, DC, MC, V. Tues–Sun 11am–midnight. AMERICAN.

This place deliberately revels in the cross-cultural differences that have contributed so much to Monaco's recent history. Modeled on the sports bars popular in the States, it features two distinct dining and drinking areas devoted to American-style food, as well as a third-floor space, The Club, which is a sports bar with memorabilia donated by many athletes of note and even a disco every night after 10:30pm (sometimes with live performances). No one will mind if you drop in just for a drink—they cost 40F to 80F ($8 to $16) each—but if you're hungry, menu items read like an homage to the macho American experience. Try an Indy 500 or a Triathlon salad, a Wimbledon or a Slam Dunk sandwich, or a Breakfast of Champions (eggs and bacon and all the fixings). If your children happen to be in tow and are feeling nostalgic for the ballpark back home, order a little leaguer's platter (for those under 12). Unless an artist of international note appears, there's never a cover charge.

MONACO AFTER DARK

The **Sun Casino,** in the Loews Monte-Carlo, 12 av. des Spélugues (☎ **93-50-65-00**), is a huge room filled with one-armed bandits. It also features blackjack, craps, and American roulette. Additional slot machines are available on the roof starting at 11am—for those who want to gamble with a wider view of the sea. It's open daily from 4pm to 4am (to 5am for slot machines). Admission is free.

A speculator, François Blanc, developed the ✪ **Monte Carlo Casino,** place du Casino (☎ **92-16-21-21**), into the most famous in the world, attracting the exiled aristocracy of Russia, Sarah Bernhardt, Mata Hari, King Farouk, and Aly Khan (Onassis used to own a part interest). The architect of Paris's Opéra Garnier, Charles Garnier, built the oldest part of the casino, and it remains an extravagant example of the 19th century's most opulent architecture. It's rather schizophrenically divided into an area devoted to the casino and others for different kinds of nighttime entertainment, including a theater (see below) presenting opera and ballet.

Unlike the jaded roués whose presence here became a cliché during the belle époque, the new grand dukes are likely to include fast-moving international businesspeople on short-term vacations and a crowd that's infinitely more democratized than in days of yore. Baccarat, roulette, and chemin-de-fer are the most popular games, though you can play *le craps* and blackjack as well.

The Salle Américaine, containing only Las Vegas–style slot machines, opens at noon, as do doors for roulette and *trente-quarente.* A section for roulette and chemin-de-fer opens at 3pm. Most of the facilities inside are operational by 4pm, when additional rooms open with more roulette, craps, and blackjack. The gambling continues until very late/early, the closing depending on the crowd. The casino classifies its "private rooms" as the more demure, nonelectronic areas devoid of slot machines. To enter the casino, you must carry a passport, be at least 21, and pay an admission of between 50F and 100F ($10 and $20), depending on where you want to go. In lieu of a passport, an identity card or driver's license will suffice.

After 9pm, the staff will insist that gentlemen wear jackets for entrance into the private rooms.

The premises also contains a **Cabaret** in the Casino Gardens, where the show is usually preceded by the music of a well-rehearsed orchestra. A sexy cabaret featuring lots of feathers, glitter, jazz dance, ballet, and Riviera-style seminudity is presented at 10pm Wednesday to Monday from mid-September to the end of June. If you want dinner as part of the show, service begins at 9pm and, with the show included, costs 420F ($84) per person. If you want to see just the show, your drinks will cost from 150F ($30) each. For reservations, call ☎ **92-16-36-36.**

In the casino's **Salle Garnier,** where lots of gilt and belle époque accents evoke the l9th-century opera house of Paris, concerts are held periodically; for information, contact the tourist office (see "Essentials," above) or the Atrium du Casino (see below). The music is usually classical, featuring the Orchestre Philharmonique de Monte Carlo.

The casino also contains the **Opéra de Monte-Carlo,** whose patron is Prince Rainier. This world-famous house, opened in 1879 by Sarah Bernhardt, presents a winter and spring repertoire that traditionally includes Puccini, Mozart, and Verdi. The famed Ballets Russes de Monte-Carlo, starring Nijinsky and Karsavina, was created in 1918 by Sergei Diaghilev. The national orchestra and ballet company of Monaco appear here. Tickets may be hard to come by; your best bet is to ask your hotel concierge. You can make inquiries about tickets on your own at the **Atrium du Casino** (☎ **92-16-22-99**), open Tuesday to Sunday from 10am to 12:15pm and 2 to 5pm. Standard tickets are 100F to 600F ($20 to $120).

Tiffany, avenue des Spélugues (☎ **93-50-53-13**), is a favorite of the 25- to 40-year-old crowd who like a glamorous modern setting. On Sunday a bevy of showgirls is featured. **Le Symbole,** rue du Portier (☎ **93-25-09-25**), is a hot spot for those over 30. The decor glitters in a high-tech gloss, and the music is disco.

Les Folies Russes, in the Loews Monte-Carlo, 12 av. des Spélugues (☎ **93-50-65-00**), is a dinner-dance cabaret. Many viewers like its shows much more than those staged at the cabaret of the Monte Carlo casino. Vaudeville acts are thrown in to ease the "monotony" of all those nude dancers. There's a dinner dance on Friday and Saturday with food served from 8:30 to 9:30pm, and a floor show, *La Folie Russe,* is presented Tuesday to Sunday at 11pm. Jackets for men are mandatory. The show with dinner is 550F ($110); 250F ($50) gets you only the show.

14 Roquebrune & Cap-Martin

Roquebrune: 592 miles S of Paris, 3 miles W of Menton Cap-Martin: 3 miles W of Menton, 1¹/₂ miles W of Roquebrune

Roquebrune, along the Grande Corniche, is a charming mountain village with vaulted streets. It has been restored, though some critics have found the restoration "artificial." Today its **rue Moncollet** is lined with artists' workshops and boutiques with inflated merchandise.

Three miles west of Menton, **Cap-Martin** is a satellite of the larger resort that's been associated with the rich and famous since the empress Eugénie wintered there in the 19th century. In time the resort was honored by the presence of Sir Winston Churchill, who came here often in his final years. Two famous men died here—William Butler Yeats in 1939 and Le Corbusier, who drowned while swimming off the cape in 1965. Don't think you'll find a wide sandy beach—you'll encounter plenty of rocks, against a backdrop of pine and olive trees.

ESSENTIALS

GETTING THERE   Cap-Martin has train and bus connections from the other cities of the Mediterranean coast, including Nice and Menton. To reach Roquebrune, you'll have to take a taxi or bus from the small train station at Cap-Martin or the nearby hamlet of Carnoles. From Cap-Martin or Carnoles, buses to Roquebrune travel at 15-minute intervals along the length of R.N. 7, stopping in Roquebrune en route. They're marked DIRECTION MENTON; buses from the train station of Menton headed for Roquebrune are marked DIRECTION NICE. If you arrive by TGV from any other city in France, you'll be routed through Menton and not through Cap-Martin or Carnoles. For more **information and schedules,** call ☎ 08-36-35-35-35.

VISITOR INFORMATION   The **Office de Tourisme** is at 20 av. Paul-Doumer in Roquebrune (☎ 04-93-35-62-87).

SEEING THE TOP ATTRACTIONS

IN ROQUEBRUNE   The only one of its kind, the **Château de Roquebrune** (☎ 04-93-35-07-22) was originally a 10th-century Carolingian castle; the present structure dates in part from the 13th century. Dominated by two square towers, it houses a historic museum. From the towers there's a panoramic view along the coast to Monaco. The castle gates are open daily from 10am to noon and 2 to 6pm (closed Friday off-season); admission is 20F ($4) for adults, 15F ($3) for students, and 10F ($2) for children 11 and under. From mid-September to mid-June it's open Saturday to Thursday from 10am to noon and 2 to 6pm (to 7pm the rest of the year).

It'll take you about an hour to explore Roquebrune. You can stroll through its colorful covered streets, which still retain their authentic look even though the buildings are now devoted to handcrafts, gift and souvenir shops, or art galleries. From the parking lot at place de la République, you can head for place des Deux-Frères, turning left into rue Grimaldi. Then head left to **rue Moncollet,** the town's most interesting street. This long, narrow street is covered with stepped passageways and filled with houses that date from the Middle Ages, most often with barred windows. Rue Moncollet leads into **rue du Château,** where you may want to take time to explore the château (above).

Rue du Château leads to place William-Ingram. After crossing this square, you reach rue de la Fontaine. Take a left. This will lead you to the **Olivier millénaire** (millennary olive tree). This olive tree is said to be one of the oldest in the world, having survived for at least 1,000 years.

Back on rue du Château you can reach the **Eglise Ste-Marguerite,** which hides behind a relatively common baroque facade. But this exterior merely masks the church from the 12th century. It's not entirely from that time, however, having seen many alterations over the years. The interior is of polychrome plaster. Look for two paintings by a local artist, Marc-Antoine Otto, who in the 17th century painted a Crucifixion (in the second altar) and a Pietà (above the entrance door).

IN CAP-MARTIN   Cap-Martin is a rich suburb. At the center of the cape is a feudal tower that's today a telecommunications relay station. At its base you can still see the ruins of the **Basilique St-Martin,** the only evidence remaining of a priory constructed here by the monks of the Lérins Islands in the 11th century. After repeated pirate raids in the centuries to come, notably around the 15th century, it was destroyed and abandoned. If you follow the road (by car) along the eastern shoreline of the cape, you'll be rewarded with a view of Menton set against a backdrop of mountains. In the far distance looms the coastline of the Italian Riviera, and you can see as far as the resort of Bordighera.

Although it takes about 3 hours, you can take one of the most interesting walks along the Riviera here. The coastal path, called **Sentier Touristique,** leads from Cap-Martin to Monte Carlo Beach. If you have a car, you can park it in the lot at avenue Winston-Churchill and begin your promenade. The path is marked by a sign labeled PROMENADE LE CORBUSIER. As you go along you'll be able to take in a view of Monaco set in a natural amphitheater. In the far distance, you'll view Cap-Ferrat and even Roquebrune with its château. The scenic path comes to an end at Monte Carlo Beach.

If you have a car, you can also take a scenic **6-mile drive,** taking about an hour. Leave by D23, following the signs to Gorbio, a perched village standing on a hill and reached by this narrow, winding road. Along the way you'll pass homes of the wealthy and view a verdant setting with pines and silvery olives. The site is wild and rocky, the buildings having been constructed as a safe haven from pirate attacks. The most interesting street is rue Garibaldi, which leads past an old church to a panoramic belvedere.

ACCOMMODATIONS

Hôtel Victoria. 7 promenade du Cap, 06190 Roquebrune/Cap-Martin. ☎ **04-93-35-65-90.** Fax 04-93-28-27-02. 32 rms. A/C MINIBAR TV TEL. 418F–588F ($83.60–$117.60) double. Rates include breakfast. AE, DC, MC, V. Closed Jan 5–31.

This rectangular low-rise building is set behind a garden in front of the beach. Built in the 1970s, it was renovated in the mid-1990s in a neoclassical style that weds tradition and modernity. It's the "second choice" at the resort for those who can't afford the lofty prices of the more spectacular Vista Palace. The casual bar/lounge near the entrance sets a stylishly relaxed tone. Breakfast is the only meal served.

✪ **Hôtel Vista Palace.** Grande Corniche, 06190 Roquebrune/Cap-Martin. ☎ **800/223-6800** in the U.S., or 04-92-10-40-00. Fax 04-93-35-18-94. 42 rms, 26 suites. A/C MINIBAR TV TEL. 1,250F–1,850F ($250–$370) double; 1,250F–6,000F ($250–$1,200) suite. AE, DC, MC, V. Parking 100F ($20) in garage.

This extraordinary hotel/restaurant stands on the outer ridge of the mountains running parallel to the coast, giving an "airplane view" of Monaco that's spectacular. And the design of the Vista Palace is just as fantastic: Three levels are cantilevered out into space so every room seems to float. Nearly all the rooms have balconies facing the Mediterranean. If you don't want to stay here, at least consider stopping by for a meal—it's expensive but worth it. Le Vistaero is open daily from 12:15 to 2:15pm and 8 to 10pm; three fixed-price menus are available featuring Mediterranean cuisine envied by the region's other restaurateurs. Facilities include a pool, a sauna, a masseuse, an indoor squash court, a fitness center, a boutique, a helipad, and a 9-acre landscaped Mediterranean garden.

DINING

You might also like to try **Le Vistaero** at the Hôtel Vista Palace (see "Accommodations," above).

Au Grand Inquisiteur. 18 rue du Château. ☎ **04-93-35-05-37.** Reservations required. Main courses 77F–140F ($15.40–$28); fixed-price menus 145F and 215F ($29 and $43). AE, MC, V. Tues–Sun noon–1:30pm and 7:30–10pm. Closed Nov–Dec 25. FRENCH.

This culinary find is a miniature restaurant in a two-room cellar near the top of the medieval mountaintop village of Roquebrune. On the steep, winding road to the château, this climate-controlled building is made of rough-cut stone, with large oak beams. The cuisine, though not the area's most distinguished, is quite good, like the chef's duck special or scallops meunière. Most diners opt for one of the fresh fish choices. The wine list is exceptional—some 150 selections, most at reasonable prices.

Hippocampe. 44 av. Winston-Churchill. ☎ **04-93-35-81-91.** Reservations required. Main courses 100F–130F ($20–$26); fixed-price menus 155F–225F ($31-$45). AE, MC, V. Tues–Wed and Fri–Sat noon–1:45pm and 7:30–9:30pm, Thurs and Sun noon–1:45pm. Closed Oct 15–Nov 15 and 10 days in Jan. FRENCH.

Opened in 1963, this fine restaurant along the seafront has a full view of the bay and even the Italian coastline. Made safe by a thick stone wall, its terrace is shaded by five crooked pines. The "Sea Horse" is a stone-and-glass garden house with a tile roof and scarlet and pink potted geraniums. Specialties include filets de sole en brioche, coq au vin (chicken cooked in wine), terrine of salmon in basil sauce, and duck with peaches.

15 Menton

596 miles S of Paris, 39 miles NE of Cannes, 5 miles E of Monaco

Menton is more Italianate than French. Right at the border of Italy, Menton marks the eastern frontier of the Côte d'Azur. Its climate, incidentally, is the warmest on the Mediterranean coast, a reputation that attracts a large, rather elderly British colony throughout the winter. Because these senior citizens form a large part of the population of 130,000, Menton today is called "the Fort Lauderdale of France." Menton experiences a foggy day every 10 years—or so they say.

According to a local legend, Eve was the first to experience Menton's glorious climate. Expelled from the Garden of Eden along with Adam, she tucked a lemon in her bosom, planting it at Menton because it reminded her of her former stamping grounds. The lemons still grow in profusion here, and the fruit of that tree is given a position of honor at the **Lemon Festival** in February. Actually, the oldest Menton visitor may have arrived 30,000 years ago. He's still around—or at least his skull is—in the Musée de Préhistoire Régionale (below).

Don't be misled by all those "palace-hotels" studding the hills. No longer open to the public, they've been divided up and sold as private apartments. Many of these turn-of-the-century structures were erected to accommodate elderly Europeans, mainly English and German, who arrived carrying a book written by one Dr. Bennett in which he extolled the joys of living at Menton.

ESSENTIALS

GETTING THERE   There are good bus and rail connections that make stops at each resort along the Mediterranean coast, including Menton. Many visitors arrive by car along one of the corniche roads. Two trains per hour arrive from Nice (trip time: 35 min.), and two trains per hour from Monte Carlo (trip time: 10 min.). For **rail information** and schedules, call ☎ 08-36-35-35-35. A local company, **Autocars Broch** (☎ 04-93-31-10-52), runs buses between Nice and Menton, one almost every hour. The same frequent bus service is offered between Monte Carlo and Menton.

VISITOR INFORMATION   The **Office de Tourisme** is in the Palais de l'Europe, 8 av. Boyer (☎ 04-93-57-57-00).

SEEING THE TOP ATTRACTIONS

On the Golfe de la Paix (Gulf of Peace), Menton, which used to belong to Monaco, is on a rocky promontory, dividing the bay in two. The fishing town, the older part with narrow streets, is in the east; the tourist zone and residential belt is in the west.

The writer/artist/filmmaker Jean Cocteau liked this resort, and the **Musée Jean-Cocteau,** Bastion du Port, quai Napoléon-III (☎ **04-93-57-72-30**), in a 17th-century fort, contains the death portrait of Cocteau sketched by MacAvoy, as well as MacAvoy's portrait of Cocteau. Some of the artist's memorabilia is here—stunning charcoals and watercolors, ceramics, signed letters, and 21 brightly colored pastels. The museum is open Wednesday to Monday from 10am to noon and 2 to 6pm. Admission is free.

At **La Salle des Mariages,** in the Hôtel de Ville (town hall), rue de la République (☎ **04-92-10-50-50**), Cocteau painted frescoes depicting the legend of Orpheus and Eurydice, among other things. A tape in English helps explain them. The room contains red-leather seats and leopard-skin rugs and is used for civil marriage ceremonies. It's open Monday to Friday from 8:30am to 12:30pm and 1:30 to 5pm. Admission is 5F ($1).

The **Musée de Préhistoire Régionale,** rue Lorédan-Larchey (☎ **04-93-35-84-64**), presents human evolution on the Côte d'Azur for the past million years. It emphasizes the prehistoric era, including the 25,000-year-old head of the *Nouvel Homme de Menton* (sometimes known as "Grimaldi Man"), found in 1884 in the Baousse-Rousse caves. Audiovisual aids, dioramas, and videocassettes enhance the exhibition. The museum is open Wednesday to Monday from 10am to noon and 2 to 6pm. Admission is free.

The **Musée des Beaux-Arts,** Palais Carnoles, 3 av. de la Madone (☎ **04-93-35-49-71**), contains 14th-, 16th-, and 17th-century paintings from Italy, Flanders, Holland, and the French schools, as well as modern paintings, including works by Dufy, Valadon, Derain, and Leprin—all acquired by a British subject, Wakefield-Mori. The museum is open Wednesday to Sunday: June 15 to September 15 from 10am to noon and 3 to 7pm and September 16 to June 14 from 10am to noon and 2 to 6pm. Admission is free.

A DAY AT THE BEACH

Menton's beaches stretch for 2 miles between the Italian border and the city limits of Roquebrune and are interrupted only by the town's old and new ports. Collectively, they're known as **La Plage de la Promenade du Soleil** and with rare exceptions are public and free. Don't expect soft sands or even any sand at all, as the beaches are narrow, covered with gravel (or more charitably, big pebbles), and notoriously uncomfortable to lie on. Don't expect big waves or tides either. Who goes there? In the words of one nonswimming resident, mostly Parisians or residents of northern France, who are grateful for any escape from their urban milieux. Topless bathing is widespread, but complete nudity is forbidden.

Unlike in Cannes, where tens of thousands of chaises pepper the beaches, there aren't many options in Menton for renting mattresses and parasols; most people bring their own. Two exceptions are **Le Splendid Plage** (☎ **04-93-35-60-97**) and **Les Sablettes** (☎ **04-93-35-44-77**), both charging around 80F ($16) for use of a mattress. They're immediately to the east of the Vieux Port.

ACCOMMODATIONS

Hôtel Aiglon. 7 av. de la Madone, 06505 Menton. ☎ **04-93-57-55-55.** Fax 04-93-35-92-39. 27 rms, 3 suites. A/C MINIBAR TV TEL. 415F–735F ($83–$147) double; 745F–1,005F ($149–$201) suite. Half board 363F–673F ($72.60–$134.60) per person extra. AE, DC, V. Closed Nov 4–Dec 20.

A nugget along the coast, this three-star hotel was converted from a stately Riviera villa. In a large park filled with Mediterranean vegetation, it offers a more intimate and homelike environment than any other hotel in Menton in its league. The former private residence has been skillfully converted to receive guests, and each room is tastefully furnished. The magnet of the hotel is a heated pool around which is a 1900 veranda. The garden setting is beautifully maintained, and other facilities include a solarium and a children's game area. An excellent Provençal and international cuisine is offered with view windows opening onto the pool and garden.

Hôtel Chambord. 6 av. Boyer, 06500 Menton. ☎ **04-93-35-94-19.** Fax 04-93-41-30-55. 40 rms. A/C MINIBAR TV TEL. 530F–580F ($106–$116) double. AE, DC, MC, V. Parking 40F ($8).

Located on the main square next to the casino, this is a well-maintained hotel with rows of balconies and awnings. The streamlined modern guest rooms are tastefully and comfortably furnished. Breakfast is the only meal served.

Hôtel Le Dauphin. 28 av. du Général-de-Gaulle, 06500 Menton. ☎ **04-93-35-76-37.** Fax 04-93-35-31-74. 30 rms. TV TEL. 350F–520F ($70–$104) double; 620F ($124) triple. Rates include continental breakfast. AE, MC, V. Closed Oct 20–Dec 20.

This affable hotel lies just off the beach. The double-insulated rooms are bright and uncluttered, each with a balcony opening onto the mountain range or the sea. The multilingual owner/director Jacques Ridés is a classical-music buff who has created a unique hotel feature: two acoustically inviting practice studios—the Apollo, with a grand piano, and the Dionysos, with a baby grand piano, for round-the-clock rehearsal. The attentive staff is welcoming. Three meals per day are served, featuring many specialties of Provence. In the afternoon the restaurant becomes a tea salon.

Hôtel Méditerranée. 5 rue de la République, 06500 Menton. ☎ **04-93-28-25-25.** Fax 04-93-57-88-38. 90 rms. MINIBAR TV TEL. 350F–450F ($70–$90) double. Children 4 and under stay free in parents' room. AE, DC, MC, V.

This white-and-salmon hotel is 3 short blocks from the sea. A raised terrace with a view of the water, chaises longues, and potted plants are on the premises. The rooms are attractively decorated and include radios. The hotel also has a restaurant offering veranda dining in fair weather.

Hôtel Napoléon. 29 Porte de France, 06503 Menton. ☎ **04-93-35-89-50.** Fax 04-93-35-49-22. 40 rms. A/C MINIBAR TV TEL. 350F–600F ($70–$120) double. AE, DC, MC, V. Closed Nov 12–Dec 20.

Built on a palm tree–shaded avenue, this recently renovated hotel has a pool set in a small garden and stone terrace. Furnished with 18th-century English and Italian pieces, the main lounge, which has a bar, is really like a large living room. The guest rooms, decorated in vivid colors, have mahogany furniture and balconies overlooking the sea and the old town. There are a rooftop terrace and an air-conditioned restaurant with great views. Nonguests are welcome to visit for lunch or dinner.

Hôtel Princesse et Richmond. 617 promenade du Soleil, 06500 Menton. ☎ **04-93-35-80-20.** Fax 04-93-57-40-20. 44 rms, 2 suites. A/C MINIBAR TV TEL. 335F–560F ($67–$112) double; 610F–810F ($122–$162) suite. AE, DC, MC, V. Parking 40F ($8). Closed Nov 5–Dec 17.

At the edge of the sea near the commercial district, this hotel boasts a facade of warm Mediterranean colors, with a sunny garden terrace. The owner rents comfortable soundproof rooms with modern and French traditional furnishings and balconies. Drinks are served on the roof terrace, where you can enjoy a view of the curving shoreline. A restaurant in the garden of the nearby Hôtel Aiglon, under the same ownership, offers lunch and dinner beside a heated pool you may use as well. There's also an open-air Jacuzzi, plus a small fitness room in the solarium. The staff organizes sightseeing excursions.

DINING

✪ **La Calanque.** 13 square Victoria. ☎ **04-93-35-83-15.** Main courses 65F–95F ($13–$19); fixed-price menus 97F–140F ($19.40–$28). AE, DC, MC, V. Tues–Sun noon–2pm and 7:15–9:30pm. FRENCH/SEAFOOD.

Of the restaurants along the port, La Calanque is the best for the budget. In fair weather, tables are set under shade trees in full view of the harbor. We recommend the spaghetti napolitaine, tripe niçoise, soupe de poissons (fish soup), and fresh sardines (grilled over charcoal and very savory), with the focus on locally harvested seafood. Two specialties are bouillabaisse and *barba giuan,* small biscuits cooked in olive oil after having been stuffed with a variety of local greens.

L'Albatros. 31 quai Bonaparte. ☎ **04-93-35-94-64.** Reservations recommended. Fixed-price menu 100F ($20). MC, V. Mon–Sat noon–3pm and 7pm–midnight, Sun noon–3pm. Closed Mon in winter. FRENCH.

This charming little bistro along the port specializes in fish dishes from the Mediterranean. On the second floor and on the terrace you can enjoy a view over the old harbor and bay while sampling fresh fish purchased directly from Menton fishers. Many regional dishes also are featured, and meat-eaters will enjoy filet de boeuf (beef) Charolais. The fixed-price menu changes every 2 or 3 months.

Petit Port. 1 place Fontana. ☎ **04-93-35-82-62.** Reservations recommended. Main courses 110F–140F ($22–$28); fixed-price menus 80F–140F ($16–$28). AE, MC, V. Thurs–Tues noon–3pm and 7pm–midnight. FRENCH.

Small and charming, employing many members of an extended family, this restaurant serves well-prepared portions of fresh fish in a century-old house near the medieval port. Everything is homemade, even the bread. Specialties are grilled sardines (succulent and increasingly difficult to find), fish soup, several kinds of grilled meats and fish, and (in honor of the northern France origins of its owner) tripe in the style of Caen. The place prides itself on its location—less than a mile from the Italian border.

Rocamadour. 1 square Victoria. ☎ **04-93-35-76-04.** Reservations recommended. Main courses 45F–130F ($9–$26). AE, DC, MC, V. Tues noon–2pm, Wed 7–9:30pm, Thurs–Mon noon–2pm and 7–9:30pm. FRENCH.

This pleasant restaurant overlooks the port. You dine at tables set under a canopy where colored lights are turned on at night. Some specialties offered by the chef are from the Périgord region, including foie gras. Magret de canard (duckling) is another specialty. But basically the cookery is grounded in the rich tradition of the Côte d'Azur, with an emphasis on fresh fish. The restaurant was founded almost a century ago by a chef from Rocamadour, and the name of that town has stayed with the place.

Index